PUBLICATION

OF THE

NAVY RECORDS SOCIETY

VOL. XCVII

DILLON'S NARRATIVE

VOLUME II

1802-1839

THE NAVY RECORDS SOCIETY was established in 1893 for the purpose of printing rare or unpublished works of naval interest.

Any person wishing to become a Member of the Society is requested to apply to the Hon. Secretary, Royal Naval College, Greenwich, S.E. 10, who will submit his name to the Council. The Annual Subscription is Two Guineas, the payment of which entitles the Member to receive one copy of each work issued by the Society for that year, and to purchase back volumes at reduced prices. The subscription for those under the age of 30 is One Guinea.

———————

MEMBERS requiring copies of any volume should apply to the Hon. Secretary.

Subscriptions should be sent to Hon. Secretary (Admin.), Crown House, Aldwych, W.C. 2.

THE BRIG *Childers*

A NARRATIVE OF MY PROFESSIONAL ADVENTURES

(1790–1839)

BY

SIR WILLIAM HENRY DILLON, K.C.H.,

VICE-ADMIRAL OF THE RED

EDITED BY

MICHAEL A. LEWIS,

C.B.E., M.A., F.S.A., F.R.HIST.S.

VOLUME II

1802–1839

PUBLISHED BY ROUTLEDGE FOR THE NAVY RECORDS SOCIETY
1956

First published 1956 for the Navy Records Society

Published 2019 by Routledge
2 Park Square, Milton Park, Abingdon, Oxon OX14 4RN
52 Vanderbilt Avenue, New York, NY 10017

Routledge is an imprint of the Taylor & Francis Group, an informa business

ISBN 13: 978-1-911423-22-5 (pbk)
ISBN 13: 978-0-85354-022-9 (hbk)

MIX
Paper from
responsible sources
FSC   FSC™ C013985
www.fsc.org

Printed in the United Kingdom
by Henry Ling Limited

CONTENTS

ILLUSTRATIONS

VIII

CALAMITY

INTRODUCTION

THE Impress Service, which W.H.D. joined just before the renewal of the war, was still something of a novelty, even then only nine years old. It arose out of that same chronic shortage of seamen which had been responsible for Pitt's Quota Acts of 1795 (see Vol. I, p. 174), and represented an earlier, and less drastic, attempt at solving the problem. The idea was to co-ordinate the operations of the independent press-gangs sent out from individual ships. So long as these were the ordinary means of securing recruits, there was much waste of energy and overlapping of effort as between captain and captain, all of whom, bent upon securing an adequate complement for their own ships, found themselves in competition, not only with their common prey, but also with one another.

To minimise this, therefore, the Admiralty gradually began to intervene, in an effort to reduce the cut-throat competition, and the final result was, in 1793, the appearance of the Impress Service, a specialising body, commanded by captains and lieutenants who belonged to no ship and therefore had no particular axe to grind: but whose whole-time duty it was to comb the likeliest land-localities—the sea ports. Here they roped in all the men they could, and brought them to recognised depots or rendezvous on land, whence they could be distributed as required to the fleet. It was not, obviously, an appointment which gave much scope for either honour or profit, and it was naturally far from popular with young and ambitious officers. It even carried with it, at first anyway, a definite slur—as W.H.D. puts it, 'a degrading appointment: none but worn-out lieutenants were employed in that service.' Indeed, it was probably always so regarded, though W.H.D.'s *amour propre* seeks to make out that, when *he* was appointed to it, Lord St. Vincent 'was nominating young and active officers to it instead of old ones.'

The picture which he paints of this despised duty, though all too brief, is instructive, if only because very few first-hand accounts survive of an Impress Officer's activities. He reveals enough, however, to show not only how unpleasant the job was, but also how astute the officer must be in conducting an operation in which 'the enemy' was indeed the quarry, but also very nearly everyone else in the port.

From time to time in these pages the debatable and complicated question is raised as to who may be pressed, and who not. The true answer, of course, is that it depended upon the demand—and the supply. In theory, only 'persons using the sea' could be taken: but when any serious crisis occurred, necessity knew no law, and Theory, *per se*, came to mean very little. Even the words 'the sea' were subject to various interpretations at various times—and by various interests. Thus, though the earliest-known statute on the subject—15 Richard II, cap. 2—limited the Admiralty's jurisdiction to 'the main streams of great rivers nigh the sea,' there were wide loopholes here for interpretations favourable to the Impress Service. For 'great' and 'nigh' are clearly relative terms. Gradually, indeed, and especially in wartime, 'great' came to differ but little from 'any,' and 'nigh' became all but synonymous with 'at any distance from'. Moreover, when canals began to appear, even the word 'stream' lost its early meaning.

Yet some sections of the community did in fact enjoy a real, though not a completely safe, immunity. Harvesters, for instance, usually escaped: so did gentlemen—but only if they looked the part. Among truly seafaring persons there were privileged folk too, not only legally but also, usually, in fact. For instance, by law (13 Geo. II, cap. 17) no sea-user could be taken during his first two years afloat. The ordinary merchant officers—masters, mates, boatswains and carpenters—were also exempt, so long as they were on board, so long as their ship was of fifty tons burden or upwards, and when in port, provided they had appeared before a local justice and taken an oath that they were what they professed to be. A pilot too was exempt, unless or until he ran a ship aground, when his exemption instantly lapsed. There was point, if not irony, in this. Doubtless it made him the more careful when piloting H.M. ships: for, being (by hypothesis) on board at the moment of the mishap, his chances of escaping impressment were exactly nil. All this helps to explain W.H.D.'s astonishment (p. 18) at the conduct of his captain, Manby, in June 1803, when he grabbed indiscriminately both masters and pilots. He had to give them up, and was distinctly lucky, as Dillon remarks, to escape being sued for illegal detention—a remedy always open (theoretically) under common law to a man who deemed himself wrongly impressed.

The case of the big carpenter at Hull was rather different. Presumably he was not a ship's carpenter: if he had been, he would have said so, and claimed exemption on that ground. Probably, too, he was not regularly employed in a shipyard, for such men, in England though not in Scotland, were entitled to be left alone. He was almost certainly, then, a perfectly ordinary landsman following the craft of carpenter: therefore not a 'person using the sea,' and therefore untouchable—in theory. But it was not theory which saved him from W.H.D.'s clutches.

It is interesting to note the very diverse interests which combined to thwart the Impress Service. Their methods range from crude rescues, pistol shots and brickbats, *via* mere bribery to the more subtle devices of the cleverer seamen with their decoy letters, and to the stratagems of the merchants themselves, who try to distract the officer's attention from his job by laying on elaborate dinners, luring him to dances, etc. W.H.D. is not altogether deceived. He suspects an underlying cause to explain why

he 'never dined alone': he pats himself on the back for seeing through
these blandishments, and even matches guile with guile, thereby revealing
the interesting fact that he often went 'pressing' in plain clothes. Yet he
did not always have the best of it. It would be intriguing to know, for
instance, just what his host at the Grand Ball whispered in the ear of the
fair one who would not dance with W.H.D., and which made her change
her mind (p. 13). One theory undoubtedly would be, 'Keep the little
nuisance occupied while we . . .' If this be so, she succeeded admirably.
By all accounts the Impress Gang was not out that night.

Though possibly inclined at times to overstress his hard luck, W.H.D.
is certainly not doing so when he comes to the account of his arrest under
Flag of Truce. That it was a blatant breach of good faith is certain, and
that every Briton, up to the very highest, thought so is abundantly
shown, not only, this time, by the sufferer himself, but also by the correspondence printed in Appendix II below (pp. 61–64), which, copied from
Lord Keith's letter-books, nowhere appears in Dillon's pages. Again, that
the Authorities remembered it, and did their best to mitigate W.H.D.'s
personal misfortune, is clear from the correspondence (this time reproduced
by Dillon) which is printed as Appendix III to Part IX below, pp. 64–66.
    It was indeed a shocking thing to do, and must, along with Napoleon's
arrest of the 'détenus,' be regarded as an early, but very important step
in the gradual degradation of war from the—comparatively—gentlemanly
affair which it once was to the 'total'—and altogether ungentlemanly—
affair which it has now become. It was at any rate a death-blow to the
whole age-old institution of '*paroles d'honneur*,' which obviously could not
breathe for long in an atmosphere like that generated by Dillon's arrest,
and still less, if possible, in that surrounding the negotiations for his
release.
    There can also be no doubt that his captivity spelt grave loss of
seniority and opportunity to him, if only because it most probably retarded the all-important date on which he was made post. Yet a study of
the Navy Lists of the period will show that it did not, as things turned
out, make a great deal of difference to his sea-career. He could not, captivity or no captivity, have risen really high, or received really important
appointments, during the war. He could not, indeed, have become even
a rear-admiral before the war ended. He had entered a little too late. The
key-year here is 1795. No one of course was to know it, but, in the event,
the last captain to attain wartime flag-rank was the officer made post
on the 7th December of that year. And not even W.H.D. could have hoped
to become a captain at fifteen. Still, though he could not have flown
his flag in wartime, he might have escaped part of the dreadful post-
war block in promotion, and at any rate would not have had to take,
as he did, thirty-nine years to work his way from the bottom to the top
of the Captains' List. For instance, had his wish been fulfilled to join

Nelson in the Mediterranean, where there was much doing, and where promotion-opportunities were good, he might well have been a commander in 1803 and, quite possibly, a captain by 1804. He would then have obtained his flag, at earliest, in January 1837, or nearly ten years before he did.

VIII

CALAMITY

(1) BOULOGNE (Summary)

SEPTEMBER TO NOVEMBER 1802

Summary of fourteen pages of manuscript omitted

AFTER a few weeks at home W.H.D. paid a short visit to France, staying with a Mr. Adams, principal banker at Boulogne. Reaching Calais at 2 a.m., he was welcomed at Meurice's hotel by the original proprietor and Madame—'M. Meurice with a cocked hat and large wig, with only an overcoat, his wife with a large drop cap, long curls hanging down—and her night gown.'

Reaching Boulogne next day, he noticed 'the labours going on in the port at low water. So soon as the tide was out, a great number of men were set to work clearing away the mud, to deepen the harbour. That proceeding,' he goes on, 'had not a very peaceable appearance. The definitive Treaty was not yet signed, and many suspicious opinions were the consequence.' During his stay he heard several things which forced him to the conclusion that the First Consul did not intend a lasting peace. He also heard many tales of atrocities committed, mainly upon the Royalists, during the republican régime.

Meanwhile he continued serenely outshining everybody everywhere. His host tried to upset his judgment and balance by overloading him with wine, but, to his chagrin, W.H.D. outdrank him and all his friends, and the attempt was abandoned—'Nous avons fait notre possible pour vous mettre dedans, mais vous avez la tête trop forte.' Then he was inveigled into a disreputable fencing-school and tavern—a very dangerous haunt—kept by a crack swordsman named Coste, who was also a billiard shark and the shadiest bully in Boulogne. Lured first into a fencing-bout with this undesirable character, he took him on, 'not having had a foil in my hand some years,' and 'having on top-boots and leather tights—not exactly the thing for fencing.' He defeated—and disarmed—the professional, however, without much difficulty, and then, challenged to billiards by the angry and humiliated Frenchman, defeated him there too. He half promised to return in the evening for the supper which he had won by his triumphs, but, on recounting his adventures to his host and hostess, was prevailed upon not to do so, as he would certainly be murdered if he went.

There follows the first of the erased passages which refer to his future wife: 'Next door to my friend's house resided an English surgeon who took in boarders, and invalids travelling to improve health. He had with him an English gentleman with his wife and another married lady. With these I became acquainted—(erased) *little thinking that the fair one without her husband would on a future day become my wife.*' He returned with this party, stopping at Rochester to visit the lady's daughter who was at school there, and reached London early in November.

(2) LONDON AND HULL (Impress Service)

NOVEMBER 1802–MAY 1803

ON my return, I had one day taken a stroll in the Strand, where, to my extreme surprise, I met the officer who stood next to me on Ad. Duckworth's list for promotion. He had arrived in England with the rank of commander. He acquainted me with all the changes that had occurred shortly after I left Jamaica. It seems that six of the line of battleship captains, anxious to get home to their families after the fatigues of the war, threw up their commands. Consequently they placed their appointments at the Admiral's disposal, and he filled them up with his own friends: by which arrangement he promoted six of his lieutenants to the rank of commander. This was a truly distressing account to me, as, had I remained three months longer with the Admiral, promotion would have been my lot. My unlucky star, for the third time, predominated,[1] and I was most keenly annoyed at what appeared a persecuting fate.

Soon afterwards my friend Ad. Gambier came home from Newfoundland. He had established himself at Iver, and invited me to

[1] For what he probably considered the first two times, see Vol. I, p. 423, note 3, and p. 300, note.

see him there. I lost no time in attending to the summons. He and Mrs. G. received me most graciously. I passed the day with them, and had a bed. I made known to him all the particulars of my disappointment and loss of promotion. He could not, he said, be of any great use to me at that moment, but assured me that, if any opportunity offered, he would not forget me. I generally rode down every three weeks to dine with him, returning the next morning.

It had been settled with my Father that I was not to accept any naval appointment unless with a certain prospect of promotion. The winter passed on, but nothing turned up in my favour. It was therefore agreed that I should go over to Ireland in the spring and establish myself upon that small estate in the neighbourhood of Drogheda adjoining Lord Netterville's properties,[1] my Father intending to assist me in making myself comfortable there. My father was very anxious to see me married. There was a very amiable young lady who was sincerely attached to me. Her parents also gave me encouragement with many friendly hints. However, I thought that I ought not to commence an establishment until I obtained post captain's rank, if I remained in the Navy. Consequently the fair one sought for a partner in another direction.

On my next visit to Ad. Gambier at Iver, he told me that, when he returned to Newfoundland, he would want a couple of armed cutters to visit the different stations there. If I chose to have the command of one of them he would apply for me, and it would lead in the end to my promotion. He made this offer, he said, under the supposition that I had nothing better in view. 'If you have not,' he said, 'you had better be employed in your profession than remain idle on shore.' I made known to my Father the Admiral's proposal, but as some time would elapse before he would quit England, no decision was fixed. In the meantime, my last captain, of the *Juno*,[2] had been appointed to the command of one of our finest frigates, fitting out in the river. From him I received an indirect message offering me the appointment of the Senior Lieutenant. I understood perfectly from whence it came, and, in thanking my friend for the communication, I told him that my mind had been made up not to accept any appointment unless certain of promotion. There the matter ended. However, I went down by invitation to the ship, the *Africaine*, and received some hospitable entertainments from my former captain. His cabin was most splendidly furnished. He was at that period much noticed by the Princess of Wales, and various rumours were in circulation relating thereto.

---

[1] See Vol. I, p. xvii. [2] Thomas Manby. See Vol. I, p. 445.

All my plans were suddenly thwarted by the Prime Minister's celebrated message to the House of Commons on the 8th of March, alluding to some armaments in the ports of France. This threw the whole country into a state of excitement which no doubt you will remember; and we began to prepare for war. I was walking the next day, very leisurely, up Piccadilly when a naval acquaintance accosted me. 'You seem to be taking it very easily,' he said. 'You are wanted at the Admiralty.' I could scarcely believe the assertion, but he repeated it with such positive assurances that I hastened thither: and, sure enough, in the hall I saw a sheet of paper stuck up, and my name on it—'Wanted, Lieut. D.—' Upon inquiry, I was ordered to proceed to Hull, upon the Impress Service. This news was so astounding that I was completely taken aback, as I thought it a degrading appointment. None, generally speaking, but worn-out lieutenants were employed in that Service. Therefore, without taking any further notice of it, I made the best of my way home to consult my Father. He also was very much annoyed at this unexpected call upon me. However, as the Second Secretary, Mr. Marsden,[1] was well known to him, he desired me to see the gentleman and try to have my destination changed. Upon my calling at the Admiralty and sending up my name to him, I experienced a very gracious reception. He told me that Lord St. Vincent had changed the whole system relating to the Impress Service by nominating young and active officers to it instead of old ones. 'His Lordship,' he said, 'has heard a great deal about you, and has selected you accordingly. You must go. Do not refuse, as you may be sure it is to lead to something better.' Upon these assurances I yielded to his advice, and, thanking Mr. Marsden, withdrew.

The next day I left home for Hull, where I arrived in due time. I had not been out of the stage one minute when I met one of my shipmates of the *Crescent*, the sailmaker. He hailed me with a cheerful countenance, but when he heard the reason for my presence in that town, he took to his heels and was out of sight in no time. I was to place myself under the orders of a Commander Grey,[2] and with that officer I soon put myself into communication. I had to select my gang and establish a rendezvous.

Lord Hawke, who resided at Scarthingwell Hall in Yorkshire,[3] was in a position to be useful. When his Lordship heard of my appointment,

---

[1] William Marsden (1754–1836), Second Secretary, 1795, First Secretary, 1804–1807: a distinguished orientalist and numismatist.
[2] Edward Grey, Lt. 29/9/1793; Cdr. 29/4/1802; Capt. 4/12/13.
[3] Brought into the family through his mother, Catherine (*née* Brooke), the wife of the great Admiral.

he wrote to the Mayor of Hull, to one of the leading members of the Corporation, to the Collector of Customs and one or two other influential gentlemen of the town, requesting them to show me attention. In consequence thereof all these individuals called upon me, their houses were thrown open, and I experienced a most cordial and hospitable reception. I soon commenced operations, and picked up many men. I will not enter into all the details of my adventures in the dark and out of the way corners that I was obliged to visit on this, to me, unpleasant service, but I will mention two or three of them where I narrowly escaped with my life.

The Admiralty sent a vessel to receive such men as were pressed or that voluntarily entered for the Navy. When I had my doubts of the safety of any in my lock-up room, they were sent off to the vessel. But all my proceedings were under the inspection of my superior. There was also a surgeon appointed to inspect the men, as to their being in sound health, wind and limb. This examination took place in the apartments of my rendezvous every morning about 9 o'clock. On one occasion I had stopped a strong powerful man as he was coming to his labours in the dock (I have often wondered that he did not throw me into it). He replied to my questions that he was not a seaman but a carpenter, and took a ruler out of the slash pocket of his trousers to prove his assertion. 'Carpenters,' I observed, 'are wanted in the Navy as well as seamen. Come along with me.' When he resisted, I made the agreed signal to my men, who were watching my action. They instantly closed, and four of them took hold of the carpenter. In taking him to my place of security, they unluckily passed through the street where this man resided. He called out to his wife while passing under the window. She made her appearance and, when she saw him under the power of the press-gang, burst out in wild lamentations. Her screams brought a large number of persons to the spot, some of whom made an attempt to rescue her husband: but they failed. When I reached the rendezvous, I lodged the carpenter safe. Shortly afterwards I was called upon by an individual who came from a firm of merchants, a clerk I suppose, who offered me £300 to liberate him. I told this gentleman that he had made a sad mistake, his proposal being useless. He had better retrace his steps, as the pressed man would be sent to serve in the Navy. It appeared that he was a clever, useful man, much valued by his employers. His being taken had made some stir, and my quarters were surrounded by many of his friends.

When the Surgeon came for the usual examination, the room was nearly full, as several seamen had been taken that night. Just at this moment the carpenter's wife was heard in the street calling her husband. My attention being taken up with my official duties, I did not hear them: but I noticed this powerful fellow drawing towards the window. I instantly changed my position, and got near to him. However, the Surgeon putting some question to me relating to the person then before him, I naturally in replying closed towards him. The instant my eyes were turned to another object, the carpenter, aware of my attention being drawn off from him, with an exertion beyond all description threw open the window and leapt out. He fell upon all fours, then, taking off his shoes, ran off, effecting his escape. There were two bird cages under the window which were broken down, and the man in falling hit one of my gang, but without doing him any injury. The noise made by the opening of the window and the sudden disappearance of such a powerful man out of it caused a surprise in the room not to be explained. His hat and shoes were brought to me, those articles being all we had of the carpenter.

In thus performing my unpleasant duties I soon experienced the ill will of the mob. On one occasion I was assaulted by a shower of brickbats: on another, a volley of either musket or pistol balls was fired into my room one evening as I was reading at my table. Fortunately I escaped any serious injury; but it became necessary for the Mayor to interfere, and some constables were directed to watch over the safety of my person. In my expeditions in quest of seamen I scarcely ever wore the same dress, and I managed to pick up men in greater numbers than expected. Whether my proceedings were reported to Lord St. Vincent I never knew, but it soon became necessary to send a frigate to receive the seamen. When she arrived, a party of marines was landed to prevent any attempt at a rescue. This event caused considerable excitement. All the labourers at the various docks turned out, and at one time their shouts and threats gave reason to apprehend some serious disturbance. But the Mayor, assisted by all the Corporation, showed much spirit and determination, which kept all quiet. I had my share of abuse that day, but no one dared to lay hands on me.

The presence of a frigate, the *Caroline*, Capt. Page,[1] was of importance to me, for whilst she remained off the port, I in some shape felt safe. From the upper classes, I rejoice to say, I experienced nought

---

[1] Benjamin William Page, Lt. 20/11/1784; Cdr. 12/4/96; Capt. 25/12/96; R-Ad. 12/8/1819; V-Ad. 23/11/41; Died, 3/10/45. Fought in all five of the Hughes-Suffren actions.

but marked attention and kindness. The colonel of the regiment quartered here and several of his officers were equally sociable. This bearing towards me from all the parties mentioned encouraged me to persevere in my professional labours. The numerous invitations sent to me proved that my conduct was favourably reviewed. I never dined alone. I was fully aware that many of the merchants who were extremely hospitable expected that I would be lenient, and avoid visiting their ships. But I did not in the least change my plan of operations. I generally attended these pleasant dinners in uniform, my host placing me between two amiable young ladies, supposing that their attractions would ensure my company for the remainder of the evening. However, on those occasions I directed the leading man of my gang to call at the house where I dined at about 8 o'clock, and to send up a note to me. He also brought with him a bag containing a change of dress.[1] Then I hastened away, in spite of all the entreaties of the fair ones. Below, the contents of the bag were turned to account, and in the course of a couple of hours I had probably secured seven or eight fine seamen. The number would depend upon circumstances. Sometimes I might be out till 2 o'clock in the morning without any success: at others the men would be caught very suddenly. All depended upon the secret information brought to me. My plans were never two nights alike, at one house passing the evening at cards, at another departing immediately after dinner. By these variations no one could be certain of my whereabouts.

One evening I was invited to dine with one of the leading merchants. He kept a princely table. The ballroom was to be opened that night. Some of the principal characters of the town were present, and also the captain of the frigate. A vast quantity of choice wines were in circulation, many of which went round after the removal of the cloth. The ladies having retired, our host challenged us repeatedly for not doing justice to the various bottles going round. I had selected some delicious burgundy, and I noticed that no one partook of it but the master of the house. He had also made the same observation, that it was only touched by himself and me. When the bottle was empty, he insisted upon opening another for our own special beverage. 'They don't understand it,' he said. 'It is the choicest wine on the table, and as you seem to appreciate its quality you are the proper person to relish it.' When our party broke up, he inquired if I intended going to the ball. I answered in the affirmative. 'Very well,'

---

[1] From this and the evidence on the preceding page, it seems that he wore plain clothes on his 'pressing' expeditions.

he replied. 'If you want a pretty girl for a partner, let me know. I'll take care to provide you with one.'

I opened the ball with the Lady Mayoress, a regular beauty. But after I had taken her to a seat, I could not persuade any of the other young ladies to dance with me. Therefore for some time I remained an idle spectator. However, my host now made his appearance, and enquired why I was not dancing. I told him the reason. Then, taking me by the arm, he led me round the room, and, stopping opposite to five or six beautiful girls, 'Did you ask her?' he demanded. 'Yes,' said I. 'I have asked the whole of them, but they are engaged.' 'Now then,' said he, 'decide which you prefer.' I pointed her out. 'Very well,' he replied. 'Leave me for a moment.' I followed his instructions. In a few seconds he rejoined me. 'Now go,' said he, 'to the fair one. You will not be refused.' I did so accordingly, and the young lady gave me her arm. So much, thought I, for being a judge of good burgundy. I wanted no more partners during the evening. When we were about to leave, I offered my arm to the daughter of one of the gentlemen already mentioned. The Colonel of the Regiment wished to lead her to her carriage, but she gave me the preference, and when I handed her in she requested me to accompany her home to supper. The gallant soldier (Brisbane)[1] appeared sadly annoyed. I passed a very pleasant evening with this young lady's family.

I had now been nearly six weeks at Hull. I encountered many unpleasant annoyances in my official duties. Letters were constantly coming to acquaint me with the news that seamen would enter if I would call with my boat at a certain place at an hour fixed. I attended to several of those letters, but found they were written to draw off my attention where more wanted.

Never was I so completely taken by surprise when the post announced to me my appointment as Senior Lieutenant to the *Africaine*, commanded by my late captain. I was fully sensible that by doing so I might interfere with all my Father's plans for my advancement in the event of war. My friend Lord Hawke was on the look out for me, and Ad. Gambier had promised to take me with him. He had already written to me, to advise my remaining quiet at Hull, that he might know where to find me when wanted. Weighing all these prospects in my mind, I determined to write to Lord St. Vincent, to explain my Father's wishes to his Lordship, and to request the annulling

---

[1] (Gen.) Sir Thomas Brisbane, 1773–1860: Soldier, Governor and Astronomer. Served with distinction in Peninsular War and American War of 1812–15. Governor of New South Wales, 1821; gave name to the capital of Queensland.

of my appointment. To my astonishment the First Lord of the Admiralty complied with my application by cancelling my commission. Delighted with his Lordship's consideration, I thought myself safe: I had not written to the captain of the frigate. However, my calculations for the future were soon set aside by the next day's post bringing me a peremptory order from the Admiralty to join the *Africaine* without delay.[1] This sudden change in Lord St. Vincent's intentions so completely upset me that I saw no remedy. It was evident that his Lordship kept me in view: nothing could be done but comply. I therefore made my arrangements accordingly, and packed up for my departure.

I had my accounts and the expenses of the rendezvous to settle. The month of April had just terminated, the time for sending them up to the Navy Office. As I did not exactly understand the form in which they were to be made out, nor was I cognizant of the allowances granted to me on the Impress Service, I was obliged to consult my superior officer's clerk, and he set me in the right way of these things. When I presented them to the Commander for his signature and approval, he drew his pen across my charges for stationery, amounting to half a crown. The clerk had clearly established my right to them. Whilst the chief was examining my accounts, his own were lying on the table before me, and I could not help seeing the charges he had made. Those that instantly attracted my notice were for 'stationery, £4-0-0!'[2]

Fortunately for me the *Caroline* was on the point of quitting the roads, and her captain offered me a passage to the Downs. This I willingly accepted. Having therefore bid a friendly adieu to all my hospitable friends, I embarked on board that ship. I confess I left Hull with a heavy heart, as I felt convinced that, had I remained there, a very advantageous match would have been arranged. But, suddenly called away upon active duty, with the prospects of a war, all my thoughts were turned to another direction. I had procured 150 seamen for the Navy in six weeks, which must have proved that I had not been idle. I had two or three very narrow escapes of my life on that unpleasant service, and upon the whole I did not, on more mature reflection, see much cause to feel any keen disappointment in the change of my destiny. At three and twenty there were still prospects in the distance, and I placed confidence in them.

[1] This curious incident is never explained.
[2] A passage here, and several smaller ones later, are omitted. They tell how he persisted in this claim for expenses, and finally received his half-crown.

We had a boisterous passage to the Downs. Captain Page had his wife with him. The ship was not in first-rate order, but as I experienced nothing but kindness on board, it would not be fair to offer any ill-natured remarks relating to her. I soon found my way to London. My Father detested the Impress Service, and did not regret my having been removed from it, hoping for the best. It was the universal opinion that we could not remain at peace with Bonaparte. Our expenses had already been enormous, and ill-forbodings were prevalent of the consequences of entering into another war which no one could tell how it would terminate. My Father felt the pressure of the taxes most seriously, and this feeling was general. But we could not, as a powerful nation, submit to the overreaching policy of France under the Consuls.[1]

My equipment was soon completed. In taking leave of my town friends, I received a message from the celebrated Lady Hamilton, with whom I had been acquainted.[2] She was extremely anxious—in short, pressingly so—to send me with Lord Nelson, assuring me that, if I would go with him, I might rely upon early promotion. However much I might feel for that lady's kind intentions in my behalf, I declined her proposal. Her early character was not unknown to me, and I preferred relying upon my own family connection which I thought would stand by me to the last. I was much blamed afterwards by some very influential men for not having accepted that offer. I wrote to Capt. Manby, acquainting him of my being on my way to join him, then called at the Admiralty for instructions. I there was informed that the *Africaine* was cruising off the coast of Holland, and was directed to proceed to Deal, where the Senior Officer would find me a vessel to convey me to my ship. Upon my arrival there the first person I met was Ribouleau,[3] who had been sent to raise seamen there. I turned my back on him.

(3) H.M.S. *AFRICAINE* (North Sea)

May 1803–July 1803

I soon embarked upon a small armed vessel and, the next day, it blowing nearly a gale, I reached the *Africaine*. When I made my bow

---

[1] *I.e.* Bonaparte, First Consul, and the nominal Second and Third, Cambacérès and Lebrun.

[2] W.H.D. never tells us how. Later he reveals a considerable degree of intimacy. For his subsequent dealings with her, see Index.

[3] John. *Cf.* Vol. I, Index.

to my captain, he kindly expressed his apprehension that his interference in my behalf had damaged my Father's views relating to my
promotion. I told him it had. 'Very well,' he replied. 'I will try and
make it up to you. I hope you will not have cause to repent joining
my ship. You shall soon know the results of my exertions in your
favour. I think I shall succeed.'

When I had time to look about me and make the acquaintance of
my messmates, I was informed that the Captain and the late Senior
Lieutenant did not agree: that therefore there had been a court of
inquiry upon his conduct, and its result obliged him to quit the ship.
They told me that the Captain was constantly alluding to me, saying
that when I joined the ship all would be set to rights. They appeared
a very gentlemanly set. Our ship, in company with the *Leda*, frigate,
was employed in watching the port of Helvoetsluys. There were two
French frigates lying there, a Dutch one also and other armed vessels.
It was these vessels to which Mr. Addington alluded in the King's
message to the House of Commons.[1] There were also several transports with troops embarked on board of them. They were supposed
to be bound to Louisiana,[2] which territory had been made over to
France by Spain. I had not been long on board when Rear-Ad.
Thornborough came and took command of the squadron in a 64,
accompanied by another frigate, the *Hydra*, Capt. Mundy.[3] On the
18th the war was declared. I believe I am correct as to the date. In
the newspapers received by the Packet we were informed of Prizes
being taken daily. Bonaparte was terribly annoyed at not being able
to humbug us any longer, and the capture of two vessels in
Hodierne[4] Bay became the subject of severe controversy, as he
insisted that we had taken these vessels previous to the declaration
of war. Therefore in retaliation (as he said) he laid hands upon all the
English travellers and residents in France, who thought themselves

[1] *Cf.* above, p. 9.
[2] The district, not the State, of Louisiana—a vast and vague territory to the west
of the Mississippi and Missouri, ceded by France to Spain in 1762 and re-ceded to
France in 1800. Napoleon's expedition here mentioned never sailed, because in this
year (1803) he sold the whole area and all its rights to the U.S.A.
[3] (Sir) George Mundy (K.C.B.), Lt. 11/3/1796; Cdr. 24/12/98; Capt. 10/2/1801;
R-Ad. 22/7/30; V-Ad. 23/11/41.
[4] Audierne Bay, south of Brest. This episode was, as W.H.D. states, Napoleon's
excuse for the inexcusable act mentioned. The ships were in fact seized on the day
that war was declared—18th May. Much later, Dillon tells us, the French Government
half-abandoned the pretext, or, rather, declared that it was only one of many. In the
autumn of 1805, some of the illegally-held prisoners sent a petition to the French
Minister of War, offering to pay the value of the disputed vessels in return for
freedom. He replied that the said seizures were 'only one cause out of many too
numerous to mention' for the reprisal.

safe while in possession of their passports. He did not care what he said, if it answered his purpose, the press and the *Moniteur* being solely under his control. The Admiral's ship, not being in very good order, was sent into port to refit, and he came on board the *Africaine*, but did not remain long with us. Lord Keith[1] became the Commander-in-Chief of the North Sea Fleet. Sir Sidney Smith also made his appearance here, but was soon off again. Our Minister from Amsterdam passed us in a Packet, and we were at war with Holland as well as France. We chaced an enemy privateer one day, but she escaped.

Our first overt act was against the enemy's fishing boats. We were suddenly ordered to repair to the Downs, where my Jamaica friend, Rear-Ad. Montagu, had his flag flying. The Captain left me in command of the ship. He did not return till the middle of the night, when we made for Boulogne, and in the morning we captured two and twenty of them. Their crews were fine powerful men. As we could not spare any more seamen to take possession of more boats, we hastened with our Prizes to Portsmouth, where all above a certain tonnage were condemned and the smaller ones liberated. As Bonaparte had threatened Lord Whitworth with an invasion, it was thought advisable to take all the largest boats to prevent their being employed in conveying troops to our shores. We in the Navy did not much like seizing these poor inoffensive fishermen, but we were bound to obey orders.

At Spithead we went through a thorough refit in our rigging. Capt. Manby placed the greatest reliance upon all my proceedings, and in one sense I felt myself uncomfortable, as I was referred to upon every part of the ship's duty. We were not fully manned, and at times our labours were not slight. But as we were anxious to have the ship in good order extra work was unavoidable. The Captain kept a good table. Here again his partiality was shown, as he scarcely ever entertained without my being present. Our labours usually commenced at 2 o'clock in the morning and ended with darkness, and after eight days of incessant toil, leaving out Sunday, I had the satisfaction to have refitted the ship thoroughly: every shroud, every rope, block and sail underwent an examination; the hull painted, the rigging blacked, the boats put into repair: all the stores and provisions, water, etc., on board. These exertions were noticed and much spoken of by the senior naval officers present—a proof of what can be done with good management.

I cannot pass over in silence the constant theme in our naval

---

[1] George Elphinstone, Viscount Keith. See *D.N.B.*

circles—the injury inflicted upon our dockyards by Lord St. Vincent's ill-judged economy.[1] He had sold all the surplus stores at the termination of the war, and boasted of having saved the country upwards of a million sterling. When hostilities were renewed, no stores could be had, and it is a notorious fact that those which we had only a short while before disposed of were repurchased at four times the price they had produced. Here was a regular wasteful economy. All the small vessels had been sold, so that, when any were wanted, we were obliged to hire them from the merchants. Some of them were known to prove useless in comparison with those we had formerly possessed. All this for Economy—an economy very ill-suited to a great and powerful nation like England.

Our ship being completed for war service in all save crew, we left Spithead to return to the North Sea. On our way thither our Captain pressed every individual he could get hold of. He even took pilots and the masters of small vessels. What his object might be I could not make out. He annoyed a great number whom he detained on board his ship for a few days, but he was obliged to liberate them upon our coming to an anchor. Luckily for him, none of them prosecuted him for illegal detention.[2] We were bound for the Downs, but he thought proper to stay a few days in Dover Roads. The Princess of Wales came there to see him, which gave rise to many sayings. Her Royal Highness put up at the Castle, and at one time I expected her on board the *Africaine*, but some unforeseen event prevented her coming. My Father, who kept watch upon my motions, hearing of our being at Dover, wrote to the principal merchant there to show me attention. I called upon him, and experienced a most friendly reception: but a sailor's *ubique* prevents, by his perpetual motion, much intercourse with the shore. The Duke of Rutland came on board under the expectation of seeing our Captain, but as he was in attendance upon the Princess he was disappointed. I did the honours as well as circumstances would permit. His Grace lunched with us in the gunroom.

So soon as the Admiralty heard of our being in Dover Roads, we were ordered to sea. Next came Ad. Montagu's displeasure at our Captain's proceedings. In his absence I had visited Dover, and called upon the master of the hotel where I had put up on my way to France in the preceding autumn. It appeared that, the previous morning, when we fired a gun as a signal to two or three merchant vessels under our convoy to put to sea without us, the gun, owing to the carelessness of the Gunner, had not been unshotted. Consequently,

[1] See also Vol. I, p. 437.   [2] See Introduction, p. 3.

that shot lodged in the beach. Had it been high water, it would have gone right into the hotel, the master and mistress of which did not fail to load me with complaints. However, luckily, no accident happened. But I gave the Gunner a regular scolding for his neglect, desiring him in the future to fire the guns from the broadside away from the shore.

The Princess of Wales left Dover, and our Captain returned to the ship. He regretted, he said, having lost the opportunity of presenting me to Her Royal Highness. We were soon under way, and made sail for the Downs. The instant our ship became visible to the Admiral, up went our signal not to anchor, but proceed without loss of time to our destination. All this clearly proved to us that our Captain had taken some improper liberties with his professional duties. We were in consequence apprehensive of some unpleasant result.

It so happened that I had become acquainted in Town with the relations of an officer, an acting lieutenant, whom we had in the *Juno*. It was principally through my influence with Capt. Manby that he was confirmed to his rank, and his connections in London were anxious to show me hospitable attentions. The senior of these came to me one day and requested me to introduce him to Capt. Manby, that he might have the satisfaction of expressing his grateful acknowledgments to him for having secured promotion for his relative. I accordingly promised to take him to the *Africaine* the first favourable opportunity. Scarcely a day had elapsed after this promise when I received an invitation to partake of a *déjeuner à la fourchette* on board the *Africaine*, and that I was at liberty to bring my friend. Accordingly, we left Town in his gig (snow was on the ground) and reached the frigate in due time. We had a regular spread, the party consisting of about twenty. My companion soon found an opportunity of making known to the Captain the object of his visit, and Manby was much pleased with the expressions delivered to him by my friend. The table was splendidly adorned with plate, and choice wines abounded. As the party broke up, the cabin furniture attracted notice—to me in particular as, when in the *Juno*, I had observed that the cabin made but a very sorry appearance, with, at table, scarcely any plate to be seen. The whole establishment was the humblest I had as yet met in a captain's apartments. Consequently I could not help making my inward reflections upon the change; but made no remarks. Whilst my friend and I were examining the fine things before us, he stopped before a very handsome hand-organ, and drawing my attention to it, 'Look here,' he said, pointing to his name on it; 'this was sold to the Princess of Wales at my warehouse only a few days ago. I was not prepared to meet with it here,'—my companion being the proprietor of a pianoforte establishment. When he made that circumstance known to me, I was as much surprised at hearing of his profession as he was at the discovery of the organ. On all other occasions I had met him at his residence in the Adelphi, where he entertained most hospitably, and was in other respects a perfect gentleman.

When I became acquainted with the officers of the *Africaine*, they told me that the Captain had daily communications, when fitting out in the river, with the Princess of Wales, who resided at Blackheath.[1] There was a certain servant who came from that residence very often, but never empty-handed. There were also two youngsters on board, supposed to be protégés of H.R.H.'s, for whom things were sent: so it was said, but what became of them is another affair. One day a messenger of the Princess's called upon Capt. Manby's agent and left £300 to his account, declaring it publicly in the office before all the clerks. I mention those things that you may understand how much my Captain relied upon that lady's influence to obtain my promotion.[2]

Our Captain put in to Solebay to set up the rigging, and he, being a regular sportsman, went on shore with his fowling piece and his spaniels to try his luck, but left orders that no one else was to go out of the ship. In the afternoon four or five of the Mids came to request I would allow them to take a ramble on shore. I told them I could not. However, they entreated me to place the jolly boat at their disposal for only a couple of hours, and made such fine promises that, having imposed upon them a promise upon honour that they would not be away more than the time mentioned, I let them take the boat. One of the Mids in particular made himself responsible for the whole party—*i.e.* four to row and one to steer. Away they went and, as the landing place was not far from the ship, I could see with my glass all that passed. Not long after they had been on shore, the Mid who was left in charge of the boat quitted it, and the boat was left exposed to the surges of the sea on the beach. I had no other boat out, and was obliged to make a signal to the Captain's boat, then on shore, which

---

[1] As titular Ranger of Greenwich Park, she had, for residence, Montague House, at the extreme south-west corner of it, and facing on to Blackheath. This house, since demolished, should not be confused with either its neighbour, the present Ranger's House, or the present Montague House on Dartmouth Hill.

[2] What W.H.D. has to say about the Princess and Capt. Manby may be tittle-tattle: but he was not the first, and by no means the only, contemporary to link their names together.

luckily was attended to. It came alongside, and I directed it to go and tow off the jolly boat. That service was scarcely performed when the Captain made his appearance, and when he returned to the ship 'Up anchor' was the first order given. The Mids found their way on board in a shore boat, and you may suppose they received from me the censure they deserved. 'This, gentlemen,' I said to them, 'is Honour. How can I ever trust you again?' I told the one who had made himself responsible that he should not again go on shore, and if he attempted to obtain leave of absence from the Captain without my knowledge, I would try him by a court martial. That settled him. Had the jolly boat been stove, I should have had some words with the Captain for disobedience of orders. How is it possible when you meet such conduct to trust to any about you? These were gentlemen!

From Solebay we repaired to our old station off Helvoetsluys, where we found the two French frigates in the same position in which we left them. I had been on board the *Africaine* about two months, and was becoming daily better acquainted with the crew I had to control. The Captain scarcely ever gave any orders, but left the whole management of the ship to me. On one or two occasions I nearly got into a scrape by steering too near to the Flemish sands: once I scarcely prevented her from running on the shoals of the Lemon and Oar. In the midst of all these doings I could not help noticing sulky looks occasionally from both the officers and ship's company. They thought I had too much influence, more than became my station. All this I could not help. However, I watched for an opportunity of mentioning the subject to the Captain, and requested him to let it be known that all my arrangements were sanctioned by him. In compliance with this hint he seized a favourable moment for doing so. But he acted on that occasion in a very strange manner. The ship's company was ordered up, and he appeared on deck with a brace of pistols in his belt. Then, addressing the seamen on a very different subject from what I expected, he blustered away in a most extraordinary manner. No one knew, scarcely, what he meant, excepting that he was captain of the ship, and cautioned them to be very guarded in their proceedings towards him. They were then ordered below and, after a few more capers from our chief, he retired to his cabin. He gave ample proofs that pomp and vanity controlled him.

The *Leda* was still with us, her Captain (Honeyman[1]) being the senior officer. We continued to watch every motion of the enemy's

[1] Robert Hon(e)yman, Lt. 21/10/1790; Cdr. 13/8/96; Capt. 10/12/98; R-Ad. 27/5/1825; V-Ad. 10/1/37; Ad. 19/2/47.

port. I boarded a great many neutral vessels coming out of it, and by degrees obtained very correct information of the position of the two French frigates. This induced me to propose to Capt. Manby to secure four of the largest fishing vessels with which we were in daily contact, and, by placing 50 British seamen on board of each, well armed and with a certain proportion of officers under my orders, I engaged to go in and cut out the two French ships of war, with 100 men from the *Leda* and an equal number from our own ship. When I communicated my plan to the pilot, who was an Englishman, he said it was perfectly practicable and that he would attend me on such an occasion. Volunteers soon came forward, but our Captain could not be persuaded to take any active part in the undertaking. The wind at that time was favourable, continuing in the north quarter for several days. There was a small channel that led into the port by the north, and easily entered at night by small vessels. Under such circumstance there would be no difficulty in laying them alongside the enemy. 100 brave fellows from each ship would board them and, cutting the cables, would drift out to sea to the southward. If Sir Sidney Smith had been there, I make no doubt, he would have encouraged th attempt.

We had not been long here when Capt. M. communicated to me the substance of a letter he had received from the Princess of Wales, wherein she stated she had applied to Lord St. Vincent for my promotion, and he promised to follow up H.R.H.'s influence. I too had written to my Father requesting him to obtain an interview with the First Lord of the Admiralty through the medium of Mr. Marsden. He did so, and was well received by his Lordship, who promised not to lose sight of me. As I was afterwards informed, he told my Father that he could not promote me in England at that moment without an action: but, if he chose, he would send me to Lord Nelson, to whom he would send instructions to provide for me the first opportunity. However, time passed, and we continued at our usual avocations, taking a view of the Frenchmen every other day. We also sent our boats inshore to try and pick up some straggling vessels, but without success. As the Captain was in constant correspondence with the Princess, he would at times read some of these letters to me. They were written in French, and as he was not wel. acquainted with that language, he would frequently apply to me for an explanation of certain expressions. By that means I ascertainec that H.R.H. was exerting herself in my behalf.

I am now arrived at the period which threw all my prospects as it

were into oblivion: at an event so totally unexpected that I fear I
shall not be able to relate it in a manner sufficiently strong to point
out the injury I have sustained by it. About the 18th of this month a
Packet came to Capt. Honeyman of the *Leda*. Capt. Manby was
signalled to attend on board of her. When he returned, he brought us
our letters, and I received a message from Lord St. Vincent, through
his private secretary, Mr. Parker, wherein he proposed to send me to
Lord Nelson for promotion. Capt. Manby and I had a long consultation on the subject. The Packet had left us, and I required a couple of
days to decide what had better be done. I naturally concluded that,
when the First Lord of the Admiralty took so much interest in my
behalf, I could not long remain without the desired object. I had lost
my advancement three times in the former war by being on a foreign
station. Consequently I was not overanxious to be sent there again.
However, in this instance, appearances were more favourable. Lord
St. Vincent's patronage with Lord Nelson, I thought, was not likely
to fail. Moreover, I was certain of Lady Hamilton's influence in my
behalf. It was then finally settled between my Captain and myself
that I was to accept Lord St. Vincent's proposal.

The next day, after these arrangements had been made, another
Packet hove in sight, bringing despatches to the senior officer. The
signal was again thrown out for our Captain to attend on board the
Leda. Lord Keith had sent a letter addressed to the Dutch Commodore lying in Helvoetsluys. He directed that an intelligent officer
should be selected, and sent in with it under a Flag of Truce. On that
occasion Capt. Manby insisted upon my being the most efficient
officer to perform that duty, having, as he said, so often been employed on that duty before. It was accordingly settled between the
two captains that I was to be the bearer of the said letter; and when
our Captain returned to the ship I received my instructions to quit
the *Africaine* the next morning at 6 o'clock.

(4) 'FLAG OF TRUCE'

July 1803–September 1803

At the hour fixed I left my frigate in the *Leda's* boat. The Mid who
had received orders to attend me not being punctual to his time, I
shoved off without him.[1] I had provided myself with something like a

---

[1] His name was Hunter. See below, p. 42.

sandwich, and a volume of Shakespeare's plays, expecting to be away altogether about four hours. Over the foresail I spread the Dutch flag and over the mainsail the English. My boat sailed inshore in capital style with a fine breeze, and I had got well inside of the anchorage before there appeared to be any notice taken of me by the Dutch frigate. However, all at once I observed a stir on board both the Dutch and the French ships. Two boats approached in great haste. The French one boarded me first. But when I showed the Frenchman that my despatch was addressed to the Dutch Commodore he saw it was not for him. Having lowered my sails, I handed it over to the Dutch officer, who invited me into his boat, and by him I was conveyed to his chief. By him I was courteously received in his cabin. When he opened the despatch, he remarked that it was not of much consequence[1] but that he should send it to the Hague, and I was to wait for an answer.

He ordered some lunch for me during which, in his conversation, he made use of some very strong language against the English Government for going to war. Some expressions were so offensive that I asked him if he intended to insult me. 'I came here,' I said, 'on a sacred duty, but not to hear my Sovereign abused. If I were not in your power you would not dare to use such language.' I pointed to my sword, and gave him to understand that I knew how to use it, and that I should not submit to any further remarks of that nature. The tone in which I addressed him had its weight, but, although he changed his bearing, he frequently repeated we should soon repent our having commenced hostilities. I merely replied that I was not sent to discuss politics with him. Having taken some refreshment, I was informed that I was to be sent to await the reply to my despatch on board a small schooner lying in the outer part of the Roads. The weather being extremely sultry, I objected to the size of the vessel. 'If you cannot allow me to remain here,' I said, 'send me to the French frigates.' 'Very well,' he said, 'I will send you there.' Previous to my leaving him he remarked, 'You have come here to see what is going on. I hope you will not be disappointed.' 'You are quite mistaken on that head,' I replied. 'I have been off here some time, and know all your forces as well as you do. I have obtained all the information required from the numerous vessels I have boarded.' I then took my leave of Commodore Valterbeek—that being his name. He sent me to the French Commodore, who would not receive me. All the seamen of his ship hissed me when alongside, and made

[1] For its nature, see below, p. 61.

use of plenty of abusive language against England and the English.
I was finally taken to the Dutch schooner, Lieut. De Mann, where I
was kept in a sort of confinement. The weather was oppressively hot,
and, to prevent my seeing anything, the Dutch officer spread canvas
curtains all round his vessel, which increased the heat by preventing
the circulation of air. I was, I confess, much vexed at this detention,
and, not having any change of linen, I suffered in bodily comfort.
The officer under whose charge I was placed was a portly person.
Having served some time in the West Indies, he appeared desirous of
soothing the annoyance I could not help expressing at what appeared
to me a useless delay, as the answer to my despatch might as easily
be sent to the English Commodore by one of their own boats. I
passed a very unpleasant night. My boat and crew had been sent in
some other direction quite unknown to me.

Lieut. De Mann, who said he had taken a passage in one of our
West India ships to England, thought he knew a great deal of our
naval discipline, and was fond of making remarks on it. He was quite
certain that if he fell in with one of our ships of war on a Saturday
night he would capture her, under the conviction that the whole
crew, being in a perfect state of inebriety, would not be able to defend
themselves: to which I replied, 'If you are so certain of success on a
Saturday night, I hope you may attack the vessel I command. I
think you will find yourself woefully mistaken.'

Two or three days having passed, my mind was not much at ease
under such detention. The sultry weather continuing, the officer in
command, being himself, I suppose, a sufferer by it, did not surround
the schooner any longer with curtains. Their removal was a great
relief to my confined position. The Dutch Commodore one day
exercised his boats, manned and armed, at boarding vessels. They
came to the schooner and, I thought, cut a very ridiculous figure.

After eight days passed in the most uncomfortable confinement,
its termination appeared at hand. About 3 o'clock on the afternoon of
the 28th, I saw my boat being towed towards the schooner, and it
soon came alongside. Next my crew was brought. There was also a
small galliot in motion, which was anchored close to us. Shortly
afterwards a Dutch officer came on board and delivered to me the
answer to my despatch, telling me that I was at liberty to return to
my ship. So soon as my men had stepped the masts in my boat and
were ready for making sail, I took leave of the lieutenant under
whom I had been placed, and, stepping into it, ordered the bowman
to shove off. But somehow or other, whether by intention or not I

had not time to inquire, the painter was still fast on board the schooner. As he could not loosen it, I rushed forward and, drawing my sabre, which was a very sharp one, was in the act of cutting it when I was boarded by a large French launch full of armed men, the officer of which ordered me to lower my sail and surrender. When he saw me hesitate, he ordered his crew, some of them soldiers, to point their muskets at me; then said he should fire if I attempted any resistance. Under such circumstances, my seamen not being armed, and seeing no chance of getting away, I was obliged to yield. I was then handed into his boat and conveyed on board the galliot already mentioned where the Flag of Truce was hoisted, the French officer acquainting me that I was to remain on board of her until further orders. I found that there were no provisions in this vessel, or any accommodation suitable to myself and crew. I remonstrated upon the impropriety of such proceeding towards an helpless officer: that I had no money nor wearing apparel, and that to be placed in such a position was totally at variance with the usage of civilized nations. The officer at length returned to his Commodore, and delivered to him the objections I had made of being kept on board of the galliot.

About an hour afterwards I was removed with my men to the French frigate, *la Furieuse* of 46 guns, the commandant's name, Topsent. After the usual presentation, he informed me that the French Government had communicated to ours their wish that all intercourse by Flags of Truce should take place through the port of Morlaix. Moreover, he explained, such a notice had been sent to England the day before I had made my appearance. In reply I acquainted him that the British Government did not know it, as the vessel which passed us on the day to which he alluded could not have reached London in time to make that arrangement with the distant naval ports of the Kingdom. Consequently I had been sent in trusting to the usual courtesy observed towards Flags of Truce. 'Besides,' said I, 'I came to the Dutch and not to you.' After a few more observations on both sides, the Second Captain—as he was called: with us the Senior Lieutenant—invited me below, and I became acquainted with his messmates. This was an act so diametrically opposed to the customs of war that I could only await patiently the result of the French Commodore's report to his government of my detention. The Flag of Truce was kept flying on board the galliot. The Packet that had passed the *Africaine*, coming from Helvoetsluys the day before I was sent on this duty, contained the remaining part of our Minister's establishment. We had boarded her, but obtained no information relating to Flags of Truce from that vessel. The official despatches on board, if any, were of course under seal.

Here then I was, detained in the most uncomfortable position imaginable. When I quitted the *Africaine* I had left all the property in my cabin unlocked, a gold watch and chain hanging up, a portable library, loose cash in my drawers which were not secured, all at the mercy of my servant. When I returned to England no watch was to be found, or the cash; and a considerable quantity of things were missing. That loss, never being recovered, must, I should think, give me some claim upon my country. But more serious losses were to befall me afterwards.

In my new unpleasant position the days passed away without any apparent change in my fate. The French officers with whom I lived were agreeable companions only in a certain sense. When they talked about the invasion of England they were not very nice on that subject. Their enthusiasm on these occasions, whether real or pretended, I could hardly make out. The First Consul was the absorbing idol, and there was no end to the repetition of 'le premier Roi fut un soldat heureux.' So they alluded to him, and also under the soubriquet of 'Le Petit Caporal,' which was constantly bestowed upon him. The post brought the letters and newspapers generally about 4 o'clock in the afternoon. The officers would then assemble in the Captain's cabin and discuss the contents. It was also an anxious moment for me, but disappointment was my lot. When they had made up their minds what stories they were to circulate, they would surround me and commence a long detail of their naval successes in various quarters. These daily repetitions became extremely unpleasant to me. On one occasion, they acquainted me that our frigate, the *Juno*, had been captured. As I happened to know that she was well officered and manned, having been on board of her during her fitting out, I asked a great number of questions. Unfavourable replies were made to all of them: which in the end annoyed me most seriously, and I could not help exclaiming in angry tones, 'That frigate is one of our best manned. Her captain is a gallant officer, and if she is taken as you say she is it must have been by an overwhelming force.' 'No,' was the answer, 'One of our small frigates captured her.' 'Then,' said I, 'it was probably a merchant ship of that name.' 'No,' they said, 'It was a ship of war.' 'Well then gentlemen,' I observed, 'there must have been a great change come over my country in a few days; for since I have been here you have related to me nothing but a series of—to me—most painful disasters.

If they be true, old England is no longer the same as when I left it. To tell you that I do not believe your statements would be rudeness, but in reality I cannot place any confidence in them, and I have to request in future that you will keep all these tales to yourselves.' I then withdrew, in a temper which they noticed was not of the best. A day or two after this, as they perceived I kept aloof from them, one of the lieutenants came and apologized for all that he had said about the *Juno*. It was all a mistake, he said, and hoped I would not think any more about it. I afterwards ascertained that the whole string of captures and events were infamous falsehoods: and I in consequence regulated myself accordingly. The Commodore invited me occasionally to dine with him. He had been brought up in the Merchant Service. He was a lusty man, and although on all occasions he had plenty to say for himself in behalf of his own country, which was to humble ours to the lowest pitch of degradation, I could not make him out a gentleman.

Continuing so long among these officers, I became acquainted with their plans and arrangements. They were better paid than our naval officers. Table money was allowed them, and each individual in rotation received at the end of the week the overplus of that allowance: this in addition to their pay, which was quite distinct from their mess expenses, whereas with us our mess money absorbed the principal part of our pay. There was no regular breakfast. Everyone found his own just as it suited his convenience. There was always a very comfortable good dinner, which when ended, the officers would say 'Voilà encore un dîner que les anglais n'auront pas.' The French ships of war also were allowed charts, nautical instruments and spy glasses: not so with us, at that period, though latterly the Admiralty found it necessary to allow charts and chronometers for the naval service. Having had plenty of opportunities to observe the discipline of this French ship, I became thoroughly convinced that, had I been allowed to make the attempt of boarding them during the night, I should have succeeded and brought them out. I passed the nights in a cot slung up close to the cabin windows, and as I could not sleep much I heard all that was going on. The fishing vessels which I intended to use in that expedition were passing close to the *Furieuse* every night, and as they were accustomed to their sailing by there was no suspicion. They were hailed, but no further notice taken of them, a clear proof that my plan was a feasible one.

The troops that had been assembled here in the transports already alluded to—two regiments, the 92nd, I recollect, being one of them—had been landed: but the officers frequently came to visit those of the frigate, accompanied by ladies (their wives, I had reason to believe). However, the French Revolution had left so many of its evils behind that I saw nothing to admire in the freedoms adopted towards those females. My idle hours were generally occupied with books, and occasionally piquet, in which game, to the annoyance of my opponents, I was generally successful. The month was drawing to a close, but no notice, as far as I could discern, had been taken by the French Government of my detention. The purser, Mons. Querelle, had for some time shown a disposition to establish a friendly intercourse with me. When he began to suspect that I should be detained and sent into France, he made many confidential communications to me. He had been in the Royalist army, and was staunch to that cause in which he had been wounded. He suspected that I should be sent to Paris. He highly disapproved of the measures adopted towards me, and appeared anxious of putting me in the way of effecting my escape. He had a brother residing in Paris who, he said, would be useful to me in such an undertaking, and he gave me several notes in cypher to give to him should I be sent there. A friend in need is a friend indeed. The other officers suspected him, and we were obliged to be very circumspect in our meetings.

As the subject daily turned upon the invasion of England, the French officers hoped I would, at parting, give them certificates of their friendly bearing towards me. In the event of being made prisoners in London, they might produce them, to induce my friends there to be attentive to them in return. Whether this was a joke or a reality I did not trouble myself to ascertain, but the remark was frequently repeated, evidently because they expected having a chance of being made prisoners in England: for, with all their bombast, there were moments when they would let out expressions indicating strong doubts of their success in such an undertaking.

My boat lay under the stern of the frigate, and I often thought of lowering myself down into her at night when the tide was running out, cutting the painter and taking my chance by drifting seawards. Once I nearly did this, but as I could not ascertain the exact course of the current I thought the risk too great, and held back. But it was impossible to be insensible to my fate. What a change had suddenly been cast upon my prospects! The day before I left the *Africaine* I had received a proposal from the First Lord which was to lead to early promotion. What could I reckon upon now, on board of an enemy's ship? In the midst of all this ill luck I was attacked with a violent fit of the Walcheren fever and confined to my cot. Two days having passed without there appearing any chance of its leaving me, I began to doubt the abilities of the French surgeon. My teeth rattled frightfully, and I was determined to try a remedy of my own. Feeling reduced to extreme weakness, I sent for the steward and asked if he could supply me with a bottle of good bodied wine. He said he could do so. I then directed him to have it well spiced and mulled, making him promise not to let the Doctor know. All this he faithfully performed. I asked for a good lump of bread, then, mixing them together, swallowed the whole. Its effect was to send me into a sound sleep and perspiration. The next morning I awoke in perfect health, but in extreme debility. When the Surgeon came to visit me, 'you have,' he said, 'deviated from my orders, and if any unpleasant consequences are the result, it is your own fault. I shall not be responsible.' 'Certainly not,' I said. 'I am getting well, and I have no fault to find.'

An hour or two later, a small Dutch schuyt, elegantly fitted, was noticed coming towards *La Furieuse*. She bore a Dutch gentleman, who inquired for me. I was still in my cot. He delivered to me a letter from my Father, who informed me that, no sooner had he heard of my detention, than he had established a pecuniary remittance for me at Rotterdam with the House of Messrs. Havart and Plemp. The gentleman who gave me this letter was one of the firm, and had hastened down to offer his assistance. This unexpected intelligence brought the tears to my eyes, and I at length thought that my prospects were brightening. I lost no time in relating to the amiable person my real position. However, he felt uneasy whilst the French officers were present. He put his finger to his lips, and I, taking the hint, changed the subject and explained my wants. The first was some port wine, to help me recover my strength. He then supplied me with cash, and, giving me the address of his house, departed, assuring me that all my wants should be punctually attended to. The arrival of this vessel made a strong impression on the whole of the French officers, and I noticed that their entire deportment towards me was changed for the better. They were more respectful, thinking me a person of some consequence. But with all this I was still in detention. To me, the most remarkable event of that period was Capt. Manby's sending to me, by one of the fishing boats, a parcel of English newspapers. Our two frigates were still cruising off the port, and we saw them daily. In looking over these papers, I saw a full account of my detention related. So far so good: but if my Captain had found it easy to send me a bundle of newspapers, why not, I thought, send me a few shirts and a suit of clothes? One could have been done as well as the other. But it was certainly satisfactory to know that a proper statement had been made public of the way my Flag of Truce had been received and captured.

Having quite recovered the effects of my fever, I left my cot with the knowledge that I had letters of credit at Rotterdam, and my spirits were in the ascendant. I began to hope for better things. A couple of days after this, orders came to the French Commodore to move his ship up one of the small rivers, or canals, in the neighbourhood as the ship was wanted for more active service. I witnessed all the preparations for this change of position. All the guns were taken out, lightening her considerably. When they had brought her to the line of flotation necessary, she prepared for sailing and I was removed to the other frigate, *La Libre*, 36 guns, Capt. Bourdet. When the Commodore's ship passed us, the crews of both manned the shrouds and cheered each other, but very tamely, nothing like the hearty hurrahs of the British seamen.

Capt. Bourdet was more attentive to me than the Commodore. He was a different character, and appeared to have more feeling. So soon as our ships outside noticed the disappearance of one of the frigates, they came very close in one morning: so near that the *Libre's* captain expected to be attacked. He hove up one of his anchors and prepared to move higher up the harbour. Whilst these operations were going on, the fearful anxiety of the officers and French seamen was so clearly depicted in their countenances that I could scarcely refrain from laughing, and my boat's crew, not being able to control their contemptuous feelings, launched out into satirical jack-tar jokes. These offended Capt. Bourdet, who spoke to me, and I advised him to send them below, to prevent any further acrimony. He did so, and I admonished them, desiring them not to commit any further act which would cause irritation. They accordingly kept quiet. The Frenchmen on that occasion cut but a very sorry figure: much more than I could suppose, as that nation has at all times been noted for bravery. When they ascertained that our ships were not coming in, their usual moorings were reoccupied.

When Lieut. De Mann heard of my being removed to *La Libre*, he came to see me and expressed a very lively interest in my fate. But he felt obliged to conceal his real sentiments while in the presence of the French officers. The month of September had now come, and no appearance of my release: the Flag of Truce still kept displayed on board the galliot. My life was one of extreme discomfort. I had several conversations on this subject with Capt. Bourdet, but to no purpose. At length, when I had been with him about a fortnight, I proposed to him to allow me to go on shore on my Parole of Honour. He entered kindly into all my views and, the next day, acquainted me that arrangements had been made by the authorities, and that I was to be allowed to reside at Breda on my Parole of Honour. A written document to that effect was drawn out, which I signed: and shortly afterwards a military officer came on board to take charge of me and escort me to Rotterdam. The senior lieutenant of *La Libre* had formed a sort of attachment towards me, and requested permission to accompany me to the said town. When De Mann knew that I was going to Breda, he gave me a letter of introduction to two of his sisters, maiden ladies residing there. I was soon put on shore, and in the course of the day arrived at my destination.

One of *La Libre's* lieutenants, who had been directed by her captain to attend to all my wants, had so far ingratiated himself in my good opinion that, previous to leaving the ship, I requested a favour of him, upon honour, at the moment of my departure. He faithfully promised to comply with my wishes. I begged him to deliver to the Dutch Commodore the despatch sent to me from the Hague. It had been in my pocket the whole time, the cover nearly worn out, and I thought it had better be returned than kept any longer in my possession.

IX

CAPTIVITY

SEPTEMBER 1803–SEPTEMBER 1807

(*aet.* 23-27)

IX

CAPTIVITY

SEPTEMBER 1803–SEPTEMBER 1807

(*aet.* 23–27)

Summary of the 323 pages of Manuscript omitted here

POOR Dillon was destined not to set eyes upon the sea again for almost exactly four years. In the interests of economy it is necessary to summarise his adventures during this period, on the grounds that the great majority of them cannot be regarded as sea-adventures. This course is inevitable, but it is in many ways a pity; for the 323 pages of his manuscript here epitomised contain a picture of life in wartime France in general, and in the prison town of Verdun in particular, which is full of interests of widely differing kinds. Here only the main *general* features are summarised: but, in accordance with the spirit of the whole work, a rather greater proportion of space is allowed for topics which touch upon naval affairs and naval personalities.

He did not stay long in Rotterdam, but was moved in the course of this same month of September to Breda. Here he met many Dutchmen who were strongly anti-French, and he had several schemes of escape put to him by such people. On the whole he resisted them, mainly because of his Parole of Honour: but in one case he weakened, and continued somewhat desultory preparations, until the Dutchman, not he himself, backed out.

Early in October he was moved, under escort, to Antwerp, no reason for the change being given. Hence, after a mere day or two of residence, he was sent on to Valenciennes, still in October and still with no reason for the move mentioned. He was now in France, and here he first met the true English 'détenus'—'not Prisoners of War, but detained while travelling upon the faith of the passports granted to them by the French Government—an act totally at variance with the usages of all civilized nations.' (The Mayor of Antwerp had already defended this act of Napoleon's, so abhorrent to the British, in this ingenious, though hardly ingenuous, way: 'He dwelt with strong expressions upon the hospitable kindness of Bonaparte in keeping all the English in France, instead of turning out the French, as we had done.') Here he met Capt. Miller, whom he knew in the West Indies (Vol. I, pp. 262, 292), and Col. Abercromby, son of the famous general with whom W.H.D. had served at St. Lucia (see below, pp. 45–6). Both later shared his captivity at Verdun.

He now tried writing to Tallyrand, asking him to attempt to secure his release, but all that happened was that the letter was forwarded to Berthier, the War Minister. The only result of all this seems to have been that Dillon was sent to Lunéville, to join the true prisoners of war. This pleased him at the time because he thought it much more likely that, from there, he would obtain a formal 'exchange'. What he did not yet realise was his danger of falling between two stools: which, as we shall see, was at least one factor in his long detention. He was certainly not a 'détenu', but, in the eyes of the British Government, at any rate, he was not a 'prisoner of war' either: in their view he was in a category all by himself—an 'illegally-detained officer.' And once they allowed themselves to negotiate his exchange for a *legally*-detained officer they were seriously weakening their case: as it were 'condoning a felony'.

He now had a great chance of escaping. He obtained leave from the Governor of Valenciennes to travel unescorted to Lunéville, and that officer made him sign an undertaking that, if he escaped while en route, he would hand the agreement to the British Government 'to claim the release of an officer of equivalent rank.' He realised—afterwards—that 'this document was the equivalent of an exchange'; but he seems to have been so sure that, on reaching Lunéville, he would be the subject of a regular one, that he failed to act upon it. This he bitterly regretted later, as the months of his captivity turned into years.

He never reached Lunéville. But he had a long and adventurous journey, first to Verdun, and then to Metz. Here he conceived the project of going off his scheduled route to visit the relatives of his mother-in-law, who resided at Thionville. Their family name was Dinot. He applied for leave from the general in command at Metz, a certain Ferino, an Italian by birth. On discovering that W.H.D. was the nephew of Col. Frank Dillon of the Cuirassiers of the Austrian army (see Vol. I, pp. XII, XVI), the veteran 'closed upon me, threw his arms round my shoulders and exclaimed, "Frank Dillon was the warmest friend I ever had in this world."' So W.H.D. was allowed to go to Thionville, where he made the acquaintance of M. Dinot. Both

Ferino and Dinot sympathised heartily with Dillon's fate, and both held out hopes of securing his release. With that end in view, Dinot accompanied him back to Metz. Unfortunately, however, it transpired that the general had no use for Dinot, and when he found that he was W.H.D.'s friend he washed his hands of the whole matter. Dinot wanted Dillon to come back and live with him at Thionville— for a prisoner in the heart of enemy territory the latter still had remarkable freedom. But he was still bent upon Lunéville, with its prospect of a regular exchange. So he refused, and, taking the next (which should have been the last) stage to Lunéville, he found himself at Nancy.

Here he had a relatively enjoyable time, meeting three very congenial Englishmen, one of whom was destined to be his close companion for a long time—a certain Mr. Sevright, who had been our Agent of Packets at Helvoetsluys. Like all other British subjects under sixty, this gentleman (a civilian) had been arrested: but in his case the cause was rather a special one. His own account of it, as given by W.H.D., was this:

> He then related to me that it was he who apprized our Minister of the destination of the troops on board the French transports lying in that port (Helvoetsluys): and upon that information Mr. Addington based the Royal Message to the House of Commons on March 8. Herewith I transmit his own statement of the affair. The Mayor and civil authorities of Helvoetsluys gave a public dinner, to which the commanding officer of the French troops was invited. During the repast he was asked when he would quit for his destination, the impression being that he was bound for Louisiana. In his reply he jocosely said, 'I know you all think I am going there, but that is not the case. I'm going to India. My soldiers are all choice men, and when we get there they will be made officers, to instruct the Indian troops in the European method of warfare, to act against the English.' That assertion caused a sensation, but, the conversation taking another turn, it was not further noticed. 'However,' said Mr. Sevright, 'as I happened to be one of the dinner party, I thought it my duty to send an account of what I had heard to my Government. When Bonaparte read our Minister's assertion in the House, he desired his Agent of Police to find out the origin of it. That individual in due time reported the French colonel's speech at the dinner mentioned. He was soon removed from his command. I was arrested soon after, and here I am. But fortunately I had time to secure all my papers of importance and send them by my servant to England. I expected some further enquiries to be made, and I acted accordingly. My house was searched

by the *gens d'armes* in the night. They secured all my remaining papers and finally made me their prisoner.' As these details were never generally known to the British nation, I have related them to the best of my recollection, and, if they are not correct in every detail, you may rely upon the substance being so.

Their gay time at Nancy was suddenly cut short when Sevright and Dillon received peremptory instructions to proceed (in W.H.D.'s case to return) to Verdun, since the Governor had just had a general order to send to Verdun 'all the Englishmen under the denomination of gentlemen,' to be concentrated there. This, it seems, was because so many were contriving to escape from isolated prisons elsewhere in France.

Again they obtained leave to proceed to Verdun unescorted. This time it was Sevright who 'engaged his word of honour that we would find our way thither free from surveillance.' Once again an escape, this time across the German border, was mooted— by Sevright, 'the language of that country being well known to him. But no measures were taken. I thought it would have been a hazardous affair. He had most solemnly engaged to surrender himself at Verdun. I had made no promise of the kind.'

It is gradually, but inevitably, borne in upon the reader that Dillon was very far from being 'escape-minded.' Indeed, though he naturally never admits as much, his attitude to any such form of adventure was positively timid. Sometimes, it is true, he sheltered himself behind his impeccable 'honour' in the matter of parole, but not by any means always: for sometimes he was not strictly held by it, and sometimes he toyed with a project even when he was. What seemed a heaven-sent chance came his way in July 1805. A faithful French servant of his—a stout Royalist—had a relative who was accustomed to making regular trips into Holland with loads of wicker baskets. This man offered to take Dillon as one of his 'gang.' Those friends in whom he confided all thought it a good and safe scheme, and he himself, considering that his French was good enough to enable him to pass himself off as a native, at length agreed to try. Whether he was free to do so, as far as Parole of Honour was concerned, is not clear—he does not mention the matter. Certainly that was not why he relinquished the plan at the last moment: that looks much more like a failure of nerve. The basket-maker, thinking no doubt of his own safety, would not take him into his company until the party was clear of the town itself, so that W.H.D. was left to find his own way out. This prospect proved sufficient to daunt

him, and he very suddenly records: 'After one or two more delibera-
tions, the attempt appeared surrounded with so many dangers that
I finally abandoned all idea of entering upon it.'

He can hardly have it both ways. Either he is greatly exaggerating his linguistic powers, or else he is very over-careful. Mixing with a
crowd of basket-carriers, disguised, and speaking in accent and in-
tonation indistinguishable from a Frenchman, he would seem to
have run but small risk of detection. But he would not try: indeed,
from first to last never did.

Again, in November 1806, a chance came his way. His remarkable
old friend, the Abbé Feulat (see below), made what, for one of his
cloth, can only be described as a remarkable suggestion, and proceeded, with W.H.D.'s concurrence, to put it into operation.
Numbering among his friends a very respectable Verdun printer, the
Abbé persuaded him, for a fee of twenty louis (paid by W.H.D.), to
print a complete forged passport. This was in the summer, and Dillon
—according to himself—proposed to await the dark days of winter
before making the attempt. In November—again according to himself—he was on the very point of carrying out the scheme: had
indeed assembled a complete disguise and hired a peasant as a guide,
when he was assailed with another bout of his cutaneous complaint:
then suspected the honesty of his peasant, then thought he was being
watched by a gendarme—and then gave up the scheme altogether.

We must return now to 1803. With nothing attempted, and
perhaps a little tamely, on December 4 he and Sevright reached
Verdun, a town destined to be his enforced home for three and a half
years. He was the first naval officer to appear there, but Capt.
(afterwards Ad. Sir Jahleel) Brenton,[1] captured when his frigate
Minerva grounded off Cherbourg harbour (2/7/1803), soon joined him,
and became the prisoner-representative of the Senior Service. W.H.D.
and Sevright found comfortable lodgings in a widow's house in the
lower town: but the whole place, he records, was dull, mean and
desperately poor.

He now devotes ten pages to a description and discussion of
Napoleon's action in detaining all Britons, including a 'true copy' of
the decree ordaining it:

St. Cloud, 2nd Prairial, 11th year of the Republic.

All the English enrolled in the Militia, from the age of 18 to 60,
holding a commission from his Britannic Majesty, who are at present

[1] See Vol. I, p. 156, note 1.

in France, shall be made Prisoners of War, to answer for the citizens of the Republic who have been arrested and made Prisoners of War by the vessels or subjects of his Britannic Majesty before the declaration of war.* The Ministers, each as far as it concerns him, are charged with the execution of the present decree.

BUONAPARTE, the First Consul.

He quotes instances of how the official French press, right up to the issuing of this edict, deliberately encouraged the British tourists to stay in France, pooh-poohing the timidity of those who feared possible arrest. The order, it seems, was implemented with remarkable suddenness, secrecy and efficiency:

> Scarcely had Lord Whitworth quitted Paris before the telegraph spread the order for the detention of his countrymen, and in one night, from Brussels to Montpelier, from Bordeaux to Geneva, all the British subjects were arrested. Travellers on the road to Spain, Germany or England, even those who were waiting at Calais for a favourable wind, shared the same fate. Some were called out of the theatres, others were waked in their beds to sign a paper declaring themselves prisoners of war.

He gives the circumstances of a number of these detentions, including those of Englishmen under eighteen and over sixty: including too the very bad case of Lord Elgin, returning home from his embassy in Constantinople. Yet, for all his treachery and efficiency (says Dillon), Napoleon was disappointed, expecting to seize many thousands 'whose expenses in France he naturally supposed would be beneficial to the tradesmen, etc.' He thinks that the actual number seized was less than 800. Much later, on hearing of his impending release, he discusses the whole subject of detention and prisoner-treatment again, giving many contrasting examples of the bad French and the good English attitudes to the subject. Nor is it surprising to find that he considers the British Government wrong and weak in not exacting reprisals—as, he says, other belligerents did. He was, he informs us, only the fourteenth officer to be exchanged in the first four and a half years of the Napoleonic War.

Inevitably a personage who looms large in his narrative is the French officer in command of the prisoners at Verdun, and he paints, gradually, a close-up portrait of him. It was a certain Wirion, a

---

* 'It is a notorious fact that no French vessels were captured before the declaration of war. But Bonaparte ruled the press in France, and cared not what appeared in the *Moniteur*, so long as it answered his purpose. He was always right, and everybody else wrong.' [See also above, p. 16, note 4.]

'general of the *Gens d'armerie*'—not, in W.H.D.'s eyes, a military officer at all. Both he and his wife were, according to our captive, products of the scum thrown up by the French Revolution. He was of mean birth and habits—he had started life as an attorney's clerk—and possessed no background at all: easily corrupted by his sudden and unlooked-for rise to power: a cad, now a bully, now a toady: venal in the extreme, and always 'on the make.' Though his high-spirited and well-educated charges no doubt made his task a very difficult one, there is so much body and inherent probability in Dillon's description of him and his wife, that it is hard not to believe it to be in the main true. One illustration of his normal procedure, typical of a score of others, must suffice. It concerns the General's conduct when asked to sanction a race-meeting organised by the *détenus*:

> When the day for the races was fixed, and some considerable sums staked on the different horses, he would unexpectedly give an order forbidding its taking place. The jockeys [amateur *détenus*, of course] were then obliged to assemble and consult what ought to be done: then depute one or two of their number to prevail on him to sanction their proceedings. The gendarme in waiting would reply that His Excellency was indisposed and he could not be seen—often an insolent answer was returned.
>
> A second deliberation takes place: a fresh deputation is the result. They call upon the aide de camp. He hems and hahs, laments the General's bad state of health, that he is quite out of temper: he should fear to incommode him by his intercession, etc., etc. At length, by degrees, having gained some ground, they venture to speak more plainly; and they agree to give fifty louis for the permission required. The folding doors are now opened. The General receives them graciously, but complains of ill-health not allowing him to receive them sooner: and while he is in conversation with one of the deputies, the other, having put fifty louis into his glove, contrives to drop it slyly into the General's hat, which, from its position, appeared to be placed to receive it. Now all the difficulties are at an end. The General wishes them good sport, and they retire.

Many of the *détenus* had their wives, and even daughters, with them, and they contrived to make the best of their captivity by setting up what was in effect a microcosm of English 'society,' with its various clubs, balls, gaming saloons, race-meetings, theatricals; even Church of England services, highly organised charitable committees, and schools for child prisoners—all as smug and class-conscious as though they were really back in dear old London. Here, needless to say, W.H.D. is in his element, and behaves exactly to type: resigning from at least two clubs because they have ceased to be as exclusive as he would like: explaining away, to his entire satisfaction, how he was blackballed from another; and purring with pleasure when introduced by Col. Abercromby to his nephew Lord Yarmouth, who 'received me with great kindness, and a familiar intercourse was the result.' Yet the unpredictable rudeness and blusterings of General Wirion, and the incredible vulgarities of his lady, combined with the inevitable restrictions and frustrations of a closely-watched captivity, kept them from being either happy or even comfortable for long at a stretch. He gives in full the official regulations of 'surveillance,' and they are far from formalities. Moreover, Wirion made them even worse by his capricious and even dishonest interpretation of them, deliberately adding vexatious rules, such as reporting regularly, carrying lanterns at night, and threatening dire penalties when he said his regulations had been broken: penalties, however, which could usually be avoided if the offender was prepared to satisfy his greed with a cash payment.

It is gratifying to learn that the General came to grief in the end. After Dillon's departure, Wirion's conduct was reported to the Emperor, who summoned him to Paris to stand his trial: and, on the day before it began, he blew his brains out in the Bois. His wife had all his worst traits, if possible in an even greater degree, coming, it would seem, from an even lower walk of life than her husband. What happened to her after his disgrace we are not told.[1]

Meanwhile more naval officers arrived—all the officers (except Capt. Philip Wilkinson[2]) of the frigate *Hussar*, wrecked near Ushant (February 1804); Capt. Edward Leveson Gower[3] and the officers of his frigate *Shannon*, wrecked off La Hogue (December 10, 1803); Cdr. Henry Gordon,[4] a *Thunderer* messmate of W.H.D.'s, captured by a French privateer when in command of the *Wolverine*—'an

---

[1] Wirion's disgrace occurred in 1808, and he was succeeded by a certain Courcelles —'a creature,' writes a sufferer in the *Naval Chronicle* (Vol. 31, p. 308), 'who trod in the vile footsteps of his predecessor.' He remained till 1811, to be succeeded by the Baron de Beauchesne, whom all the prisoners loved and respected. Lastly, when he died early in 1813, came Major de Meulan, of whom they had, if possible, an even higher opinion.

[2] Philip Wilkinson, Lt. 22/10/1790; Cdr. 30/3/94; Capt. 5/9/94; R-Ad. 4/12/1813. Had commanded the *Hermione* immediately before Capt. Pigot. For a very biased account of his character, and of the loss of the *Hussar*, see *The Adventures of John Wetherell*, ed. Forester.

[3] Edward Leveson Gower, Lt. 19/3/1793; Cdr. ?; Capt. 1/6/95; R-Ad. 4/6/1814.

[4] Henry Gordon, Lt. 13/7/1798; Cdr. 29/4/1802; Capt. 8/4/05; R-Ad. 17/8/40.

apology for a sloop of war' (March 1804); his old shipmate—one can hardly say friend—Macdougall, 2nd Lieutenant of the *Crescent*, captured in a merchant ship when invalided home from the West Indies; Lieut. (afterwards Capt. Sir) James Lucas Yeo (K.C.B.),[1] who was to make a name for himself in the American War of 1812–15; Lieut. Douglas, son of an admiral,[2] whom W.H.D. saved from imprisonment at the hands of Wirion; Dillon's old friend Dr. Grey of the *Glenmore* (see Vol. I, p. 337); Midshipman Hunter, the young man who ought to have accompanied W.H.D. on his 'Flag of Truce' mission (see p. 23); Spence, 3rd Lieutenant of the *Crescent*; and several others whom he knew but has not previously mentioned in his Narrative. It is a curious coincidence, as he remarks, that all three of the lieutenants of the *Crescent*—himself, Macdougall and Spence— found their ways separately to Verdun.

W.H.D. was not the man, however, to waste all his time on such frivolous pursuits as gambling and horse-racing. So he engaged the services of a certain French abbé named Feulat, with whom he read French and Latin classics. Of this old gentleman he became, rightly, very fond, and he leaves an admirable portrait of him. Later he learned German too, and used his linguistic acquirements in getting to know some of the local gentry, indulging also in their country pursuits. The most interesting one which he describes, perhaps, is an unusual form of lark-hunting with nets, in which sometimes as many as 1,200 birds were caught in an evening.

It is only too well known in our own day that the nerves of active-minded men are apt to become frayed beyond endurance under conditions of captivity: and W.H.D. records a number of incidents stemming from this cause. There were many insults, real or imaginary, and not a few duels. Even the naval officer contingent was not free from such squabbles among themselves, especially as the senior, Capt. Brenton, seems to have been a man of uncertain and rather dictatorial temper. Thus he took it upon himself to represent to the French authorities that Dillon was not entitled to the pitiful allowance of £2 per month made by them to prisoners of war of Dillon's rank, on the grounds that he did not strictly belong to that category. Brenton may have been technically in the right, but, under the

---

[1] Born 7/10/1782; made Acting Lieut. Sept. 1796 (while still 13), and confirmed 20/2/1797 (when 14). A *détenu*, not a P.O.W. Neither the *Naval Chronicle* (XXIV, 265) nor the *D.N.B.* mentions his imprisonment. Cdr. 21/6/1805; Capt. 19/12/07; d. 21/8/18.

[2] Billy Douglas—a real name this, apparently, not a nickname—who became full Admiral (of the Blue), 4/12/1813. *Cf.* below, pp. 84.

circumstances of Dillon's undoubtedly illegal detention, it sounds a mean and small-minded step to have taken. To W.H.D. it seemed, naturally, like adding insult to injury, and a long-sustained coolness sprang up between them. On another occasion Brenton, aided this time by Cdr. Gordon, committed an act which must seem worse than odd to the modern reader. A certain Sir B. Dixie, 'who had originally been in the Navy, but, inheriting a title and a fortune, had quitted it,' formed an ingenious scheme of escape:

> He went to bathe in the river. His clothes were left on the bank, he wishing it to be supposed that he had been drowned. Those friends who knew his plan, lamented his fate and were loud in their grief at his misfortune, wishing to mislead the gendarmes on the watch. And I have no doubt, if no informer had interfered, he would have succeeded in getting out of France. But I regret to say my friend Capt. Gordon, who happened to be of the bathing party that morning, and suspecting Dixie's motives, gave information to Capt. Brenton, who transmitted the same to General Wirion. Had Dixie been under his command, he would have been justified in following up the measure as a part of his duty. But, our Government having refused to acknowledge the *détenus* as lawful prisoners of war, it was not to be expected that a British naval officer, whose character is that of open-hearted generosity, would have assisted Wirion in violating the lawful usages of civilized nations against a countryman. . . . Wirion, upon receipt of the information, issued his orders accordingly, and his myrmidons were soon in quest of Dixie, who was overtaken in his flight and brought back to Verdun, then confined to the Citadel.

The *détenus*—and Dillon—protested formally to Brenton, and much bad blood was caused. Dixie, who was sent off to Bitche (the dreaded fortress for recaptured prisoners, where he was confined in a room with a Hanoverian Jew), determined to challenge Brenton when he got the chance: but whether he did W.H.D. never learned.

Later, when several more unsuccessful attempts had been made, Wirion caused a notice to be pinned up declaring that the French Government had ordained death by shooting for escapers who were caught. But W.H.D. does not make it clear whether this was really an edict of the Government or merely a whim of the General of Gendarmes. Nor is Dillon so shocked by it as might be expected. His comment is that, formerly, such an order might have been considered justified, but that, in more polite times, a more liberal plan was adopted by all civilised nations. Much later in the war, he adds, the French of all classes began to take pity on the wretched *détenus*, 'and many of them winked at, and in some guarded shape assisted, them in getting away.'

Later still (January 1805) Brenton and our author were reconciled. The occasion arose out of an effort by the British Government to get justice done to the Verdun captives. On August 20, 1804, it issued a strong demand for the liberation of all *détenus* in general, and of Brenton and Dillon in particular. It seems that, in Brenton's case, a French officer of equivalent rank had actually been released in exchange for him, but Brenton himself had not even been informed of it, still less liberated. W.H.D. then gives, verbatim, the Government's demand for his own release:

> I am next to advert to the capture and detention of Lieut. Dillon. Lieut. Dillon, of H.M. Frigate *L'Africaine*, was sent into Helvoet on the 20th July, 1803, in a six-oared cutter with a Flag of truce, and was there seized and detained with his crew. Upon a representation being made on the subject, a letter was received from the Officer commanding in the Texel, under date October 16th, 1803, to the Officer commanding His B.M. ships off that port,[1] stating that orders had been issued by the Council of the Batavian Navy to the Commanding Officer at Helvoet, on the 30th July preceding, for the entire release of the said Lieut., Flag of truce, and equipage: in consequence whereof he departed the same day: but that he was on his return carried back by a French armed boat, and transported on board the ship of the Commandant of a French Division stationed in the same port. It appears that remonstrances have been made by the Batavian Republic to the French Government for the liberation of Lieut. Dillon. But, notwithstanding these circumstances, Lieut. Dillon is still retained a Prisoner in the Territory of France, in open violation of every privilege in relation to Flags of truce, established and acknowledged by civilized nations. . . .
>
> It must be obvious to Mons. Rivière and to the French Minister of Marine under whom he acts how deeply His Majesty must be impressed by the already lengthened and unjust captivity of his subjects, and by the circumstance of Lieut. Dillon's detention and Capt. Wright's imprisonment, and how reasonable it is to expect an honourable redress in these points, previous to the establishment of a Cartel.
>
> (signed) Edward Cooke.
> Downing Street, August 28th, 1804.

When the English papers containing a copy of this remonstrance reached Verdun in the following January, these two highly injured

---

[1] In spite of a ten-day discrepancy in the date, this is almost certainly the letter printed below at p. 63.

men met by chance and made it up. W.H.D.'s comment on the
reconciliation is not uninteresting: 'It was certainly desirable to be
upon a good footing with the leading naval officer, as he was in some
shape or other in constant communication with the Admiralty and
the Transport Board.' It would be interesting to learn the channels of
communication, but here W.H.D. is silent.

In December 1804 Dillon began to consider the possibility of
applying to the Admiralty for promotion, even though he was still
in captivity—'as I was not placed in the same position as the officer
captured in action or wrecked upon the enemy's coast. I had therefore
no responsibility.' Here he was right in distinguishing himself from
the true prisoner of war. The rule was that the latter, having lost his
ship, would have to submit to a court martial upon return to England:
so that, unless or until formally acquitted, he could not be promoted.
But W.H.D. had no such ordeal to look forward to. He had lost
nothing but his liberty.

In February 1805 he took the next step, and very characteristic
it is:

> I sketched out a statement of my services, which Sevright put into
> an official form, and the document was completed. Lord Melville [1]
> was then at the head of the Admiralty. I referred his Lordship to my
> friend Lord Gambier for further particulars. But, previous to closing
> my despatch, I thought I should do right by showing it to my two
> influential friends Lord Yarmouth and Col. Abercromby. The former
> was much pleased with the contents of my memorial, and promised
> to urge his father, the Marquess of Hertford, to assist me with his
> powerful interest. The latter expressed himself very warmly in my
> favour, advocating my claims in the most pointed terms. 'I think,'
> said he, 'I can settle that matter for you. My brother has married
> Lord Melville's daughter. Give me a copy of your memorial. I will send
> it to him with full instructions how to manage the affair.'

This time we are left in no doubt how the precious memorandum
was transmitted home: and that, in another sphere, is characteristic
too:

> The most fortunate part of this event was the opportunity that
> offered at this moment of my sending by a safe conveyance the
> memorial. Sir Thomas Wallace, with whom I was on most friendly

---

[1] This, of course, was Henry Dundas, Viscount Melville, First Lord 1804–5,
and not to be confused with his only son, Robert Saunders Dundas, 2nd Viscount
Melville, who was First Lord from 1812 to 1830, with one short break in 1827–8,
and who figures so prominently in the later pages of the Narrative.

terms, was obliged to send home his paid mistress on urgent affairs. She kindly took charge of all the letters relating to me, undertaking to deliver them, herself, at the Admiralty. That promise she performed with the strictest punctuality.

In April they learned at Verdun of the fall and impeachment of Lord Melville, and poor Dillon began to fear that his memorial had been all in vain. On applying to Col. Abercromby for the latest news, he was merely told that he should rely upon the efforts of Lord Yarmouth, and, if any favourable result materialised, to give him all the credit for it.

Then, one day in June 1805, it happened. W.H.D. was moping in his lodgings in very low spirits, suffering from a recurrence of his West Indian skin-trouble, when Lord Yarmouth burst in upon him with the great news. He had been promoted Commander. The long-hoped-for, long-deferred step had been achieved, and instantly he became a different man. The promotion was dated April 5, 1805. Dillon profusely thanked the young lord, under the impression—not disavowed by Yarmouth—that the Marquess had wielded the decisive interest. Later, however, he discovered that the commission had been signed before Hertford's letter reached the Admiralty: also—and here for once Dillon was lucky—just before Melville's spectacular fall. The interest that accomplished it, apparently, was Col. Abercromby's, *via* his brother, the First Lord's son-in-law. If indeed this was the case, then the Colonel is deserving of every credit. For those times, he must have been an altruist of the highest order, unique in performing a service without seeking any reward, or even the beneficiary's thanks. But we should not overlook the possible intervention of Dillon's old patron, Gambier, now once more at the Admiralty.

There is one feature of this commission which is worthy of comment. Up to a few years before—1794 is probably the crucial date—it would not have been possible to give it, even to a man who was not due for a court martial. For, before that time, a man was promoted only by being appointed at the same time to a definitive *post*, of corresponding importance—*i.e.* to command an actual and named ship, too small to be a full captain's command. This was what was known as a 'Ship Commission.' In W.H.D.'s case, of course, such a thing was not possible, since he was clearly in no condition to take up an actual command anywhere. What he did receive, therefore, was a 'General Commission'—*i.e.* the modern sort, which appoints a man to be 'a Commander of Her Majesty's Navy', and not 'the

Commander of' a named ship. It is in fact an early example of this modern kind, which came into universal operation only in 1860. It may be noted, if we may look ahead, that when, in 1808, he obtained his next step, to Captain, he was once more posted without being appointed to a ship: he was, in fact, once more incapable of taking any command at all, though for a different reason. It is evident that, already, the modern idea of 'rank' was gaining rapidly over the old idea of 'post,' though the old word was still retained.

There are naturally in these pages a number of allusions to the progress of the war, the more significant because they emanate from the heart of enemy territory. Dillon hears from time to time some interesting enemy comments on passing events. Thus, in 1804 (September), he found himself at a party with a young artillery officer attached to the Army of England, then waiting at Boulogne:

> One of the company inquired what he thought of the plan of the invasion. 'Do you think,' he demanded, 'that it will succeed?' He hesitated, and the question was repeated. 'It is impossible for me to judge, but if I am to form an opinion from what passes almost daily under our batteries, we shall find sharp work when we land. Truly imagine,' said he, 'that the small British cruizers stationed off the coast watch for the flowing tide, then come in, ranging so close to us that we can see the whites of their eyes. If they act thus against us upon our own shores, what have we to expect when we debark upon theirs?'

Sometimes, too, the ripples of war reached Verdun itself. Native troops, foreign prisoners or prominent French personalities passed through the town or broke their journey there. In October 1805, for instance, Verdun was a nightly halting-place for troops, when Napoleon was moving his Army of England eastwards. W.H.D. saw, among others, Soult and Oudinot. A number of Englishmen who knew the latter called upon him, and were well received. Dillon notices the extreme youth and smallness of stature of many of the men. Some 50,000 passed through the town.

Nearly a year later, when the Prussian War had started, Napoleon himself passed through with Josephine, and W.H.D. has this to relate:

> My lodging was close to the Post House, and one morning early I was awakened by the shouting in the streets and the report of artillery. I jumped out of bed and, to my surprise, beheld Bonaparte's carriage changing horses. It was surrounded by the inhabitants crying

out 'Vive l'Empereur, vive Napoléon!' A number of English seamen had collected near, with their arms folded over their hats, fearing they might be pulled off by the French. Luckily, however, no notice was taken of them. One of the inhabitants of Verdun arrived at Metz just after the imperial couple had left the hotel there. The mistress thereof asked him if he should like to take a cup of coffee of Her Majesty's making. So apprehensive was Napoleon of being poisoned that, instead of ordering any refreshment where he stopped, Madame Bonaparte produced a coffee machine, and prepared it herself.

He had another opportunity of seeing the great man, who passed a night in the town in August 1807. This time, apparently, he took no such precautions.

In both 1805 and 1806 droves of prisoners, first Austrian and then Prussian, passed through after Austerlitz and Jena. Contrary to Wirion's express orders, both parties were received and succoured by the English with the utmost kindness. Both were harshly treated, but the Prussians far more so than the Austrians.

> They arrived in the most miserable state on their way to Chalons, shivering with cold and hunger [it was in November] many half naked, without shoes or stockings. A Prussian officer of illustrious family was seen without a shirt. Though it had been intimated that it would be taken amiss if we spoke to or noticed them . . . we entertained the officers at our messes and in private families, and supplied them with clothes and money. To the privates also we distributed cash and tobacco. The gratitude of these poor fellows who had been driven across the country like a drove of cattle cannot be easily described. They kissed the hands and garments of their benefactors and shouted 'Long live King George!' and 'George, Francis and Frederick William for ever!' The next day, when they had to quit, those English who had carriages stationed themselves on the high way, and made them over to the Prussians, to those who were lame in particular. These kind acts were reported to Wirion, who had the effrontery to call many of the *détenus* to account for the attentions they had bestowed on these distressed warriors: among the number a Major Burke, who had formerly served in the Austrian army, severely reprimanded for having given to a soldier an old hat and a pair of shoes.

In October 1805, the prisoners heard of the death of Capt. John Wesley Wright,[1] of the brig-sloop *Vincejo*, captured off Morbihan on May 8, 1804. The mystery surrounding this officer's death in the Temple is well known. W.H.D. has his contribution to make.

---

[1] Lt. 29/3/1800; Cdr. 7/5/02. Died (by suicide or murder?), 27/10/05.

Nor is it entirely hearsay, for, though not of course first hand, it stems partly from the officers of Wright's ship who were sent to Verdun, having shared the beginning of their Captain's captivity. The *Moniteur* of that period, he writes, announced:

> . . . that Captain Wright, whose vessel had been captured some time previously, had cut his throat, in the Temple where he had been in close confinement. Lieut. Wallis,[1] and other officers of that sloop of war were at Verdun, having been in the Temple for a short while with their Captain. He had not much opportunity of communicating with them, and they were soon sent to our depot. But Capt. Wright, at parting, declared to them that he felt convinced he should never quit the place alive. In fact the very circumstance of keeping him in prison whilst his officers were allowed their parole had a most suspicious appearance. Moreover, he assured them that no consideration should induce him to put an end to his existence during his incarceration. 'Therefore,' said he, 'if you hear of my death, depend upon it I shall have been murdered. I make this statement to you that you may repeat it should you hear of my having quitted this life.' The article in the *Moniteur* stated that he was found dead in his bed, having cut his throat whilst reading the bulletins announcing the victories of the French Army over the Austrians. What, in God's name, had the victories of the French in Austria to do with Capt. Wright, an English officer? The whole story must convince anyone remembering the events of that day that he was murdered.
>
> Capt. Wright had been confined in the Temple with Sir Sidney Smith during the previous war. But they effected their escape. On the next occasion he was locked up in the same apartments he had formerly occupied, and in examining the locality he found some files which had been hidden by him, and with which he intended to sever the bars of his window. When I related this case to Lord Mulgrave on my return to England, his Lordship assured me that our Government tried to ascertain what had been done to him but that they never could obtain any satisfactory information. If they could have been certain that he had been put to death, they would, in return, have visited a similar act upon a French officer.

To the last Napoleon denied all knowledge of the affair, saying, however, that, if he had acted at all, he might have had Wright tried and shot as a spy. For he was hardly the ordinary type of officer. He had spent some five years in Russia, and may well have been used for intelligence work. Until given a commission as lieutenant, he was acting as Sir Sidney Smith's confidential secretary. Upon his second

---

[1] James Wallis, Lt. 7/6/1797; Cdr. 3/11/1813.

capture, the French authorities accused him of landing royalist agents in France, and when they failed to elicit any confession from him by cross-examination, threatened him with all sorts of ill-treatment. But to this day the problem of his death remains unsolved.

In October 1805 there arrived vague accounts of Calder's action with Villeneuve off Finisterre, but no details, and W.H.D. had a bet with Lord Yarmouth, the terms being that the nobleman should hand over to Dillon five louis d'or, and receive back one for every ship taken by the British—'I being—unluckily in this case—the gainer of three.' A little later in the Narrative Dillon inserts long extracts from a letter written to a French resident of Verdun by a relative serving in the French fleet, 'containing a circumstantial statement of its proceedings from the time it left Martinique.' By far the longest extract concerns the Battle of Trafalgar, and is here printed verbatim at p. 57. But a shorter passage refers to Calder's action, and reads as follows:

> Dès ce moment [*i.e.* of the action off Ferrol] commence à se perdre la confiance qu'on avait en Mons. Villeneuve, qui, dans son rapport, s'est excusé sur la brume. Mais le lendemain il pouvait bien prendre sa revanche, s'il ordonna même de se préparer au combat. Point du tout. Nous eûmes la douleur de voir l'ennemi ayant deux vaisseaux de moins, qui étaient allés se reparer, traîner dans son escadre les deux vaisseaux espagnols, sans qu'on les eût attaqués, sans même en avoir fait le simulacre. Nous entrâmes quelques jours après dans le port de Vigo, Espagne.

W.H.D.'s comment upon this—in English—is:

> This statement corresponds with Sir Robert Calder's. The fog prevented his following up his first success, and the next day the French admiral, being to windward, had it in his power to attack the English. But he did not do so, or even, as this officer says, make the attempt. Sir Robert Calder was censured by a court martial for not renewing the engagement. It is quite evident circumstances would not permit him.

The two enemy ships referred to as going off for repairs are presumably the *Windsor Castle* and the *Malta*; the two captured Spaniards are the *San Rafael* (80) and the *Firme* (71).

It was not until December that the news of Trafalgar arrived:

> I happened to enter the Caron Club about 11 o'clock one day when one of the committee came in with the English newspapers containing

the account of Nelson's victory over the combined fleets of France and Spain. Lord Yarmouth, Col. Abercromby and several others of my friends seized hold of me as if by one accord, and, lifting me on the table, desired me to read in a loud voice the official report of that splendid victory. The most perfect silence having been secured, I communicated the details of Collingwood's letter to the Admiralty. When I had finished it, three hearty spontaneous cheers were given by at least one hundred members present, and those who were not near the table closed up and requested me to read the account a second time, which I readily agreed to do. I was then requested by Lord Yarmouth to explain the manner in which that battle was fought, as they did not understand the nautical description of the disposal of the two fleets. I did so by placing a parcel of books that were lying on the table in the position of the adverse fleets. We separated then, but, going out to the street, we met a crowd of French gentlemen who were anxious to know the reason of all that cheering. I told them of our splendid victory, and they were sadly cast down on the occasion. My French friends overloaded me with questions. They allowed they could not contend with us upon the ocean. 'We do not doubt,' they said, 'that you have triumphed. But that you should have taken and destroyed so many ships without your losing any is a case we cannot admit. Our seamen can fight as well as yours, and surely you do not mean to maintain that our shot has not sunk *some* of your ships?' My only reply was that they might see Lord Collingwood's official report for themselves, by which it was perfectly clear that they had lost twenty sail of the line: but not one on our side, either lost or taken, a British admiral not daring to send home a false report.

Two other passages give a strictly French view of the battle. The first is the letter quoted above, and printed in full below, at p. 57. The second is a conversation which W.H.D. held with a French naval officer who had occupied in the battle the most responsible position of Villeneuve's Chief of the Staff:

He had been wounded at the battle of Trafalgar, and had been sent to take the waters of that place (Barège), which had been beneficial in curing him. This gentleman's name was Prigny. He was Adm. Villeneuve's flag captain, and I do not recollect at any period of my life having enjoyed a more interesting conversation than I did in that officer's company. I found in Capt. Prigny an amiable and well-informed officer who did not, at the meeting which took place between us, conceal any of the facts or principal incidents which occurred between the hostile fleets on that important occasion. His ship, the *Bucentaure*, was taken possession by the *Mars*, 74, commanded by my former captain, George Duff of the *Glenmore* (who was killed on that glorious day). After a conversation that lasted until 2 o'clock in the morning, wherein the gallant Frenchman made the most satisfactory replies to all my questions, I at length, fearing that I had made too many, said in conclusion, 'I am truly sensible of your polite attention in conveying to me the interesting details which you have so frankly given.' 'Not in the least,' he replied. 'We did not gain the victory, and the truth will out in due time. Therefore it would be absurd to conceal the events as they really happened.' 'Well,' said I, 'one more question before we part. What was the act on the part of the British Fleet that made the greatest impression on your mind during that battle?' 'The act that astonished me the most,' he said, 'was when the action was over. It came on to blow a gale of wind, and the English immediately set to work to shorten sail and reef the topsails, with as much regularity and order as if their ships had not been fighting a dreadful battle. We were all amazement, wondering what the English seamen could be made of. All *our* seamen were either drunk or disabled, and we, the officers, could not get any work out of them. We never witnessed any such clever manœuvres before, and I shall never forget them.'

In February 1806 they heard that Pitt was dead, and that Fox had succeeded him. The latter was on comparatively good terms with Napoleon, having recently warned him of an attempt on his life. An indirect result of this was that a number of English *détenus* succeeded in securing their release. Col. Abercromby was of the number: so were Dr. Grey, and Capt. Brenton, whose place as Senior Naval Officer was taken by Capt. Sir Thomas Lavie;[1] so too was Lord Yarmouth, who was also sent back to Paris at once as a negotiator in the abortive peace-parleys: and he contrived to procure passports for several more, among whom was Col. Phillips of the Marines— that same Lieut. Molesworth Phillips who was present at the death of Capt. Cook:

> I have often heard it mentioned in the naval circles (writes W.H.D., for what it is worth), that if he (Phillips) had acted with more energy on that unfortunate occasion Cook's life might have been saved: at all events his body might have been brought off to the ship instead of remaining in the possession of the natives.

It should be added that this judgment, though supported by Capt. Bligh, is in direct opposition to all other extant accounts. These, on the contrary, praise Phillips's conduct throughout.

---

[1] Sir Thomas Lavie, Lt. 4/11/1790; Cdr. 9/11/95; Capt. 1/1/1801. Knighted in 1806 for his capture (in the *Blanche*) of the *Guerrière*, 19/7/06. He was captured when the *Blanche* was lost off Ushant on 4/3/07.

W.H.D. corresponded at some length with Lord Yarmouth, and was at first very hopeful that his release was at hand. For several months

> my small portmanteau was packed up, all my bills paid, expecting every post would bring me a passport for England. But disappointment was my lot.

And a further blow struck him in June, when he learned that his Father, the amiable (Sir) John Talbot Dillon, was dead. In July he heard that the other Sir John—of Lismullen—was no more: and, in the same month, his patron, the second Lord Hawke, upon whom he had so long relied for a step in promotion. As a result of these losses, of the successful efforts of so many of his fellow-prisoners and of his own hopes deferred, he became very much depressed.

About this time, too, there were several successful escapes, notably of four midshipmen (Hunter of the *Africaine*, Cecil, Gordon, and one unnamed), who first got themselves imprisoned in the Citadel for some minor offence, thereby renouncing their paroles, and thence made a clean escape. Another and infinitely worse case was that of Mid. Temple, who not only broke his parole, but also left behind debts to the value of £4,000. It was a bad business, and Sir Thomas Lavie, very rightly, sent a letter, *via* the French Minister of Marine, to the Admiralty at home. This led to Temple's dismissal with ignominy from the Navy. (See below, p. 71.)

But though many left, a few new officers arrived. One such was a Col. Stack, who, first and last, had a strange career. As a member of Dillon's regiment, he had met, many years before, the celebrated Paul Jones, then a guest in the regimental mess. On the latter asking for some officer to go afloat with him and train his men as marines, Stack volunteered, and was present at the famous action of the *Serapis* and the *Bonhomme Richard*. Returning to the regiment, he rose high in the French army: but, leaving the country before the Terror, he was received into the British army, and died a major-general. Before reaching Verdun this gentleman had been confined at Bitche, and hereabouts W.H.D. gives us some details of this much dreaded place. The fortress, near Strasbourg, was the prison for ratings and other ranks of the Army, but also the place of detention for officers who had been caught escaping, or who had, for one reason or another, got on the wrong side of Wirion and his opposite numbers elsewhere. He gives a harrowing description of the life led by the prisoners. But here there may well be some exaggeration: and even his worst accusations amount rather to gross and unimaginative neglect than to calculated cruelty. Even for the ratings—though characteristically he does not say much about them—conditions can hardly have been intolerable. His own boat's crew were there, and seem to have kept their morale remarkably well. They were still there when he left, and he does not mention their ultimate fate.

In October 1806 there were not wanting signs that his captivity might really be drawing to a close. One of the difficulties to be over-come, as we saw, was that the British Government had hitherto been unwilling to recognise his status of prisoner of war—quite rightly, on moral and public grounds, since in so doing they would have, by implication, acknowledged the legality of his detention. But at last W.H.D. got a letter through to his father's old friend, and colleague at the Board of Agriculture, Mr. Arthur Young, who actually per-suaded the Admiralty to issue a certificate of exchange between Dillon, a mere junior commander, and one Millius, a full *capitaine de vaisseau*, then on parole of honour in France. But even then the French Government refused to sanction it, on grounds untenable in both law and honour—that Millius was already in France. (In the old accepted code, of course, this made no difference at all: and in fact the French capitaine was—up till then anyway—playing according to the rules, and not serving anywhere against the English.) So this effort also came to nought, for the time being. Yet it pleased Dillon, not only because an officer of one grade higher than himself was proposed as a fair exchange, but also because he thought, probably rightly, that his Government had at last realised the hardness of his individual case, and would no longer persist in regarding him as an 'un-exchangeable': and he hoped that, once this point was conceded, it would try again.[1]

But still he had to wait. In the spring of 1807 his skin disease grew so bad that he applied for, and obtained, leave to reside in the country. He was taken in by a wealthy French widow called Emart, at the Château de Moulainville five miles from Verdun. Here, in very pleasant surroundings, he was well cared for: but not happy, for the endless waiting for what never came was clearly getting on his nerves. In July 1807 he was informed by a friend in Paris that, if he could persuade the Admiralty to exchange him for a certain Soleil—not only a senior *capitaine de vaisseau*, but actually a commodore—the French Government would consent. Not very hopefully, therefore, he wrote to that effect to the Admiralty. But two months passed, and

[1] For the correspondence arising out of his case, see below, p. 64.

nothing happened. Then, according to his own account, one day in September, despair seized him, and, taking a razor, he went down to the bottom of the garden,

> then, stowing myself away behind some bushes, I placed the sharp blade to my throat, and was in the act of drawing it across when the emotion of the moment led me to desist for a few days longer.

Again, in reading what follows, we have alternatives to choose from. Either he was once more the victim of the same kind of indecision of character which had marred all his escape-projects, or else he is somewhat overdramatising the situation. The sequel, indeed, inclines one to the latter view; for, upon returning to the house, he found a letter from Wirion 'announcing that my passport and certificate of Exchange had arrived: that I was free—"franc comme l'air!"' And an additional reason for suspecting drama—nay, melodrama— lies in the fact that, apparently, the bearer of the good news had already been trying to deliver it about an hour before W.H.D. took his razor with him down the garden. He had been exchanged for Soleil.

He hurried to Verdun, where he was well received by Wirion (not yet fallen), had a few farewell dinners, and set out in a travelling cabriolet bought for the occasion, reaching Paris the following evening. Here, a little unexpectedly, he remained for a whole week, sightseeing and being entertained by both British (of whom there were still many) and French people—among the latter, Madame de Genlis. He tried at first to get the port of departure mentioned in his passport changed from Morlaix to Rotterdam. But after seven days he became rather anxious, especially when asked to give up the precious document in order that a change of venue might be effected. So he decided to make for Morlaix after all, and finally left Paris for Versailles in a panic and a one-horse *chaise-de-poste*. Thence, without a break, he drove to Rennes, putting up at the very hotel (as he puts it) 'where Admiral Villeneuve had either been murdered or had put an end to his existence.'

The next stage brought him to St. Brieuc (spelt by him Brieux), where, to his intense delight, he saw the sea again. Here he was detained—socially—by a General Bowyer, the local commander, who at first mistook him for a French officer sent to relieve him. After another wasted day, at length he reached Morlaix, where he sold his carriage and, not without difficulty, chartered a small schooner. But a final fright was in store. He had been charged with the delivery of many letters to people in England, and, very unwillingly, he undertook to bring away some trunks belonging to Capt. Brenton which had been left behind when that officer was repatriated. The police commissaire took his passport and would not return it, and, in the Customs, Brenton's trunks were opened. They contained all the money accounts relating to the English prisoners at Verdun, and the Customs officers could not understand what they were, or why they were in Dillon's possession. He was cleared, however, by the good offices of a friendly French merchant, and allowed at length to embark. But what really scared him was that all the time he had, sewn in the collar of his greatcoat, some secret information[1] given to him in Paris: and he was in terror lest he should be searched.

He was scarcely out of harbour before his schooner was spoken by the *Sharpshooter*, gunbrig, Lieut. Goldie,[2] who took him on board:

What a delight and relief to my senses to find myself once again on board a British man of war. Lieut. Goldie's attentions and hospitality can never be effaced from my memory. He made all sail for Plymouth, and the next day, the 19th September, the *Sharpshooter* anchored in the Sound. When I landed I could scarcely believe my senses, and remained for some time in a sort of doubt whether I really was on British ground. But my misgivings were soon relieved by being accosted, as I arrived at the house of the Admiral, William Young,[3] by his secretary, Mr. Procter Smith,[4] who had been my shipmate in the *Alcide*. His congratulations were of the warmest, and he introduced me to the Commander-in-Chief, who, having heard all that was necessary, allowed me to proceed to the inn, where I made instant preparations for London by the mail.

One of my friends at Verdun had put into my hand on the day of departure a ten pound Bank of England note, in part payment of a sum due to me. When I took it I had lost all confidence in that sort of paper. However, when I offered it to the master of the house he instantly gave me cash for it. . . . I set off by the mail that night, and reached London by 6 o'clock on the 21st. I put up at the Salopian Coffee House, to be near the Admiralty.

[1] See below, p. 70.
[2] John Goldie, Lt. 7/1/1802; not promoted.
[3] (Sir) William Young (K.B.), Lt. 12/11/1770; Cdr. ? ; Capt. 23/9/78; R-Ad. 1/6/95; V-Ad. 14/2/99; Ad. 9/5/1805. Rear-Admiral of Great Britain.
[4] See Vol. I, Index.

THE FRENCHMAN'S ACCOUNT OF THE BATTLE OF TRAFALGAR

Le général ordonna d'appareiller le 19 octobre, non pas dans un coup de vent, comme il avait promis, mais dans un calme. La flotte était composée de 33 vaisseaux dont 3 à trois ponts, de 5 frégates et 2 bricks; elle était en bon état. En louvoyant toute la journée 10 vaisseaux purent à peine sortir de la rade. Le lendemain 20, tous sortirent en gagnant le large, et ce ne fut qu'au soir seulement que l'armée rallia. Le lendemain 21, jour à jamais mémorable pour le combat qui eut lieu et par ses suites désastreuses, il était écrit dans le livre du destin que nous serions témoins de la plus terrible catastrophe dont les annales de la marine d'aucun peuple aient jamais parlé.

L'armée aperçut l'ennemi à trois lieues d'elle vis à vis Trafalgar qui a donné son nom à ce terrible combat. Leur armée n'était composée que de 26 vaisseaux,* mais elle avait le vent; mais elle avait les canonniers très habiles à démâter; mais, enfin, elle était commandée par Nelson. Notre général, insouciant, apathique et peut-être malintentionné (car il était désperé d'avoir appris que le général Roselli était en route pour le remplacer) parvint à peine à former la ligne depuis le matin jusqu'à midi; encore fut elle bien mal formée: aucun vaisseau n'était à son rang de bataille. L'ennemi, au lieu de se former en ligne, vint fièrement et à toutes voiles fondre sur nous, sur deux colonnes. Une se dirigeait sur le centre et l'autre un peu sur la gauche où se trouvait notre vaisseau. Les français qui étaient le plus à portée firent feu sur l'avant des premiers vaisseaux anglais qui se présentèrent. Ils continuèrent leur marche sans riposter, mais quand ils furent près ils se mêlèrent parmi nous et le combat devint opiniâtre. Notre vaisseau de 74 canons avait déjà canonné depuis trois quarts d'heure, quand vint se mettre sur son travers le vaisseau anglais, le *Tonant*, de 80 canons.[1] On se battit de si près que les canonniers pouvaient prendre les écouvillons[2] des ennemis. On demanda les hommes destinés à la fusillade sur le pont. Etant destiné à la faire sur la dunette,[3] je m'y rendis avec mes soldats, quand un boulet, perçant la seconde batterie, tua trois hommes et en blessa

* He has miscounted, there being twenty-seven.
[1] The *Tonnant*, 80, Capt. Charles Tyler.
[2] Sponges. 'Escauvillons' in text.   [3] The poop.

plusieurs autres, du nombre desquels j'étais. Je tombais, baigné de mon sang et de celui des tués. Je restai quelque temps sans connaissance. Quand je revins à moi, je reconnus un de mes soldats à la voix que je priai de me conduire au poste du chirurgien. Il me dit qu' il l'eût déjà fait s'il ne m'eut cru mort. En arrivant on me pansa. Je n'avais heureusement aucune fracture. J'avais reçu trois blessures, une à l'oeil gauche que j'ai cru perdre, mais qui est ouvert depuis quatre jours; une à la main gauche qui sera le plus long à guérir; et—celle qui m'a causé les plus vives douleurs, mais qui s'avance d'être guérie—c'est le coup que j'ai reçu sur ma frêle poitrine près de la clavicule, en prenant d'une épaule à l'autre. Je l'ai eue enflée pendant 5 jours de 4 à 5 pouces.

Après cela, quand je fus étendu sur un matelas, je fus de nouveau blessé à la tête en deux endroits par les éclats que fit un boulet en traversant le faux pont, et qui tua un chirurgien—ce qui prouve la mauvaise qualité du vaisseau quoique neuf. Ce qui me fit le plus de mal, c'est que d'abord je n'y voyais pas, et qu'ensuite une douzaine de blessés me tombèrent sur le corps, et me firent souffrir considérablement. L'on fut obligé de me panser de nouveau, et l'on me plaça dans la chambre d'un officier de marine. Si je ne fus plus témoin oculaire du combat et des suites terribles, je ne pus sans frémir en entendre le récit. J'appris que mon sous-lieutenant a été tué, ainsi que mon premier sergent, mon tambour et deux autres soldats, et 23 furent blessés, la plupart grièvement. Le nombre des tués et des blessés sur notre bord fut porté à 400. Dans cette journée la plus grande partie de nos vaisseaux furent démâtés, deux coulèrent bas, et un sauta, le feu ayant pris à son bord. Très peu de personnes de ces trois vaisseaux échappèrent.

Dans la nuit l'escadre fut dispersée. Quelques vaisseaux au nombre de 5 ou 6 revinrent mouiller près de Cadiz. On prétend que 4 sont rentrés dans la Méditerranée.* Les autres, démâtés, sont restés sur le champ de bataille et amarinés par les anglais, qui ne purent les garder, étant eux-mêmes bien avariés; la mer étant d'ailleurs trop forte, ces vaisseaux échouèrent presque tous, et s'engloutirent dans les abîmes. L'amiral Villeneuve fut fait prisonnier, plutôt que de se brûler la cervelle, ce qu'aurait dû faire tout homme de coeur, ayant été cause d'un si grand désastre. Il y a cinq jours qu'un courrier de l'empereur est venu apporter l'ordre de ne pas faire sortir l'escadre— ordre malheureusement trop tardif. Le contre-amiral Magon fut tué,

---

* These four were afterwards captured by our squadron under Sir Richard Strachan.

et trois généraux espagnols perdirent chacun un membre, et un d'eux fut noyé avec son équipage.

Le lendemain on vit échouer à la côte le *Bucentaure*,* mais l'on sauva l'équipage. Le vaisseau avait été abordé et amariné par les Anglais qui, n'ayant pu le tenir longtemps à la remorque, le coupèrent. Les Français dirent alors aux Anglais qu'étant près de Cadiz ils étaient leurs prisonniers, et qu'étant les moins forts ils ne devaient opposer aucune résistance. Ils sentirent de ce raisonnement et s'y rendirent. Dans la nuit notre vaisseau avait eu les câbles de trois ancres cassés. Il ne nous restait plus qu'une, dite de miséricorde.[1] Nous mîmes à la voile avec trois autres vaisseaux et trois frégates, et nous fûmes rechercher la *Ste Anne*, vaisseau espagnol à trois ponts, que traînait une frégate anglaise qui la lâcha dès qu'elle nous aperçut. Apres avoir été sauvé, ce vaisseau alla s'échouer. Nous rentrâmes dans la rade, où nous mouillâmes avec notre dernière ancre. Pendant deux nuits nous fûmes dans des transes horribles. Notre ancre ne tenait pas, nous chassions dessus. La mer était grosse; la secousse qu'avait essuyée le vaisseau pendant le combat s'était entr'ouverte et lui faisait faire 26 pouces d'eau à l'heure: et, par surcroît de malheur, le feu prit à notre bord, de sorte que nous craignions à chaque instant ou d'échouer ou d'être submergés ou de sauter. Heureusement, à force d'activité et d'intrépidité, on parvint à nous sauver de ce mauvais pas.

Pendant ces jours et nuits malheureux on n'entendait que des coups de canon de minute en minute, de distance en distance. On me dit que c'était des vaisseaux démâtés qui, jetés à la côte, demandaient du secours. Mais on ne pouvait leur en porter. On avait essayé de le faire; plusieurs chaloupes et canots qu'on avait envoyés à cet effet avaient chaviré ou coulé. Les pauvres infortunés étaient condamnés à périr. Très peu d'hommes échappèrent au naufrage. Les blessés poussaient des hurlements épouvantables. Quand la mer était basse ils se traînaient sur les membres qui n'étaient point mutilés, et cherchaient à éviter la mort qu'ils trouvaient plus loin. Tout cela offrait le spectacle le plus affreux et le plus déchirant. Enfin, la plume la plus éloquente, le pinceau le plus habile ne peuvent donner qu'une esquisse très imparfaite d'une pareille horreur, et cela avait lieu pendant la nuit. Un de ces malheureux vaisseaux dont l'équipage et les troupes formaient un total 1,400 hommes, il ne s'en

---

* Admiral Villeneuve's flagship.

[1] According to Jal, the sheet anchor, also called *ancre de salut* or *ancre maîtresse*. But, according to Witcomb and Tiret, the sheet anchor is *ancre de veille*, and the *ancre de miséricorde* is the waist anchor.

échappa pas 150, et sur les 24 officiers deux seulement se sauvèrent du naufrage. Enfin, juge des pertes par celle des troupes expédition-naires. Nous avions deux fort beaux bataillons. Le 67eme en avait un qui en valait presque deux. Il y avait le premier bataillon de la demi-brigade suisse, des dépôts coloniaux. Tout réuni ne forme aujourd'hui qu'un total de 756. La perte des marins est dans la même proportion. Le reste est ou tué ou noyé, ou amputé et languissent dans les hôpitaux.

Finissons cette esquisse effroyable, et rafraîchissons nos idées par ce tableau touchant de l'humanité et de la commisération, et du secours des Espagnols de Cadiz et des endroits environnants envers nos blessés et nos naufragés. On voyait sur le Port le Capitaine Général, le Marquis de Solano, environné des officiers les plus marquants, s'empressant à donner des ordres pour le débarquement des blessés. Des brancards, des chaises à porteur, des calèches, des équipages même étaient tout prêts pour le transport de ces mal-heureux aux hôpitaux. Le transport se faisait avec toutes les pré-cautions imaginables au milieu du peuple qui regardait en pleurant passer cette triste procession. M. de Solano lui-même a aidé à porter un brancard jusqu'aux portes de la ville. Il a visité et consolé les malades, offert du secours et même sa bourse. Combien de marquis en France feraient ce qu'a fait ce brave homme, dont les traits d'humanité, de générosité, attendrissent, soulagent et élèvent l'âme? Nos naufragés ont partout reçu des vêtements, des vivres et même de l'argent des habitants des endroits près desquels ils avaient échoué. Enfin, je doute que dans aucun département maritime de France on fasse pour les espagnols ce que ces braves gens ont fait pour les français.

This letter was dated November 5 from Cadiz, 1805, and signed,
Ton Frère, Pernot,
Capitaine au 16me Régiment de ligne. J'étais rapporteur du conseil de guerre de l'armée, mais, hélas, qu'est devenu de cette armée?

[The evidence seems to show that Pernot was in the *Pluton*, 74. The *Tonnant*, as she entered the fight, would have attacked the *Pluton* first had not the latter's gallant captain, Commodore Cosmao Kerjulien, pressed on to prevent the *Mars* from breaking through. The *Pluton* was one of the survivors which the Spanish Admiral Gravina led out of the battle and back to Cadiz; and it was Cosmao in the *Pluton* who, as the author relates, led the sortie two days later which retook the *Santa Ana*.]

EXCERPTS FROM LORD KEITH'S LETTER-BOOKS

(In National Maritime Museum. Dates as per letter-headings.)

1. *Capt. Robert Honyman of the* Leda *to Ad. Robert Montagu.*

H. Majesty's *Leda*, off Helvoet,
July 30, 1803.

Sir,

I beg leave to inform you that on the morning of the 26th inst. I sent Lieut. Dillon of H.M.S. *Africaine* with a six-oared cutter from this ship into Helvoet as a Flag of Truce to deliver Lord Keith's letter and to return immediately.

I am sorry to say the boat has never returned, nor can I hear anything of her. I am very apprehensive the enemy have detained her, as this is the fourth day since she left the ship. I enclose the copy of my letter to the Commanding Officer of the Batavian ships of war at Helvoet. . . .

2. *Lord Keith to Sir Evan Nepean, Bart.*

Ceres at the Nore,
August 4, 1803.

Sir,

Be pleased to acquaint their Lordships that R-Ad. Montagu has been informed by Capt. Honyman of H.M.S. *Leda* that he is apprehensive Lieut. Dillon of H.M.S. *Africaine*, whom he sent into Helvoet with a six-oared cutter on the 26th ult. as a Flag of Truce, has been detained by the enemy, as he has been four days absent from the ship: and I think it necessary to explain to their Lordships the circumstances which occasioned this Flag of Truce being sent in.

When Capt. Pool of the Batavian brig *Ajax* arrived at the Nore to receive Madam Schimmelpenninck on board, he either sent a bill to London for cash, or wrote to his correspondent to send it down to him by post: but the letter with the expected remittance not having appeared, he applied to the General Post Office in London on the subject, and, previously to his sailing from hence, he requested that I would pursue the enquiry and let him know the result. Some time after his departure, the Post Master of this place brought the letter in question to me, alleging that it had been sent to a merchant vessel called the *Ajax* by mistake: and, considering, under the existing circumstances of the two countries, that the national character was in some degree implicated in the transaction, I lost no time in forwarding the letter to R-Ad. Montagu, and instructed him to take the earliest opportunity in sending it into Helvoet by a Flag of Truce from one of the ships before that place, for which port I understood the *Ajax* had sailed, little apprehensive that the enemy would have requited an act of civility and attention in the ungracious manner which they appear to have done. I regarded the business, in the first instance, as a matter of little consequence, and did not consider it necessary to trouble their Lordships with any report upon it.

I have the honour to be, etc.

KEITH.

Sir Evan Nepean.

3. *Sir Sidney Smith to Lord Keith.*

H. Brit. Maj. Ship *Antelope*,
off the Texel, October 15, 1803.

My Lord,

Capt. Manby of H.M. *Africaine* having acquainted me that Lieut. Dillon, who had been sent with a Flag of Truce, was still detained at Helvoet, I took an opportunity by the Dutch fishermen returned on the 12th inst. of addressing a letter to the Commanding Officer of the Navy at the Texel, to reopen the communication by claiming his release: a copy of which I have the honour to send enclosed for your Lordship's information. I am in hopes from what the fishermen said that the Dutch Commodore will either send out a Flag of Truce or allow one of them to bring an answer.

W.S.S.

Ad. Lord Keith, K.B. etc.

Enclosure.
H. Brit. Maj. Ship *Antelope*,
off the Texel, October 12, 1803.

Sir,

[Para. I. I restore the twelve fishermen and their nets.]

[Para. II. Pilot boats will not be interfered with.]

[Para. III. We are not waging war on individuals.]

(IV) I should have sent *these* poor people in by a boat from this ship, but I am discouraged from so doing by the circumstance of

Lieut. Dillon being detained at Helvoet. I hereby formally claim his release according to the laws of war, and the usage of civilized nations, and I hope for a satisfactory answer on this subject, which I shall be happy to receive by a more *direct* conveyance than this mode which I am obliged to adopt, under my assurance that I will not follow the example of detaining a Flag of Truce.

W. SIDNEY SMITH.

To the Commodore commanding the Navy of
the Batavian Republic at the Texel.

4. *Capt. Thomas Manby to Lord Keith:* H.M.S. Africaine, *off Goree, October 29, 1803.*

. . . Lieut. Dillon was sent into the interior three weeks ago, as were the boat's crew. A Flag of Truce yesterday came to me from the Texel with a letter from the Dutch Commodore respecting Lieut. Dillon, which I forward for your Lordship's information. . . .

Enclosure.

Commodore Albert Kikkert to Commodore, H.M. Ships off the Texel.

On board the *Brutus*
at the Texel,
October 26, 1803.

Sir,

The informations which I was obliged to take concerning Lieut. Dillon have put it out of my power to give an earlier answer to the letter which your Honour was so kind as to write to me.

[Thanks him for returning twelve fishermen, and hopes that the rest of those detained will follow.]

It is extremely painful to me to be deprived of the satisfaction to give your Honour some favourable account about Lieut. Dillon's situation, but it is in the meantime comforting for me to assure you that the Government of this republic has acted in this matter in such a manner as possibly could be desired by the same Lieutenant, orders having been issued by the Council of the Batavian Navy to the Commanding Officer at Helvoet, on the 30th of July last, for the entire release of the said Lieutenant, Flag of Truce and equipage: in consequence whereof he departed on the same day, but was on his return carried back by a French armed boat, and transported on board the ship of the commandant of a French division stationed at the same port, and is, I am informed, conducted since to Nancy or Valenciennes by a French officer, where probably he stays to this moment, on his parole. Sir Hotham, at that time commander of a British squadron off Helvoet, has been already informed of this accident, in the month of August last, by the Batavian officer commanding at Helvoet. . . .

I flatter myself that your Honour will be perfectly sensible, by the foregoing account, that Lieut. Dillon's detaining can by no means be ascribed to the Batavian Government, but that, to the contrary, every method has been tried to effect his free departure: and I can moreover assure your Honour that the most energical (*sic*) remonstrances are still made to the French Government in behalf of this case, which, I am confident, will not remain ineffectual; . . .

A. KIKKERT

Commodore commanding the Navy of the Batavian Republic at the Texel.)

To the Commodore of His Britannic Majesty's
Ships off the Texel.

APPENDIX III

LETTERS CONCERNING HIS EXCHANGE

(Copied by W.H.D. from the records of the Transport Office.)

1. *From Commissioners of Transport to Mons. Rivière, Paris.*

Transport Office,
January 27, 1807.

We have now to propose to you the exchange of Capt. Wm. Hy. Dillon of the British Navy, at present detained at Verdun, for Capt. Millius, taken in the command of the *Didon*, French frigate, who was allowed to proceed from this country to France on his Parole on the 13th of May last. As we take it for granted that the Minister of the French Marine can not possibly have any objection to this exchange, we inclose the usual certificate, liberating Capt. Millius from his Parole; and we request that Capt. Dillon may be furnished by you with a corresponding certificate as soon as possible, and a passport to enable him to return to this country. Should, however, the French Government prefer exchanging any other French officer of equal rank for Capt. Dillon, a certificate will be sent to you for such officer immediately upon your informing us of his name.

[On 30/1/1807 the Transport Office writes to W.H.D., informing him of the contents of the above letter. As its substance is exactly the same it is hardly worth reproducing. W.H.D.'s comment is:— 'The Commissioners considered my proposal, which came direct from the French Minister of Marine, so certain that they instantly liberated Capt. Millius. But what was the result? I was still retained in France!']

2. *From Mons. Rivière, Sec. to the French Minister of Marine, to Coms. of Transport.*

(Extract) . . . la troisième de même date, qui contenait l'acte de liberation du Capitaine Infernet contre Mons. Brenton, renferme une demande d'échange de Mons. Wm. Henry Dillon contre le Cap. Millius, ou tel autre officier qu'il plaisait au Gouvernement français de designer . . .

[This is dated April 8, 1807, and, as W.H.D. says, 'merely acknowledges the application for my exchange.' But it would seem that, in the portion not quoted by him, there must have been a more concrete proposal. For the next letter, the Transport Office's reply (No. 3 below) refers back to Rivière's letter of April 8, and seems to reveal the game which that gentleman was playing. What he must have added in his letter of April 8, I think, was, in effect:—'I propose to take advantage of the option which your letter of January 27 gives, and to propose substituting the name of Capt. Soleil for that of Capt. Millius.' By this time, of course, both Capt. Millius *and* the certificate liberating him from his Parole were, by the simplicity of the Transport Office, safely in France!]

3. *From Commissioners of Transport to Mons. Rivière, Paris.*

Transport Office,
July 16, 1807.

We have received your letter of the 8th April, and acquaint you that we have accepted the exchange of Captain Soleil for Capt.

Dillon, as proposed by you. The former has been furnished with the usual certificate, and will return to France by the vessel which will convey this letter. We shall therefore expect the return of Capt. Dillon to this country immediately. It is proper to observe that our adoption of this exchange must prove clearly to the French Government our disposition to do everything possible to forward the exchange of prisoners, Mons. Soleil being a Capitaine de Vaisseau and Capt. Dillon at present only a Commander in our Navy, and who was actually at the time of his detention no more than a Lieutenant.

[W.H.D. again gives the Transport Office's letter to himself, reporting their action—again omitted here, and for the same reason as before. He also has two comments to make: (1) 'This letter'—*i.e.* the one to himself, here omitted—'never reached me in France: another proof of the cold-hearted proceeding of the French authorities,' and (2) 'These official documents are of value as they fully prove the interest our Government took in behalf of the prisoners of war.'

Our comments also may be two: (1) They certainly do prove our Government's interest in British prisoners, but they also show (2) how very trusting the Transport Office was in parting with the body of Mons. Soleil (which, this time, they actually held) before they were quite sure that the old trick on them was not to be repeated. In fact, we know, it was not: W.H.D. was duly returned.

One curious feature is that the Transport office does not even suggest that Capt. Millius's certificate should be forthwith destroyed or returned. Whether this was because, trusting to the last, they assumed that the honourable Mons. Rivière would automatically refrain from using it, or whether they felt it would be a mere waste of time and ink to insist upon it, I do not know. Nor do I know whether Capitaine Millius himself used it. But we cannot altogether dismiss a suspicion that cunning M. Rivière had secured two French capitaines in exchange for one English commander—one moreover who in international Law and equity alike, was not a prisoner of war at all!]

X

POST CAPTAIN

SEPTEMBER 1807–APRIL 1808

(*aet.* 27–27½)

INTRODUCTION

W.H.D.'s encounter, in the ramshackle *Childers*, with the powerful Danish brig *Lougen* is, in one important sense, the highlight of his naval career. It was the only occasion on which he commanded in a single-ship action—indeed, the only time he commanded any ship which was in action against other ships. It is certain that he emerged from this most unequal contest with considerable credit: and, this time, we have not to take the fact from his evidence alone. There is plenty of extraneous proof. The Admiralty officially congratulated and promoted him: the Patriotic Society at Lloyd's presented him with a 100-guinea sword: the *Naval Chronicle* thought fit to publish his dispatch (reproduced below, p. 105); and James, in his *Naval History*, gives two and a half pages to the action.

In his day, in fact, and in his own small way, Dillon became something like the hero of the hour. The action was just of the sort to grip the generous imagination of the British public, which is always apt to count odds before results, and whose warriors, if they would make absolutely sure of a niche in the hearts of their countrymen, have but two alternatives—to fail against odds, or to fall in the hour of victory. The history of the Napoleonic War teems with examples. There was a good one three months later, when that same *Lougen* was again engaged with a British sloop, the *Seagull*. This time the Dane put up a much better show and, when joined by six gunboats, secured the surrender of the *Seagull*, which sank immediately afterwards. Yet the latter's commander, Robert Cathcart, was, like Dillon, immediately made Post. It is indeed a good example of this most English trait. W.H.D. did at least beat off his formidable antagonist and bring the leaky *Childers* home. Cathcart did not—his ship was lost. Yet he too received his superiors' full recognition and his countrymen's grateful praise, because they deemed—rightly—that he had failed gloriously.

James brings out very clearly what a death-trap the *Childers* was, and criticises the policy of employing such ships in trade-protection:

> Notwithstanding the fate of the 'sloop of war' *Lily* [a ship of strength, or rather weakness, exactly like the *Childers*, captured (15/7/1804) by a French privateer of much greater force after repelling boarders eight times], vessels of that denomination, inferior in force to a gun-brig, were still suffered to remain in the British Navy. One of the 'cruisers' of this class was the *Childers*, a brig of 202 tons, built as long ago as the year 1778; a vessel so unseaworthy as to have been obliged, on more than one occasion, to throw overboard her guns, 4-pounders, in order to save the lives of her crew. The brig at length

became so crazy, that 18-pounder carronades were found too heavy for her, and she was fitted with fourteen 12-pounders. In this state, and manned with a crew, nominally of 86, but really of 65 men and boys, including only one lieutenant (there not being accommodation for more), the *Childers*, Captain William Henry Dillon, in the month of January, lay in Leith Roads, waiting to give her 'protection' to the trade proceeding to Gottenberg. But the merchants, as soon as they knew the force and qualifications of the *Childers*, objected to place their property under her care; supposing, very naturally, that so small and ill-armed a vessel was incapable of beating off the privateers that infested the northern waters. . . . What vessel the merchants obtained at last we do not know [W.H.D. says it was the *Snake*, sloop]; but the *Childers* proceeded by herself to the Baltic, to effect as much, in the way of annoying the enemy, as her small powers would admit.

A pleasant feature of the whole episode is that W.H.D., riding his little wave of fame, does not, as readers might fear, spoil things by excess of vanity: he does not seriously over-dramatise, nor even overwrite. For once, too, in his dispatch we have a chance to view Dillon the professional officer, as opposed to Dillon the man-writing-to-his-cousin. Neither account overstates the case, but they state different, though complementary, things. The dispatch gives the straight story, with little personal detail. The Narrative gives many more details but, oddly enough, omits to record much of the actual manœuvring in the fight itself. Whereas from the dispatch one can deduce—as James clearly did—the whole course of the action, such deduction is not possible from the Narrative alone. A probable explanation of this is that W.H.D. was assuming his cousin to be familiar with the dispatch, and was seeking in the Narrative merely to supplement it with more intimate detail.

Dillon, then, richly deserved all the credit he won. But there is the reverse of the medal. He paid heavily for it in the wounds which he sustained. Their effects lasted for many years, leaving a legacy of much suffering and long-term, if sporadic, discomfort from which he was never fully released.

The old *Childers* had been 'in the news' once before. She was the very first ship in the long wars to be in action with the French, having been fired upon, and hit with a 48-lb. shot, from the Brest forts on January 2, 1793, a month before war was declared. It was no doubt for this reason that Nicholas Pocock painted a fine water-colour of the scene, part of which is reproduced as the frontispiece of this volume.

X
POST CAPTAIN
SEPTEMBER 1807–APRIL 1808
(*aet.* 27–27½)

(1) HOME

SEPTEMBER 1807–JANUARY 1808

MY arrival in London was a new era in my existence. I lost no time in presenting myself to the Hon. Mr. Pole, the Secretary to the Admiralty, first of all delivering to him the secret information I had received in Paris relating to a certain number of troops collected in the neighbourhood of Brest, which were intended to be landed on the coast of Ireland. Our conversation was a long one, during which I acquainted him that I had ascertained while in Paris that the French Government had obtained our private naval signals. He admitted the fact, and remarked that, when he had taken office, the private signals were kept in an outer room, open to any person who chose to enter it. Consequently they found their way to our enemies. 'However,' said he, 'I have altered all that. They are now secure.' He then desired me to call on Lord Mulgrave, the then First Lord of the Admiralty, about 12 o'clock. He would, he said, apprize his Lordship of my return to England, and ensure my being received.

I accordingly presented myself at the hour mentioned. My audience was a gracious one, but very cold. Many subjects were discussed, particularly the detention of Capt. Wright in the Temple, where he terminated his existence.[1] His Lordship positively assured me that, if our Government could have ascertained the real facts of his case, a French officer would have been similarly treated by us. But all inquiries led to nothing certain. Some years afterwards Sir Sidney Smith visited the Temple, and devoted much time in trying to find out the fate of that officer, who had served under him and become his personal friend. But all his exertions failed.

---

[1] See above, p. 48.

His Lordship made many inquiries about Mr. Temple's escape,[1] and I stated what little I knew of it. He then assured me that he had been dismissed the Navy—the Board could not sanction such conduct. The most extraordinary thing was, after what had passed between Lord Mulgrave and me about him, he was the first person I met upon coming out of the Admiralty. He made his bow and offered his hand. In doing so he had mistaken his man, as I turned my back upon him and passed by without acknowledgment. With Lord Mulgrave I left a memorial, stating what I suffered during my captivity, and my loss of promotion. He admitted that I had very strong claims on my country. I could not help mentioning the interest my friend Gambier took in my advancement. He was then before Copenhagen in command of the British Fleet. 'When he returns,' said I, 'your Lordship will hear more of me than I can state myself.' As I was retiring his Lordship invited me to dine with him on the 24th.

My next duty was to present myself at the Transport Board. The Secretary, Mr. McLeay's, reception I shall never forget. He greeted me with the warmth of an old friend. 'Welcome to England,' he said. 'I wish you joy! We have had trouble enough about you, and I'm heartily glad to see you at last. Your trial has been a severe one. Let us hope all will be right in good time.' When I was requested to attend the Board, I was very kindly received, Capt. Sir. Rupert George[2] of the Navy being the chairman. I was overloaded with questions, and replied to them as far as my abilities would admit. They acknowledged that my confined position at Verdun would not admit of my communicating any intelligence of consequence. They expressed a proper feeling in behalf of our unfortunate countrymen, prisoners of war and those detained in France, at the same time frankly declaring that our Government had done its best to effect an exchange; but all had failed. They cordially congratulated me upon my having obtained mine, and, after a very interesting conversation relating to our political position, I retired.

[Several passages omitted. He visits his stepmother at Brompton, and meets Mr. Loveden, the member for Shaftesbury and his father's executor. He decides that Lady Dillon—and Brompton—are a little too dull and 'out of the swim' for him: so he returns to his London hotel. Then in an ill moment for himself, he calls on Mr. Voller, 'my

---

[1] See above, p. 53.
[2] Sir Rupert George, Bart., Lt. 13/9/1770; Capt. 29/11/81. One of the few officers on the 'Superannuated and Retired' List.

old friend whose wife I had met in Boulogne,' only to find him recently deceased. But 'Mrs. V.' insists on renewing the intimacy, and very evidently lays siege to his affections. Many of these references are erased, but it is clear that during this period he succumbed and reached an 'arrangement' with the lady, whereby he was to marry her when he obtained post rank. Thereafter they spent much time in each other's company.]

At Lord Mulgrave's table I met many men of rank and fashion. I was seated next to Lord Palmerston, who had just commenced his political career. Sir Richard Bickerton[1] managed the naval affairs in Gambier's absence. Many questions were made to me by the company when they knew that I had just returned from Verdun. Sir Richard in particular failed not in inquisitiveness, and in conclusion remarked, 'You don't appear the worse for your detention in France.' I replied that I should feel sincere regret if any friend of mine underwent the same trials I had endured. He then drew in, without any further remarks.

I next applied to Lord Keith to interpose at the Admiralty in my behalf, as it was by being the bearer of his despatches that I was detained by the enemy. His Lordship instantly replied that my case gave me a claim upon the Government, and I ought to be employed without the assistance of any influence. I next went to the Board of Agriculture, where I was informed by Mr. Arthur Young[2] that Lord Carrington had been the principal means of getting me exchanged. His Lordship had rendered some very essential service to Sir Rupert George, the Chairman of the Transport Office, but that Board could do nothing in my favour until a proposal came from France. When my application arrived, requesting to be exchanged for Capt. Soleil, it was instantly granted. He advised me to lose no time in seeing his Lordship, who had been sincerely attached to my Father. Mr. Young persuaded me to stay and dine with him, and the kind attentions I experienced from this gentleman and his family I can never forget.

When I went to Hampstead, I did not fail to call upon your worthy Father[3] and Mother. Nothing could exceed the warmth of their reception. Your Father more than once repeated, in terms highly gratifying to me, how much he approved of my conduct towards my

---

[1] This is W.H.D.'s first meeting with the man who was destined to be, perhaps, the worst enemy he ever made. For his career, see below, p. 112.

[2] The great agriculturalist, whose writings raised agriculture to the status of a science: appointed, 1793, Secretary of the new Board of Agriculture.

[3] William Mervyn Dillon. See Vol. I, p. xii.

Father. Then, alluding to the Irish estate,[1] he remarked that it had
been disposed of for less than one sixteenth part of its value—not
very pleasant information for me: but the deed was done, and I
could not recover what was lost.

The next gentleman who expressed great anxiety to entertain me
was Mr. Falconer, my friend the Major's brother. The latter's case
was certainly a hard one. He was on his way home from India, as
Aide de Camp to General Sir David Baird. When captured by an
enemy's privateer, the Major went on board the Frenchman to be
answerable for his General's person, who was allowed to remain in
the Indiaman. One of our cruizers shortly afterwards recaptured the
ship, and Sir David arrived safe in England. But the privateer
escaped, and Falconer was sent to Verdun, where he remained
many years, to the serious injury of his advancement in the Army.

Gradually I was allowed more leisure, and the sudden appearance
of my old messmate Dr. Grey[2] was a sort of relief to me, as I wanted a
friend to consult. He had just left his ship, fully determined not to go
to sea again. When he accompanied Capt. Brenton to England, it was
understood that Grey was to go with him as his surgeon. He had done
so, to the serious annoyance of his wife. Capt. Brenton, who had been
appointed to the command of a fine frigate, was sent to the Mediterranean, Grey accompanying him. Brenton's ship, while watching
Toulon, was one day surrounded by several of the enemy's frigates
and nearly taken: but a gallant defence and clever manœuvres
cleared him of the danger. That event shook Grey's nerves, and he
succeeded in quitting the ship, to retire upon his half pay, to resume
practice on shore, Mrs. Grey having a fair dowry.

I now demanded of the Transport Office whether they would
sanction my claim for the lodging money which the Government had
authorized the officers of the Navy to draw whilst prisoners of war.
In reply, they advised me to write to them officially for the said
allowance. On that occasion Capt. Bowen,[3] with whom I had sailed
under Ad. Sir H. Christian, being one of the Commissioners, came
down and kindly told me how to act, remarking that I was fully
entitled to it. I accordingly sent in my application, which they forwarded to the Admiralty. In the course of a few days I received an
answer refusing the lodging money! Our Government had, in the
first instance, after having failed in establishing a regular cartel for

---

[1] Laytown, near Drogheda. See Vol. I, p. xvii.
[2] See Vol. I, pp. 337 and 343, and below, Index.
[3] Capt. James Bowen. See Vol. I, Index.

the exchange of prisoners, ordered the Senior Naval Officer at Verdun to draw for lodging money, every officer being allowed so much a day according to his rank. I as a lieutenant was allowed one shilling per diem. Consequently I had nearly five years' payment due—upwards of £80! My application not being acknowledged gave me a shock, which I confess was not an agreeable one. I had hitherto formed such an favourable opinion of the Government that I never would allow anyone to abuse its liberality. I had several times risked imbroiling myself in a duel when I heard illiberal words said against it. But now I could not help remarking that, if the French Government had not prevented that lodging money's being distributed, I should have received it. But as my official application had been refused, our Government was sanctioning the oppressive act of the enemy.[1] I in consequence again wrote to the Admiralty, pointing out in strong terms the injustice of the measure. But Grey urged me not to send it. 'You are applying for employment,' said he. 'Take care not to give offence, or they may turn their backs on you. Make your mind up to lose the money. It is a most shabby act, but you had better submit than make them your enemies.' I followed his advice, and remained silent.

From my Agent (Mr. Ommanney) I received some confidential information relating to a very fine sloop of war about to be launched, it being his opinion that if I applied I should be appointed to the command of her. I lost no time in sending in my application accordingly.

Meanwhile, I accepted an invitation from Mrs. V. to accompany her to Portsmouth, and I found myself again at that celebrated naval station. With her I visited Winchester, where I met several French officers, prisoners of war. They were very anxious to hear my reports of Verdun, but as I could not make any flattering statements of what I had undergone there, I was not a very welcome guest. On my return to Portsmouth, I met my friend Capt. Manby, then in command of a frigate, the *Thalia*. He did all, and said all, that an officer in his position could after my unfortunate captivity, and assured me that he had represented in the strongest terms at headquarters the unjustifiable act visited upon me by the French Government.

Just as we were on our return to London, Mrs. V. heard of the arrival from Sicily of the wife of the late Lord Nelson's steward to the

---

[1] A possible, and more charitable, explanation is that they were still regarding him, officially, as being in a category all by himself—an 'illegally detained' person, and not a prisoner of war at all.

Bronte estate, Mrs. Graeffer. She sought her out, and offered to take her to Lady Hamilton's at Merton. Mrs. V. had a son and daughter with her, also a niece. Therefore, instead of returning by mail, it was arranged that the hotel keeper should supply us with a private carriage that would hold six, which was to take us to Merton instead of London. We left Portsmouth that evening, and were the next morning, by 7 o'clock, at the place mentioned. From Lady Hamilton, although only partially known to her previous to my captivity, I experienced a hearty welcome. I examined all the curiosities of the gallant Nelson's residence, and in a couple of days returned to Town,* taking up my residence at Brompton.

Weeks passed on, but I heard nothing of an appointment, and my spirits began to feel the effects of disappointment. However, one satisfaction attended me. The change of scene from Verdun to England and the change of diet produced wonders in my health. I found my strength recovering daily. Port wine quite renovated me. But the arrival in Town of Admiral Gambier, who was created a peer for the capturing of the Copenhagen fleet, was for me an event of the utmost consequence, and my hopes began to revive, as I had placed the fullest reliance upon his powerful influence in my favour. So soon as his Lordship had re-established himself in his official situation at the Admiralty, I called, and was received with all those expressions that convinced me of my possessing in him a friend. He invited me to dinner and presented me to Lady Gambier, who also let drop many words highly gratifying from such a virtuous and distinguished character. After I had dined, he desired me to renew my visits at breakfast, whenever I wanted his assistance, at the same time assuring me that he would take care to let Lord Mulgrave know all about me. I could only await patiently the result of his Lordship's influence in my behalf.

The year came to a close, and I was still waiting anxiously the result of his interest: and I occasionally renewed my application at the Admiralty for employment. I went to breakfast one morning with his Lordship, who received me with his usual kindness, but I could not

---

* During my sojourn at Lady Hamilton's, I could not help noticing her affectionate attentions shown to Horatia, then about seven years old. She had been adopted by Lord Nelson, her maiden name supposed to be Thompson. Her real mother, I was told, would never be known. 'That may be,' was my reply. 'But as far as I can judge from what I have witnessed, her real mother is Lady Hamilton. Her whole proceedings towards the child are those of a mother, and no mistake.' My judgment in the end proved correct.[1]

[1] The ink in which this last sentence is written is that used, throughout, in the latest corrections. The rest of the note is in the same ink as the ordinary text of the Narrative.

help noticing his extreme taciturnity. Scarcely a word escaped from his lips. Therefore, conceiving that his mind was occupied with matters of more importance than my presence, I was in the act of retiring when he desired me to wait. Lady Gambier instantly withdrew. When we were alone, the following conversation ensued.

'Well, D.,' said his Lordship, 'are you going to be employed?' 'I hope so, my lord,' I answered, 'but I know nothing as yet for certain.' 'Have you seen Lord M.?' 'Yes. His Lordship is kind in inviting me to dinner, but I would rather be left out of the dinner party, and be appointed to a command.' 'Have you seen the private secretary?' 'I have, my lord; only a few days since. His reception was so cold that I was anxious to beat my retreat.' His Lordship hesitated. 'What else have you done?' he demanded. I then stated that I had drawn up a memorial which I had sent to the Board, and appealed to their Lordships for an act of justice towards me, by employing me after I had undergone so much in the cause of my country. His Lordship stopped me rather sharply. 'What's that you say? Justice, did you say?' Then, holding his right hand up in the air and snapping his fingers, said, 'There's justice for you at the Admiralty! I have two connections whom I have mentioned to Lord M. for employment. He has not as yet taken any notice of them. I have not yet seen your memorial, as I was not at the Board at that time. However. I shall take a look at it. But you can do nothing here without parliamentary interest. Where is your parliamentary interest?' 'I have none, my lord. I have lost all that I had by my Father's death. When he was alive I was in a very different position.'

His Lordship listened very patiently to all I said, but, still showing by his actions some uneasiness, he at length addressed me as follows:—'You have certainly great claims on your country. No one can deny that. I have spoken to Lord Mulgrave about you. He can not plead ignorance. What are you going to do today?' 'I have nothing in view, my lord,' was my reply. 'I advise you then,' said his Lordship,' to go to the Secretary in my name, and tell him to let Lord M. know that I am interested in your welfare. I shall be here, and, if you are not satisfied, come and let me know.' I then tendered my grateful acknowledgments to his Lordship and retired.

A few minutes after 11 o'clock, I presented myself to Capt. Moorsom,[1] Lord M.'s private secretary, and said, 'I do not come to pester you on my own account. I am sent here by Lord Gambier.'

---

[1] (Sir) Robert Moorsom, Lt. 5/1/1784; Capt. 22/11/90; R-Ad. 31/7/1810; V-Ad. 4/6/14; Ad. 22/7/30. C.-in-C. Chatham, 1824–27. Died, April 1835.

The instant I mentioned his Lordship's name, the Secretary became quite an altered person. He rose from his seat with an anxiety that I could not help noticing, and requested me to take a chair. 'I am directed by his Lordship,' I said, 'to call upon you and request you to explain to Lord M. his Lordship's anxiety to see me employed. Should the First Lord wish to know more about me, Lord G. is ready to answer any questions in my behalf.' Capt. Moorsom opened a large book lying on his table: then, running his finger across the page, said, 'By this report you are the first for employment. But the ship you have applied for is not yet ready.' I could only reply that the friend who had confidentially advised me to ask for that ship intimated that she would be ready in the course of a few days; that upwards of three months had passed, and my not hearing of anything made me conclude that I was forgotten. 'Moreover,' said I, 'younger officers than I, who have not seen half of the service that I have, are receiving appointments every day. Such a trial can not well be endured.' The Secretary could not say when that ship would be ready. It was therefore settled between us that he was to deliver Lord Gambier's message to the First Lord, and that I was ready to accept any other appointment which might be selected for me.

Returning to my hotel, where I had again taken up my quarters, I found an invitation from Lady Hamilton, requesting me to pass a few days at Merton, which I willingly accepted. I soon reached Lady Hamilton's, where I passed nearly a week most agreeably. Upon my return to Town, my landlord acquainted me that Capt. Moorsom had called for me the day after I had left Town. I hastened to the Admiralty, it being the 18th of the month, the Queen's birthday. I was instantly received by Capt. Moorsom, who acquainted me that Lord M. had offered me the refusal of the *Childers*, brig of war.

When that vessel's name was mentioned, a sort of horror overcame me. 'What,' said I, 'you don't mean the old *Childers* that used to run alongside of Lord Howe's ship last war, and take charge of the dispatches?' 'Yes,' was his reply. 'Oh no,' I rejoined, 'I cannot accept that old worn-out craft. Only recollect, Capt. Moorsom, I am three years a commander, and am in every sense entitled to something better than that!' Much hurt at such an offer, I was in the act of retiring, having opened the door and made my bow, when the Secretary called me to him. 'Now, Capt. D., pause well,' said he. 'Recollect the interest that has been exerted for you. You have declared that you were prepared to take any command at a moment's notice, and proceed to any part of the world. Here is a vessel full manned and ready for sea. You have only to put yourself into a post chaise, take the command, and God knows what may happen in the next 24 hours!' Those words produced their effect. I acknowledged that I had been rather taken aback when I heard the name of the old *Childers*, but that I had recovered from the shock, and would accept the command of her. 'You have no time to lose,' he replied. 'Capt. Innes,[1] who now commands her, is not in very good health. He has applied to be superseded, and Lord M. has pitched upon you to relieve him.' In a few more words I agreed to leave Town that night: then, thanking the Secretary for his advice, requested him to tender my acknowledgments to Lord Mulgrave for the appointment.

I retired, and had scarcely left his room when I was accosted by one of the Admiralty messengers. 'Pray, sir, is your name Dillon?' he said. 'Lord Gambier wishes to see you.' Thither I hastened. It was then about 2 o'clock. 'Well,' said his Lordship, 'have you accepted the command of the *Childers*?' 'I have, my lord.' 'Very well. I am glad of it. I was fearful you would not take her. But it is all right. It is a stepping stone to something better. You are stationed at Leith. You will go in the first place to Sheerness, where you will be ordered to Scotland. But before long I am in hopes of removing you to a superior command.' With these assurances his Lordship renewed his expressions of the warmest feelings for my advancement and welfare, shaking me by the hand in confirmation of all he said. I took my leave of him.

As I passed through the hall of the Admiralty, several officers of my acquaintance accosted me in the following terms:—'Is it true that you have accepted the command of the *Childers*?' 'Yes,' I replied. 'Then go and insure your life without loss of time. She has returned to port having thrown her guns overboard to prevent her sinking. You will never come back again!' 'Very satisfactory news,' I observed. 'However, I shall try what I can do with her.'

(2) H.M.S. *CHILDERS* (North Sea)

JANUARY 1808–APRIL 1808

As I had promised to quit Town that night, I had enough to do, not having any uniforms or anything ready. I hastened to my stepmother's, in the meantime writing a note to Mrs. V., acquainting her

---

[1] Thomas Innes, Lt. 22/11/1790; Cdr. 26/12/99; Capt. 21/10/1810.

that I hoped to be at her house in a couple of hours. Lady D. assisted me as much as she could. I then called upon my Agent and requested an advance of cash to fit me out. Mr. Ommanney, who was in attendance, remarked in reply to my demand, 'You have some property in Ireland?' My reply acquainted him that the Irish estate had been sold to pay my expenses at Verdun. 'If that is the case,' said he, 'I can not assist you. There is a certain sum which we generally allow to officers taking a command. That will be at your disposal, but I cannot let you have more.' I took a part of that sum, then made the best of my way to Mrs. V. She had ordered a tailor to be in waiting who undertook to make me a coat and waistcoat in a few hours. We then repaired to the sword cutlers, where I fitted myself with an article of that kind according to the regulations: next a cocked hat. Then I went to Wedgwood's China Establishment and bought a tray that contained four dishes with a small soup tureen in the middle. Other articles were obtained, packed up and paid for. They were to be at Sheerness next morning. I had performed wonders in the course of a few hours. We then sat down to dinner, during which, as if an inspiration had seized Mrs. V., she made up her mind to accompany me to Sheerness. Her daughter, niece and maid were to be of the party.

A travelling carriage was ordered, and by 10 o'clock it came to the door with four horses. The tailor had not kept his promise, but he declared that my coat, etc., would be at Rochester before 4 o'clock in the morning. We then started for that town accompanied by a deep fall of snow. We were too much taken up with our own affairs to attend to the brilliant illumination which everywhere appeared to our view. When we got off the pavement, and were proceeding at a rapid pace, the young ladies entertained us with some songs. However, just as we had passed the Elephant and Castle, I thought I heard a noise at the back of the carriage—something like a screw. I put my head out of the window, and to my astonishment beheld a man on the seat. His left hand had hold of the spring. With my stick I gave him a hearty thump over his knuckle which obliged him instantly to drop himself to the ground, accompanied by a partner. In their dress they had the appearance of chimney sweeps. I then called out to the postboys to stop, but it was useless. They did not, or, more properly speaking, would not hear me. Shortly afterwards, another person got up behind. However, I made him drop off—in appearance a gentleman in shoes and stockings. By 2 o'clock we were at Rochester, where we were obliged to wait till the tide would allow us to proceed to Sheerness. All my questions to the postboys ended in nothing; but I am fully persuaded that they were leagued with the fellows who got up behind. In the attempt made to wrest my portmanteau out of the back panel of the carriage a sort of large gimblet had been employed. When we stopped at the inn we saw a large hole bored by such an instrument. It had penetrated through the side of my portmanteau which had been placed in the back seat. Had I not heard the working of the screw, it would have been carried off in a few seconds. It contained my commission appointing me to command the *Childers*, some linen and cash. At 4 o'clock the stage arrived bringing me a parcel containing my uniforms, and after that delay we proceeded to Sheerness, putting up at the inn there.

My first duty was to present myself to the Port Admiral, Thomas Wells, Esq.[1] This was the officer under whom I had served in the *Defence*. Consequently I was well received by him. After the etiquette usual on such occasions, he insisted upon my immediately putting to sea. However, when he heard of my having nothing ready, and that I had quitted London the day of my appointment, he agreed to allow me two days, that indulgence being obtained with great difficulty: but I was obliged to act accordingly. He invited me to dine, then sent for Mrs. Wells and his daughters, to whom he presented me. They recognized me although we had not met for fourteen years. They were extremely affable, and I was astonished that those fine girls still remained without husbands.

I next—it being the 19th—proceeded off to the *Childers*, where Capt. Innes was waiting to receive me. My commission having been read to the crew and all the officers introduced to me, I became installed in the command of the brig. I agreed to take many articles from Capt. Innes which I thought would answer my purpose until I reached Leith, where I had directed all my luggage to be sent from London. Capt. Innes then went on shore, where we were to meet to settle other matters. I then bent my steps round the vessel, and was surprised at her diminutive dimensions. There was only one lieutenant,[2] although she was allowed two: in fact, there was no cabin fitted for a second. My inspection was not of a nature to be pleasing, but I made no remarks, not wishing anyone to suppose that I was disappointed. However, I was most seriously annoyed at all I saw. When I entered the Cabin, I met the youth who was there in attendance, to whom I put some questions. This lad, anxious to please his

[1] See Vol. I, p. 163 *et seq.*
[2] Thomas Edmonds, Lt. 28/4/1807; Ret. Cdr. 17/1/1843.

new captain, let out a number of things that had better never have
been mentioned. The Cabin was very small and not very clean, which
made me make some remarks on that score. 'Very true, sir,' said the
youth. 'We have been labouring heart and soul these two days to put
the vessel to rights to please you.' The more I saw the more I had
reason to regret having accepted the command. When the officers
felt themselves at liberty to offer their remarks, I found them all discontented. They could not help alluding to the throwing of the guns
overboard. I made no replies, but listened patiently to all they said.
After remaining on board two or three hours to ascertain the exact
condition of the brig, I went on shore. In my conversations with
Capt. Innes, I tried to discover the real cause of his giving up the
command. He did not appear inclined to say much on the subject.
He had been in the brig some time, and had made £15,000 Prize
money. He thought he was entitled to a larger vessel. However
he assured me that, with proper management, I should take Prizes,
as the Norwegians and Danes had constant communications by sea,
and a good look out would ensure success.

On the following day I mustered the brig's crew and exercised
them at the guns—carronades, I should say. She mounted 14 of
them, 12 lbers, with a crew of 63 men and boys, her proper complement being 86. The carronades, being new, were sealed, and I did all
I could to inspire confidence in the men I had under command. The
weather was cold, and we were visited with snow storms—not a
pleasant season of the year to put to sea with an unknown crew, as
it was probable that many of my regulations differed from those of
the late captain. However, I had undertaken the task: therefore
perseverance was my motto. I met several acquaintances among the
captains. One of them, with whom I sailed in the *Prince George*,
Baker,[1] commanded a fine sloop of war.[2] I had some long interesting
conversations with him. He assured me that I should not be able to
keep up the respectability of my station under £500 a year. 'Why,'
said I, 'I have already spent that sum in my outfit!' 'Very true,' he
replied. 'It's what we all do. And if you have not something beyond
your pay the case is desperate.' That literally was mine; but I did not
like to tell him so. The *Childers'* pay was about £250 per annum, out
of which there were many deductions, such as the Agent's charges
and the income tax. I confess I pondered a good deal over the position I was placed in. However, hopes of good luck buoyed me up. I

[1] John Baker, Lt. 9/7/1794; Cdr. 29/4/1802; Capt. 21/10/10. Died, March 1845.
[2] The *Kangaroo*, 18.

met here a Capt. Sturt,[1] in command of a fine brig of war. This officer made himself known shortly afterwards by carrying off a nun from one of the convents at Madeira. This was a regular sailor's frolic.

My hours were counted, and I found there would be no peace for me until I left Sheerness. I had taken with me a fine youth of the name of Parker[2] as a naval cadet: also a Mate, Mr. Knight, whom I appointed as an acting lieutenant. I was exerting myself to the utmost to make the best of a bad bargain. I had only one day more to remain at anchor, and I devoted it entirely to the brig. I had her thoroughly washed below, cleaned and smoked. While this operation was proceeding, I saw the smoke coming out of the seams, which indicated her crazy state. The officers pointed to many parts of the vessel, proving that she was worn out: in short, I began to be seriously impressed with the awkward situation in which I found myself. The *Childers* was in fact an inferior command to the gunbrigs under lieutenants, which mounted 18 heavier guns than those on board my craft. Turning all these matters over in my mind, being alone in my Cabin whilst the crew were at dinner, I was suddenly seized with a fit of despair, and I thought it my duty to let Lord Gambier know all the difficulties I had exposed myself to in taking command of such a rotten vessel. I wrote my letter accordingly, and requested his Lordship to have me removed to a better one. I have often thought of that act since. It was, probably, lucky that I had not written the letter on shore, as if I had it would have been instantly sent to the Post Office. What the result would have been no one knows. But, on board the brig, I waited until the boat's crew had dined, and in the meantime I reflected upon the contents of my letter to the leading naval Lord of the Admiralty. He had acknowledged to me that he expected I would refuse the command: consequently he might be prepared for receiving my letter. However, upon more mature reflection I tore it up. I treated all the difficulties made by the officers with contempt, and finally made up my mind to brave every danger. I had not been accustomed to the management of a brig, but my own conscience led me to believe that I should succeed in my undertaking. I had not much confidence in the First Lieutenant—he was very young and had not much experience—but I had a better opinion of the crew. There were some stout fellows amongst them, and my knowledge of that class of man inclined me to place reliance upon

[1] Henry Evelyn Pitfield Sturt, Commanding the *Skylark*, 16. Lt. 20/2/1800; Cdr. 29/4/1802; Capt. 21/10/10.
[2] Charles Parker, Lt. 17/9/1816.

their exertions. Therefore the die was cast. I had come to the conclusion that it was more manly to trust to my fate than to make
difficulties. Under these feelings my future conduct was regulated.

On the 22nd, being ready for sea, I took leave of Ad. Wells and
his family. I had lent the young ladies some caricatures which were
returned: then, off to the *Childers*, and removed from the Little Nore
further out. My whole thoughts were now taken up with my official
duties. I had two pilots for the North Sea: they were very uncouth
fellows. I slept on board for the first time. The following day, at half
past 2, the brig was under sail; but I cannot pass unnoticed what
appeared to me an unpardonable neglect on the part of the late
Captain. The capstan bars were so long that they overlaid the tiller.
I was all astonishment to perceive that this tiller was lashed on one
side to make room for the bars to go round. Consequently, the instant
the anchor was out of the ground the brig lost the use of her helm.
Upon my mentioning this bad contrivance to the First Lieutenant
and the Master, they said that they always had managed in that way.
'It is a very lubberly act,' I replied, 'and it shall be instantly
remedied.' So soon as the sails were trimmed I sent for the Carpenter,
and ordered him to shorten the capstan bars so many inches; next,
to curtail the tiller, that it might be used free of the bars. These
orders were instantly executed, and everybody appeared to wonder
why such a measure had not been thought of before. The safety of a
vessel depends upon the motion of the rudder. So long as it remains
unmanageable no one can tell what accidents may occur. This
improvement for the better caused some remarks, which I could not
help overhearing. It was thought that the Captain knew what he was
about.

In passing the *Namur*, the Flag Ship, at the Great Nore I received
nine seamen for a passage to Yarmouth. In the evening, a fog
coming on, I was obliged to anchor. The next day, Sunday, I read the
Articles of War to the crew. I then acquainted them that, in so small
a vessel, every precaution was necessary to prevent surprise; in consequence whereof the brig's company were never to quit the deck all
together, but one watch was to be constantly on deck, and to be
armed. That regulation was instantly put in force, and a number of
others, the details of which I shall not dwell upon, were adopted.
But I gave the crew to understand that I did not mean to be captured without a sharp defence, and every soul on board was to
practice, as often as circumstances would allow, the broadsword
exercise. The Marines I ordered up, inspected all their muskets, and

saw them put into order fit for use. They had scarcely reported them as such when a vessel was seen nearing us. She was instantly hailed, but as the answer was not satisfactory a volley of musketry was discharged at her by the Marines of the watch—a very lucky warning, as, if the stranger had not been alarmed, he would probably have run on board of us in the fog. The vessel was an English fishing craft, and the chief received a jobation from me for not keeping a better look out. That act of mine proved to my crew that I was in earnest.

On the following afternoon the fog cleared and, the wind being fair, the brig was soon under way with studdingsails set. The crew were exercised at the guns. At dinner time one watch remained on deck till relieved by the other, having had theirs. At nightfall I was again obliged to anchor with a fog, but the next morning a fresh breeze sent it off, and by daylight we were making the best of our way towards Yarmouth. At night Lowestoft lights were seen. Shortly afterwards a lugger closed upon us. A shot was instantly fired at her, and repeated till she brought to. I sent a boat to board her. She was from Rochester bound to Yarmouth. On the afternoon of the 26th we anchored in Yarmouth Roads.

I lost no time in presenting my respects to the Admiral, B. Douglas.[1] His son, who was still at Verdun, had written to him about me, and I was most courteously received. The supernumeraries were sent to the *Amelia*, and by 10 o'clock the next day the *Childers* was under sail, bound to Leith. At night the weather had a threatening appearance, and as we were now more out to sea I issued night orders. The officer of the watch was astonished that I did not hand the square mainsail. He came to me to request that I would do so. It had, he said, always been done before. 'Then,' said I, 'that custom will be changed. Should a gale of wind come on, you may furl it, but not before. If we can't fight we must be prepared to make sail.' That order, and others, were very different from those they had been used to act under. One of the most unpleasant duties of a captain is to train the crew of a vessel which has been disciplined by another commander. If his regulations differ from what they have previously been used to, it occasions unpleasant occurrences, murmurs, and sometimes even mutiny. In this case, however, luckily for me, every one became aware that my orders were based upon good principles, not upon whims, and the officers and crew soon began to understand my ways.

I was anxious to be acquainted with the qualities of the *Childers*.

[1] See above, p. 42.

The little experience I had of her led me to believe that she was over-masted, as she appeared to sail better, and be more easy, under reduced canvas. I made many enquiries relating to her guns being thrown overboard, and concluded that it was all through bad management. She was lying to in a gale of wind, with the helm lashed alee. That old system, by which many of our ships had been injured by getting sternway, I thought had been abandoned. But it was not so in the *Childers*, for it was while she had sternway that the sea came in and nearly swamped her. Therefore, to prevent her going down, away went the guns. If I recollect rightly, those which had just been shipped were of a lighter calibre than those thrown away, and no doubt the brig had not so much stability on the water as formerly. Turning the officers' statements to account, I sent for all of them and pointed out the evil consequences of lashing the helm to leeward, and forbad its being done again. I next had the seamen and Quarter Masters aft, explaining to them that, in future, the brig was to be constantly kept under command of the helm—that is, to have head-way. I threatened the steersmen with punishment if it ever came to my knowledge that the helm was lashed to leeward. I ordered a card to be stuck on the binnacle with written instructions on it directing the helm to be kept amidships during stormy weather. This plan, on being followed out, proved that I was right: for, instead of laying the vessel to in a gale of wind, I kept her under the storm staysails, always forging ahead and under control of the helm. The change for the better became evident to all on board. The Gunner,[1] who had been nine years in the brig, and who had charge of a watch at sea, was the first to notice the improvement in the ease of her motions. There was no sudden jerking, but the vessel yielded gradually to the pressure of the wind and, with the assistance of the storm staysails, went slowly through the water, to the astonishment of all the seamen who wondered that no other officer had thought of such a system before. The Gunner, who proved to be a thorough good seaman, repeated over and again his regrets that this plan had not been put in practice sooner, as it would have prevented many a sail being blown away and eased the wear of the hull. All my orders, I now observed, were attended to with alacrity: it was evident the crew had confidence in their Captain.

When the officers knew I had been so long detained at Verdun, they inquired if Mr. Temple was an acquaintance. When they heard my reports of that gentleman's proceedings, they were astonished,

---

[1] M'Nicholl.

as they had formed the highest opinion of him. They had received him on board as a passenger when in the Baltic. He had, after his escape from France, visited Russia and, luckily finding his way on board the *Childers,* came to England in her. He had by his lively disposition and other attractive qualities completely captivated their good feelings towards him. However, I requested them not to bring his name again under my notice.

We were 13 days getting to Leith, during which we encountered a great deal of stormy weather. It had been my object to keep near the land, expecting by so doing to make better progress. I was right in my judgment, but the unruly pilots lost by night what I had gained by day. So soon as they knew that I was in bed, they would shape the brig's course out into the middle of the ocean. Consequently we encountered tremendously high seas: the vessel laboured woefully and shipped immense quantities of water, the leeside being constantly submerged. All this rolling about woke me, and, inquiring of the officer of the watch, I was informed that the pilot had stood away from the land. I finally put a stop to these whims. One night I went on deck to see what was going on. The vessel was rolling to an alarming extent. I was suddenly jerked from one side to the other, and fell on the cap of one of the carronade screws. The pilot who witnessed this accident, a stout lusty fellow, never came to my assistance: nor did anyone till I called out for help. I thought one of my ribs was broken, as the pain was intense. I could not keep my body upright for a long while afterwards. The crew were seized with colds and coughs: in short, the whole of us were laid up by the mismanagement of the pilots. The Master was a young officer, and only acting. I therefore found myself obliged to interfere and take upon myself a responsibility not usual in such cases. The pilots kept out to sea at nights because they felt no uneasiness when at a distance from the land. But when it was near they were fidgety. The consequence of all this was that the rigging became so slack from the labouring of the vessel that I was obliged to run into Berwick Bay to set it up. Putting to sea the next day, we found the foretopmast sprung, and I had to shift it for a sound one. Finding my arguments had no effect on these obstinate pilots, I assumed the charge myself, and gave written orders at night for the management of the brig. We soon benefited by the change. By keeping at a moderate distance from the shore we had smoother water, and gained ground rapidly. On our way we boarded only two vessels—English ones—nothing like an enemy being seen.

On the 9th of February we anchored in Leith Roads. Never in my life did I feel greater relief from anxiety, as every soul on board was a martyr to coughs, hoarseness and alarming colds, so severe had been the weather. When I reported my arrival to Ad. Vashon,[1] who held the naval command, and represented to him the state of the *Childers'* crew, he expressed a very proper feeling in their behalf. It was not only their case which required consideration, but also my own: I was completely knocked up. He assured me that time would be given for rest, etc., and that he should not think of ordering the vessel to sea till the crew had recovered from their fatigues. He also expressed his astonishment at such a useless vessel being kept in the Service. So far I had reason to be satisfied, as I now knew for certain that I should have time to fit out my brig; and I hoped to make all on board comfortable, as far as circumstances would allow. Our arrival made the fourth brig of war stationed here to cruize against the enemy. The Admiral had his Flag on board the *Texel*, a 64. There was a sort of depot at Leith for naval stores, but nothing in the shape of a Dock Yard.

Having now time to look about me, my first object was to make my cabin more comfortable. There was only room for the half of a round table in it, which was placed against the fore bulkhead. This arrangement would only admit of three, but I was determined somehow or other to find space for four. There was a stove against the after bulkhead, which I could not well do without in the winter: but it was much in the way. At last I contrived to cut away the bulkhead, making a grove to receive it. By that means I gained nearly 24 inches in length, which enabled me to fit up a small round table, with four chairs conveniently placed. I could now invite a friend or two to dine with me. I had to set all my wits to work to turn to the best account a cabin scarcely deserving the name of one. The officers were astonished at my perseverance and ingenuity in overcoming obstacles that no other captain had hitherto attempted. The other brigs on the station could easily have hoisted mine in, so much superior were they in size and dimensions. They were armed with 16 32 lb carronades and two long nines, with a crew of 120 men. The names of their commanders were G. Andrews,[2] F. Baugh[3] and my

---

[1] James Vashon, Lt. 1/6/1774; Cdr. 5/8/80; Capt. 12/4/82; R-Ad. 23/4/1804; V-Ad. 28/4/08; Ad. 4/6/14.

[2] George Andrews, Lt. 9/3/1797; Cdr. 29/4/1802; Capt. 22/9/09; commanding the *Ringdove*, 18.

[3] Thomas Folliott Baugh, Lt. 2/11/1793; Cdr. 29/4/1802; Capt. 21/10/10; R-Ad. (Ret.) 1/10/46; commanding the *Clio*, 18.

old shipmate of the *Alcide*, Sanders.[1] My again meeting him was a rencontre for which I was not prepared. However, on our acquaintance being renewed, he conducted himself very properly, and a friendly intercourse was established. The four of us formed a mess at the principal inn, on the pier of Leith. There was a naval club which met occasionally in Edinburgh, which I attended once or twice. I there made the acquaintance of several naval officers of distinction, among the number Capt. George Hope,[2] who at that time was Captain of the North Sea Fleet under Ad. Sir James Saumarez, and who afterwards, when a Lord of the Admiralty, became a useful friend.

As the crew were recovering from their complaints, I employed them in making such improvements as I thought necessary: but the more I examined the contents of the vessel under my command, the more I had reason to despond. The stores were in a most neglected state, and, after weighing all these defects in my mind, I thought it my duty to lay the case before the Admiral. He gave strong symptoms of displeasure at having such a vessel under his Flag. He ordered the Master of the *Texel* to take a survey of the brig's condition. That officer in the performance of his duty gave the strongest signs of dissatisfaction—even of disgust—at all he saw, and he did not hesitate to declare that he thought the *Childers* unfit for sea service. He accordingly made his report to the Admiral verbally, upon which I was directed to apply for a survey of the vessel's capabilities. I was not prepared for such a proceeding, but as the Commander in Chief seemed determined that something of the kind should be done, there appeared to me no backing out of the position in which I unexpectedly found myself. I thought the requesting of a survey of a vessel to which I had just been appointed might offend the Admiralty. Consequently, in my official letter, which, in the first instance was addressed to the Admiral, I began by saying, 'Acting under your directions, I have to report the defective state of the sloop under my command.' Admiral Vashon noticed its commencement, and appeared inclined to disapprove of the sentence: but, without allowing me time to make my reply, he said, 'Very well. I don't mind. I shall send it.' I was considerably annoyed. The brig, everybody knew, was a worn-out craft, but I should have taken my chance in her. When I thought it my duty to represent her inefficient condition, I had not contemplated the consequences. I thought the Admiral

---

[1] George Sanders. See Vol. I, p. 15 *et seq.* Now commanding the *Bellette*, 18.
[2] (Sir) George Johnstone Hope, Lt. 29/2/1788; Cdr. 22/11/90; Capt. 13/9/93; R-Ad. 1/8/1811. Died, 1818.

would order a supply of better stores, and direct the other defects to
be made good on the spot. But when the case took the turn mentioned,
I felt myself justified in placing the principal responsibility on the
Admiral. He was an odd-tempered man, and a stranger to me; and I
felt embarrassed in my early dealings with him. However, I thought
it prudent to write to Lord Gambier and explain all that had passed
between the Admiral and self.

Whilst employed in improving my cabin I could get no assistance
from the naval depot. I was consequently obliged to buy plank and
other things. The First Lieutenant of the Flag Ship, Mr. Peake,[1] had
been my shipmate in the *Alcide*. When he heard that I had been
buying the articles mentioned, he hastened to the naval yard, and in
strong terms pointed out to the authorities there the impropriety of
making an officer in my situation purchase deal boards for his cabin.
His representation produced its effect, and one of the clerks from the
office came and requested me to send my bill to him. He also made a
sort of apology for what had happened. I could not help reminding
him that my application for a supply of the articles had been refused.
I shall here state that I was obliged to buy log lines, as there were
none in store, and the Admiral carried his ideas of economy to such a
pitch that he would not allow any to be purchased. Therefore the
brig's speed through the water was reckoned at my expense.

It took three days to convey a letter from Leith to London. On
the seventh day an order arrived from the Admiralty, directing that
the *Childers* should be examined, whether sound or not. In the
meantime all my traps had arrived from London, and I had the means
of making my preparations. The Admiral did not invite us often to
his house. His son[2] commanded the Flag Ship. Mrs. Vashon appeared
an amiable person, but as there was not much sociability I was left a
great deal to my own resources. Capt. Sanders resided at a different
inn from mine, but he came to us to dine. He had nicknamed my
brig 'the Half-Moon Battery,' and was not backward in passing
severe strictures upon her inefficiency, as the brig that he commanded
—the *Bellette*—was one of the most powerful in our Navy. At one of
our mess dinners he proposed that the whole of us should share
Prize money together: but nothing was decided. The *Childers'*
defective sails were sent to the *Texel* to be repaired, and the officers
from the Yard were employed in examining our timbers, but as the
vessel was afloat the survey could only be partial.

---

[1] Thomas Ladd Peake, Lt. 8/5/1805; Cdr. 8/5/12; Capt. 1/3/22.
[2] James Giles Vashon, Lt. 13/1/1794; Capt. 28/5/1802.

As time passed on, I invited my brother officers to come and dine with me. The tray which I depended on so much had not yet been used, but now was the time for displaying it. We were all seated in my cabin waiting the appearance of dinner, when my steward announced that the passage leading into it was so narrow that the tray could not be brought in. Here was a disappointment! The dishes were handed in separately. The casualty did not interfere much with our dinner, which proved a very sociable one, and Sanders was so anxious to see the tray that it was produced. He was so much pleased with the construction of it that he purchased it. In a few days he became my constant companion, and would not let me rest until I wrote a letter to Lord Mulgrave in his behalf, reminding his Lordship of a promise that he had made to Lord Chatham to promote him. Hitherto I knew nothing of Sanders. At times he gave himself consequential airs, wishing it to be understood that he possessed considerable influence. He assumed importance from the circumstance of his commanding so fine a vessel. However, not having much faith in this gentleman's assertions, I demanded explanations, which proved him to be the son of a surgeon who had for many years been attached to Lord Chatham's household. Thereat Mr. Sanders did not rise much in my estimation. His authoritative bearing, with other freaks, were not suited to his connexions. I had supposed him, by his sayings and doings, to be a member of some high aristocratic family. He was fond of the bottle, and during our rambles he had frequently indulged in that failing. It fell to my lot to carry him home one night in a hack carriage, but he never refunded to me my expenses therefor, or even thanked me for my care of him. Therefore, instead of an agreeable companion, I found him a regular bore.

The builders, having terminated their examination of the *Childers'* timbers, declared them to be sound—a result no one expected. However, so it was, and I, her Captain, lost no time in completing all that was required. I fitted a boarding netting to the brig, and had the boats, such as they were—a cutter and jolly boat—well repaired for cutting out work. The first orders I received were to take charge of a convoy for Gothenburg. When the merchants heard that the *Childers* had been appointed to perform that duty, they protested against placing their property under the care of such an inefficient vessel of war, and they remonstrated. Consequently a sloop, the *Snake*, with 32 lber carronades, was ordered round from Sheerness to relieve me of my charge. This was no great compliment to my brig!

In a short time all the provisions were on board, a few volunteers came from the Rendezvous, and I was anxious to try my fate on the briny waves. I hove up one anchor to be ready to start at a moment's notice. The Admiral had arranged that the four brigs should put to sea at the same time, and we, the commanders, agreed to have a parting dinner at the inn. Here the proposal was renewed to share Prize money together. Sanders made use of some very ill-timed expressions relating to my brig, remarking that she would be taken by the smallest enemy privateer: and that, the others' vessels being so much superior to mine, the risk was not a fair one. I retorted upon Sanders, stating that, as he had been the first to moot the question of sharing, he ought to be the last to make such out-of-the-way observations. 'If I am attacked,' I said, 'I shall not be so easily captured as you imagine. Therefore, to close the bargain with you, I will agree to share Prize money with you for three months, or not at all. It is now for you to decide.' In conclusion no agreement was made. The party broke up, and we repaired on board our separate vessels. I had received a clerk recommended by Mrs. V., also a steward who had been employed in her establishment. When Ad. Vashon gave me my sailing instructions, he authorized me to seek shelter against stormy weather wherever I might find it convenient, and not to expose my crew to chances of sickness. I was to cruize off Gothenburg to annoy the enemy to the best of my power. Having settled everything satisfactorily, I took my leave.

On the 10th of March, by 11 o'clock in the morning, the *Childers* was under sail, favoured with a good breeze and fine weather. So soon as we were clear of the land I exercised the seamen at the guns and the sword exercise. The boats were also put into good order, with a certain number of men fixed upon ready for boarding ships at anchor. I explained to the crew my determination to be constantly ready for action, by night or by day, directing them to keep their cutlasses and pistols in fighting condition. The next day I boarded a whaler bound to Davis Straits, but nothing of consequence occurred till the 14th when we made the land, and I saw the coast of Norway, of stupendous height, for the first time. I had suited my dress for sea service in a small vessel—a round jacket, etc. When exercising the seamen at the guns and the Marines with muskets, I appeared on deck with my sabre drawn and pistols in my belt. This proceeding seemed to be approved of by all under my command, as I noticed cheerful countenances in every direction. My orders were obeyed with alacrity and apparent good will. All these indications gave me confidence, which led me to rely on their support in the event of meeting an enemy.

It was about 1 o'clock of this day that a vessel was seen from the mast head. Sail was instantly made in chace of her. The stranger closed in with the land, by which means we lost sight of her. My dinner hour was ½ past 2, p.m. By ½ past 4 we had closed this mountainous coast and again got sight of the chace. We were now in smoother water, but the stranger disappeared among the rocks. Not thinking it prudent to stand too near to this high land, I hoisted out the cutter. Volunteers offered themselves with an animated spirit that was truly gratifying. A certain number having been selected, I gave the command of her to the Master, Mr. Wilson,[1] directing him to proceed inshore and bring out the vessel. He had no sooner left the brig when more volunteers came forward, anxious to assist the cutter. Not wishing to thwart their bold intentions, I had the jolly boat lowered and soon manned, the Purser[2] requesting to lead her. He evinced such determination that I complied with his wishes. All this time my dinner remained on the table. I had been so often interrupted during the chace that I had not finished the necessary meal. The two boats that had gone away contained 24 of my best men. They were soon out of sight, and the *Childers* lay to, waiting the result of their exertions.

More than an hour elapsed, and no boats were to be seen. I became anxious, as the day was closing: and this feeling was considerably increased when the man aloft on the look-out, shouted in a loud voice, 'A large vessel coming towards us from under the land!' All our attentions were instantly directed to the object. Opposite to that part of the coast where I had hove to, the land trended to the North East. A long inlet extending to some distance was discerned, which the pilots informed me led to the port of Hitteroe. It was from thence that this stranger was approaching under topgallant sails. The two lusty pilots gave symptoms of extreme alarm, declaring that the enemy's vessel was a very powerful one, and that I should either be taken or sunk. I desired them to keep silence and attend to my orders: but they became so refractory that I was obliged to order them below, as their sayings made a strong impression upon the seamen.[3] I then called the crew to their guns, and prepared for action.

As the stranger drew out from his apparently confined inclosure,

[1] William Wilson (Acting). Confirmed, 3/7/1813.
[2] A. W. H. Le Neve, 1st Warrant, 29/4/07.
[3] W.H.D. mentions their names—Drummond and Gordon—in his dispatch and praises their conduct!

he was still end on, and I could not see his rig. But the size of his bows indicated a vessel of some dimensions. Then, as he shaped his course towards the *Childers*, we saw the length of his hull: he was a large brig, mounting nine long heavy guns upon his broadside. This was not a very agreeable visitor, and I now found myself in a most awkward position. The boats had not yet hove in sight from the N.W.—that is, on my right—and I was, I confess, almost at a loss how to act. If I attempted to draw further off from the land, I exposed my boats to capture. Therefore, after a few seconds of meditation, I determined to bring my opponent to action. He continued to near me, and when he was about a mile off upon my starboard bow, I fired a shot at him. At the same time up went the colours of Old England. My firing obliged him to alter his course: therefore, instead of closing nearer, he hauled off. This was a most critical moment for me. When he changed his plan, which at first seemed to be one of attack, he hoisted the Danish Ensign and kept aloof, whereby the advantage instantly turned in my favour: which had its effect on my crew. Fortunately for me, I had now time to make my arrangements.

But before I could make sail, to bring the enemy to action, my boats hove in sight, coming from a deep creek on our left, with a galliot in tow, under sail. Its crew, not being armed, had been unable to resist the attack of my boats, but had fled on shore, where they hurled down from the rocks huge stones. But fortunately no one had been injured by them. My crew were firing their muskets, and a similar fire was noticed from the Prize, which circumstance led me to believe that my men were still contending with the Danes. However, the firing soon ceased, and the boats neared us rapidly. Yet notwithstanding these favourable appearances I was still in a very embarrassed position, because it lay in the power of the enemy to capture my boats and retake the galliot. Why the Dane did not make that exertion is no affair of mine. By his not doing so, my boats finally rejoined me, my opponent looking quietly on all the while. I now gave directions for the security of the Prize, placing an officer in command of her. The boats were hoisted in, and I made sail to attack the Dane.

The day had just closed. I had therefore to beat to windward to reach him. He kept so close to the land that I could not get inshore of him. My broadsides were directed only as often as they could bear, I was obliged to shorten sail, and I could only aim at him as the flash of his guns indicated his position. Darkness now came on, which for a short while interrupted our fire. Many broadsides had been exchanged, but as yet the *Childers* had not received any injury of consequence. There was only a light air so close to the high land, and the water was as smooth as a millpond. Under these circumstances all the advantages lay with the enemy. He could see us as we were outside, but we could not see him. I therefore ceased cannonading till the moon enabled us to see what we were about. It was during this interval that we heard sounds very similar to the rowing of boats, and an impression naturally arose that the enemy was receiving men from the shore. Our quietness did not last long, for the Dane, profiting by his position, opened his fire in slow succession. One of his shots went clean through both sides of the *Childers* just above the line of flotation. Another shot lodged in the Lower Deck. It weighed 22lbs English, so that I was led to believe that he had long 18 lbers—overwhelming odds against 12lb carronades. The moon at last, being at its full, shone forth in all imaginable splendour. Being now enabled to ascertain my exact position, I thought myself rather too near the land, upon an hostile coast. Judging it imprudent to expose my vessel to such unusual dangers, I directed the pilots to widen our distance, and, having placed her about 3 miles from the shore, I again hove to, waiting the proceedings of the Dane.

The heavens were cloudless; the stars and planets were seen in all their brilliancy. The enemy set his square mainsail, and, shaping a diagonal course, gradually increasing his distance from the land, he neared us. I was on the watch for a favourable moment to tack. I now ascertained that all the captains of the guns were on board the Prize, which, in a certain way, was a loss. At about 11 o'clock I thought I had obtained the object I had been endeavouring to realise. I instantly set the courses and tacked the *Childers*. When round, I had the enemy on the lee bow. I then made a short speech to my crew, telling them that I meant to lay him on board on the weather bow and that they were all to follow me. They instantly armed themselves and patiently waited for orders. My clerk attended me carrying my sword. We were favoured with one of the finest nights I ever beheld. Every object could be seen as plainly as by daylight.

We stood on towards our opponent, and for a time all my plans bore the appearance of success. But, at the critical moment of weathering the Dane, the wind headed us two or three points. He, taking advantage of that circumstance, luffed up as close as he could, and my expectations were foiled. Instead of gaining the wind I was obliged to bear up to prevent the jib booms of the two vessels coming in contact with each other, and pass along to leeward, as near as it could be done without touching the enemy, myself directing the motions of the man at the helm.

When the two jib booms were clear of each other, I ran forward to ascertain that the steersman was acting properly. Then we poured a broadside of round and grape shot into the enemy's deck. His vessel leaning over into the wind, not one of the shot, I imagine, failed of doing mischief, and the groans of his men were distinctly heard. Then, coming aft and still directing the man at the helm, I had reached the lee side of the capstan when I was hurled down by it with such violence that I felt as if life had departed. My left arm was jammed against the edge of the lee carronade slide and my body smothered underneath the capstan. I lay in that position a few seconds till the smoke cleared away, when, my person being missed by the First Lieutenant, he set to work to ascertain what had become of me. When he discovered my helpless position, with the assistance of some of the seamen he lugged me out from under the capstan, and as they were raising me from the deck my senses returned. The first words I heard were, 'The Captain is killed!,' repeated several times. Moving my arms and opening my eyes contradicted that assertion. My clerk had received a shot in the body which killed him outright, and I was covered with his gore. Altogether I was in a shocking plight, suffering great pain in both my legs and left arm. Having been removed to the weather side, I was seated on one of the carronade slides. At that moment the Dane fired two stern guns, but they missed us. I now ordered the First Lieutenant to tack and lay the enemy on board on the weather quarter, but whilst he was preparing to do so the Gunner called out from below that the magazine was afloat and the brig sinking. This report was confirmed by the Carpenter.[1] Consequently, renewing the action was out of the question. The enemy widened his distance by keeping on the opposite tack, and all that I could do was to close with the Prize to save my crew. The enemy's last broadside killed two and wounded nine, including myself, severely.* When the Surgeon, Mr. Allen,[2] came to my relief, I desired him to dress the wounded men first of all, then return to me. In the meantime he sent me some wine and water. When we got near the galliot we hove to. The pumps were at work

---

[1] Mason (Acting).

* *Killed*, Mr. Joseph Roberts, Captain's Clerk; Wm. James, Boatswain's Mate. *Wounded*, W. H. Dillon, Esq., Commander, severely in both legs and left arm; —— Boatswain, slightly; Mr. Batterst, Midshipman; Mr. Parker, Volunteer; —— Allender, Corporal of Marines; J. Halding, Seaman; D. Burke, ditto; J. Constable, Marine; J. Marshall, Boy.

[2] Henry Allen, 1st Warrant, 1807.

and the dead were committed to the deep. Meanwhile, the Dane, standing on on the same tack, closed in with the land and we soon lost sight of him. This brought on 2 o'clock of the morning. The jolly boat was lowered, to communicate with the Prize and then to examine the damages sustained by the enemy's fire. There were eight shot between wind and water on the starboard side, seven of which penetrated the hull.

The Surgeon, having dressed all the wounded, repaired to me again. I was taken down to my cabin, which I found in a wretched condition. My steward had not removed a single article from the table on which my dinner had been laid. Most of them had been smashed to atoms. I had not returned to my cabin from the moment I left it to direct the motions of the *Childers*, about 4 o'clock in the afternoon. It was afloat, and the prospect was anything but agreeable. The Surgeon found my left leg most severely contused. The right one was cut open from the knee, down the bone to the ankle, by a splinter. Had it penetrated the thickness of a wafer deeper, the bone would have been broken to pieces. My left wrist was bleeding freely and the arm below the shoulder in acute pain. Whilst he was dressing me, the First Lieutenant came to report that one of the pumps was choked and the brig sinking. 'Well,' said I, 'if that is the case I cannot help you. We must all go down together. Give me your hand, and God bless you. I have done my duty and am resigned to my fate.' Whether the cool and determined manner in which I delivered these words had any effect upon the Lieutenant, I know not. But he hastened on deck and in the course of a quarter of an hour returned to acquaint me that the pump had been set to rights and that there was a chance of saving the *Childers*. At that moment the water in my cabin was about 6 inches deep, and as clear as the sea without. The Surgeon quitted me, and I attempted to get some sleep.

After a few hours the Surgeon renewed his visit, and reported favourably. He expected from the severity of the contusions that an inflammation would ensue. Fortunately for me that was not the case, but he entreated me to remain quiet. The report of the injuries we had received in the action was now laid before me. Both the lower masts were struck by shot, also the bowsprit. The rigging and sails were very much cut, and several shots had struck the hull. However, by the afternoon of the 15th the damages were repaired, and the shot holes under water stopped, so that we were able to shape a course for Leith Roads. The action had lasted, with intervals, upwards of seven hours against an enemy of vastly superior force.

Twenty guns were counted plainly on his deck—that is, twenty on the sides and two in the stern. When I reflected upon the conduct of the enemy, he appeared, during the whole proceeding, to have been deficient in energy, as I always attacked him. He had the advantage of the weather gage, and might at his convenience have closed upon me. But instead of doing so he allowed me to bring him to action, waiting very quietly the result. Had he, when I attempted to cross his bow from the leeward, borne down upon me, the consequences might have been most fatal to the *Childers*. I have often thought of it. His vessel, being of considerably more burden than mine, when coming in contact would probably have overpowered her, and she would have gone down. After I had poured my last broadside into him, he never altered his course, but permitted me to close with the Prize and make all my arrangements without annoyance. Consequently, I beat off an enemy after a very severe contest of long duration, and bore away in triumph the vessel which he evidently intended to recapture.

In the afternoon I directed the galliot to be taken in tow. She was called the *Christina*, and had only a part of her cargo in—45 casks of fish, some iron and other materials. She did not sail well: she was accordingly taken under our stern. The damages inflicted upon my property were very serious. Three trunks containing my wearing apparel were shot through; my writing case—a very handsome one—shattered to pieces. A small pocket book containing £25 in bank notes was never recovered, but my purse with 11 guineas in it was brought to me, as well a diamond pin. Altogether my losses by the engagement could not easily be replaced. The next day I was carried on deck to breathe some fresh air. As we were proceeding towards the coast of Scotland, we passed the convoy which I had taken charge of at Leith but afterwards delivered over to the *Snake*. We exchanged the Private Signal with that ship. Her captain would not be liable to any annoyance from the Dane that I had engaged.

On the 18th we anchored in Leith Roads. I had dictated to the Purser my official report of the action as I was in too much pain to write. When he had completed it, I sent for the officers that they might hear the statement of our proceedings. They appeared not satisfied with it, saying that I had not done myself justice, as the action was one of the hardest fought of the war, the odds being immense and that I had not sufficiently explained the enemy's vast superiority. The officers and crew repeated over and over again that the late captain never would have done anything of the kind. He would not have gone so close inshore. My only reply was that I preferred underrating the action to making a boasting report. The truth would soon be known and our exertions would be appreciated accordingly.

Not long after the *Childers* had anchored, in the forenoon, I was carried on shore and took up my quarters at the Britannia Inn on the pier of Leith, on the second floor, that I might be out of the way of all interruption. On my leaving the *Childers*, the crew gave me three hearty cheers.

My principal anxiety, now, was to learn what light my action would be viewed in by the Admiralty. The next was to recover the use of my limbs. I could not walk without crutches and my left arm was nearly useless. The following day the Admiral called to see me. As I was in acute pain, he did not stay long, merely asking a few questions as to the state of the weather and the number of hours the action lasted. He then withdrew. So soon as the public became acquainted with the particulars of this engagement, all sorts of reports were in circulation—among others that the vessel I had fought was not a man of war but a privateer. Many officers of the Navy called. One in particular passed some very appropriate compliments upon my exertions, assuring me that I should receive promotion. 'You command,' said he, 'the very worst craft in the Navy, and you have fought a vessel of vastly superior force, bringing away a Prize. You are entitled to reward, and I am sure the Admiralty will place that construction upon your conduct. Promotion will be the result.' I differed with him on that part relating to my advancement, as I had not captured the Enemy, and told him so. 'Well,' he replied, 'recollect what I tell you. You have performed wonders under the circumstances, and you will be noticed accordingly.'

The reports to which I here allude no doubt made some impression upon Ad. Vashon as in two or three days he called again, and appeared in very ill temper. He overloaded me with questions and found fault with my report of the injury done to the rigging: in short, seemed inclined not to believe any of my statements, and refused to approve of my demand for the proper quantities of rope to replace those which had been shot away, unless I altered it. This was one of the most unpleasant official interviews I ever had in my life. I submitted patiently to all he said. I was in pain, suffering from the wounds, and therefore allowed him, without making any replies, to settle the fate of the *Childers* as he thought proper. Among other questions, he demanded in peremptory tones, 'How do you know that your enemy had long 18 lbers? The Prize you have taken is not worth two pence.' I told him that I saw, and very nearly touched, the guns, that the shot on board weighed 22 lbs English, and that I would send him one. After he took his leave, I directed that one of them should be sent to his house.

On the 24th, in the morning, the Surgeon had dressed my wounded limbs, it being about 8 in the morning. He retired, and I set to with my razors. In the course of five minutes he returned. 'What has brought you back again, Doctor?' I demanded. 'I merely called to inquire whether you had received your letters from London,' said he. 'Not yet,' was my answer. He kept pacing the room behind my chair, which made me look round, and I noticed an expression on his countenance that gave rise to an opinion of something having happened. 'Will you have the goodness, Capt. Dillon,' said he, 'to lay your razor down?' I did so. He instantly caught hold of my right hand with considerable energy, saying,

'*I wish you joy, sir. You are a Post Captain!*'

'I was,' he went on, 'anxious to be the first to congratulate you, and I have succeeded! Shortly after I left you just now, I met the Admiral's secretary in the street, and he communicated to me all the particulars. You will receive an official letter from the Admiral announcing your promotion, and there will be another one, to be read publicly on the *Childers'* Quarter Deck. I am delighted beyond measure. You are now an independent officer, and will rise to your Flag. All the Admiralty can do against you now is not to employ you!'[1] He then renewed his congratulations and retired.

So soon as I had finished dressing, I hobbled into my room, rang the bell for the waiter, and inquired if he had any letters for me. 'Ay, guid sir,' he replied in a Scotch twang, 'my pocket is fu' o' letters for you. I've had them there these twa hours!' He then deposited a handful of letters on the table, among the number one from Lord Mulgrave, merely acquainting me that I was promoted for my spirited action with the Dane, one from your father, another from Col. Abercromby, remarking what a crazy vessel I had commanded. Lord Yarmouth also wrote, stating that my action was everywhere talked of, and many others upon the same subject, all very gratifying

[1] Not quite a certainty but, barring accidents, a *near*-certainty. There existed a very short list of Superannuated Captains—in 1808 there were only 33 of them alive, consisting mostly of either officers holding good shore-posts like Commissioners of Dockyards or (a very few) notorious failures who had been censured by court-martial. If W.H.D. could avoid this list and—perhaps a more serious "if"—if he could survive long enough, his promotion was certain. In fact he did avoid both pitfalls, and became Rear-Admiral of the Blue on 9/11/1846, 38¾ years later!

and complimentary. I took my breakfast, waiting in extreme anxiety for the Admiral's letter, which at last arrived. I send a copy of it:—

Texel, in Leith Roads, March 24, 1808.

Sir,

I have received directions from the Lords Commissioners of the Admiralty to signify to you, the officers and crew of His Majesty's brig *Childers*, their Lordships' high approbation of the gallantry and able conduct displayed in the severe action you sustained with a Danish Man of War Brig of very superior force off the coast of Norway: and I am further commanded by their Lordships to acquaint you that they have been pleased to promote you to the rank of Post Captain.

I am, sir,

Your most humble and obedient Servant,

J. VASHON,

Rear-Admiral of the Red.

When I had perused this letter several times, I felt an exaltation of spirits better understood than described. I had obtained the grand desiratum (*sic*) of my profession, and a sort of contentment prevailed with a relief from anxiety that set me perfectly at ease for the future. I had not reached my 28th year, and all my rank had been obtained, chiefly under fire, by merit, without any undue influence. Under these circumstances, I thought, no one could grudge my advancement, and my Father's prediction was verified in every sense, that I should not rise by favouritism, but by my own exertions.

When this official letter was read on the *Childers'* Quarter Deck to the officers and crew, it was received with three vociferous cheers. The tars were in high spirits to hear that their conduct had been approved of by the Admiralty. One of the officers now called upon me, and requested my sanction to publish my official report of the action, but I would not do so. 'If the Admiralty will not gazette my letter,' I said, 'we must remain satisfied. My promotion is sufficient proof that we have done our duty.' Nevertheless, in the course of two or three days, my letter appeared in the Edinburgh newspapers.[1] Who inserted it I never could find out. Being apprehensive that the Admiralty might be offended at its publication, I wrote to your

---

[1] Also in the *Naval Chronicle*, from which the full transcript on p. 105 below is taken.

father, requesting him to see Mr. Barrow[1] on the subject, explaining that I had no hand in laying it before the public. In his reply, he assured me that their Lordships were not in the least displeased. They considered my action equal to a victory, but they did not think it of sufficient consequence to have it gazetted. Therefore there had been no act of impropriety. All's well that ends well.

By the arrival of some of our trading vessels from Gothenburg we received an account of the Dane we had engaged. She was called the *Logen*,[2] carrying the number of guns already mentioned, with a crew of nearly 200 men;* and was represented as a vessel of very heavy burden for a brig, commanded by a Capt. Wholfe.[2] The various reports that were now in circulation, brought in daily by our merchantmen, not only confirmed every particular of my report, but proved that in no instance had I overrated the force of my opponent. On the contrary, I had not availed myself of that opportunity of displaying the energies of those under my command in a more favourable light. When my officers mentioned their regrets at my not having done so, I repeated what I had before said—that it would be more to our honour, when the particulars became known, that a plain and truthful statement had been made, in preference to one that might be considered bombastic and liable to be contradicted.

Being without a clerk to keep the books in order, I sent round in all directions, but failed in obtaining one. However, strange to say, the jail-keeper came to me one morning and produced some very nice writing from a young man in his keeping. He spoke in the highest terms of his abilities, good temper, and the Lord knows what. But the poor fellow was in debt, and £5 would clear him: I should be amply repaid in trying him. I agreed to see him. From his appearance, there was not much gentility about him. Yet he promised to conduct himself so properly that I engaged him, paid down the cash, had him liberated, and made him deposit a silver watch as some sort of security for my outlay. Whether the turnkey thought me an easy good-natured person I cannot say, but a few days after this transaction I received another visit from him, representing that he had in his possession another and much superior youth of some connections and with a good name: and he begged me to give him a trial as my Clerk. 'I suppose,' said I, 'when I have set him free, you will find someone else still more talented.' After rather a long discussion,

---

[1] Later Sir John; at this time Second Secretary.

[2] *Sic.* All other authorities call her *Lougen*; James calls her captain 'Wulff.'

* Some time later I was told by a shipmate who had been captured by the *Logen* that her guns were equal to English 24 lbers.

however, I agreed, in the meantime having inquired what sort of a hand the youth made whom I had lately taken. The report was favourable as to his willingness, etc., but he was only fit for a shop, and not to live among gentlemen. In that respect my original opinion was confirmed. The officers, however, wanted a steward for their mess, and proposed to engage him as such if I could obtain a more suitable person to do the Clerk's duty. I consequently desired the jailer to produce his protégé. The youth's name was Hood,[1] rather good-looking. £10 were required to set him free. I paid the money, and accepted him as my Clerk. The professions he made, for my generous proceedings towards him, led me to place some confidence in all his assertions.

When the officers knew that I had lost my pocket book with bank notes to the value of £25, young Parker wrote to his father, who held a situation in the bank. He in reply desired his son to acquaint me that if I could transmit the numbers of the missing notes to the bank I should be reimbursed the amount. But, as I had not taken them down, I could not do so. I forwarded to the Committee at Lloyd's the names of the killed and wounded, who in consequence received gratuities, each according to his rank. To myself they voted the sum of £250. When that was announced to me, I requested a sword. The Committee very handsomely ordered me a similar one to that given to the captains who fought at Trafalgar, valued at 100 guineas, and the remaining sum was sent to my agents for a piece of plate. I had sustained, by the damage to my private property, a loss equal to £300. Mr. Lavie, of the Old Jewry, was a useful friend to me on that occasion. He called upon the Committee and represented my losses. There was some satisfaction in receiving that attention from my countrymen.

The Purser had sustained a heavy loss by the damage inflicted upon his stores: consequently his messmates entreated me to get him nominated joint Agent. I had in the first place included the Admiral's secretary in conjunction with Ommanney, but, yielding to their wishes, I wrote to acquaint him with my reasons for inserting the Purser's name in the Agency. This produced a very ill-tempered reply from Mr. Ommanney: so intemperate that I immediately settled my account with him and appointed another Agent.

The *Childers* was now brought into Leith harbour, and lashed alongside of the pier, where she was visited daily by persons wishing

---

[1] Thomas Hood. He became a purser (1st Warrant, 6/10/1812), and, we learn much later, prospered. See below, p. 403.

to see the effects of the enemy's shot. Most of the crew were removed
to the *Texel*, the Flagship. Days passed, and, as the brig was beginning to make progress in her repairs, the Admiral contemplated
sending her to sea under the acting command of his First Lieutenant,
Mr. Peake.

In the meantime he performed one of those acts of curiosity that
men in office now and then commit. He watched his opportunity,
when the *Childers'* crew was away at dinner, and, muffling himself
up in his great coat with a round hat on, he slipped down the steps of
the pier, making his appearance on board of her. The Master happened
to be there but, not knowing Ad. Vashon, he took him for one of the
inhabitants wishing to see the vessel. He was confirmed in that
opinion by the simple manner of his address. 'Pray, sir,' said he, 'is
this the *Childers*? May I be allowed to go round her? I have heard a
great deal of an action she has had with a Danish man of war.' The
Master instantly offered to escort him, and showing him every part
of the brig, on deck as well as below, pointed out and explained all
the damage done by the shot. He asked a great many questions,
particularly about the Captain, to all of which the Master made
suitable replies. When the Admiral was satisfied with his inspection,
he paid the Master some handsome compliments. Then, waiting for
a favourable moment, he gave a hearty slap on his shoulder, saying,
'You are a set of very fine fellows. I am glad I have seen this vessel.'
Next, catching hold of the manrope that led up the steps, he ascended
with rapidity and made off. The Master, astounded at this proceeding
of the stranger, instantly followed him, suspecting that he was not a
landsman. The Admiral was going at a quick pace, and had nearly
reached the end of the pier when two or three passers by took off their
hats to him. The Master, noticing that act of respect, accosted one
of these persons and inquired who he was. He was told that the
gentleman was Ad. Vashon. He then hastened on, and tried to close
with him, but failed in doing so, as he entered some premises and
disappeared. He next bent his steps to me and related all that had
passed. From the questions put, it was obvious that he doubted many
parts of the *Childers'* exertions, but, in the conclusion, it became
perfectly evident that he was convinced of her having performed, in
the fullest sense, all that had been stated to him. I cannot say much
for such a proceeding on the part of the Admiral.

It was about this time that Capt. Sanders, in the *Bellette*, returned
from his cruize. He lost no time in calling upon me, and overloading
me with compliments for my gallant conduct, saying he would not,

had we agreed to share Prize Money, have received his portion. He next announced to me that the letter I had written to Lord Mulgrave for him had produced its effect, that he was ordered to the West Indies for promotion, and was satisfied. Some of the *Childers'* officers had communication with his, from whom they learnt that the *Bellette*, instead of keeping the sea in quest of the enemy, put into Loch Swilly in the Orkneys where the Captain enjoyed himself in smoking and drinking. However, I had obtained my Post rank before him.

My communications with the Admiral after my promotion had been carried on by a third person. He had not expected that the *Childers'* action would have merited that distinction. He never invited me to his house, all our intercourse being by official formality. I now received a message from him expressing a wish that I should relinquish the command of the *Childers*, that he might be enabled to appoint an acting captain in my room. Not exactly understanding the fairness of this proceeding, as it would place me upon half pay whilst my expenses at the inn were serious, I objected to the proposal. This led to several other messages assuring me that the Admiralty would not be displeased at my retiring, and I finally wrote an official letter requesting to be superseded. In a few days the Admiralty sanctioned my giving up the command, in consequence whereof the Admiral appointed his first lieutenant to the acting command of the *Childers*. Not long afterwards we heard that Capt. F. John Nott[1] was appointed to relieve me in command of her, and he soon made his appearance at Leith. This officer was an old acquaintance of mine whilst he was a lieutenant of the *Sans Pareil*, with Lord Hugh Seymour at Jamaica. Our meeting was an agreeable one. He had been eight years a commander, having by the death of Lord Hugh lost his principal friend and patron.

After having settled all my affairs with my successor, and recommended to him the officers, etc., I made preparations for my departure. I was allowed to take my new clerk, Hood, my young friend Parker, my steward and my coxswain. The crew of the *Childers* at my parting addressed to me a letter. Herewith a copy:

Captn Wm. Henry Dillon Esqr., we humbly petition from H.M. Sloop *Childers* crew—

Sir,

    that your petitioners has served on board the said sloop for 2 years but under your Command for a short time but the Ships Company

---

[1] See Vol. I, pp. 403 and 407.

in general understands you are going to leave the said sloop but if by permission you get the grant from the right honourable Lords of the Admiralty for the said Ships Company to go along with you unto another ship we will take it as a very great favour if it could be done. We hope that these few lines will not make you take any anger but if it meets with your approbation your addition will be greatly accepted.

Dated on board the said sloop the 8th day of April 1808. Leith.

Captn Dillon Esqr.
at the Britannia Inn, Leith.

If these honest tars did not cut any figure in the elegance of style by the above epistle, they were not devoid of courage, as their conduct under fire could not be surpassed: and it would have been a most gratifying circumstance to me to have had them under my command in another ship. But there was not the least likelihood of such a chance. The Clerk, Steward and Coxswain were sent round to Portsmouth to join the *Royal William*, the Receiving Ship, and wait there till I obtained another command, which everybody thought would soon be my lot. But we were all out in our expectations.

APPENDIX

(From *The Naval Chronicle*, 1808, Vol. XIX, pp. 282–284.

CAPTAIN DILLON'S OFFICIAL ACCOUNT OF AN ACTION, BETWEEN THE *CHILDERS*, SLOOP OF WAR, AND A DANISH SHIP, OF SUPERIOR FORCE

From the circumstances of the case, the following letter of Captain Dillon's, to the Admiralty, has not appeared in the Gazette. The Board, however, have signified their highest approbation of his conduct, as well as that of his officers and crew, by official letter, and have conferred on him the rank of post captain:—)

Leith, March 18, 1808.

Sir,
I have the honour to acquaint you that on the 14th inst. at four p.m. when standing in for the coast of Norway, a sail was discovered in-shore, and, on seeing us, appeared to be seeking a port in safety. We instantly gave chase, with a fresh breeze from the eastward. As we neared her, she

was hauled among the rocks, out of our sight, to take shelter in the small port of Misbe. Immediately a number of boats came out to her assistance, I suppose with the intention of removing her cargo. I dispatched Mr. Wilson, acting master, accompanied by Mr. Knight, mate, with the cutter well armed, to bring her out: the jolly boat was also sent, with Mr. M'Nicholl, gunner, and Mr. Le Neve, purser, who volunteered his services. This duty was performed by Mr. Wilson with the utmost gallantry; for when mixed with the boats, they were dispersed in all directions, leaving him at liberty to board the vessel, in doing which he was opposed by the inhabitants with musketry, whilst others hurled down stones upon our men from the top of the precipice under which she lay secured; however, she was carried without any loss, to the astonishment of an increasing multitude, who crowded together on the surrounding heights. She is a galliot (name unknown, her crew having deserted her), with only part of her cargo, consisting principally of oil and fish.

Scarcely had the galliot hove in sight from under the rocks, when a large brig was observed coming out of Hitteroe. He bore down on us with confidence, indicating a vessel of force, and apparently with a design of rescuing the prize. About six, he got upon our weather beam, and judging him to be within reach of our guns, I sent a challenge, by firing a shot over him. He hauled his wind close, and kept in shore. Finding he would not join us, I made sail for the purpose of bringing him to action, which soon commenced at half gun shot range, distant from the shore half a mile, passing each other on different tacks. When he received our first broadside, he caught fire forward, and, had we been closer at the moment, to profit by his confusion, I have no doubt of the result. He kept so near the land that he was held from our view, so that we could only be guided in our fire by the flash of his guns, and were also, from this circumstance, prevented weathering him. We continued engaging him in this manner for three hours, but found he had a decided advantage over us. The Dane was a man of war, well appointed in every respect, carrying long 18-pounders, and seemingly had taken fresh courage after a few of our broadsides, as if aware of our inferiority to him in weight of metal, the *Childers* bearing only 12-pounder carronades: latterly, his guns were so well directed that every shot did us mischief, particularly between wind and water. Observing that nothing could be done whilst he kept so near his own port, from whence he might at pleasure draw fresh supplies of men, I conceived the plan of enticing him out to sea, where the contest would be more equal, by giving us an opportunity of forcing him to close action, which he had hitherto so repeatedly avoided.

In order to effect this, I stood out under easy sail. It was some time before he relished the idea of following us; but in the end he did so. At 11 he was about three miles off the land. I set the courses and tacks, intending to weather him. As we approached, the wind unfortunately headed us and foiled our attempt. I therefore passed under his lee, as close as it could be done without touching, and poured round and grape upon his decks, which I imagine did the Dane much damage, for we distinctly heard the groans of the wounded; his guns also did us material injury, most of his shot taking us between wind and water; and when on the point of renewing battle, it proved impossible. In the meantime the enemy tacked, and made sail to regain the shore, and we shortly after lost sight of him. I was mortified that our situation would not admit of our pursuing the enemy. We had five feet of water in the hold, the magazine afloat, the lower masts wounded, bowsprit and mainmast badly, and the pumps increasing on us in such a way as to make it doubtful whether we should be able to prevent our vessel sinking under us. In this position we bore up to secure our prize, with the only satisfaction left us of having drove a man of war, of much superior force, off the field of action, which we kept during the space of six hours, in the very entrance of his own harbour.

I therefore trust that when the above particulars are seen in their proper light, it will be found that, although not successful in capturing the enemy, the *Childers* has supported the glory of the navy, and the honour of the British flag.

I am happy to have this opportunity of testifying the spirited conduct of my first lieutenant, Mr. Edmonds, as well as the other officers and crew, who on this occasion behaved with that determined courage which at all times distinguishes the bravery of English seamen. Mr. Drummond and Mr. Gordon, pilots, deserve much praise for the able manner in which they conducted us among the rocks. The acting carpenter, Mr. Mason, has rendered himself worthy of his appointment, by his ability in stopping the shot-holes. Not being able to keep at sea, from the nature of our leaks and wounded masts, I could not put into execution the remaining part of your orders; have in consequence judged it proper to return to this anchorage with my prize. I am, &.

W. H. DILLON.

Rear-Admiral Vashon, &.

P.S. We could not possibly ascertain the number of guns on board the Dane, but having measured his length, in which he had considerably the advantage of us, we are all of opinion that he had at least nine ports on a side; the shot on board us weigh 20 pounds. Enclosed is a list of killed and wounded, as well as an account of the damage we sustained during the action.

A list of killed and wounded on board His Majesty's Ship Childers, in the action with the Danish Brig, off the Nase of Norway, on the 14th of March, 1808.

KILLED.—Mr. Roberts, captain's clerk, shot through the body; William Jones, boatswain's mate, through the belly, and left leg and arm off.

WOUNDED.—Captain Dillon, badly in both legs, his arms and shoulders very much contused; Mr. Batters, midshipman, slightly on the thigh and hand, by a splinter; Mr. Parker, midshipman, slightly on the belly and right arm; Corporal Allander, of Marines, slightly on the head; John Holding, seaman, badly on the hand, lost one finger; Dennis Bark, seaman, badly on the face and head; John Constable, private marine, slightly on the forehead; and John George Marshall, boy, slightly on the thigh.[1]

[1] Both this casualty-list and that from W.H.D.'s own MS (see above, p. 95) are correctly transcribed. In the many discrepancies of spelling we have evidence, probably, of the " pirating " of Dillon's official report. We know from his narrative that he did not himself see any printed version prior to publication.

XI

TEMPORARY COMMANDS

April 1808–March 5, 1811

(*aet.* 27½–30½)

INTRODUCTION

THIS section covers an uncomfortable and unprofitable period in W.H.D.'s professional career. He had three temporary commands in succession. It was clearly frustrating to be only 'acting', and the Narrative, while confirming this again and again, serves incidentally to stress the very proprietary nature of a permanent captain's command, and to show how much the general efficiency and happiness of the ship depended upon the Captain's personality and method.

Very early on, two important subjects are introduced: without, however, the author making much attempt to fit them into a wider context.

The first—on p. 114—concerns the institution of Half Pay. The action brought by Beauclerk against the Admiralty was a much more decisive landmark in the story of the Navy's development than would appear from the text. The system of Half Pay had started from small beginnings in Charles II's time, when all employment for officers was still sporadic, and when there was no real professional corps of naval officers in existence. Its primary object—then—was simply to ensure that the Government had the services of its temporarily-unemployed officers when they were required. That is, Half Pay was—then—purely a 'retaining fee'. During the eighteenth century the practice of giving Half Pay spread, until it came to be received by all unemployed officers, whatever the reason for their unemployment. But there were always two quite different categories of recipients. One was 'the unemployed'—the officer just waiting for a job—the other was 'the unemployable'—the officer who by virtue of age, wounds or even incompetence, was not under consideration for employment.

These two sorts, we know well enough nowadays, represent quite different principles. Half Pay given to one of the former class was essentially a 'retaining fee': but, given to the latter class, it was what we should now call 'retired pay' or 'pension'—*i.e.* 'reward for past services'. It was in this last-named direction that no advance had ever been made. An overwhelming preponderance of officers never 'retired' in anything like the modern sense: for the State had not yet even realised that it had any 'after-care' responsibilities at all.

The judgment mentioned here, by recognising the existence of 'reward for past services' (*i.e.* the State's responsibility for 'after-care') as something distinct from support during unemployment periods (*i.e.* 'retaining fee') was one of the first and most important steps towards a true system of Retirement. Yet nearly a century was destined to elapse before the full and modern principle of Retirement was properly established.

The second point concerns the important question of Prize Money, which loomed so immense in the eyes of contemporary naval officers. So we find (p. 119) W.H.D. waxing eloquent on the iniquity of Lord Mulgrave in reducing the Captain's share. This, as the Narrative has so often revealed already, was such an important factor in the finances of the naval officer in general, and the Captain in particular, that his anger need cause no surprise. Yet, considered in terms of equity, the reform, we may well think, was admirable as well as overdue, and we may regard Lord Mulgrave as moving in quite the right direction.

Until the change was made on 15th June, 1808, the distribution was as described in Vol. I, p. 75 (note). To facilitate comparison, these figures are now set out alongside the new ones:—

Category	*Before* 15/6/08	*After* 15/6/08
a. The Captain or Captains	$\frac{3}{8}$ths*	$\frac{2}{8}$ths†
b. Capt. of Marines and Army, Sea-Lieutenants and Masters. . . .	$\frac{1}{8}$th	$\frac{1}{8}$th
c. Lt. of Marines and Army, Sec. of Admiral, Master's Mates, Principal W.O.'s and Chaplain	$\frac{1}{8}$th	$\frac{1}{8}$th
d. Mids, Inferior W.O.'s, Principal W.O.'s Mates, Sergeants of Marines and Army	$\frac{1}{8}$th	$\frac{4}{8}$ths (*d.* and *e.* together)
e. The rest	$\frac{2}{8}$ths	

* Flag Officer to have one of the Captain's $\frac{1}{8}$ths.

† Flag Officer to have $\frac{1}{3}$rd of the Captain's share.

Thus Lord Mulgrave's change was twofold:—

(1) he docked one-eighth off the Captain's share, though leaving him still a whole and undivided quarter of the proceeds, and

(2) he scrapped Category *d.* as such, bringing its occupants into a new and enlarged Category *e.*

Having thus 'saved' two eighth-shares, he added them both to the (now enlarged) *e.* category—'The rest'. This he subdivided as follows:—

Mids, etc. (as *d.* above)	$4\frac{1}{2}$ shares each
Inferior W.O.'s Mates, Capts. of Tops, etc. . .	3 shares each
Able and Ordinary Seamen	$1\frac{1}{2}$ shares each
Landsmen, Servants, etc.	1 share each
Volunteers per Order, Boys, etc.	$\frac{1}{2}$ share each

This distribution held, substantially, until the end of the war. On October 14, 1816, however, the Captains temporarily regained their lost eighth. But not for long: on March 19th, 1834, they sustained a heavy reverse, when it was laid down that the Flag Officer should have a one-sixteenth share, and the Captain one-sixth of the remainder. All the rest —officers and men alike—took shares of the new remainder. These ranged from 55 for the Commander down the whole scale to Boy, 2nd Class, who received one.

As it happened, W.H.D. did not lose much by this change, since he was never very fortunate with his Prizes. But we can understand his complaining: and indeed it *was* a little hard on him as an individual that the scheme favouring the Captains, which had prevailed for so long, should come to an end just when he was in a position to profit by it.

W.H.D. secured his temporary command of the *Aigle* just in time to sail with the famous 'Grand Expedition', the largest Combined Operation hitherto attempted by this country. Finding that the really 'close' blockade instituted by Lord St. Vincent had, to all intents and purposes, put the port of Brest out of business, Napoleon had been industriously developing the port of Antwerp to take its place, hoping to use its enlarged facilities, *via* the estuary of the Scheldt, to turn the Straits of Dover, the natural British defence line, and to develop his superior military potential in the North Sea. It was to neutralise this effort—to unload Napoleon's 'pistol pointed at the heart of England'—that the Grand Expedition was launched.

It failed, largely through our inexperience in such combined operations. And its historical importance today lies mainly, perhaps, in its value to subsequent military planners as an example of how *not* to conduct such enterprises. No overall account of the affair is called for here, for reasons explained on p. 139. The interest of the Narrative hereabouts lies in W.H.D.'s eyewitness and detailed account of the initial operations, before failure began to stare us in the face. It also gives us an admirable—indeed somewhat startling—reminder that War was, still, far from the vicious business it has since become. There is a good deal of unconscious humour in the picture that Dillon draws of himself landing from an open boat into a front-line trench, in complete uniform and accompanied by two trunks containing all his personal effects: not to mention the portrait of Alderman Curtis arriving at Middleburg as soon as it is captured, accompanied by a large turtle (p. 136).

We now make the acquaintance of an officer upon whom W.H.D. evidently made a lamentable impression. Unfortunately, he was an important naval personage—Sir Richard Hussey Bickerton, (1759–1832), K.C.B., 2nd Baronet—at this time 'the leading Naval Lord of the Admiralty', and later to become C.-in-C., Portsmouth. From the first he became a thorn in the side of Dillon, and, if we are to believe the latter, he was never weary of thwarting and insulting him. W.H.D. seems to hint that the quarrel arose from the episode narrated on p. 151, but, on the Admiral's side anyway, the antipathy appears to have existed already.

On p. 72 we have seen the Admiral being almost offensively terse with the Commander; and thereafter he goes out of his way to slight and humiliate him.

The relations of the two being what they were, it is hard to come by the truth: nor must anything like an objective judgment be expected from W.H.D. Yet Sir Richard was unquestionably a distinguished officer, with a good (rather than a great) record. Son of a Vice-Admiral of the same names, he was made Lieutenant 16/12/1777, Commander, 20/3/1779, and Captain, 8/2/1781, and was present two months later at Hood's action with de Grasse off Martinique. In the next war, after service in the North Sea and the Channel, he received his Flag, 14/2/1799, and in the following May went to the Mediterranean, where he blockaded Cadiz and (1800) the coast of Egypt. During the Peace of Amiens he was C.-in-C., Mediterranean, and then Second in Command to Nelson there. When the latter sailed for the West Indies in 1805, Bickerton was left behind as C.-in-C., but was soon recalled to the Admiralty, where he remained till 1812. He then went as C.-in-C., Portsmouth, to plague W.H.D. again till 1815. He became Vice-Admiral, 9/11/1805, and full Admiral 31/6/1810.

Of his personal character little seems to be known, the biographies in Ralfe, Beatson and the Gentlemen's Magazine being of that adulatory type which is not particularly helpful. Yet there can be no smoke without fire: and though it would be unwise, from the one-sided nature of our evidence, to put all the blame on Sir Richard, it is equally impossible to conclude that all the faults were Dillon's. After all, he was not in the habit of quarrelling with his superiors: indeed, very much the reverse, his relations with all the others—though he often criticised them privately —being of the best. It would seem, in fine, that there existed between the two one of those personal and inexplicable incompatibilities not unknown in all professions and in all ages.

Later in this Part, an even better-known figure comes into the Narrative —Sir Edward Pellew, later Lord Exmouth. With him W.H.D.'s relations conform much more to pattern. He has plenty of criticism to set down, and it is by no means to Sir Edward's credit. Yet he never gets near to quarrelling openly, let alone engaging in a shouting match with him. Nor does Sir Edward appear to have had a 'down' on W.H.D.

W.H.D.'s difficulty in procuring a permanent appointment, and Capt. Hartwell's warning words (p. 165), furnish a significant foretaste of what was in store for Naval Officers after 1815. If there were not enough commands for all while the war was still at its height, and the Navy still swollen to its largest, what would happen when the inevitable reductions came, if nothing were done about clearing the lists by some system of Retirement? Yet the Admiralty failed to do anything. Instead, they gave more and more Lieutenant's commissions, and promoted more and more officers to Commander and Captain, thereby ensuring the most terrible 'block' in the Navy's history.

XI

TEMPORARY COMMANDS

APRIL 1808–MARCH 5, 1811

(*aet.* 27½–30½)

(1) CONVALESCENCE

APRIL 1808–JUNE 1809

(*Note.*—Those parts which are Summaries are printed within square brackets. The portions not so printed are Narrative.)

[With his young friend Parker, also wounded, W.H.D. first went to Harrogate to take the waters. He was still a cripple, unable to walk without crutches.]

HERE I met the Duke of St. Albans, formerly Lord Amelius Beau-clerk,[1] who, as a Lieutenant in the Navy, had brought an action against the Admiralty for striking him off the naval list of half pay officers, for refusing to serve when called upon in the Peace after the first American War. The 12 judges decided in his favour relating to the half pay, declaring it to be a reward for past services, and not a retaining fee.

[In May, somewhat better, he went up to London, and was very handsomely received by the First Lord, Lord Mulgrave, who presented him to the King.]

As I felt very infirm upon my legs, I asked the Master of the Ceremonies whether it signified on which knee I bent to the King upon my being presented. He replied that I must do so upon the right one. I showed him my feeble pins, and remarked that I was very much feared I should not be able to acquit myself properly upon that leg, but could do so in safety upon the left. It was contrary

---

[1] W.H.D. here confuses two brothers. Lord Amelius, who had quite a distinguished naval career and rose to be Admiral of the Red (see below, p. 130), was the third son of Aubrey, 5th Duke of St. Albans. The 6th Duke, whom W.H.D. says he met at Harrogate, was the 5th Duke's elder son, also Aubrey, and elder brother of Lord Amelius.

to established rules of Court etiquette, he said, and could not be. We were soon ushered into the presence chamber, where we beheld the King attended by his ministers. My turn came, and the Lord in Waiting spoke out in a clear voice, 'Capt. William Henry Dillon of the Royal Navy, for having fought an action against a Danish vessel of war of very superior force.' As I approached the good old King, he addressed me, inquiring whence I came. I replied accordingly. I was then desired by the said nobleman to kneel down: in doing which my right leg slipped from under me, and down I went upon my left side. But the King, who instantly noticed my reclining, caught hold of me with both his arms. I seized them, and righted myself. His Majesty laughed, and I could not help doing the same. But I met Lord Mulgrave's countenance, and he appeared much displeased at the occurrence.

My next duty was to undergo an examination before the College of Surgeons, to ascertain whether my wounds were such as to entitle me to a pension. I never thought of applying to any friend for a letter or two of introduction to some of these worthies. The College was situated in Lincoln's Inn fields, where I was directed to attend before them at 8 o'clock in the evening. I was introduced into a spacious room, where they were in consultation by candle light, and I thought that I observed some rosy cheeks among them, rather inflated by the juice of the grape. My name having been called, I was suddenly addressed by the Chairman, Dr. Chandeller, an intimate friend of my Father's. 'Why did you not let me know of your being wounded?' he asked. I told him that I was perfectly ignorant of all the forms attending such examinations: moreover, that I did not know of his being Chairman of the College. After the examination, I was told that no decision would be given until one year had passed. They thought I should recover the use of my limbs as I was young and hearty, with a good constitution.

[Having been told that he was entitled to full pay and expenses while undergoing cure, he applied for £100 for the latter, and was told to his disgust that he could have only £4—which he returned with thanks. But now he learnt that 'Interest' was as potent in the Medical profession as it was in the Naval. Dr. Chandeller intervened, and got the £100 paid . . . 'Had I known where to lay my hands upon that gentleman in the first instance, my meeting at the College would have taken a very different turn.' He then visited the Board of Agriculture, and met all his father's old friends—Mr. Arthur Young,

Lord Somerville, Lord Sheffield, Sir John Sinclair—the President—
and especially Lord Manvers and his father's executor, Mr. Loveden
of Buscot Park—who all paid him the most flattering attention.]

Mr. Loveden related to me all that had passed between my
Father and Mr. Pitt on the subject of my unjustifiable captivity.The
Prime Minister did not hesitate to declare that, upon my return, he
would make up to me all my losses of every description. All this
proved the consideration bestowed upon me by that distinguished
statesman. 'But,' I remarked, 'he is no longer of this world, and I
am in want of powerful influence to rise in my profession.' 'All that
will come,' replied Mr. Loveden, 'now that you have obtained your
post rank in a most satisfactory manner. Have patience.'

[With Lord Manvers he struck up a real friendship, going to stay
with him at Thoresby in August.* Meanwhile, however, he had consulted Sir Astley Cooper, who recommended a course of sea bathing
at Margate. Thither he proceeded, and put himself under the care of
his old friend of the *Glenmore*, Dr. Grey.]

The Agent at Leith now sent me an account of the sale of the
Danish Galliot. She produced about £400, my share amounting to
£28! The charge that astonished me the most was that of the Proctor
of the Admiralty Court, which was within a fraction the same as
mine. Why the individual in the office should receive, though not
exposed to any danger or responsibility, the same sum as the Captain
who fought the action, I could not comprehend. Lord Cochrane,
some time afterwards, published a pamphlet exposing all these
charges to the nation.†

---

* Since my visit to Thoresby Park I have seen a great deal of the world, and
mixed with Royalty—I am a member of the Duke of Sussex' Household, his Equerry.
But I have nowhere seen the honours of the table so well supported as at Lord
Manvers'. There were never less—often more—than 20 servants in attendance, and
with every course a table-cloth was removed, there being four laid on, always with
changes of the most costly china ware, wines and an abundance of every other luxury.
After the third had been served, coffee was brought for the ladies when they retired.
Then the fourth cloth was removed, and the gentlemen drank their wine upon the
mahogany. The upper servants lived in better style than many of our gentlemen.
They were served at dinner with Port and Sherry. Thoresby had been the property
of the Duke of Kingston, which the Earl inherited. He had for neighbours two other
Dukes, of Portland and Newcastle.

† The Proctor's charges: for condemnation . . . £24 18 4
registering, etc. . . . £6 18 4
£31 16 8

The Prize realised . . . £244 15 2
Charges amounting to . . £128 13 11
Balance distributable to Captors £116 1 3

[He called once more on Lord Mulgrave, who informed him definitely that there was no chance whatever of an appointment for one year.]

I then wrote to my shipmates on board the *Royal William* at Spithead, desiring them to look out for other ships. Young Parker soon found one. The Coxswain and Clerk I had assisted with money. The Clerk went with my old messmate Sir Thomas Hardy, Captain of the *Triumph*, and the Coxswain to a frigate, still hoping to join me again when I hoisted a pendant. My *Childers'* shipmates were constantly making applications to me of various kinds, but at length, finding that I could not assist them, they ceased plaguing me.

[It is at this point that the extensive excisions (see Vol. I, Intro., p. XXII) begin. The moment he had returned to Town from the north, Mrs. Voller had descended upon him, insisting on his fulfilment of his promise to marry her as soon as he was made post. She constituted herself the guardian of all his movements, and procured for him first a house in Russell Square and then rooms at Margate. He escaped for a moment to pay his visit to Thoresby in late August, but not for long. Curtailing his visit, he hurried back to London, and married her at St. Pancras Church on the 22nd or 23rd of September. Thence they travelled at once to Chester, and resided there till the following March. All this, and a good deal more on the painful subject, is deleted. In substitution for some three pages of MS. he afterwards inserted six words:—'I soon afterwards went to Chester.' The narrative covering this Chester period is overwhelmingly non-naval in content. The following, however, throws light on both the vagaries of promotion, and the attitude of officers (especially wealthy ones) to the Service.]

Another of my neighbours in the Square was a retired Naval Officer by the name of Townsend,[1] brother of the Colonel of that name. As we were often together, I heard his naval history, which will

---

[1] Thomas Townsend, Lt. 4/3/1759; Ret. Cdr. 12/10/1801. Note that, for all his *factual* retirement, his name appears in all Lieutenants' Lists up to 1801. The story teems with inconsistencies. No *Suffolk* took part in any of Pocock's E. Indian actions. Nor does the situation described seem to fit the story of any other ship. The only Captain killed was Michie, of the *Newcastle*, in the third battle, but the *Newcastle* was not isolated from the fleet. Townsend was not a Lieut. in the first two actions, and even in the third—10/9/59—only just one. Lastly, Sandwich was First Lord 1748-51, 1763 (for a brief period), and 1771-82: not, as the story seems to make out, for a considerable and consecutive period starting from 1759. Perhaps the whole yarn is the product of a long-cherished, oft-reiterated 'grouse'.

prove the uncertainty of a gentleman's career who adopts the
naval profession. He was Third Lieutenant of the *Suffolk* in the
East Indies, attached to Sir George Pocock's squadron. In an action
with the French, the *Suffolk* received very serious injury. The
Captain and First Lieutenant were killed and the Second took the
command. The ship had been driven out of the line, and anchored on
the coast, unable to rejoin the Admiral, who thought she had been
either sunk or wrecked. The trials of this ship were beyond the usual
occurrences of naval actions. However, those remaining proved
themselves equal to all their dangers, and, after extraordinary exertions, the ship was saved, repaired and brought back to her station
in the port where the squadron had anchored. Sir George Pocock,
fully sensible of the abilities displayed and the labours endured by
her officers and crew, made his report to the Admiralty accordingly.
The Senior Lieutenant received promotion. When Mr. Townsend
returned home, and made his appearance at that Board, the Chief,
Lord Sandwich, acknowledged his claims and sent him on board the
Flag Ship stationed at the Brazils for advancement. He remained
there 27 months without a vacancy occurring. When the squadron
returned to England, it was paid off. Townsend again laid his claims
for promotion. Then Lord Sandwich, having patiently listened to
him, addressed him as follows:—'What good will a Commander's
Commission do to you, Mr. Townsend, with your fortune and family
connection?' The applicant, astounded at this remark, retorted,
'What has my connections and fortune to do with my service? Even
if I am the person your Lordship describes, I have surely some right
to expect an equivalent for the number of years devoted to my
country's cause?' In conclusion, the First Lord told him that he
could not do anything for him. He then made his bow, acquainting
his Lordship that he should not trouble him again. About 10 days
later he received a message from the Admiralty requesting his attendance. But he declined going, came into Cheshire and fitted up the
establishment of an independent gentleman. He was now 74 years
old, in perfect enjoyment of all his faculties. The Navy lost by
Lord Sandwich's proceedings one of its most able officers. In our
intercourse I used to call him Admiral. He had been risen to the rank
of Retired Commander, but I usually avoided naval subjects, which
were not agreeable to him.

[A more modern instance of a similar incident follows. It concerns
another lieutenant with private means named Hunt, and his inter-

view with Lord Spencer, 1st Lord in 1797. I have not been able to
trace this officer at all. Nor does his story illustrate the point so well,
for Hunt's only claim to promotion was 19 years' service as lieutenant; and Lord Spencer is not made to say anything so outrageous as
the words attributed to Lord Sandwich. He merely says that Hunt's
'time has not come.' Thereupon Hunt asks to be relieved of his post,
and retires to his patrimony.]

It was about this period that Lord Mulgrave reduced the share of
the Captains' Prize Money, which occasioned a universal feeling of
dissatisfaction throughout the Navy. In consequence of this proceeding many meetings took place among the seniors, when it was decided
to present a remonstrance. Capt. Sir Joseph Yorke[1] took the lead, and
presented it to the Port Admiral, George Montagu,[2] who approved
of the measure and transmitted it to the Admiralty. That Admiral
was shortly afterwards superseded, a measure which made a most
unfavourable impression amongst naval officers. The consequence
was that the captains, generally speaking, left off keeping tables, as
their pay would not admit of their doing so. The Prize Money, such
as it was—and which fell to the lot of very few—made up in some
cases for the expenses to which the captains were liable. Lord
Mulgrave had been brought up in the Army, and proved in many
instances that he did not understand the liberal spirit which animated
the officers of the Navy. Many ruined themselves in keeping up the
respectability of the profession. Lord Cochrane exposed to the country
in a pamphlet all the outlays to which the naval captains were
subjected. Lord Mulgrave lost ground by that arbitrary measure, and
the Navy was much pleased when he left the Admiralty.[3]

However, the time was now approaching for my appearance in
Town, to be examined by the College of Surgeons. My wounded limbs
became extremely troublesome and I suffered intolerable pain. The
Surgeon (Rowlands) who attended me applied electricity, which
finally gave me relief. Having witnessed the excruciating torment
which I endured, he made a very able statement of it to be shewn to
the College. When I arrived in Town, I put up at the Spring Garden
Coffee House to be near the Admiralty. On the 7th April I underwent
an examination at the College, and, to my inexpressible disappointment, they did not consider the wounds equal to the loss of an eye

---

[1] Joseph Sidney Yorke, Lt. 27/6/1789; Cdr. 19/11/90; Capt. 4/2/93; R-Ad.
31/7/1810; V-Ad. 4/6/14.
[2] See Vol. I, p. 119 et seq.
[3] See above, p. 111.

or a limb: therefore no pension was granted. On my mentioning this
to Lord Manvers, he regretted I had not made him acquainted with
the intended examination, as he thought he might have been able
to assist me. I was not up to the ways of the world, nor did I suppose
that any influence would be required. Dr. Chandeller was no longer
the Chairman. I yielded to my fate, my spirits keeping me in expectation of some good appointment.

[A much more serious affliction—this time domestic—was now
assailing his spirits, and making employment even more necessary.
There follow four pages of deletions: he was discovering the besetting
weakness of his wife—her senseless extravagance. He visited the
First Lord again, but 'he gave me no hope.' Then he met, for the first
time, Charles, 12th Viscount Dillon, the head of the whole clan.
This nobleman, of whom an admirable portrait is drawn, was an
elderly but generous and warm-hearted man, who kept open house to
all and sundry, including, hereafter, W.H.D., to whom he seems to
have taken a great fancy. He interested himself actively in the latter's
search for an appointment, and tried very hard to exert his influence
upon Lord Mulgrave (who was his brother-in-law). He even told
Dillon at one point that he had obtained the promise of a command
for him in the course of the next three weeks. But it all came to
nothing, and W.H.D. was soon afterwards informed by another
friend (and probably also a distant connection)—Ad. Sir Charles
Nugent[1]—that in fact Lord Dillon had no influence at all. On the
contrary, he probably injured his protégé's cause, quite inadvertently:
for, armed with an introduction from the peer, W.H.D. twice called
on Mulgrave, who finally snubbed him soundly.

Interspersed between his visits to Lords Dillon and Mulgrave,
there appear several passages about Ad. Gambier and Lord Cochrane
at Basque Roads, where the famous action was taking place. These
have considerable interest in that they view the incident from an
angle which is unusual today. In considering the controversy which
split the Navy at the time, the modern view leans heavily on the side
of Cochrane. But W.H.D., who was inevitably a whole-hearted
'Gambier Man,' takes quite the opposite view. He is no admirer of
Cochrane—he could not afford to be.]

I was dining one day with Lord Manvers. The conversation naturally turning upon the operations of our fleet against the enemy in

---

[1] Charles Edmund Nugent, Ad. of the Fleet, 24/4/1833. See *D.N.B.*

Basque Roads, Ad. Bentinck,[1] who was one of the party, had a great deal to say. Whilst we were listening to him, we heard an arrival with post horses next door, where resided Mr. Cochrane, Lord Cochrane's uncle. It was well understood that, at that particular moment, Lord Gambier had not acted in a manner to please his subordinate officer, Lord Cochrane, who, in the command of a large frigate led the fire-ships and others to attack the enemy in Basque Roads. Everybody being anxious to hear how that matter would be settled, Lord Manvers ordered one of the servants to inquire who had arrived next door. He was informed that it was Lord Cochrane, from the fleet. Upon this information, Ad. Bentinck rose from the table and hastened out. He had a short interview with the naval lord, who did not say much, but gave a hint that something would be said in the House of Commons. Sure enough, Lord Cochrane made his charge against Lord Gambier, the particulars of which I need not repeat here. Lord Gambier with a squadron had attacked a French one in Aix Roads on the 11th April and operations were continued to the 12th. The whole of the French ships were either burned or driven on shore. Only one, I believe, was brought away—the *Calcutta*, 50, which had been some years before captured from the English. Several of the French ships by dint of perseverance got up the river Charente. The operations were not terminated till the 28th, all this time close in upon the enemy's coast: but none of our ships suffered, excepting by killed and wounded. Some time afterwards Lord Gambier told me that Lord Cochrane was disappointed at not having been sent home by him in charge of the official despatches, which would have put £500 into his pocket. But he, in justice, had sent a Flag Officer who had a prior claim to that Captain.[2]

[Later in May]. When Lord Cochrane understood that the thanks of the Houses of Parliament were to be voted to Lord Gambier and the squadron under his command, he declared that he felt it his duty to oppose any such vote of approbation on that occasion. That declaration produced a wonderful sensation throughout the country, and when Lord Gambier heard of it he demanded a Court Martial upon himself.

[1] William Bentinck. As a scion of the house of Portland, and great-grandson of William III's adviser, he enjoyed an unusually smooth promotion-passage. Lt. 12/7/1782 (when barely 18); never a Commander; Capt. 15/9/83 (when barely 19); R-Ad. 9/11/1805; V-Ad. 31/7/10. But, on 21/2/13 occurred the only event which could stop his rise—he died.

[2] Not only a remarkably one-sided version of the story, but also an entirely unsupported slander upon Cochrane and his motives.

I

[This Court Martial, which is reported in its correct place later, was the indirect means of obtaining an appointment—albeit a temporary one—for W.H.D. But, meanwhile, Lord Dillon and he visited Portsmouth to attend, out of curiosity, another Court Martial in which Gambier was concerned, but, this time, as prosecutor and not defendant. Ad. Eliab Harvey, one of the Trafalgar captains, furious at Gambier's lack of enterprise, and even more so at the appointment (by the Admiralty) of Lord Cochrane—a mere Captain—to lead the fireship attack, had insulted Gambier on his own Quarter Deck, and had left the Flag Ship with (among others) the following words:—' . . . I'm no canting Methodist, no hypocrite, no psalm-singer, and do not cheat old women out of their estates by hypocrisy and canting.']

We attended the trial upon Ad. Harvey, who was dismissed the Service, but some time after reinstated.[1] Lord Dillon having brought a note of introduction to the Port Admiral, Sir Roger Curtis, and another to the Commissioner of the Dock Yard, Sir George Grey,[2] he was received by them with the attentions due to his station. Fortunately, too, Capt. Macnamara's[3] ship happened to be in port. He knew Lord Dillon, and kindly placed his barge at our disposal. He dined with us. The discussion at one of these dinners I shall never forget. The subject of conversation turned upon Nelson and Lady Hamilton. Who was the Father of Horatia? That was the question that could not be easily solved. I maintained that Lady H—ton was the Mother. Macnamara denied it in the strongest terms, and was rather heated on the occasion. I told him that I had no intention of disputing the case, but that I should reserve my own opinion. Time proved that I was right.

Not many days after this, I was at breakfast in the Coffee House (in Town again) where two or three Captains of the Navy whom I knew took theirs in the opposite box. One of them who had just come from the Admiralty said he had been offered the command of a fine frigate, but had refused it, the Captain of that ship being wanted to attend the Court Martial on Lord Gambier. I put some questions to him, and he said he thought no one had been appointed. If such a command suited, he thought I might have it. Weighing in my mind what he had said, I determined to call on the First Lord's private

[1] And rose to be full Admiral. Lt. 26/2/1779; Cdr. 21/3/82; Capt. 20/1/83; R-Ad. 9/11/1805; V-Ad. 31/7/10; Ad. 12/8/19.
[2] Lt. 2/1/1781; Capt. 1/11/93. See note, p. 191.
[3] See Vol. I, p. 338 and Index.

secretary to ascertain the real state of the case. He gave me a hearty shake by the hand, and when I inquired whether there was any chance of being appointed to the *Aigle*—that was the name of the frigate alluded to—'No doubt of it,' he replied. 'Her Captain must resign his command of her to be present at the trial of Lord Gambier.' 'Can I have a three months' cruise in the Bay?' I demanded. 'No. I cannot insure you that,' he replied. 'But the ship is ready for sea. All you have to do is to go down and take the command of her.' I soon settled this affair, and accepted the temporary command of the *Aigle*. When I acquainted Lord Dillon with what I had done, his Lordship thought that Lord Mulgrave had nominated me to that ship in consequence of his recommendation. But I most fully explained to him the nature of my appointment, which might not last more than a month, and that I should be at some expense by accepting it, merely to prove to the Admiralty that I was anxious to serve my Country.

(2) H.M.S. *L'AIGLE* (The Grand Expedition)

JUNE 1809–SEPTEMBER 1809

MY preparations were soon made. I left London for Plymouth, and reached that Naval Station by the 13th June. The Captain of the *Aigle*, Wolfe,[1] did not much like resigning the command of his ship, but the naval Commander in Chief, Ad. Young, soon settled that point. Next day I went on board, and the ship was delivered over to my control. But instead of being ready for sea, as reported to me, all her lower masts were out, and, what was still more unpleasant, a new First Lieutenant was appointed to her, the effective officer being a perfect stranger to the crew, and the regulations of the ship, whatever they might be, were unknown to him. I found her in a most dirty, slovenly state, the cabin full of rolled-up sails, without any circulation of air. Capt. W., being a married man, lived on shore, totally neglecting his cabin. I saw at a glance that extraordinary exertions would be required to get the ship ready for sea. In short, my professional character was at stake. I gave instant orders for the purifying of the cabin. Next day I took up my abode in it, and superintended every operation going on. It happened that there were 50 of the Ship's Company who had sailed with me in the *Juno* when she returned

[1] George Wolfe, Lt. 24/12/1794; Cdr. 1/9/97; Capt. 10/12/1800.

to England from Jamaica. Seven years had elapsed since then, but they had not forgotten the rapid changes I had made for the better when I joined that ship. These men told the others what they might expect, advising strict obedience and prompt execution. So far all this told well: but Capt. W. had the mania of placing himself upon a very familiar footing with the seamen, giving them the preference to his officers. On the first day that I went on board I had noticed one or two seamen entering the cabin with as much freedom as if in their own homes, and speak to their Captain in the most familiar tones. He seemed to encourage all that, as he styled them Tom, Jack, Bill, etc. My plan of proceeding was diametrically opposed to this, my opinion being that familiarity breeds contempt, and the officer in command ought, by his conduct to all under him, to insure respect. There is a certain deportment which, regulated by firmness and moderation, never fails to produce its object. Upon that principle, I avoided abusive language, but never failed to rebuke the negligent. I allowed 25 men to go on shore daily, and Capt. Wolfe had his boat, with 10 men, all the while he remained at Plymouth. Notwithstanding these indulgences, the three lower masts were got in, six months provisions on board, and the ship ready for sea in eight days. This exertion made an impression upon all, the Admiral in particular who, being a strict officer, was not in the habit of paying compliments if they were not due.

I met some old acquaintances here—Mr. Smith, the Admiral's Secretary,[1] who greeted me so kindly when I landed from Morlaix; and my old messmate of the *Alcide*, Carpenter,[2] who had just been made a Commander. But my anxious duties would not allow me to attend them much. I slept on board every night, so that nothing passed without my knowing it.

A Court Martial had been assembled to try a Marine for an unnatural crime. It was a question of mine that led to his conviction. Upon summing up, the President agreed with me, and the criminal was condemned. The President and I, without having any communication with each other, were both sensible of this responsibility. The Marine was a Romanist, and confessed his guilt to his priest. The Holy man kindly waited upon the President to let him know it. The President then came to me, saying that he supposed I laboured under the same anxiety as he did himself. I acknowledged it. 'Then,'

[1] W. Proctor Smith—a very old and useful friend. See Vol. I Index, under P. Smith: also above, p. 56.

[2] John Cook Carpenter, another very old friend. See Vol. I, p. 68 and note, and Index.

said he, 'we are both clear, for the prisoner has confessed the whole.' That certainly removed a considerable oppression of mind which had annoyed me for two or three days.

One morning the crew had been turned up at 4 to scrub the decks, when, to my astonishment, the First Lieutenant, Holcombe,[1] came to report that the seamen refused to do their work. 'What do you mean?' I demanded. 'They won't turn out,' he said. 'Did any one particular individual refuse to obey your orders?' I asked. 'No, Sir,' was the reply. 'Then you have not done your duty,' I said. 'Go down among them and secure the first one who will not obey you: bring him to me, and I will settle accounts with him. Order the Marines on deck instantly.' He did as I directed. I was dressed in no time, and hastened on to the Quarter Deck. The Lieutenant had seized one of the crew who would not obey him, and brought him aft to me. The hands were directly turned up for punishment. The Marines had come aft armed with cutlasses. I ordered the culprit to strip, read the Articles of War and awarded him 24 lashes upon his bare back.[2] He was then released, and I made a suitable speech to the Ship's Company upon the impropriety of the delinquent's behaviour, and cautioned them for the future, remarking that it was a very bad termination to their labours which had drawn upon them the approbation of all the squadron in the Sound. That punishment, and the decision with which it was performed, made a strong impression upon all hands. The officers were not prepared for it, declaring that Capt. Wolfe would not have acted so.

By 8 o'clock I was with the Admiral who acquainted me that the Ship's Company would be paid that morning, after which I was to proceed to Spithead. It was the established custom of the Navy that when the crew of a ship received their wages they were to be allowed 48 hours in port, to spend their money and provide themselves with necessaries. 'As the *Aigle* is going to Portsmouth,' said he, 'they can lay out their cash there. You will explain that to them before you weigh anchor.' When I returned to the ship, the pay officers were on board. Plenty of Jews occupied the Main Deck: there were many women on board: nothing to be seen but confusion. I had considerable difficulty in getting rid of Moses and his party, but perseverance drove them all out. The hands were ordered to unmoor, and when they were ready I had them aft, and told them that, by the ship's being ordered to Portsmouth, they would not be deprived of their

[1] Essex John Holcombe, Lt. 7/1/1802.
[2] The official maximum that a Captain could order.

usual indulgence. I hoped they would show their good will, and I would, in return, make up to them what might be required. They then gave three vociferous cheers, and unmoored ship in double quick time. These fellows were fractious at 4 o'clock in the morning, and 12 hours afterwards they were ready to do anything they were ordered. Such is the material of a frigate crew.

I was soon at Spithead, where Sir Roger Curtis held the naval command. As I had not long before been presented to him by Lord Dillon, I was well received. Preparations were going on for the trial of Lord Gambier. It occasioned many remarks. The enemy's squadron had, in a certain sense, been rendered useless, attacked close in with their own shore.* Whether Lord Mulgrave acted with correct judgment on that occasion has often been questioned. His Lordship held the rank of Lieut. General at that period. His having sent Lord Cochrane to take an active part in Lord Gambier's plans of attack was also not much approved of by the profession, as the Admiral was maturing all his plans, and would no doubt have succeeded without his assistance. But Lord Cochrane, as a Member of Parliament, had great influence, upon which he acted, it was thought, rather spitefully towards his Commander in Chief.[1]

The discipline of the *Aigle* was not of the highest order. One of the young Mids had been refused permission to go on shore, for misconduct. Determined, however, to have his swing, he persuaded the Bum boat woman to allow him to hide himself beneath her petticoats, by which contrivance he escaped the notice of the Master at Arms, the chief police-officer on board. When this youth's proceedings were reported, I would not allow him to return on board for some time. Capt. Wolfe was very much annoyed at my having noticed that boyish trick (as he called it): but if you allow one act of irregularity you must wink at others. This was an extremely improper one for a young gentleman rearing up to become an officer. Not long after my arrival at Spithead, the Admiralty ordered me to place one of the Midshipmen in irons. He was accused of an act of Piracy. This, to me, created a new sensation. Piracy committed by an English ship of

---

* The French Captain of the *Calcutta* was afterwards shot for cowardice, and most of the other Captains were sentenced to long imprisonment, while many of the officers were placed under close arrest.

[1] A remarkably partisan statement, ignoring completely not only all those features of the affair to which Cochrane took exception, but even the possibility that his patron, Gambier, may have been in error : yet—and here the modern view is much more nearly with him—allotting blame to the First Lord, for what was certainly rather a tactless appointment, offensive to many of the senior officers, of whom Harvey was but one.

war was a most serious charge, and did not say much for the *Aigle's* plan of operations. She had captured, while cruising off the French coast, a large French boat without a deck, employed going from one port to another, keeping close inshore. This boat was on board the *Aigle* when I took command, and was by the officers and crew generally designated 'The Privateer'. She was always manned by the same crew of about 16, under the command of the Mid in question. Capt. Wolfe would send her away to prowl along the shore, often out of his sight. She would then return, sometimes bringing a neutral for examination. Upon further inquiry, I found that the fewer questions asked the better, and evasive answers were made. The investigations created uneasy feelings on board that I could not help noticing. The delinquent was examined in my cabin by one of the Judge Advocate's clerks, my clerk writing down the depositions. I took care to have one of my officers constantly present, that he might hear all the questions put. The complainant was the Master of a Prussian vessel that had been boarded close in with a French port. He had been plundered of his money by the Mid, but he had ascertained the name of the frigate and all particulars relating to her. He then complained to the Admiralty, who acted accordingly. When the examination terminated, I asked the officers if they had any objections to make about the investigation, pointing out how awkward it was for me to be ordered to direct the examination of an officer who had not been under my command when the act was committed. They all expressed themselves fully satisfied at the delicacy of my proceedings, and said that they would report it to their Captain. The delinquent was dismissed the Navy. He was not a gentleman.

A youth now arrived from Ireland—the young friend that Lord Dillon had spoken about. Upon his making himself known to me, he delivered the following note:

London, June 10th, 1809.

My Dear Captain,

The bearer is Thomas Parker McDermott, the young man whom I recommended to you to be entered as Midshipman in His Majesty's Navy.

I am, my Dear Captain,
your obedient Servant and Kinsman,
Dillon.

Every attention was shown to this youth, but the next day he entreated me to allow him to leave the ship. He had taken a strong dislike to the Navy. Whether any of the Mids had frightened him I know not, but at last I got rid of him, and wrote to Lord Dillon representing that young McDermott was not a fit subject for the profession.

Troops were now ordered to assemble at Portsmouth to assist our allies the Austrians. We were also exerting ourselves in the cause of Spain, and there appeared some prospect of humbling Bonaparte. Reports were in circulation that an expedition amounting to 40,000 men would soon be fitted out. Sir Richard Strachan[1] was mentioned as likely to command the naval part, with Sir Home Popham[2] under him. One day, going to the sally port, I met Sir John Duckworth, who had behaved so kindly to me in Jamaica.[3] His Flag was flying, and he invited me to dine with him.

Now for the Grand Expedition. Its destination was all a matter of speculation, excepting with those who were in the secret. Troops were arriving daily. In the meantime Bonaparte was carrying all before him in Germany. Our fleet was divided into four squadrons. I was under the orders of Ad. A. Otway,[4] and received on board 150 men belonging to the 35th Regiment under Major Armyt. One day an old shipmate of the *Thunderer* (in the West Indies) came on board. He had left the Navy, and was in the Commissariat department attached to this armament. When he heard that I commanded a ship in it, he told his colleagues that he would provide them with a comfortable berth with me. He said that he had come to make arrangements, and would take care that a round sum of money in dollars should be brought on board, which would give me a good freight. Having listened to all this gentleman had to say, I explained to him that an official list of embarkation had already been issued by the Commander in Chief, and that my portion was already shipped. 'I should be most happy to have your company, as well that of your companions, if I had my will. But as it is I fear you will be doing wrong to come here. And as to the dollars,' I said, 'you may rely upon it they will not be sent to me, only an acting Captain.' But my arguments had no effect on the Commissary, who returned to the shore and brought back with him one of the Chiefs of his establishment and another associate. These gentlemen I received, and did my best to make comfortable. I felt it my duty to

---

[1] Sir Richard John Strachan, Bart., K.B., at that time R-Ad. of the White. See *D.N.B.*
[2] See Vol. I, p. 415 and note.
[3] See Vol. I, pp. 434–446. His Flag was in the 112-gun Spanish Prize, *San Josef.*
[4] William Albany Otway, 2nd in command of the Grand Expedition. Lt. 25/8/1773; Cdr. 29/3/81; Capt. 1/12/87; R-Ad. 2/10/1807; V-Ad. 1/8/11.

communicate my doubts again, but they cared not. Three or four days later I called upon Ad. Otway, and reported my having three Commissariat officers on board. Having sent for the embarkation list, and ascertained that they ought to have been in a line of battle ship, he thanked me in marked terms for having received them, but informed me that the individuals mentioned would be instantly removed. 'It is well,' said he, 'that you have made this communication to me, for had they been wanted we should not have known where to lay hands on them.' They were instantly removed to a certain 74. They were highly displeased, and supposed I had been the cause of it from very different motives than those which really actuated me. The principal officer of the party never forgave me afterwards. The dollars were placed on board of some favourite officer, who received his freight accordingly.

Our division proceeded to the Downs at the end of the month, where we joined the other part of it under Sir Richard Strachan. Lord Chatham had arrived. Our fleet from Portsmouth consisted of 18 sail of the line, many frigates, sloops of war, gunboats etc., and innumerable transports, the whole force of the two Services supposed to amount to 80,000 effective men, of which 40,000 belonged to the Army. So large an assemblage caused considerable alarm on the enemy's coast. Sir Richard Strachan, thinking that such a large fleet would not be easy to manage sailing together, went off with one part to make himself better acquainted with the locality. Sir Home Popham, who had in the peace, when a lieutenant, fitted out a merchant ship at Ostend, was supposed to be the fittest officer to assist him in the operations on this coast. Sir Richard Keats, my old Captain,[1] commanded a division of the fleet. My messmate of the *Hêbê*, now Capt. Cockburn, held a distinguished position in it.[2] Several frigates stationed off the Scheldt instantly communicated with the Commander in Chief upon his appearance, and there was a squadron of six sail of the line at anchor off the entrance of that river, under the orders of Lord Gardner.[3]

Our division sailed, and anchored off the enemy's coast on the 29th. The troops were under the direction of Sir Eyre Coote. This was the left wing of the Army. As it blew a gale of wind, we were prevented from having any communication with Sir Richard

---

[1] In the *Niger* in 1792. See Vol. I, p. 45.

[2] (Ad. of the Fleet, Sir) George Cockburn. See Vol. I, p. 33. He figures a good deal later in this volume. He was here employed in the *Plover*, 18, commanding a division of sloops, bombs, brigs and gunboats for close-in bombardment of Flushing.

[3] See Vol. I, p. 126.

Strachan. The next day we were ordered to move closer inshore, into a place called the Room Pot. Sir Home Popham,* who had selected this anchorage, had shown good judgment in doing so. The next day we commenced landing the troops, and I had the charge of landing the Portsmouth Division on the Bree Sands. In performing that service, I frequently came in contact with Sir Eyre Coote. I had known Lady Coote during the Irish Rebellion, and had danced with his daughter, who was a great beauty, at Mr. Bury's of Little Island, Cove of Cork. Sir R. Strachan had in the first instance placed himself in a frigate to direct operations, but he found he could not proceed without the Commander in Chief of the Army, and returned to his ship, to be in constant communication with Lord Chatham. Whilst disembarking the troops, I was ordered to weigh anchor, and take up a commanding position along the beach, to protect them from any sudden attack of the enemy. I did not return to the *Aigle* till past 2 o'clock in the morning, the soldiers having by that time all been put on shore. There was a constant fire of artillery kept up the best part of the night, but it was evident, from the report of the guns, that our men were advancing. The first naval attack was led by Lord Amelius Beauclerk[1] and Capt. Cockburn. The fire from our mortar- and gunboats drove the enemy from the Oerhaak[2] battery, on the island of Walcheren.

The first object having been accomplished, we next attacked Cambere [sic]. The ensuing morning, August 1, Campvere† was assailed by the gunboats, but it held out. The fire did much damage to the town. Three of our gunboats were sunk. The weather being unfavourable, a pause took place in our fire, but the attack was renewed at night, and the enemy sent an officer to capitulate. The division under Sir John Hope had landed in South Beveland this day, and the island soon fell into our possession. In the meantime, the French fleet in the Scheldt, alarmed at the presence of such a powerful force, moved up above Fort Lillo; the most advanced had reached Antwerp. The signal was now made for all the Captains to repair on board the Admiral. The *Aigle* had, after landing the troops,

* He was no favourite with the Senior officers of the Navy, as the two senior Captains of Gambier's fleet objected to his being appointed Captain of the Fleet at the attack on Copenhagen. He had been in the Merchant Service, and the Agent of Transports in attendance upon the Duke of York's army. It was through that Prince's influence that he obtained his Post rank, and generally bore the soubriquet of 'the D. of York's Admiral'.

[1] W.H.D. has the right man this time—Lt. 21/9/1790; Capt. 16/9/93; R-Ad. 1/8/1811; V-Ad. 12/8/19; Ad. 22/7/30.

[2] Illegible: perhaps 'Terhaak'. There is a Fort Tenhaak.

† Campvere the name of the town and Te Vere the battery.

removed further from the shore, and was surrounded by an immense number of transports which had come into this anchorage for safety. When I presented myself to Sir Richard Strachan in the *San Domingo*, finding him alone, I delivered to him a letter of introduction from Ad. Nugent. This was not the time for any complimentary speeches, and he merely acknowledged it. Five other Captains now came on board and we were assembled on the Quarter Deck, under the instructions of Sir Home Popham, who handed to each of us a good-sized card on which was a plan of the coast. We were to guide our motions by it. Sir Home entered into some details relating to the frigates' proceedings. Some of them were not sufficiently clear, and when I consulted my companions, they could not supply the information I required. I then, pointing with my finger to the parts of the shore unsufficiently designed, requested his instructions how to act in that locality. He examined the premises, and, after a short hesitation, he candidly declared that he could not give me any instructions as he had never been there. This made its impression upon the other Captains, who let out a few remarks. However, I turned towards Sir Richard, who was listening, but as I approached him he turned off. Here was a dilemma of rather an unpleasant nature. But when we found we could not obtain the information we sought we each made our bow to the Admiral and retired to our respective ships,* with orders to proceed forthwith off Flushing.

When I got on board, some of my crew were employed with the Army. I directed them to be sent for, and ordered the ship to be got under sail. The Pilots declined lifting the anchor. I was fully sensible that our position was one of extreme difficulty, but after the most mature consideration, as my orders were positive, I told the Pilots that I should get the ship under way and that I should hold them responsible for the rest. Up went the anchor, but there was scarcely space for the ship to manœuvre in. At last by keeping the ship before the wind we picked out some room. Fortunately the wind was against the tide, which was running out to sea. I was thus enabled to hold the ship in a sort of balance, and by degrees to clear our

---

* The frigates employed were increased as follows:—The *Lavinia* (Lord Wm. Stuart[1]), *Heroine*, *Amethyst* (Sir M. Seymour[2]), *L'Aigle* (Capt. Dillon), *Euryalus*, *Statira* (Boys[3]), *Rota*, *Nymphen*, *Dryad* and *Perlin* [*Pearlen*?], 10.

[1] Lt. 11/10/1797; Cdr. 24/12/98; Capt. 9/11/99.

[2] Sir Michael Seymour, Bart., K.C.B., Lt. 28/10/1790; Cdr. 20/8/1795; Capt. 11/8/1800; R-Ad. 27/6/32. Lost arm at First of June; commanded the *Amethyst* in famous duel with *Thetis*; C. in C. S. America, 1833. Died, 9/7/34.

[3] Charles Boys. W.H.D.'s fellow-midshipman in the *Thetis*, see Vol. I, p. 84, note and Index.

difficulties. It took us two hours, backing and filling. Once the jib boom just grazed one transport, and presently the driver boom scraped another. As we passed many compliments were paid to our extraordinary exertions in finally getting clear of such a multitude of shipping. I do not recollect ever passing such anxious hours as those. None of the other frigates attempted to stir. When I had cleared the Room Pot, I anchored for the night.

The next morning the other frigates came out. The transports had moved further up, which left them plenty of room to manœuvre. Had I been aware that those vessels would change their position, I should have avoided a couple of hours of extreme danger. The tides on this coast were very strong, and twisted about in various directions. I was much annoyed to find that the other frigates were gaining upon me, as the *Aigle* was considered a good sailer. However, as they neared the wind freshened, and I kept my distance. But I had a very exciting trial with the *Amethyst*, Capt. Sir Michael Seymour. The unpleasant part was the stupidity of the Pilots, who were in constant fear of grounding. I kept the lead going, and there was plenty of depth to move in. When I found them objecting to my setting the mainsail, I gave them to understand that, as Captain, I would set what sail I chose, and that they were to apprise me when in danger of touching bottom. The mainsail was accordingly set. The Pilots were both out in their soundings. On one occasion they wanted me to tack in 10 fathoms water. I would not do it: in fact I navigated the ship that day myself, regulating my proceedings entirely by the lead, and made them appear perfectly useless. When the struggle between my ship and the *Amethyst* had risen to its utmost, it was in doubt which was the better sailer—the other ships we had distanced. But, not choosing to take any advantage of my senior officer, as we were not chasing an enemy, I backed the mizzen topsail and allowed him to go ahead. In the evening we anchored off Flushing, where we found Commodore Owen,[1] lying in the Wieling Passage with his broad Pendant on board the *Clyde*.

During the day we noticed several of the inhabitants on the sands, watching our motions, on horseback. The officers wanted to fire upon them, but I would not. 'No occasion,' I said, 'to kill these poor fellows. Besides, they appear to me to be Dutchmen.' Our frigates anchored in a line, out of the range, as we thought, of their batteries. They did not fire at us, and we in return remained perfectly quiet.

---

[1] Edward William Campbell Rich Owen, Lt. 6/11/1793; Cdr. 19/9/96; Capt. 23/5/98; R-Ad. 27/5/1825; V-Ad. 10/1/37.

However, the mortar battery occasionally sent a shell to Commodore Owen, but without doing any serious damage. We now waited for the operations of the Army, during which I generally took my station aloft in the main top, whence I had a commanding view, with my spy-glass, of the movements of our attacking detachments and the enemy resisting them. At high tide it was a most interesting sight, but we were subjected to strong gales with dark clouds, which impeded my vision of the proceedings on shore. In one of these gales a large boat put off from Cadsand, the shore opposite to Flushing, and passed over to that fortress in defiance of the Commodore, who had no guns ready in his stern ports. The channel was not very wide, and did not occupy many minutes in crossing. However, the Commodore took his measures to prevent a repetition of such an occurrence. That boat no doubt conveyed some important intelligence to the enemy. The Admiral was anxiously employed in preventing supplies being sent in to Flushing. The Rammekens, a strong battery on the N. side of Walcheren which commanded the water intercourse in that direction, was after a short resistance carried by us; and from that moment our approaches on Middleburgh, the capital of the island, were not so difficult.

Capt. Lord William Stuart was the Senior Officer in command of frigates, acting in separate instructions from the Commodore. The *Statira* was commanded by my old messmate of the *Thetis*, Charles Boys. We could not exchange visits, our whole thoughts being taken up with the operations against the enemy.

On the side of the Army, Lieut. Gen. Sir John Hope began the attack with the reserve. This was the part of the Army that we sailors thought had to be literally kept in reserve, to fill up vacancies: but in fact they were in advance. Lieut. Gen. Frazer carried ter Vere, assisted by Capt. Richardson[1] of the Navy. Sir Eyre Coote led on the attack towards Middleburgh, which surrendered without resistance. Lord Huntly acted with Commodore Owen. Lord Paget and Major Gen. Graham held commands: the Light Division was led by Brig. Gen. Baron Rottenburg: Lieut. Gen. Grosvenor and the Earl of Rosslyn had divisions. Our troops having taken possession of Middleburgh, Lord Chatham established his headquarters there, and the Army was making rapid strides towards Flushing. But the enemy did not yield one inch of ground without resistance—considerable reinforcements had been sent to them at intervals—and the rainy weather

[1] (Sir) Charles Richardson (K.C.B.), Lt. 4/8/1794; Cdr. 9/10/1802; Capt. 27/9/04; R-Ad. 10/1/37; V-Ad. 17/12/47.

considerably retarded our operations. The position of the *Aigle* was as near as could be in a line with the right of our entrenchments on shore, as I could at times distinguish the fire of musketry from them, as well the opposing fire of the enemy under the walls of Flushing.

About the 9th of the month I was surprised at the appearance of Capt. Wolfe, who had returned from the Court Martial on Lord Gambier to resume the command of his ship. This placed me in rather an awkward situation, as we were blockading Flushing, and I had no means of quitting the ship, but was obliged to remain on board. Capt. Wolfe did not fail in his attentions, but I could not help noticing the familiarity of the seamen who came in to the cabin as suited them, to compliment him upon his return. So soon as he made himself master of the ship's position, he thought she was not near enough to the forts. I told him that she occupied the station ordered by the Senior Officer, but, to make known, I suppose to the Ship's Company that he had resumed the command, he contrived to place the ship a few fathoms nearer to the batteries of Flushing.

He brought the report of Lord Gambier's trial, and, out of consideration to that noble friend of mine, I will quote one or two passages of his defence. In his address to the President his Lordship says, 'When I first entered this Court, it was with a mind perfectly at rest as to the issue of my trial, confident of having asserted myself to the utmost for the honour and advantage of my King and Country. The result of these proceedings has confirmed me in this state of mind. I now retire, committing to your protection my professional honour, with full persuasion that I shall receive at your hands ample retribution for the aspersions on my character which have led to this inquiry.' When the sentence was pronounced, adjudging him to be most honourably acquitted, Ad. Sir Roger Curtis, the President, desired Lord Gambier's sword to be handed to him, and returned it saying, 'I have peculiar pleasure in receiving the command of the Court to return you your sword, in the fullest conviction that, as you have hitherto done, you will on all occasions use it for the honour and advantage of your Country, and to your own personal honour. Having so far obeyed the command of the Court, I beg you will permit me, in my individual capacity, to express to you the high gratification I have upon this occasion.' His Lordship replied, 'I cannot sufficiently express the sense I feel of the indulgence of the Court, and beg to return thanks to you, Sir, for the obliging manner in which you have conveyed the sense of the Court.'

On the 11th, Capt. Lord Stuart made the signal to prepare for action; also for getting under way. It was my wish to remain on board, to witness coming events, and to contribute what little assistance I could in the action that was about to take place. However, Capt. Wolfe thought it would not be proper for me to run the risk of being killed, for no earthly advantage. It was at last agreed that we should both call upon Lord William Stuart and consult him. To the *Lavinia* we went, and found him most decidedly against my going into action. After some discussion I was obliged to yield; then, retiring to the *Aigle*, packed up a couple of trunks. I was taken to the beach and landed at the point which I had calculated was our advanced post. I left my cot, spy-glasses and other heavy articles on board to their fate. When I ascended the sand hills, I found I had exactly hit upon the right spot. An officer of our Army who was here on the watch, seeing me, called out in extreme anxiety, 'For God's sake, drop down, Sir, or you are a dead man. Slide down, roll yourself down. You have not the slightest idea of the danger you are in.' Perceiving by his countenance, as well the agitated tone of his address, that I had unknowingly exposed myself, being in uniform, cocked hat, etc., I slid down instantly as the officer advised. When I had reached the ground, and explained who I was, he told me that he commanded at that particular post, being a Major. 'That you may understand the danger you have escaped, look here,' said he, drawing his sword and holding it up above the parapet. Instantly came a volley of musket balls. 'What a lucky fellow,' he remarked, 'not being seen by the enemy's look-out! Nothing could have saved you from death.' After a few explanations, my trunks were brought over by the boat's crew, with the greatest caution. They returned to the ship in safety, with a douceur which I gave them, and I then, with the Major's assistance, hired a cart from a Dutch boor who promised to escort me in safety to Middleburgh. In passing along, I met Lieut. Robert Dillon, Sir Charles's brother,[1] who was serving in the 32nd. His appearance was very acceptable. He detained me a short while, to give me some account of the proceedings of the Army. Whilst we were in conversation, Lord Paget came to reconnoitre, attended by his brother Capt. Paget,[2] who commanded a 74 in the Expedition.

[1] Of Lismullen. See Vol. I, p. xix.
[2] Hon. (Sir) Charles Paget, commanding the *Revenge*. Born 10/7/1778; Lt. 12/12/96; Cdr. 27/6/97; Capt. 17/10/97; R-Ad. 9/4/1823; V-Ad. 10/1/37; Died, 27/1/39. An illuminating example of what Interest (a) could, and (b) could not, do for an officer:— Made Lieut. at 18½; promoted Cdr. after 6 months; promoted Capt. after 16 weeks; but promoted R-Ad. after 25½ years! He was made Post when just 19, though the rule that no one could be a Lieut. until he was 20 was still in the regulations: but not even Interest could hurry him up the Captains' ladder.

The enemy had cut one of the dykes, and the water was nearly level with the bottom of the tents. In fact, the appearances were anything but agreeable, the worst of all being that the coming in of the sea would spoil the drinkable water. My position was one of too much anxiety to remain long with my friend. He directed my Dutch conductor where to lodge me. I was accordingly taken to one of the best hotels, where I established myself for the time being in tolerably comfortable apartments. Reports of guns firing now caused considerable anxiety. Our frigates were passing the batteries of Flushing. I contrived to ascend to the roof of one of the buildings, whence I had a perfect view of the whole proceeding. The *Aigle* was the fourth frigate in the line. The wind being light was much to the disadvantage of our ships; nevertheless they rounded the strong forts of Flushing in gallant style, taking up a position in the Scheldt[1]. A shell fell on board the *Aigle* and went through her decks into the bread room where it exploded, and shattered her stern frame. My spy-glasses were injured by the bursting of this shell. Thus, in passing those batteries mounted with heavy guns, mortars, etc., only 2 men were killed and 9 wounded. Had there been a strong breeze, probably not a casualty would have occurred.

I now became a perfect idler, my time being taken up with sight-seeing at Middleburgh and its environs. English travellers were arriving daily to witness the exploits of our Army: among the number Alderman Curtis, whom I shall never forget. He paid great attention to gastronomy, and came in a pleasure boat, bringing with him a fine large turtle which I believe was presented to Lord Chatham. Among the strangers I was agreeably surprised to meet my friend Lord Yarmouth. These gentlemen were longing to have a view of a siege of a fortified town, and Flushing was considered one of the first order: it was therefore expected that it would not easily surrender. A Col. Congreve,[2] with whom I became acquainted, had invented a rocket of destruction, which bore his name. They were in high request on this occasion. Combined with the capture of Flushing was the taking or destroying the French Fleet. Sir Home Popham commanded a squadron of sloops of war with which he was forcing his way up the Scheldt. One of them was fitted to fire the rockets. This officer acted in conjunction with Sir Richard Keats who held his station at Bathz. An attack was made upon six of the enemy's gunboats: five were

---

[1] W.H.D. here inserts a table of casualties in the individual ships of the squadron. The *Aigle* leads easily with 1 killed and 4 wounded.

[2] William Congreve. For his early experiments with rockets, and the Navy's early opposition to them, see *N.R.S.* vol. XCII, p. 423 *et seq.*

destroyed and the other taken. We had cleared all this part of the river, but, the enemy having a flotilla of 50 vessels, it required some caution in approaching them.

The General and the Admiral having completed their arrangements for attacking Flushing by land and sea, the batteries opened fire on the afternoon of the 13th. It was returned with great vigour. At night the rockets and the bomb shells had a most splendid effect. The wind would not allow Sir Richard Strachan to lead his squadron to the attack on this day, but he did so on the 14th. The *St. Domingo*, Flag Ship, led, followed by the *Blake, Repulse, Victorious, Denmark, Audacious* and *Venerable*, all ships of the line. The bombs and gun vessels were under the direction of Capt. Cockburn in the *Belleisle*, and were most judiciously placed at the south east end of the town: and to the south west Commodore Owen in the *Clyde*, with equal skill, placed his bomb- and other vessels. The fire from these light squadrons was maintained with great precision. The *St. Domingo* having grounded, Lord Gardner came to her assistance, but, keeping too near inshore stuck fast. However, they were again afloat in due time. By the evening the enemy's fire slackened considerably, and the town was on fire in several places. A summons was sent in during which our fire ceased; but, as it led to no result, it was again renewed with all energy and without intermission until 2 o'clock in the morning of the 15th, when Gen. Monnet offered to surrender. Commissioners were accordingly nominated, Lord Gardner and Capt. Cockburn on the part of the Navy, with Sir Eyre Coote and Col. Long of the Army. The terms of the capitulation were concluded late in the evening. The total loss to the Navy during the capture of Flushing amounted to 9 killed and 47 wounded. I do not report the casualties of the Army.

So soon as we had taken possession of Flushing on the 17th, I hastened over to see the place. It would be difficult to describe the devastation that one meets in a fortified town that has been bombarded both by sea and land—the ruined houses destroyed by fire, the haggard countenances of the inhabitants, the deserted streets. In the Dock Yard I saw a large frigate on the stocks. Passing through a storehouse vacated by its attendants, I could not help being guilty of plundering the printed regulations of the French Gunnery Exercise: also I carried off a paper knife made of wood. These relics are still in my possession. Thence I repaired to the Ramparts, to examine the batteries. Our squadron, with flags of truce flying, were still lying at anchor before the walls. A sudden shower of rain coming on,

I sought shelter under a sort of wooden shed. Here I was accosted by a French artillery blacksmith, who had been at work in his department. I obtained more information from him than from any of the better-classed individuals. He was extremely intelligent, and stated that the authorities had been expecting our attack six weeks earlier. Preparations for defence had been made in all directions, but as our ships did not appear it was conceived to have been a false alarm. The rain having passed off, I requested this person to show me the way to an hotel, where I obtained some refreshment and champagne. The house was full of English officers of every description. I had arrived in a chaise, but could not get one to return. I had been so much on my legs that I was in great pain. Luckily I met an old shipmate of the Marines, who promised me his arm on the road back to Middleburgh. We sallied forth, he under the impression that we should meet some cavalry who would assist us. We nearly succeeded two or three times, but in the end failed. I reached my apartments thoroughly knocked up, and went to rest with serious forebodings for the morrow. However, thank Heaven, next morning I was able to move about, but with great care. There being a fair in the neighbourhood, I attended it, and purchased some beautiful Holland linen, with which I had shirts made that lasted many years.

The garrison at Flushing amounted to 5,803 men when it surrendered. At our landing on the island of Walcheren, there must have been at least 9,000. Many were killed at our landing, or taken prisoner. Their ships of the line that had assembled near Flushing were about nine, but their frigates and flotilla were very numerous. There were also ships of the line at Antwerp, and some on the stocks in a forward state of building.

Having satisfied my curiosity at Middleburgh, I applied to Sir Richard Strachan for a passage to England, as the prisoners, the sick and the wounded were being conveyed there. I was advised to reside at Tervere, near our fleet, that I might be ready to embark at a moment's notice. Whilst occupied in looking for a lodging there, I met my shipmate of the Commissariat, Mr. Damerum, who kindly entreated me to take up my quarters with him. I willingly accepted his invitation, and passed a few days, until I heard that Capt. Rowley,[1] commanding the *Eagle*, had orders for England. I requested a passage home, and he, in a most friendly manner, offered me the

---

[1] (Sir) Charles Rowley (Bart., G.C.B., G.C.H.), Lt. 8/10/1789; Capt. 1/8/95; R-Ad. 4/6/1814; V-Ad. 27/5/25; Ad. 23/11/41. C. in C. Nore, 1815–18; C. in C. Portsmouth, 1842–45: Died (Ad. of White) 1845.

use of his cabin. At this period our advances against the enemy were very slow, and our Army was attacked with much sickness, by which many died, afterwards so well known as 'the Walcheren Fever'. Lord Chatham had removed to Bathz, preparatory to proceeding on to Antwerp.

I now embarked on board the *Eagle*, 74. In the cabin there were two passengers besides myself. One, Col. Petol (*sic*),[1] who commanded the 35th, had unluckily been wounded in the wrist by one of his own men by mistake. He never recovered his spirits afterwards, but died upon arriving in England. The other was a Major in the Army who had lost his arm, but, notwithstanding such a serious deprivation, was in a constant flow of good humour. The difference between these two officers was extraordinary.

When we arrived in the Downs, I had some anxiety to pass my Dutch purchases. The Major volunteered to take charge of them as belonging to his military equipments, and he passed them for me with the greatest facility. I met here Capt. Tomlinson.[2] During my residence at Tervere a party of seamen were employed in raising one of our gunbrigs that had been taken by the enemy. She was restored finally to the Navy.

I made a very short stay at Deal. From Capt. Rowley, one of our distinguished officers, I had experienced the kindest hospitality. I left England in the *Aigle*, and returned in the *Eagle*. After presenting my respects to Admiral George Campbell,[3] I hastened up to Town.

(3) H.M.S. *CAMILLA*

SEPTEMBER 1809–DECEMBER 1809

Summary (SEPT.–OCT.)

[W.H.D. narrates, in four pages of MS., the subsequent history of the Grand Expedition, and Lord Chatham's reasons for calling it off. His account is not inaccurate, but is omitted here since, in this context,

---

[1] Probably P. H. Petit.

[2] W.H.D. here repeats the whole of the Tomlinson-Hawke story, with substantially the same comments, reported in Vol. I, pp. 323–24.

[3] (Sir) George Campbell, Lt. 6/6/1778; Cdr. 27/8/80; Capt. 9/11/81; R-Ad. 1/1/1801; V-Ad. 25/10/09; Ad. 4/6/14. As C. in C. Portsmouth figures prominently in W.H.D.'s later story.

it is 'secondhand history' which can readily be studied in *James, Brenton, the Naval Chronicle, Laird Clowes* and *Fortescue.* He records that his innocence was again exploited over his just allowance for the entertainment of Army officers. He then went to stay with Lord Dillon at Ditchley, and heard the adventures of that peer's eldest son, Col. Dillon, in Spain:]

We were elated to hear of Sir Arthur Wellesley's victory at Talavera. Col. Dillon had gone out as a Volunteer. He had tried to persuade me to accompany him, but I declined turning soldier in a foreign country. By the Spanish Government he was made a Brigadier. I several times cautioned him not to place too much confidence in that nation, and I foretold what happened. He arrived in time to be present at the defeat of the Spaniards at Aucagna[?], and would have been made a prisoner had he not been mounted upon a good blood horse that carried him far away beyond the Frenchmen's pursuit.

[He made his routine visit and application to Lord Mulgrave at the Admiralty, without meeting with much encouragement; then returned to his home and wife at Chester. This time, however, he had not long to wait.]

I had not been a week at home when I received a letter from Lord Mulgrave acquainting me that he had appointed me Acting Captain of the *Camilla*, a 20-gun ship stationed off the Texel. The contents of that letter led me to believe I should become permanent Captain of that ship. I packed up and hastened to North Yarmouth, where I reported myself to Ad. Douglas. No vessel being ready to convey me to the *Camilla*, I had to wait a few days in this seafaring town before a small brig arrived and took me to the Texel, where I was installed into the command. Her Captain, Bowen,[1] had requested leave of absence and, as I understood, did not intend to rejoin her. He was the son of Capt. Bowen, with whom I had served in the *Prince George, Glory* and *Thunderer.* I had made the son's acquaintance at Walcheren, for he was still under the orders of Sir Richard Strachan. We soon came to a friendly understanding respecting the changing of positions, and the vessel that brought me out took him home. He had with him a kept mistress, a companion that did not do much honour to his station. Here again I had to work against the prejudices

---

[1] John Bowen, Lt. 13/4/1802; Cdr. 2/5/04; Capt. 22/1/06; see Vol. I, p. 140 and note.

of the crew, by the regulations I might feel it necessary to adopt, in opposition to those to which they had been accustomed. All the officers were strangers to me. However, they invited me to pass the evening with them below, and we talked over the doings of the Army and Navy at Flushing.

The *Camilla* was an old crazy ship of 20 guns, 9-pounders with a few carronades. She sailed badly, and was painted all black, but, such as she was, I felt it a compliment from the First Lord that he had himself selected me to command her. I was at sea, watching an enemy port, and I was determined to lose no opportunity of annoying him. I had no one to interfere with me and was entirely master of my own actions. The officers appeared well inclined. There was a very clever Pilot on board, with one failing—he was fond of grog. The Ship's Company showed every disposition to exert themselves on all occasions. I had them exercised at the guns, making sail, etc., and was satisfied. I examined the coast off the Texel, but scarcely ever saw anything like an enemy cruizer. One or two of our sloops of war occasionally joined me. If I happened to be Senior Officer, they entreated me not to detain them. I yielded to their wishes. Consequently they chose their cruizing ground as I selected mine. Many neutral vessels were boarded, all their papers being so carefully arranged that detaining a doubtful one was rather a ticklish affair. However, one morning on the Dogger Bank, I chased a small vessel which proved to be a Dutch fishing vessel. I had not as yet met any so far out from the land: I therefore detained him and sent him into port for adjudication. The other fishing vessels which I constantly met when closing in with the coast I never interfered with. Shortly after this a large schuyt[1] came off the Texel under convoy of one of our gunbrigs, from the Thames laden with treasure, to be escorted to that port. The Lieutenant commanding that vessel showed me his instructions—to see this vessel in safety inside of a particular buoy leading into the entrance. This I thought would afford a good opportunity of sending my boats, armed, into the Texel, to try and bring out any enemy vessel that might be ready for sea. Volunteers presented themselves, and having enlisted the Lieutenant with his brig into my plans, I attached three boats, well manned and armed, to the schuyt, and sent them in under the charge of the brig, who had my orders to wait outside the buoy for their return. They were away the whole night under the command of the Master, who rowed well into the Texel without meeting anything worth his notice. The next

---

[1] 'Schuytz' in text.

day they all returned in safety. I then liberated the Lieutenant and his brig, which had brought out a considerable sum of money, principally in gold, for the use of the Dutch. This supply to the enemy gave room for ample speculation as to the manner in which it was to be employed. This month completed the 50th year of our good King's reign, and, as a Jubilee was held in celebration thereof, I gave the Ship's Company a dram each to drink His Majesty's health.[1]

The next vessel that I fell in with was also a fishing vessel, on a larger scale. She was fitted with an open well, and as the proceedings of her Master were very suspicious I detained him, my chief reason being that he had a good round sum of gold on board, to be smuggled over to the enemy. This traffic had been forbidden by our Government, and I was determined to send this knowing Dutchman into port that his conduct might be judged by the Admiralty Court. He had caught a very fine sturgeon, which he sent to me. As I had been some time at sea, I thought it prudent to take a peep into Yarmouth and consult with the Admiral. He had that day a large dinner party, to which I was invited. That gave me the opportunity of displaying the sturgeon. When Mrs. Douglas heard that I had given it to the Admiral, she came and thanked me for having supplied the only dish wanting to complete the dinner. There were no fish to be had in the market, owing to blowing weather: moreover, a sturgeon was not to be had every day. Therefore my company was the more acceptable. I was now informed that the vessel I had previously sent in, being a regular fishing craft, would not be condemned as a Prize: but as she had exceeded the sea-limits allowed to them, one half of the value of her cargo would be awarded to the *Camilla*. The Dutchman was in consequence ordered to make the payment. He was very glad to get clear upon such easy terms, and deposited £200 in my Agent's hands. This sum, small as it was, had its effect upon my officers and crew. It was a new event to them, their former Captain not having been in any way successful in the way of Prizes.

I was soon at sea again off the Texel. The winter was setting in and I expected some gales, but I had fine weather. An enemy Privateer kept watching our motions. She sailed too well for the *Camilla*, and all my attempts against her failed. At last I thought of an expedient by which I very nearly succeeded in capturing him. I got hold of two of the Dutch fishermen of that part of the coast, and

---

[1] An odd mistake. George III ascended the throne on October 25, 1760—*i.e.* had reigned only 49 years.

placed 25 men in each, under the command of the Master, an active, intelligent seaman. These I sent into the Vlie Passage. They were to watch for an opportunity of laying the Privateer on board and carrying her sword in hand. I anchored the ship for the night, to be sure of my position, getting under sail next morning with the dawn. Soon we noticed the two vessels standing inshore. By and by the Privateer came out. Our spy-glasses were now at work, watching every motion of the fishing vessels. At one time the Privateer passed between them, and we made sure of their laying him on board. But this did not happen. The whole day was passed in anxiety, but no success attended our seamen. I could not approach nearer, as that would cause suspicion to the enemy. The following morning the Master returned with his party. He declared that the only plan which could have succeeded was to fall alongside of the Privateer as if by accident. When nearing him, he had kept all his men under cover, but the Privateer's Commander was so much on the alert, and the vessel kept with such fresh way on, that he never had the slightest chance of grappling with him. I was now assailed by the Dutch fishermen, with tears in their eyes, begging to be set free. Their wives and children, they said, were in despair at their absence. In short such doleful tales were poured out that I let them go.

We were soon afterwards visited by a strong gale. Knowing that there was good holding ground, however, I anchored and rode it out in safety. One vessel now gave me a hard day's work and obliged me to fire upon him. The Master was drunk, but a shot through his fore topsail brought him to his senses. I reported his conduct at Lloyds. Not long afterwards I boarded a large ship from Norway, deeply laden with timber. The Master gave out that he was bound for the Thames, but there were wooden trucks for gun-carriages in abundance upon his deck. This circumstance naturally led me to believe that the cargo consisted of warlike stores. When boarded, this ship was not steering a course for England, but for Holland. I had the Master on board and explained my suspicions. He had plenty of reasons to justify himself. I released him, at the same time warning him that, if he did not alter his course towards England, I should certainly detain him. Upon his return to his ship, he gave proof of his not minding the warning. I allowed two hours to elapse, during which he continued to near the Dutch coast. I then closed upon him, and sent the 2nd Lieutenant on board with a party of seamen to navigate her into Harwich. The Danish Master wished to make it appear that he was steering as he did to avoid the Lemon and Oar, a dangerous reef in the North Sea. But the position he was in falsified that danger. I had placed some confidence in the 2nd Lieutenant, who was only Acting, from his previous conduct. I gave him this opportunity of exerting himself, and, if he had done to my satisfaction, should have felt much pleasure in recommending him to the notice of the Admiralty. But the result will show that I could not have made a greater mistake than by employing him on such responsible duty.

As the provisions were getting short, a few days after parting from the Norwegian, I returned to Yarmouth, where the news I received was anything but agreeable. The ship I had detained had anchored off Yarmouth, had lost an anchor and had received assistance from the Pilot boats of that place, for which upwards of 100 guineas were demanded. The whole proceedings of that party appeared to have been so shameful that I appealed for another decision. I was warned that my appeal would not lead to any favourable result, as the feeling towards all naval officers, under circumstances like mine, was so inimical that the charges would be augmented instead of reduced. However, I came to the conclusion that it would be proper to call the parties together, to be present myself, and hear the arguments made use of. The meeting took place, and the falsehoods I heard quite satisfied me what lengths those men would go to in supporting charges that had not the slightest foundation. I was so disgusted at all I witnessed that I withdrew from the meeting horrified beyond description.

The Pilot had of late been so often intoxicated that I intended bringing him to a Court Martial, and I had forbidden his going on shore. When he heard of my feeling towards him, he turned the whole into ridicule. 'The Captain,' said he, 'may try me if he pleases. But I have been tried by a Court Martial already. They cannot do without me, and the Captain has rendered me very essential service by not allowing me to land, as I was drunk and should have been noticed as such by my friends. But now I am sober, and quite prepared for anything.' Upon inquiry, I found that all he said was true. He had been repeatedly before a Court Martial and censured, but notwithstanding that was still continued on the list of Pilots as he knew the coast of Holland so well. However, I finally had him discharged, receiving another in his place.

Ad. Douglas reported my return to the Admiralty, who ordered the *Camilla* to Sheerness to refit. But I requested permission, on my way thither, to look into Harwich that I might ascertain what proceedings were necessary relating to the ship detained. All the accounts forwarded to me about her were of the most unfavourable description, and the consequences, to me, assumed rather an alarming appearance as to damages. The Admiral kindly sanctioned my request, and promised if necessary to explain to the Admiralty the awkward position in which I was placed. The newspapers now gave out that I had sent three vessels into port, causing an impression that the Captain had made some Prize money, and my friends in Town concluded that I had been lucky. Capt. Bowen's father, I was told, had called his son to account for having requested leave of absence, as I had turned his ship to such advantage. He little knew the scrape I had got into.

I was soon under sail, but was obliged by stormy weather to anchor outside of Harwich. The fates seemed against me. A thick fog came on and clapped a stopper on all my operations. It now turned out that all the ship's rum was expended. Here we were in cold weather, and no grog for the tars. What was to be done? After some deliberation, I ordered my boat to be hoisted out, an empty puncheon being placed in it. Then taking my pocket compass, I shoved off from the ship and groped my way into Harwich, where I had never been before. I got hold of the individual who supplied the King's ships with provisions and desired him to fill the cask with rum. Whilst he was doing this I hastened to the Norwegian. When I stepped on board, I noticed that all the gun trucks had disappeared. I inquired of the Lieutenant what had become of them, and he coolly replied that the seamen had burned them. That information went through me like an arrow. 'What?' said I. 'Have you allowed the articles which were the principal cause of my detaining the ship to be destroyed? Those trucks were the same as implements of war. You have been guilty of the most unpardonable neglect. What the consequences to me may be I cannot judge, but you have done me a most serious injury.' I then inquired for the Master of the ship. 'He is gone to London,' was his answer. 'Worse and worse!' I said. 'What could have induced you to allow a Master of a neutral, detained on suspicion, to go to Town, until you had the authority to do so? He will now place his papers in the hands of those who are on the look out for such events, and who will frustrate all the charges I may bring against the ship.'* In fact, by his ignorance (for the more

---

* In those critical times most of the Masters of the neutral vessels had two sets of papers, to be used according to circumstances. In this instance, when the Dane found himself in an English port, he declared that he was consigned to a London merchant, and, having persuaded the Lieutenant to allow him to proceed thither, he laid his plans to counteract the cause of his detention.

I saw of him the greater fool he appeared to be) he had completely set at nought all I had done.

I now quitted the ship and went in search of the Admiralty Proctor, with whom I had a long conversation. He felt most keenly the ill-judged act of my Lieutenant, but promised to represent the whole case in such terms to his superiors in Town that it would not fail to make an impression in my favour. I then embarked in my boat, with the cask full of rum, and started back in a thick fog. When I got outside the harbour, the attempt seemed a desperate one, as I could not see an object three yards off. However, I shaped my course by the pocket compass, in an opposite direction to the one I had come in by. At last I thought I saw something like a ship, and fortunately was correct. It was 4 o'clock in the afternoon, and the officers expressed themselves in terms of respect at my undertaking: and afterwards the Ship's Company gave many proofs of their feelings towards me that were truly gratifying. When the fog cleared, the ship was taken into the harbour, where I devoted all my energies to remedy the consequences of my Lieutenant's neglect and ignorance. I brought him on board with the other seamen, and placed the detained ship under the care of the Admiralty Court.

Now again the fates seemed to frown on my endeavours to quit this place. The entrance is very narrow, which requires a favourable wind to conduct a ship through it. As I had been some days here, I became anxious to get away, but the winds were contrary. Then the First Lieutenant came to me in behalf of the whole Ship's Company to offer their utmost exertions to warp the ship out to sea, saying that they were ready to sacrifice their lives for a Captain who had shown so much consideration for them. After weighing this proposal, I at last accepted it, and preparations were made for the next morning, should the wind still be against us. All the boats and hawsers were placed in readiness, and by 4 o'clock in the morning all hands were at work, and the ship unmoored. Here I had another escape similar to former ones. A seaman fell from the main yard whilst loosing the sail, and came down on deck. I happened to be standing immediately under, but, hearing something like a jerk aloft, moved a step inwards. That act saved my life, as the man's right heel came in contact with my right shoulder, struck the rounded part and grazed my arm. When he reached the deck, the poor fellow was instantly taken to the Surgeon, perfectly senseless. He died in the course of a few hours.

The anchors were soon up, the hawsers laid and the ship hauled along with every prospect of getting out to sea. However, when we were abreast of the harbour point, one of the hawsers broke in two, and the ship drifted on the beach. As I had no assistance but my own boats, all sorts of difficulties presented themselves. But by dint of perseverance the ship was hauled off, the seamen exerting themselves in a wonderful manner. These hawsers were worn out—in fact rotten. I was most reluctantly obliged to retrace my steps to the place I had left, and the ship was again in safety.* The officers and men were all exhausted: they required rest. It was a sad disappointment.

Another day of anxiety passed, but on the following one a fine breeze sprang up, fair for sailing, and the ship was soon going along with as much rapidity as there had been difficulty on the former attempt. When clear of the port all anxiety ceased, and we soon reached Sheerness, where the *Camilla* was ordered into harbour to be paid off. I was not prepared for such an event. It was a sad disappointment: and what caused another was the appearance of Capt. Bowen, who came to resume the command of his ship. I did not expect him. However, he acknowledged that his father had insisted upon his returning to his duty. He allowed me to suit my own convenience in giving over the command to him. My preparations were soon made, and in the course of a few days I quitted the *Camilla*. The officers and Ship's Company, rather to the annoyance of Capt. Bowen, proved in marked terms their respect and attachment towards me. I was soon in London.

(4) HOME (Unemployed)

DECEMBER 1809–AUGUST 23rd, 1810

(*Summary and Narrative*)

[HAVING paid his routine visit to the Admiralty, to be coldly received by Lord Mulgrave, he returned to Chester. Here or hereabouts he relates the final proceedings at, and the evacuation of, Walcheren, mentioning that the French who occupied that area were, no less

---

* There being no plank on board—the stores were all expended—I ordered some of the hammock boards to be cut up to make a coffin, then sent the body on shore for burial. That act of attention from the Captain made an impression upon the Ship's Company, which they expressed in most grateful terms. Their former Captain, they said, would never have bestowed so much consideration upon one of his crew. I mention this merely as a proof that seamen know how to appreciate those who are considerate towards them.

than the British, victims of the 'Walcheren Fever'. He ends with his
own—indifferent—version of the famous Walcheren epigram:—

> Sir Richard Strachan with his sword drawn
> Was waiting for Lord Chatham:
> Lord Chatham, waiting for Sir Richard Strachan,
> Was anxious to be at 'em.

W.H.D. was now in low spirits all round—in great pain from his
wounded leg (for which he was 'advised by the Surgeon Mr. Rowlands
to repair to Bath and undergo a regular system of friction'): in low
water financially, and on the verge of a complete breach with his
wife whose mad extravagance was ruining him. Further, a stranger
to him—the Right Hon. Charles Philip Yorke—now became First
Lord; and W.H.D., in despair of further employment, being without
'Parliamentary Interest', toyed seriously with the idea of throwing
up his commission for good. With that intention in view, he wrote
to Mr. Malony in Jamaica to ask if the latter's promises still held
good. (See Vol. I, p. 432.)

He went to Bath—by himself—and put up at a boarding house
in Abbey Square. The celebrated waters failed him, but massage
did not. Though, strictly speaking, irrelevant here, his account of
that cure is inserted, since it seems to run contrary to the usually
accepted history of massage: viz., that, though practised in classical
times, at *least* from the period of Hippocrates, it fell into total disuse
during the dark ages, to be revived only after the middle of the
nineteenth century by physicians like Mezser.]

The pumping and bathing had no good effect on my unfortunate
limb. At last, however, my medical attendant recommended the
rubbing. A female came to me for that purpose. She laboured the
first time for two hours, and I felt relief. She applied the powdered
flour to prevent carrying off the skin, but without success. However,
there appeared some chance of improvement. The next day two
hours more rubbing restored the circulation. I can never forget my
feelings of that hour when I placed my foot on the floor, and attempted to walk. I was astonished beyond description to find that I had
again, in a certain sense, recovered the use of my leg. The warmth,
the flow and the circulation which took place, for the first 10 minutes,
caused an elasticity in my limbs that I can not explain. I felt myself
quite another person. When the Doctor heard the result of my second
operation, he was equally pleased, satisfied that success would

finally result. I continued the rubbing system every other day. My leg became perfectly scarified, but that I did not mind. I knew my limb was improving.

[At Bath he met several old friends, including Sir James Lucas Yeo (see above, p. 42), and Capt. Prigny of the French Navy, now himself a prisoner of war (see above, p. 51). A very long erased passage follows. He met, and for a time lived with, his cousin (Sir) John Dillon, the recipient of all the letters which form the text of the Narrative. The latter, a lawyer, gave him valuable advice on his relationship with his wife. He also introduced him to the Duke of York—an event destined to be something of a turning-point. The prince exerted himself strongly in W.H.D.'s favour, and, though nothing came of it at the time, it served to wean him from his idea of emigrating to Jamaica: which indeed was fortunate for him—and for the remainder of this Narrative—for he now ran into Mr. Malony in person in London.]

. . . From him I heard the particulars of the fate of the *Richmond*, which I had been the cause of detaining when First Lieutenant of the *Crescent*. The American, it seems, had appealed against the first judgment given in our favour, but, finding that the feeling of the Admiralty Court was against him, offered Capt. Lobb £10,000 to be clear.[1] That meant giving up half the value of the *Richmond*, but the Captain, being certain of having the whole, would not accept. Then the Yankee, who had all his wits about him, bribed one of the officials about that Court, who contrived to slip the *Richmond's* papers into those of a vessel that was acquitted: by which means he got away, laughing at Capt. Lobb for having declined the sum offered. As Capt. Lobb was at this time at Gibraltar, the Commissioner there, I had no communication with him except by writing. His wife I dined with once or twice in Sloane Street, but had no information from her.

[Malony renewed his offers, 'but the interference of the Duke of York in my favour had changed the position of affairs.']

Among the events of the day, I received an invitation from Lady Hamilton to dine with her. When I went there, she told me that she had requested my company as the Duke of Sussex intended to pass

---

[1] See Vol. I, p. 444, where, however, the sum offered to Capt. Lobb was only £8,000.

the evening with her. This was all right, as you had already written to H.R.H. about me. At that period Lady Hamilton resided in Piccadilly. We had a very nice sociable dinner. In the evening the Duke made his appearance with Mrs. B .[1] There were other ladies and gentlemen who dropped in, and amongst the number (who should present herself but my wife. That was a sad event, for which I was not prepared, as I naturally supposed her to be at Bristol. Lady H. and Mrs. B. interfered, and persuaded me to try once more. I again yielded).[2] H.R.H. was very gracious, and at parting invited me to pass a few days with him at his country residence near Fulham. I accepted the Duke's proposal, and in a couple of days repaired to the premises. H.R.H. received me with great condescension, and was very anxious to hear all my professional services, taking a very lively interest in all my concerns. Knowing that I suffered from wounded legs, he would not allow me to stand in his presence. In short, I found him an amiable, well-informed Prince and a most interesting companion, I passed two or three days at this mansion, and when I took my leave he invited me to see him at Kensington Palace, and I availed myself of the first opportunity to do so.

[There can be no doubt that the Duke of Sussex was greatly taken with W.H.D., whom he later appointed to be his Equerry. At Kensington Palace he went to the pains of writing out in his own hand a long statement of Dillon's services, and sent him with it to the Duke of York.]

I had some difficulty in getting admittance to the Duke of York's residence in the Palace Yard, St. James's. However, by feeing the servant, and telling him that I had a letter to deliver from the Duke of Sussex, I finally obtained an audience of the Royal Duke, who received me without ceremony and took from me his Royal brother's letter. He told me that the First Lord had replied to his application in my behalf, expressing his satisfaction at my being again able to serve: to this he added a few courteous words, with a smiling countenance. 'I am obliged to be off,' he said. I then withdrew, full of expectation for the future.

[1] The rest of this name is not, as usual, scored out in ink, but carefully erased with a pen-knife. The lady may well be Lady Bugge, with whom the Duke had an affair which lasted for many years. She is mentioned by name later on in connection with him.

[2] The words in brackets are erased in the text: but the obvious interest of the intervention of so historic a figure in W.H.D.'s affairs seems to justify a departure from the rule of not printing erased matter verbatim. This is one of the very few exceptions in the whole Narrative.

[He attended a big dinner given by the Duke of Sussex at the Neapolitan Club, where the latter, who had a high opinion of his own musical attainments, 'gave us a song in a good voice: but I could not contribute my share.'[1]) W.H.D. now had his first serious brush with his ill-wisher, Bickerton.]

I cannot pass unnoticed an incident of a very unpleasant nature that I had with the leading Naval Lord of the Admiralty, Sir Richard Bickerton. It is the custom for these gentlemen to fix the hour that suits them to admit applicants. Calling one day at the time appointed, I was shown up to the receiving room. When Sir Richard entered, he fixed his eyes upon me in such a pointed manner that I could not help feeling it, as indicating no good will. By his look of surprise at seeing me, I imagined that he would not deign to acknowledge me. Yet, thought I, he must know me, as he has often met me at Lord Mulgrave's table, and spoken to me. However, the reception made its impression, and I acted accordingly, merely asking a question or two relating to some reports. In reply, he said they had no foundation. I withdrew, determined to let this official Lord know that I was somebody. I lost no time in calling upon an influential M.P. to whom I was well known, Sir John Sinclair, to inquire if he knew Sir Richard B. 'Yes,' he replied, 'perfectly well.' 'Could you give me a line of introduction to him?' 'Most certainly,' said he. 'Explain what you want.' I then stated that I had been informed of an expedition upon a small scale to act upon the coast of France, and that I thought I could be usefully employed in it. Sir John instantly put pen to paper, expressing himself as follows:—'The bearer is a friend of mine, and I shall feel obliged by your having the kindness to forward his views.'

Two or three days later I presented myself at the Admiralty, requesting an interview with Sir Richard. The messenger who took my card up told me that he was at leisure and would see me. A long half hour passed, but no notice was taken of my being in waiting. I inquired of the porter if Sir Richard was engaged. 'No,' he replied. 'He means to see you.' After the lapse of an hour, I sent my note to the Admiralty Lord, with a message that I was waiting. Another half hour passed without my being admitted. My patience was exhausted, as the proceeding appeared intended. I then mounted half way up the stairs, and in a loud voice called to the messenger,

---

[1] It is well-known that the Duke was particularly proud of his vocal powers—especially his 'three-octave compass'. Hereafter he figures frequently in these pages.

'Does Sir Richard Bickerton mean to see me or not?' The words were scarcely out of my mouth when the messenger said, 'I was coming to acquaint you that Sir Richard is ready to receive you.' I ascended, and in the passage leading to the receiving room met Sir Richard, his lips quavering, neither of us, I imagine, in the very best temper. He demanded what was my object in calling. 'I hope,' I replied, 'that Sir John's note will have its weight with you in my behalf. I am anxious to be employed, and I trust your influence here will be useful to me.' He made some excuses. 'All the reports you have heard take their origin in the newspapers. You must not be led away by them.' I then withdrew.

Another circumstance turned up shortly after this that led me again to the Admiralty. I sought for another interview with Sir Richard, which was granted. He now gave me plainly to understand that he never interested himself in behalf of any officer with the First Lord unless he had served in his ship, and whom he knew. That declaration I thought a very strange one from the Naval Officer placed in his position to assist the Chief of that Board in his selection of individuals best suited to serve the Country. I thought my friend, Sir John S., would not be much pleased to have heard this. However, such are the difficulties in the way of a half-pay officer seeking a command. Sir Richard B. never forgave me for calling out on the staircase, and I shall have to bring him in again in due time.

It was only a few days later that I received a note from the First Lord's private Secretary, acquainting me of his having appointed me Acting Captain of the *Bellerophon*, but that I was to understand that it gave me no claim for a permanent one beyond the ordinary chances of the Service. The ship was stationed off the Scheldt, watching the French fleet, and as there was no probability of that fleet putting to sea, I saw no chance of going into action: which would no doubt, if I were not killed, give me a claim for a command in my own right. Therefore I resolved not to accept it, and repaired to the Admiralty to see the First Lord. He was not there. I then presented myself to Sir Richard Bickerton, acquainting him that I should decline the employment. He replied in a passion, 'If I were the First Lord of the Admiralty, and you refused such an appointment, I would never employ you again.' 'Thank you, Sir Richard,' I rejoined. 'I cannot believe that it is the intention of the Admiralty that an officer should ruin himself in serving his country.' 'How so?' he demanded. 'I have lately held two acting commands,' I replied. 'They were, in the first

place, very unpleasant ones: and, in the next, they were very expensive, as I had to do all the honours, keep a table, and was sent in all
directions at considerable expense for nothing—as this note (showing
it to him) plainly states. My accepting the acting command gives me
no claim for a permanent one, and I am already more than £200 out
of pocket by accepting the first two.' '£200,' he exclaimed: 'how so?'
'I can show you the bill,' I replied. He then lowered his tone. 'I
advise you to accept that ship,' he said, 'but do not keep a table.
Mess with the officers in the Ward Room.' An explanation now took
place which ended in my accepting the command of the *Bellerophon*.

(5) H.M.S. *BELLEROPHON* (Blockade)

AUGUST 23, 1810–NOVEMBER 4, 1810

I hastened to Deal, where I presented myself to the Port Admiral,
George Campbell, on August 23. He placed a boat at my disposal to
convey me on board the *Bellerophon*. Her Captain, Samuel Warren,[1]
I had known in the West Indies, where he commanded a sloop of
war. Ad. Gardner had, not long before, had his Flag flying on board,
but he had removed to another, and Capt. Warren was appointed to
command one of our large frigates. Here I met an old shipmate of the
Prince George, Mr. Robert Pilch,[2] the First Lieutenant. My arrangements were easily concluded, and I was installed in the command of
a line of battle ship. In a couple of days I was at sea, to join Vice-Ad.
Sir Edward Pellew, commanding the fleet off the Scheldt. I took with
me cables, and all sorts of stores for the ships there. On the afternoon
of the 26th I discovered the fleet at anchor, and when I closed it my
signal was made to anchor near the *Bellona*. We made the 8th two-
decker lying here. The next morning I called on board the *Christian
VII*, of 80 guns, the Flag Ship. I was highly gratified at the Admiral's
reception. I had brought out with me a lieutenant, a passenger, to
join his proper ship, the *Aboukir*. He had given a strange account of
himself, but it turned out that he had just before offered to Mr.
Yorke £2,000 for his promotion: upon which he had been ordered to
appear before the Admiralty to give an account of such proceeding.
However, he had sufficient good sense to acknowledge the error he
had committed, and appealed for mercy. He was an Hibernian, John

---

[1] Lt. 3/11/1790; Cdr. 1/3/97; Capt. 29/4/1802.
[2] Lt. 22/12/1796; Cdr. 4/12/1813; thereafter unemployed: Died, 1846.

Heally.[1] In consequence of that submission he received directions to retrace his steps and rejoin his ship: but in the first instance he was to be reprimanded by Sir Edward Pellew, who did not mince the matter with him. He received a jobation that must have stung the coldest heart in existence.

Sir Edward invited me to dine with him, and when he heard of my detention at Verdun there was no limit to his inquiries. The squadron was anchored upon a bank of good holding ground called the Broad Fourteens, as that was the general depth of the water upon it. Attached to the squadron were some frigates and smaller vessels stationed inshore, watching the enemy's motions. I here met my old acquaintance Capt. Macnamara,[2] who had just been appointed to a new 74, the *Berwick*. I often dined with him, and passed some agreeable hours in his society. I had established myself in the Ward Room Mess, which I found tolerably comfortable. The Captain of Marines was an old acquaintance of the last war: but there was a certain caution which I could not help feeling on the part of the officers. The captain is a different person to themselves in an official point of view, and the general tone of conversation was guarded. There was not much occupation for the squadron. The usual exercise at anchor, of the great guns, etc., was in practice when necessary. I knew most of the captains, who frequently invited me to dine, to relieve the monotony of the Officers' Mess. The squadron occasionally got under way, and after a day's sailing anchor again at night.

Our Admiral was a first rate seaman, but he did not cut a conspicuous figure in manœuvring the squadron. One morning I noticed something going on on board the Admiral's ship, and desired the First Lieutenant to keep his eye in that direction. I had scarcely done so when out flew our signal to weigh the anchor. The *Theseus's* was also made. There was a strong breeze with a very heavy rolling sea and a lee tide. As we noticed the *Christian VII* heaving in cable, we understood that we were to have a day's trial. With such a strong lee tide and sea running, the weighing of the anchor was no easy job. In truth, the signal was ill-judged, and ought not to have been made until slack water. However, we set to work, and when the difficulty became apparent by the snapping of the nippers, and the cable running out again, a consultation took place between myself, the First Lieutenant and the Master, when we decided to hitch the messenger round the cable till the anchor was out of the ground. By

---

[1] John Healy, Lt. 26/2/1802; Cdr. (ret.) 12/9/39.
[2] James. See Vol. I, Index.

adopting that measure, the anchor was brought up to the bows. Meanwhile the ship drifted away with the tide a long distance to leeward, and in time made sail. But the Admiral's ship and the *Theseus* were still fast. They could not weigh their anchors until the tide had slackened, and set to windward. On the other hand, my ship, by weighing, had lost at least three miles to leeward. After a day's trial, which could not be a fair one, we anchored in the afternoon and the Admiral made my signal to dine with him. When I got on board, he demanded, 'How did you manage to weigh your anchor?' I told him. 'That was a dangerous experiment,' he remarked. 'I could not weigh mine. I have 17 men wounded at the nippers: consequently I waited till the tide turned.' That saying was his own condemnation, because every seaman knows full well that in attempting to weigh under such disadvantages you are exposed to serious accidents, which literally befell his men. The *Theseus* did not stir till the tide became favourable for moving, and so none of his men were hurt. Had I not acted as I did, many of mine, no doubt, would have been injured. When Sir Edward began to reason on the subject, I replied, 'I have just taken the command of a ship known to be in the very highest state of discipline. Had I failed in obeying your signal, I should probably have lost ground in the estimation of the officers and Ship's Company. Therefore at all risks I got under way: and luckily not a man was hurt.' He expressed himself much pleased with the tact I had shown. At parting, he invited me to breakfast next morning.

On that occasion he asked me if I was fond of boat sailing. 'Yes, Sir,' I replied, 'when I have a good one that I can depend upon.' 'Suppose,' said he, 'that you try your barge against mine.' I agreed, and it was settled that I was to hoist out my barge and come to the *Christian VII* to meet him. On reaching the *Bellerophon*, I found that there were two on board. When I asked the First Lieutenant which would be best, there was a pause. Then one of the junior Lieutenants stated that he knew the qualities of one of them, and requested me to allow him to steer that one. The boat, he said, sailed well, and had a good chance of beating the Admiral's. Being myself a perfect stranger, I had no choice but yield to the Lieutenant. That boat was instantly hoisted out, and when all the sails etc. were in proper condition we went to the *Christian VII*.

It was a fine day with a commanding breeze, but a long rolling swell of the sea. The boat was an old one, with lateen sails which were nearly threadbare. Noticing these disadvantages, I thought there

was no likelihood of outsailing the Admiral. However, it was pass-
time, and a challenge from the Commander in Chief. When I got
alongside, I beheld Sir Edward in a round jacket, with a leather hat
on, making his preparations in a systematic manner. His boat was
a large one, lugger rigged, the sails all new. On seeing this, I directed
my crew to dip my sails overboard and soak them well. The Admiral
now asked if I were prepared. 'All ready,' I replied. 'Here go, then,'
said Sir Edward. His barge shoved off, and away we went. Two or
three other boats had joined us to watch the proceedings. At the
start he was to windward, which was an advantage. However, in
less than a quarter of an hour, I forereached, and gradually crossed
his bow, gaining the wind. After an hour I was at least two miles
to windward of my opponent. The Admiral now made my signal to
pass under his stern. I obeyed, and when I got close I lowered my
sails, at the same time telling the men to hoist them whilst I was
speaking to Sir Edward, who was evidently trying to put me off my
guard. After exchanging a few words, during which I was a few
fathoms to leeward of him, he called out, 'Now let us try again.' Up
went my sails, and I passed him in exactly the same way as before.
The wind freshened and the sea rose. In about an hour he threw out
the signal of distress. I hastened down to him. His boat was full of
water. He had placed several 32-lb. shot in her to give her stability,
but by the violent pitching motion one of them went through the
bottom, and his boat was near sinking. All further attempts were at
an end. We returned to our ships, my boat having performed
wonders. I complimented Lieut. Mawle[1] who had steered with
excellent judgment. This event caused some conversation in the
squadron. The next day my barge was out in the afternoon, and I
saw the Admiral in his, standing under sail towards me. As I had had
so much superiority the day previous, I did not like to try again,
and ordered my barge to be hoisted in: which Sir Edward must have
noticed as he closed the *Bellerophon*. He said nothing, but passed on.

On one occasion when we received a supply of provisions, three
men were drowned, I thought, in a very lubberly way. Neatness was
studied on board of this ship to a fault. I could not, as Captain,
become acquainted all at once with all these whims—for such they
really were. It has always been an established custom on board ships
of war to have rope ladders suspended over the stern, one on each
side, for the men to go down and come up, in and out of the boats
generally lying there. But in this ship these ladders had been

---

[1] George Maule, Lt. 30/8/1806.

removed, as they were considered unsightly. It so happened one evening, when the labours of the day were closing, the boat that hung over the stern was in the act of being hoisted up. There was a heavy swell, and one of the tackles became unhooked. This not being known on the Poop, the men hoisted away: but instead of bringing it up horizontally, they brought it up on end, the other end hanging in the sea: and the swell swept off three of the crew. Being in my cabin, I heard an alarming noise, and, hastening to the window, beheld the boat hanging by its bow tackles, one poor fellow in great alarm holding on by it. The boat's position, of course, occasioned to me extreme anxiety. Upon my questioning the seaman as to how all this had happened, he gave a clear account of the accident, stating that three men were drowned. I instantly ordered another boat to be lowered, to search for these poor fellows: but, though we were favoured with moonlight, there was a very strong tide, and all attempts to recover them failed. Meanwhile measures were taken to get the stern boat properly secured. 'Where are the stern ladders?' I demanded. I sent for the First Lieutenant and inquired what had become of them. He very coolly replied that they were hanging up in the wings. I launched out on some remarks of dissatisfaction, conveying the impropriety of their being kept there, and that these unfortunate men would have been saved had they been in their proper places. I descended to the wings, and, sure enough, saw two very well constructed ladders triced up. I could not help expressing my astonishment. How could so excellent officer as the one I had replaced have allowed such a system? Then I instantly ordered the ladders to be removed and hung in their proper place. But three men had died because the ladders had been stowed where they could be of no service whatever. I often wondered afterwards whether the Captain or the First Lieutenant was most to blame. The next day the order came for Lieut. Pilch's discharge into the ship now commanded by Capt. Warren, as well for the discharge of other of his followers.

Just after this a fog came on, very thick. We could not see one end of the ship from the other. All the Captains had received an invitation to dine with the Admiral, but as the hour approached his ship could not be seen. However, as the *Bellerophon* lay nearly abreast of the *Christian VII*, I determined to make an attempt to reach her. My boat was hoisted out, and my favourite pocket compass brought into play. I desired the Lieutenant in charge to fire a few muskets after I had been away a quarter of an hour, to enable me to judge of my whereabouts. I made allowance for the tide, etc., and, acting with every caution, reached the bow of the Flag Ship, where Sir Edward received me with great cordiality. Only two other captains made the attempt. Dinner was served, but the fog continued in one dense mass all the evening. As night set in the Admiral would not allow us to attempt returning to our ships. We therefore remained on board until 4 o'clock in the morning when, the fog gradually clearing, I returned to the *Bellerophon.*

On the 22nd we had a general exercise of the great guns, and fired several broadsides in commemoration of the King's Coronation. At the end of the month our duty was deranged by one or more of the Ship's Company cutting and rendering useless several of the breechings of the maindeck guns: several of the tackles were also injured. Such a wanton act led me to believe that there were some ill-disposed men on board, and I was obliged to report this unexpected occurrence to Sir Edward, who immediately ordered two of the senior captains, Parker[1] and Douglas,[2] to examine the Ship's Company. These were ordered aft, on the Quarter Deck, and an oath, as follows, was administered:—'I do most solemnly swear that I did not myself, nor have I any knowledge of any other person who did, cut the gun breechings, tackles or rigging of this ship last night. So help me God.' All inquiries failed. All the seamen's bags and hammocks were examined, but nothing was found that could lead to any result. We had on board a Mulatto as a lieutenant. He was a sort of relation to one of our distinguished naval captains. Whether the Ship's Company had taken a dislike to him I never knew, but it was an unusual occurrence to see an officer of that description on board of one of His Majesty's ships. Not being the permanent captain, I could not interfere with the appointments I found.

The fore rigging was found to be defective, being nearly worn out, and additional shrouds were employed to secure the mast. Two lieutenants, Messrs. Couch[3] and Luckraft,[4] joined the ship to replace those who had left some time previously. Soon afterwards Sir Richard Strachan joined the squadron in the *Marlborough*, then removed to the *St. Domingo.* The ships took their turn to go inshore, and at last

---

[1] (Sir) George Parker (K.C.B.): nephew of Sir Peter Parker, Lt. 13/3/1782; Cdr. 4/11/93; Capt. 7/4/95; R-Ad. 4/6/1814; V-Ad. 19/7/21; Ad. 10/1/37. Died, 1847.
[2] John Erskine Douglas, Lt. 21/4/1778; Cdr. 24/5/94; Capt. 10/6/95; R-Ad. 4/6/14; V-Ad. 27/5/25; Ad. 28/6/38.
[3] James Couch, Lt. 6/9/1800; Cdr. 6/9/17; Capt. 24/1/24.
[4] Alfred Luckraft, Lt. 3/9/1810 (*i.e.* promoted to the *Bellerophon*); Cdr. 28/10/28; Capt. 28/6/38. He was (13/7/35) chosen by W.H.D. to be his Commander (by then 2nd in command) of the *Russel*, and in his narrative of that commission, Dillon tells how he helped to get him made Post.

it was ours. On the afternoon of the 16th we got under way and made sail to close in with the land, not only to watch the enemy's motions but also to supply the smaller ships with water. I now had several interviews with Commodore Owen of the *Clyde*. Next day I noticed three sail of the line of the enemy under sail. They were evidently exercising their crews. The squadron got under way and stood towards the coast of England. On the 17th I had completed the duty I was sent upon, and the Commodore made my signal to proceed to the Downs. We made sail in that direction, having strong breezes, and on the following afternoon sighted the North Foreland. Soon after, the squadron was seen at anchor, and the Admiral made my signal to anchor as convenient. The ships at anchor were the *Christian VII, St. Domingo, Berwick, Aboukir, Marlborough, Monarch, Theseus, Defence, Defiance, Bellona*. We made the 11th two-decker.

On the morning of the 19th we weighed anchor by signal, and the Fleet was formed in two divisions, beating to windward, to reach the Downs. There were heavy squalls, and in the afternoon we were obliged to anchor. It now came on to blow a strong gale: two cables were veered out and the top gallant masts sent on deck, then veered to three cables. On the 21st the wind moderated and we prepared to weigh: by 9 o'clock in the morning the Fleet was under sail, in two divisions. I must again notice rather an ill-judged signal on the part of our Chief when he made the Fleet beat into the Downs through a narrow channel in two divisions. The lee division was constantly coming in contact with the weather one. There was a very strong breeze, and accidents might have happened, which would have been avoided by sailing in a single line. The *Bellerophon* was the sternmost ship in the weather line, and the *Defiance* the last in the lee one. That ship interfered with me two or three times, exposing me to a signal from the Admiral. I was therefore determined to yield no more. The Captain of the *Defiance* was my senior officer, and evidently assumed in consequence thereof: whereas in other respects he had no right to impede my progress in the order of sailing, so long as I was in my station. Coming up from to leeward, he attempted to weather the *Bellerophon*, which I could have prevented. When he noticed my keeping the wind on the starboard tack, he threw out, as signal, a red pendant, meaning that I should open for him. But I would not. However, as the ships were approaching at the rate of 5 knots in opposite directions, with the certainty of boarding each other, when close to the South Sand head, sooner than run that risk, I put the helm up and allowed the *Defiance* to pass to windward.

Her Captain, Ekins,[1] hailed, alluding to the red pendant he had shewn. I replied that I was in my station. We continued tacking as necessary and reached the anchorage by 4 in the afternoon, when we were ordered to anchor according to the order of sailing. That put the *Bellerophon's* station a long way out towards the northern part of the Goodwin Sands. My signal was then made to strike foremast, and put on the new rigging which I had been preparing. So soon as the *Christian VII* had anchored, Sir Edward Pellew went to London, leaving Sir Richard Strachan in command.

Another gale now came on, which retarded the rigging of the foremast. Sir Edward had issued instructions for the whole of us to complete water and stores, and to be ready for sea at a moment's notice. However, the weather would not permit our having any communication with the shore. I now found myself obliged to punish several of the seamen. I had a very unruly set, requiring a very taut hand to keep them down.

When the weather moderated I went on shore. At my landing, I met Capt. Macnamara on the beach, accompanied by Capt. Ekins. The former, taking me by the hand, said, 'My friend here is anxious to make it up with you, as he suspects that you are displeased at his having the other day taken the weather gage of you.' I merely replied, 'I did my duty. If the Admiral takes no notice of what has passed, the matter falls to the ground. But should he say anything, Capt. Ekins must be responsible, as I am clear in every sense, Capt. Ekins held out his hand, which I accepted. They then invited me to dine with them and we passed a very pleasant evening together: I became acquainted with Mrs. Ekins. I was greatly surprised to meet Lord Carrington here, who held his residence in the Castle. I dined there, his party consisting of his own family, Lord and Lady Mahon, the Admirals Sir R. Strachan and Graham Moore,[2] to whom he presented me as an old friend. I was the only Captain present, which was noticed by the two Flag officers.

Sir Edward Pellew now returned, and was all anxiety to be off to sea. He was rather astonished when informed that none of the Fleet had taken in water or provisions. Rumours were in circulation that the enemy fleet in the Scheldt was coming out, and the *Clyde*,

[1] (Sir) Charles Ekins (K.C.B.). See Vol. I, p. 188. W.H.D.'s memory is slightly at fault here. Ekins was at this time Captain of the *Defence*.
[2] (Sir) Graham Moore (G.C.B.), Lt. 8/3/1782; Cdr. 22/11/90; Capt. 2/4/94; R-Ad. 12/8/1812; V-Ad. 12/8/19; Ad. 10/1/37. Here W.H.D. has made a mistake very rare in his Narrative. From the above-named dates it will be noticed that, at the moment here reached (Oct. 1810), Moore was still a Captain, with nearly two years to go before obtaining his Flag.

Commodore Owen, was instantly ordered to sea to watch their motions. The Fleet was increased to 15 of the line, by which arrangement a Captain of the Fleet was to be appointed, also a Master of the Fleet. Sir Edward sent for me and acquainted me that the *Bellerophon* was to proceed to Spithead to be converted into a Flag Ship. On this occasion I had a long conversation with him. He had scarcely spoken to any of his captains, nor was he at all aware of the state of the Fleet, till I told him. He asked me if I could recommend a Master, as the one then serving with him was to be promoted to be Master of the Fleet. Mr. Bates,[1] Master of the *Bellerophon*, was a very clever, intelligent seaman, and knew the coast of Holland well: I thought he would be just the person for Sir Edward. I was right, and I rejoiced to have had it in my power to recommend this officer, who was appointed to the *Christian VII*, and proved an acquisition.

On the 30th I put to sea, and reached the Owers on the 31st. Next morning we made the best of our way to St. Helens and anchored. In the afternoon, with fine weather, the Ship's Company made one of those extraordinary exertions that occasionally occur when all hands are acting with an animated spirit. The *Bellerophon* was at single anchor with only half a cable out when orders were given to get under way. The anchor was weighed and the royals set in 22 minutes. Not a single delay intervened from the first motion of the capstan till the ship was under full sail. By 6 o'clock we were safely moored at Spithead. I had given a passage to Capt. Newcombe[2] of the Navy, who had been acting in command of the *Monarch*, and we landed together that morning, enjoying a friendly dinner together. The next day he went to Town whilst I was expecting an officer to relieve me in the *Bellerophon*. On the afternoon of the 4th, Capt. Halstead[3] came on board and took the command, after which I lost no time in returning to London.

[He joined his wife in a 'very roomy set of apartments in Chelsea'. He has—for the only time—omitted to edit the following passage, which indirectly concerns his wife and her father.]

She entertained me by relating what had happened to one of the seamen of the *Bellerophon*. He was, it seems, an American of good connections, but serving on board in the capacity of common sailor, and he had been punished by me for drunkenness. Shortly after that

[1] John Bates, 1st Warrant, 10/12/1807.
[2] Francis Newcombe, Lt. 7/2/1794; Cdr. 15/9/1801; Capt. 11/4/09.
[3] John Halsted, Lt. 20/9/1793; Cdr. 22/6/98; Capt. 21/11/1808.

punishment, I had received orders to discharge him as a native of the United States. His relations knew my Father-in-law, and wrote to him to obtain his discharge from our Navy. Mr. Roberts[1] succeeded in his application, then directed his daughter to supply the individual with money, fit him out, and ship him off to America. She accordingly applied at the Navy Office, where she was informed that, when he applied for his pay, he would be directed to call upon her. He accordingly made his appearance at Chelsea. She gave him an apartment, but he took his meals in the kitchen. The premises led to the banks of the Thames, and the seaman, wishing to have a swim there, repaired to the sands early in the morning to do so. It so happened that the maidservants could from their room see the river. They witnessed his going into it, and noticed that his shoulders bore the marks of the lashes he had received from the cat of nine tails. When they told him what they had seen, Jack explained what had been the cause of those marks. When their mistress was told, she inquired what he had done to merit the castigation. He very good-naturedly stated all that had passed, and fully acquitted me of any improper feelings towards him. 'We were inshore,' he said, 'watching the French Fleet. The Captain had told the Ship's Company to keep themselves ready for action at a moment's notice: and I got drunk, and was reported to him. Consequently I merited the 24 lashes inflicted upon me. The Captain did his duty. Everyone on board said so.' The lady represented this young man as being well disposed. She fitted him out and forwarded him to America. We never heard of him afterwards.

(6) UNEMPLOYED AGAIN

NOVEMBER 4TH, 1810–MARCH 5TH, 1811

[ON his routine visit to the Admiralty, he had a revealing talk with Mr. Yorke, the First Lord:—]

'I suppose,' said Mr. Yorke, 'you will allow that there are many old officers applying for employment whose claims are superior to yours, and who are entitled to a preference.' 'Most certainly, Sir,' I replied. 'But I am not an old officer. I am aware that you have three classes to provide for—the old captain for the line of battle

---

[1] His father-in-law, it will be recalled, was himself American by birth. See Vol. I, p. XXII.

ship, the one of next standing for the large frigate. Then comes my class, to command a small one. If any officer of my standing can produce fairer services than mine, I am silent. But I believe there are none.' Mr. Yorke, who listened attentively to all I had to say, took up a scrap of paper and wrote some remarks on it. Then we parted.

[Sir James Yeo now tried to get W.H.D. taken on as Sir Sidney Smith's Captain. Dillon was invited to dine with that officer, and did so: but for some reason (not stated) the project came to nothing. He next met General Sarazin.]

The arrival of a Gen. Sarazin from France made some stir at this period. I accidentally made his acquaintance. The General had packed up his traps and left Boulogne, where he was stationed, in an open boat: then, when in England, published an abusive article against Bonaparte. I lost no time in acquainting Lord Dillon, who advised my seeing Mr. Hamilton of the Foreign Office. I accordingly called, and communicated to him what little I had picked up in my intercourse with the General, who, afterwards, communicated some useful intelligence to our Government, for which he was pensioned.

[By February 1811 W.H.D., partly through his wife's extravagance, was again in desperation, and felt obliged to approach the First Lord once more, though he had been informed that, by doing so just then, he ran a serious risk of being appointed to a very unpopular type of command—that of a troop-ship. He also tried again to solicit the interest of the Commander in Chief, the Duke of York, and once more had some hopes of success from that quarter. Meanwhile, in February 1811, Lord Dillon took him to the public levée held by the Prince Regent to celebrate the increase in the latter's powers. A much-abridged account of this curious occasion is inserted.]

The crowd that day surpassed all that I have seen at a Levée. His Lordship was suffering under a slight attack of the gout, and fortunately for both of us everybody gave way, and made room for him as he approached the door of entrance to the Presence Chamber. But a few gentlemen pressed in between his Lordship and me, in consequence of which, when the door was opened, Lord Dillon got in and was presented to the Regent. He then informed the Lord in Waiting that he had a friend to present to H.R.H. My name was called several times. I requested those in my way to allow me to pass on. Most of them did so: but one gentleman, a civilian, showed no such inclination. I spoke to him, explaining that I was the officer called. That information making no impression, I was obliged to make use of main strength. Then, using my elbows, I forced myself past him. In that act my sword, a weighty one presented to me by Lloyds, came in contact with the belt of his which, being made of light leather, instantly gave way, and his sword fell right across the Regent's feet. This caused an impression, but everyone present saw that it was not my fault. Lord Dillon then told H.R.H. who I was. The Regent gave me his hand to kiss. The white glove upon it was a soiled one, and I confess I was not much gratified at such an occurrence. H.R.H. in a few words said he was glad to see me. As I passed on, I happened to turn round, and there beheld Mr. Yorke who had his eyes fixed upon me. The Duke of York acknowledged me, and the Duke of Sussex neared and shook hands with me. We had to wait a long while for the carriage, and I had time to notice many of the pictures. The one that attracted me most was that of the Duke of Orleans, the celebrated Mons. Egalité, whom I had met on the racecourse at Vincennes in the year 1788. As he walked by, he had trodden on my foot, and made his excuses for so doing. When he heard I was a native of England, he desired one of his attendants to take me to his wife the Duchess, who was close by in a handsome phaeton. You will hear more of her by and by. I now entered into the Grand Salon, which had contained such an innumerable set of distinguished characters. The scene I there beheld is beyond relation. There were strewed upon the carpet hundreds of feathers, gloves, hats torn in pieces, belts of swords, several flaps of coats, handkerchiefs, shoebuckles, knee buckles without number. In short, what I looked upon had more the appearance of a ragged fair than the palace of a Sovereign Prince. Retiring from this scene, I went home. I there found a letter from the Admiralty, acquainting me that I was appointed Captain of the *Leopard*, a 50-gun ship.

The keenest mortification now ensued, because I suspected that the ship would be employed in the conveyance of troops, the service I had been trying so anxiously to avoid. Had I been nominated to hoist my pendant in a small frigate, I should have been overjoyed, but as it was I retired to bed with wounded feelings, and passed one of the most unpleasant nights of my life.

The next morning I hastened to the Navy Office, Somerset House, to consult my old friend, Capt. Sir Francis Hartwell.[1] He told me at

---

[1] W.H.D.'s Captain in the *Thetis*. See Vol. I, Index.

once that the *Leopard* was lying at Chatham and was to be turned into a troop ship. When he noticed my depressed spirits, he said, 'I can perfectly understand your disappointment. But if you knew what I do, and the number of officers trying for employment who can not succeed, you would not refuse the *Leopard*. Let me beseech you to accept her. There are many that would rejoice at the command of an old tub, provided they could only hoist their pendants.'[1] I next went to Kensington Palace and was received by the Duke of Sussex. He advised me by all means to accept the appointment, and promised to keep a look out for me, as he was sure this command would lead to another. Under these circumstances, nothing could be done but make the best of a bad bargain. I acknowledged Mr. Yorke's letter, and, in accepting the command, regretted that he had not selected me for more active service. I also wrote to the Duke of York, expressing my grateful acknowledgments for his kind and powerful influence in my favour, and hoping that my pendant would soon be removed to a better ship. Whether Mr. Yorke had selected me as a friend of the Duke, who was Commander in Chief of the Army, I never knew. But the appointment, occurring just when H.R.H. renewed his application in my behalf, led me to believe it.

I now lost no time in making my arrangements to assume the command of the *Leopard*. Some cash was required, and I called upon my Agent to ascertain how far he was willing to oblige me. I regret to say he held back on that occasion, but, after an explanation, we came to an understanding, and a small sum was placed at my disposal. I had quite forgotten—or rather never knew—the Admiralty Regulation which authorized an officer of my rank drawing three months' pay in advance when he hoisted his pendant. However, having obtained what I thought necessary for the moment, I hastened away to Chatham, and on the 5th of March commissioned the *Leopard*. When my London friends heard of my appointment, I received many applications to take youngsters with me. But when I explained the nature of the service on which I was to be employed, they did not trouble me further. Mr. Loveden, however, wished me to provide for the son of one of his bailiffs, and, when I assented, he sent me a fine stout youth, whom I tried to turn into a Clerk. In the end, he was no use, and after a trial of a few months he left the ship.

[1] See above, p. 113.

XII

TROOPSHIP

INTRODUCTION

THIS long Part is devoted, mainly, to Trooping and Convoy work—essential duties which were yet apt to be dull in a war wherein Great Britain held so absolute a mastery of the seas: duties, moreover, not very likely to lead to professional honour or advancement. This, of course serves to explain W.H.D.'s impatience at the conduct and (as he thinks) the prevarications of Sir Edward Pellew.

Though Dillon nowhere mentions the fact, it is perhaps worth recalling that his ship the *Leopard*, now reduced in status to a troopship, had played a prominent part in the earlier stages of the long Anglo-American dispute. It was she who, in June, 1807, had had the celebrated 'affair' with the U.S. frigate *Chesapeake*, in which action she killed and wounded 21 of the latter's crew, and took out of her four men whom the *Leopard's* captain considered to be British deserters. That captain, incidentally, was W.H.D.'s old friend of *Aimable* days, Salusbury Pryce Humphreys.

At page 172, the avowed policy of omitting erased passages is partially departed from. His account of how he came to take his wife and step-daughter to sea with him should be included, if only because it was the only occasion upon which the current of his professional career actually commingled with that of his private life. Whether he was, strictly, entitled to take such a course I am not sure. Had the *Leopard* been in full fighting commission it would certainly not have been allowed—though that is not to say, of course, that he would not have done it (*cf.* p. 140). But, as she was, officially, only 'trooping', he could probably have made a case for himself if challenged. Even as it is, a good deal of the erased passage (in which he says hard things about his wife) is omitted. The daughter stayed on board for some 10 months, and then, on marrying one of the lieutenants (named Arnold), left the ship with him. But I have not been able to discover when Mrs. Dillon did so. All that is sure is that she did not stay till the end of the commission, for, while still the *Leopard's* captain, W.H.D. reports his judicial separation from her (p. 265). Save for one early reference to mother and daughter and the above-mentioned allusion to the daughter's marriage, he ignores the existence of both of them.

On page 179, there is included (in the text) a long note dealing with the operations against the Boulogne Flotilla in September 1811. W.H.D. was not present himself, but he arrived in the Downs a few days later, and no doubt received a 'hot' report of what had occurred. These episodes are dealt with by James (V. 336-9) and, in rather less detail, by Brenton (II. 384-5), but W.H.D. adds just sufficient new material to warrant the inclusion of his version. The piquancy of the situation lay, of course, in the presence of Napoleon himself—an eyewitness all the time, and for part of it actually afloat. He can hardly have been gratified by the performance of his navy, even when he conferred upon it the spur of his presence.

The *Leopard's* 'non-trooping' operations off the east coast of Spain (p. 203 *et seq.*) call for little comment. The only one of any importance was the first—the proposed landing at Palamos Bay on August 1st, 1812. The troops to be landed were from General Maitland's army in Sicily, which had been ordered, much against the General's will, to make a diversion at Palamos, north of Barcelona, in order, primarily, to occupy General Suchet's attention and prevent him from sending reinforcements to Marmont, facing Wellington in Leon. Maitland's reluctance led to much delay and, as we learn here, his troops were not in the end landed at all. Yet, though on the short view he was too late, for the decisive battle in Leon had already taken place (Salamanca, 22nd July), the very threat of his presence had achieved the principal object for which the diversion was intended. Suchet sent no troops to help Marmont.

The triviality of the rest of W.H.D.'s activities—his 'campaign' in defence of Altea—can hardly be concealed even by a gallant attempt to write it up. There is indeed a faint aroma of comic opera about it all, of which even W.H.D. seems at times aware; though he does conclude his account with an unsolicited testimonial of competence from a nameless French officer (p. 209). It will not escape notice, probably, that, while he was there, the defenders of Altea never saw an enemy, and such firing as took place was all 'in the air'. Yet, for all its operational insignificance, the episode does furnish a firsthand picture of at least one guerilla leader, and of the very real problems and exasperations which confronted the British officers who had to co-operate with these picturesque people.

W.H.D.'s dealings with—and remarks on—the Gibraltar smugglers provide a local illustration of a far wider historical phenomenon, of whose very existence he seems barely conscious. A well-known result of the long bout of 'economic' warfare between France and Great Britain, beginning with the Berlin Decrees and the retaliatory Orders in Council, was an immense growth in the smuggling of British manufactured goods on to the continent. But those who practised this kind of smuggling were not, as even W.H.D. seems to be dimly aware, quite ordinary practitioners of that traffic; or, if they were, they were certainly viewed by our authorities with a far more lenient eye than usual. It was Napoleon's expressed intention to ruin Great Britain by closing the whole of the European market to her trade, and, had he been able to do it, the result would have been disastrous to us. But he failed, discovering, too late in the day, that he could not keep out British goods for which there was a real demand unless he could substitute for them equivalent goods made elsewhere: and these he could not find. The result was that, not only did the people of his 'satellite' states defy him *sub rosa* (as one might expect, seeing that they had nothing to gain, and much to lose, by obeying him), but even his own people—even, as we see here, his own Army—defied him too.

The fact was that these 'traders of the Rock', whose activities Dillon was so shocked about, and so anxious to curb, were busily (and no doubt profitably) engaged, in their own small corner and their own small way, in breaking down Napoleon's Continental System. So it is not nearly so surprising as W.H.D. found it that 'the authorities of Gibraltar winked at it.' It was indeed essential to our economy that such people, and others like them up and down Europe, *should* succeed in their trading. Thus, when he informs us that the Governor of the Rock was convinced by his arguments that the traffic was wrong; that he would put a stop to it, and that 'in due time' this was done, we must assume one of two things:— either that Dillon was exaggerating his influence over men and events (as he is often prone to do), or that 'in due time' must be read to mean 'when, by the course of military events, the Continental System had tumbled about Napoleon's ears.'

W.H.D. was in Zante (p. 245 *et seq.*) during the early days of the British occupation of the Ionian Islands. This group had had a chequered career. For nearly 400 years up to 1797 they were in the hands of the Venetians, but in that year were ceded to France. Two years later they were seized by Russia, and placed under the 'protection' of Turkey. But not for long: in 1807 they were handed back to France at the Treaty of Tilsit. Two years later the British seized Zante, Cephalonia and Cerigo, and, after Napoleon's fall, Corfu. In 1815 they became the United States of the Ionian Islands, under the protection of Great Britain: and so they remained until 1863, when they were ceded, at their own request, to Greece.

XII

TROOPSHIP

MARCH 5, 1811–DECEMBER 1813

(*aet.* 30½–33¼)

(1) H.M.S. *LEOPARD* (Trooping to the Tagus)

MARCH 5, 1811–JUNE 16, 1812

OFFICERS and men came slowly, but the ship was rigged by contract, and the shipwrights from the Dock Yard were at work fitting the accommodations for the troops. The Admiral resided at Sheerness, an awkward distance to have frequent communications with. The *Leopard* was lashed alongside of a Hulk, in the cabin of which I established myself. There was a 74, the *Swiftsure*, paying off here, and another, the *Colossus*, refitting, so that I was not badly off for society. The lieutenant who had charge of the Dock Yard a Mr. Calcraft,[1] I had known as one of the Elderly Mids of the *Saturn*, and he made himself useful in the Dock Yard duties. But my most agreeable meeting in this place was with my old messmate of the *Crescent*, George Browne[2] of the Marines. He was adjutant of the Barracks and, being a married man, had a very comfortable establishment where I often dined, and through him became acquainted with some amiable families. The ship's fitting was principally managed by men lent from the two 74's, and from another, the *Warrior*. By their assistance I made good progress. On the 22nd April the ship was loosened from the *Utrecht*, hulk, and warped to Gillingham, where she was secured alongside the *Terrible*. At this place I was reminded of the many happy days I had passed at Mr. Dan's, when in the *Prince George* in 1795.[3]

[Since then he had fallen on evil financial days. W.H.D. sought him out, and describes at some length their pathetic meeting, and

---

[1] Not identified.
[2] 1st Lt. 1801; Capt. 15/2/09; not promoted. See Vol. I, p. 398 and note, where W.H.D.'s *Crescent* friend is called *E.* Browne.
[3] See Vol. I, pp. 178, 182.

the very frugal repast that he was persuaded to take with him and his wife.]

On the 28th a Pilot came to take charge of the ship. We made sail down the river, passed Sheerness and anchored at the Nore, the *Namur* being the Flag Ship of Sir E. Stanhope.[1] Men were now sent to complete the complement—marines were already on board. Several changes had taken place among the officers: Lieut. Small[2] became the First Lieutenant, Vickery the Second,[3] Merrick[4] Master, Preston[5] Purser, Mr. Conisby[6] Surgeon. Some affairs required my immediate presence in Town. On that occasion I performed one of those rapid motions that seldom occur. The Admiral, on granting me leave of absence, invited me to dine with him on the Friday. I started on Wednesday from the Nore and reached London that night. My signing was over by 2 o'clock on the Friday: at half past 2 I left London in a post chaise and arrived at Chatham by 6 o'clock, just in time to save the Sheerness Packet. There my boat was in waiting, so that I reached my ship by 9 o'clock. This was considered an extraordinary exertion. We had no steamers in those days. The trip [from London to the Nore?] was performed in about 6 hours.

After mature deliberation upon my state of affairs, I thought it would be advisable to take my wife to sea, and, by uniting the two incomes together, we might live within our means. . . . I wrote to propose to her to accompany me, judging that, in the command of a troopship, I should not have much cruising against the enemy. Consequently my. wife would not be much in the way. She accordingly made her appearance, accompanied by her daughter and maid. I remarked that the officers were pleased at the arrival of the ladies, anticipating an amusing change in the monotony of a sailor's life.[7]

When the ship was nearly ready for sea, I received from the Admiralty some instructions relating to the treatment of the troops that would be embarked, as well a set of regulations signed by the Duke of York directing the Commanding Officer of any detachment sent on board to conform to the discipline of the ship. In plain terms, they were to consider themselves during the passage under the naval

---

[1] Sir Henry Edwin Stanhope, Bart., Lt. 10/3/1777; Cdr. 6/8/79; Capt. 16/6/81; R-Ad. 1/1/1801; V-Ad. 9/11/05; Ad. 12/8/12.
[2] Francis Small, Lt. 1/12/1800, not promoted.
[3] Robert Caryer Vickery, Lt. 25/3/1809, not promoted.
[4] Not identified, but almost certainly Stonestreet Merritt, 1st Warrant, 23/4/1799.
[5] Abraham Preston, 1st Warrant, 2/2/1801.
[6] Richard Coniby (not Conisby), 1st Warrant, 15/9/1808.
[7] The whole of this paragraph is erased in the original. See above, p. 168.

Articles of War. These documents were satisfactory as, by them, my authority as captain was not interfered with, and in the event of meeting with any troublesome characters, I had the power of controlling them. I was employed upon a service altogether new to the Navy. Consequently it was necessary to be armed with sufficient authority for the occasion.[1]

The usual ceremony of paying the Ship's Company two months advance, and bounty to the volunteers, having been performed, we unmoored on the afternoon of the 12th, and made sail with a merchant ship under convoy, reaching the Downs after a tedious passage on the 15th. The next day we left, with four more merchant vessels added, and arrived at Spithead on the afternoon of the 17th. I reported myself to Ad. Sir Roger Curtis,[2] the Commander in Chief. The *Leopard*, as a troopship, was not fitted with the rigging allowed to a 50-gun ship, but with that of a frigate of 28 guns, and a crew suitable to that class. However, we had the allowance of boats, the launch being a very heavy one. The lower yards, not being of sufficient strength for that weight, were sprung in hoisting her out. I had therefore to represent this to the Powers above, who ordered stronger lower yards to be supplied. On the 30th we embarked a battalion of the Guards, and sailed next day for Cadiz. We were obliged to anchor in Cowes Roads, but then went through the Needles. When out fairly to sea, I met strong contrary winds which obliged me to anchor in Torbay. On the 4th June the King's Birthday was celebrated by a salute of 21 guns. On the 7th the weather moderated and we made sail. On the 9th, assailed again by strong westerly winds, we had to anchor in Falmouth.

Whilst detained here, I found myself the Senior Naval Officer. Lord Melville and Levin[3] was here in command of a sloop of war. I invited his Lordship to dine with me, and as we heard of a Ball in the evening, we went to it. I attracted some notice, and the Master of the ceremonies failed not in his attentions.

[Here he met the daughters of the Rector of Falmouth, the Rev. Robert Dillon, whose brother (now deceased) Capt. John had offered to take W.H.D. into the Packet which he commanded in 1792.]

---

[1] This represents a complete victory for the naval officers who, it will be recalled, reacted so vigorously to the Duke of York's earlier effort, in 1795, to create a dual hierarchy on board. See Vol. I, pp. 176–7.

[2] See Vol. I, p. 136.

[3] *Sic.* This is David, Earl of Leven and Melville, but still known in 1811 as Lord David Balgonie: Lt. 8/8/1806; Cdr. 16/9/09; Capt. 28/2/12; R-Ad. 1/10/46.

The next morning, whilst we were at our breakfast, the Reverend gentleman made his appearance accompanied by his wife and eight children, none under 15 years of age. This was an event little expected on my part. They were anxious to receive me that day at dinner. But the sudden appearance of a Midshipman with a letter from the First Lieutenant acquainting me that the wind had become fair and that he was getting the *Leopard* under way made me return to the ship.

By noon on the 12th we were under sail and making the best of our way to Cadiz. The officer in command of the troops, Col. Lambert, who had a brother in the Navy commanding a 74, was an agreeable gentleman. He had brought a note of introduction from Capt. Cockburn, my old messmate of the *Hêbê*. He came repeatedly to dine with us. His companions, I found, expected the same attention. But I declined, on the score of not being able to afford receiving much company. That act of mine brought on some coolness with the rest of the officers, which I cared little about. It was not my intention, in command of such a ship, to be entertaining the officers of the Army, whom I might never meet again. I accepted Col. Lambert's invitation to dine with his mess, where they complained of not having been supplied with good wine.

On the 18th we made the land, at night, Corunna lighthouse being plainly seen. On the 22nd we passed Cape St. Vincent, and were safely moored in Cadiz harbour on the evening of the 23rd. The next morning the Guards were landed with all their accoutrements and baggage. I paid my respects to the Hon. Mr. Wellesley,[1] who held a high diplomatic position here. The British Consul, Mr. Duff, came off to the *Leopard*, and as he happened to be an old acquaintance of my Father's, a friendly intercourse was established between us. On my arrival I found myself the Senior Officer, so that all the Port duties had to pass through my hands. I was placed in the most responsible position. The French Army was blockading the place: four of our bomb sloops were moored opposite to the batteries of Port St. Mary: all the dispatches passed through my ship: I had to attend to the Spanish Admiral, Don Villaricencia: all the Masters of our transports came to me for instructions, and the guard boats watching the enemy acted according to my orders; so that, with the attendance to Civil and Military affairs, I had not a moment that I could call my own. The next day the *Caledonia* was seen at anchor outside of Cadiz. I hastened off to her, taking with me some informa-

---

[1] Henry Wellesley (later Baron Cowley), younger brother of Wellington.

tion which I thought might be useful to Sir Edward Pellew, who had just been appointed to command the Mediterranean Fleet. He gave me a most friendly welcome, asking how it happened, after all my services, that I had not received a more eligible command. To that question I could make no answer. He afterwards went on shore at Cadiz, and I again called to receive his orders. But he would not interfere with the Port duties.* He returned to the *Caledonia*, then onwards to take command of the Fleet.   .

So soon as I could, I invited some of the Commanders to dine with me. Just as we were seated, the Senior Officer in the Bomb ships made the signal that reinforcements were arriving to the enemy. On such occasions it was usual for the Bombs to send in shells for his annoyance. When I made the signal for them to do so, their commanders who were with me were obliged to repair to their vessels, and the fire commenced, the enemy returning it. This was a most interesting scene. The shells were falling and bursting in the enemy's lines. Theirs were also dropping among us, some very close to my ship.† At last, after an hour's fire, the Spanish Admiral sent an officer requesting that the action might be discontinued. I in consequence made the necessary signal to cease firing. Among my guests was a Capt. Searle,¹ who was a few down the list my junior. During the bombardment he kept up a volley of jokes, intimating what a lucky event my sudden arrival had been for him. 'If you had not been here,' he repeated, '*I* should have had all this anxious responsibility.' Luckily no lives were lost on our side during the affray. Whilst it lasted, I had frequently fixed my spy-glasses upon the enemy's batteries, and could easily distinguish the bristling bayonets coming into the Fort. The next morning a boat crossing the harbour was sunk by the French batteries. Such were the difficulties surrounding me. We were never certain of a moment's rest.

I went to our lines of defence, to inspect the advance post on the Cadiz side, but all was quiet during my inspection. The sentinels frequently cautioned me not to show myself above the walls as, if I did so, volleys of grape shot would be poured in. I attended to their advice, but, by sinking on my knees, fixed my glass upon the embrasure to watch what was passing in the Fort opposite. Not a soul

---

* An article relating to Sir Edward Pellew is to be inserted here. [It is not. This is the first of two examples in the whole MS. of incomplete 'editing' by W.H.D.]

† (erased) The ladies conducted themselves with complete calmness under the circumstances. [This is W.H.D.'s only allusion to Mrs. Dillon after she came on board.]

¹ Thomas Searle (C.B.), Lt. 19/8/1796; Cdr. 26/11/99; Capt. 25/4/1808; R-Ad. 9/11/46. He was three below W.H.D. (21/3/1808) in the Captains' List.

stirred, whereupon I returned to my ship. An application was now made to me to send a Flag of Truce over. That was not at all to my liking, having been myself so great a sufferer in performing that sacred duty. However, a Capt. Carrol[1] of the Navy came to explain that frequent Flags of Truce had been sent to the enemy, who had been received with respect, returning with suitable replies. He was therefore selected for that service, but I remained uneasy till I saw his boat coming away from Port St. Mary. Just after this I received an official letter from Sir Richard Keats, then cruising at sea, desiring me to turn over the port duties to Capt. Searle of the *Druid*. I accordingly sent for him and, in delivering over my charge, retorted with interest all the sallies with which he had belaboured me. I did so with considerable relief, as I had not till then had an opportunity of examining such an interesting town as Cadiz.

[He now did so. The four pages of the Narrative describing the place are omitted, save for a note of genealogical interest.*]

All my perambulations were interrupted by the arrival in the Bay of Sir Richard Keats in the *Milford*, 74: also the *Revenge*, with the Flag of Rear Ad. Legge.[2] As I had sailed with Sir Richard in the *Niger* in 1792, I experienced a most kind reception. He approved of all that I had done during the four days that the port duties fell under my direction, invited me to dine with him, and expressed an anxious desire to be useful to me. He had as Master of his Flag ship Mr. McCleverty,[3] who had been my messmate in the *Africaine*. This gentleman had committed a breach of discipline with me on board that ship, and I naturally supposed that he owed me a grudge. But I was luckily mistaken. After many hearty sayings, he told me that he heard in all directions expressions of surprise at my being appointed to such a command. Sir Richard intended to send me to Lisbon, to convey there Gen. Graham, his staff, and a detachment of the German Legion. This officer was the theme of universal conversation at that period, having not long before had an action with a superior

---

[1] William Fairbrother Carrol(l), just appointed to command the whole Cadiz flotilla. Lt. 15/5/1804; Cdr. 4/3/11; Capt. 6/12/13.

* Cadiz was taken by storm in Queen Elizabeth's reign by the English forces under the Earl of Essex, Sir John Wingfield, Quarter Master General of the Army, being the only Englishman of note killed in the expedition. He was the immediate ancestor of Sir Mervin Wingfield, Bart., who dying without [male] issue, his only daughter Mary married, as you know, Francis Dillon of Proudston in Ireland, our mutual grandfather, your Father's name being Mervin. (See Vol. I, Intro., p. XII.)

[2] Hon. (Sir) Arthur Kaye Legge (K.C.B.), Lt. 3/8/1789; Cdr. 19/11/90; Capt. 6/2/93; R-Ad. 31/7/1810; V-Ad. 4/6/14; Ad. 22/7/30.

[3] Henry McCleverty, 1st Warrant, 1793.

force, and extricated himself with glory. I made his acquaintance, and was making my preparations accordingly. Through the intercession of our Consul, it was decided to place some treasure on board the *Leopard*. The freight of it would have put a few hundreds into my pocket. This was unexpected, and I was in high spirits. On the morning fixed for receiving the Dollars, my launch was at the landing place. Some of the casks had already been stowed in her when, to my surprise, a signal was made to countermand all proceedings, and to send the troops I had embarked to H.M.S. *Latona*, also a troop ship, which had just arrived from Lisbon for the purpose of executing the duty for which I had been selected. Sir Richard Keats wrote a note wherein he explained that he regretted being obliged to rescind the orders he had given me, as the *Latona*, belonging to the Lisbon station, was the proper ship to receive the cash, etc. Thus ended all my expectations. I had reckoned upon receiving a sufficient sum to have reimbursed the expense of my outfit.[1]

Sir Richard now decided that I was to embark the invalids from the Army and some French prisoners of war, and proceed with a convoy of transports to England. A Gen. Disney of the Guards was to take passage in the ship and live in my Cabin. There were several Army officers also to be accommodated, and separate apartments were fitted for their use, which they disposed of as they thought best. On the morning of the 3rd we left Cadiz, with nine sail under convoy. Among the officers embarked was a Major McLean, who had distinguished himself against the French lines of Matagorda. His first act when we were at sea was to tamper with my Cook. This came to my knowledge, and produced a coolness between us that was never made up. He had what you call a Bee in his Bonnet, and was inclined to assume authority where he had none. It was necessary to keep the gentleman at a distance.

We soon boarded an English merchant vessel from London bound to Cadiz, who informed me that orders had been issued to detain all Americans. Our political affairs had been for some time in a doubtful state with that country, and I thought a rupture would be the consequence. As there happened to be an American vessel in my convoy, I lost no time in taking possession of her.[2] A day or two afterwards I detained another American, and the following day a third. However, the last one I liberated. The detention of these

---

[1] For freight money, see below, pp. 270–3.
[2] 'Her' written, in later ink, over an erased word which I think was 'him'. See Vol. I, pp. 62–3.

vessels was rather an awkward affair. On the 13th we fell in with the *Tigre*, Capt. Hallowell,[1] from whom we heard that there was no foundation for detaining American ships. Consequently I allowed the two which I had taken possession of to proceed on their voyage. Luckily there was no act brought against me for having detained them. On the 18th we saw the Rock of Lisbon, and I detailed some of the convoy into that port. We were making very slow progress, and our voyage became a tedious affair. Light and contrary winds were a great drawback. On the 28th we fell in with H.M.S. *Niemen*. We were now in the 20th degree of West Longitude, and my patience nearly exhausted. However, at last the winds appeared inclined to favour us, and we were able to shape a course for England. Gen. Disney was a very amiable person, but he complained bitterly of the length of our voyage. On the 1st of August we fell in with two ships whose motions were very suspicious, and at one time I thought we should have to contend with an enemy. But the private signal exchanged between us showed them to be H.M. Ships *Chiffone* and *Saldanha*, and all our anxieties vanished. On the evening of the 3rd we sounded in 76 fathoms, and on the afternoon of the 4th made the Land's End. The next day we were entering the Needles Passage and about 7 that evening anchored at Spithead. On the 7th we disembarked all our invalids, prisoners, etc.

Having refitted the ship and set all to rights, we put to sea on the 29th, but in passing H.M.S. *Denmark* carried away the Flying Jib boom, owing to a hawser being kept fast on board the *Royal William*.[2] Next day we exchanged numbers with H.M. Ships *Egmont* and *Royal Oak*, and on the 2nd of September anchored in Plymouth Sound, the ship having touched the ground near the buoy of the Shovel, but received no damage. We were now fitted to receive French prisoners of war, and a new Master, named Lamb, was appointed. On the 11th we got under way with 457 French prisoners on board bound to Leith. An officer and a party of Marines were sent on board. As we got clear out to sea we encountered adverse winds. We chased a vessel that proved to be a smuggler, but, there being a heavy sea, he landed his cargo in spite of all that I could do. The gale increased, and I was obliged to anchor in Torbay. In making my report of the smuggler's proceedings to the Admiralty, I remarked that it appeared to me that if the look out men at the signal station had exerted

---

[1] (Sir) Benjamin Hallowell, Nelson's friend, and the donor of the famous coffin. Lt. 25/4/1783; Cdr. 22/11/90; Capt. 6/2/93; R-Ad. 31/7/1810; V-Ad. 12/8/19.
[2] This is the oft-quoted example of longevity in wooden ships: still Guardship at Portsmouth, and nearly a century old, having been built in 1719.

themselves, the cargo could not have been landed. But, with all
our precautions, such things are. There were no revenue vessels at
hand.

In watching the motions of the French prisoners, we ascertained
that they had sailors' trowsers and jackets which they put on at
night, and mixed themselves amongst the seamen of the watch,
evidently forming a plan to get possession of the ship. However,
those thus cloathed were instantly secured and put in irons. Whilst
we were at anchor in Torbay, the heat was so oppressive there was
no keeping the men below at night. One of them pretended to faint,
in appearance insensible. I had him aft on the Quarter Deck and
soused him well with a few buckets of sea water, which soon brought
him to his senses. Many other acts were attempted, but they all
failed. I kept all the Marines under arms, with two loaded field
pieces on the Poop, ready to fire upon the appearance of any rising.
By these and other regulations they were kept in order. On the 19th
I left Torbay, the wind being favourable. The anchor, on being
heaved up, broke at the shank, and the flukes were left behind. We
came to an anchor in the Downs on the evening of the 22nd.

At that period Bonaparte with his Imperial Consort visited the
Flotilla at Boulogne. Capt. Carteret[1] of the *Naiad*, with three brigs
of war, was watching the enemy's motions. The Corsican Hero,
anxious to make a display, ordered out several of his praams to
attack the English. In the first engagement the frigate lay at anchor
and nothing of consequence took place. But the next day, the *Naiad*,
being under sail, was watching for a favourable moment when the
French came out again, to close with one of the largest ones and
board and carry her. This she did. It was a most dashing affair, and
she was brought into the Downs. The other enemy vessels got so
rapidly inshore, under the cover of their powerful batteries, that they
escaped. The vessel captured was the *Ville de Lyons*, mounting
12 long 24-pounders, with a crew of 112 men, 60 of them being
soldiers of the 72me Regiment. She was commanded by Commodore
Jean Baptiste Coupe and Capt. Jean Barbaud. On our side, Lieut.
Cobb[2] of the *Castilian* was killed and several wounded. Capt.
Carteret, an old acquaintance, displayed much professional skill and
judgment. On the second day the French force consisted of 7 praams
of equal force to the one taken, and 15 smaller vessels, chiefly brigs,
under the direction of a Flag Officer, Rear Ad. Baste, who took care

[1] Philip Carteret, Lt. 8/10/1795; Cdr. 7/5/1802; Capt. 22/1/06.
[2] Charles Cobb, Lt. 1/5/1807.

to tack inshore the instant he observed the *Naiad* stand towards him. The First Lieutenant of that ship, Mr. Greenlaw,[1] was promoted.

Ad. Foley,[2] who now held the command, invited the French officers to dine with him. I happened to be one of that party, and my knowledge of that language was brought into play. The Frenchmen took me for one of their countrymen, but were told that they had made a sad mistake. This being made known to me, I acquainted those Gaulish gentlemen with the cause of my familiarity with their native tongue—a 5-year detention in France when sent with a Flag of Truce. There was some difficulty in persuading them of that fact. 'No civilized Power,' they said, 'ever detained a Flag of Truce.' However, in the end they were convinced of such an outrage having been visited upon me by Napoleon's Government.

In the Downs I got another anchor and a Pilot. We left on the 26th, and moored in Leith Roads on the 2nd of October. We met the *Diadem* here, also a troopship, and the *Adamant*, Flag Ship to Rear Ad. Otway.[3] The French prisoners were landed. What a relief to get rid of them! We left the place on the 6th, and by the 10th I was again at anchor in the Downs. It now appeared that great anxiety had been expressed by the Admiralty on the *Leopard's* account, rumours having got into circulation that the prisoners had risen and succeeded in carrying the ship into a port of France. All a fudge.

I got away from the Downs on the 17th. On the 18th we were running through St. Helens, where we passed three sail of the line, and anchored at Spithead at noon. At this time I was suffering so much pain from my wounded limbs that my life was a perfect burden to me, and I seriously began to think of retiring from the arduous duties of the Naval Profession. I took lodgings on shore, but all I could do brought no relief.

The Admiralty had all of a sudden changed their plan of proceeding towards the Captains in command of ships, and any anonymous letter sent to that Board, by any dissatisfied seaman, was attended to without inquiry as to its veracity, and a court of inquiry was ordered upon the Captain. These anonymous letters had hitherto been transmitted to the Captain of the ship, by which proceeding he had an opportunity of clearing himself or demanding an inquiry, as the case might be. I came down one day to the Sally Port, to

---

[1] John Potenger Greenlaw, Lt. 4/5/1804; Cdr. 15/6/14 (N.B. *not* 1811!).
[2] (Sir) Thomas Foley (G.C.B.), Lt. 25/5/1778; Cdr. 1/12/82; Capt. 21/9/90; R-Ad. 28/4/1808; V-Ad. 12/8/12; Ad. 27/5/25. Commanded the *Goliath*, Nelson's leading ship, at the Nile.
[3] See p. 128.

embark in my boat for my ship; but, instead of finding the crew there, only one man was to be seen. It was a swift 4-oared gig. My Coxswain and two other men had made off, leaving my boat thumping on the beach to its fate. Luckily I saw a brother officer passing by and waved to him. He pulled in to the shore, kindly took me into his own boat, and towed off mine to the *Leopard*. A few days after this, without any notice from Sir Roger Curtis, the Port Admiral, he directed a court of inquiry to assemble on board my ship to investigate her state of discipline, etc. It appeared an anonymous letter had been written to the Admiralty, I suppose by my Coxswain who had deserted, stating that the tyranny and oppression on board the *Leopard* was beyond all endurance. The Mid who came with the boat that morning acquainted me of the inquiry, that would be held on board at 11 o'clock. I found the Senior Lieutenant seriously alarmed. 'Three Captains will soon meet here, Sir,' he reported, 'to inquire into the discipline of the ship.' 'Very well,' said I. 'Let them come and make such inquiries as they think proper. I certainly did expect that the Admiral would have given me timely notice of his intentions, but as he has not shown that consideration, I am not the least alarmed at the result of any investigation.'

At 11 o'clock three Captains, Pat[t]erson,[1] Prescott[2] and Hodgson,[3] came on board, acquainting me with their having been directed by the Commander in Chief to inquire into the discipline of the ship. I instantly ordered the Ship's Company aft on the Quarter Deck. The Senior Captain, I saw, was astonished at this decided proceeding, and demanded if I were prepared for the event. 'Most certainly,' I replied. 'Men have been punished here according to the Articles of War, and I am prepared to answer any question relating thereto. Your presence here, gentlemen, does not cause me the slightest uneasiness.' Capt. Patterson then made known to the Ship's Company the reason of his coming on board, and that, if they had any complaint to make, now was the time to do so. No one replied. He then read aloud the anonymous letter. The seamen still kept silent. Upon being questioned, they declared it had been written unknown to them: that they had no complaint to make; on the contrary, they thought themselves better off than in most ships in the Navy. 'We all know,' they said, 'what we have to trust to here. Our Captain is always the same. He does his duty, and we must do ours.' Thus

---

[1] Charles William Paterson, Lt. 3/2/1777; Cdr. 8/4/82; Capt. 20/1/94; R-Ad. 12/8/1812; V-Ad. 12/8/19.
[2] Henry Prescott, Lt. 28/4/1802; Cdr. 4/2/08; Capt. 25/7/10; R-Ad. 24/4/47.
[3] Brian Hodgson, Lt. 11/12/1799; Cdr. 8/4/1805; Capt. 22/1/06; R-Ad. 28/6/38.

ended the inquiry. The Captains returned to the Admiral, made their report, and by the return of post, next day, the Admiralty expressed their satisfaction at the state, condition and discipline of the ship under my command. When Sir Roger Curtis communicated this message to me, I could not help remarking that fair play had not been attended to in my case: then, making my bow, retired.

A large American frigate had arrived at Spithead. She was inspected by many of our Naval Officers, and was considered equal to one of our 64-gun ships. Our affairs with that country were in a very unsettled state at that period.[1] The size and armament of that ship was the subject of much conversation. Her crew consisted of 500 picked men—no boys—and as they were of the same flesh and blood as ourselves, it was natural to suppose that some caution would be adopted by our Admiralty in the event of a war, to be prepared to act against such powerful frigates. Mr. Croker, the Secretary of the Admiralty, visited Portsmouth at this juncture, and took a short cruise in the *Cleopatra*, Capt. Sir John Pechell.[2] When that American frigate was alluded to, Pechell vauntingly remarked that he would take her in half an hour. It will not do to be overconfident. The Americans proved that their heavy frigates were too strongly armed for ours.

By the 17th all our refitting had been completed. I was directed to receive a Flat Boat, to be employed in the landing of troops, and to prepare for sea. I had not the slightest idea where I was to be sent, but I received orders to place myself under Capt. Phillimore.[3] The squadron was to consist of six troopships, including ourselves, as follows:—*Diadem, Latona, Sanfiorenzo, Mermaid* and *Brune*. We got under way on the 17th, to proceed to Lisbon. There was a Mr. Mackenzie embarked on board the *Diadem*. With that gentleman I became acquainted. He had not long before been sent to Morlaix, to attempt to effect an exchange of prisoners of war. But the account he gave me of the unbearable impertinence of the French officials he had to deal with is past all imagination. They wanted him, among other proposals, to exchange Lord Wellington's army. 'You must first of all take it,' he replied. It was quite evident that Bonaparte had not the slightest intention of agreeing to an exchange. It was merely a pretext, to deceive the French, then make them believe

---

[1] The U.S.A. declared war the following 4th of June.
[2] Sir Samuel John Brook Pechell, Bart. (C.B., K.C.H., F.S.A.), Lt. 1/4/1803; Cdr. 23/3/07; Capt. 16/6/08; R-Ad. 9/11/46. A gunnery expert and author of a well-known pamphlet on the subject.
[3] John Phillimore, Lt. 4/4/1801; Cdr. 10/5/04; Capt. 13/10/07.

that he could not accept our terms. Therefore Mr. Mackenzie soon returned to England.

The agonizing pain of my limbs continued. However, on the morning of the 23rd, we made the land, Cape Finistere. The heavy clouds disappeared suddenly, and we were relieved by a clear sky and brilliant sun. We had arrived in another atmosphere, and to me the change was most acceptable. All my sufferings vanished, as if by a miracle. I recovered the use of my limbs, and felt myself an altogether different person. I had not, from the period of my wounds, felt myself so supple and active. When we arrived near the rock of Lisbon, as soon as the Pilot came off to us, we had to beat into the Tagus against a strong N.E. wind on the 26th. The Hon. Ad. Berkeley[1] held the command here. His Captain, Sir Thomas Hardy,[2] had been my messmate in the *Hêbé* in 1791. Through his friendly intercession, I soon established a good understanding with the Commander in Chief, and at a suitable opportunity had a long conversation with him. He commanded the *Marlborough* in the action of the 1st of June, 1794. My having been present on that occasion had its influence with him, and when he understood the interest which the Duke of Sussex took in my behalf, I found him perfectly willing to render me any service that lay under his control. I explained, most fully, all the sufferings I had endured, and the relief experienced by the change of climate: and I then requested him, if it were in his power, to retain the *Leopard* during the winter months at Lisbon. He most readily entered into my views, and promised to do all he could for me. 'From this hour,' he said, 'there is a bed in my house at your service, and I will try to make your stay here agreeable.' I confess I was highly gratified, the more so because this officer was not a favourite in his profession, and I had been prepared for a refusal.

There were a great many French prisoners at Lisbon, and it was necessary to get rid of them. The Admiral ordered the *Mermaid* and *Latona* to England loaded with Frenchmen. Capt. Sotheby[3] of the latter invited most of the captains to dine with him previous to quitting the Tagus. He had embarked in his cabin a French general, Brun, who had been captured by one of our distinguished generals, Hill,[4] at Molinos del Rey in Spain, who had pounced upon a French division when it was not prepared. Our success was a very brilliant

[1] See Vol. I, p. 135 and note.
[2] Thomas Masterman (Nelson's) Hardy. See Vol. I, p. 33 and note.
[3] Charles Sotheby, Lt. 25/1/1802; Cdr. 8/1/10; Capt. 28/2/12; R-Ad. 20/3/48.
[4] Rowland (1st Viscount) Hill. At Arroso-dos-Molinos (28/10/1811) he had surprised the enemy on parade!

affair, and Prince Staremberg of Belgium was included among the captives. I became acquainted with the Prince at Sir Charles Stuart's table, and he dined with me on board the *Leopard*. I made one of the party at Capt. Sotheby's dinner, and was the only one who could keep up any conversation with Gen. Brun. He at first—mark the French vanity—thought that the dinner had been given out of compliment to him, and drily observed that he did not notice any officer present suitable to his rank. I requested an explanation. 'Why,' said he, 'as a General I expected to have met here officers corresponding to that rank, whereas the company is composed of naval officers of an inferior grade.' 'I regret,' I replied, 'that you should have formed such expectations: for nothing of the kind has been intended. The Captain of this ship has been suddenly ordered to England, to convey you and a portion of your countrymen there. He has invited us here to a sociable farewell dinner; and, as you are his guest, you are of course included. That is the long and short of the matter.' At the termination of the repast he was annoyed that the Emperor Napoleon's health had not been proposed. 'I cannot conceive why such an omission can offend you,' I remarked. 'We are all English naval officers. We know nothing of the Emperor except that he is our enemy. And England has never acknowledged him by that title.' Thereupon he completely lost his temper, vociferating a lot of abuse against our King. 'I will not drink his health,' he said. 'We don't ask you to do it,' I replied. 'He is a Guelph,' he continued. I rejoined that that was his family name. 'Monsieur Brunswick,' he added sarcastically. 'Well,' said I, 'what do you obtain by all this? It ill becomes one in your present position to make these remarks, or to utter any expressions of derision against our Sovereign. They will not be allowed.' My companions, who had been listening, clapped their hands and highly approved the rebuff which the Frenchman had brought upon himself. The General, perceiving he had the worst of it, remained silent. Then, our conversation having resumed its former flow, I watched for an opportunity, and said to him, 'As you appear so sensitive on the subject of the Emperor's health not having been drunk, out of compliment to you—it being my own act—I will now fill my glass: and here's to the health of Napoleon.' That act quite revived the drooping spirits of General Brun, who followed my example, and in turn toasted King George the Third.

I now had a very long conversation with this officer on the subject of plunder. I remarked that I thought Napoleon, with his influence over his army, ought to put a stop to it. 'Wellington,' I said, 'will not allow such doings.' 'Bah!' he replied. 'Nous ne pillons pas. Nous prenons.' I leave you to judge the difference between the two.

[He now met again two Verdun companions, Capt. Gower (see above, p. 41) and Mr. Jackson: also Robert Dillon of the 32nd (see above, p. 135). Of the six troopships which had entered the Tagus with him, the *Leopard* alone was retained there. The Admiral was being obliging. The *Leopard* was sent to lie at the mouth of the Tagus, off Belem Castle, to act as a guardship, but W.H.D. was often ashore, participating in a gay round of entertainments, dinners, balls, etc., given by the Admiral, the Minister (Sir Charles Stuart), the Consul (Mr. Geoffrey), and various generals from Wellington's army when they returned from the front.]

My idle moments were generally devoted to exercise on horseback, in company with the Admiral, who had proposed to me to join him in his rounds. I was highly amused with his naval anecdotes. From Sir Thos. Hardy I received equal attention. He had married one of his Chief's daughters. Among the amusements of the winter, one deserves to be mentioned. An English officer of the Army circulated a great number of handbills, in print, giving notice to the inhabitants of Lisbon that he intended to pass the Tagus at low water on a certain day in a pair of cork boots.

[W.H.D. relates what happened as a result, at very great length. As a practical joke, it was, it seems, a huge success. On the day advertised thousands of boats put out to see the spectacle, completely blocking the river. More than 100,000 people, of all classes and both nationalities (including Marshal Beresford and the whole Portuguese Cabinet) turned out to line the shore. The officer responsible did not put in an appearance. W.H.D. who, while coming ashore, got caught in the press of boats—and therefore twitted by his friends as being among the dupes—strives, with almost pathetic earnestness, to prove that he was not deceived.]

On our right [as we lay off Belem Castle] were the sands of Cascaes, on which was established a colony of fishermen who were governed by their own laws and had very little intercourse with Lisbon excepting to sell fish. We had plenty of nets on board, which I thought might be turned to account to supply our seamen with an occasional meal of the finny tribe, and I desired the First Lieutenant to find out from the Portuguese opposite the best place to lay them. All his inquiries produced nothing. We therefore managed as well

as we could, submerging them overnight and sending to draw them
next morning. But they were not to be found. It was quite evident
that they had been stolen. Upon that impression I had my boats
out the next night, to try and find my nets among my fishing neighbours. But the officers found the Portuguese so much on the alert
that there was no approaching them. I had no remedy but to submit
to the loss. However, when it was least expected, some friendly
genii assisted us. Several of their fishing boats were observed laying
out their nets close to us. At times, the tide here runs most rapidly,
at nearly 5 miles per hour. These nets were driven by the strength
of that current right across our cables. As it was my duty to keep
them clear, I gave directions to haul the entangled nets off. It was a
long job, but finally accomplished in a most able manner: and—
what was more satisfactory—the Portuguese nets proved of a
superior quality to those we had lost. The next day several fishermen
came aboard to claim them. I would not listen to their demands.
Finding they could obtain nothing from the *Leopard*, they repaired
to their Bishop, who receives 36 per cent. upon their earnings. The
Prelate, accompanied by his countrymen, laid the complaint before
Ad. Berkeley. I was in consequence ordered up to account for my
proceedings. At the Admiral's door I saw the same persons who had
been on board my ship, with the Bishop in waiting. When I was
admitted to the Admiral, I explained all that had passed: how my
nets had been carried off, and the lucky circumstance of some others
becoming entangled with the cables. He candidly approved of all I
had done, but added that it was necessary to send him a written
statement. 'Then,' said he, 'you may keep them.' I soon sent that
letter, and so became the gainer by the accident.

The Portuguese generally did not cut much of a figure at our
Minister's hospitable table. On one occasion, one of the party belonging to that nation, watching his opportunity, contrived to pocket a
chicken, as he thought unobserved. However, he was mistaken. An
English officer had seen the whole transaction. Rising from the table
with a sauce-boat in his hand, he approached the Portuguese and
poured the melted butter over the chicken saying, 'You cannot take
the bird without the sauce belonging to it.' That act of course was
noticed by all, and the purloiner withdrew, sadly disconcerted.

[At the very end of the year W.H.D. had a recurrence of the pains
in his wounded limbs, which for a time kept him from the gaieties of
Lisbon.]

As my ship lay opposite to Belem Castle, I thought I would examine the premises. Here I fell in with two Portuguese noblemen, detained there under suspicion of being attached to the interests of Bonaparte. They were full of anecdotes, of which I recall two. At the period when Soult occupied Oporto, he was intriguing to establish himself as King of Portugal. Bonaparte heard of his intention, but not wishing to cast off so fine an adherent, was yet determined to make him feel his power. Prince Kurakin had just been appointed Embassador from the Emperor of Russia to France. The Hotel generally occupied by the Russian Embassy was under repair, and the French Minister, at a loss where to place the Prince, consulted with Bonaparte. Just what he wanted. Napoleon asked if Marshal Soult had not a splendid Hotel in Paris, and, the reply being in the affirmative, 'very well,' said he: 'place Prince Kurakin in Soult's Hotel till his own is ready to receive him.' Soult was annoyed beyond measure, but he submitted.

The next relates to Murat. When Napoleon appointed his brother-in-law King of Naples it was agreed between them that no commercial intercourse was to be allowed with England. This was enforced by the King during the first year of his reign: but, the Exchequer being nearly empty from the failing of duties on trade, Murat found that he could not maintain his army or his establishments without more revenue. Consequently he threw open all his ports, and the result realized all his expectations. Napoleon, however, hearing of his proceedings, taxed him with this breach of promise. Murat stated that he could not support his military expenditure without the aid of traffic: but, upon that answer, Bonaparte sent for his Minister, and inquired whether the King of Naples maintained a Royal Palace in Paris. Being told it was so, he then exclaimed, 'Confisquez-moi tout cela. Je n'entends pas qu'un Prince étranger tient un Palais dans la Capitale de mon Empire.' His orders were obeyed. How Joachim settled his accounts with the Emperor was not known.

The duties of a Guard Ship in a foreign country I found to be no trifling affair. Ad. Berkeley, who was Generalissimo of the Portuguese Navy, had been requested by the Portuguese Authorities to cause all vessels arriving in the Tagus to be examined, as many spies had arrived, as well several ill disposed persons. Consequently, I had instructions to that effect. When the wind assisted the tide, I was obliged to have a boat a couple of miles outside, to board vessels coming in: but no suspicious characters had turned up. I found more difficulty with the Masters of my own country's ships, the transports in particular. One gave me particular trouble. It happened to be a flowing tide, the wind fair into the Tagus. The officer in my boat attempted to board a ship entering, but he would not shorten sail. This was reported to me. I instantly attended on the Quarter Deck and, noticing the merchantman's evasion of my boat, ordered the bow gun to be fired, shotted. But the vessel came in very rapidly, and I called to the Marines to load their muskets. By now the stranger was within hail, and I desired him to wait for my boat. He paid no attention. A musket shot was sent over him. It had no effect. As he was passing our broadside, I saw a boat slung between his fore and main masts, which was being painted. I ordered the Marines to fire a volley into that boat. They obeyed, and the clattering of the shot was distinctly heard. I now called out, and ordered him to come to an anchor under my stern. Another boat with an officer was instantly sent to him, which at last seemed to produce a change in the Master's proceedings, for as the boat was in the act of boarding, down went his anchor. Having rebuked him for not having hove to when required, I took from him two good seamen. The vessel was a transport. I reported what had passed to Sir George Berkeley. The Agent of Transports came forward to reclaim his men. But the Admiral approved my conduct, and desired me to keep the men. Here again I was supported by my Chief. In fact, I could not have fulfilled the duty imposed upon me had I not been properly supported.

[With Capt. Gower he made a trip, which he describes, to a hill-top monastery beyond St. Ubes.]

I had expected to stay in the Tagus till the month of March, but all my castle building was suddenly set aside by the arrival in Lisbon of five or six influential officers from Lord Wellington's army. They had given out that they were going to England. I had heard nothing, but, a day or two afterwards, I dined with the Admiral. Upon my taking my place, he addressed me, and inquired if I was going to England. I replied that none but he could answer that question. 'It is very strange,' he said, 'that neither of us knows anything about it. If the Admiral don't know, and the Captain don't, who is to decide?' 'It is strange indeed,' I observed. 'But I am ready to obey orders.' I returned to my ship under the impression that I should remain in the Tagus, but next morning my signal was made to attend the Admiral, and I was admitted to a private audience. He then told me that he had made up his mind to send me to England, and that

the officers alluded to, six in number, had applied to be conveyed
home in a ship of war. Lord Anson, Sir Loury Cole[1] and Col. Murray[2]
were the three for whom he felt most interest. He inquired how many
I could receive in my Cabin, and remarked that such an acquaintance
under such circumstances might lead to a friendly intercourse which
in the end might be turned to account. I explained that my establishment was but a small one, that I could not accommodate with
comfort more than six, and if four of the number would embark with
me, I should be happy to receive them. I did not, I said, like to
receive more, wishing always to have at least one of my officers at
my table: but if I took the six, I must exclude them from it. Sir
George approved of my proposal, observing, 'If you consider your
officers, you may rely on them feeling your attention, and you will
not be a loser by so doing.' He then undertook to communicate with
the Army officers, and let me know the result. Lord Charles Manners[3]
had arrived in a sad state of health, having been attacked by a
violent fever. He was anxious to go with me: and as Capt. Walpole,[4]
R.N., one of my Verdun companions, was on a visit, being an invalid,
to Sir Charles Stuart, he requested me to receive him. But I would
not commit myself till I knew what arrangements the Admiral had
made. When Lord Anson heard of the limited size of my table, he
gave in his claim and determined to take the Packet. Therefore I
made room for Lord Charles Manners. Sir Thomas Hardy took a
lively interest in the arrangements, so that there was little left for
me do to, except to receive them. The next day I went to a good
market in Lisbon to lay in plenty of stock. But I met there Sir
Thomas, who would not allow me to lay out a single dollar. He
explained himself so decidedly in the matter that I took my boat,
leaving him to order what he thought fit.

   The names of the officers having been selected, viz. Lt. Gen. Sir
Loury Cole and his aid de camp, Lt. Col. Murray, the confidential
friend of Lord Wellington, and Lord Charles Manners, I prepared for
sea, and was ordered to take charge of a convoy. Several invalid
officers were embarked, and about 70 soldiers from different regiments.

   [1] Sir Galbraith Lowry Cole, 1772–1842. The advance of his fusilier brigade had
saved the day at Albuera in the preceding year.
   [2] Sir George Murray, 1772–1846. Q.M.G. to the forces in Spain and Portugal under
Wellington.
   [3] 1780–1855, 2nd son of Charles Manners, 4th D. of Rutland.
   [4] The Hon. William Walpole, Lt. 11/10/1802; Cdr. 22/1/06; Capt. 9/11/09. Died
1813 or 14. He had been captured with Capt. Jahleel Brenton in the *Minerve*
(2/7/1803) and with him sent to Verdun.

On the morning of the 8th (Jan.) I got under way. I happened to have a tolerably good cook, and was glad to perceive that my guests enjoyed themselves. The General's aid de camp did not join, so that I had only three. Lord Charles, who had been considerably weakened by copious bleeding, made his six meals a day, and constantly repeated that he owed his life to me. Three intelligent gentlemen made an agreeable change in the monotony of a sea life, and many entertaining anecdotes were related, with interesting details of the proceedings of our Army. We had made but slow progress, having a convoy and contrary winds, when suddenly our methodical routine was interrupted by the appearance of a stranger. On the afternoon of the 15th, I made all sail in chace, directing the convoy to close upon each other. The vessel I was chacing, I observed, had fired several guns, and the look out at the masthead reported that three other strange sail were seen to windward. Evidently something was going on. Before 3 o'clock, I exchanged private signals with the chace, and when I had neared her to bring her hull in sight, she proved to be the *Endymion*, Capt. Sir Charles Bolton.[1] He was watching the motions of two frigates and a brig to windward. I instantly altered course and stood towards them with all the sail I could carry. In the course of time I closed upon the frigates to about eight miles. In the evening I lost sight of the *Endymion* and the enemy. However, I stood on after him with all sail set, and the ship was prepared for action. All the officers of the Army and the soldiers came to offer their services. We passed a most anxious night. The next morning the enemy were not to be seen, but the *Endymion*, after exchanging the private signal, joined us about 9 o'clock. I went on board of her, and her Captain told me that the frigates and brig were French. He requested me to keep company, and if possible bring them to action. Having promised to support him, I returned to my ship, but we could not regain sight of the enemy. After another anxious night without seeing them, I parted company from the *Endymion*, and, having also lost my convoy, made the best of my way towards the English Channel.[2]

We sounded in 105 fathoms on the 24th. The islands of Scilly were seen on the next afternoon, and before noon of the 27th we anchored at Spithead. My guests now departed with the warmest

---

[1] Should be Sir *William* Bolton, Lt. 28/10/1790; Cdr. 27/4/1801; Capt. 10/4/05.

[2] The enemy ships were the 40-gun frigates *Arienne* and *Andromaque* which, having shaken off the *Endymion*, did considerable damage to our shipping until brought to action by the *Northumberland*, Capt. Hotham, and others. They were driven aground off the Isle de Groix and destroyed, 22/5/1812. See James VI, 48–51.

thanks for the attentions they had received. I made an official report to the Admiralty of my having parted from my convoy in chace of an enemy, but they all, I believe, arrived safe.

I must mention the scandalous act of one of my servants, which proves how little you can depend upon that class. The Captain of a ship of war can not go down to his store room for wine in the same way that a private gentleman can go to his cellar on shore. Consequently I trusted to my servant to bring up wine as it was wanted. The First Lieutenant had already mentioned to me that he had noticed empty bottles lying about my store room door, and at last I placed a person to watch it. The next day my valet went down for the wine, took what was required for me, and sold six bottles to a seaman who was in waiting! The individual on the look out could identify the servant, but not the seaman. That chap was severely punished, but I could not obtain the slightest information from him of any of the particulars. When my store was examined, discovery was made of a deficiency of 16 dozen of wine!

I was now favoured with a letter from Lord Manvers, who had heard of my hospitable attention to the Army officers I had brought home, complimenting me upon the occasion. Lord Charles Manners, I suppose, lauded me on that account, as I had taken him as my personal friend, whereas the General and the Colonel were ordered on board by the Admiral, and the Treasury finally refunded my expenses for their entertainment.

The Dock Yard officers, having examined the state of the ship, reported that she wanted a thorough refit. She was in consequence ordered into Portsmouth harbour. On February 16th she was secured there alongside of a hulk. I now drew up a plan for the improvement of the crew's accommodation, as well for the troops when embarked. My plan was approved by the Commissioner, Sir George Gray,[1] and then by the Admiralty who issued instructions accordingly. Thus the principal part of my time was occupied in supervising them.

You no doubt recollect the calamitous losses sustained this winter by our Baltic Fleet. It had been detained there this year later than usual. The first ship that became a victim to the storms was the *Hero*, 74, Capt. Newman. She was lost on the Haak Sand off the Texel. I knew it well in the *Camilla*. Only eight of the crew were

[1] Sometimes so spelt, but more usually Grey—Hon. Sir George, Bart. He was a Capt. of 1/8/1793, but, as a Commissioner, was not promoted when due for his Flag, 1/8/1811, but put on the superannuated and Retired Captains' List. He was still Commissioner of Portsmouth Dockyard in 1825.

saved. Shortly afterwards[1] the *St. George*, 98, Admiral Reynolds, and the *Defence*, Capt. Atkins, were both stranded on the coast of Jutland. Only six men belonging to the three decker were saved, and 12 from the *Defence*. The *Minotaur* had been lost in the winter of 1810 off the Texel. The *Cressy*, being in attendance upon the *St. George*, had a narrow escape. These losses made a lamentable impression upon the whole nation. Mr. Yorke, the First Lord, it is said, never recovered the shock occasioned by that disaster. All the Navy were called upon for a subscription to relieve the widows and relatives. At Portsmouth all the officers and seamen contributed two days' pay to their assistance.

While I was walking through the Dock Yard, one of those strange events that occasionally occur in our lives turned up. Passing between two docks, I found myself under the stern of the *Africaine*, which ship I had not seen since I left her as the bearer of a Flag of Truce. Immediately opposite to her lay the French frigate *La Furieuse*, in which I was detained at Helvoetsluys after quitting the Dutch Commodore.[2] I could not help pausing for a few minutes between these objects: but, after some meditation upon the extraordinary ups and downs of this sublunary planet, I passed on to my avocations.

I had selected comfortable lodgings outside of the town. But how shall I express my astonishment, when entering them after the fatigues of the day, to find, stowed away behind the door, my friend and fellow prisoner of Nancy and Verdun, Charles Sevright. He had been liberated by Bonaparte, and had come, not only to see me, but to inquire into the state of the French prisoners of war detained at Forton and Portchester Castle. It seems that Napoleon had been detained by the overflow of one of the rivers in the neighbourhood of Bitche, and the Authorities could not extricate him. There were several English prisoners belonging to our Packet Service in the place. They volunteered their services, and contrived to pass him over the river in safety.[3] Bonaparte was so much pleased with their exertions in his behalf that he demanded what he could do to serve them. Anyone would naturally suppose that he could grant them their liberty at once, without asking any questions. However, so it was. When the Englishmen were requested to say what could be done for them, they unanimously begged the liberation of Mr. Sevright, whose care and attention to all their wants had been

---

[1] Actually just before—Christmas Eve, the *Hero* being lost on Christmas Day. See James V, 349–50. The *Defence* was W.H.D.'s ship at the First of June, 1794.

[2] See above, pp. 26 *et seq.*

[3] According to John Wetherell (see above, p. 41, n.) he was himself one of this party.

unceasing during their captivity. Their demand was granted, and thus my friend returned to England after a nine-year unjustifiable detention. He remained with me a few days, then went to Town to solicit some employment. We did not meet for some time to come.[1]

On the 25th March the *Leopard* was undocked, and again secured alongside the hulk. Every effort was now called forth to prepare the ship for sea. About this period Sir Richard Bickerton[2] relieved Sir Roger Curtis in the naval command at Portsmouth. And a change took place at the Admiralty, Lord Melville[3] having replaced Mr. Yorke.

On the 20th April the *Leopard* left Portsmouth Harbour for Spithead, and by the beginning of May was in every respect refitted and ready for any service. As I had attended daily to all the operations going on, I wrote to the Admiralty for five days' leave of absence, which, to my annoyance, was refused. It was stated that it was not the practice to allow Captains to be absent when the ship was ready for sea. On my part, I had not thought of being away during the alterations, but when they were finished I had some family affairs to settle in Town. But as that indulgence could not be obtained, my stepmother came to Portsmouth to see me, remained 3 days and returned to Brompton.

Anxious to ascertain my destination, I wrote a confidential letter to Ad. Domett,[4] one of the Lords of the Admiralty. In reply, he laconically said, 'it is probable you will visit Gibraltar. Thereupon I went to Sir Richard Bickerton, to demand charts for the Mediterranean. I had not as yet had much communication with him, and was not prepared for what followed. When I said I had reason to believe the *Leopard* would proceed to the Straits, 'How do you know that?' he inquired in a very sharp tone. I showed him Ad. Domett's letter. 'That has nothing to do with it,' he remarked. 'I shall not sign your demand. I don't see why Captains are to be indulged in their whims. You have not yet got your orders.' I explained that I had no charts of the Mediterranean,* and that I was convinced, from

---

[1] (Erased) During these operations my wife's daughter married one of the Lieutenants, a Mr. Arnold, who not long afterwards left the ship.

[2] See above, p. 112.

[3] Robert Saunders Dundas, 2nd Viscount and son of Pitt's Henry Dundas, First Lord 1804–5. The former now began the longest-ever tenure of the office (1812–27, and 1828–30).

[4] (Sir) William Domett, Lt. 27/12/1777; straight to Capt. 9/9/82; R-Ad. 23/4/1804; V-Ad. 25/10/09; Ad. 12/8/19. B. of Admiralty, 1808–13; C. in C. Plymouth, 1813.

* The supplying of ships of war with proper charts was only a late regulation. Formerly the Captains and the Masters found them at their own expense. As some ships were lost owing to the want of correct ones, the Admiralty, under the Government's authority, issued them to the Navy.

what I knew of Ad. Domett, that he would not have written as he had, if he did not know that I was to be sent there. To all I said, however, he turned a deaf ear, and I withdrew, fully persuaded of Sir Richard's having no kind feelings towards me.

On the 6th of May I gave instructions to four transports which were to accompany me to Cork Harbour, and next morning we got under way. One of the transports came to anchor in disobedience to my signal. We reached the Cove of Cork on the evening of the 9th, where we anchored with three transports. Here Ad. Thornborough[1] held the command, whom I knew when he hoisted his Flag on board the *Africaine* cruising off the coast of Holland. He had afterwards rebuked the Dutch authorities at the Texel for my unjustifiable detention. He was extremely kind during my short stay in harbour. On the 12th we embarked 450 of the 5th Regiment of Foot, and left the harbour on the 16th with some transports under convoy. The Colonel of this Regiment had been introduced to me by some of my Irish friends, and many acts were extended to his officers, by which some of the *Leopard's* Lieutenants deprived themselves of their usual comforts. The instant the ship was fairly at sea, I sent an invitation to the Colonel to dine with me. He declined it, and as he kept his distance, all intercourse between us ended. The Army officers noticed his coolness and spoke to mine on the subject. They coolly replied that 'our Captain always has a reason for his conduct.' By the 27th we were near the land, making our way towards the Tagus. The Colonel now requested an interview, and I was astonished to hear him launch out in a rhapsody of apologies for not having accepted my invitation. I listened patiently to all he had to say, and could only reply that I concluded he had had the worst of it by keeping aloof: for if he had chosen to make himself agreeable my cabin would have been at his disposal: and that all his officers had in rotation been sufferers by his coolness. He had evidently mistaken his man. Explanations took place and he became an altered person. He had, I suspect, supposed that he was entitled to a great deal of consideration. But he was not the Captain of the ship. He found out his error late in the day, but we became friends and met again many years afterwards.

We had to beat into the Tagus against a strong N.E. gale. When inside of Belem, the First Lieutenant did not tack the ship properly. She missed stays, and the Portuguese Pilot, alarmed beyond measure, went down on his knees exclaiming, 'Jesu Maria, somos perdudos.'

[1] See Vol. I, p. 343.

—' Jesus Maria, we are all lost.' At that moment I took the command, and ordered all the sails to be braced flat aback. That manœuvre gave the ship stern way, her keel scraping over the sands on the Cascaes shore, discolouring the water. The anxiety was so intense that not a word could be heard. However, I kept cool, and, watching our progress under stern way, I braced the yards round and filled upon the opposite tack. The danger was over. It happened that Sir George Berkeley and his Captain, Hardy, were looking on, and in great anxiety waiting the result. When I reported myself to the Admiral, I was complimented upon the seamanlike manner in which the ship had been handled. They both thought she would have been lost. Nothing but cool determination saved the ship that day. All the officers and the crew were fully aware of it.

The next day the troops were landed. Here I remained a few days, then embarked 258 of the English artillery under the command of Col. Holcombe, the brother to Lieut. Holcombe, my First Lieutenant while I was acting in *L'Aigle* in 1809. Shortly afterwards I received 150 Portuguese artillery. There was great anxiety expressed by the Admiral to get the *Leopard* to sea, as the artillery were wanted by Lord Wellington. The usual Pilot would not undertake to go out in the dark, which was considered dangerous. However, at last the Portuguese Admiralty Pilot made his appearance. The anchor was weighed at half past 6, and away we went down the Tagus, scarcely able to see any of the leading marks. There was also a scarcity of wind. The lead was kept going on either side. I several times asked the Pilot if he knew where we were. He constantly assured me he did not. In fact our way out was one of those extraordinary events that occasionally occur without accident. The ebb tide had run out by 10 o'clock, and there was no wind. The ship was anchored for the night in 9 fathoms. Soon afterwards one of my convoy came close to me, and I desired the Master of it to anchor. The next morning the remainder joined. The unexpected appearance of a three-decker now drew my attention, and we received the news of Mr. Perceval's being killed at the entrance of the House of Commons by a man named Bellingham. We got on our way to Gibraltar with the convoy. As we passed by Cape Trafalgar and Tarifa we were assailed by contrary winds, and on entering the Straits we had strong easterly winds.

It was on this occasion that some ill disposed men threw a couple of 12 lb. shot at the Surgeon one evening as he was visiting the sick. About 9 o'clock in the evening, my steward was attending the

Surgeon with a plate of stewed poultry for a suffering seaman on the Lower Deck. In passing along, my Steward carrying a lighted candle, the Doctor was saluted with a 12 lb. shot which grazed him. In a few seconds another followed. However, he administered relief to his patient. The Steward instantly hurried up to my cabin and reported what had happened. I was undressing, preparing for bed. I could not believe his statement: it sounded so unlikely. However, soon afterwards the Surgeon himself came and verified it, with additional particulars. This was not an affair to be trifled with. I therefore hastened on deck and ordered the hammocks to be piped up. Fortunately it was a fine moonlight night. So soon as the hammocks were stowed, and all the crew on the Quarter Deck, I inquired who had thrown the shot, and told them that I would not allow them to have their hammocks piped down until the defaulter was delivered up. All that I could say made no impression. However, to convince them that I would not submit to anything like insubordination, I ordered eight men who were in the Black List for various breaches of discipline to be brought out, and told them that there was a chance of their not being punished if the offender on the present occasion were produced. But from the Ship's Company I could get nothing. So the Black List men were punished for their offences according to the usage of the Navy: after which the watch was called, but the hammocks remained in the netting. Upon further consideration, it appeared that the watch on deck could not have been concerned with what had happened on the Lower Deck. They were in consequence cleared of all suspicion, and permitted to take away their hammocks at midnight. Then, upon further inquiry, there were 17 men who could not give a satisfactory account of themselves. Therefore the blame of this transaction naturally fell upon them. Amongst the number was one of my boat's crew. I was thoroughly convinced from his attachment to my person that he was not the delinquent. But where such a serious act had been committed against an officer, it amounted to a mutiny, and required stringent measures. Therefore those 17 men's hammocks were kept up, and the remainder restored to their owners. Three weeks passed, and as I could not find out who had been the guilty man, they were allowed in the end to take them out of the netting and the offence was forgotten. But this was an example to the Ship's Company that was not lost on them, as they never afterwards committed any similar disorderly proceeding.

The following morning the Rock of Gibraltar was in sight, and after a toilsome day against an easterly wind the ship anchored on the evening of June 14th. The next day I waited upon the Naval Officer in Command, Commodore Penrose, by whom I was received with much cordiality: but he was very silent as to my future destiny, telling me that I should know when I was at sea, as I was then to open my orders, which were secret. This was the officer who had been Lord Hugh Seymour's Captain in the *Sans Pareil* at Jamaica, and who first announced to me that my name was the last word pronounced by his Lordship when he died, with pen in hand to sign a commission for my promotion.[1] There were many ships lying in the Bay, which obliged me to anchor in deep water, 24 fathoms. Upon my landing in this extraordinary place, where I had never been before, I met Major Rutherford, whom I had so often seen at Ad. Nugent's house. He held an appointment under the Governor, and proved a useful acquaintance as I was a perfect stranger. He most kindly installed me in his apartments.

[An eight-page account of the Rock and its history follows. Later, under the date March, 1813, another six pages are devoted to the same subject, and W.H.D. suggests that the two be brought together. This direction I have followed, but only to omit the bulk of both. This has been done with real regret, for W.H.D.'s style and descriptive ability, not always impeccable, are here at their very best. There are, however, a few historical incidents included, mainly concerning the famous siege, which seem to warrant inclusion, in that they add picturesque details, some of which, probably, are known to but few readers, while others I have not seen recorded anywhere.]

. . . There are still some apes to be seen, but very rarely. They retire to the precipices on the eastern side beyond the reach of man, where they find plenty of grass. But when the strong easterly wind assails them, they are driven from their caves to take refuge among the bushes to the westward. On those occasions they are seen hopping about, cutting the most extraordinary antics. They have no tails. The general impression is that they came over with the Moors, as Apes' Hill on the opposite shore still bears that name. I was often amused by a story still related about these animals. During the Siege, the enemy had contrived to make an irruption at a considerable height to the right of our lines, but was repulsed with great slaughter. The apes of that day seized the cocked hats from the dead bodies and wore them. Our lookouts noticed a parcel of cocked hats

[1] See Vol. I, p. 425 and note.

in motion and gave the alarm, supposing that the enemy had again penetrated in that direction. A detachment was ordered out to meet the imagined assailants, whom they ascertained to be monkeys. Those now remaining being harmless, orders have been issued not to molest them. . . .

. . . The principal [forts are] casemated, and traverses are constructed to prevent mischief from the bursting of shells. The flanking fires that may be brought into play against an attack are tremendous. The most extraordinary works are the galleries excavated from the solid rock, in which loopholes are formed for the reception of guns of heavy calibre. They are pointed towards the narrow causeway which alone admits of a passage to the town. I have been inside of St. George's Gallery, from which I had a good view of the remains of the Spanish lines, twice set on fire by Gen. Elliot during the siege. There are cisterns, bomb-proof, capable of containing 40,000 tons of water. I was told that, at the period of the great siege, there were only 80 guns mounted, with a few mortars and howitzers, but when I was there, I understood, upwards of 1,000 were in battery, since which many improvements have been made. . . .

. . . It is the general opinion that the guns of Gibraltar command the entrance to the Mediterranean. But such is not the case, as the Rock is at least 20 miles from the Atlantic, and the batteries, instead of pointing to the South, are all directed towards the Bay in the West. Vessels may easily enter the Strait by keeping close to the Barbary shore. . . .

. . . Beneath the walls may be seen an assemblage of small craft. Amongst them lay the Spanish smugglers, felucca rigged, with a heavy gun concealed under their deck hamper. . . . These vessels take in their cargoes at the Rock, and watch their opportunity of landing it on the neighbouring coasts, where they are met by a daring body of contrabandists who carry the goods into the interior: assisted, it is said, by Spanish officials of a certain character. The Spanish Government maintains a number of fast sailing Guarda Costas or revenue vessels, which keep a sharp look out from Algesiras, and will sometimes cut out the smugglers from under the very batteries of Gibraltar: at the risk, however, of being sunk by our guns if caught invading the jurisdiction of our waters—a fate which has befallen more than one. This system is not approved by our military authorities, and is said to be on the wane. Endeavours have often been made by us to do away with this temptation by inducing the Spaniards to admit our goods at a reasonable duty. But the influence of the Barcelona manufacturers, who are anxious for a protecting duty, has hitherto prevented this desirable result. This traffic increases the bitter feelings of the Spaniards at our possession of Gibraltar. . . . I have often wondered at our allowing these fellows to carry on their underhand work against a friendly country. It is beneath us as a great nation to permit their using this station for such purposes. Such is my opinion: but I am not a statesman. . . .

. . . . I must allude to the heroic and extraordinary exertions of one of our naval officers, who distinguished himself by saving the lives, during the memorable siege, at the repeated risk of his own, of many of the Spaniards in their floating batteries, which were sunk and burned by the red hot shot from our lines. In spite of every obstacle among the flaming wrecks, he dashed in with his gunboats, to the wonder and amazement of the enemy, and rescued them from inevitable destruction. . . . With that officer I became well known during the naval command he held at Portsmouth, and experienced many acts of kindness from him—Sir Roger Curtis. . . .

. . . When the Grand attack was about to commence, two French Princes of the blood, the Comte D'Artois[1] and the Duc de Bourbon, arrived at the camp to witness the operations. I made the acquaintance of the former not very long since. Many of the Moors also were present, and many visitors from various parts of Europe. Nothing could surpass the courtesy of the Duc de Crillon, Commander of the Allied forces. He wrote to Gen. Elliot to inform him of the arrival of the French Princes, who joined him in expressing their high respect for his character and valour, and requested his acceptance of a present of some fruits, vegetables and other refreshments for the use of his Staff, adding that he was well aware that His Excellency lived entirely on vegetables, and he was desirous of knowing what sort he preferred, as he wished to send him a daily supply. The Governor's reply was in accordance with the romantic gallantry of those days. But, in receiving his present, he begged him to abstain from sending him any more, as he made it a point of honour to share in common with his garrison either plenty or scarcity as the case might be. . . . [On conclusion of hostilities, the Duke and the General exchanged presents and visits]. . . . When the Duke came to the Rock, he was saluted with 17 guns. The soldiers received him with loud huzzas, with which he was at first confused, until their meaning was explained to him, when he was highly pleased at the

[1] Afterwards Charles X. See below, p. 428.

good old English custom. When the artillery officers were introduced
to him, he observed, 'Gentlemen, I would rather meet you here as
friends than on your batteries as enemies, where you never spared
me.' . . .

 . . . Prince William Henry, afterwards, as King William IV,
our mutual friend, was serving as a Midshipman with Ad. Digby in
the *Prince George* in that war. The Spanish Admiral, Langara, then
a prisoner of ours,[1] visited the ship, and our Admiral introduced to
him the young Prince, who after that ceremony withdrew during the
conference. But when it had terminated, he reappeared as the Mid
on duty, respectfully informing the Spanish Admiral that his boat
was ready. 'Well does Great Britain merit the empire of the Sea,'
exclaimed the Spaniard, 'when the humblest stations in her Navy
are occupied by Princes of the blood.' . . .

 . . . On the opposite coast of Africa we noticed Ceuta, which is
to Spain what Gibraltar is to England, being held by them in spite
of the Moors, just as we maintain the Rock in spite of the Spaniards.
It is a solitary fortress in the Kingdom of Morocco, strongly fortified
and garrisoned by 5,000 men. During the Peninsular War the French
nearly succeeded in capturing it, had not an English detachment
been promptly thrown in. At the Peace, we were politely requested
to evacuate the fortress. This was rather provoking, as it was not
of much use to the Spaniards, but to us it would have been important,
to give us the entire command of the Straits. However, it was
restored to Spain, and serves for a place of banishment to convicts,
etc. . . .

(2) H.M.S. *LEOPARD*. (The Mediterranean)

JUNE 16, 1812–DECEMBER 1813

On the 16th I issued instructions to my convoy to weigh anchor.
The position of the *Leopard* was one of extreme difficulty—in deep
water with a strong head wind, and a ship right under my stern.
It appeared impossible to extricate her without some accident. I
waited a couple of hours, but my orders were so peremptory that I
could no longer delay making the attempt. I accordingly addressed
a few words to the Ship's Company pointing out the necessity of the
utmost exertion in heaving up the anchor. The Commanding Officer
of the artillery placed all his men at my disposal. They were useful

---
[1] Captured by Rodney in the Moonlight Battle, 16/1/1780.

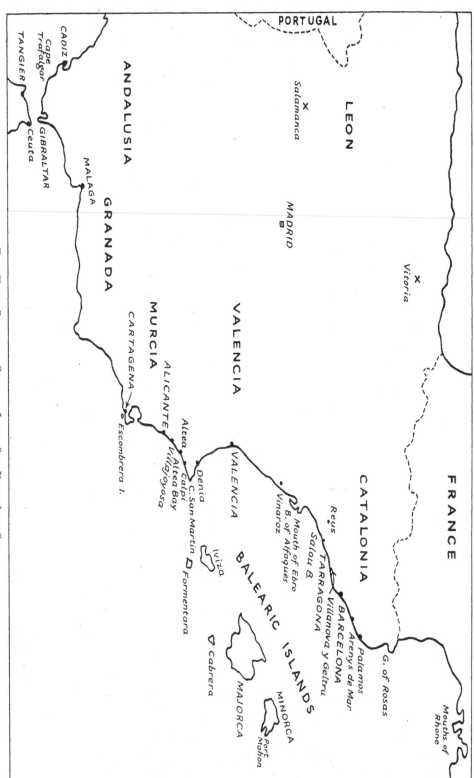

PORTUGAL

LEON

ANDALUSIA

GRANADA

MURCIA

VALENCIA

CATALONIA

FRANCE

BALEARIC ISLANDS

TANGIER
CADIZ
Cape Trafalgar
Ceuta
GIBRALTAR
MALAGA
Salamanca ×
MADRID ■
Vitoria ×
CARTAGENA
Escombrera I.
ALICANTE
Altea
Altea Bay
Villajoyosa
Calpi
C. San Martin
Denia
VALENCIA
Vinaroz
B. of Alfaques
Mouth of Ebro
Salou B.
TARRAGONA
Reus
Villanova y Geltru
BARCELONA
Arenys de Mar
Palamos
G. of Rosas
Mouths of Rhone
Iviza
Formentera
Cabrera
MAJORCA
MINORCA
Port Mahon

at the Capstan, at which they laboured manfully. The ship was loosened from her strong hold, but before the anchor came to the bows, to enable sail to be made, she drifted on board of the vessel alluded to. However, good management on both sides prevented any damage to either party. At that moment the Commodore,[1] and all the officers of the ships in the Mole, were watching our proceedings, fearing some mishap. Fortunately the *Leopard* came out perfectly clear, and, having reached an outward position, hove to for the convoy. The Masters of those ships behaved with extreme neglect, and I waited, firing guns, several hours before they joined late in the afternoon. So soon as I had cleared the Rock, I opened my orders, which directed me to proceed to Minorca.

On the 18th I fell in with the *Hyacinth*, Capt. Ussher,[2] my old messmate, who came to dine with me. From him I obtained some useful information concerning the Greek Polacres many of whom traded with enemy ports and so were liable to capture. On the 23rd I fell in with one and chaced her. The Greek manœuvred with skill, but as I had the weather gage his attempt to escape failed. He then bore up, and ran into a small bay in the island of Cabrera. I followed, boarded him and brought him out, determined to detain him owing to his suspicious conduct. However, his papers were cleared at Minorca and I allowed him to depart. On my arrival in this harbour on the 24th, I found myself under the orders of Ad. Pickmore,[3] whose Flag was flying on board the *Royal George*. I had taken a good position opposite George Town. There were some Spanish ships lying here dismantled. The harbour of Port Mahon, as it is called, is a very safe place, but not easily entered. It is strongly fortified, and was very useful to us, as all our fleet could resort there when necessary. It contained a good Dock Yard, and a very capacious Lazaretto, to receive those attacked with the Plague, or to perform the quarantine established in this climate. Our ships stationed off Toulon used to winter here, and refit when required. In this port I enjoyed all the comforts of the Italian climate, and as there was the appearance of my remaining here some time, I determined to devote my leisure moments in learning the Spanish language.

I increased my acquaintance daily with the Captains of the

---

[1] A note here reads:—'Examine Navy List of that date for his rank.' It is the second, and last, occasion in the Narrative when the careful W.H.D. has failed to finish his editing, and it throws light on his high level of accuracy in such matters. Here no correction is necessary, for Penrose did not obtain his Flag till 4/12/1813.

[2] See Vol. I, p. 228 and Index.

[3] Francis Pickmore, Lt. 18/12/1777; Cdr. 27/6/82; Capt. 21/9/90; R-Ad. 28/4/1808; V-Ad. 12/8/12.

men of war, coming and going in succession. Here I found the
Swiftsure, *Rodney*, *Union* and *America* of the line, with several
smaller vessels. On the 28th the *Malta*[1] arrived with Rear Ad.
Hallowell,[2] with whom I became acquainted. I had reason to believe
that I should be placed under his orders. I found him a very intelligent officer with great cordiality. Among the persons of note residing
here was the Dowager Duchess of Orleans, widow of the celebrated
Mons. L'Egalité. As I had been presented to her in the year 1788 at
Vincennes, where the Prince her husband had established a Horse
Race upon the English system, I requested Ad. Hallowell to introduce
me to Her S. Highness.[3] He very readily complied. When this
Princess heard me relate the manner in which I had the honour of
making her acquaintance, she recollected the circumstance most
minutely, and from that hour I was admitted as one of her friends.
She invited me to dine at her table, and I became acquainted with
the principal persons of her establishment, among whom must be
noticed the Marquess and Marchioness de Castras. When this
gentleman, a distinguished officer in the Spanish Army, perceived
the marked attention shewn to me by the Princess, he sought my
acquaintance, and often visited my ship.

I now received orders to discharge the Portuguese artillery men
into H.M.S. *Brune*. Active preparations were going on to assemble
troops from Sicily. The *Malta* left us next day, and the *Implacable*
and *Imperieuse* came in accompanied by several transports full of
soldiers. On the 23rd *L'Aigle* frigate arrived with Sir Edward Pellew.
When I presented myself to this gallant officer, he acquainted me
that Ad. Hallowell (to whom I had already spoken, requesting him
to advocate my cause in obtaining a remove from the *Leopard* to
the command of another ship) had brought me under his notice:
and, if in his power, he would appoint me to a more active command:
but he had already promised to two captains the first vacancies that
might occur. He expressed much feeling in my behalf, and his desire
to serve me. 'How is it,' he demanded, 'that you are appointed to
a troopship? Have you no interest?' I replied that the Duke of York
was my friend, to which he expressed astonishment at my having
been selected for that service. He left Minorca in a couple of days
to return to the Fleet off Toulon.

---

[1] The *Malta* was the rechristened *Guillaume Tell*, last French survivor from the
Battle of the Nile, captured by the *Foudroyant* when attempting to escape from
Malta just before we captured it.
[2] See p. 178, note.
[3] See above, p. 164.

On the 29th, all the preparations for the expedition having been completed, the squadron and transports put to sea under the orders of Rear Ad. Hallowell. On the 1st August we anchored in Palamos Bay. All the boats were instantly out and loaded with soldiers. The arrangement of landing them was confided to me. The Bomb *Strombolo* and a small frigate were ordered to take a station inshore. Just about the time that I had drawn up all the boats ready for a dash on shore, the French troops, to some amount, were seen advancing towards the beach.* On it there was a rising slope of about 10 or 12 feet, which prevented my noticing them. The Admiral now made the signal for recall, so that all my plans were annulled. The boats having returned to the ships, I proceeded on my own, accompanied by a Gen. Mackenzie who held the command of the troops that day, to reconnoitre the beach. Upon my landing, a Spanish peasant hastened down to me. Being able to ask a few questions, which were satisfactorily answered, I took him on board and conveyed him to Ad. Hallowell's ship, where he underwent a strict examination. I was sadly disappointed: but I suppose, from what little I could learn, that the Admiral had expected to find this part of the coast unguarded, and to have disembarked on it without opposition. But, as he found the enemy prepared, he abandoned his plans. The *Invincible*, 74, joined us here, and on the 3rd, after alarming the whole coast, we put to sea early in the morning. On the 5th the *Malta* drew out from the convoy and made my signal to close. We then parted from the squadron and proceeded towards Alicant, where we anchored on the 8th—my birthday.[1] On the 10th, all the transports having joined, the troops were landed. The *America* came to us, and increased our strength. The artillery, after having been on board upwards of two months, were removed to the shore.†[2]

On the 20th I received orders to proceed with several transports to Altea Bay, where there was a good spring of water. The *Fame*, 74, had been watching this place, but I relieved her. I had instructions to act in concert with a Spanish officer in command of a detachment of 200 men, to annoy the enemy. On the 21st I anchored in the bay, and next day the *Fame* left us. More transports arrived, and the watering

---

* Gen. Suchet, Duc D'Albufera, held the chief command of the French troops in Catalonia.

[1] See Intro., Vol. I, pp. ix and xiii.

† Alicant is defended by a strong castle deemed impregnable. It was taken from the Moors in 1264, and by the English in 1706, when it stood a siege of two years against the French and Spaniards. It surrendered upon honourable terms after a part of the rock on which it stood had been blown up, the Governor being killed.

[2] For the significance of this disappointing operation, see above, Intro. p. 169.

was carried on with great activity. On the afternoon of the 25th a small column of troops was seen coming down the road from a high mountain. I directed the *Bristol* lying in that direction, to fire on them. When the shot whizzed over their heads, they began waving white handkerchiefs. In consequence of this display of what was intended for a Flag of Peace the firing was discontinued. I then hastened to the shore in my boat, and came in contact with the officer in command of the column. He had received instructions to unite his efforts with mine to keep the enemy out of Altea. But he made so many excuses that he had no powder, and resorted to so many shuffles, that he convinced me there was no reliance to be placed upon him. However, I took one of his subordinates back to the *Leopard* and gave him a supply of powder. When he returned to his party, they retired in the near (*sic*), and, during my stay in that place, never reappeared, so that I had only my own resources to depend upon to protect the town from the French. I proposed to the Admiral to erect, at a trifling expense, a scaffolding on the beach, which would have been of the utmost use to the watering party, enabling them to collect larger quantities in a purer condition. He approved of all I had done, but would not sanction any expenditure relating to the watering.

I examined the locality, which was surrounded by lofty mountains, and found there was no danger of consequence from the interior, as there were no military roads in that direction. The main one communicating with Altea came close to the beach, so that my boats armed with carronades, as well the broadside of my ship, had the full command of it. The chief of the Guerillas, Orosco, and the Alcade (the mayor) came on board to consult me as to the most efficient means to keep out the French. They were stationed at Denia, about three leagues off on the other side of the mountain. Their force consisted of 1,200 men, under the command of a Gen. Judin. Before admitting these Spaniards to any confidential intercourse, I mentioned that I had noticed several articles in the Spanish newspapers wherein some very ill natured abuse appeared against the English. Therefore, until I was certain that I should not be exposed to similar reports, they could not expect much sincere co-operation. But if I could rely upon their joining, heart and hand, in supporting my plans of defence, I would do all in my power to drive away the enemy. They most readily agreed to yield to all my wishes, promising to communicate every intelligence of the French General's motions, and declaring themselves ready to make any sacrifice that might be required to repel their invaders. A signal was then agreed upon to be made by them when they wanted my assistance.

Not many hours after this, the Guerilla leader came to acquaint me that there were 12 lurking spies who had come over from the enemy to prepare the disaffected, if there were any, to assist the French in capturing the town, and that if I would land a party of men to apprehend them, he would assist. Fortunately there were two other men of war lying at that moment in the bay. I instantly summoned their Captains to my ship and directed them to prepare their Marines for acting on shore. By 8 o'clock in the evening, about 80 of them, with a certain proportion of seamen, were on the beach under my immediate command. They were then distributed in detachments, with officers, to follow the Guerillas in quest of the spies. The heat was most oppressive; so much so that I could not bear my coat on. In the course of a couple of hours eight of the men had been secured, the inhabitants having indicated their hiding places. Orosco now came to me, declaring that he gave up all hope of capturing the other four. I pointed to several buildings, as likely to be their secret resort. He assured me that they had all been strictly searched, without success. Then I inquired if he had looked into a large residence with a sort of square attached to it. He replied with great solemnity, 'El Obispo.' It was, he said, the Bishop's, and he dared not go in. 'What,' said I, 'will the Bishop forbid your entering his premises to secure your enemies?' He appeared to have lost all his energy. 'Very well,' I rejoined. 'Come along with me. I don't know the Obispo, but I shall examine his dwelling and take my chance for the rest.'

He accompanied me into the square. We had fine moonlight. I made my way to the principal door and knocked, but no notice was taken of the intrusion. The Chief told me that the Bishop was inside, and thought I should not be admitted. I called in the Marines who now filled the place. Orosco pointed to an open space on my right. Its door not being shut, I went in, and saw before me a staircase, which I ascended with my loaded pistol in hand. When I reached the landing, I heard the footsteps, as I supposed, of two men. I called to them, but all remained quiet. As I advanced on the floor, feeling about with my left hand, I came in contact with a loose shutter which I burst open. The instant the light came in, I saw three men close together in a corner. I desired them to surrender, then fired one pistol over their heads. The other was let off outside, and I ordered my men up. The three strangers were instantly secured.

They were connected with the spies already taken, so that 11 out of the 12 had been secured.

On descending into the square, I found the door of the Bishop's palace (if such it might be called) open. I was invited into it, and to my astonishment beheld a table spread with a good supper, wine, etc. Two fine Spanish girls who were seated there, were represented as the Holyman's nieces. I partook of some refreshment. His Holiness complimented me upon my exertions in the cause of his country. I requested him to send some wine to my party outside, which he readily complied with. The officers were called in and supplied with the needful, after which we all returned to our ships. Next day I sent the 11 detained Spaniards in a ship of war to Alicant, giving an official account to the Admiral. That act of apprehending the men gave the enemy some idea of what he might expect if he made his appearance in the bay, and no immediate attempt was made by him to attack the place.

[In a long note W.H.D. gives a verbatim copy of a dispatch dated August 25, 1812, sent by him to Ad. Hallowell. He states that 'a part of the Spanish Army on the retreat to Villajoyosa' had arrived, with (he was informed) the French close on their heels. He had ordered the *Bristol* to stay with him, and had landed both his and her Marines, to hold the passes leading to the town. 'At this moment, ¼ past 8,' he concludes, 'I learn from some guerillas come on board that the advanced guard of the enemy, 60 in number, is at Calpi, a few miles hence.' The note is clearly an afterthought, being altogether unconnected with the text. Thus we never learn what, if anything, was the outcome of the affair. It was all, probably, a false alarm. Otherwise, in a narrative hereabouts so lacking in serious action, he would hardly have left off in the middle of such a comparatively promising theme.]

As I was anxious to be better acquainted with the neighbourhood, Orosco lent me a horse, and attended me. We agreed to cut a deep ditch on the top of the mountain to the north, which led to Denia, to prevent the enemy from crossing in that direction. Strong planks were placed over it during the day, but withdrawn at night. The guerilla showed me a watch case inside of which was a small cross made from the bones of a Saint. While he had it about his person, he said, he was invulnerable, and feared nothing. I told him I did not possess such a relic, yet had very often been exposed to the enemy's fire without being killed. So much for superstition. It was now settled that the guerillas were to guard the mountain pass all night, and my boats, manned and armed, were to take station close to the beach, where the high road is near to it: by which arrangement the French could not pass without being exposed to our fire.

Orosco came on board every morning to report what had happened in the mountains during the night. We often heard the report of musketry in that direction, which led me to inquire the cause. He would reply that the French, while reconnoitring, had come in contact with his men, who had killed several of the enemy. This question was renewed every morning, and Orosco would quietly say, 'We have shot 4 or 5 Frenchmen.' But as I never heard any further particulars, I considered it all a hum, and refrained making further inquiries. However, one day, the guerilla chief announced that Gen. Judin had sent in a summons to prepare quarters and rations for 3,000 men. The Frenchman's summons threw all the inhabitants of Altea into great alarm, and at sunset, to the number of at least 150, they hastened off to the *Leopard* for security. I ordered some canvas to be spread in my cabin, to which place they generally resorted— Spaniards of every station in life, from the landed proprietor to the beggar. Wine and biscuit were distributed during the night, and they left the ship with the dawn. This visitation was continued so often that it became a serious annoyance. One individual, who spoke English, made himself useful to me with his countrymen, and he procured ice from the peaks of the mountains, being always paid for the supply. He also frequently attended me when a consultation was necessary, but when he found that he did not receive a gratuity he kept aloof. Upon my inquiring the reason, I was told that he was taking care of his wife. Most of that class looked to me for remuneration when they were required to prepare to meet the enemy. Having discovered this, I altered my system, and told them that, if they would not exert themselves to defend their own homes, I should leave them to their fate. Once the Authorities requested my meeting them on shore to discuss a plan for the protection of the place. I attended, having, luckily as it turned out, taken a party of Marines to guard the premises against surprise, for I was aware that the enemy had many spies, watching to take advantage of any careless neglect. As I was closeted with the Mayor, a couple of peasants outside contrived to abstract my telescope and boat cloak, with which they were making off. But my Marines, observing their proceedings, hurried after them and brought them back. Of course I presented these patriots to the Mayor. This act broke up our meeting: but at parting I promised to receive all the Church plate on board for the better security thereof. I had a queer set to deal with.

All my proceedings were much approved by Rear Ad. Hallowell, who promised to relieve me at the first opportunity. I had explained to him the plans I had adopted, as well the expense to which I was exposed by receiving so many Spaniards every night. The priests had deposited three large chests under my care containing the Church plate. They availed themselves of every opportunity to turn my ship to account. I had 40 men laid up from being exposed all night in the boats, and I began to be weary of this unpleasant duty that produced nothing but toil.

Among the many ships that came here to water was the *Ganymede*, Capt. Purvis.[1] He expressed an anxious desire to go to the advanced post on the brow of the mountain. I advised him to be well attended, in case of accidents: then, finding him determined to be a witness of the doings of the guerillas, I introduced Orosco to my friend, telling him that Capt. P. wished to pass the night with him and his party on the cliff. He most readily offered his services, and they went on shore together. Nothing of consequence occurred that night. The report of the muskets was frequently heard, which I concluded was Orosco quietly shooting a few Frenchmen. About 2 o'clock the next day, Capt. P. came to report his adventures. He had reconnoitred the locality, stationing his men where he thought the enemy might attempt an intrusion. As the hours passed on in stillness, he thought he might venture to take a nap, requesting Orosco to watch over him. The Spaniard agreed to do so. But when he noticed the English officer close his eyes, off went a musket. This alarmed Purvis, who was instantly on his legs expecting an attack; but no more firing being heard, he resumed his former position. Instantly off again went a musket. He then rose and prepared accordingly, but no change took place. Thus the firing was continued at intervals all through the night, which prevented my friend from obtaining a moment's rest. He inquired the reason of it, but had no satisfactory answer from Orosco, except his desire to alarm the enemy. With the dawn he returned to his ship, annoyed and disappointed at all that had passed, and determined not to visit again the advanced post.

As it had become the custom for the inhabitants of both sexes to come off to my ship, many out of curiosity and others, no doubt, to watch and report my proceedings to the enemy, I made no restrictions, but allowed them full liberty to pass to and fro.

[1] John Brett Purvis, Lt. 1/5/1805; Cdr. 9/8/08; Capt. 16/9/09; R-Ad. 9/11/46.

[He describes at some length how the Spaniards danced their national dances on board, to the entertainment of the British officers, who were also entertained by the arrival of a local heiress of outstanding beauty, also described at length. There follows a very long note on how W.H.D. dealt with the natives when they failed to produce the meat, bread, fish, etc. for which he had asked and which they had promised. He appealed first to their good feelings—'I have entertained you freely. What about you doing *your* share?' Next, he threatened to sail away and leave them to their fate, and finally said that he would sink any fishing boat leaving the bay, if his demands were not satisfied. The last-named threat succeeded; provisions poured in, and amity was restored.]

Whilst our leisure moments were thus passed, Orosco brought me a summons from Gen. Judin, and the bearer of it. The Frenchman gave warning that he should make his appearance at the head of 3,000 men, and desired that preparations be made to receive him in the town with rations, etc. I wrote a note to Mons. Judin, acknowledging the receipt of his summons, and assuring him that it would afford me the greatest satisfaction imaginable to receive him in Altea, and that he might rely upon being welcomed with all the honours of war at my disposal. I heard no more of Gen. Judin at that period. But, many years afterwards, when travelling in France, at Amboise near Tours, I heard some French officers talking of their adventures in Spain. One of them alluded to his Chief, Gen. Judin, at Denia, he being Second in Command. The arrangements, he said, of the English naval officer in Altea Bay had baffled all the French General's plans for an attack on the place. He eulogized that officer's conduct in marked terms. I could not resist addressing him, and inquiring if he recollected the year when he was stationed in that part. He replied with much civility, 'The year 1812.' 'Then,' said I, 'you now see before you the English officer who acted against you on that occasion.' A few more particulars were mentioned, which confirmed my assertion. The Frenchman then rose from the table and offered me his hand, as a proof of his admiration of the measures I had adopted to prevent his countrymen entering the town of Altea. This officer proved to be the Adjutant Major of the town of Tours. He with extreme affability invited me to his house.

Having reason to suspect that I had dropped anchor on a rocky bottom, I became anxious to ascertain the fact. We had a very laborious day, as it proved that the anchor was embedded in foul ground. All our purchases failed in moving it. Consequently I was obliged to cut the cable, lost my anchor and removed the ship into a better position. Our monotony was relieved by the unexpected arrival of the *Prince of Wales*, a three-decker commanded by an old acquaintance, Capt. J. E. Douglas.[1] He had as a passenger the Hon. Mrs. Cadogan, wife to the Captain of that name. I hastened on board, and he requested me to stay and dine, which invitation I readily accepted. Capt. Douglas was anxious to see the guerilla Chief. I sent for Orosco, whose costume made an impression upon my friend and the lady, just from England. Over his head was wrapped a large handkerchief, one end of which hung down upon his shoulder: above that a large slouching sombrero, in his hand a musket, and his waist encircled with a sash, out of which might be seen the handle of a stiletto: his feet guarded by a species of sandal peculiar to that part of Spain. In the evening I procured more of the Alteans, whom I persuaded to dance the sapatio in the cabin. Then the Spaniards retired, but Capt. Douglas requested me to remain on board until his ship was fairly under sail to join the Fleet under Sir Edward Pellew. I complied most readily.

Shortly after this the *Bristol* came into the bay, as I thought to relieve me: but she had been sent by Ad. Hallowell to supply the *Leopard* with provisions. However, led to believe that I should soon be recalled, I requested the Spanish Priests to receive back all their church plate. Shortly afterwards I received orders to repair to Alicant. I left the bay on the 26th, and fell in with the *Tremendous*, 74, having on board Sir Sidney Smith.[2] I saluted with the number of guns due to his rank.[3] When I presented myself on board the *Malta*, Ad. Hallowell informed me that he intended to detach me with a small squadron under my command to Carthagena, to protect that place from the French. They were losing ground in Spain, and Soult, who had for so long blockaded Cadiz, had commenced his retreat from that neighbourhood. But it was deemed proper to prepare for such an event. I received a small detachment of the 2nd Minorca regiment, who were destined to assist their countrymen, and on the 30th anchored in Escombrera Bay, just outside of the harbour, accompanied by some transports. The *Leyden*, 64, and the *Brune*, frigate, both troopships, and the *Thunder*, Bomb, formed the squadron under my command. I was requested by the Spanish Authorities

[1] John Erskine Douglas, Lt. 21/4/1778; Cdr. 24/5/94; Capt. 10/6/95; R-Ad. 4/6/1814; V-Ad. 27/5/25; Ad. 28/6/38. Still living (Ad. of the Red) in 1849.
[2] See Vol. I, p. 184, note.
[3] V-Ad. of the Blue.

to visit the fortifications of the place, and a plan was arranged in case of attack from the French. Carthagena was in a sad state of melancholy owing to much sickness that infested the town. Col. Prescott was stationed here with part of a regiment for the protection of this important place, but his quarters were in a wretched condition, as there were no regular barracks. My first occupation was to fit out a Spanish frigate as a Hospital Ship. We could not have much communication with the shore while the epidemic lasted: in short, I forbade it. We were visited by a succession of gales. The *Brune* drifted from her anchors, and would probably have been lost had I not sent a cable to her assistance. A flash of lightning set the *Leopard's* flying jib boom on fire. It was cut away to prevent further injury.

We soon ascertained that Soult had left Carthagena in his rear and, as there did not appear to be any chance of his attacking the place, I was recalled, and by the 9th October was again at anchor in the bay of Alicant. We were at this season exposed to very sudden changes of heat and cold. One night I was seized with a shivering fit, and my limbs nearly petrified with cold, so much so that I had great difficulty in re-establishing a healthy circulation. On the 12th I put to sea with some transports, bound to Oran, Coast of Africa, to procure cattle for the Army and our squadron. Ad. Hallowell requested me to purchase a good saddle horse for him. When I made the African shore, the storms were so violent that we made 40 miles leeway in the 24 hours. Under these circumstances, I thought it advisable to anchor in the bay of Algiers. It was a lucky event that I did so.

Not far from Algiers is a prominent headland called Cape Casines. In those days it was a celebrated rendezvous for all French Privateers. When we saw it, I desired a strict watch to be kept for the enemy. On the evening of the 20th we were under easy sail, with my convoy close up. I happened to go on the Quarter Deck about 8 o'clock. There being moonlight and scarcely time to look about, I saw a strange settee close on my larboard bow. I inquired of the Officer of the Watch how she came there. He did not appear to be aware of her presence. I instantly ordered a musket shot to be fired at her, and one of the cutters to be lowered, by which means I hoped to be able to send the boat on board the stranger. But I can hardly express my astonishment when I saw the settee making more sail, and attempting to cross my bows to get inshore of me. The hands were instantly turned up to make sail, and a hawser given in to secure the boat, in tow. Out went the reefs of the topsails, and up went the studdingsails. A course was shaped to prevent the chace nearing the land, which lay under our lee and not far off. It was a critical moment, with no time to lose as there was now reason to believe that we had an enemy to deal with. The forecastle nine pounders was (*sic*) removed and run out of the Bow Port. The ship was going 11 knots. More muskets were fired at the stranger, which were not noticed. Presently the bow gun drove a shot into him. I had the satisfaction to perceive that we were gradually nearing the chace. Another shot was sent into this vessel, from which they called out in Spanish, 'Algerine, Algerine.' I desired the sails to be lowered down, but as they did not obey, another shot was fired, which told on board of the settee. Then, instead of putting his head to starboard, which would have kept him clear of the *Leopard*, he put it to port, so that we nearly ran over him. I ordered the helm hard aport, by which our bow took the hull of the chace instead of our cutwater. In that position I called the boarders, intending to lead them myself, being armed for that purpose. When the Ship's Company saw me, sword in hand, desiring them to follow me, they called out, 'We will carry her, Sir. It is not your business to board this vessel, but to command us to do so. We will soon take possession of her.' Many of them closed near me, amongst the number the Chief Boatswain's Mate, Hastings, whom I shall never forget, entreating me in most suppliant terms not to quit the Quarter Deck. They were ready to sacrifice their lives sooner than I should be exposed to any danger. I of course allowed them to proceed.

The supposed enemy was now on our larboard broadside. The seamen boarded her, but before she could be cleared of the ship, her foremast came down and her bowsprit carried away. She proved to be an Algerine from Cape Tres Forcas bound to Algiers with grain. One of his men was killed, a Marabout or Priest. He had about 30 men on board who were brought into the *Leopard*. As none of us understood their language, we could only communicate by signs. We took her in tow, but she was so much injured by the crash she sustained in boarding us that she sánk two or three hours after we had taken possession of her. This was a most unfortunate event, and had occurred entirely by the bad management of the Algerine. What business had he, as a merchant vessel, to come out from the land into my convoy at night? He must have been aware of there being a ship of war protecting the vessels among which he had mixed himself: and by attempting to escape exposed himself to the misfortunes that unluckily befel him, and which no one regretted more than I. When I asked the Master what had induced him to act as he had, and expose himself to my fire, I could only make out that he had taken my ship for an American, and his crew would not obey his orders.

The next morning we anchored in the outward part of the Bay of Algiers, the weather being very boisterous. The usual salute of three guns was fired from the Fort, which indicated a friendly welcome. The salute was returned, and shortly afterwards a barge came alongside containing our Consul, Mr. McDonald, accompanied by one of the Bey's staff officers who came to tender the usual compliments, and to assure me that His Highness would be glad to see me: also that the official present of some cattle and vegetables would soon be alongside. I was glad to receive so amicable a greeting, as I was apprehensive that my having sunk an Algerine would lead to some unpleasant remonstrances. All that had happened was communicated to Mr. McDonald, who requested a written statement, that he might act upon it at the Divan. The unfortunate Algerines were then allowed to make known their case to their officer, who I must say behaved with great command of temper when he heard the account rendered by his unlucky countrymen. He promised that boats should be sent for the crew of the sunken vessel, then demanded whether I would receive on board any of the Christian slaves who might escape from their confinement. 'If you intend doing so,' he said, 'we shall lock them all up. But if you will not, they will be allowed their usual liberty.' Before answering that question, I consulted Mr. McDonald, who was of the opinion that, under the circumstance of the unlucky event that had taken place, it would be prudent on my part to refuse receiving any runaway persons from the Bagnios. I accordingly made that promise to the Bey's officer, who left the ship with our Consul, whom I saluted with 11 guns.

I had long been anxious to visit this place where Christian Slavery with all its horrors still existed, but little thought that I should do so under such unfavourable circumstances. I had apartments in the house of the Vice Consul, Frankovitch, Mr. McDonald's residence being outside of the town. The town has a most imposing effect, all the buildings being perfectly white, and rising one above another from an extended base up a sloping hill covered with verdure till it ends in almost a sharp point on which rests the Castle. The fortifications also are of some magnitude. Batteries are to be seen, wel mounted with heavy calibre in various directions.[1] The streets of this slaving emporium are very narrow. A mule with paniers generally filled up the whole space, and the windows of the houses were placed inwards, looking upon a small yard not sufficiently large to be called a square, which gave the outward walls a sombre appearance. The Dey, Hagi Ali, now sent word that he was too unwell to receive visitors. Whether this sudden illness arose from my having sunk one of his trading vessels did not transpire: but as I could not be admitted to an audience, it was decided that the encounter with the settee should be discussed at a meeting of the Divan. In the meantime many hints were given to me by the officers of the Government that it was not a friendly act to sink a poor merchant vessel, and I might, under proper feelings, make up the loss to the owners. To all these allusions I replied that it was not my fault, and that I was ready to attend the Divan to explain how the accident had occurred. Mr. McDonald made the same declaration. However, he had it in his power to distribute a sort of charitable donation to the distressed seamen of the sunken vessel, which he sent to them.

As I was expecting some unpleasant negotiations relating to this event, I took care to place my ship out of the reach of the guns of the batteries. She therefore lay far out, anchored in 28 fathom water where, luckily for me, there was good holding ground. Some very heavy storms commenced, and serious damage was entertained. The sea broke over all the lower batteries in a frightful manner. These were the gales named Tramontana, which frequently caused shipwreck and disasters on the coast at this season. But the ship rode out all the tremendous weather without accident, having three cables ahead.

The day was at last fixed for my attending the Divan, but I insisted upon no foreigners attending, which was after some difficulty granted. Upon my entering the Divan, I was placed on a sopha near to the Algerine Admiral, Hazi Braim (?Braine?). He had received a desperate wound on his left arm, which was bare below the elbow. He was in appearance a fine old man with an open countenance. He was squatted in the Turkish fashion. Mr. McDonald and his deputy were seated on his left. Whilst the members were preparing their papers on a round table not far from us, the Admiral entertained me

---

[1] A long note, in a later hand, gives more elaborate details of the defences, stating that 500 guns could be brought to bear against an enemy. 'Notwithstanding all these,' he concludes, 'Lord Exmouth, as you know, very soon humbled the pride and the power of those Barbary Pirates.' This occurred on the 27th August, 1816—less than four years after W.H.D.'s visit.

with some amusing accounts of the attentions he had received from our ministers when he had been sent to England, dwelling particularly upon Lords Spencer and Grenville. He had noticed my anxiety, and evidently intended to remove any unpleasant feelings in my mind. No doubt he was aware that I had only done my duty and should be cleared of blame. I could not, of course, understand one word that was spoken by the Counsellors, but watched the expressions of their varied countenances. One of them pointed at me repeatedly, and in a loud tone gave utterance to what I thought was abuse. I instantly turned my back towards him, intending that he should notice my displeasure at his proceeding. I then requested a sheet of paper, pen and ink, and drew an outline of the position of the settee and that of the *Leopard* with her convoy.

[He then restated his case, already described.]

Having succeeded in making myself understood, I withdrew and seated myself near the Admiral. In the course of a few minutes the Council broke up, acquitting me of any blame in the sinking of the Algerine. Then the officer who had pointed at me came to shake me by the hand, explaining through the medium of an interpreter that he had from the commencement advocated my cause; but, having noticed my turning my back upon him, he supposed that I was offended. We shook hands, I thanking him for his good offices. The remainder of the Council also offered their hands, and the Admiral very courteously wished me all health and success. Thus terminated my attendance before the Divan.

During my leisure hours I had visited the grounds where the Christian slaves were set to work. It was a painful sight to behold those poor fellows under the lash of a Moor, watching all their actions and inflicting a cut with his whip if he noticed anyone idle. Several spoke to me, but I could not give them any hopes. Whilst listening to their misfortunes, a fine youth came and caught hold of the skirt of my coat. At first, from his handsome and feminine appearance, I thought it was a female addressing me; but he soon undeceived me. He was an American, a lad of about 17, most beautifully limbed: in other respects the most exquisite shape I have ever beheld. Never had I seen before such a lovely figure of the male sex. However, painful as it was to refuse the supplications of this Adonis, his being subject of the United States, I explained to him, prevented my interference in his behalf, and I hurried away from the spot, regretting that I had been near it. The next thing that deserved notice were the projecting iron hooks upon the outward walls of the bastion, upon which are hurled from the upper part those victims who are sentenced to death. The sight of this place filled my mind with horror, and I hastened away. It was not considered safe for an officer of my rank to walk about in the town. Consequently, I did not show myself much. Nevertheless, before leaving this extraordinary place, I went to the Shampooing Bath, and I can only say that I derived great benefit from the proceedings of the blacks who performed that operation upon me. My attendants handled me rather roughly, as I have a delicate skin. They literally scarified both my thighs, taking away a great deal of the cuteous (*sic*) membrane.

It so happened that the Bey of Oran was in the town, and I requested our Consul to let that Governor know that I was bound to his province to purchase cattle, and that I should feel obliged if he would send his orders there to have them in readiness for me when I arrived. The Bey's answer was civil, but he took no measures whilst in Algiers.

I had to deal with a nation not far removed from pirates: therefore I had regulated my proceedings that no opportunity should be given to the Algerines to commit depredations upon our merchant ships. The whole of my proceedings was communicated to our Consul in an official document which was transmitted to England.

[He gives it in a note. It is omitted here, as it retells exactly the same story for the third time.]

On the 26th, having taken my leave of Mr. McDonald, I put to sea with my convoy for the Bay of Oran, which I reached safely on the morning of the 2nd of November. I anchored in a place called Mazazuvere Bay, opposite to a small fort. The town was about two miles distant, but could not be seen from the ship. Upon landing, I was much disappointed at being informed that the Bey had not yet arrived, and that no cattle could be obtained till he made his appearance. In the meantime the Vice Consul, Mr. Sedgovitch, a foreigner, made himself very agreeable, giving me a bed in his house. The Bey was a noted character, and had, it was well understood, put to death at least 40,000 men in various ways. Such information prepared me for some uncourteous proceedings from this Satrap.

Shortly after my arrival I received a message from the Bey's son, 'the Prince' as he was called, requesting me to allow the Surgeon to visit him as he was suffering from some illness. I fixed an hour, and the Surgeon was punctual to his time, accompanied by the Vice

Consul to the residence of His Highness. The dragoman not being in attendance, no admittance could be obtained. Mr. Sedgovitch, who knew the Prince, attempted an entrance, but was instantly thwarted by a sentinel, a Moor who placed himself across the doorway. The Vice Consul remonstrated with the guard, then tried to get into the palace. The Moor immediately drew a dagger, but, previously to using it, struck him with his hand. Mr. Sedgovitch, knowing with whom he had to deal, instantly left the premises and reported to me all that had passed. The Surgeon also returned to the ship. This brought on 4 o'clock, when the dragoman reappeared, and in a sad melancholy tone complained that the Doctor had not been to visit the Patient. I explain the way in which the sentinel had insulted the Vice Consul, and that the Surgeon had returned on board; upon hearing which the individual positively denied the whole of the transaction. I sent for Mr. Sedgovitch, who related all the particulars of the affront. The dragoman, all astonishment, left us to inquire into these particulars, then returned to intercede with me in a most gloomy mood, representing that, if the Doctor did not visit the Prince, he would lose his head. 'I have nothing to do with that,' I replied. 'His Highness's wishes have been complied with, and in return the English Vice Consul has been grossly insulted. The Surgeon shall not call again until the sentinel be punished for his offence, or that the Prince make an ample apology to the Vice Consul for what has happened. That is my final determination.'

In the course of the evening the dragoman reappeared with a message from his master promising to punish the guard, with a thousand apologies for the mistake that had happened. These expressions were conveyed in such respectful terms that I agreed to direct the Surgeon to proceed to the palace next morning. Accordingly the Doctor, with one of the lieutenants and the Vice Consul, presented themselves. But I had arranged with them that they were not to enter, or see His Highness, until the guard had received his punishment. The dragoman had requested my attendance, but that I declined. The sentinel underwent the Bastinado on the soles of his feet, receiving 100 blows. Then the Surgeon and his party entered the palace and administered relief to the Prince, who expressed himself truly thankful for the attention shewn him, and all unpleasant feeling vanished. I had maintained the honour of my Country in resisting the affront offered to the Vice Consul.

A day or two later one of the Moorish Princes dined with Mr. Sedgovitch. I sat next to this hero. He contrived to make known who he was, and assumed consequential airs. At first he drank wine with me, but some of his sect, watching at the further end of the hall, called out lustily at this act: which had its effect, for he drank no more of the juice of the grape. But a bottle of rum was placed by his side, which liquor he swallowed, to my astonishment, pure, with as much facility as I did the wine. During the entertainment he made frequent eruptions of wind from his throat, which, I was told, was considered an accomplishment among the upper classed Moors. He attempted to give a tune to these noises, all of which were of course to me unintelligible. I think by appearance the Prince had taken his 'quantum suf.', as at parting he covered himself with his bernous that he might not be known, mounted his horse and made off.

One day I was induced to visit the Court where justice was administered, but I noticed that my presence was not very agreeable to the Moors, and I soon retired. A culprit was sentenced to have his right hand cut off for stealing. After the operation I met the man, who had just returned from having dipped his wrist into a tub of hot pitch. The whole proceeding appeared to be regulated by extreme cruelty.

[An account of the womenfolk and another one of the town are omitted.]

The Bey at last made his appearance, and the Vice Consul set to work to purchase the cattle required. But he was informed that nothing could be done until the money was paid. It was, I thought, unusual to pay for an article before it was delivered. I now consulted the Army Commissary, whether he would consent to do so. He replied that he had been instructed to attend to my orders, and he depended entirely on me. My next resource was Mr. Sedgovitch. After some deliberation, he stated that it was the custom of the country, and he had no apprehensions of the Governor's failing in producing what he promised. The dollars were taken to the Bey's palace, who no doubt reaped a good harvest in the bargain made with his underlings. I was told that some days would elapse before the arrival of the horned animals, as they were not yet caught. I inquired of the Vice Consul if there was any chance of my being admitted to an interview with the Governor. He told me that he thought not, as he was not in the best humour. Moreover, I had not made him the usual present, of a certain quantity of gunpowder. As all these points of etiquette had been explained to me by Mr. McDonald at Algiers, I felt myself able to act for myself, and, as I knew from him that this present had been discontinued for some time, I was justified in not making it. 'However,' said I, 'you may explain to His Excellency that it is one of the principal parts of a Mussulman's duty to be hospitable, and charitable to strangers. As I am the stranger and visitor, he is bound by the articles of his faith to commence that ceremony towards me. Should he make me a present suitable to my station, he may rely upon receiving an equivalent. Please to mention this to him.' The Vice Consul complied accordingly: but no notice was taken of the communication by the Bey.

I tried to purchase a good saddle horse for the Admiral, but could not find one suited to my purpose. I then began to bargain for a good stock of poultry, but the Governor in some measure thwarted all my purposes, and gave directions to the people in the market not to supply me with more than one fowl per day, saying, 'The English Captain cannot, as a man, require more than one fowl a day.' I therefore had to devise some plan of my own to procure all that I wanted. I made an arrangement with the market people to supply every man belonging to the *Leopard* with a fowl daily instead of beef, saying that the cattle would be kept for the other ships and our troops, and that my Ship's Company preferred the poultry. This plan was at last agreed upon, and I had at my disposal nearly 200 of the feathered tribe per day, in spite of the Bey's orders.

On the 18th information reached me that the cattle were coming, and preparations were made to receive them. As I had sent my linen to be washed, my servant went to the Vice Consul's house to receive it. As he came away, my trunks were seized and secured in the Custom House by its officers. The next morning I called upon Mr. Sedgovitch, requesting him to accompany me to the Bey's. When we reached the palace, he took off his shoes: such is the custom of the country. But I had boots on which could not be slipped off so easily. The officer in attendance desired me to take them off. The Vice Consul very kindly explained to him that it would be an annoyance to me, at that moment, to do so. After a few moments of parley, I finally made up my mind not to take them off, stating that the Captain of an English ship of war had come to His Excellency on affairs of importance, and, whilst he had his sword on, he should present himself in full attire. I then advanced into the hall, where I saw the Bey sitting crosslegged on a mat, waiting to receive persons on business. Mr. Sedgovitch explained the object of my visit. He desired me to approach and, evidently with reluctance, gave me his hand. He remarked that there were Custom Houses in our ports, and that luggage was detained there for examination. 'Most certainly,' I replied, 'under particular circumstances': but that my trunks did not contain merchandise: that they had never been detained in any friendly port in such an abrupt manner as they were yesterday, and that they contained nothing but my linen, which had been washed a few days before. He hesitated. At last Mr. Sedgovitch told him in my name and behalf that, if he would not liberate the trunks, I should in a couple of hours bring my ship abreast of the town, and lay it about his ears with a few broadsides. It was therefore for him to consider whether he would run the risk of offending such a power as England upon such trifling grounds. Not receiving any reply, I was in the act of retiring, fully determined to act as I had stated, when he consented to set them free. I next requested him to send one of his officers to the Custom House to convey his commands to those on duty there. To that he assented also. I then again took his hand in token of amity, and instantly retired. When I reached the beach, I directed my boat's crew to enter the Custom House and take possession of my effects. The guard, seeing this, allowed them to do so without impediment. I now took my leave of the Vice Consul, saying that he would not see me on shore again, as I had had quite enough of the Moors.

By the 19th the bullocks had arrived under the convoy of an officer commanding a detachment of about 150 men. All the boats were now employed to embark the cattle, provender, vegetables, etc. My communications with the shore were carried on through a Jew who understood Spanish, but, to keep order, I had as usual landed a strong party of Marines. As it was dark by 6 o'clock, I directed lanterns to be used on shore, wishing if possible to complete the embarkation that night. But the work did not proceed so quickly as I expected, and I was going on shore to expedite them. When I reached the Quarter Deck, the effect of candlelight still operating upon my eyes, I could not distinguish any object. I had not made more than three or four paces, when I came in contact with an individual and demanded who he was. No answer being made, I began to handle him. Judge then of my surprise when I beheld a white turban close to my face. There was no officer on deck. I called out for one, then, seizing the turbaned fellow by the shoulder (who had already saluted me with a whiff of the smoke of tobacco in my face) I turned him round and kicked him forward till we reached the gangway. By this time I had recovered my sight. An officer approached, but no account could be given to me how this person had got on board. I ordered the sidesmen to hand him down into a shore boat that lay alongside. They obeyed, and the turbaned hero left the ship. The Officer of the Watch received a jobation for not keeping a better look out.

I hurried on shore, it being then past 7 o'clock, when the Jew contractor came to acquaint me that I had given great offence to the Moorish Commanding Officer by kicking him out of my ship: who, knowing of my being on shore, would instantly take his revenge. This information, I confess, staggered me with apprehensions. 'Do you know the officer?' I demanded. 'Yes,' he replied. 'Then go instantly to him from me,' I said, 'and explain that I did not know he had been aboard of my ship. The annoyance which he has experienced has been occasioned by his not having sent me a message to prepare me. He came alongside in a little shabby boat in the dark. Had he given me notice, I should have received him with the attentions due to his rank.'—I understood he was a Major—'Therefore it is all his own doing, and he must take the consequence. However,' I added, 'should this statement not satisfy him, you see that I have soldiers, all armed and ready for any event, and my seamen on the beach are numerous: so that he had better be cautious in his proceedings.' The Jew, who had already heard how the sentinel at the Prince's palace had been bastinadoed for his conduct towards Mr. Sedgovitch, probably thought he had better exert himself to prevent an hostile meeting, and hurried off to the fort, about 200 yards distant. He had scarcely left me when loud shouting was distinctly heard in the fort, torch lights were in motion, and the blades of bright scimitars were plainly seen waving in the air. The Moors were coming out and forming into a body of attack. It now became my duty to prepare for the worst. I collected all the seamen belonging to the transports and my own, and drew them up in a line, with the oars and boathooks stretched out. The Marines, with fixed bayonets and muskets loaded, were ranged a few steps in advance, and the lanterns divided in such a manner as to show a good line of defence. Then, addressing both seamen and marines, I desired them to be ready to charge when I gave the word. I decided that, if the Moors came on, the Marines were in the first instance to take good aim and fire: then we were to rush on in a close body.

By this time the Moors appeared to be at a stand, and presently the Jew returned, acquainting me that my explanation had in a great measure pacified the Moor. 'Very well,' said I. 'Let him come and shake hands.' Off went the Jew and soon came back to say that the Major was satisfied. He could not speak English, and thought it would be useless coming down to me: but he should feel much obliged if I could supply him with some water, as his men had not had any since they occupied the fort. Very fortunately the seamen had several kegs of it, which I placed at the disposal of the Jew, who took them to the Moors. Thus ended all our warlike preparations. I did not find out how many men the Major had, but they appeared about 100. They were only armed with sabres, and therefore had not much chance of driving us off the beach. Having superintended the embarkation of several head of cattle, I returned on board, and all the bullocks, with provender, etc., were taken into the transports during the night.

On the morning of the 21st I got under way and shaped my course towards Alicant. We encountered some very heavy weather, and the ship laboured in a most extraordinary manner, the water coming in through the seams. I scarcely ever recollect seeing a ship feel the effects of a gale more. However, by care and attention no injury of consequence occurred, and we anchored in the bay of Alicant on the afternoon of the 25th. The *Malta* and the *Fame* were lying there. When I paid my respects to the Admiral, he apprehended that my coolness with the Bey would have led to some disagreeable personalities to myself. One of our naval captains had been some years before put in irons in one of the African ports. I knew that officer well, Capt. Dunn.[1] 'I suppose,' said the Admiral, 'you have been Dicky-Dunned?' 'No, Sir,' said I. 'Nothing like it. I have managed my affairs better, and have carried my point in all cases of necessity.' He dwelt a long while upon the duration of my absence. 'You have been away 6 weeks,' he often repeated. He made no complaint: at the same time I could not help perceiving that there was a slight change in his usual cordiality. No time was lost in landing the cattle for our troops, and I supplied all my naval friends with poultry. All complimented me upon my proceedings among the Algerines, and maintaining with spirit the honour of my country.

Whatever may have been the private opinion of Ad. Hallowell, he very soon ordered the *Leopard* to Altea upon a very responsible duty. He selected me to act in conjunction with an English officer, Whittingham, who held the rank of General in the Spanish army. He had been pitched upon by Gen. Campbell, who held the chief command of our troops here, to drive away the French at Denia. When I waited on my Admiral, I was, I confess, startled when I heard the complimentary address which he bestowed upon me. 'Since you have

---

[1] Richard Dalling Dunn, Lt. 17/11/1790; Cdr. 24/12/98; Capt. 29/10/1801.

left the bay of Altea, the French have entered and plundered the place. We don't feel easy for the safety of that town, and the General is determined to send a strong detachment to clear out these troublesome Frenchmen. As you have so ably kept them at bay whilst stationed there, you are the proper officer to assist Gen. Whittingham in putting these fellows to the rout. He has 1700 men under his command. You are to assist him in all his operations as far as it can be done by your ship. The Captain of the *Brune*, now at Altea, will receive instructions to put himself under your orders.'

When I heard this, my heart bounded for joy, and I at last thought that an opportunity had turned up to render some important service to the cause in which I was engaged. The arrangements were soon settled. Gen. Whittingham was to quit his quarters that night, and I was to keep up a communication with him as he marched along the coast until he reached Altea. We were then to unite our forces and act together. I took my leave of the Admiral under excited feelings, expecting soon to be able to send him a report of having cleared this part of the coast of the French.*

On the afternoon of the 28th I got under way. So anxious was the Admiral to expedite my proceedings, there being scarcely any wind, that he ordered all the *Malta's* boats to tow us out to sea. Shortly afterwards a light breeze sprang up, which enabled me to shape a course along shore. My first object was to place myself in communication with Gen. Whittingham, to whom I sent a letter by one of the lieutenants to Villajoyosa, where I understood he was to be found. He returned to it a verbal answer that he would meet me at Altea the next day by 11 o'clock.

[This letter is given in full in the MS., but omitted here since it merely repeats the orders which W.H.D. has just received from Ad. Hallowell.]

On the following morning I anchored in Altea Bay. I instantly sent on shore to Orosco and the authorities, desiring them to prepare for attacking the enemy, as a detachment of the army would soon

---

* An old friend, an officer of the artillery, called to see me. The details he gave of the retreat of our Army from Burgos I shall not easily forget. He had been under the Duke of Wellington during his successful entry into Madrid, and also present at the attack upon the firstnamed town. Our Army, it seems, suffered during that retreat not only from the inclemency of the weather, but equally so from want of food, and no tents. When the Duke made his official report, he coolly stated 'that under all these trying circumstances the Army had not experienced any privations.' This was so decidedly opposed to what that Army literally did undergo that all hands were vexed that their sufferings had not been made known to the Country.

make its appearance. From Capt. Badcock[1] of the *Brune* I was informed that the enemy had sent in one night 25 of his cavalry, and had plundered the Mayor's house of some hundreds of dollars which had been secreted under the sill of his door. That proceeding proved to me that there was a constant communication between the town and the French, by spies: but I had kept such a sharp look out when formerly stationed here that the enemy never could take me by surprise. The Captain of the *Brune* had not followed my plan. The pass on the hill had been neglected, and instead of having his boats armed at night watching the beach, he had placed a few men in a . mill not far from the main road, whence he thought he could obstruct the advance of the French. But they seized the opportunity of a dark night, and marched in unobserved by his men. They reported next morning that they thought they heard something moving on the road, but could not see anything. Could they only have made a stir it would have frustrated the enemy's plans, as it was evident they never intended to expose themselves to the fire of a ship's broadside. However, the mischief had been done, and we were now to prevent a recurrence. Having prepared Capt. Badcock for the part he would have to act, I hastened ashore and found all the authorities assembled at the Bishop's residence, where a collation was prepared for the General. Orosco was in attendance with several guerillas, himself cutting a fine figure, his horse in good order and another in readiness for me. The inhabitants had crowded round the mansion, waiting in anxious suspense the arrival of Gen. Whittingham, who, they thought, would free them from all further annoyance from the French.

At last he arrived, in splendid regimentals, accompanied by an officer and about 15 horsemen. I naturally inquired for the remainder of his force—the 1700 men. He coolly replied that they were in the rear. He expressed a desire to partake of some refreshment, which was served. The conversation did not take any very interesting turn. All this time the crowd remained on the premises watching the event. The General, having satisfied his appetite, with great composure smoked a cigar. Time passed on, and I became anxious to commence operations. He at length rose and, looking out of the window, inquired in what direction the enemy lay? I pointed to the high road

---

[1] William Stanhope Badcock, Lt. 29/1/1806; Cdr. 13/8/12; Capt. 21/8/15. He was thus, at this time, not only not a Captain, but also barely a Commander. He changed his name in 1840 to Lovell. It is amusing to note that, in O'Byrne, it is claimed for him that he performed the very task which W.H.D. accuses him of not performing —'preventing a French foraging party, 300 strong, from levying contributions on the inhabitants of Altea.'

and the hill which led to Denia. What instructions the General had received were of course unknown to me, but in all that passed between us not one word dropped from him expressing any desire to come in contact with the enemy. What his object had been in coming to Altea he never mentioned. I naturally expected something would be done without loss of time. I urged him to advance, and offered to lead him over the mountain, although that was not my duty, which was on board of my ship. At last he exclaimed, 'If they would come into the plain, I would cut them into pork pieces.' 'They won't come there,' I said. 'You may rely upon it. They will not come in contact with the fire of our ships. If you will not go to them, they won't come to you.' But the General, having satisfied his curiosity, remounted his horse and rode off with his attendants.

Never shall I forget the disappointed countenances of all present. The crowd gradually retired. Then up came Orosco and the guerillas. Their looks expressed more than I can convey. They appeared humbled beyond description, and seemed to indicate that their hopes now lay on me. I was completely puzzled how to act with these Spaniards. I talked with one, listened to another, and by degrees persuaded them to take care of themselves. I then made some calls on my acquaintances, and contrived to bring on 4 o'clock. That being my dinner hour, I told those who still hung about that I must retire to dine. They, understanding me, withdrew under feelings of the deepest depression, while I took to my boat and returned to the *Leopard*. I then sent for the Captain of the *Brune* and acquainted him that, as our warlike preparations were at an end, I should return to Alicant. From Gen. Whittingham I learnt nothing, and never saw more of him. As he never indicated any intention of coming on with his 1700 men—they were not all English—I felt myself justified in quitting Altea and reporting to my Admiral.

As soon as it became dark, and the Alteans could not see what was passing, I up anchor and sailed out. The next day I rejoined Ad. Hallowell, who was all astonishment at seeing me. 'Well,' said he, 'what have you done with the Frenchmen?' 'I have not seen them,' I replied. 'I met the General according to agreement'—then recounted all that had occurred between us. There being nothing to do, I thought it my duty to come to him for further orders. He expressed the keenest disappointment, then approved all I had done. 'It is quite clear,' he said, 'you could not act without the troops. So there's an end of this glorious transaction.'

I now received instructions to give a passage to a Spanish Major to Villa Nova in Catalonia. Previous to my putting to sea, the *Thames*, Capt. Napier,[1] put in. On the afternoon of the 2nd (Dec.) I quitted Alicant. The *Leopard* required a regular refit. Consequently, after landing my Spaniard, I had orders to repair to Minorca for that purpose. Nothing occurred while bound there. By the 9th I reached Villa Nova, where I found the *Blake*, 74, Capt. Codrington.[2] He had made himself extremely useful to the Spanish cause. He took charge of my companion, the Major, whom I found a very intelligent person. At parting he insisted upon my receiving a broken sword, which he had used in the war. As a soldier, he said, it was all he could give, and entreated my acceptance of it. I had it repaired. But, somehow or other, it disappeared from my cabin.

Taking my leave of the *Blake*, I made sail for Port Mahon, where I anchored in safety on the 11th. I found lying here the *Caledonia*, with Sir Edward Pellew's Flag, and most of the Fleet, with Ad. Sir Richard King[3] and Sir Sidney Smith, taking shelter during the winter months, a small squadron remaining off Toulon, watching the enemy's motions. As I had come in to refit, the ship was moored into a sort of cove called by the Spanish 'Calo.' Sir Edward Pellew entertained the captains and officers of his Fleet: Sir Sidney Smith also, and Ad. Pickmore. Several captains, among the number your humble servant, formed a kind of Mess at the principal inn of the town. Sir Sidney Smith generally attended it, and never failed in wit and anecdotes. Others were incessant in relating the most entertaining events in the foreign countries they had visited, and I came in for my share. Many pleasant hours were passed on those occasions. From the *Caledonia* I received a large packet of letters, two or three from the First Lord of the Admiralty, who had directed our Commander in Chief to give me the first vacant frigate. His Lordship had taken interest in my cause, and I had every reason to be satisfied. I had many conversations with my Verdun friend Capt. Gower[4] of the *Elizabeth*. Whenever the subject of Prize Money was mentioned, he would constantly repeat, 'Whatever you make, they (alluding to the Admiralty) will have it out of you.'

[1] This is the famous Admiral 'Charlie' Napier, who, during his command of the *Thames*, performed many of those brilliant land-sea operations which were the foundation of his reputation. See O'Byrne and *D.N.B.*

[2] (Ad. Sir) Edward Codrington, (G.C.B., etc.), the victor of Navarino. Like Napier in the *Thames*, he made a great name for himself during his long command of the *Blake*, 1808–13. See O'Byrne and *D.N.B.*

[3] Sir Richard King, Bart. (K.C.B.), Lt. 14/11/1791; straight to Capt. 14/5/94; R-Ad. 12/8/1812; V-Ad. 19/7/21. Died, C. in C. Nore, 4/8/34.

[4] See above, p. 41, note.

[He was well received at the Hermitage, the temporary home of the Duchess of Orleans: and, as he knew her to be hard up, he was, when he dined there, 'permitted the liberty of introducing my own wine.' He also ordered his Joiner to make 'a very handsome reading desk, which proved very acceptable when the Duchess went to prayers.' Sir Sidney also entertained her (and W.H.D.) very lavishly in his ship, and 'never failed to attend the dancing parties on shore, figuring away at them with more spirit, grace and ease than the youngest man present.' At one of these Christmas festivities, 'Sir Edward Pellew took an opportunity of assuring me that he was anxious to place me in a more active ship, if any vacancy occurred.' . . . 'I passed in Port Mahon some of the most pleasant hours of my life.']

When the *Leopard* had completed her refit, I was not allowed to remain long an idler, as the Admiral, about the 10th of this month [January 1813], gave me instructions to take charge of three transports. The next morning I received an invitation to breakfast with him. When it was over, he took me into his private cabin, and I expected some confidential communication, which came out as follows:—' I am directed by the whole Fleet to appeal to your feelings in behalf of the Spanish Governor of this Island. He has resigned his command in consequence of his advanced age, and has accepted, as a sort of retirement, the Deputy Governorship of the island of Majorca. He is a Grandee of Spain, and the particular favourite of the King. All the captains here say that you are the proper person to convey him to his destination. I therefore address you in their names.' In replying to Sir Edward, I assured him that I felt the compliment, and that I willingly accepted the office required. At the same time I clearly pointed out that my cabin was most homely, and probably not suitable for an individual of such high rank. When this affair was settled, he took me in his boat to the Government House, and presented me to the Don, I. Gregorio. The family consisted of himself, his wife, three daughters, rather young, and a son of maturity—an officer in the Army—so that, with servants of both sexes and the priest, I had to receive 25 persons on board of my ship: also a good lot of furniture. I took him to the *Leopard*, that he might give such directions for his personal comforts as he thought fit, and no time was lost in receiving his luggage, furniture, etc. Sir Edward now sent for me to breakfast, and kindly said that he was aware of the difficulty of my position—mind this—and he would in consequence give me an official order, that my expenses might be defrayed. This was an agreeable surprise. I had willingly, to oblige my brother officers, exposed myself to a considerable outlay by carrying so large a family.

By 11 o'clock in the forenoon of the 13th I weighed anchor, and made sail out of Port Mahon with my transports. Three fine seamen came from these vessels and entered for my ship. This occasioned some unpleasant correspondence with the Government Agent, which ended in Sir Edward Pellew taking those men out of my ship and putting them on board of the *Caledonia*. The island of Majorca was at no great distance from Minorca, but I had scarcely cleared the harbour than I was assailed by unfavourable winds. Therefore, instead of reaching it in one day, I was four getting there. The ladies were seasick, and my poultry were speedily reduced in numbers to supply them with broth, etc. But the worst of all was the General's son who, being nearly blind, cut off all the points of my silver forks. You may in some shape understand what one is exposed to in receiving passengers. My crockery and glasses were broken so rapidly that I had few left for use.

On the afternoon of the 17th we anchored in Palma Bay, Majorca. Next day, being the Queen's Birthday, I fired the usual salute. The Spanish Governor could not understand the meaning of this cannonade until it was explained to him. As there were no houses ready for the Deputy Governor, he still continued on board, but the ladies were landed, and the baggage and furniture. Having brought a Spanish Grandee to the island, I experienced the utmost attention from the Marquis, the Governor. I dined with him, and accompanied him to the theatre. Whilst in his box, I was requested by a lady whose husband was residing at Alicant to give her a passage there: and I ascertained that her family consisted of 19 persons. 'How long will it take you to get ready?' I inquired. She was not in any way ready, it seemed, to leave at a few hours' notice.

[The story, long even for W.H.D., of how he contrived to escape taking her, is omitted. He returned without her to Alicant, arriving on the 21st January.]

Not many days after my Grandee had left us, my Steward brought me a blue bag, which he said belonged to the Priest of the Spaniard's establishment. When it was opened we there found some loose papers and a few prayerbooks. But what was my astonishment when out came some Conjuring Boxes? The Holy Man evidently made use of these upon particular occasions to deceive the credulous.

Whilst I was at dinner one day with Admiral Hallowell, one of our brigs of war came in with a few thousand dollars on board, intended for the use of the Spanish Army stationed in Catalonia, and the Admiral proposed to me to take them there. I was shortly afterwards at sea. One evening, the weather being fine, I was close inshore when a boat was seen coming towards us, with some ladies in it, accompanied by gentlemen (in appearance). They wished to come on board, but as this part of the coast of Spain was occupied by the French Army, I did not admit them, naturally supposing that they were anxious to obtain some information, or to ascertain my ship's armament. However, they were not indulged, and when they found that no notice was taken of them they returned to the shore. Probably they were spies, as the French in Spain resorted to all manner of means to obtain intelligence.

On the evening of the 27th I saw some suspicious vessels inshore, and sent my boats manned and armed, to examine them. Meantime the ship was anchored in the Bay of Alfaques. At 10 o'clock the boats returned, having detained two settees from Gibraltar; but, as they were manned by Spaniards who were in constant communication with the enemy, and their papers not in correct order, I took possession of them. It appeared that they were selling their goods, English manufactures, to the French Army. Those gentlemen not being able to supply their wants from France, adopted this plan. It was a lucrative transaction for the traders of the Rock, but as the account given by the principal Spaniard on this occasion, who it seems was a smuggler, was not satisfactory, I was determined to retain them until I obtained further information. Very fortunately, shortly afterwards I fell in with one of our brigs of war, the *Merope*, whose Captain, Roberts,[1] knowing all that was going on, explained to me that the Authorities of Gibraltar winked at it, and encouraged this sort of smuggler, who carried on an extensive traffic with the coast of Spain. Consequently I liberated the vessels. They had plenty of gold doubloons in their cabins, being what they had realised on the articles sold. Some time after, when at Gibraltar, I pointed out to the Governor the impropriety of these vessels not being properly registered, that their papers did not correspond to the description of them, and, as this irregularity was at variance with our Navigation laws, every ship of war that fell in with them was justified in their detention. He acknowledged this neglect of the officers of the Customs,

---

[1] John Charles Gawen Roberts, Lt. 12/10/1805; Cdr. 23/7/12; Capt. 13/6/15; Ret. Capt. 1846.

thanked me for the information, and promised to have it remedied: which, I learnt, in due time was actually fulfilled.[1]

On the evening of the 31st I anchored in Salou Bay, Catalonia, not far from Tarragona. I lost no time in communicating with the Capt. General of the Province, the Baron D'Eroles. This distinguished patriot found his way to the *Leopard* and was received with a salute of 13 guns. He dined with me and enjoyed himself. He gave directions for the disposal of the dollars. At parting, I agreed to proceed to his headquarters and pass a couple of days with him. The next day he sent his own favourite charger, to carry me to Reus, over 5 or 6 miles of open country. Half a dozen Spanish cuirassiers were in attendance to escort me free of all dangers from the enemy. I never felt myself so well mounted as I was on this dark bay, beautifully limbed and with splendid action. The Spaniards, I soon noticed, were anxious to discover how I should acquit myself as an equestrian. An English Naval Officer in their company was something new. I had dressed in a blue morning coat, not uniform, and had slung inside of it my sabre, to be prepared for coming events. Noticing the French sentinels on the fortified walls of Tarragona watching my motions, I preferred going at a slow pace, thinking it would not do to pass in a hurry, as if in fear: and I suspect that we passed within musket shot of the enemy's lookouts. When we were well clear, we increased our speed to a hand gallop. I slackened the bridle, and my steed, being homeward bound, dashed on with spirit, leaving the cuirassiers in the rear. As we proceeded, we unexpectedly came in contact with a row of donkeys, coming out of a pass with skins of wine hanging on their sides. I was apprehensive of some mischief, but my charger, sooner than be pulled in, literally leapt over two or three of them with as much ease as a cat would over mice. No accident occurred. We soon entered the town, and found our way to the Captain General's residence.

I was much entertained with all I saw in Reus. Every hour almost, news came in relating to the French, and many anecdotes of the difficulties they met with. It required an escort of 1200 men to send a courier into France: their officers were constantly being killed or plundered.

[The account of the remainder of his visit to Reus is omitted.]

I had been informed that an English merchant ship had been captured by the French, and lay close in with the beach of Tarragona.

[1] See Intro., p. 169.

It appeared that the officers of that army seized every opportunity of fitting out small sailing vessels or large boats, with which they sailed out to sea and frequently caught some of our stray merchant ships, brought them in, and disposed of their cargoes to advantage. They managed these affairs with extreme dexterity, cunning and secrecy. I was anxious to make an attempt to bring away the vessel mentioned, but the more I weighed the chances of success, the difficulties became so apparent that I gave up all thought of engaging my crew in such a desperate undertaking, merely in order to bring away an empty merchantman. Therefore I left Salou Bay on the morning of the 7th, little thinking of what was about to happen.

The Spanish Government, such as it was, or the Junta's, aware of the services rendered by our Navy in protecting their coasts, showed some anxiety to remunerate the British Captains for their exertions. They in consequence established regulations authorizing our cruizers to capture all Spanish vessels, trading or having communication with the ports occupied by the French Army; and in some instances placed their Navigation laws upon the same footing as ours, intending by that arrangement to prevent our Naval Officers making other claims, as the Spaniards would naturally say, in case of an appeal, 'We allow you the same claims as those granted by your own Government. You have no right to complain.' On my way back to Alicant, I fell in with the *Blake, Invincible*, 74, and three sloops of war at anchor off a place called Arans del Mare,[1] and I anchored there, anxious to obtain from the Senior Officer, Codrington, information of passing events. On the evening of the 9th, however, I parted from the squadron. The following day I passed so close to the town of Barcelona that all the French troops turned out, expecting that we intended attacking the place. I had a good view of those gentry with my glass from the Main Top. As night came on, the enemy no doubt returned to his quarters.

On the morning of the 14th, about 3 o'clock, having very light airs, I boarded a Spanish brig in ballast, from Villa Nova bound to Vinaroz. When I heard of this destination, I sent for the Master and warned him against going into that place, as if he attempted to put in there, I should seize his vessel, as the French Army had possession of that town and his brig would be liable to seizure as a Prize. He finally promised not to go in. Strictly speaking, I might if I had chosen have taken possession of this brig on the Master's own assertion, as he acknowledged being bound to a port occupied by the

[1] Arenys de Mar.

enemy. However, this vessel was in ballast, and not of sufficient consequence to lead me to any decided measures. I allowed the Spaniard to return on board, cautioning him to mind what he was about. We were about 10 miles from the place (Vinaroz). During the day we still had light airs with scarcely steering way, the brig being close to us. In the afternoon he availed himself of a few light puffs to draw inshore. As the evening advanced, he widened his distance, and I hauled towards him. A sudden breeze sprang up in his favour, and with that advantage he instantly crowded all sail inshore. The breeze did not extend to my ship: nevertheless I had wind enough to manage the *Leopard*. I made sail after him, but as I had no pilot I dared not stand too close in. I therefore anchored and sent in two of my boats, well armed, under the Second Lieutenant, Vickery,[1] with orders, if he could not bring out the brig, to set her on fire: but by no means to land, or run the least risk of coming in contact with the French troops who were in some force at Vinaroz. All these motions were seen by the French and Spaniards. Fortunately we had moonlight. My boats had not been long away when we not only heard but plainly saw the fire of musketry. As I naturally expected that some of my men would be wounded, the Surgeon received orders to prepare. The firing ceased at about ½ past 9 o'clock, and a most awful suspense hung over us.

About ½ past 11 o'clock one of the boats returned with a wounded seaman, and I was informed that, just as the boats had got near to the brig, they observed several hawsers from that vessel leading to an immense crowd of men on the beach, who succeeded in hauling her on shore. The French troops were drawn out in a long extended line, and kept up an incessant fire upon the boats. The Lieutenant, in compliance with his orders, did not land, but he noticed two settees close to the shore which he thought he might as well bring out. In the midst of the enemy's fire he boarded them and, finding no one in possession, cut their cables and brought them away. By 1 o'clock the two settees anchored close to us. When Mr. Vickery made his report, it appeared perfectly miraculous that he and all his party were not killed. There were many bullets in the boats, and the blades of the oars were shot through in a most extraordinary manner: but the sails of the settees were still worse, for so soon as the Frenchmen noticed our boats towing them out, their whole fire was directed upon them. The owners of the vessels brought out had to thank the Master of the brig for their loss. They were loaded with dried beans,

[1] See above, p. 172 n.

arubas, for the French cavalry. No papers were found on board. They were lawful Prizes cut out from under the enemy's fire.

At daylight I got under way. Weighing in my mind what to do with the Prizes brought out from Vinaroz—they were not of any value—I supposed that the circumstances alone of their having been cut out was sufficient proof as to their being enemy property, and that taking them to Gibraltar would not be sanctioned by my Admiral, who wanted the services of my ship. I therefore thought I should be justified in selling them to the highest bidder when an opportunity offered.

On the afternoon of the 17th we were close to Cape St. Martins, not far from Denia. A rakish schooner was observed close in under the Cape. Many of the crew expressed a desire to be sent in to attack her. Noticing this spirit, I hove the *Leopard* to. We plainly saw hawsers from what we took to be a Privateer, leading to the shore, and the vessel was sheltered inside a low craggy rock which covered the hull from our view. She was too securely moored to be easily captured. The risks appeared too serious, as the loss of many lives would have been the consequence had I sent my boats to attempt cutting her out. I therefore gave up all idea of attacking her. But I had scarcely rounded the Cape when a strange brig was seen standing towards us. We were soon afterwards becalmed, but now I witnessed what often happens in this climate. The strange vessel had studding-sails set, and we had them out, nearing her, both of us having the wind aft. However, in a few minutes we were both without a breath of air. She was about 8 miles off, evidently a merchantman. The evening was setting in, and I thought it too far to send my boats to her, but left directions for a sharp look out on her motions. The calm continued during the night, but when, at dawn, I inquired for the stranger, I was told she was no longer to be seen. ' You say it has been a calm all night,' I said. 'We are in the same position we were last evening, and the brig was outside of us. Where is she now? Has she sunk or been burned?' I hastened on deck with my spy-glass. I swept the horizon to seaward, but saw nothing. Then, directing it inshore, I beheld the brig being towed by a boat. I instantly ordered one to be sent to her, and the others were got out. Mr. Vickery hastened away and boarded the stranger when she was so near the beach that she would soon have been on it. The crew had made off. The Lieutenant took her in tow, and prevented her striking on shore. There was scarcely any wind, and I ordered the other boats to go and assist in towing out the brig.

In a couple of hours she was brought close to us, and proved to be a Spanish brig deeply laden with cocoa that had been captured by the French, who had taken to their heels when they saw my boat approaching. No papers were found, but there was a part of a log book not connected with our present time. A few scraps were picked up with French writing, and some buttons belonging to the French regimentals. The only living animal on board was a cat. Properly speaking, therefore, this was an abandoned vessel, a derelict. The officers and Ship's Company were in high spirits at our having taken a Prize. This vessel had been captured by a party of French soldiers who had sailed out in a boat. They had landed when mine got near, and had no doubt joined their regiment under Gen. Judin. I instantly shaped a course for Altea. The winds were light, so that we made slow progress. I had now three Prizes in company, quite an event. The next morning we noticed a large boat full of soldiers standing towards the brig, which lay at some distance from us. I instantly sent mine, manned and armed, to capture them, but they were so rapid in their motions towards the shore that they escaped. On the afternoon of the 20th I anchored in the Bay of Altea. When Orosco came on board, hearing what had happened, he offered to purchase the settees. I at last agreed to sell them. He put down 1200 dollars, which I distributed to the officers and seamen.

On the 21st I up anchor and, taking the brig in tow, let it go in the Bay of Alicant the next morning. Ad. Hallowell was quite astonished at my bringing in a Prize. He was also excited at the entertainment I had given to the Captain General of Catalonia. As he did not understand foreign languages, he could not make allowances for those who did. I gave him a full explanation of all my proceedings, and of my having sold the vessels cut out from Vinaroz. He had his doubts of the propriety of that proceeding. I dwelt upon the Spanish decree. However, to set matters right, the case was laid before the Spanish authorities of Alicant, who approved and confirmed all I had done. All these acts, I noticed, made an impression upon the Admiral, and he laughed at my hoisting the English flag over the French on board the brig. 'What am I to do?' I demanded. 'It is quite plain that the French had captured her, and I have retaken her.' Many Spaniards came on board to offer the portion allowed by their Government for recapturing the brig. But, thinking that my Admiral would be inclined to make some remarks, I refused them all, then requested him to allow me to take her to Gibraltar, where the Admiralty Court would decide what was usual. Shortly

afterwards I was ordered to take 4 vessels in convoy. My Prize not
being in very good order, I was obliged to take out some of the cargo
to lighten her.

[In a long note W.H.D. illustrates the rudimentary nature of
'Security' at this period. A certain French gentleman, M. de Montron,
had been arrested in Alicant, and sent on board the *Malta*, where,
'having an engaging appearance', he was admitted to the Admiral's
cabin and table, and permitted to dine with the captains of other
ships, W.H.D. included. On that occasion he boasted openly of being
'one of the Admiral's Privy Council, as, when anything of consequence was going on, he was sure to be present.' After being thus
lightly 'detained' for some time, 'he was allowed to return to the
shore, where he joked and turned into ridicule all he had witnessed
on board the English Flagship. It turned out afterwards that de
Montron was a gentleman of fortune who was travelling for his
amusement.' But, equally, he might have been something much more
dangerous.]

I left on the afternoon of the 23rd, taking 40 Sicilian soldiers, the
convoy and Prize in company. The next day I fell in with the
Aboukir, 74, commanded by my old friend Capt. George Parker.[1]
He came from England with Sir John Murray, who was to take the
command of our troops in this part. I was presented to the General,
as well to his lady, whom I had met at Lord Mulgraves'. In passing
Carthagena I met the brig of war *Charger*. On the 1st of March I was
close to Gibraltar, but the weather was dreadfully stormy, and as I
stood in to the Mole my ship took the ground. At that moment the
storm was raging with all its fury. I made the signal for assistance.
The Government Pilot came on board, but fortunately the ship was
blown off. I then anchored. However, it would not hold in the ground.
The Pilot left the ship, considering he could not be of any use to us.
Our case appeared a hopeless one. The anchor was weighed with
difficulty. We noticed the twirling gale drawing up the sea in columns,
upwards of 100 feet in the air. Altogether the scene was an awful one.
These storms at Gibraltar are what they call the Levanters, and
generally happen every winter. So soon as I was able to set some sail,
the fore topsail was split by the violence of the wind and the yard

---

[1] (Sir) George Parker (K.C.B.), Lt. 13/3/1782; Cdr. 4/11/93; Capt. 7/4/95; R-Ad.
4/6/1814; V-Ad. 19/7/21; Ad. 10/1/37.   Died (Ad. of the Red), 24/12/47. Nephew of
Sir Peter Parker, who took him to sea when he was 6 years old, and promoted him to
Lt. when he was under 15.

was carried away. This accident rendered the ship not very manageable. Therefore, instead of renewing my attempt to anchor under the Rock, I stood towards the Orange Grove, on the coast of Spain, St. Roque overlooking it. Soon after 12 o'clock I had placed the *Leopard* in a better position and let go the anchor in deep water, 34 fathoms, and veered out plenty of cable. On this trying occasion my crew behaved uncommonly well. A new topsail yard was soon crossed. The Prize had reached a safe anchorage in the Mole. I noticed a merchant brig that had several of her sails torn away by the gale, driving about in the centre of the Bay in a most helpless situation. No boats from the Rock went to her assistance, fearing, no doubt, the effect of the storm. In the end she reached Algesiras. In my new anchorage I lay under the neutral ground. I struck the topgallant masts and made all snug. The anchor held in spite of the gale, and the ship rode in apparent safety all the next day.

On the 3rd, the storm having moderated, I weighed the anchor, which we found, to our astonishment, had gone down foul, one turn of the cable round the stock. But as it had well performed its duty, it was so far a lucky event. I stood in for the Mole, and anchored half a mile from it. Ad. Hood Linzee[1] had replaced Commodore Penrose in the command. I had scarcely made my bow to the Rear Admiral when he informed me that I was appointed Captain of the *Undaunted*, one of our finest frigates in the Mediterranean. I could scarcely believe this good news. However, he repeated his assertion, describing how the Captain of the frigate had been obliged to resign his command on account of his health, and how Sir Edward Pellew had nominated me in his room. After quitting the Admiral, I received a letter from Sir Edward Berry,[2] who commanded a three-decker in the Fleet, acquainting me that the Commander in Chief had proposed my health at his public dinner as Captain of the *Undaunted*. The toast had been well received by the company, and he lost no time in writing to compliment me upon the auspicious event. This was all very satisfactory, but I wondered I had not a letter from Sir Edward Pellew on the subject. I shortly afterwards made this remark to Ad. Linzee. 'Oh,' he replied. 'Make yourself easy. The *Undaunted* will soon make her appearance here. Then you will take command of her.' However, I heard no more about the *Undaunted*, excepting that she was given to my old messmate, Capt. Ussher. Why Sir

[1] Samuel Hood Linzee, nephew of Samuel Lord Hood and son of W.H.D.'s first Captain in the *Saturn*. Lt. 21/7/1790; Cdr. 5/11/93; Capt. 8/3/94; R-Ad. 12/8/1812.
[2] Sir Edward Berry, Bart., Lt. 20/1/1794; straight to Capt. 6/3/97; R-Ad. 19/7/1821.

Edward Pellew should have committed himself in such a public manner was never explained to me.

During my stay at Gibraltar, I received much friendly attention from the officers of the Artillery. There has always been a very sociable feeling between that Corps and the Navy. They elected me an honorary member of their mess—an agreeable compliment, for instead of going to dine at the inn, I repaired to the Artillery quarters, paid my share of a very good dinner and enjoyed interesting society. My Prize was favourably judged at the Admiralty. That matter had scarcely been settled when I found myself obliged to try the Master and the Boatswain by a Court Martial for drunkenness. The Admiral ordered the Court to assemble on board of my ship, and the charge was proved against the Master, who was sentenced to lose 5 years' rank, and dismissed the ship. The Boatswain was reprimanded, and the Third Lieutenant, Burgh,[1] who behaved contemptuously to the Court, while giving his evidence, was sentenced to one month's imprisonment in the Marshalsea. He was from Ireland, and I believe not much attached to Old England's cause. Five minutes were allowed him to correct his evidence and apologise to the Court for the impropriety of his conduct. I attempted to advise him, but my time and counsels were entirely thrown away. He acted upon wrong principles. The Master and Lieutenant were removed from the *Leopard*. Another Master, Mr. Medland,[2] came to me.

It was whilst in company with five naval Captains that our attention was drawn to an article in one of the newspapers, attempting to prove what a lucky set of men the Captains of the Navy were in taking Prizes and making fortunes. This article was so pointed, and so false in its assertions, that we drew up a reply to it which was signed by the whole six. We stated that we had been so many years serving our Country, that we had commanded ships a long while, that the whole of us had been wounded, and that none of us had, up to that period, received £100 Prize Money.[3] We stated many other facts, explaining our expenses in keeping a table, to support the respectability of our stations which our pay never did cover. Moreover, we alluded to an act of Lord Mulgrave's when First Lord, by which he mulcted the Naval Captains of a certain share of their Prize Money.

---

[1] Thomas, Lt. 3/1/1810.
[2] Robert Medland, 1st Warrant, 26/3/1811.
[3] Presumably he refers to his receipts since becoming a Captain. Before that he had received *much* more: *cf.* Vol. I, p. 306 (£500), Vol. I, p. 101 (£105), and, *passim*, many smaller sums.

[W.H.D. here repeats, in almost identical terms, the passage printed at p. 119 above.]

What the Editor did with our statement I never heard. But it is a notorious fact that not one Captain in 20 realises sufficient by Prize Money to establish an independence. Very many are ruined in endeavouring to keep up the honour of the Profession.

[Here follow the further six descriptive pages of Gibraltar, mentioned at p. 197, and there summarised.]

Having received my men from the Prize, as well orders from the Admiral to take six merchantmen under my convoy, I left Gibraltar on the 14th, on my way to Alicant. My convoy was troublesome, and neglected making sail. We arrived at the destined port on the morning of the 19th, where I found the *Malta* with two or three sloops of war. Upon presenting my respects to my Admiral, I learnt I was to proceed to Malta, giving a passage to Gen. Campbell and his suite. He, being relieved in the command of the Army by Sir John Murray, was appointed to the Governorship of Zante, with other influence in our Ionian Islands. He invited me to dine with him that I might meet the General and make such arrangements as might suit him. It was on this occasion that I obtained an insight into the proceedings of those in power. We had a very sociable dinner, and at its termination, observing the two Chiefs in deep conversation together, I quietly withdrew. Whilst in the act of leaving the cabin, I was caught by the arm by the Admiral's Secretary, Mr. Murray,[1] who entreated a few words of confidential chat. The tone, and the whisper, led me to suppose that he had some good news in store for me. The evening was very dark, and we selected a retired corner of the Quarter Deck. 'I must be brief,' said he, 'for my time is precious. I must prepare you for a shabby proceeding towards you. But let me most solemnly urge you to keep secret all that I am about to mention. Act upon it to your advantage if you can, but for God's sake do not commit me.' I promised the most profound secrecy. 'Well,' said he, 'there is a plan laid to get rid of you. When you get to Malta, you will be appointed the Senior Officer of some troop-ships there, and proceed with them, accompanied by some transports full of troops, for America. You were a great favourite with Ad. Hallowell when you first came under his command. There was nothing like you. But now all is altered. As I have witnessed your

---

[1] Archibald Murray, 1st Warrant as Purser, 29/1/1794.

exertions I cannot allow you to be imposed upon. The Admiral
knows that the Admiralty has interfered in your behalf. You are to
have the first vacant frigate on the station should you be on the spot:
but if you are sent away you will lose that chance. There is some
dirty work in progress against you. I am so thoroughly shocked at
all that has come to my knowledge that I was determined to let you
know it, that you may be on your guard.' I thanked the Secretary
most sincerely for this proof of his friendly feeling. Then, shaking
me by the hand, he said, 'I shall sleep quietly tonight, as I was
anxious to let you know the plot at work against you.' The time of
parting having arrived, as my boat was alongside, I took leave of
Ad. Hallowell, his Captain and others: then, handing the General
over the ship's side, we left the *Malta* for the *Leopard*.

When on my pillow, my whole thoughts were occupied with the
information conveyed to me, and of the underhand work in operation
to my prejudice. It was now proved that Lord Melville determined
that I should not be passed by a second time. No doubt his Lordship
had heard how I had been treated with regard to the *Undaunted*.
But Sir Edward and his Lordship were not on good terms. The act
of sending me off to America, at this, to me, critical moment was,
to say the least of it, an act of decided injustice, as my claims were
of the first order. When I took up my commission for the *Leopard*,
it was understood that I was to be removed into an active frigate in
18 months. I had now been in her two years.[1] After a couple of days'
intercourse with Gen. Campbell, I found him an agreeable, friendly
gentleman. As I experienced from him the utmost courtesy, I determined to have some confidential communication with him. I told him
the plan laid down to my prejudice, and requested him to advocate my
cause with Sir Edward Pellew, whom he intended to see at Minorca,
previously to going to Malta, and urge him to keep me in the Mediterranean. He very kindly promised to do all he could, but remarked
that his interference might do harm. 'However,' said he, 'I will try.'

When we had reached the east end of Minorca, and I had lowered
a boat to take the General on shore, a sudden change in the weather,
frequent in this climate, assailed us. It came on to blow a gale in a
few seconds. I had just time to hoist the boat in, then to prepare the
ship for the coming storm. I was obliged to haul off from the land,
to wait till the gale had passed. By the 26th I again stood in for
Minorca. Whilst signals were passing between my ship and Cape

---

[1] If there was any truth in what the Secretary told W.H.D., this is another illustration of the clash between 'on-the-spot' and 'Admiralty' interest. *Cf.* Vol. I, p. 308.

Mola, soon after 9 o'clock, I observed Sir Edward Pellew standing towards my ship in his barge. There was still a strong breeze, and I did not feel very comfortable in the position of the *Leopard*. The Admiral made the signal from his own boat to prepare to anchor, and, seeing that he wished to board me, I hove to. He shortly afterwards came alongside. When he reached the Quarter Deck, my ship had got into an awkward place where there was no safe anchoring. Consequently I was obliged to run right into the harbour and let go an anchor. Very fortunately I was on the Forecastle, watching the anchor, which did not hold, and instantly made them let go another. That one just brought up the ship, only 18 inches from the rocks. The entrance is very narrow, and of difficult access without a fair wind. I now hastened aft to Sir Edward, and told him that the ship was in danger. He directed me to make the signal to the Fleet for assistance, and plenty of boats came from the different ships. The Admiral now took his leave, and invited me to dinner, most frankly declaring on the Quarter Deck that if any accident happened to the ship, he would bear me clear of all blame, as he was the cause of my ship being so awkwardly placed. The boats supplied us with plenty of hawsers. We weighed the anchors, and hauled the ship over to the other shore, securing by them to the Lazaretto point.

After dinner Sir Edward Pellew took me aside and said he thought the Admiralty had already made their arrangements relating to the embarking of the two regiments from Malta to America, and that the *Leopard* would not be wanted. 'This is my opinion,' he said, 'and I hope I am correct. But I cannot guarantee you against unforeseen events.' So far I was satisfied, more especially when he assured me that he would not interfere to my prejudice. We had a very sociable dinner, previous to which I had just time to present my respects to the Duchess of Orleans. Sir Edward ordered all the boats of the Fleet to attend upon the *Leopard*. He again, in very handsome terms, complimented me upon the seamanlike way in which I had managed my ship in the morning. Then, with a friendly shake of the hand, we parted. With the assistance of so many boats, the *Leopard* was soon loosened from the rocks, and made sail out of the harbour on the evening of the day we entered it. When we got fairly to sea, we felt the effect of the late gale; the swell coming down from the Gulph of Genoa was tremendous, and the ship rolled all night most uncomfortably. I had been authorized to take the General to Palermo. That change in my route to Malta, I thought, would, by the delay, prevent my being sent to America. The light and variable winds also retarded our progress. On the evening of the 31st, when off the southern end of Sardinia, I fell in with the *Cephalus*, one of our cruizing brigs of war, to whom I turned the convoy over, then made sail, free of my charge, for the island of Sicily.

On the 3rd of April we saw that island, but we made slow work with such light airs. Several turtle were seen floating about, and I sent my boat after one that appeared of a good size, and which the crew succeeded in catching as he was asleep. The next day we anchored in Palermo Bay, and I sent the turtle to the Governor, Lord William Bentinck.[1]

[A description of Palermo is omitted.]

Lord William Bentinck held here the chief position relating to Great Britain, and entertained in good style. The Duke of Orleans[2] was residing here, and mixed much with the English. He invited me to the christening of one of his children. Not long after my anchoring, a violent gale came on, and at one time it was doubtful whether the ship would hold at her anchors. A tremendous swell set in, and all eyes from the shore turned towards the *Leopard*. However, with three anchors ahead she weathered the storm, the lower yards and topmasts struck. But there was some damage done to the merchant shipping in the Mole. We had a strong military force here to protect the island from Murat, the soi-disant King of Naples. He had made one attempt, and landed 1200 men, who were soon captured. We had gunboats and a good garrison at Messina, which kept a lookout on the opposite shore. The Neapolitan Royal Family resided here in quiet retirement. The arrival of the *Furieuse* frigate and the *Termagant* made a change in the appearance of the bay. The former was the ship in which I had been detained at Helvoetsluys. She had been captured when bound to France from Guadeloupe by one of our sloops of war. She had not all her guns on board, having a cargo of sugar, but made nevertheless a stout resistance against Capt. Mounsey,[3] of the *Bonne Citoyenne*, who, after a long and spirited action, made her his Prize, and was afterwards promoted and appointed to command her.

After an agreeable pass-time in this delightful place, whither we had come to suit the convenience of Gen. Campbell, of about 10 days, I prepared to quit Palermo. But an unexpected charge brought

---

[1] Lord William Cavendish Bentinck, Governor-General of India, 1828–35. W.H.D. calls him 'Bentick' throughout.
[2] Later King Louis Philippe.
[3] William Mounsey, Lt. 22/5/1793; Cdr. 29/4/1802; Capt. 6/7/09.

against the Purser by the Master, in which he was supported by all his messmates, brought on a great change in my deportment towards the Purser, who had kept a long series of notes against me. It is mentioned upon my being appointed to the *Horatio*.[1] On the 14th we left Palermo, bound to Malta. I found Gen. Campbell such an agreeable companion that his society was an acquisition, and highly valued. On the 19th the ship anchored in Malta harbour. I saluted the Admiral, Laugharne,[2] according to the regulations, but when this officer heard all I had to say, he without ceremony warned me that, if I remained in the harbour more than three days, he should attach me to the troopship squadron destined to convey our regiments to America. That was not a very pleasant decision as far as I was concerned. I therefore hastened to communicate with my friend the General who lost no time in calling upon the Admiral to acquaint him that three days was not sufficient to enable him to transact the affairs in hand. The Admiral made a courteous reply which pacified the General, but not me: and I told him so. Mind the result.

Shortly after my arrival the *Bacchante*, frigate, came in, commanded by the gallant Capt. Hoste.[3] The appearance of this officer made an imposing impression upon the Governor, Hildebrand Oakes, and the garrison: in consequence of which His Excellency determined to give a splendid ball out of compliment to this naval Hero. When the hour drew nigh, I received a letter from Capt. Hoste stating that he was too unwell to go on shore to the Governor's ball, and requesting me to supply his place. As, from my wounded limbs, I had long given up dancing, this request was anything but agreeable. I replied accordingly. However, another note came from the *Bacchante*, entreating me in pressing terms to present myself, as I was the only other naval Captain in the harbour; that it was necessary for me to attend, as the entertainment was given in honour of the Navy. On receipt of this billet, I instantly made my arrangements; but, not intending to trip it on the light fantastic toe, I put on a stout pair of military boots.

[W.H.D. describes at length how he 'opened the Ball' with the 'first lady of the place, the Hon. Mrs. M.': but, after acquitting

[1] This passage is inserted in a much later ink. The episode referred to will be found, summarised, below at p. 282.
[2] John Laugharne, Lt. 25/6/1776; Cdr. 1/12/87; Capt. 22/11/90; R-Ad. 31/7/1810; V-Ad. 4/6/14.
[3] Sir William Hoste, Bart. (K.C.B.), victor of the famous action off Lissa, 13/3/1811. Lt. 8/2/1798; Cdr. 3/9/98; Capt. 7/1/1802: died (for all his great services still, of course, a Captain) 6/12/28.

himself with credit (in spite of the twin handicaps of wounded legs and military boots), he was allowed to sit out for the rest of the evening with the Hon. Mrs. M. and her husband, 'the Hon. Col. M. of the 44th.' He also met the French colonel captured in Murat's attempt on the island (see above, p. 241), who, wearing himself '7 or 8 stars on his left breast', wondered at Dillon having no decorations. To this W.H.D. replied 'that it was not the custom with us,' and adds, in a note:—'Mr. Pitt had often contemplated establishing some military honours for those officers of the Army and Navy who distinguished themselves in action against our enemies. At the end of the war the Prince Regent increased the Order of the Bath into three grades: the highest, Knights Grand Cross; the second, Knight Commander, and the third, Commander of the Bath.' For further discussion on this subject, see below, p. 425. The first Naval General Service *medal*, however, was not issued till 1848, though veterans surviving from actions back to the First of June received it. See Vol. I, p. 152, note.]

I now heard that the Admiralty had applied to Sir Edward Pellew to explain who the Spanish Governor was that I had escorted from Port Mahon to Majorca, and requested him to state what he thought I ought to receive in compensation for entertaining an official of his rank. He in reply, I was also informed, stated that I was entitled to nothing. The Commander in Chief had given me a public order to receive the Grandee with his suite, and by such an act he had authorized my applying for the regulated allowance. 'Sir Edward,' I observed, 'has not shown much regard for me in this case. I shall renew my demand the first opportunity.'

The next day I received an invitation to dine with the Governor and, as Hoste could not attend, I took the post of honour on his right hand. I found His Excellency a very intelligent person, and quite *au fait* with all the gastronomic dishes suitable to a good entertainment. Here I made the acquaintance of Capt. Hamilton,[1] who had distinguished himself in the Navy. As his Mother was a Dillon, he claimed a kinship with me.

On the 3rd day of my being in port, the Admiral, rather sharply I thought, acquainted me that if I made any longer stay in the harbour he would follow up his original intention of ordering me to take command of the troopships in Malta. I observed that he had promised my passenger, the General, more time. 'That may be,'

---

[1] Not identified, but probably Capt. Edward Hamilton, the hero of the cutting-out of the *Hermione*, 24/10/1799. See Vol. I, p. 368 and note.

said he, 'but I advise you to quit this port if you do not wish to go to America.' I instantly wrote to General Campbell, telling him what had passed, and that I intended sailing out of the harbour next morning by daylight, and waiting outside for him. The General, with the kindest intentions towards me, had already sent on board some thousands of dollars wanted at Zante, upon which I was to receive the freight. Accordingly, on the morning of the 24th, with the dawn, I moved my ship out of the harbour, and lay with the maintopsail to the mast for the appearance of the General, who came on board about 12 o'clock, very much annoyed at the Admiral's proceeding. 'Another day,' he said, 'would have answered my purpose. However, considering that your interest has been at stake, I don't much care about it.' My apprehensions relating to a trip to America now vanished and all sail was set towards Zante.

[There follows a brief history, and a very long and detailed description, of Malta, covering 19 pages of MS. It is almost entirely omitted here, for there is very little in it of naval import. There is, however, one description of an interesting gun which he saw in the Governor's palace:—'Small, about the size of a six-pounder, made of wood, with several iron rings to support it from bursting, the inside being lined with a sheet of that metal.' And one anecdote, relating to the French surrender of Malta in 1800, is retained:—'The Commandant, with his garrison in a state of famine, surrendered on honourable terms to Gen. Pigot, scarcely a day's provisions remaining in la Valetta when taken possession of by us. The English Commissioners were courteously received by Gen. Vaubois, who entertained them to dinner. To their surprise, the various dishes appeared to be a select choice of animal food, dressed in the superior style of the cuisine. They could not refrain from expressing their astonishment at this unexpected display, when they expected, at the utmost, a loaf of bread. The French General, in reply, assured them that the repast consisted merely of some tame rabbits, with a couple of quails accidentally caught upon the ramparts, the whole skilfully disguised by the tact of his Cook.' W.H.D.'s account concludes as follows:—'Its occupation by us is highly advantageous to the Maltese, by our commercial intercourse and the sums of money spent by our travellers, as well by the Government in the improvement of the works. The importance of Malta to us cannot be overrated, and while in the possession of Great Britain, it will prevent the Mediterranean from becoming a French Lake.' Here W.H.D.

proves himself more enlightened than some of his contemporaries—including even Lord Nelson, who wrote to Lord Spencer, in 1799, 'But, as I said before, I attach no value to it (Malta) for us.']

Nothing of consequence occurred during the run to Zante. We had fine weather, and I enjoyed the agreeable society of the General. On the evening of the 29th we cast anchor in the bay of that island. The next day Gen. Campbell landed with his suite. On his quitting the ship he was saluted with 15 guns. Mr. Forresti, a Zantiot, who held the responsible position of Political Minister and British Consul, was the gentleman to whom we addressed ourselves; but his functions ceased upon Gen. Campbell taking up the management of the colony as Principal Commissioner of the Ionian Islands. Ceremonial dinners now took place. I gave one on board the *Leopard* to the principal inhabitants, but on that occasion an unlucky event happened to one of my boats which had been sent to bring on board some of the most noted senators. When she had shoved off from the shore, with the sails up, one of those sudden squalls which so frequently happen in this climate burst upon her with such violence that she was capsized. Fortunately only one of them was embarked. He got a ducking, but the boat righted itself without any serious injury. This gentleman had just married a very amiable young lady, who was watching the motions of her husband when he stepped into the boat. When it was upset, she instantly sent forth loud lamentations, ran down to the boat, and caused considerable alarm. When the senator had recovered himself, seeing his wife almost frantic, he requested the officer to land him. Then the lady caught him in her arms, and both retired home: so that I was one short of my number at the banquet.

I being the Senior Naval Officer, I was invited to all the entertainments so liberally bestowed upon the General. Some of them were splendid for such a retired spot, and did honour to the Zantiots, who on all occasions manifested their attachment to Great Britain. Some of the senators were anxious to display their court dresses, and figured away with elegant smallswords, laced frills, jewelled knee and shoe buckles and ruffles of great value; many of them well shaped, good looking men. But one who cut a conspicuous figure was pointed out to me as having caused the murder of 40 individuals, at the rate of two dollars a head. It was an established fact that, previous to the island becoming in possession of the English, a man's life could be sacrificed for that trivial sum. However, the case was now altered, and no murders were heard of.

My stay at Zante depended in some measure upon the will of the General, to whom I had received instructions to show every consideration. Among the gentlemen of note here I became acquainted with the Hon. Frederick North, afterwards Lord Guilford.[1] So soon as the General became free of his ceremonial engagements, he requested me to give Mr. North and his suite a passage to Malta. I readily consented, but I then ascertained that he could not be ready to embark for some days: upon which I made no further inquiry, but asked him to give me timely notice when he would be ready to quit.

In my passage to and fro, between my ship and the shore, I noticed a small islet, only a few yards from the beach, upon which a tent was pitched. One morning when passing, I noticed it open. Inside, I saw a Turkish gentleman smoking his hookah, sitting cross-legged according to the Eastern custom. I made my bow to him. He returned the compliment by touching his turban with both hands. I then landed, entered his tent and offered him my hand, which he accepted, evidently much pleased with this attention. I could not speak his language, but by signs I proposed to him to come into my boat. He instantly complied, and I took him to the town. When we reached the shore, he took hold of my arm, and we thus walked up the street together to the astonishment of all who beheld us. Mr. Forresti, informed of my having taken the Turk in tow, came and invited us to his house. From him I learned that the Mussulman was a Colonel of the Turkish Army, sent by the Sultan to collect recruits. I next took the Colonel on board the *Leopard*. He was much delighted, and examined the ship with great pleasure. After he had remained a couple of hours, I conveyed him to his tent. We perfectly agreed in all the forms of a first acquaintance, and I now found that a gentleman makes himself known as such in every clime. We perfectly comprehended each other, although our intercourse had been established only by signs and motions.

[He met the Turk on several other occasions, never communicating with him by word of mouth. They exchanged invitations, the Colonel to Constantinople, Dillon to London. He now attended a Greek wedding, on which he spends no less than six pages: omitted

---

[1] 5th Earl, 1766–1827. A Hellenist, famous in his day for his wit and linguistic ability, especially in classical Greek. A successful Governor of Ceylon (1798–1805), but spent most of his life travelling, mainly in the Near East, where he was received into the Eastern Church. Founded an Ionian University in Corfu, and became its first Chancellor.

here. He next visited the mainland of Greece with a certain 'Dr. Hd.' and two of his own officers. Warned that real risks accompanied such an excursion, he armed himself with 'a brace of pocket pistols and my sabre.' The former he did not have to use, but the latter came in very useful when he was attacked in a narrow defile by a ferocious dog. They visited the Plains of Olympia, and saw Ossa and Olympus: but the plain was otherwise empty. This does not prevent him, however, from giving a six-page description of what *was* there in classical times. He had left his boat on the beach, apparently to cover his retreat if things went wrong. In the event he was glad he had done so.]

I reached the beach at sunset. The Doctor's attendant had arrived. My boat was in order and ready. As I was hastening towards it, I was accosted by two powerful Greeks, both armed with large pistols and other weapons. They had been watching for my arrival, and wanted to obtain money from me. By the assistance of the attendant they were given to understand that I had paid for the use of my steed and that all affairs had been settled. But these chaps were not satisfied, and began to give symptoms of an appeal to arms. Out came my sabre again, and I called to my boat's crew to hasten up with their muskets. The tars were up in an instant. 'Now,' I said to the attendant, 'you had better explain to these fellows that I am not to be trifled with. They will not obtain any money from me.' My crew consisted of seven stout men, myself making the eighth, and we were ready for a brush. But the Greeks changed their tone, sneaked off, and left me in possession of the beach.

Upon questioning my men how they had fared during my absence, I was informed that they had had a row. One of the crew wanted to get hold of my money; but he who had charge of it would not part with it. A fight ensued, and the one who attacked received the cut of a sword over his right arm, which settled him. This was an unpleasant affair, but the delinquent having exposed himself to the infliction he had received, I did not take any further notice of what had happened. When the remainder of my party arrived, we embarked, and made our way to the *Leopard*, reaching it about 11 o'clock.

[He now found, to his surprise, that he had committed himself to embarking, not only the Hon. Mr. North, but also Dr. Hd., '13 servants of different grades . . . and a large quantity of marble statues . . . amounting to 60 cases,' that the firstnamed had collected in the course of a year's travel and archaeological excavation in and around Athens. He consented, but without enthusiasm. He now describes some of the articles, mainly statuary, brought to light (and to Zante), especially 'the combat between the Amazons and the Centaurs . . . a frieze reported by Pausanias.']

The next day, being Sunday the 9th, with fine weather, the anchor was weighed, and sail made out of the roads. We took a good look at Cephalonia as we passed along. The climate of Zante is delightful. It is in size about 24 miles in length and 12 in breadth, is extremely fertile, and produces an immense quantity of currants, cultivated on the plains, which are sheltered by the mountains: the population, I think, above 50,000. The houses in the town are low, on account of its being subject to frequent earthquakes. The natives speak both Greek and Italian. The only fortified place here is a castle upon an eminence. In a certain part of the island is an extensive quagmire which, when shaken by the earthquake, throws out a quantity of bitumen which answers the purpose of pitch. With it the bottoms of their vessels are payed. The island formerly belonged to the Venetians. It is near to the Morea and about 19 miles to the S.E. of Cephalonia. The bay in which I anchored has good holding ground, and is considered safe.

I found Mr. North a mild tempered, accomplished gentleman. As the principal part of our conversation turned upon Greece and his excavations, I obtained from both him and Dr. Hd. much interesting information. The former had some of his cases opened to show me the beautiful sculpture of them. One in particular I shall never forget—the bust of a female broken from the body just below the breast. Its softness was the most perfect representation of nature that could be imagined. The face and the hair were all, or more, than one could suppose possible to be carved out of marble.

Delightful weather attended our passage to Malta, and by the 15th we were safely anchored in the harbour of that island. But all our plans were frustrated when I received the unpleasant news that the plague had broken out in Valetta, and all communication with the shore at an end. This was a sad blow to Mr. North, as he could not land to hire a vessel in which he could proceed further down the Mediterranean. I soon received orders to hoist the Quarantine Flag, a yellow one. The next day I had an interview with the Port Admiral, Laugharne, at the Pratique Office, during which he told me that I should be sent to Palermo to take charge of a convoy. He desired me to call in my boat, every morning, alongside of a line of battle ship lying in the harbour, whose Captain would convey to me such orders as might be necessary. At that period I had not a sick man on board. On the following day I took Mr. North with me to the Senior Officer, Capt. Hollis.[1] He from his cabin window spoke to me under the stern in my boat, as we were not allowed to come in personal contact with one another. He particularly addressed himself to Mr. North, pointing out to him the immediate necessity of his removing, with all his effects, from the *Leopard*. It was a great relief to me that Mr. North had been thus warned, as I felt a certain degree of reluctance in acquainting my guest that circumstances required his quitting my ship. He wrote some letters to merchants at Valetta, but they produced no result. I was now placed in a very awkward position in regard to a gentleman in so respectable station in life. Plainly speaking, he became an incumbrance, being unable to procure a vessel into which he might transship himself, his attendants and property.

I had brought some turkeys from Zante for the Admiral, which were conveyed to him through the Pratique Office, but no payment returned. I was then informed that I stood no chance of receiving any. It was a weak point of his to request the Captains going to Zante to bring him a supply of that breed. I had complied with his wishes, and naturally expected to be refunded the money laid out on his account. I heard no more on the subject at that moment. However, after leaving Malta, the Second Lieutenant, Vickery, acquainted me that he felt extremely uneasy at not having been able to land, to pay a bill due at one of the hotels. I demanded the amount. Strange as it may appear, it corresponded with what the Admiral owed me for the turkeys. I told him that I would soon settle his account. 'You have only,' I said, 'to pay me what you owe at the inn, and I shall write to Ad. Laugharne to discharge it, instead of forwarding to me his debt for the birds supplied.' I wrote accordingly to the Admiral, who, I suppose, complied with my request, as I received no answer to my letter.

After staying a few days and receiving some seamen and some casks of dollars, I obtained a clean bill of health, and on the 19th took my departure from Malta, Mr. North and his party still with me, bound for Palermo. With light winds, our progress was not of the quickest. The first thing that came under our notice was the island of Pantellaria, where the Spaniards kept all the French

[1] Aiskew Paffard Hollis, Lt. 22/1/1781; Cdr. 28/10/96; Capt. 5/2/98; R-Ad. 27/5/25; V-Ad. 10/1/37.

prisoners of war. By the 25th we were close to Sicily, and, entering the bay of Palermo, ran foul of a transport, but without any serious injury occurring. Capt. Dundas[1] of the *Edinburgh*, 74, was the Senior Officer. My having been at Malta prevented me from having any communication with the shore: consequently my pass-time could only be to take an airing in my boat close in to shore, taking a view of all the dashing belles and beaux in carriages on the Marine Esplanade of Palermo. Many transports lay here, having on board the 44th, and I was taken by surprise one day when I heard that the Hon. Col. M. and his amiable wife had come alongside. They could not be persuaded to enter the ship, but I went down into their boat and passed a few moments with them. The *Leyden* was also here, commanded by my old friend Capt. Davy,[2] who very kindly devoted much of his time to me.

I was informed that the Queen of Naples had been mixing herself so much with Politics that Lord William Bentinck had been obliged to have her removed, and I believe she was sent to Constantinople. His Lordship had a difficult game in hand. The *America*, 74, arrived, and on the 28th took away Lord William to take command of our army assembled at Tarragona. I made an attempt with Mr. North to see his Lordship, but after waiting on board the *America* until past midnight I returned to my ship. Mr. North remained an hour or two longer, and had his interview with the Peer. Shortly after this a brig of war commanded by a lieutenant came in, and Mr. North at last contrived to make some agreement with that officer, who took him, with his servants, Dr. Hd., and all the marbles. This was a lucky turn up for that gentleman. However, at parting, I could not help noticing a slight coolness on the part of the Honourable and his companions: for what reason I could not imagine, as I had afforded them every accommodation within my power. Besides, I had saved Mr. North a considerable expense.

[W.H.D. is evidently incensed at this treatment, and spends half a page in stressing all the services he had rendered Mr. North. He concludes as follows:—]

Some years afterwards I met him in Town. He scarcely knew me. So much for kindness shown. In those days there were many English gentlemen travelling about the Mediterranean. They were in con-

---

[1] Hon. George Heneage Lawrence Dundas, Lt. 23/3/1797; Cdr. 26/12/1800; Capt. 3/8/01; R.-Ad. 22/7/30.
[2] John Davie, Lt. 2/9/1793; Cdr. 6/9/1800; Capt. 22/8/09.

stant intercourse with the Navy, from whom they received marked
attention on all occasions. When these wanderers called and left
their cards, there were on them the letters 'T.G.', which meant
'Travelling Gentleman'. Those cards became a password amongst
us, and it was a common question, when we met a naval friend,
'Have you got any T.G.'s?'

So soon as Mr. North and his party had entirely removed from
the *Leopard*, I offered the Hon. Col. and Mrs. M. accommodation in
the Ward Room,[1] and the use of my cabin and table. They accepted
this act of kindness, and on the 9th June came on board with their
children, a boy and a girl, the lady's by a former husband. Although
I passed three weeks here without being able to land, the intercourse
that we established with the ships of war in the bay in some shape
made up for the annoyance of performing quarantine. The Palermi-
tans were terribly alarmed at the idea of the plague. Though I had
not a sick man on board, they would not permit anyone to put a foot
on shore. Under such circumstances I did not regret taking my
departure, with a few soldiers and my convoy, on the 10th. The
'heavy battery' (as it was called) of the 44th was embarked.

We made very slow progress owing to light winds and calms.
Maritimo was many days in sight. On the 20th, being near to Sardinia, I ran in with the convoy to Pulo Bay, wishing to supply the
troops with some vegetables and water. Having obtained fresh
supplies, I left the island. It was beautifully wooded, but we had no
communication with the town. Such of the natives as made their
appearance were more like savages than a civilized race. By the 24th,
Cape Mola, on Minorca, was in sight. When I got close into the entrance to the harbour, I had intercourse with the Pratique officers,
who, when they knew whence I came, although without a sick man
on the medical list, decided that I should anchor in the Quarantine
harbour, Cala Taulena as it was called—a cove over which the
Lazaretto was situated. Accordingly next day the ship ran into that
place and was safely moored, the transports near. The day after, all
the Spanish Authorities, the Governor, etc., with his medical advisers,

---

[1] These last four words are added in a later hand. In an ordinary fighting ship the
Captain's guests, especially when feminine, would not—probably could not—have
thus invaded the domain of the Lieutenants. But here was no invasion. The *Leopard*,
fitted as a troopship, would have a much more liberal allowance of cabins than most,
and the extra ones would certainly be situated, though not actually in the Ward
Room, yet on the same deck, and sufficiently near to it for their locality to be called,
generically, 'the Ward Room.' They would normally be occupied, of course, by Army
officers and, often, their families. It is to be noted, too, that the 'M' family were only
to sleep there. They were to *live* in the Captain's cabin.

came to the Lazaretto all in military attire. They requested my attendance, but when I made my appearance they would not allow my approaching them within 10 feet. I explained to them the space wanted for the accommodation of the Regiment, and they promised to give me timely notice when the soldiers could land.

The time was now drawing near for my parting with my friends. An unfortunate accident had hurt one of my legs and obliged me to keep it in an horizontal position during several days. The Lt. Col. and his amiable wife would in turns sit near, and read to me by the hour. They were determined to devote their time to me, in spite of all my objections. The young daughter would generally accompany her Mother, and by way of relief would sing a song. She was only eight years old. You can consequently comprehend that the subjects upon which she sang occasioned more laughing than any other sensation. Nevertheless they were extremely entertaining.

On the 30th I received intimation that the Lazaretto was ready to receive the Regiment, and that the Governor, accompanied by the Junta, would be present when the soldiers landed. Our officer in command lost no time in landing his men on the beach, where there was a large fountain. There they washed, and dressed in regimental order, the band in readiness to strike up the usual tune on such occasions. At 2 o'clock the Spanish Authorities appeared, and I hastened to meet them. I had no reason to be satisfied respecting the directions the Governor had given for the accommodation of our soldiers. Some discussion ensued, in which I reminded him that they were going to fight the battles of Spain, and ought to receive every comfort the place would allow. The Spaniard is a stubborn fellow, and I, not being in the least concerned in it, sent a message below, requesting that the Colonel would attend. When he came, I acquainted him with all that had passed, and told him I could interfere no further. The Colonel, who could not speak any language but his own, made sad work of it with the Spaniards. Consequently the whole brunt again fell on me. When the Governor found that the Regiment would not quit the sands until the room required was granted, he gave in. I then told the Colonel that he might order his men to march in to their quarters. In a few seconds we heard the band playing The British Grenadiers. Up came the men. The foremost files had just entered the gates when the intelligence reached us that a soldier had dropped down dead on the ascent. This was a sad event at this critical moment. The band stopped playing, the men halted, and the Governor sent two of his medical officers to find out the cause of the

man's death. It was then ascertained that the unfortunate individual
had drunk a large quantity of water at the fountain, which, it seems,
occasioned his demise, as he had no disease. The Governor was
satisfied, and the Regiment entered the Lazaretto in solemn step,
as fine a set of men as could be seen.

I had not seen the Port Admiral, my only communication with
him having been by letter: but he contrived to acquaint me that the
Spanish Governor was highly offended at the part I had taken at
the Lazaretto. I explained to him in writing the principle on which
I had acted. My ship was now in Quarantine. I was not allowed any
intercourse with my friends in the Lazaretto: no communication with
any part of the island. But I had the privilege of rowing about the
harbour in my boat, with a yellow Flag stuck up on the bow. My
naval friends would come near in their boats, and convey intelligence.
The Duchess of Orleans would come down, almost every afternoon,
on the opposite side of the harbour, and wave her hand as a signal
for my attendance. I instantly made towards H.S. Highness, and in
my boat would enjoy an hour's conversation with her.

The ship being terribly infested with rats, I availed myself of this
opportunity to get rid of them. Having obtained the Admiral's
consent, I set to work. It was whilst this duty was going on that one
of the seamen, John Read, would not work. When he was in the act
of being punished, he declared himself an American, then requested
to be considered a Prisoner of War and placed in confinement. He was
placed under arrest until I could get rid of him. An empty transport
came alongside to remove the powder, and the work of clearing the
hold went on rapidly. The ship was smoked below. The rats, of
immense size, were smothered and lugged out of their hiding places.
I soon got clear of them, but that was no sooner accomplished than a
nest of mice was discovered in my cabin. The ship was set to rights,
and I waited patiently.

A series of unjust annoyances were now imposed upon me.

[The 44th received pratique after 11 days, but the Junta took no
notice of W.H.D.'s application for it. He now approached the Port
Admiral (Pickmore), who refused to intervene. Then he heard that
a brig of war, the *Carlotta*, had arrived—from Malta—and instantly
been granted pratique by the Junta. He thereupon wrote angrily to
them—a very natural act which led to trouble with Ad. Pickmore.]

It so happened that the officer commanding this brig was at
dinner with the Admiral when the Authorities received my letter.

One or two of them hastened thither, and saw the officer in question. He was obliged to quit the Admiral's table, and the other officers were secured and sent off to their vessel. Admiral Pickmore was terribly annoyed at this act of mine. A correspondence ensued, the long and short of which was that I made good my statement: and I dwelt in the strongest terms upon the Admiral's listening to the reports of foreigners in preference of giving me a hearing. He in his turn found fault with my corresponding with the Junta without its passing through his office. I thought the remark rather too late, as he had known from the commencement that I had been constantly writing to them, and had offered no objection. However, he transmitted the whole to the Commander in Chief, and, after a great deal of fuss too ridiculous to be inserted here, Sir Edward Pellew advised my making to Ad. Pickmore an apology. All the Fleet took my part, but as the *Leopard* was not a cruizing frigate, her being kept in Quarantine, right or wrong, was of no consequence. I consented to make the apology, as I had no intention of doing anything out of order. It was now that my old friend Capt. Dilkes[1] of the *Castor* came to my assistance. He saw Ad. Pickmore and settled everything for me upon an amicable understanding. However, the Quarantine was not removed. This was inflicted upon me to please the Spaniards, who kept three guards on board.

I was frequently annoyed too by the Captain of the Lazaretto, who took it into his head that my ship was under his control. He would come off in his boat, and order the seamen's bedding to be aired, or any other whim that he fancied. The fellow was a black. None of his orders was attended to by me. On one occasion he gave directions to hang up the seamen's clothing. It was then raining, and I told the negro that if he repeated his conduct I would sink his boat. Away he went, but I represented his conduct in such terms to the Spanish Authorities that the hero received a regular jobation and never came near me afterwards. This brought some of the pratique officers alongside. They were respectful, but no release was granted from Quarantine.

At last, on the 3rd of August, the officers came on board to fumigate the ship, as they said, after which pratique would be granted. We were all ordered below, under hatches, where a quantity of sulphur, gunpowder and straw, mixed together, was prepared for ignition. When the Spaniard was satisfied that every individual had come down, he sprang the combustible on fire. This lasted five

---

[1] Charles Dilkes, Lt. 6/1/1797; Cdr. 20/3/1805; Capt. 18/1/09. Died, 1846.

minutes, and my eyes suffered dreadfully. We were then ordered on deck, and the chief told me that I might haul down the Yellow Flag, as pratique was given to the ship. I requested this gentleman to look at my eyes. 'I am now in a worse state,' I remarked, 'than before the fumigation.' 'Why did not you tell me that you would suffer?' he demanded. 'How could I tell,' I replied, 'never having before undergone such a trial?' 'Had I known it,' he observed, 'I would have left you out of this ceremony.' 'Thank you,' said I. 'There is not a sick man on board. The ship has been 40 days under your laws of Quarantine. What good have you done?'

No time was lost in removing the ship out of the cove into the open harbour. I dined with the Admiral, who lived in the country. It passed off very well, but I believe he never thoroughly forgave me, as I had told him some home truths which he could not deny. When the caulkers had done their work I received provisions for the Fleet off Toulon. Capt. Hoste came off the harbour, and with him I had some very interesting conversations. I found that 50 head of cattle were to be embarked, and all sorts of stores. The ship was deeply laden when, on the 24th, I sailed out of Port Mahon with a transport under convoy.

Nothing of consequence occurred on my way to Toulon. On the 29th I made the coast of France in the neighbourhood of Poquerolles, but I saw nothing of our Fleet off the entrances to the harbour. On the 31st I exchanged numbers with the *Mulgrave* and *Revenge*, 74. The next day, the 1st September, I saw the British Fleet at anchor off the mouths of the Rhone. I soon brought my ship up in a good position, and paid my respects to the Commander in Chief, who invited me to breakfast. When that repast was over, he took me into his sanctum, where we had a long conversation. He told me that he had received repeated instructions from the First Lord of the Admiralty to place me in the command of a frigate, and that he had at one time the intention of giving me a 20-gun ship. 'But,' said he, 'that would not have suited your standing, and you would have lost pay. I have not had a vacant frigate to dispose of. However, I expect there will soon be a promotion. In the meantime, I shall send you to Gibraltar, where you will find a frigate in waiting for you.' He overloaded me with flummery compliments, and invited me to dinner. I made but short replies to his observations, although I had it in my power to recall to his memory his having toasted my health at his own table in the presence of the Captains of the Fleet as Captain of the *Undaunted*. He demanded if I had not on board 3 or 4 seamen

that came to me when at Minorca from the transports. I acknowledged that I had. 'Very well,' said he. 'I have had a long correspondence with the Transport Board relating to them. You will send
them to my ship.' The correspondence had produced no beneficial
result to the seamen, and, instead of remaining with me, where they
were very comfortable, they were removed into a strange ship where
they knew nobody.

After quitting the *Caledonia*, I had a large packet of letters
delivered to me. Some were of nine months' date; three from Lord
Melville who, I was happy to find, had paid every fair consideration
to my applications to his Lordship, and had written three times to
Sir Edward Pellew, desiring him to remove me into an active frigate.
When I was appointed to the *Leopard*, I was led to believe that I
should be removed from it in 18 months, whereas I was then border-
ing upon a three years' occupancy. Although I had met with continual disappointments, I felt some satisfaction in knowing that the
First Lord of the Admiralty took an interest in my favour. I had
never seen him, nor had any influential friend of mine spoken to him
in my behalf, as far as I knew.

Whilst the boats of the Fleet came to take away the cattle, I
visited my friends. One in particular, Capt. Robert Rolles,[1] offered
to receive me as his guest until a vacant frigate might be disposable.
That was certainly a tempting and friendly offer: but upon more
mature reflection, I could not place much confidence in the assurances
of Sir Edward P. Therefore I preferred remaining in command of a
trooper. 'If I give her up,' I said, 'I am nobody but an idler in your
ship, whereas by holding on I am in active employment.' The next
officer who noticed me was Sir Sidney Smith, who invited me to
dinner. I passed a very pleasant evening. However, he had his object
in view, which was to request me to give a Spanish gentleman a
passage in my cabin to Minorca. There was no refusing, and the Don
was soon on board the *Leopard*. I now ascertained that Sir Edward,
or at least some of his officers, had found out the secret of all the
enemy's signals along the coast. That was an important acquisition
whilst watching the motions of an enemy off his own port. The
French Admiral who then commanded the Fleet in Toulon, Le Comte
Emerieux, I afterwards met in France. We often dined and went
to the theatre together, conversing on the naval events of that
day.

[1] Robert Rolles, Lt. 26/3/1782; Cdr. 10/5/93; Capt. 12/8/95; R-Ad. 4/6/1814;
V-Ad. 19/7/21.

On the 4th I left the Fleet for Minorca, having a convoy of transports. Nothing worth relating occurred, and I anchored in the harbour there on the 7th. After my conversation with the Commander in Chief, it was natural to suppose that I should not be much longer in the Mediterranean. Consequently, I took my leave of the Duchess of Orleans, from whom I had experienced so many acts of attention, kindness and hospitality. She particularly requested that I would write to her when opportunity offered. I promised to do so. The Spanish Junta had visited their authority upon me with useless and unbecoming severity. Consequently none of those Dons were called upon by me. On the 13th I left the island of Minorca.

[A five-page description of the island follows. It concludes with a brief summary of Ad. Byng's action, trial, sentence and execution on March 14, 1757 on board the *Monarque*, quoting Voltaire's famous comment. The only comments which he himself makes are:—'Why he did not follow up the advantage gained by his next in command, Rear Ad. West, does not appear. His sentence was often discussed in the naval circles when I commenced my career, and the general opinion of that day was against his execution. But those times are gone by. My Father was present at that trial.']

I do not know whether you ever heard my Father's reason for quitting the Navy. As I have just alluded to him, I shall relate it to you. He entered the profession with Capt. Dennis,[1] in the *Mermaid*, a small frigate of 20 guns. After a long cruize, the ship returned to Portsmouth. My Father having obtained leave to visit the shore—he was then about the age of 15—the Parade Coffee House attracted his attention. It is still in existence. He entered it and ordered some refreshment: but he had scarcely opened his mouth when he was accosted by two or three naval captains present, who desired him to quit the premises. He objected, observing that it was a public Coffee House which he considered was open to any gentleman for his money. Consequently, he would stay and make use of it. Those officers would not listen to his argument, and, as they found he would not retire, caught hold of him by main strength and shoved him out of the house. He instantly wrote to his Father, stating what had happened, and requested to be removed from the Navy. By return of post his discharge arrived: so there terminated my Father's professional services. He never forgot that act, and, though he had the

---

[1] Probably Sir Peter Denis, one of Anson's Lieutenants in the *Centurion*, Lt. 12/11/1739; Cdr. 25/6/44; Capt. 9/2/45; R-Ad. 24/10/70; V-Ad. 31/3/75.

warmest attachment for the Navy, and was always loud in its praises, he would often say, 'It is not the profession of a Gentleman.' The Parade Coffee House was in those days kept by a widow who devoted all her means to the entertainment of the Captains of the Navy. Consequently, no other person was a welcome guest in her house. My Father did not know of that arrangement. The captains who put up there suited their own convenience in the payment of their bills. They paid, or did not, just as it might be in their power. However, those who took long credit made handsome remunerations, and the result was that the widow, by her liberality to those officers, realized an independent fortune.

A couple of days after leaving Minorca, I fell in with the *Castor*, commanded by my friend Dilkes. The next day I met the *Iphigenia*, Capt. Andrew King.[1] In the evening, as I neared the coast of Spain, I saw the *Malta*, Rear Ad. Hallowell, at anchor. I hastened on board to receive the Admiral's commands. He had taken up a position to the eastward of Tarragona (where Lord Bentinck held the military command), as he expected a detachment of the French Army to pass in this direction. He had sent his boats, armed with carronades, to keep up a constant fire on the beach and among the bushes. I now had an opportunity of learning all that had passed during my absence from Capt. Inglefield,[2] who had on all occasions taken a lively interest in my behalf. The first expedition against Tarragona had failed, under Sir John Murray. Lord Bentinck replaced him, and that town finally fell into our hands, the *Malta* being stationed off the place to protect it against any sudden attack. The Secretary, Mr. Murray, did not fail to shake me by the hand. I received instructions to take a station a few miles to the eastward, there anchor, and act in concert with the *Iphigenia*, to prevent the enemy coming up that road. I made all sail to close upon that frigate. It was a beautiful sight to see the blaze and fire of the *Malta's* boats, but it struck me as a strange proceeding to maintain it in such a state of uncertainty. A small detachment of Marines might easily have landed to reconnoitre the passes in the neighbourhood. Had the enemy advanced, our men could have taken shelter in the boats, informing the officer in command how to direct their fire with effect: whereas an immense quantity of ammunition was expended to no other purpose than exercising the men. However, knowing that I should not remain long

[1] Andrew King, Lt. 11/8/1797; Cdr. 22/1/1806; Capt. 13/10/07. Fourth Lieut. in the *Victory* at Trafalgar.

[2] Samuel Hood Inglefield, son of Capt. John Nicholson Inglefield (see Vol. I, p. 69, note). Lt. 26/7/1798; Cdr. 29/4/1802; Capt. 6/10/07; R-Ad. 23/11/41.

upon the station, I did not feel the same interest in the proceedings as formerly.

There was moonlight, and about 2 o'clock I got sight of the *Iphigenia*, anchored close to her, then went on board. Her Captain received me cordially, stating that he had not expected me till 8 o'clock. I replied that the enemy was expected, and I was anxious to assist him in driving them away. But I declared that they would not expose themselves to the broadsides of two British ships of war, and I was convinced we should have nothing to do. I then retired to my ship, and to bed. The day brought fine weather, and the first thing we saw was a very nice farm opposite to my ship. I determined to examine it and, if possible, procure poultry, eggs, grapes, etc. I was soon on shore, the boat's crew, 10 in number, being armed. The instant I put my foot on the beach, I was accosted by a Spanish peasant. I inquired for the enemy. He replied in his native tongue, 'They are here.' 'Where?' I demanded. He pointed eastward. 'There they are,' said he. On my right I observed two hillocks of sugar loaf shape, one on each side of the main road. I instantly directed two of my seamen to mount on each with their muskets, and to fire if they saw anything like the French approach. The tars immediately did so. I then addressed the Spaniard, who was without exception the most muscular man I ever beheld: in stature about 5 feet 6, but extremely square in frame, his arms of immense circumference, legs and thighs of equally strong dimensions: a perfect Hercules. I could not refrain watching all his motions. But he was trembling, his face pale, and he was evidently in dread of some awkward event. It turned out that he was a regular coward. It was evident on his countenance. 'Who does that farm belong to?' I demanded. 'It is mine, Señor,' he replied. 'Have you any poultry, eggs, fruit, etc. to dispose of?' I inquired. 'Plenty, Señor,' was the reply. 'Let us go towards it then,' said I. Having ordered the boat's crew to load and prime, I accompanied the Spaniard to his farm, about 300 yards from the sea. We passed through a splendid vineyard of muscatel grapes. He gave orders to a little girl—I supposed his daughter—and she, with the assistance of a woman, soon produced baskets full of grapes, eggs, almonds and raisins. But as to poultry, there occurred some bargaining. His demands were out of all reason. I told him that he ought to recollect that he was dealing with an English officer acting in the cause of his country. However, he being regardless of all I said, I put down the dollars for the fruit, etc., and embarked without seeing the enemy. At parting I said, 'Adieu. I hope the French will visit your quarters and help themselves to the poultry that you have refused to me.' The extraordinary part of this story is that, some months later, the Spanish farmer was plundered by the French soldiers, who carried off all his cattle, etc.

Next day Capt. King wished me to accompany him on shore. I confess I hesitated, as I had every reason to believe that the enemy was in the neighbourhood. I thought a stroll on shore rather imprudent. However, we landed, not near my friend the farmer's, but in another direction, and proceeded towards a small village about a mile up country. I was delighted to notice here some cavalry outposts, which we learnt were attached to the German Legion, being a party of the Brunswick Oels' Corps, who bore the soubriquet of the 'Death and Glory Boys.' They had the crossbones upon their military caps, and bore the appearance of a set of fellows not to be trifled with. A sergeant addressed me, and as I judged by the twang of his English that he was a German, I spoke a few words in that language: whereat he sprang off his horse, and offered it to me, saying that he would attend me in examining the locality. However, I declined the foreigner's kind intention. We rambled about a short while on the skirts of the village, and I made many inquiries relating to the enemy. 'They are not far off,' he said, 'but we have not yet seen them.' He advised us not to go beyond the village, as the French were in the habit of disguising themselves as Spanish peasantry, and would frequently pounce upon an officer lounging about his quarters for recreation. In short, he recommended our returning to the beach, then on board, as his party would not remain long in their present position. He attended us to the shore, and we took leave of this good fellow.

The *Malta* was now seen under sail, returning to Tarragona, and on the 17th my signal was made to join the Admiral in that bay. My predictions had been verified—the enemy had not made his appearance. The next day I presented my respects to Lord William Bentinck, by whom I was most kindly received, as I had made the acquaintance of his brother Lord George. When I waited upon Ad. Hallowell, he acquainted me that I should have to convoy some transports to Gibraltar, and asked if I would give a passage to a Gen. Hineberg to Valencia. 'Most readily,' said I. 'I am ready for all services.' We immediately agreed that he should embark on the *Leopard* the next day. He was most anxious to send some wine on board, as well a couple of sheep. But I entreated him to do no such thing, Valencia being only one day's sail away and my stock in good order. The Admiral invited us to dine with him that we might become acquainted.

The next day I took leave of Ad. Hallowell, his Captain, Secretary, etc. Gen. Hineberg made his appearance on board, and on the 19th I sailed from Tarragona. We had not been long out when we were assailed by one of those violent storms of rain, thunder and lightning usual in the climate. Fortunately no accident befell us. My Steward now acquainted me that the General's servant had handed over to him a small case of wine and a couple of sheep. At my parting, the Admiral, very much to my surprise, had given me an official order to receive the General for a passage to Valencia. The wind now failed us, and I was obliged to anchor off the coast. However, by the 23rd I was in the bay of Valencia. Gen. Hineberg particularly requested me to be his guest at that town for two or three days. I at length yielded to his entreaties, and on the following day, when I landed, I met a dragoon with a steed for my use, and was piloted to the General's headquarters, 'La Marquesa de las Aquas'—the Marchioness of the Waters. The General devoted himself solely to be my cicerone. We had pleasant drives and dinners, and we went to the Opera. But I could not prolong my stay beyond the second day. It was very gratifying to meet such a friendly attention from an officer whom I could hardly consider as more than a stranger. On the 25th I took leave of him, and rode back to the beach on the same charger that had previously been at my disposal.

[A short description of Valencia is omitted.]

On my arrival on the shore, there was all the appearance of a gale, it being the equinoctial period. Many of the transports' boats were in waiting, and I gave notice that I should soon be under way. On the afternoon of the 25th I left Valencia with my convoy. On my way I met the *Ganymede*, Capt. Purvis, and the next day anchored in Altea Bay with the transports. I called upon the Spanish Guerrilla Chief to bid him adieu. We had had a great deal to do together, and in conjunction had bid the enemy defiance. He was a fine wellshaped manly fellow. He could not, he said, take leave of me without requesting me to accept a small hamper of wine which had been in his possession 20 years. When I tasted it, there could be no doubt of its age, and it was well flavoured, being probably made from his own grounds. All the other Spaniards, the Alcade, etc., came to bid me goodbye. The next day, the 27th, I left for Alicant. I now found out that my Steward had left the wine sent me by Orosco on the beach. About 18 months later I met Capt. Purvis at Portsmouth, who asked my reason for having left a hamper of wine on the beach of Altea. I explained to him. 'You had no loss,' he said. 'It was sour.' 'I did not find it so,' I replied. 'Your having tasted it is a proof of your having drank it.' The fact was that my friend *had* turned the contents of the hamper to his own account, which produced many a pleasant tale in our future meetings.

On the 28th I came to anchor in the bay of Alicant, well known to me. Here I had to receive some French prisoners. When taking leave of my Spanish friends here, I was requested by a lady of high rank to give a passage to an officer's widow. There was no refusing the Donna, and her friend soon found her way on board. On the 1st of October I took my departure from a place where I had passed many a happy hour. The last person I shook by the hand was Mr. Athy, to whom I had much to say relating to the vessels I had captured. As an old acquaintance of my Father's he had made himself not only useful, but had acted as a kind friend.

During my passage to Gibraltar my mind was frequently directed to the parting words of Sir Edward Pellew, that I should find a frigate waiting for me at the Rock. 'What ship could that be?' thought I. However, upon mature reflection I had my doubts. As he had deceived me on one occasion, he might do so again. Moreover, one or two of my naval friends had confidentially communicated to me some parts of his conduct to others that led me to suspect that all he had said was not fair above board. All went along quietly till daylight of the 7th, when I found myself close to a strange ship of war. Signals were of no use, and I hoisted the British Flag and pre-pared for action. The stranger displayed the colours of Spain. I then sent my boat with an officer on board, who soon returned having been very courteously received by the Don. On the 13th I anchored in the Bay of Gibraltar. The ship was not allowed pratique: never-theless the Prize Agent came on board to settle accounts with Mr. Preston, the Purser, whom I had appointed to attend to these affairs. There was no frigate waiting for me. I requested a friend who called alongside to inquire of the Admiral, Hood Linzee, if he had heard anything about it. He had not. So much for the sayings of Sir Ed. P——w!

One of the French prisoners having caused some serious injury to one of the Lower Deck ports, I had him up, and he received corporal punishment, giving warning to his companions to be cautious in their proceedings. They were soon landed—a happy riddance. The winter season had set in, and the weather was very unsettled. On the 14th I left Gibraltar with my convoy. My fair guest intended to leave the ship in the Tagus, whither I was now bound. On the 21st I made Cape St. Vincent, and, as the weather had a very threatening appearance, I caused a certain signal to be made to the convoy: but not one of them would obey it, though repeated with a gun. Consequently I lost sight of my charges during the night. However, one I got hold of, after firing several shots at him. When my officer returned from boarding the transport—called the *Nelly*—he informed me that her Master was drunk. I sent him back, ordering him to bring her, a brig, close under my lee quarter. Then I hailed the Master and told him, if he attempted to widen his distance, I should make him repent his conduct. I then made sail, and the *Nelly* kept within half a stone's throw on my lee quarter all night—a proof of what can be done with proper attention. On the 23rd I anchored in the Tagus below Belem, to perform a few days' quarantine. Wherever I went I had to undergo that visitation because I had been at Malta: but not a sick man on board. My convoy dropped in in rotation. On the 27th I received pratique, removed the *Leopard* up near Lisbon, and presented my respects to Sir George Martin,[1] the Admiral, to whom I represented the irregular conduct of my convoy. Shortly afterwards, I met the Master of the *Nelly* in the streets of Lisbon. He was extremely abashed when I inquired what he thought would be the consequence if I reported him to the Transport Board. He merely made his bow and sluked [*sic*] off.

I received from the Admiral the most courteous and hospitable attention. The boats were kept watering, etc., and on the 1st of November I moved down below Belem. The next day, having a large transport storeship and a merchant brig under my convoy, I left the Tagus for England. We were accompanied by strong winds, heavy clouds and rain. This was an awkward time of the year to enter the British Channel, and I had my anxiety on that head. The Master did very well in the Mediterranean, but I had been cautioned as to his knowledge on the coast of England. We soon lost sight of the brig, but the ship behaved well, and kept close to us. On the 11th we made the land with clear weather, and in the evening were close in with the Lizard lights. It was my constant practice when near the land to have the chart laid out upon my cabin table, with the compasses, ruler, etc. to refer to in case of need; and the Master had his instructions

---

[1] Sir George Martin (G.C.B., G.C.M.G.), Lt. 16/7/1780; Cdr. 9/3/82; Capt. 17/3/83; R-Ad. 9/11/1805; V-Ad. 31/7/10; Ad. 19/7/21; Ad. of the Fleet, 9/11/46. Died, 28/7/47.

to bring me the ship's reckoning at 8 o'clock every evening. On this occasion he did not appear, a message being brought to me that he was unwell. Consequently I navigated the ship myself. In the first watch it came to blow a regular gale from the S.W., with a thick mist: so much so that I could no longer discern the land. I shortened sail to a closereefed main topsail and foresail, then shaped a course for Portland lights. When that distance had been run, not seeing them, I hove to. At 7 o'clock the day began to dawn. There was a tremendous sea running, and the ship rolled about most deeply. The Officer of the Watch who called me, stated that the thick mist still continued, and that there was the appearance of land under our lee, against which the sea was breaking in immense surges. 'I wish you would come on deck, Sir,' he said. 'The Master has been up. He wanted to send me aloft. He seems to be lost.' I hurried on my clothes, took a good look at the chart, then to the Quarter Deck. I noticed the heavy breaking waves on the rocks, the ship still laying to. I ordered the hammocks to be instantly stowed, and all hands to their stations. Presently a lighthouse was seen, but no fire burning in it. At first we thought ourselves off Portland. As the day broke, another lighthouse became visible, without any lamps alight. The Master was still in doubt of our position. However, in the course of a few seconds a third lighthouse was discernible. In that one the faint glimmering of a lamp could be seen. So soon as we had a good sight of these lighthouses, the mist lightened a little, which enabled us to see the land. Then, to our utter astonishment, we found ourselves off the Caskets,[1] and very close to the one on which stood the buildings mentioned.[*]

There was now not a moment to be lost. I caught hold of my speaking trumpet, but, before giving any orders, addressed a few words to the Ship's Company, telling them that the safety of the ship, and their lives, depended upon their punctual obedience to my directions. Then I set the foresail: up went the helm, and the ship, in wearing, passed so close to the rocks that the spray of the sea came on board. It was a most critical and awful moment: but, thank Heaven, the ship was saved. When we got out into the mid Channel, we saw our convoy going on in good style. It was supposed that the tide had driven us out of our direct course whilst lying to. All the

---

[1] Some 7 miles west of Alderney—*i.e.* on the wrong shore of the Channel.

[*] It was a most serious neglect on the part of those persons who had the management of the lights. Had we seen, in the first instance, the whole three alight, we should have known our true position. Only the light in the third one pointed out the danger we were in. Another minute's delay might have been fatal.

officers came in succession to thank me for having, by my management, saved their lives.

In the evening we were off St. Alban's Head, the weather still hazy and the lead kept going. On the morning of the 13th we were off St. Catherine's Point, and by ½ past 2 in the afternoon the ship was anchored at the Mother Bank, being obliged to perform Quarantine under the Yellow Flag. The ship under my convoy did not in this instance follow my example. Consequently it was my duty to report her proceedings to the Quarantine officers as she came from Malta. Some of her passengers were walking about the town of Portsmouth, but they were ordered instantly to return to their ship.

I lost no time in sending an official statement to the Health Office in London, from which, on the 18th, I received orders to haul down the Quarantine Flag, having been 100 days under it without a sick man on board. No consideration had been bestowed upon me during this trial. The *Leopard* was removed the same day to Spithead, and I presented my respects to the Port Admiral, Sir Richard Bickerton.

[In an erased passage W.H.D. records that he now secured a separation from his wife, 'and you will not hear of her again in the Narrative'.]

After having attended to all my professional duties, I applied to the Admiralty for 10 days leave of absence. In all the naval circles I heard but one opinion in my behalf, that an act of injustice had been done me in keeping me so long in the command of a troopship. My application was granted, and I was soon in London, at my old quarters, the Salopian Coffee House.

XIII

NORTH AMERICAN STATION

DECEMBER 1813–JULY 1815

(*aet.* 33¼–35)

INTRODUCTION

INSTALLED at length in an operational command—Captain of 'one of our crack frigates'—W.H.D. came at last into his own. His commission proved a long one, from January 19, 1814 to January 10, 1817, and in the course of it he visited every continent, save only Australia, and of that he passed within a few miles. Africa he visited twice, North America twice and South America once: Greenland and the Arctic Circle, the East Indies, China, India and St. Helena. His only regret was that, from the start, the war with France was practically over. Yet he could console himself somewhat by participating in the Anglo-American war which was still on, and in the brief crisis of the Hundred Days. He even had a sporting chance, in the summer of 1815, of 'nabbing the fallen Emperor' (pp. 335 *et seq.*).

On p. 276, occurs his account of his last rencontre with Lady Hamilton, in December, 1813. It is a pity that he never divulges how he came to know her in the first place, but he has already made it clear that he did know her quite well. So, though he does not stress the fact, he must have been a witness of her sad fall in the social, or rather, perhaps, financial world.

She was now drifting fast downhill, and, with only a bare year to live, had no one but herself to thank for her misfortunes. Nor, it should be emphasised, was she to the last in real financial want. For three years after Trafalgar she lived quite happily—and very extravagantly—at Merton (where W.H.D. had visited her after his return from captivity). In November, 1808, that estate was taken over by faithful friends in an attempt to free her from her financial difficulties. On leaving Merton, she was offered a villa at Richmond by the eccentric Duke of Queensberry, who seems to have been fond of, or at least kind to, the rapidly ageing beauty, and who, it was rumoured at one time, toyed with the idea of making her his Duchess.

But nothing could save her from herself. In 1810 she moved from Richmond into Town. W.H.D. has already recounted (p. 150) how he went to see her 'in Piccadilly' in June of that year, and the company she kept then can hardly be described as 'low', seeing that it included a Prince of the Blood—though the Royal Brothers hardly, had the reputation of being exclusive in their circle of acquaintances! Two things here are news (to the Editor anyway): first, her familiarity with the Duke of

Sussex, who is there twice when W.H.D. calls (see also p. 277); and, second, her residence in Piccadilly in 1810. She had, of course, inhabited No. 23 in that street much earlier, when both Sir William and Lord Nelson were alive; for at that house Horatia was born and Sir William died. But perhaps, in 1810, she was merely lodging in Piccadilly, as she was certainly, a year later, in rooms at 150 Bond Street.

In 1813 things went seriously wrong. She was arrested for debt, and sent to the King's Bench prison. But even this was not quite so bad as it seems, for as W.H.D. found, she was not actually in gaol, but in the 'precincts'—as Dillon tactfully puts it, 'at an address in the neighbourhood of the King's Bench.' It was in fact No. 12, Temple Place. In the spring of 1814 she was released from even this mild detention. But her affairs were in hopeless confusion, and in July of this year, France being now open to her, she embarked at the Tower Wharf for Calais, taking Horatia with her.

She went no further. Again she started in the best hotel, but descended to indifferent lodgings in a farm near Calais. And here she died on January 15, 1815, certainly not penniless, probably not even in serious financial straits.

In W.H.D.'s account of the evening there are significant pointers. There is quite an ostentatious dinner—but no carvers. He asks for some trifling memento of Nelson, and she promises to oblige him. But he does not record that he received anything: and the probability must be that there was nothing left for him to have. Everything of realisable value had already been—realised.

The passage about Lord Cochrane (p. 287) has a melancholy interest of its own. But it also exposes two of W.H.D.'s personal weaknesses. Our author, though he does not know Cochrane personally, never has a good word to say for him, and the reason is not far to seek. After the Aix Roads affair, and Cochrane's rash opposing in the House of the Vote of thanks to Gambier, there was something of a split in the Navy between 'pro-' and and 'anti-' Gambiers. Nor could it be in doubt on which side W.H.D. would align himself. He was always, unashamedly, a 'Gambier Man', and that alone would make his judgment suspect: that alone would make him sure that Cochrane could do nothing right. The second revelation concerns Dillon's own passion to appear right. This has been revealed already on many occasions, and here he is at it again. He is asked for his views by his acquaintances, and gives them in no uncertain terms, entirely against Cochrane. Then, by inference, he claims as usual how right he was proved to be: how the Government, by its subsequent actions, exactly bore out his opinion. For once, however, he has not had the last word. History has entirely reversed the verdict, not only of the Government but also of W.H.D.

We may perhaps be inclined to question his rightness again when he chronicles his strange quarrel with Sir Richard Keats (pp. 314 *et seq.*).

Indeed, as he narrates it, it is not even easy to understand exactly what the Admiral had against him. The two most likely theories are, perhaps, that he was accusing Dillon of deserting his convoy in the storm, and making for safety on his own at 8 or 9 knots, while the lame ducks of the party laboured on at 3: or (perhaps *and*) that the *Horatio's* damage did not justify him in departing from his Admiralty orders, and in making for St. John's instead of seeing the Quebec ships safely into the St. Lawrence. We know enough of Dillon's character and standards by now, probably, to enable us to acquit him freely of the first charge. But the second must remain more a matter of opinion, and of contemporary and technical evidence which is no longer available to us. As usual, of course, we are hearing one side of the case only: a case—as usual too—in which the other party is 100 per cent in the wrong and W.H.D. 100 per cent right. So it is perhaps worth noticing that, of all the great naval names of the period, none stands higher than that of Keats for just that sort of quality of which he reveals a total absence here. His habitual courtesy, urbanity, under-standing and equability made him beloved among all his contemporaries: so that, of all his seniors whose conduct W.H.D. criticises—and that means, sooner or later, almost all of them—this account of Sir Richard Keats rings least true. In fairness to Dillon, however, it should also be mentioned that Keats, during his command of the American station, was in a very poor state of health.

Towards the end of this Part, there looms up the old, vexed but exceedingly important question of 'Freight'. It is a long story, dating from the days before the inception of the naval profession. We shall readily recall the—to us—scandalous activities of some of Charles II's captains (*vide* N.R.S. Vol. LXXIII), who liked to regard 'trading' as one of their most important duties, as it was certainly one of the most lucrative of their perquisites. Pepys, we may remember, set his face against it, since in his eyes it detracted from the efficiency of H.M. ships. He did not fail entirely, for he contrived to kill the *general* tendency of the captains to turn H.M. ships into merchantmen. But he did not—almost certainly could not—abolish Freight altogether. It remained throughout the eighteenth century one of the two great sources of a captain's remunera-tion. His wages were never one: the other, of course, was 'Prize'. Yet, by W.H.D.'s time, Freight had narrowed itself down to one particular type of goods—precious metals, or, to use the technical term, 'Treasure'. That remained as a very profitable 'vested interest', affecting far too many powerful and interested parties.

Along with the payment of a percentage to the captain of the carrying ship, there had always existed the corresponding interests of the admiral under whose flag the captain was serving at the moment. Here again the parallel between Freight-Money and Prize-Money (see Vol. I, p. 75, note) was noticeably close. By the end of the eighteenth century, custom had crystallised the Admiral's share at one-third of the total payable by the owner. But there were two further complications: the first, which need not concern us much, the division of the Admiral's third between himself and his subordinate Flags: the second, and more important, the distinction between 'Public (*i.e.*, state-owned) Treasure' and 'Private Treasure' (the property of individual citizens). The real trouble, in both cases—and indeed implicit throughout the whole problem—was that the rights of all parties, captains and admirals alike, were based, not upon Law, but upon ancient usage. There was thus a fruitful field for disputes, and such were constantly occurring, especially as the sums at stake (as in W.H.D.'s case) were often large.

No official move, apparently, was made before 1801. But relentless things were happening, in the fields both of 'public' and of 'private' Treasure. In the first case, with the ever-growing elaboration of the economies of states, the carriage of bullion and specie became more and more imperative, and so it became commoner and commoner for the governments concerned to have it conveyed by the safest possible means, especially in wartime—that is, in the armed ships of the state. But, this being so, it was quite inevitable that, sooner or later, the Government would notice that it was not only paying for its own ships, but also paying extra for using one of its own ships for one of its own purposes: and it would—ultimately—object to such a curious arrangement.

The case of the private treasure-owner was clearly somewhat different, and less likely to become acute so soon. In view of the century-old French policy of 'Guerre de Course'—attack upon our trade—and the still world-wide prevalence of piracy, he too found it eminently desirable to have his treasure conveyed by the safest possible means, the warship. But, in this case unlike the other, he might expect, and be expected, to pay for the additional protection afforded him. So the real crux here was not the fact of freight-money itself, but the question of who was to receive it.

Thus the first move came on the 'Public Treasure' side. It was taken in 1801, when all allowance for its carriage was stopped. But, here as elsewhere, the Vested Interest—the age-old *usage* of a freight-percentage finding its way into a captain's pocket—remained uncomfortably strong: so strong that, in 1807, it was powerful enough to force a partial reversion to the old practice. In that year a 'gratuity' of one-half per cent. was allowed for the carriage of all 'public treasure.'

All the old and prolific grounds for dispute remained, however, whether between owner and captain, captain and admiral, or senior and junior flag officer. Indeed, so many cases came up before the courts that at length both the Courts of Common Pleas and the King's Bench decided that Flag Officers had no legal rights at all, even by 'custom', to any share either in the 'public treasure gratuity' or the 'private treasure freights' (Montagu v. Janverin, 1811).

There followed an even more drastic decision by the Court of Common Pleas—that in *Law* no captain had any such rights either: not even in 'private' freights, since it could not be legal to use a King's ship for any private purpose (Brisbane *v.* Dacres, 1813). Yet—and this is a highly characteristic feature in the story of all vested interests in this, and other, countries—these decisions in no way killed the practice, for they still left open an immense practical loophole. They all recognised the Admiralty's power to make its own regulations on the subject, which, though not upheld by the law of the land, could yet govern the relations between the Admiralty and its own officers. The result was that, in *fact*, everything went on very much as before.

This was the stage reached in 1815, when W.H.D. received his offer. He had, therefore no right, in law, to accept any freight percentage, but he was entitled to do so by Admiralty regulation. His case proves a good illustration of how much the whole system stood in need of clarification. There was clearly plenty of scope for 'business manoeuvring': *e.g.*, for the private owner, in this instance the E.I.C., to exploit the natural desire among captains to obtain a freight, and to secure cut-throat terms. We see the Companys' Agent doing it, and W.H.D. struggling—unsuccessfully —against it. He can urge that 1 per cent. is unfairly low, being far under the $2\frac{1}{2}$ per cent. 'which was the general rule for going to India'—*i.e.*, the current rate obtaining at the moment. But the Agent can—and does— apply the squeeze of competition. 'All right! Take it or leave it. But remember: there are dozens of other captains who will snap it up if you don't!' So W.H.D. is duly squeezed—yet for all that makes a very comfortable £2,000: and a good deal more later.

Dillon's behaviour under this pressure is interesting. There was evidently a conflict in his mind. Conscience told him that, by accepting the cut rate offered, he might be spoiling the market, and establishing a precedent unfavourable to the whole body of naval officers. So he squirmed a little before succumbing to the temptation. Nor was he wrong in supposing that his action might bring on him his colleagues' censure, and we find that he was taken to task, pretty severely, by at least one of them (see p. 398).

In a Service gradually becoming regularised in every direction, such a state of things could not last. So it was that, in 1819, an Act of Parliament (59 Geo. III, cap. 25) authorised the Crown to take the whole matter over and fix, by proclamation, the rates for the conveyance of treasure, both public and private, in H.M. ships, in both war and peace, as well as the proportion which was to go to the various recipients. And it is to be observed that, in spite of the decisions of the courts which found that the whole business had no standing in law, the new legislation went all in favour of the officers who now, *for the first time*, found that they had statute law behind them.

The following, in slightly simplified form, are the rates laid down by the relevant Order in Council of July 12, 1819, which implements the Act:—

Length of Carriage	'Public'	'Private'	
		Peace	War
Under 600 leagues . . .	¾%	1½%	2 %
Over 600 leagues. . . .	1%	2 %	2½%
Beyond Capes of Good Hope and Horn	1%	2½%	3 %

It is very probable that these 'crystallising' figures represent pretty faithfully the uncrystallised 'custom' prevailing at the moment. If this be so, W.H.D. is shown to be right in the main. A mere 1 per cent. for 'private' freight was certainly a 'squeeze' on the part of the E.I.C.: and his 2½ per cent. suggestion was just about right since, with Waterloo safely won, the E.I.C. might make something of a case for 'Peace' rates

The same Act, too, settles the other vexed question of the 'share-out'. One-fourth of the total received was to go to the admiral (or admirals): two-fourths to the captain, and—a complete departure this—one-fourth to Greenwich Hospital.

The rest of the story may be briefly told. As the nineteenth century proceeded, there were several revisions of the percentages laid down in 1819. All were in a downward direction, perhaps because the far-flung shield of Pax Britannica made the risks less. In 1831, though the figure for 'public treasure' remained the same, those for 'private treasure' fell steeply, to one-half of the former figure, or nearly. In 1881 they moved still further down—to a flat rate of 1 per cent., irrespective of distance.

Thus they stood when the twentieth century dawned. But clearly the whole principle was doomed, and the end came, suddenly, just after the outbreak of the 1914–18 war. On October 26, 1914, a laconic Order in Council simply cancelled all previous orders, thus terminating the whole business. By then the official view clearly was that all payment for carrying public goods in public ships, and all private perquisites for naval officers were like anachronisms.

One more important 'vested interest' comes under discussion at the end of this Part, and W.H.D. chronicles what was practically the first move towards demolishing it, though he does not stress its significance—if, indeed, he was aware that it *was* significant. This vested interest was the custom whereby naval officers, usually captains, were the real and only selectors of the material from which their next generation was to be produced. This had always been so hitherto. It was the Captain who made all the arrangements for, and received on board—or rejected—all aspirants wishing to become naval officers. The Admiralty had had, as yet, nothing to do with it. It is true that, in 1794, a nominal change had taken place when the old, and truly descriptive, name of 'Captain's Servant' had given place to that of 'First Class Volunteer'. But it was no real change, since after it, in most cases, it still lay with the captains to make the choice, picking or discarding at will all save the few 'Volunteers-per-Order' or

'College Volunteers'. These, having been nominated by the Admiralty to pass through the Royal Naval College at Portsmouth, had to be accepted by the captains. (Nor was this little entry itself a novelty: it had been invented by Pepys.)

It was now, in July, 1815, W.H.D. tells us (p. 339) that the order went forth 'that the youngsters could no longer be received into the Navy, and entered in the Ship's Books without the sanction of the Admiralty.' This was the beginning of that governing body's assault upon the vested interest of officer selection, or, as the later phrase had it 'Officer Nomination'. It met with Dillon's approval for just the kind of social reasons which we should expect of him. He held that it elevated the *ton* of the naval officer. It is quite possible that this was the Admiralty's immediate reason too. The fact that they seem to have used their new power of veto quite sparingly for the next score or so of years perhaps bears this out. Or again, it may be that, foreseeing the dreadful officer-block about to develop, they wanted to keep a more careful eye on the sheer number of entrants. But neither of these motives was the one which was of long-term importance. That was—or rather, probably, became—a determination first to reduce, and ultimately to break, the officers' vested interest of 'Nomination'. This is in some ways a parallel case to that of Freight, just discussed, marking the same phase of naval development. Any *modern* service must be run, to an overriding extent, from the top. And just as the Authority and not the individual must decide the principles and even the details relating to the carriage of treasure, so also—and even more so—must the Authority secure the right to select all its officer-recruits.

The struggle for this right, waged between the Admiralty and its own more senior officers, was in fact long and stern: and, though the former gradually—and inevitably—won, it took all but a century to do so completely. The last vestiges of 'officer-nomination' died out only in 1913. Herein, too, lies another curious parallel. 'Freights', as we have seen, lasted a bare year longer. And it is perhaps a fitting conclusion to this discussion of 'vested interests' to recall that 'Prize' outlasted them both, surviving, albeit in modified form, even the Second World War. This survival-order was probably right, for these three 'interests' are, in one respect at anyrate, hardly comparable. Prize, in its very nature, implied at least some degree of risk, where Freight involved very little, and Nomination none at all. Indeed, there are those, even now, who would uphold the principle of Prize. Still, rightly or wrongly, it is dead.

XIII
NORTH AMERICA
DECEMBER 1813–JULY 1815
(*aet.* 33–35)

(1) H.M.S. *LEOPARD* AND *NEWCASTLE*
DECEMBER 1813–MARCH 3, 1814

My first duty was to call at the Admiralty, to have some conversation with the Senior Naval Lord. That station was then occupied by Sir Joseph Yorke,[1] but Rear-Ad. George Hope[2] was the person upon whom I depended. I had a great deal to say after the absence of 18 months, and having saved so many villages on the coast of Spain from the ravages of the French army. Ad. Hope, whom I had known in Scotland, received me with great kindness, and promised to take up my cause with Lord Melville. I consulted him upon my claim for remuneration for having given a passage from Minorca to Majorca to the Spanish Governor. 'Write to me,' said he, 'and give me all the particulars. Have you an official order to receive him'? I showed it to him. On all other subjects I found him quite willing to be useful. I told him that I had not as yet the honour of the First Lord's acquaintance. 'Very well,' he replied. 'Call here tomorrow at 12 o'clock, and I will present you to his Lordship.'

I attended accordingly, and was highly gratified by the kind manner in which he presented me to Lord M., with whom I had a long conversation. His Lordship put many questions relating to the duties of a troop ship. 'I hear,' said he, 'that it is expensive.' 'Why,' said I, 'there is a great deal to be said on that subject.'

[There evidently was. The interview followed the usual course of such audiences. W.H.D. enlarged upon the unavoidable expenses, and Lord M. sympathised, or appeared to. Then W.H.D. gave some account of his services in the *Leopard*, saying how much he had

---

[1] Sir Joseph Sydney Yorke, (K.C.B.), Lt. 27/6/1789; Cdr. 19/11/90; Capt. 4/2/93; R-Ad. 31/7/1810; V-Ad. 4/6/1814; Ad. 22/7/30; accidentally drowned, 1831.
[2] See above, p. 88.

done, and how much more he would have done had the ship had her full 50 guns instead of 28. Then he asked for the command of the *Tiber*, a large new frigate. Lord M. 'promised to think of me'. On reaching the hall below, he was advised to call on the Private Secretary, Mr. Robert William Hay, and did so. He again urged his case for consideration to something better than a troop ship, and Mr. Hay 'promised to make a note of my application.']

The next day I called upon Rear-Ad. Hope again, taking with me the printed regulations of the Admiralty relating to the allowances made to Captains receiving passengers of high rank at their tables, which showed that I was entitled to upwards of £100. He explained that, by his intercession in my behalf, the Board had awarded me £50. I was sorely vexed at that decision. I remarked that the Don's party consisted of 25 individuals. I maintained them for 9 days, and surely the least that could be allowed would be £100. He was not prepared for my appeal, and hesitated for a few seconds. Then he remarked, 'You have received lately some orders on the Treasury for entertaining officers of distinction, and I do not think you will get more. You had better make up your mind to be satisfied. Take my advice.' 'I only claim,' I observed, 'what is fairly pointed out in the Regulations. I have performed my part of the contract, and am in justice entitled to the sum mentioned. These regulations allow £100 for the entertainment of an officer of his rank, and suite. But I shall follow your advice.' Afterwards, having had some satisfactory talk with him, I withdrew.

Upon my return to the hotel, I found a letter from Lady Hamilton, inviting me to dine with her the next day. Three years had elapsed since I had seen her. The address given was in the neighbourhood of the King's Bench, which caused me some anxiety.[1] When the hour approached, the rain was pouring down in torrents. I engaged a postchaise for the remainder of the evening, then started for the residence indicated. Upon my arrival her Ladyship greeted me most sincerely. 'How did you know that I was in Town?' I demanded. She acquainted me that a friend who had seen me at the Admiralty had told her, and that she was highly delighted to shake me again by the hand. I noticed a splendid display of plate on the dinner table, and covers laid for four, but made no inquiries who the guests were. This lady was naturally very anxious to hear all that had happened since we last met. I gave her the information she

---

[1] See Intro., p. 269.

required, and, during the conversation, requested her to give me some small trifle belonging to Nelson. She promised to do so.

Whilst we were thus occupied, I was surprised by the entrance into the room of H.R.H. the Duke of Sussex. Shortly afterwards Mrs. B. made her appearance. The Prince was all kindness, and wondered I had not been to see him. In making my acknowledgements for his gracious condescension, I explained that I had only been three or four days in London, and my whole time taken up with the Admiralty, but the first leisure would be devoted to H.R.H. 'Come and breakfast with me,' said the Duke. I gladly promised to obey that command.

The dinner being served, the conversation turned in another direction. I had to do the honours—carve, etc. The first course went off in complete order, and I could not help thinking that rather too much luxury had been produced. H.R.H. did not expect such an entertainment from the lady who received him. However, there was a sad falling off in the second course, and a great deficiency in attendance, as also of knives and forks. I had to carve a good-sized bird, but had not been supplied with the necessary implements. Time passed on, but no servant made his appearance. At last Lady H. said, 'Why don't you cut up that bird?' I told her I was in want of a knife and fork. 'Oh,' said she, 'you must be not particular here.' 'Very well, my Lady,' I rejoined. 'I did not like to commit myself in the presence of H.R.H., but since you desire it, I will soon divide the object before me. Besides, you are aware that, as a Midshipman, I learnt how to use my fingers.' Then, looking about, I found what I wanted, and soon had the bird in pieces. My reply produced some hearty laughter, and the repast terminated very merrily. After a sociable and agreeable entertainment, I took my leave of the company.

[He visited the Duke of Sussex, who gave him a hearty reception and an introduction to the Duke of York. The latter, in his turn, 'was all kindness': but nothing more positive came of the interview. He then returned to the *Leopard* at Portsmouth.]

This winter was a very severe one. The streets of London were blocked up with large pieces of ice. One day, in a hackney coach, the motion in going over lumps of it made me sick. The river was frozen over, and bonfires lit upon it.

Our principal conversation at Portsmouth turned upon the war with America. Our large frigates were in no shape upon a par with theirs. We had lost the *Guerrière*, taken by the *Constitution*, the *Macedonian* by the *United States*, and the *Java*, also by the *Constitution*. Most of the seamen in these American ships were English.[1] The Government and the Admiralty were fitting out larger frigates, and some of our small 74's were cut down to carry 50 heavy guns. Accustomed as our Navy had been to triumph on all occasions where a foe was met on anything like equal terms—and sometimes when he was vastly superior—these measures were necessary. The French, Spanish and Dutch were roughly of the same dimensions as ours, though the former usually had more tonnage and always outnumbered us in their crews. But the American frigates were far superior in every respect: the hulls were larger, and they had heavier metal, with crews of at least 500 picked men—no boys—whereas the crew of one of our 46-gun frigates never exceeded 285, including boys. Consequently we were obliged to improve the size of our ships and increase the number of their crews.*

Not hearing anything further from the Admiralty, I wrote to Lord Melville, proposing to have the *Leopard's* number of guns increased to her proper rating of 50, but with heavy carronades. The ship sailed well, the actual crew were equal to any service, and, by adopting that plan, we could make her, with her seamen increased to 450, a match for the heavy American frigates. I received a letter of thanks for my suggestion, but nothing more. I cannot help noticing here the gallant act of a friend of mine (Cdr. J. F. Maples[2]), in the command of a brig of war, the *Pelican*, (18 guns). He boarded and carried in a most spirited manner the American brig of war, the *Argus* (20 guns).

[W.H.D. now fell foul of two Flag Officers. The first was Rear-Ad. E. J. Foote[3] who, unknown to him, had been appointed to assist the

---

[1] A statement which American historians would *not* confirm. Yet it will not surprise us unduly, perhaps, when we recall that the primary cause of the whole unfortunate war hinged on this very point, the United States accusing us of pressing American seamen, we declaring that we were only recapturing British deserters.

* (The first part—a long and accurate account of the *Shannon* v. *Chesapeake* duel—is omitted here.)

The Bold Chesapeake	Quite sure of the game,
Came out for a freak,	As from harbour they came,
And swore she'd soon silence our cannon,	A dinner and wine they bespoke.
While the yankees in port	But for meat they got balls
Stood to laugh at the sport,	From our staunch wooden walls,
And see her tow in the brave Shannon.	So the dinner engagement was *Broke*.

[2] John Fordyce Maples, Lt. 16/5/1794; Cdr. 21/10/1810; Capt. 23/8/13; R-Ad. (Ret.) 1/10/46. The action took place 14/8/13 and he was made Post as a result of it.

[3] See below, p. 280 n.

Commander-in-Chief—'my *friend*(!) Sir Richard Bickerton'.[1] Accused of neglecting the former by not paying him a routine call, he did so, and found him 'an officer who did not possess the best temper, and thought it a part of his duty to make all his inferiors feel his power.' He contrived, however, to make his peace with him.

But this was not so easy with the C.-in-C. himself. One day, while on his own Quarter Deck, Dillon was hit by some spent slugs from a ship's musket fired—at a passing gull, he said—by the master of a victualling hoy. W.H.D. promptly reported the matter to Sir Richard, who would not listen to the complaint. Thereupon Dillon went straight to the Victualling Office, sidetracking the Admiral. Here he received immediate satisfaction, and indeed thanks, for the master in question turned out to be 'the greatest scamp upon the establishment': and they welcomed—and took—the opportunity to dismiss him. When the C.-in-C. heard of this he was apparently very angry, but could do nothing official about it. He did, however, attempt to pay W.H.D. back in the following mean and undignified way:—]

On the 18th of the month, it being the Queen's Birthday, I received an invitation to dine with the Admiral. I attended at the hour fixed, but was disappointed at not meeting any ladies, not even the mistress of the house. It was a regular bachelor's reunion, all in naval order, seniority, etc. When the cloth had been removed, and the ceremony of toasts commenced, they went off in quick succession. I then expected a little respite. I was seated by an old shipmate of the *Alcide*, and we naturally had a good deal to say. My position was on the Admiral's left, about half way down the table. My friend and I were in deep conversation, and the bottles were standing before us unnoticed when the Admiral, calling me by name in a loud voice, said, 'Pass the Wine.' This order drew the attention of the whole company towards me, and my companion very properly rejoined, 'I am more to blame than him.' The wine went on, and all was quiet. However, after two or three rounds, there was another short delay, if such it could be called, the bottles being before us. Another loud call again brought us into notice. I was the person fixed on again, which certainly bore the appearance of a desire from that quarter to annoy. However, I made no observation. Shortly after the second call, at the very instant the wine came to us, the Admiral burst out a third time, in a louder voice than ever. As he had all along called to me,

---

[1] See above, p. 112.

without noticing my neighbour who was nearer to him, it appeared evident he fixed upon me: which was not, at a gentleman's table, correct or proper. Such was my feeling at the time, therefore, that, taking hold of the bottles in succession, I moved them on, then withdrew, leaving my seat vacant. Thence I went to the Ball where, shortly afterwards, my dinner companions joined me. Some of them remarked, 'Sharp work with the wine!' But I avoided saying any-thing on the subject. I then mixed with the ladies of my acquaintance. The remark of one of them I shall never forget—'You are the only sober man in the room.'

The next morning at 10 o'clock a messenger came to my lodgings announcing that the Admiral wished to see me. What's in the wind now, thought I. Anything more unpleasant to turn up? However, I lost no time in attending to the summons. When I saw Sir Richard he was in his dressing gown, and, advancing towards me, he said, 'I have some good news for you.' I waited patiently. Then he placed in my hands a letter from the Admiralty, acquainting him that I was appointed to the command of the *Horatio*, one of our finest frigates. 'You must have the first interest in the country,' said the Admiral. He was in the morning a very different person from what he had been the previous evening. He repeated frequently the superior qualities of the *Horatio*, clearly intimating that she was a ship destined to be commanded by an officer of considerable parliamentary influence. He put several questions to me on that subject, to all of which I could not give him a satisfactory answer. However, it was a truly gratifying event to me, and it was a proof that my long and faithful services had not been forgotten at the Admiralty.

An appointment at the Dock Yard led me thither, where I came in contact with the Admiral[1]. This officer accosted me with all sorts of compliments, and repeated all the remarks made by the Comman-der-in-Chief. Whilst I commanded a trooper, he had already given proof that he did not care much about me, but when I was a captain of one of our crack frigates I was a different person.

On this subject I cannot omit my observations. The troopships had been introduced solely for the accommodation of the Army, because so many accidents had happened to the transports. All the naval captains out of employ dreaded the idea of being appointed to one of them. However, whatever the feelings of the whole Service towards those officers who accepted the commands of them, the

---

[1] (Sir) Edward James Foote (K.C.B.), Lt. 12/8/1785; Cdr. 1/10/91; Capt. 7/6/94; R-Ad. 12/8/12; V-Ad. 19/9/21.

Admiralty had selected for the Captains of the frigates men of title and of the first families in the kingdom. They were in rank Commanders, and in accepting their appointments were sure in the end of obtaining promotion. Among the Post Captains chosen for that duty I noticed some of our most distinguished officers—your old friend Chetham[1] in particular. Therefore, though not overpleased when I received my appointment to the *Leopard*, I found officers, my seniors, in a similar position: which circumstance in some degree enabled me to bear with patience the chances of my profession. Now I had gone through the ordeal, and in consequence thereof had received a distinguished appointment. I had now to commence a new career, but the thought that plagued me most was that the war had nearly reached its termination in Europe. But there was still America open for a chance. I could not see my way clear, and I felt all sorts of misgivings.

When I returned to my ship, I came in contact with my officers, who were delighted beyond description at my new command. It now came out that the Master was drunk when the ship was off the Lizard coming up channel. That was the reason he had not attended with his reckoning in the evening. 'However, Sir,' said they, 'you saved us. We owe our lives to you.' But not one of them had given me that information when it was so essentially required. What would they have done had the ship been lost on the Caskets? The next day I began making my arrangements—packing, etc.—and I selected one or two of the most deserving petty officers whom I recommended for promotion, which in the end was granted. All my establishment, Coxswain, Steward, Cook, Clerk and others, were directed to hold themselves in readiness to quit the ship for the *Horatio*. The First Lieutenant, being partially deaf and not long with me, had no claim. The Third, only Acting, had already committed himself, and therefore had no right to expect any attention from me. The Second[2] had no desire to quit the ship, as he could not take his wife with him in a cruising frigate. He had been with me the longest, and regretted that it would not suit his plans to follow me into my next ship. But he was evidently most sincerely attached to me, and said; 'I have been with many Captains, but you surpass them all by your correctness and attention to duty. Whenever the ship is in port, we always know where to find our Captain—I could not say so much

---

[1] (Sir) Edward Chetham (K.C.H.), Lt. 18/8/1794; Cdr. 7/11/1800; Capt. 13/10/07; R-Ad. 23/11/41.
[2] Vickery.

of other ships I have been in. You were always the same, and three years' experience under your command has taught us that we could always place the utmost reliance in you.' This declaration, although from an inferior, had its merit because all the others joined him in the assertion. The conduct of the Purser was also mentioned. . . .

[Omitted here is a long account of how the Purser,[1] while the *Leopard* was in the Mediterranean, had kept a notebook in which he had set down, and commented adversely upon, every act of W.H.D since he had taken over the command. This book was brought to his notice by all the other officers. Dillon had refused to read it himself, but the officers had insisted upon the Purser reading it aloud in the presence of both W.H.D. and themselves. Thereupon the former said:—'If I acted rightly, I ought to report the whole of your conduct to the Admiralty. I do not envy your feelings, if you have any, after the way in which you have been exposed by your mess-mates. I can only express to you my sovereign contempt. You are beneath my notice. Take your book of notes, and be off. You can expect no favour from me.']

Next day I was informed officially that the *Horatio* was detained upon the coast of Holland, and that her present Captain, Lord George Stuart,[2] was appointed to command the *Newcastle*, a new frigate built to match the Americans, of 50 guns, having one tier of them along the gangway. I was ordered to repair to Woolwich to fit her out: and when the *Horatio* came to England, his Lordship and I were to exchange ships. Capt. Crofton[3] was to relieve me in the command of the *Leopard*. Whilst these events were passing, I received two or three very supplicating letters from the Purser, who was anxious to reinstate himself in my good opinion. But his letters were returned to him.

Whilst my preparations for departure were going on, the death of Lord Dillon[4] was announced, and I wrote a letter of condolence to his successor,[5] from whom I received a very courteous reply. As I had been some time at Portsmouth, I had become acquainted with many naval officers. Among the number who devoted friendly attentions to me was Capt. H————r[4] of the *Bellerophon*, at that period Sir

---

[1] Preston, see p. 242.
[2] Lt. 21/3/1801; Cdr. 22/4/02; Capt. 3/3/04.
[3] Edward Crofton: Lt. 19/3/1804; Cdr. 1/2/05; Capt. 4/3/11.
[4] Charles, 12th Viscount. See Vol. I, Introduction.
[5] Henry Augustus, 13th Viscount, 1777–1832.
[4] Edward Hawker, Lt. 14/7/1796; Cdr. 29/8/1803; Capt. 6/6/04; R-Ad. 10/1/37.

Richard Keats' Flag Captain. I happened to dwell, once, upon the high opinion which I entertained of that Admiral, who then held the command at Newfoundland. I had at all times experienced kindness from him, particularly when he had the command at Cadiz. In addition to that feeling of his towards me, I had been informed that he had promised Sir Charles Dillon,[1] with whom he was intimate, to assist me when in his power. So it was natural that I should express a wish to serve under him, never supposing that Capt. H. would repeat to him any expression of mine. However, the *Horatio* was a superior frigate, and would be a desirable acquisition to any squadron.

About the 28th of January, Capt. Crofton made his appearance, and relieved me in the command of the *Leopard*. In giving up that ship I felt it my duty to make him acquainted with her state and condition, as well as the character of her officers. I pointed out the Master's propensities, and advised him to be on his guard with him.* On the 30th I left Portsmouth, and in the course of three or four days made my appearance at Woolwich, to take the temporary command of the *Newcastle*, of 50 guns. She was a splendid ship, but, having been built by a Frenchman, Mons. Barrallier, (who had been at the head of that department at Toulon when the Revolution broke out and had emigrated and been employed by us), she was upon the scantling of the ships of that nation. Close to her lay the *Leander*, also a 50-gun frigate, commanded by Sir George Collier,[2] but built by an Englishman. Whilst the fitting was going on, I had frequent personal communications with the Admiralty, and from these heard that Lord George Stuart did not wish to quit the *Horatio*. However, Lord Melville acquainted him that his refusing such a distinguished appointment would not be accepted. He could not, after such a message, refuse the honour intended.

During my intercourse with the Dock Yard officials, I could not help noticing that there was a strong jealous feeling against Barrallier, and as the stowing of the *Newcastle's* hold proceeded, it became quite apparent that there would not be room for the ballast and casks intended for her use. This failing produced in the Dock Yard a feeling highly detrimental to the Frenchman. However, the ship was very superior in her capacities, and I wrote to the Admiralty

---

[1] Of Lismullen, eldest son of Sir John (of Lismullen) and elder brother of W.H.D.'s namesake, Sir William (of Lismullen). See Vol. I, Introduction.

* The *Leopard* was afterwards (later in this same year) lost off the island of Anticosti, Gulf of St. Lawrence, by that officer's negligence.

[2] Lt. 22/1/1796; Cdr. 3/9/1799; Capt. 22/4/02. Not related to V-Ad. Sir George Collier, of American Independence War fame. See below, pp. 437, *et seq.*

requesting that Mons. Barrallier should be ordered to attend, that he might witness the stowing of his own ship. That gentleman made his appearance; but, as he was not much at ease in English, I requested him to speak French, and we soon made way on the subject at issue. The *Newcastle* had no flooring from the keel, and was as sharp as a wedge. Consequently the fullsized iron ballast could not be laid flat, but inclined. That defect took off from the height under the beams, with the result that nine inches in depth was lost. When I pointed this out the Frenchman was quite disconcerted. That loss of height prevented one tier of butts being stowed over the iron tanks.* Therefore a tier of puncheons replaced them, which would cause some diminution in the quantity of water for use. In an attempt to remedy this defect, the smaller-sized iron ballast was used. However, by that change he only gained three inches. Some small battens secured over the flooring near the kelson were next removed, but all his plans to make up the required height failed. This was a sad annoyance to him. 'Here you are,' I said. 'You can judge the cause of the want of height. The ship's bottom is too sharp, and cannot receive the casks originally intended. You must submit her to being stowed with only puncheons instead of butts. You cannot remedy the evil.'

[There follows a not uninteresting, but very long, argument between W.H.D. and Barrallier on the ideal form for a frigate. This ended in a £50 bet, W.H.D. maintaining that in the first gale of wind, the *Newcastle's* decks would sink three inches, and giving his reasons. The Frenchman insisted—hotly—that they would not budge. It will surprise nobody to learn that, in due course, W.H.D. won his bet: that Barrallier paid up, and that W.H.D. magnanimously returned the money.]

Whilst devoting all my exertions to get the ship ready for sea, I heard from the Admiralty that the *Horatio* had arrived at Sheerness, and that I was to proceed there to take the command of her. The senior Lieutenant of the *Newcastle*, Mr. Howe,[1] was to take the

---

* From that period iron tanks were brought into use in the Navy, which proved a great improvement in the stowage of water.[2] By their introduction no shingle ballast was required—another advantage, as that ballast, when wet, sent up a most offensive effluvium from what was called 'bilge water', often producing unhealthy results.

[1] Alexander Burgoyne Howe, Lt. 28/5/1803; not promoted, though he went on serving till 1844.

[2] This hardly makes clear their *greatest* advantage—that the water stored in them remained sweet, and drinkable, for much longer than when stored in wood. This, a major hygienic reform, was made compulsory in 1815.

charge of the equipment, etc. On quitting that ship, I received an
invitation to dine with Lord Dillon in Town. I there met Lord
Frederick Beauclerk who had married one of his sisters[1]: also the
Hon. Mrs. Henry Dillon[2] from the continent.

(2) H.M.S. *HORATIO* (Newfoundland, 1st Cruise)

MARCH 3, 1814–JULY 1814

On the 3rd of March, after presenting myself to the Port Admiral,
Sir Thomas Williams[3]—an old acquaintance—I hastened off to the
Horatio, and was most kindly received by Lord George. My commission was read, and I was regularly installed in my new command.
But his Lordship required a few days to pack up. He was not overanxious to move, and I had to wait. It was a fortunate circumstance
for me that the Commissioner of the Dock Yard happened to be my
old friend, the Captain of the *Crescent*.[4] We had not met for nine
years, and his hospitable attentions, although himself an invalid,
were very acceptable. I was obliged to reside at an inn, and established myself at my old quarters when I took command of the
Childers in 1808. I met here many naval acquaintances: no lack of
society: among them Capt. Donnelly.[5] I had heard a great deal of
this officer's services whilst in command of one of our active frigates.
He was a distinguished character, which made his acquaintance the
more desirable. His attentions to me were marked, whether from
my family name or because he was himself an Hibernian. 'I know
what you have to undergo,' said he, 'in fitting out your cabin. I live
on board, and shall deem it a friendly act of yours if you will come
and dine with me every day that you are not engaged.' I acknowledged in suitable terms this kind proposal. This gentleman proved
in the end that he was sincere in all he said.

In one of my morning visits to Lord George, he persuaded me to
stay and lunch with him. He was very communicative upon matters
relating to the ship, but did not say much of the crew, as he had not
been much cruising at sea. When the lunch made its appearance,

[1] Charlotte.
[2] Widow of Gen. Henry Dillon, younger brother of Charles, 12th Viscount.
[3] Sir Thomas Williams (G.C.B.), Lt. 8/12/1779; Cdr. 15/4/83; Capt. 23/11/90;
R-Ad. 25/10/09; V-Ad. 4/6/1814; Ad. 22/7/30.
[4] William Granville Lobb. See Vol. I, passim. He died in July of this year.
[5] Ross Donnelly, Lt. 27/9/1781; Cdr. 6/7/94; Capt. 24/6/95; R-Ad. 4/6/1814;
V-Ad. 19/7/21.

he inquired if I had left off keeping a table, as many captains had done since the last regulation relating to our Prize money. I told him that I had not varied from the old system, and that I contrived, somehow or other, to have a joint on my table every day, with some of the officers' company. 'You are wrong,' said his Lordship. 'You must injure your finances by so doing. All of us have given up the entertaining of young men who do not care about us. It's a mistaken notion. I have long left off blowing out their stomachs. I dine by myself, at considerably less expense, and I feel happier.' To this I merely remarked that I was fully sensible to the feeling of my brother officers on the subject, but I could not as yet give up what had been so long an established custom, and that I should go on some time longer, as I had up to that period covered my expenses.

When Lord George had taken his departure, I set to work to put my cabin to right, and was kindly assisted by Capt. Donnelly, who personally attended and gave me several very useful hints on hanging my cot, securing my table against the heavy rolling and lurching of the ship in stormy weather. I took from him a couple of Mids, as he expected soon to be paid off. When I sent for my luggage from the Flag Ship at the Nore, I was considerably annoyed to find much of it broken—a very handsome mahogany sopha table smashed to pieces, my plate chest let down into the hold by the run, and all other articles similarly treated. So what was intended to be an act of economy in sending my furniture by water proved to be one of great expense. I did not get my cabin fairly in order until I had laid out more than £200. The pay of my ship amounted to only £280 per annum, from which was to be deducted income tax, agency, etc.

The officers and ship's company appeared pleased with their new Captain. To improve such a feeling, having been called upon by the manager of the Sheerness theatre to order a play, I yielded to the application, took a box, and in addition gave him £10 for seats to be distributed among my seamen. *The Taming of the Shrew* was selected on that occasion. When the ship's company heard of the tickets to be given to them, they were much pleased. Many others went on their own account, and most of the officers: by which means the theatre was more than half filled by the *Horatio's*. That act made a favourable impression in Sheerness.

The officer who had been appointed to fill the vacancy of Senior Lieutenant expressed great anxiety to remain in his present position. He was to me a perfect stranger, but his messmates spoke of him in such high terms that I wrote to the Admiralty Lord with whom these appointments rested to have him confirmed, that nomination being allowed to every Captain on his taking command. The reply to my letter informed me that he was not of sufficient standing to fill that post, and I was cautioned not to keep him, as it would not be sanctioned by the Board. This letter was shown to the officer, Luckraft[1] by name, who thought that, if I persevered, he would not be removed.

At our inn the Captains generally messed together. One morning at breakfast the arrival at the Nore of the *Tonnant*, an 80-gun ship, under the command of Lord Cochrane, was announced. This was to be the Flag Ship of Sir Alexander Cochrane, who was appointed to the chief command of our naval forces on the coast of North America. One of our party, in reading to us the news of the day, startled us by the account which appeared of a Col. Berenger, who had stuck up a handbill on the Lord Mayor's Mansion, announcing the signing at Paris of the preliminaries of peace. Then came the transactions of that notice on the Stock Exchange. As all the details relating to that affair must be known to you, I need not enter into particulars. I only allude to it because I was called upon that morning, by the Admiral and Commissioner, to pass my opinion upon the proceeding. Lord Cochrane was implicated in it. The affidavit which he made on that occasion was the general theme occupying our attention. Our general opinion was that, in his statement of the part Col. de Berenger had acted, he had not cleared himself. Later I was obliged to call upon Sir Thomas Williams, where I met the Commissioner. I had scarcely opened my lips when each, addressing me, inquired if I had met Lord Cochrane. 'No,' was my reply. 'That's strange,' they remarked. 'He has just left the house. What do you think of his Lordship's affidavit?' I hesitated, but they urged me to give a decided answer. I finally declared that I thought his Lordship had not, in that document, cleared himself of the suspicions entertained by the public against him. They then told me that he had been with them upwards of half an hour, and made out a very plausible statement: that all would be satisfactorily explained in a few days. Of course I could only judge of events as they appeared. However the Government, in due time, took a decided part relating to Lord Cochrane's conduct. He was struck off the list of Naval Officers, and his escutcheon of K.C.B. kicked out of the stalls of St. George's Chapel, Windsor.

---

[1] This is not the Alfred Luckraft, Lt. of the *Bellerophon* during W.H.D.'s temporary command (see above, p. 158), and the Commander of the *Russel* in 1835, but —probably—his elder brother John, Lt. 11/12/07; Cdr. 27/7/25; Capt. 4/11/40.

During this interview with the Admiral, as he, as well as the Commissioner, entertained very friendly feelings towards me, I was anxious to derive some advantage from that circumstance. My ship was not well manned. The confinement on the coast of Holland during the winter had caused much sickness on board. A considerable portion of the crew was very slight and undersized, and the Admiralty had ordered its number to be increased to 315. Consequently I requested his good offices, pointing out the probability of my falling in with one of the large American frigates, and the necessity of being prepared for such an occurrence. The Commissioner advocated my cause in the warmest terms, and in the end the Admiral promised to do his best in my behalf. This was a great point gained. The conversation then turned on my being in want of a Senior Lieutenant. The Admiral wished me to take one of his, if I had not any friend in view. Not having one, I expressed a willingness to accommodate him. The Commissioner accompanying me into the Dock Yard, I had a very long chat with him, and learnt that the Lieutenant whom Sir Thomas wished me to take had been with him for some time, and had been led to expect promotion; and, the war being over, the Admiral was desirous of providing for one of his connexions. He led me to his house, where I made my bow to the ladies. At parting, the Commissioner assured me that he would take care to give directions for all the *Horatio's* wants to be amply made good.

[W.H.D. made one more attempt to keep Mr. Luckcraft, but, the Admiralty not allowing it, he had to apply for—and of course instantly got—the Admiral's choice, Mr. Marshall.[1] Thereupon the Admiral gave him '35 good seamen' to replace sickly ones. The Commissioner also helped him to defeat the obstructions of the Superintendent Painter who was difficult about painting his boats, and of the Blacksmith of the Yard who was slow in providing him with coal.]

After a fortnight's anxiety, my labours were completed. On the morning of the 17th the Pilot appeared on board, and the ship went out of harbour to the Little Nore. About this time, my companion in the troopship command, Phillimore,[2] had a gallant action with a French frigate, *la Clorinde*. He commanded the *Eurotas*, a fine new frigate. The match was nearly equal, and although the French ship did not strike her colours to the *Eurotas*, the *Dryad*, Capt.

---

[1] George Edward Marshall, Lt. 22/9/1807; Cdr. 27/5/25.
[2] (Sir) John Phillimore: see above, p. 182.

Galwey,[1] which happened to be near, obliged the enemy to surrender; and Capt. Galwey, most nobly, sent the Frenchman's sword
to the *Eurotas*, congratulating Phillimore on that fortunate event.
He was severely wounded.

The following day I was bound for the Downs. Now came the
trial of a new Ship's Company. The ship was neatly painted, and very
neatly rigged: but I soon found out that her fitting was more for show
than utility. On one occasion, having a fine breeze, I made all the sail
that could be set on a wind. The ship was going through the water
in a good style, when to my astonishment the officer of the Forecastle
called out that the fore topgallant mast was complaining. The wind
was not sufficiently strong to cause any apprehensions. However,
another alarm being given from the same quarter, I ordered the
royals to be taken in. Next, making inquiries relating to the stability
of the topgallant masts, I was informed that they were slight, more
fit for show than for carrying sail. Consequently, I had all the show
articles taken down, and replaced by others that could stand the
wear of an effective ship. Next, there was a complaint against a
seaman for neglect of duty. He was punished according to the Articles
of War, when I told the Ship's Company in decided terms that proper
discipline would be maintained. Every indulgence consistent with
naval duty would be allowed, but the *Horatio* was to be a perfect
man of war, to support in every sense the honour of England.

On the 24th we anchored in the Downs. I had brought with me a
barometer, by which to regulate the weather, and a chronometer to
rectify the reckoning. These two new companions caused considerable
anxiety on board, as neither the officers or the seamen had been used
to them.[2] I left the Downs the next day. Variable weather attended
us, with fogs, but we arrived at Spithead on the morning of the 28th.
I now had to present my respects to Sir Richard Bickerton, not as the
Captain of a troopship, but as one of our finest frigates. He received
me accordingly.

---

[1] Edward Galwey or Gallwey, Lt. 24/6/1793; Cdr. 8/10/98; Capt. 29/4/1802;
R-Ad. 10/1/37.
[2] Both these instruments had been invented, and had reached quite an advanced
stage of perfection, for many years. A marine barometer had been produced by
Dr. Robert Hooke (1695–1703), and John Harrison had earned (though not been
paid) the famous Board of Longitude prize by 1765. Conservatism among sea-users
was notorious, yet it would seem that, by 1814, the officers and seamen were more
than a little old-fashioned if none of them had really ever seen them in use. Yet,
even in 1814, they were not quite 'standard issues.' Dr. Burney, in his 1815 edition
of *Falconer*, can still write, 'Most captains of men of war have one [a chronometer]
allowed to them by Government, *when they apply for it on going on foreign service*,
[Editor's italics] and many of them have one of their own property.'

Shortly after my arrival, with the Admiral's sanction, I struck the lower yards, and turned to, to make such improvements in the rigging as were required: among other things, another pair of shrouds to the mizen mast. The *Horatio* was what they called a 'walled sided' ship, and she rolled deeply. It was therefore necessary to have the lower masts well secured with shrouds. These matters set to rights, the ship was soon all ataunt, and ready for sea, making a very good figure among the men of war lying there. I now received orders to fit for foreign service, and ascertained that I was to proceed to Newfoundland to be under the orders of Sir R. Keats. I was not overpleased with my destination. However, in consequence of my conversation with Capt. Hawker relating to that officer, it appeared that my good opinion of him had produced its effect, not in the way that I had anticipated. But there was no remedy. I was now occupied in drawing stores and completing the provisions for foreign service. I watched for an opportunity to look at the French frigate *Clorinde* lying here. She had lost the main and mizen masts, but did not appear to be so much injured in her hull as one would expect after such a severe engagement.

Letters from Sir Richard Keats informed me that I was to proceed to Newfoundland and fulfil the Senior Officer's duty previous to his arrival. I was to receive a Gen. Campbell as a passenger, he being appointed to command the forces on the island. The *Dauntless*, sloop of war, was to be under my orders. The news had reached us that the Allies had entered Paris on the 31st March, and all our conversation turned upon that important event and its results.

On the 6th the General, with two daughters, a son and an infant, with servants, came on board and was placed in possession of his apartments. Many of the senior Captains had called to compliment me upon the command of the *Horatio*. It was while one of them was in my cabin that a most ill-judged proceeding on the part of the Senior Lieutenant occurred. The Ship's Company being at dinner, I was not prepared for any interruption. My visitor was occupied in examining the various fittings for my passengers when, suddenly, Mr. Marshall came in, acquainting me that the whole of the crew had come aft to the Quarter Deck, demanding to see me. I remarked that I was engaged, and could not attend. However, the Lieutenant evidently did not show any tact on this occasion. He ought, with proper judgment, to have desired the seamen to wait till the Captain was at leisure. He let drop a few expressions which I thought, in the presence of a strange officer, most indiscreet. Consequently I was compelled to adopt a more decided tone, then, apologising to my visitor, left the Cabin to meet the men on deck. When I inquired why they came aft at that particular moment when I had an officer of rank in my cabin, they replied that a new First Lieutenant was required. Several voices repeated the same expressions. 'Upon my word, gentlemen,' I said, 'you have begun to assume authority very soon. We have not been long together, and I cannot indulge you in your request. I have not as yet had reason to be displeased with the officer to whom you allude, and he shall not quit the ship.' There was a pause. I then assumed an attitude of attack. Clenching my fists, with extended arms, I made a dash at the spokesman, who was the Chief Boatswain's Mate. He retreated in all precipitation, and, as I advanced, the seamen retreated till I had cleared the Quarter Deck. I then ordered them below, and was glad to find them obey me. Upon my questioning the First Lieutenant upon the meaning of all this outbreak, I could not obtain any satisfactory information. However, it was evident he was no favourite with the seamen. As I knew little of him, I could not take any decided step relating to him. At that period the Boatswain's Mate was drunk.

A few minutes afterwards my visitor left the ship, and I got under way. When the second anchor was nearly up to the bows, by some mismanagement of the nippers it was led down to the mud. That neglectful act, happening at this critical moment, appeared as if it had been done on purpose. I ordered the two men at the nippers to be brought aft, and, censuring them for their misconduct, directed their being put in irons: after which I went forward and addressed the seamen in decided tones. I warned them to mind their duty, and remarked, 'You have begun it by your proceedings today, and you must take the consequences. I am not to be frightened: so you had better do your duty with good will.' These words produced a good effect, for when the anchor was hove up a second time no neglect occurred, but the ship was under sail in good style. We proceeded to St. Helens, where we anchored, the *Dauntless* in company.

One of my rules was to have the sentinel's muskets loaded with powder, but the bullets kept in their pockets to be let into the barrel if required. When we had been at anchor a couple of hours, the Boatswain's Mate who had cut such a figure in demanding a new First Lieutenant jumped overboard. I hastened on deck and beheld him in the water attempting to swim away. I called to him to come back or I would shoot him, directing the sentry to run the bullet into his musket. As I suppose he heard the order, he returned to the ship and was hauled aboard. This man's conduct naturally gave cause for reflection. I had just taken command of a fine frigate, the crew of which were strangers to me. I had to cross the Atlantic, and it would not do to let these men imagine that I had the least dread of them. Besides, their dislike was aimed not at me but at the Lieutenant. The Boatswain's Mate was not much supported by the crew; he was drunk and dissatisfied. Therefore I thought the best way of acting towards him and to prevent any repetition of his mutinous conduct, would be to get rid of him. So I sent for the Captain of the *Dauntless*, and proposed that he should take one of my seamen in exchange for one of his. That affair being soon settled, the Boatswain's Mate was discharged to that sloop, and I received another man in his room.

The following morning we were under way with our consort, and proceeded down channel with variable winds. As five of the seamen had been very refractory and insolent to their superiors, I was obliged to bring the Articles of War into practice, and they were punished according to the nature of their offences. Now was the time to try what my seamen were made of. They were exercised at the guns, and acquitted themselves to my satisfaction. On the 9th we saw the lights of Scilly, and on the 10th made the coast of Ireland. A signal was made for a Pilot, and the ship was taken into the Cove of Cork that evening. In entering the harbour, I noticed a merchant brig badly managed. I sent one of my Lieutenants to assist her, and that officer afterwards received a handsome gratuity from the owners for the service rendered. I had now to take charge of a convoy for Newfoundland.

Ad. Sawyer[1] held the Port Command. I had never met him, though his professional reputation was well known to me. He received me with much courtesy and presented me to his family. The *Horatio*, having been fresh-painted, her rigging blacked, etc., made a conspicuous appearance at Cove. The Admiral seemed so much pleased with her that I invited him to come and pay me a visit. In short, it was settled that I should entertain him, his family, and a few of his friends at an evening meeting: in fact a dance.

[A long account of this festivity, reminiscent of, though more decorous than, the party he had given here when in the Glenmore, (Vol. I, pp. 337–8), is omitted. Afterwards he met again many of his former Irish friends, 'experiencing one of the most friendly entertainments of my life'.]

[1] (Sir) Herbert Sawyer, Lt. 9/12/80; Cdr. 14/6/83; Capt. 3/2/89; R-Ad. 2/10/1807; V-Ad. 1/8/11; Ad. 27/5/25.

While my convoy was assembling, a 20-gun ship, the *Cyane*, came in to be under my orders. In the midst of my preparations a violent gale came on, which obliged me to strike the lower yards and topmasts. It was upon this occasion that the use of the barometer became known to the officers and Ship's Company. I happened to be watching it about 4 o'clock one afternoon on the second day of the storm, and noticed that the quicksilver had made a small inclination upon the rise. I instantly sent for the Senior Lieutenant, to whom I gave directions to sway up the lower yards, etc. He observed, with an air of astonishment. 'It is blowing a strong gale.' 'Very well,' I replied. 'You will please to obey my orders.' He set to work accordingly, and had scarcely completed the duty when the gale was turned into a calm. He came to me to make some observations on the barometer, when I merely observed, 'You will soon become used to it.' My order, at that particular moment, and the sudden change in the atmosphere, made an impression upon all hands on board.

The unsettled weather retarded the convoy's getting out to sea. However, by the afternoon of the 23rd we were clear of the harbour with between 50 and 60 sail under our care, attended by the *Dauntless* and the *Cyane*. I now began to get acquainted with my Ship's Company. I had noticed, at their exercise at the great guns, as well as at the broadsword, many who did not cut a very good figure. There were amongst them several foreigners. I was determined to exchange them into the vessels of the convoy. To accomplish that object, whenever any particular ship was negligent in obeying signals, I ran alongside of her and sent an officer on board to examine her crew. If she was well manned, one or two good seamen were taken away, and others from the *Horatio* sent to supply their places. By that arrangement the Masters could not complain, and I improved the complement of my Ship's Company. Some time afterwards this proceeding of mine was reported to Sir Richard Keats, who would, when jocosely inclined—not often the case—say when the conversation turned that way, 'Oh, follow Dillon's plan. Send a boat on board and take a man out.' One fine ship, whose Master had been extremely inattentive to all the signals, fell under my displeasure. He was boarded, and one of his men taken out. Shortly after this he was observed altering his course. The *Horatio* was soon alongside of her, and an officer sent on board. It was then discovered that the Master, in a fit of passion, was unbending his studdingsails and unreeving all his rigging, placing his ship in a position to prevent his making sail. I had these acts taken down in writing, and made the Master understand that his conduct would be reported at Lloyds. Then, insisting upon his bending his sails and replacing the rigging, I kept by him till he shaped a proper course with the sufficient quantity of sail set. On leaving him, I warned him that if any more neglect became noticed, he might expect an 18-lb shot from the frigate. Luckily he gave no further cause for my suspicion. Our progress was very slow, the *Horatio* occasionally taking a ship in tow.

One day, it being fine weather. I invited the Captain of the *Cyane* to dinner with his guest, the Marquis of Tweeddale, who was going to America to serve in our Army. His noble father I had known at Verdun. The captain of the *Cyane*[1] was very desirous of trying his sailing qualities against the *Horatio's*, and it was settled that, the first strong breeze, the trial should be made. Accordingly, a few days afterwards, there being a commanding breeze with a long heavy swell, I inquired by signal if the *Cyane* would test our sailing qualities. Her captain complied and, at a given time, we made sail upon a wind. In the course of three hours the *Cyane* cut but a very sorry figure. Some of her spars were carried away, whilst the *Horatio*, without straining a rope yarn, was going at a rapid pace to windward, dashing over the swelling waves in perfect splendour. When I noticed the loss sustained by my opponent, I shortened sail and bore down into the convoy. No further trial was demanded.

On the 15th May the *Cyane* and *Dauntless* parted company, taking with them the Halifax and Quebec trade. The *Horatio*, with near 30 sail, kept her course towards Newfoundland. The next day the atmosphere was extremely cold, and, a strange object being seen to windward, I went in chace of it. What we had taken for a ship turned out to be an island of ice, but still at some distance. As this was the first one I had seen, I devoted some anxious moments to its examination. Shortly after this we saw more ice islands, some of them beautiful objects to look at, but very unpleasant companions to meet in the night. We were now approaching the Banks of New-foundland, celebrated as the abode of the cod fish. Our lines were soon sent down whilst the ship was lying to, and we caught plenty of them—a great treat to the officers as well as to the seamen. Fogs too were the consequence, and I lost sight of my convoy. Guns were fired occasionally, but, thinking it unsafe to carry sail, I hove to and struck soundings on the Bank in 38 fathoms. On the 20th the fog cleared a little, but none of the convoy could be seen. I made sail

---

[1] Capt. Gordon Falcon, Lt. 15/5/1800; Cdr. 8/3/11; Capt. 29/10/13. In the *Cyane* off Madeira he engaged, and was captured by, the *Constitution*, 20/2/1815.

and, when going at the rate of seven knotts, the ship very nearly ran upon a large island of ice. It was at least 400 feet in height and aground on the Bank. Its upper part had either a vapour or a small cloud hanging on its slopes. We just tacked in time to clear it. This was a very narrow escape.

At noon on the 21st the chronometer gave warning of our being near the land. Shortly afterwards Newfoundland was discovered, the reckoning proving correct. Consequently all confidence was placed on it, and those who had made their remarks upon the time-piece and barometer were silenced. The officers then told me of the uneasiness many of them felt at being subjected to the 'forebodings of the Chronometer and Barometer'. But they had by this time experienced their utility. For many months afterwards it was a common occurrence for them to apply for permission to go into my Cabin to look at the barometer. On this evening we boarded a merchant vessel bound to St. John's. From her I got a Pilot. On the morning of the 22nd we exchanged numbers with H.M. sloop *Sabine*. Many of the convoy were near the land. By 10 o'clock the *Horatio* had entered the harbour of St. John's, where she was safely anchored. In the course of the day I ascertained that all my convoy had arrived in good order. It was a very unusual event at this season of the year for a ship of war to be accompanied by the whole of the vessels under her charge, and it made a favourable impression upon the inhabitants.

I found a packet of letters, containing instructions for my future proceedings. It was now discovered that the fore yard was badly sprung. It could not be replaced in Newfoundland, but to Halifax I should be obliged to repair. At the same time I was informed that the harbour of St. John's was blockaded by an American schooner, a privateer. The next day Gen. Campbell left the ship, and I became acquainted with the authorities, and the principal merchant, Mr. Stabb, who was also the Naval Agent.

The harbour is as calm as a millpond: therefore there is no difficulty for anyone to swim on shore from the ship. On the same evening an alarm was given that some of the seamen had thrown themselves overboard, one or two heavy splashes having been heard. Being informed of this, I instantly ordered all the ship's company aft, and inquired whether any of them were discontented, promising them, if they would manfully come out with their grievances, I would attend to them, or allow them to quit the ship. The question was frequently put, but not answered by anyone. They were then mustered, without a soul being absent. So far all was satisfactory. The Senior

Lieutenant, I had reason to suspect, was not liked. He was corpulent, with a husky voice, and did not deliver his orders very clearly. Consequently, in blowy weather I had to make use of the speaking trumpet and, in fact, do his duty. This was the consequence of my taking as Senior Lieutenant an officer of whom I knew nothing.

I now prepared for sea, determined, on my way along the coast, to make a good search for the Yankee Privateer. On the morning of the 26th I made a signal for a Pilot. He came on board but, the wind failing, he could not take the ship out. I was extremely dissatisfied with the slow work of my ship's company on this occasion. All hands knew there was an enemy outside, and I did expect more exertion on their part. Consequently, I told the First Lieutenant in very decided terms to let the crew know what I expected. I now resorted to a measure which I thought would produce a good effect. I ordered all the men aft, and explained to them my displeasure at their not bringing their hammocks up quicker when they had been piped up. 'You are not,' said I, 'aware of what you can do when you choose, and I shall now show you. Hammocks will be piped down and you will all turn in. They will be piped up, and we shall see how long you will be in bringing them up. You were $\frac{1}{2}$ an hour this morning.' Down went the hammocks: the men got into them: they were piped up. The seaman who slept in the bow of the ship brought his hammock to the extreme end of the Quarter Deck. He was dressed. 'How long do you think,' I asked him, 'you have taken in lashing up, putting on your clothes and coming here?' 'I don't know, Sir,' he replied. Then, showing him my watch, I said, 'You have been $4\frac{1}{2}$ minutes at it.' I then gave directions for a five-minute glass to be prepared. When it ran out, a bell was to be struck, and all those men whose hammocks were not up were to be reported to the officer on the Quarter Deck. That arrangement having been put in force, no failures occurred.

On the afternoon of that day the Pilot came on board, and offered to take the ship to sea. The officers had invited some of the principal inhabitants to dinner, in which I was included. However, there was no remedy. There was an enemy off the harbour, and the ship, I was determined, should go. The hands were turned up to unmoor. The messenger had been, for what reason I know not, removed. It was the principal article wanted on such an occasion. However, to show what can be done when the will is suited to the action, the messenger was rove, the ship unmoored and all sail set in 28 minutes. In the morning 30 minutes had not been sufficient to stow the hammocks.

I of course expressed to the men my satisfaction for their activity. Here was an object gained of the utmost importance in the discipline of a ship of war.

Now to describe one of the most trying moments of my life. So soon as the *Horatio* got between the narrows—that is, between the two lofty mountains which form the entrance of the harbour—the wind failed. I was obliged to hoist out all the boats to take the ship in tow. When we had cleared the narrows, we were still becalmed, and felt the heavy swell of the sea which impeded the boat's progress. We were for nearly three hours close to a rock rising from the bottom, in the shape of, and at the point as sharp as, a needle. The Pilot was in the greatest state of alarm. 'Had I known,' he said, 'that we should be becalmed, I should not have offered to bring you out. But when I came to you I observed a fine breeze outside.' There was no anchoring in our dangerous position. It was extremely dark, with only a few stars to be seen. Of my state of anxiety no one who has not met with a similar occurrence can form an opinion. At last, at about half past 10, a light breeze came from the land. The boats were hoisted in, and shortly afterwards the breeze freshened. The Pilot, on leaving us, declared that he had not for many years felt such a heavy responsibility. 'Had the ship struck upon the point of that rock,' he said, 'nothing could have saved her.' However, the danger was past, the watch called and the rest retired.

With the morning we were not far from the land. Several strange sail were seen, but one of them, a schooner, at some distance in the S.W. quarter, attracted my attention, and I ordered sail to be made in chace of her. The wind favoured us, and the crew were in a state of excitement usual on such occasions. This was my first attempt, and I was highly delighted to witness the spirit displayed by the seamen. The studdingsails were soon set: the ship dashed on, turning the sea at the bows into a foam as white as snow. As the breeze freshened the haze disappeared, and we were nearing the chace. Her captain evidently became aware that a ship of war was in pursuit, as every stitch of canvas at command was hoisted where it could be most serviceable. The studdingsails had not been used for a long time. Therefore, as the wind came in strong puffs, away went their yards. This was a most perplexing annoyance. Nevertheless, they were very soon replaced, and we were gaining rapidly on the chace, whose hull was distinctly seen above the horizon. I judged her by all appearances to be the American Privateer. Other vessels were to be seen, one apparently a ship of war, but a long way off. I made the signal for an enemy. The scene was now all animation. Our motions were noticed from the shore, and the crews of the fishing vessels were observed to be waving their hats as we passed. The schooner shaped a course towards some dangerous rocks, among which, no doubt, she would try to entangle us. At last we had neared so much that we were almost within gunshot. We saw spars floating in all directions, thrown overboard from the chace: in fact we saw her crew all in motion casting out material to lighten her.

Then, unfortunately, at the moment when I thought myself sure of capturing the enemy, and was directing the chace gun to be pointed towards her, away went the maintopmast studdingsail boom in a sharp squall of wind and rain. This was a sad disaster, and, as darkness was drawing near, our chance of boarding her began to grow doubtful. Then, as the squall passed over, we were left for some time with little wind, and the chase caught the breeze. Here was a most trying and disappointing change. The Yankee, making sure of his escape, fired a gun and made off without our being able to follow. Nothing more could be done. From my observations through my spyglass I imagined the schooner to be armed with 14 guns. She was painted black. Not long after this we were joined by the *Crescent* frigate.[1] I hailed her Captain,[*] and told him what had happened. In fact he had witnessed our proceedings, but was too far to leeward to assist. So the schooner escaped, and I shaped a course towards Halifax. Such are the casualties of war. My chace frightened away the enemy's Privateer, which did not return to Newfoundland. She had not taken any of my convoy, and that, under my disappointment, was some satisfaction.

My studdingsails were sadly damaged, but as we were bound for a port where there was a Dockyard, they could be replaced. Several islands of ice were seen, and as the weather was hazy, great caution was required. As we neared Halifax, Sable Island lay in our way, a very dangerous place as the currents there are very rapid and

---

[1] Not W.H.D.'s old *Crescent*—7th of the name in the Royal Navy—which had been wrecked off Jutland in 1808. This—the 8th—was a 5th-rate of 1084 tons and 46 guns commissioned at Woolwich in 1810. She lasted till 1854.

[*] Her Captain had been one of the seamen of the *Prince George* under me in 1795. He was Lord Nelson's First Lieutenant at Trafalgar, and at the period here mentioned he was my senior officer.[2]

[2] His name, John Quilliam. It is not, perhaps, so well-known as it should be that (to use modern parlance) the Commander of the *Victory* at Trafalgar was an officer from the Lower Deck. But so it was. According to Beatson, he was Irish, and a pressed man. He secured a Lieutenant's commission, 6/10/98, and as a reward for his Trafalgar services, was made Post, 24/12/1805, skipping the intermediate grade: but not without causing heart-burnings among the other Lieutenants who considered themselves his seniors.

uncertain. On the afternoon of the 31st we struck soundings, but we could see nothing owing to a thick fog. During my absence from deck the officer of the watch, unknown to me, had made more sail, and when I again made my appearance he got a scolding for doing so, and he was ordered to reduce the sail to its original quantity. It had scarcely been taken in when I saw the land, rather close to us. The weather still being very hazy, we supposed ourselves to be near the Sambro lighthouse, but all was guesswork as there had been no opportunity to see the sun. When I inquired whether any person on board had been off this coast before, one of my Mids from Capt. Donnelly came forward and told me that he had been in Halifax, that he supposed us to be near the lighthouse mentioned, and that, in foggy weather, ships approaching this part of the coast generally fired a gun, which would be responded to by one from the lighthouse. Consequently I ordered a gun to be fired, and a few seconds later we heard the report of a gun from the shore—a proof that our reckoning was correct. We were now assailed by a gale of wind, and obliged to haul off from the land.

During the night a report was brought to me that a party of seamen had assembled and discussed, as they thought in secret, a plan for taking the ship into America. At daybreak I ordered the Ship's Company aft, and inquired into the report. I could obtain nothing connected with it. However, I let them understand in plain terms that they would not obtain possession of the ship whilst I was alive. All this did not create a very pleasant feeling. However, they retired expressing their determination not to do anything against their country, and I never heard more on the subject. But I thought it right to let them know that I was prepared for any emergency.

In the morning the gale abated, and I stood in towards Sambro lighthouse. Shortly afterwards I took a Pilot on board. He certainly was a queer chap, and his Yankee dialect caused many a laugh. In the evening we anchored in Halifax harbour, but not in a good position. Therefore, next morning, we moved the ship further in, and before 11 o'clock were moored in a good berth. I saluted the Admiral—Griffiths[1]—with 13 guns. The foreyard was soon sent on shore to the Dock Yard, as well as all the sails that were worn out. On the 4th of June the usual salute was fired for the King's Birthday.

---

[1] Should be Griffith, (Sir) Edward (K.C.B.), Lt. 15/4/1783; straight to Capt. 21/5/94; R-Ad. 12/8/1812; V-Ad. 19/7/21. Captain of the *London* in 1797, he was concerned in the famous scene on board that ship when his uncle, V-Ad. John Colpoys and his Lieutenant Peter Bover nearly lost their lives at the hands of the Spithead mutineers. He later added Colpoys to his surname.

A grand dinner was given at the Town Hall, which I attended, and was highly delighted to witness the truly patriotic spirit that prevailed at that meeting. The *Spencer*, 74, was lying here, the *Leander*, Sir George Collier, also; and—not to be passed by—the *Chesapeake*, which had been taken by the *Shannon*. I went on board and examined her very closely. The Naval Commissioner turned out to be the Hon. P. Wodehouse,[1] who had been my shipmate in the *Defence*, *Prince George*, etc.

Having received a new fore yard and replenished all my wants, I left the harbour on the 6th of June. On my way back to Newfoundland, nothing of consequence occurred. I boarded several vessels, spoke H.M.S. *Charybdis*, met plenty of ice islands and had constant foggy weather.* By the 15th we were close off St. John's harbour. Here we met the *Hamadryad*, frigate, and were then visited by such violent gusts of wind that many of our sails were split. It was one of the most trying positions I was ever placed in. The *Hamadryad*, more fortunate, contrived to anchor in the entrance of the harbour. Here I witnessed what might be called the 'Sea Mirage'. There was a calm some miles from the land, and the vessels seen on the horizon appeared to vibrate, their dimensions being reduced to the size of a miniature. I contrived at last to come to an anchor, and warped my ship in. By 10 o'clock at night she was safely moored. The next day I presented my respects to Sir Richard Keats, who had arrived in the *Bellerophon*, 74. The *Victorious*, 74, the *Crescent* and other small ships were lying here. The Admiral informed me that I was to be attached to the *Victorious*, Capt. Talbot.[3] We were to proceed up Davis Straits to protect the whale fishing, information having reached our Government that the Americans intended to send a squadron there to capture our ships. We had one or two sociable dinners at the Admiral's.

[1] See Vol. I, pp. 160–2.

* I had noticed that the sick list had increased to about 70, without any prospect of diminution. All my conversations with the Surgeon[2] led to no improvement. This was a serious dilemma, and I was determined to try a remedy. All were suffering from large boils on their legs and arms. I at last persuaded the Surgeon to give them warm baths. I then ordered six cots to be slung up under the forecastle. There was no want of salt water. Every precaution, as well as decency, being observed, six men at a time took the baths. The first batch having derived benefit, it was continued, and the complaint was completely removed. That act of mine made a sensible impression upon the Ship's Company. After this, I gave directions for the crew to take their meals constantly on the Main Deck when the weather would allow. The Lower Deck went through a partial fumigation daily. That system was kept in practice during the whole time I commanded the *Horatio*, to the advantage of the seamen's health.

[2] Thomas Bishop, 1st Warrant, 15/10/1808.

[3] (Sir) John Talbot, (G.C.B.). Lt. 3/11/1790; Cdr. 17/4/95; Capt. 27/8/96; R-Ad. 12/8/1819; V-Ad. 22/7/30; Ad. 23/11/41.

On the morning of the 20th, with fine weather, we left the harbour with the *Victorious*, the *Crescent* coming out at the same time. We passed the sloop of war *Sabine*. We were now bound for the Davis Straits with no other prospect than to encounter ice islands and whales. I was desired to take my station on the Commodore's weather beam. We fell in with numerous portions of ice, large and small, and hazy weather. Our only occupation was to exercise our seamen. On the 28th we had a glimpse of what we supposed to be Greenland, as we were about 50 miles from Cape Farewell. We had not met anything in the shape of danger, but, on the afternoon of the 29th we were nearing an immense field of ice on the lee bow, which obliged us to alter course: and when the fogs came on we had to regulate all our motions by the firing of guns. There was no darkness: consequently I seldom undressed, but reposed on my sopha, book in hand. The lead was constantly thrown, but we had not struck soundings of any light draft. However, on the 6th July we struck bottom in 110 fathoms. The next day we saw the land, the west coast of Greenland, and I made the signal to that effect to the *Victorious*. Shortly after this I received an invitation to dine with Capt. Sir John Talbot. When I went on board the Commodore, he received me with marked attention, declaring that he had never during the whole of his nautical life met with a ship which kept her station so well as the *Horatio*. 'At all hours,' he said, 'when I look for you, there I find you in your true bearing. You may convey my thanks to your officers of the watch for their strict attention to their duties, signals, etc.'

We had seen many whales. The noise they made when many of them were together resembled very much the report of heavy artillery at a distance, and their water-spouting, when acted upon by the sun, had a most brilliant effect. The sea was covered with a sort of animal-culae which, we understood, supplied the whales with food. I caught many and kept them in a glass lamp fitted for the occasion. But they did not live long. I now communicated to Capt. Talbot a conversation I had had with the Master of a whaler that I had boarded. He expressed himself completely astonished at beholding a line of battle ship in such a high northern latitude, stating his apprehensions for us both, and remarking that the charts for this region were not correct. 'You are,' said he, 'surrounded by innumerable dangers, and I hope you will quit these premises safely.' I explained to him that our reckoning was regulated by the lunar observations and our chrono-meters. He replied that the coast of Greenland was not properly laid down in the high latitudes, therefore all was uncertainty, and he repeated his anxiety on our account. This statement had some effect upon Capt. Talbot, and it was agreed that, in future, I was to keep my station one mile ahead of him. When I returned to my ship the lead was kept going every two hours, the soundings varying from 50 to 60 fathoms.

We had very fine weather, with light airs and occasionally a partial fall of snow, the ship at times sailing through drift ice. About noon of the 8th, it being nearly calm, the Commodore came to see me. We were then in nearly the 67th degree of north latitude, longitude 54 west, and I expressed my doubts of his chronometer being correct, as it did not agree with mine by nearly one degree. However, upon that subject he did not seem inclined to enter into explanation, and the conversation took another direction. Shortly afterwards he returned to the *Victorious*. The *Horatio* was then lying to, with the main topsail aback, all hands being at dinner. To my astonishment when Capt. Talbot had got on board he made all sail. It was a regular established system not to interfere with the seamen whilst at their meals, except in a case of the utmost urgency. As there appeared none, I allowed the Commodore to proceed, it being then about ½ past 12 o'clock. Knowing that my ship sailed at least a mile an hour faster than his, my proceedings were regulated accordingly. He was then about ½ a mile ahead of me, and my station was one mile ahead of him. Suddenly a fog came towards us, in the first instance covering the whole of the 74 except the stern. I could not run the risk of losing sight of my Commodore: therefore, the ship's company were ordered instantly to make all sail in the S.E. direction. As the fog thickened, and we could no longer see each other, the *Victorious* fired a gun every half hour, which we repeated. When I made sail, I reckoned that I should have to go at least 3 miles to get my proper bearing. A light breeze sprang up, which took us along at the rate of upwards of 5 miles per hour. I was soon abreast of the line of battle ship. We had sounded in upwards of 100 fathoms before 12 o'clock. Whilst we were forereaching the Commodore, the Master pointed to a dark object on the weather beam which we thought looked like land. However, we could not make anything of it owing to the fog: besides, during the forenoon, which had been tolerably clear, nothing like it had been seen. It was therefore the general opinion that it was not land.

About 4 o'clock I reached my station, as the *Victorious's* firing was now astern of us. I went to dinner, the signal book on my table. Some time after 5 o'clock, we heard the fog signal to tack. At the

same moment a Mid came down to inform me that something like
the surge of the sea upon the shore was heard on our right. The water
was extremely smooth. I instantly ordered the ship to be put about,
then repeated the signal, and sounded in 14 fathoms. That depth
alarmed me. The fog was so thick that we could hardly discern the
fore part of the ship. Presently we were in 7 fathoms. When the
ship had been tacked, I gave orders to steer on the immediate
opposite point of the compass to that on which we had previously
been sailing. Then I hove the ship to, hoisted out all the boats and
ranged the cables, etc. The boats were kept ahead, sounding. During
these operations we heard from the *Victorious* guns fired in rapidity,
then the report of musketry, which led me to suppose that some
accident had occurred. I then filled the topsails, and allowed the
frigate to go on about two miles per hour. We responded to all the
firing from the 74. To my surprise about 7 o'clock, I saw a boat close
to us. She came alongside with an officer from the Commodore to
acquaint me that his ship was on shore. The poor fellow was sadly
depressed, and by his account I could imagine only the most melancholy result. My boats had not struck less than seven fathoms. So
far my ship appeared safe. In the course of a few minutes we discovered the *Victorious* lying over on her starboard side in a most
awkward position. I passed her as close as I could without risk, and
Capt. Talbot desired me to let go an anchor under his stern, and send
him the end of my cable. This order was soon obeyed. The streams of
water, by pumping, coming out of the unfortunate ship caused a
woeful impression. I had anchored in 22 fathoms, but, luckily, before
I could send my cable to the two-decker, she floated off the small
island on which she had struck. It was then past 8 o'clock.

I then hove up my anchor and hoisted in the boats, having first
ascertained that the Commodore did not want any immediate
assistance. His ship was making between 4 and 5 feet of water per
hour. The fog now began to clear away, and by degrees we saw the
land, of immense mountainous height. We were all amazement at the
dangers we had escaped. It was not a very prudent act to have made
the sail he did in a thick fog, in an unknown region, with a line of
battle ship. Luckily it was no worse, and the warning previously
given by the Master of the whaler made its due impression on me.
The next day I called on board the *Victorious* to offer such help as
might be required. The most extraordinary thing is that, when on
the previous afternoon Capt. Talbot fired the guns which I took to
be the signal to tack, nothing of the kind was meant. His ship was

on shore, and they were fired to give warning. As we could not see each other, I could only judge by the report; but the guns, luckily for me, were let off in the exact manner directed in the signal book for 'tack the ship'. I obeyed accordingly, but had I stood on a few minutes more, the *Horatio* would have grounded. It appeared afterwards, on examining the chart, that we were approaching the entrance of a river.

So soon as the *Victorious* could fix a large portion of canvas well lined with oakum over the injured part of the ship, and properly secured with hawsers, a course was shaped towards Cape Farewell, and ultimately for England. I attended frequently on board of her, and I believe several of my suggestions were very serviceable. It was during those visits that we examined our respective charts. They proved useless on this part of the coast, as it was four degrees further westward than laid down in them. As there was six points westerly variation, and strong currents running in all directions, the *Horatio's* escape appeared quite miraculous. The coast was of stupendous height, the peaks of it reaching into the clouds and covered with snow. Capt. Talbot had had some desire, I believe, to see the Danish settlement of Disco. But all was frustrated by this unfortunate event, and we saw neither a Dane, a Greenlander or an Esquimau.

The coast of Greenland was once a thriving colony to the Danes, who settled here in the year 1721, upon the banks of a river called Baal in latitude 64 North. It was navigable some miles up country, the low lands being clothed with verdure in summer. It was named by them Groenland. The coast abounds with inlets, bays and rivers. But before the Danes a company of Icelanders, headed by one Rande, was driven here by accident. On his return, he made such a favourable report that several families accompanied him, and it became worthy of the notice of the celebrated Norwegian chief Olaf, who sent there a missionary to establish the true faith. The settlement continued to increase and prosper under his protection, with many towns, convents and churches arising under the jurisdiction of the Archbishop of Drontheim: and a considerable commerce was carried on between Greenland and Norway till the year 1406. At that period all correspondence was cut off, and all knowledge of that colony buried in oblivion. This strange and sudden change has been attributed to various causes. The colony had from the first been harassed by the inland natives, a barbarous and savage race very much resembling the Esquimaus of Hudson's Bay. These people, called Schrellings, in the end overcame the Iceland settlers to such an extent that, when their brethren in the eastern district came to their assistance, they found nothing but the cattle running wild about the country. It is supposed that these newcomers met the same fate as their predecessors. Some ruins of their habitations are still discernable, and there are reasons for believing that some descendants of the Iceland colony may yet be in existence on the eastern shore.

Anyone then visiting Greenland could not help expressing surprise at the change which has taken place in those regions. In former times there were two districts, Eastern and Western. The former is said to have contained 12 extensive parishes, 190 villages, a bishop's see and two monasteries. There was a constant trade with Iceland and Norway. But at last the ice, which accumulated in such immense fields along that shore, interrupted and totally put an end to that commercial intercourse. The eastern and western colonies had continual communications with each other across the country once. But the inhabitants of the western districts of the present day know nothing of the opposite one, although there is still reason for believing some of that race to be in existence. The immense mountains of ice that now occupy the intermediate space between them has put an end to all possible means of traversing it. No doubt, then, some considerable alteration in this part of the world has taken place since the fifteenth century. This coast—the eastern—was discovered by Sir Hugh Willoughby in 1553. The King of Denmark, Christian IV, heard so much of this colony that he ordered an expedition to ascertain if any of its remains could be found. The officer entrusted with that service visited East Greenland where he traded with some savages, but saw no signs of a civilised people. Had he been able to proceed to the original spot, he would, there is reason to believe, have traced some ruins of that ancient district. The savages are supposed to be a part of the Schrelling race.

That part of Greenland inhabitated by the Danes lies between the 64th and 68th degrees of latitude. The summer, which commences at the end of May and lasts till mid-September, is bearable. To the northward of 68 the cold is intense. This country is supposed to contain many mines, and you will recollect the account of the ore brought from it by Capt. Martin Frobisher. A strait of that navigator's name is still in existence at the southern extremity, west from Cape Farewell. The Greenlanders are employed all the year round in fishing or hunting. The fishing boats are generally managed by the women and are called 'kones'—kone meaning, in their language, a woman. They attack the whales with success. The hunting, of course, is the males' duty, the reindeer being the principal object of pursuit. They are driven into narrow defiles and slain with arrows. The sea fowl they kill with lances. This region is but thinly inhabited. They live in huts and are not longlived, of low stature, brawny and inclined to corpulency.*

The first leisure moment that I had, I drew up a written state- ment of what had passed under my observations, with our reckoning by chronometer, etc. When I showed it to Capt. Talbot, he merely perused it without expressing any wish for further investigation. His taciturnity reminding me of what had already passed between us relating to the difference of our timekeepers, I naturally thought that he cared little about the matter. However, as I thought that document deserving of notice, as it pointed out the errors of the charts, I availed myself of the first opportunity of transmitting it to the Hydrographer of the Admiralty, Capt. Hurd.[1]

In shaping our course southward, we were in sight of Greenland for several days, and the *Horatio* took her station on the Commodore's weather quarter, keeping at all times as near him as the wind and weather would allow. We encountered strong breezes, squalls and plenty of islands of ice, the lead being kept going. The *Victorious's* crew was kept at the pumps, the water coming out of her scuppers being at all hours noticed by us. On the 12th we fell in with two whalers. I spoke one of them, and her Master was as much surprised as the former one at meeting such large ships, especially the 74, in those regions. No men of war of such dimensions had ever been so far north before. We had fogs, during which we never parted com- pany from the Senior Officer, guns being regularly fired. On the 20th we sent some carpenters to our consort, and three whalers favoured us with their company. About noon on the 23rd four strange sail were seen. I was sent in chace of them, and they proved to be a small convoy bound to Hudson's Bay under the care of H.M.S. *Rosamond*.

On the 25th one of my Marine Officers, Lieut. Capel,[2] was dis- charged by his own request into the *Victorious*. That officer had, some time previously, refused to dine with me, and, as no reason or explanation ensued, he was not invited again. . . .

[Omitted: an account of an apparently pointless misunderstand- ing. W.H.D. attempts no explanation, though (as we might expect)

---

* This statement is in part taken from the work by a Danish Missionary, Hans Egede, to which I have added my own observations.
[1] Thomas Hurd, Lt. 30/1/1777; Cdr. 18/8/95; Capt. 29/4/1802.
[2] Edward Capel, 2nd Lt. 29/9/1808.

he regards his own conduct as not only impeccable but even generous. In the end Dillon invited him to return, but Capel 'aware, I suppose, that he had made a fool of himself, thought proper to remain in the *Victorious.*']

(3) H.M.S. *HORATIO* (Newfoundland, 2nd Cruise)
AUGUST 1814–MARCH 8, 1815

By the beginning of August we were clear of Davis's Straits and felt more at ease. Having got clear of the islands of ice, we shaped a course for the Lands End of Old England. On the 7th I was ordered to chace a stranger whom I boarded—a merchant ship from the island of St. Thomas's bound to Glasgow. On the evening of the 8th we struck soundings in 76 fathoms, and on the morning of the 9th saw the land—the Lizard. Shortly afterwards I boarded one of our merchantmen, from whom I heard that the Princess of Wales[1] had refused the offers of the Prince of Orange. At 9 o'clock I hove to, and sent a boat to the *Victorious* for my Carpenters, from which ship I parted company in an hour's time. Not wishing to go to Portsmouth, I made the best of my way towards Plymouth Sound. At noon, with fine weather, I saw the Eddystone lighthouse, and by 3 o'clock the *Horatio* was safely moored. I saluted the Admiral (my kind acquaintance Ad. Domett) with 17 guns. As the ship wanted a regular fitting, the seamen were employed accordingly. As to myself, I was occupied for several days from 8 o'clock till 4 attending Courts Martial.

At one of these, a question of mine led to the prisoner's being sentenced to death. The President, McKinley,[2] being of the same opinion as myself, gave the casting vote. Consequently the man's life hung upon our consciences, which caused much uneasiness to me. However, the next day the President called upon me at my lodging. 'I have,' said he, 'some good news for you. I suppose yesterday's sentence has been upon your mind. It has upon mine.' 'Yes,' I replied, 'I have been thinking of it ever since.' 'Then,' said he, 'you will now be relieved, because the prisoner has confessed himself

---

[1] This refers, not to Caroline, the Prince Regent's wife, but to Princess Charlotte of Wales; his only daughter. She was betrothed to William, Heriditary Prince of Holland, but refused to marry him unless they could live in England, where she was determined to remain.

[2] George McKinley, Lt. 14/1/1782; Cdr. 16/5/98; Capt. 20/10/1801; R-Ad. 22/11/30; V-Ad. 23/11/41.

guilty to the clergyman who has visited him.' That information was, I acknowledge, a quietus for which I was not prepared, and I cordially thanked my friend for his attention in taking the trouble to bring me the parson's report.[1]

During my absence, great changes had taken place owing to the peace with France. The seamen of a certain number of years' service were to be pensioned. This occasioned many alterations. I also perused with much satisfaction an official document published by the Admiralty on 30th April of this year, expressing to the Petty Officers, Seamen and Royal[2] Marines of His Majesty's Fleet the high sense their Lordships entertained of their gallant and glorious services during the late war. The patience, perseverance and discipline under the most trying circumstances, the skill, courage and devotion with which they have upheld the best interests, and achieved the noblest triumphs, of the country, entitle them to the gratitude, not only of their native land which they have preserved inviolate, but of the other nations of Europe, of whose ultimate deliverance their successes maintained the hope and accelerated the accomplishment. This document also alludes to their regret that the unjust and unprovoked aggression of the American Government prevented our reducing the Fleet at once to a peacetime establishment. But every attention would be paid to the claims and services of both seamen and marines.

[The incident which follows, very long in the original, is here abbreviated.]

[Ad. Domett informed him that he had received an anonymous letter from the ship's company of the *Horatio*] . . . to be sent to the Admiralty, complaining of tyranny and oppression, to such an extent that it was impossible for seamen to live or serve on board of such a ship. It alluded to her having been upon very trying service in Davis Straits, and that none of them had received leave to go on shore.

[Domett, who was evidently a good friend, expressed himself] . . . very uneasy on your account, because, having been at the Admiralty, I am fully aware of the spirit existing there in cases of this kind.

[Thereupon W.H.D. asked as a favour that the Admiral would alter the first sentence of his covering letter from ' In consequence of the *Horatio's* Ship's Company having represented to the Lords

---

[1] *C.f.* the almost identical story of what happened, also in Plymouth, in June, 1809, (p. 124).
[2] The Marines became a 'Royal' Corps in 1802, by order of George III.

Commissioners of the Admiralty' to 'In consequence of an official request made to me by Capt. W.H.D. of H.M.S. *Horatio.*' To this Ad. Domett agreed.]

That affair settled, I withdrew. So unconcerned was I that, instead of going off to my ship to inquire into particulars, I passed the evening very quietly and sociably with some of my brother officers. Next morning, however, I went on board, and mentioned what had happened to the Senior Lieutenant, who became very uneasy. I took no steps with the Ship's Company, but to one of the seamen whom I supposed by his constant attentions to be attached to me, I merely asked if he knew anything of the complaint the Ship's Company had made. He replied in a most respectful manner, upon his honour, that he knew nothing of it. That fellow, it was afterwards proved, was one of the principals in the whole transaction. How *is* a gentleman of rectitude to act?

[The three captains sent on board to investigate were Lambert,[1] Maling[2] (W.H.D.'s shipmate of the *Alcide*) and Prescott, who had appeared on board the *Leopard* on precisely the same errand in 1811. (See above, p. 181). The crew was ordered aft and the letter was read to them. Capt. Lambert then demanded who wrote it. There was a long silence, but at last] . . . out stepped, to my utter astonishment, my own joiner, by name Robert Fowler, who was no one more nor less than my servant, whose whole occupation was attending to and cleaning my furniture. Upon the question being put again, he said, 'I wrote it.' But the fact now became evident that the Ship's Company did not, as a whole, approve its contents. Then, the muster book being produced, Capt. Lambert began to examine the seamen, starting with the two captains of the Forecastle. The first, being asked if he had any complaints against me, replied that he never wished to sail with a better Captain or a better seaman. This answer caused a very marked sensation upon the officers constituting the inquiry. I confess it did so upon me, as I hardly knew the man who had spoken. I had been only five months in the command of the ship, and had not courted popularity among the crew, my principal object being to have her in good shape as an official man of war. When the next was called, and the same question put to him, his reply was rather stronger in my favour than the former. Upon hearing it,

---

[1] Robert Lambert, Lt. 1/8/1791; Cdr. 4/5/95; Capt. 11/4/96; R-Ad. 12/8/1819; V-Ad. 22/7/30. Died Sept., 1836.
[2] Thomas James Maling, Lt. 6/01/1797; Cdr. 24/12/98; Capt. 6/9/1800; R-Ad. 22/7/30; V-Ad. 23/11/41.

Capt. Lambert appeared at a loss how to act, and became convinced that there was some foul play. He inquired of me if I wished to say anything to the seamen. I merely answered, 'I have nothing to say. I have done my duty.' Again addressing the crew, he demanded if anyone had received any ill treatment. That question remained for some time unnoticed, but upon its being frequently repeated, out came one of them belonging to the Foretop. . . .

[This man claimed that he had been 'started' by the Officer of the Watch for not reporting a strange sail. On further examination, it came out that that officer had not reported the incident to W.H.D., and Capt. Lambert told the foretopman (who agreed) that] . . . he had not been severely punished: on the contrary, he had got well out of the scrape by the Mate's negligence in not reporting him to the Captain. As no other seaman came out to complain, the inquiry terminated, upon my mentioning that there were, at that time, 15 men on leave of absence—which was a direct denial of one of the charges. Capt. Lambert now wished to muster the crew, as he noticed that most of them were very slight and of low stature. That ceremony performed, he with his colleagues retired to my cabin. . . .

[W.H.D. wished to take no further steps, but the Captains persuaded him that, in the interests of all other officers, he should put his joiner in irons, and have him tried: so] . . . he was placed in limbo, and in the course of the day I wrote for the trial of the delinquent.

[The Captains' report cleared W.H.D. completely, but, as they added their remarks upon the puny build of the crew, the Admiralty ordered a survey, and 90 of the weakest men were replaced by 90 stronger ones.] . . . However, it unluckily so happened that the four ringleaders who had been the occasion of all the mischief remained behind. After the inquiry, I had allowed the Second Lieutenant,[1] who knew all the seamen well, a few days' leave of absence. Consequently he was not present at the Survey, where he might have been of great use in pointing out the refractory characters. I received a proportion of powerful men, but I had 20 landsmen more than previously. Therefore if I had less seamen, there was additional strength placed at my disposal, and I did not much regret the loss. It would only have been acting fairly with me, though, with a ship of that quality under my command, to have made up all the ratings taken away.

The Surgeon had been so frightened at our constantly meeting

---

[1] Lardner Dennys, See below, p. 404.

the ice islands in Davis Straits that he left the ship. He never could sleep whilst we were in those latitudes, but was always aloft on the look out, to give warning of the coming danger, and wrote several notes to me on the subject. This was no part of his duty. His mind had evidently been affected. An order was now sent to me to discharge my joiner into the Admiral's Flagship, there to remain until their Lordships thought proper to order a Court Martial upon him. He was accordingly removed and kept under confinement.

Odd enough, who should arrive in the Sound at this moment but Sir Edward Pellew in the *Caledonia*, coming from the Mediterranean. I went to call alongside that ship (she being in quarantine) and, to my surprise, Sir Edward came down to the last step of the accommodation ladder, and greeted me in terms extremely gratifying at my having command of such a fine frigate. Whether these gratulations were sincere was another matter. When he had it in his power to place me in one of the same dimensions, he did not do so. However, after many agreeable sayings, I took my leave of the gallant Admiral, who soon became a Peer of the realm.

On the 18th I weighed, and removed to Cawsand Bay. On this occasion the Master[1] managed the ship very badly. I was anxiously watching all his directions as we were proceeding out of the Sound, and thought that he stood too close to the Mount Edgcombe shore. Presently, whilst in the act of tacking, the ship touched, and held fast upon the rocks of that locality. When I had ascertained that it was the after part that had taken the rocks, I instantly ordered all hands to take a couple of shot, one in each hand, then hasten forward on to the Forecastle: many to go out on the bowsprit. When they had taken the positions I desired, I ordered them to rise up from their feet together by signal, and stamp down on the deck. After that act had been repeated two or three times, the ship was shaken off and got clear of the rocks without accident. Fortunately there was but a light breeze and no swell, so that the ship had no rising motion of consequence. As I had not previously much opinion of the Master's abilities, this last act did not raise that opinion. The next morning we left Cawsand Bay on our way to the Cove of Cork. A long list of complaints was now brought to me against 12 of the men for very improper conduct. After what had happened, I was determined to let the Ship's Company see that I would not sanction irregularities. They were all punished. It was then that the Second Lieutenant acquainted me of his having found out the four seamen who had been the

[1] John Mills, 1st Warrant, 3/10/1811.

principals in drawing up the letter written against me. He gave their names. We reached the Cove (of Cork) on the afternoon of the 21st, where we moored the *Horatio*. I soon received instructions to issue orders to our merchant ships bound to Halifax, Quebec and New-foundland. The *Derwent*, brig of war, Capt. Williams,[1] had orders to place himself under me to attend the convoy.

By September 4 they were, to the number of 116, ready. This was one of the most valuable convoys of its kind that ever crossed the Atlantic. I had made this circumstance known to the Admiral, and requested another ship or two to protect so much mercantile property, but all my representations failed. I experienced some difficulty in getting them all out of the harbour. We were obliged to anchor outside for a short while, but by the morning of the 7th we were all clear of the land. The cargo of four of the ships under my charge was valued at nearly a million sterling.

[He followed his usual system of keeping his convoy together by pressing prime seamen from delinquent ships in exchange for lands-men. Nothing much occurred until September 14, when a strong gale blew up.]

I had some important despatches on board, transmitted to me by the Secretary of the Admiralty, with particular instructions relating to them. They were in duplicate. I had also a Mate for the Flagship. Therefore, weighing in my mind the delays which I thought would attend us, I selected a very fine ship, coppered, which had the appearance of a sloop of war. I sent for the Master of her and pro-posed to him to receive the officer above-mentioned, with a bag of despatches, and that, in the event of his separating from the *Horatio*, he should be at liberty to make the best of his way to Newfoundland. The Master acted with strict propriety, declaring that it should not be his fault if the separation took place: but, should events so turn out, he would do his best to deliver the despatches. The Mate, to whom I gave them in charge, was to throw them overboard in case of being captured by the Enemy. Having made these arrangements, as I thought for the good of the Service, I wrote a statement to Sir Richard Keats, transmitting Capt. Talbot's report of the accident that had happened to the *Victorious* in Davis Straits. I then added a private letter, detailing the boisterous weather we had encountered and what I expected in the future, stating that, with such prospects in view, I had authorized the Master of a ship called the *Lune*, with

---

[1] Thomas Williams, Lt. 25/12/1800; Cdr. 27/6/14. Not promoted. Died 1849.

whom I had placed one of his Mates in charge of some despatches addressed to His Excellency, to proceed, in case of parting company, without loss of time to St. Johns. That letter was dated the 18th of the month, on which day I sent the officer on board the ship mentioned, stating that 30 sail of my convoy had already parted from me. My foresight and caution, I thought, would merit the approbation of the Admiral. Besides, I looked upon him as a friend, and had entered into details in my private letter which were afterwards turned against me. Such is the uncertainty of the temper of our superiors.

[The convoy gradually scattered till, after a 'gale more like a hurricane', he had, on the 25th, only two sail in sight. He found several, then lost them, as the bad weather persisted. On October 7 he was in company with three. On the 12th he had an exciting chase, in a gale, of a strange ship which, when at last overhauled, proved to be one of the convoy. Next day he 'sounded on the outer Bank of Newfoundland in 94 fathoms.']

I had now plenty of fogs but was quite alone. When the weather permitted I stood in various directions to try and find my convoy, but failed. On the 19th we fortunately got a sufficient sight of the sun to regulate the Latitude at noon. I made the position of the ship to be 28 miles from a small rock, just to be seen upon the surface of the water, not far from Cape Race. The fog now came on as thick as ever. There was a strong breeze and an immense heavy swell. I was so satisfied with the correctness of our reckoning, that I determined to stand towards the rock. Sending for the Second Lieutenant, who had charge of the chronometer, I inquired if he felt confidence in his calculations. He replied in the affirmative, but I noticed that neither he nor the Master seemed inclined to approach the land whilst enveloped in such a thick mist. Nevertheless my mind was fixed. We had lost our convoy, and I concluded that they had reached Newfoundland. We had suffered in many places from the effect of the stormy weather. The rudder coat had been washed away and the stern frame injured. Under these circumstances I thought myself justified in running towards St. Johns, instead of proceeding up the Gulf of St. Lawrence according to the tenor of my orders. The helm therefore was put up, and a course steered for the rock, the ship going 12 knots under close-reefed topsails and courses, topgallant masts struck. I calculated that we should make it by $\frac{1}{2}$ past 2 o'clock. The cables were ranged, and every precaution taken in the event of our getting into danger. We could not see more than a ¼ of a mile round us. Two o'clock struck. The ship was bounding over the waves. The Second Lieutenant was terribly nervous: he could not, he said, eat his dinner. The Master too was not at his ease: he thought I might run the ship on shore. Men were stationed in all the prominent parts of the ship. I kept· on deck with my watch in my hand, which was constructed on the time-keeper principle, and had been used as a companion to the chronometer. Fifteen minutes after two arrived: the anxiety of all on deck became intense. However, I stood on in the same direction.

At 28 minutes past two, the lookout man on the larboard fore yardarm and the one on the same cathead called out strongly, 'Rock on the larboard bow.' We had shaped a correct course, and, when seen, it was not a quarter of a cable's length from the ship. So far I was satisfied. Sail was taken in, and fortunately the fog began to clear away, which enabled us to see the coast of Newfoundland.

[W.H.D. receives the fervent congratulations of his officers with his usual complacency. They warp into the harbour of St. Johns without further adventure.]

I was soon informed that most of my convoy had arrived safely. So far, I thought, all right, and I hastened on shore to Sir Richard Keats. I was received in his private office, the Secretary being present. I shall have some difficulty in relating all that passed. Expecting to hear my proceedings approved of, I was stung to the quick to be told that I had no business in harbour, and that he regretted there were not sufficient Captains present to try me by a Court Martial. He had sent for my Admiralty orders and my log whilst the ship was being warped into harbour, so that he was prepared to receive me a full hour before I appeared. That reception was so completely at variance with what I had hoped that I cannot describe to you my sensations. However, when I heard that a Court Martial was in contemplation, I replied that nothing would give me greater pleasure than to appear before one, so thoroughly convinced was I of having acted for the best. Then, to my utter astonishment, Sir Richard addressed me with a forbidding countenance, in a downright sulky mood. 'I see what you have been about. Your own letter condemns you. Very prudent to put the despatches on board of a merchant ship. The brig's log is enough for me.' I made a suitable reply, stating that I was quite ready to answer all charges brought against me. 'Why,' said he, 'you have been going for the last 6 or 7 days at the

rate of 8 or 9 knots.' 'Yes, Sir,' said I: 'in search of my convoy, and
I am now glad to learn they are all in port. But if you will examine
my log, when with it,[1] you will perceive that 3 knots was our utmost
speed, when not having a fair wind.' 'What,' he demanded in a
blustering tone, 'do you raise your voice at me?' 'Nothing disre-
spectfully, Sir,' I replied. 'But if you prefer charges against me, you
must expect that I shall defend myself.' He then inquired if I had
been up the St. Lawrence to Anticosti. I told him that I had not:
that my convoy had separated so many days previous to my arrival,
and, having failed in finding any of them, I naturally concluded that
they had all reached their destinations. He now changed his tone,
regretting he could not try me by a Court Martial. 'You shall go to
sea tomorrow morning,' he added. 'Go on board. I shall order your
being supplied with water during the night. So lose no time in
proceeding to Anticosti.' I withdrew to prepare for sea. This was my
friend.

One satisfaction I felt—that he lowered his domineering attack
towards me, perceiving, probably, that he had not humbled or
frightened me. I hastened on board. Luckily we had only one anchor
down. The seamen worked watch and watch all night, taking water
and getting up the naval stores. I sent a message to the Captain of
the *Derwent* inviting him to breakfast next morning, that I might
learn from him what his log might produce against me. I also learned
that the *Lune*, by whom I had sent the despatches, had arrived
10 days before the *Horatio*. Capt. Williams came to breakfast, but
there was nothing in his log to my prejudice. That vessel had suffered
so much by the gales that she was obliged to throw her guns overboard. When her Captain reported his proceedings to Sir Richard, it
seems by his account, he received such a jobation that mine was
nothing in comparison. The Admiral never forgave him, telling him
that he ought to have got rid of his stores in preference. That alone
proved what blunders men will make when they cannot command
their tempers. The getting out of the stores of a brig, when in a
sinking condition, could not be effected. She would have gone down
while making the attempt, whereas the guns were on deck, and easily
got rid of.

[1] *Sic.* He means, presumably, 'those portions of my log which cover the period
when I was in touch with the convoy': and his argument apparently is:—'When you
see in the log the entry "8 or 9 knots", one of two things was happening: either the
wind was fair for the convoy and all the ships could make that speed, or I had lost
the convoy and was casting about for it. You will find that, whenever I was with
them and the wind was *not* fair, I always conformed with the pace of the slowest—
not exceeding 3 knots.'

Now for another interview with Sir Richard. The Surgeon reported that the Master had been taken so seriously ill that his life was in danger, and urged the necessity of removing him to the shore. I requested that officer to accompany me to the Admiral's where he could state the case better than I. Ashore we went, at 10 o'clock. Sir Richard had just finished his breakfast. When he saw me enter, he would not acknowledge me. However, I addressed him respectfully (in his Secretary's presence), and, holding out a copy of the *Horatio's* log, told him that I had brought it for his examination, to prove that he had taken a wrong view of the ship's rate of going whilst with the convoy. He paused for a few seconds. I then told him I was preparing for a Court Martial. His looks turned to perfect sourness. I next acquainted him with the state of the Master's health, of its being necessary to leave him behind. He would not listen. 'What has one man's life to do with the public service?' he demanded. 'I only report to you what the Surgeon has represented to me,' I replied: 'and as that officer's life is in danger, I think it my duty to make the same known to you, not wishing his death to be laid at my door.' This statement produced some effect, and he began to ask some questions about the Master. 'The Surgeon,' said I, 'is outside, ready to explain the real state of the case.' 'Very well,' he replied, 'Order him in.'* Then, addressing me in angry tone, 'if your ship is not at sea in an hour's time you shall be answerable for the consequences.' He sent a message to his Captain in the next room to make my signal to weigh. I left my log upon his table, then retired. Capt. Blamey[1] accompanied me. That officer was acting in the room of Capt. Hawker, who was at sea in the *Bellerophon*, and the Admiral's Flag was flying on board of his ship, one of 20 guns. As we proceeded down to the wharf, Capt. B. observed that the Admiral was in a sad temper. 'However,' he said, 'every minute is now of use to you, and I shall not make the signal until you are aboard of your ship.' As soon as I had reached the *Horatio*, up went her signal to weigh. The carpenters had been at work repairing the rudder coat, and the caulkers making good the damages the sea had caused to the counter. In a few minutes the ship was under sail, and when out of the harbour obliged to lay in smooth water under the land to enable the men to complete their labours under the stern: for the ship would not be safe until they had made a finish there. However, by 5 o'clock, we

* The Master was sent on shore and, as the Surgeon attended to him, he was left behind. Unfortunately for him, he met the Admiral one day, who recognized him and called him sharply to account for not having hastened off to his ship.
[1] George William Blamey, Lt. 6/9/1794; Cdr. 12/7/1802; Capt. 21/10/10.

made sail on our way up the St. Lawrence. I was determined not to mention to the Admiral one word of these injuries which the ship had sustained whilst he continued so completely out of temper. But when he proceeded to extremities he would have found that I was justified in bringing my ship into port to repair the defects.

[His cruise—from October 21 to November 8—was brief and uneventful: indeed, perhaps as perfunctory as he dared make it. He saw little shipping of any sort, and no enemy. The only incident of any note occurred when 'a tremendous sea struck the ship whilst we were shifting the mainsail, and stove in all the main deck ports on the starboard side. I was washed out of my cot. The main channels were so much injured that the mainmast was in danger. The ship trembled under its effect, which caused a general panic throughout the crew. But as daylight came we were able in due time to secure the mast.' There is also an account of how he discovered a brig—one of his late convoy—whose Master kept no reckoning at all, but 'guided his brig entirely by following us.' 'What,' he wonders, 'did that fellow do when he parted from the convoy'?]

[On re-entering St. John's harbour] I reported myself to Sir Richard, and when I had replied to all his questions, I acquainted him that I was quite prepared for a Court Martial. He had a green shade over his eyes, and did not appear pleased with the assertion. This led to a lengthened conversation, the substance being that he had written to the Admiralty, and that he had made explanations which would set me all right there. Other expressions came out that led me to believe he had altered his mind on that subject. I thought it would be imprudent to push affairs to extremities, and, as he appeared to be in pain, I retired. As I left the room he invited me to dinner, observing he wished to have some chat with me. What a change, thought I, as I left the premises.

[Relations thereafter improved, with Keats evidently trying to be friendly, and to re-establish old relations; and W.H.D. resisting in his usual cautious, prickly way. Then a further, and trivial, misunderstanding threatened. The Admiral, on the point of departing for England, invited him to a farewell official dinner. W.H.D. refused it, on the grounds that he had promised to dine with the General (Campbell). Unpleasantness was averted, however, by the Admiral's Captain, Hawker, who paid W.H.D. a personal visit, and persuaded him to put off Campbell and attend upon the Admiral. Hawker's last words give us a glimpse, if only an oblique one, of what others thought of W.H.D., and of how aggravating he could be when he sulked. . . .]

'But,' Hawker added, 'the Admiral has noticed your coldness. You were in the habit of entertaining him with anecdotes and merry stories. All that is changed, and you keep aloof from him when at his table. You must assume your usual convivial bearing and sit by him today, and do all you can to remove any unfavourable impressions which our Chief may have formed against you.' I accordingly presented myself at the Governor's at the hour appointed, and seated myself next to him at table. The dinner passed in a very sociable and friendly manner. Thus we were all right again. On the 7th (December) Sir Richard embarked on board his Flagship, the *Bellerophon*, the crews of the various ships of war cheering him as he passed.

[W.H.D. was due to depart too, having been ordered to take a small convoy to Lisbon and Gibraltar. But gales prevented the departure of both the Admiral and himself. He now gives a 3-page description of Newfoundland, in which he states, among other things, that 'the interior is scarcely known, still being occupied by the aborigines, called the Red Indians.' Also: 'The island abounds in timber, which is turned to account in repairing the fishing vessels. It is sometimes employed in building merchant ships, but the spars are not of sufficient dimensions to furnish masts and yards for a larger craft than a cutter.' And: 'Poole in Dorsetshire appears to be the principal port from which these fishing vessels arrive, and the markets are in Portugal, Spain, Italy and the West Indies.' He then relates how he 'became acquainted with a Lieutenant of the Navy, Buchan, who made an attempt to establish an intercourse with the Red Indians.' He gives a very detailed account of Buchan's expedition, covering seven pages. This though by no means uninteresting, must be omitted. The principal fact which emerges from it is the complete and virgin savagery of the natives, who for all our long occupation of the island, had clearly had no communication whatever with white men.]

As the articles of the peace with France became known, I was astonished at that country's being allowed to retake possession of St. Pierre's and Miquelon, small islands close to St. John's, which interfered with our fishing. But so it was. We gave away abundantly.

I now issued my instructions to the merchant vessels that would

sail under my convoy, and, whilst doing so, we received private
information that the Northern States of America were desirous of
separating from the Southern ones, and that some deputies who had
been selected to repair to Great Britain with that object in view were
at Boston, waiting for an opportunity to set sail for England. As the
time drew near for my quitting, I had two or three applications made
to me to take passengers in my cabin, one from a lady with whom I
had become accidentally acquainted in the society of the town. She
was the widow of an officer who had been killed at Waterloo,[1] and had
made herself conspicuous in abstracting his dead body from among
the heaps of corpses that covered the field of battle. I assented to
receive such an amiable woman. However, on the day fixed she did
not make her appearance, and her place was filled by one of the
principal merchants, Mr. R———n, who was too happy to avail himself of such an opportunity, and soon found his way into my cabin.

On the 23rd, having tolerable weather for this season, the ship
was under sail, standing through the Straits, my boats employed in
assisting some of the convoy and the *Pioneer*, schooner, being under
my orders. We had not been long out of the harbour when the weather
began to change with a most threatening appearance. . . .

[Another gale followed. The convoy was instantly lost, and the
ship considerably damaged. Two episodes are, however, somewhat
out of the ordinary:—

1. 'One heavy sea struck the ship on her starboard side, stove in
all the half ports and drove out several of the side foot steps, which
were washed in upon the Quarter Deck. That you may form some
opinion of the violence and overpowering weight of such an assault
from a long sending sea, these steps were secured by 3 nine-inch nails,
and had only a surface projection of 4 inches, the side of them being
angular. Their shape would lead anyone to believe that the wave
would wash over them, and not root them out from their fastenings.
But such was the fact.'

2. 'On the 29th we fell in with an abandoned brig with only her
mainmast standing. Had the weather not been so boisterous, I
might have taken her in tow, and probably have seen her into some
port in safety. However, I passed close to her, to ascertain if any
living soul was on board: but no one made his appearance. It was
therefore quite clear that her crew had deserted the brig.']

[1] W.H.D.'s worst 'howler' (Waterloo, June, 1815: date here reached, Dec., 1814).
See Vol. I, Introduction, p. xxix.

On the 1st of January, 1815, I was in Lat. 43 North and began to feel a change for the better in the atmosphere. By 4 o'clock on the afternoon of the 8th, we saw the coast of Portugal, Cape Mondego, distant 8 leagues, the reckoning proving correct. The next morning we saw the Barlings to leeward, and on the afternoon of the 9th I anchored near to Belem Castle in the Tagus. All the carpenters were set to work to repair the damages the ship had sustained. Meanwhile, I went up to Lisbon to present my respects to Mr. Canning,[1] who was our political minister at that court. I was most kindly received by him. On retiring, I met Ad. Sir George Berkeley, who insisted upon my dining with him. He was no longer the naval Commander in Chief, but had come over to settle some private affairs, and was in lodgings. I passed a very sociable evening with him and her Ladyship. There was an American Privateer in the Tagus, upon which I kept a sharp lookout. As my guest, Mr. R———n, intended to find his way to England over the Continent, and visit Paris, I gave him some letters of introduction to the Duchess of Orleans and her Lady of Honour the Marchioness, sending some fine furs which I had selected in Newfoundland. He afterwards informed me that Her Serene Highness had shown him every attention; but all his plans were frustrated by Bonaparte's arrival from Elba.

On the 11th I put to sea, intending to remain off the Rock of Lisbon, watching the motions of the American Privateer, as well to pick up any of my convoy should they appear. I boarded several English ships which had parted from the convoy of H.M.S. *Tiber*. On the 14th I made sail in chace of a large ship which proved to be that frigate. I went on board to wait on the Captain, Dacres,[2] he being the Senior officer. He persuaded me to stay and dine with him. I was much surprised to find that he had for a 1st Lieutenant one of my Verdun acquaintances, Lutwidge,[3] whose ship had been wrecked on the coast of France. I was boarding 4 or 5 ships daily, but none American.

Tired of boarding ships, I ran towards Tangier. As I had never been here before, I landed and waited on our Consul. He persuaded me to dine with him, during which the American Consul's son came, anxious if possible to make the acquaintance of the Captain of the

---

[1] The famous statesman, George Canning, who was Ambassador Extraordinary at Lisbon for nine months.

[2] James Richard Dacres, Lt. 15/11/1804; Cdr. 5/7/05; Capt. 14/1/06: commanded the *Guerrière* in her unequal struggle with the U.S.S. *Constitution*, 19/8/12; R-Ad. 28/6/38; C. in C. Cape 9/8/45; V-Ad. 20/3/48.

[3] Henry Thomas Lutwidge, Lt. 6/9/1800: wrecked in the *Hussar* (Capt. Philip Wilkinson), 1804, and a prisoner of war till 1814; Ret-Cdr. 26/11/30.

English frigate. In the evening my host took me over the most interesting part of the town. There was a fine prospect, and rural mountains, but, in a Mooorish fortress, not many objects to attract attention. The gates were always closed at sunset; therefore I returned to my ship. A gale had sprung up, which brought on a very heavy sea and made my passage off rather a dangerous affair. The next day, having procured some cattle, I put to sea. On the 20th, when off Cadiz, I boarded a Spanish ship from Amelia Island in America. The Supercargo was either an Englishman or an American, and made himself extremely troublesome. I had him in my cabin upwards of two hours, and, speaking that language, examined the Spanish Master and his papers. The latter made very suitable replies to all my questions, but it was quite evident that the Supercargo was trying to get me into a scrape, by hinting of there being a chance that, if I detained the ship, she might turn out a Prize. However, after a great deal of useless chatter, I got tired of the fellow, and allowed him to go into Cadiz. Some time afterwards I heard that the Supercargo had boasted in the commercial circles of Cadiz how nearly he had humbugged the Captain of the frigate *Horatio*. Ad. Fleming,[1] in command there, directed his Secretary to obtain information. It was then proved that she contained Spanish property, and I had acted rightly in not detaining her.

In my trip from Newfoundland I visited Portugal in Europe and Tangier in Africa. In the short space of 21 days (deducting stoppages) I had had my foot in three parts of the globe within a month.

[The *Horatio* now made her way home without any outstanding incident and. . . .]

On the afternoon of the 6th of February we struck soundings in 92 fathoms. On the 9th, with fair weather, the coast of England was seen, and by 2 o'clock the ship was anchored in Sandown Bay near the Culver Cliff, and at 4 p.m. under sail again, standing in for Spithead, where she was moored that evening. She now had to undergo a thorough refit. The foremast and mizen mast were both rotten. New ones were got in by the 21st.

I now received a letter from the mother of Fowler, who had written the anonymous letter whilst we were in Plymouth Sound, accusing me of tyranny and oppression, entreating me to forgive him.

---

[1] Hon. Charles Elphinstone Fleeming, Lt. 22/4/1793; Cdr. (spring) 1794; Capt. 7/10/1794; R-Ad. 4/12/1813; V-Ad. 19/7/21; Ad. 10/1/37. Lord Keith's nephew. Died, Governor of Greenwich Hospital, 6/11/40.

He had been 6 months in irons. Consequently I wrote to the Admiralty representing his long confinement and requesting that he might be pardoned. However, their Lordships decided otherwise. The culprit was brought before a Court Martial. My letter demanding it had stated that he had acknowledged himself the *author* of that letter. He, in his defence, proved that he was not the *author*, but the *copier* of what had been given to him by some of the seamen: he had written it, but with its contents he had nothing to do. However, the Articles of War are very stringent when the offence relates to a mutiny. They say, 'Anyone aiding and abetting' a transaction of that nature 'shall suffer death.' Therefore the delinquent had come under that part of the Law, and, in the strictness of that meaning, he had forfeited his life. But he was acquitted, to the astonishment of everybody. It was of no consequence to me, because I had solicited his not being tried: and I believe that the Court Martial, being aware of my having done so, acted upon that feeling. My principal annoyance was my having to receive Fowler on board again. Fortunately one of the captains, Sir James Wood,[1] remarked that it was very unpleasant for me to have to take such a man back to my crew, and very goodnaturedly applied to the Admiral, Sir Richard Bickerton, for his being removed into his ship, the *Pompée*. Fowler was therefore kept on board the *Royal William* where he had long been until his discharge to the *Pompée*. Thus I got rid of the fellow. The Admiral's Captain, Fowke,[2] had taken a decided prejudice against me during the trial, frequently questioning Fowler about the discipline, etc., of my ship, and every word that could be turned against me he brought out before the Court, under the pretence of serving the prisoner, but actually to injure his Captain. So much for honour among gentlemen, and an officer of rank. The worst part of his conduct was the difficulties that all my officers experienced in their official duties through the Flagship. My clerk, in particular, had made several applications to be examined touching his capabilities to do a Purser's duties, but they were never attended to. I at last wrote a strong remonstrance to Capt. F., declaring that the whole of his proceedings relating to the *Horatio's* officers would be laid before the Commander in Chief. He was rather astounded at that threat, and changed the whole of his bearing for the better. No more neglect occurred: the Clerk passed his examination with credit.

[1] Sir James Athol Wood, Lt. 18/10/1778; Cdr. 8/7/95; Capt. 27/3/97; R-Ad. 19/7/1821.
[2] George Fowke, Lt. 14/11/1790; Cdr. 29/9/95; Capt. 9/7/98; R-Ad. 27/5/1825. Died 1832.

The Master, who did not appear clever at his profession, left me, and shortly afterwards the Senior Lieutenant, Mr. Marshall,[1] committed such a serious breach of duty that I could not allow it to pass unnoticed. I therefore gave him the option of standing a Court Martial or of leaving the ship, and he preferred the latter. It was he who had caused so much discontent among the seamen. Consequently, I expected some improvement by his retiring. An old Verdun acquaintance, Lieut. Mackenzie,[2] replaced him.

(4) H.M.S. *HORATIO* (Spithead and the Channel)

MARCH 1815–JULY 1815

It was now understood that negotiations for a peace with America were on foot at Ghent in the Low Countries. By the 8th of March I was ready for sea. However, boisterous weather caused some delays. I was therefore very much annoyed one morning, when I called on the Admiral[3] at the usual hour, to be abruptly received. In a blustering voice he declared, 'Your ship shall be at sea by four o'clock this afternoon.' 'As far as I am concerned,' I replied, 'I would go to sea immediately if the ship were ready.' 'Your sea stores are on, board,' observed the Admiral, 'and to sea you shall go.' All this passed in his office before the clerks. 'There must be some mistake, Sir Richard,' I said. 'They were not on board last night.' However, he kept firm. In withdrawing, I told him that he would hear further particulars in the course of a couple of hours. I then hastened to the Dock Yard, but my wounded legs would not allow me to walk fast. There I met one of my Lieutenants with a party of 40 men who had come to draw the sea stores. The Admiral's Flag Lieutenant[4] was in attendance, to whom I thus addressed myself:—'Have you reported the *Horatio's* sea stores on board?' He hesitated, but made no decided reply. 'I see how it is,' I remarked. Then, taking out my watch, I said, 'It is now 11 o'clock. I shall return to the Admiral and relate to him what is going on. If anything unpleasant occurs,

---

[1] George Edward Marshall, Lt. 22/9/1807: not employed again till 1821; Cdr. 27/5/25.
[2] John Mackenzie, Lt. 8/10/1809.
[3] His old enemy, Bickerton.
[4] Henry Boyes, Lt. 14/1/1803; Cdr. 11/5/15; Capt. 23/12/42. It is interesting to observe that this officer, who 'specialised' as a Flag Lieutenant—often, but not always, with Bickerton—did not seem to benefit much from the patronage of the important officers whom he served. His last appointment (still as a Commander) was to a 6-gun steam-vessel, the *Viper* (1841).

I shall make you answerable for the same before a Court Martial.' The Lieutenant, I noticed, was completely taken aback. I then made my way back to the Admiral, and, when admitted to his presence, acquainted him that the sea stores were not aboard, that they were only being taken out of the Store House at 11 o'clock, and, taking into consideration the state of the weather, it was not likely they would reach the ship for some time. 'However, Sir Richard,' said I, 'not one second shall be lost as far as it depends upon me. But I feel that I am warranted in stating that I fear the ship will not be at sea so soon as you expect.' The Admiral made a quiet bow, but not a word escaped his lips. I then retired and went to Spithead.

I now inquired of the Master[1] when he could get the ship under way. 'The shipwrights are still at work,' he said, 'and the mainmast is not secure.' When I mentioned to him and the other officers present what the Admiral expected, they jocosely observed, 'He would not have acted in that way to Lord George Stuart.' The Dockyard officer superintending his men assured me that the mainmast would not be finished till the evening. Consequently, at 2 o'clock, I sent one of my Lieutenants to the Admiral to acquaint him that the shipwrights could not quit the *Horatio* till past 6 o'clock, and to request his further orders. It was 4 o'clock when my officer was admitted to that Chief's presence—the hour at which I was to be at sea. The Admiral, having satisfied himself of the real state of the case, merely sent word by him that I was to proceed according to circumstances. As Sir Richard had not dropped a word of anxiety about the *Horatio*'s being wanted, this sudden outbreak was, I suppose, another of his bilious fits which he vented upon me.

[He sailed next day, made a short and quite uneventful trip to the Nore, and was moored at Spithead ten days later.]

News of Bonaparte's having left Elba and landed on the coast of France was received not long after my arrival. That unlooked for event set all Europe in motion. Previous to this, I had discharged most of my Midshipmen, three of whom, having served more than nine years, were promoted by the Admiralty in consequence of the representations I made of their good conduct. One of those heroes passed me in the street of Portsmouth a day or two afterwards without acknowledging me. That was a grateful act.

When our Government reckoned upon terminating hostilities with America, circulars were addressed to several of the Naval

[1] The new Master was Charles W. Taylor, 1st Warrant, 9/6/1810.

Captains in the command of ships, desiring them to communicate their wishes respecting their being employed in the Peace. When this letter reached me, I acquainted the Private Secretary to the First Lord of the Admiralty[1] that if any ship should be wanted to serve in India I was ready to go there. I then wrote to my friend, General Abercromby,[2] begging him to forward my views. I received a friendly answer advising me to stay in England. However, I kept firm in that intention, and I have reason to believe that the General was useful to me.

The ratification of the peace with America was gazetted on the 15th March, and the proclamation declaring a cessation of arms soon made its appearance. The Treaty had been signed at Ghent on the 24th of the previous December, my friend Lord Gambier having a distinguished share in that negotiation. We had scarcely settled our affairs with America when, on the 25th, a treaty of alliance was concluded between Great Britain, Russia, Austria and Prussia, in consequence of the return to France of Bonaparte from Elba. Consequently, as fast as our troops arrived from America, they were sent over to Flanders to join the Army under the Duke of Wellington.

At that period the arrival of the American frigate, the *President*, Commodore Decatur, which had been captured by the *Endymion* in company with some other frigates,[3] caused a sensation among the naval officers. I went with many other captains to examine the Prize. She was of a much more superior scantling than ours: in fact, the Americans taught us a lesson for the improvement of our frigates.

But all attention was drawn towards Bonaparte's proceedings. I had to keep my ship manned. Several seamen were sent to me from the *Prince*, and my boats were sent away to press all the loose hands that could be got hold of. On the 30th I received my orders to proceed to the island of Guernsey, as Senior Officer of a squadron stationed there. That was a marked compliment, and so far satisfactory that it proved the confidence the Admiralty placed in me. I shipped a Pilot who was acquainted with the coast of France.

[1] Robert William Hay.
[2] Lt.-Gen. Sir John Abercromby, K.C.B., 2nd son of the famous Sir Ralph. For W.H.D.'s debt to him at Verdun, see above, p. 36. Caught travelling in France in 1803, he remained a captive till 1808. So highly thought of was he that he was promoted Major General while still a prisoner in 1805. In addition to being a most capable general, he seems to have been of a most amiable disposition, universally loved and respected by his men and his equals alike. The unobtrusive help he gave to W.H.D. both here and at Verdun seem typical of his character.
[3] Off to New York, 15/1/1815. The *Endymion*, Capt. Henry Hope, fought her to a standstill, and she surrendered to the *Pomone*, Capt. John R. Lumley, when the latter came up.

At 8 o'clock in the morning of the 31st I was under sail, with a 20-gun ship, the *Leven*, Capt. Bluett,[1] under my orders. We made sail through the Needles, the weather being fine, and anchored in Guernsey Roads on the forenoon of the 1st of April. My first duty was to wait on the Governor, Sir John Doyle.[2] A British squadron was a very agreeable sight to His Excellency just them. After settling with him in which way the ships could be employed to the best advantage, I withdrew; then sent the *Pickle*, Lieut. Figg,[3] brig of war, over to the coast of France to reconnoitre. In the afternoon the *Sapphire*, sloop of war, came in and was placed under my command. I obtained two of the most experienced Pilots that could be procured. On the 2nd, I put to sea, having detached the *Sapphire* to cruize. The next day I anchored in the bay of St. Hilliers, island of Jersey, and called upon the Governor[4] to establish a proper communication with His Excellency, to be prepared for coming events. He too was greatly pleased to have a squadron to watch over the safety of the island. In the afternoon I was again at sea standing towards Guernsey. On the 4th I was joined by the brig *Tyrian*, Capt. Baldwin,[5] making the fourth vessel of my squadron.

[Despite the threat of renewed hostilities, W.H.D., living ashore 'at the principal hotel' contrived to pass a very enjoyable month, and 'received in succession hospitable invitations to the houses of the principal inhabitants,' attended 'balls in the evenings,' and generally promoted 'most friendly intercourse between the select Society of the town, the Military and the Navy.' . . . 'I believe I do not err when I state that there were in these Channel Islands not less than 60 circles of Society, not visiting each other.' . . . 'I must not pass unnoticed the marked attentions shown to me by Ad. Sir James de Saumarez,[6] a distinguished person here and a native of the island.]

My own squadron I kept employed on the coast of France. We had information daily from thence, and were led to believe that Bonaparte was only popular with the Army. The townspeople of

---

[1] Buckland Stirling Bluett, Lt. 24/11/1800; Cdr. 10/4/04; Capt. 12/8/12; d. Nov. 1845, still Capt.
[2] Lt.-Gen. Sir John Doyle, Bart., K.B.
[3] William Figg, Lt. 30/8/1806; Ret. Cdr. 21/4/1840.
[4] Lt.-Gen. (Sir) T. Hilgrove Turner, K.C., K.C.H.
[5] Augustus Baldwin, Lt. 28/6/1800; Cdr. 19/9/08; Capt. 1/1/17; Ret. Capt. 1/10/46.
[6] James (cr., Sept. 1831, Lord de Saumarez), Lt. 25/1/1778; Cdr. 23/8/81; Capt. 7/2/82; R-Ad. 1/1/1801; V-Ad. 13/12/06; Ad. 4/6/14; R-Ad of G.B., 1819; V-Ad. ditto, 1821; C. in C. Portsmouth, 1824–27; Gen. of Marines, 1832; d. 9/10/36.

Granville refused to hoist the tricoloured flag, and some disturbances ensued against Bonaparte until put down by the military forces. At Honfleur they would not display it. The mob in Paris was bribed to obtain acclamations in his favour. (For instance, ' J'ai encore vingt sous pour boire a l'Empéreur.') The South of France remained favourable to the Bourbons. Bonaparte was in Paris on the 2nd of this month, and issued a decree for raising 300,000 men.

[Towards the end of April W.H.D. visited Alderney, the Caskets and, again, Jersey. A storm did minor damage, but the *Horatio* was back at Guernsey, repaired, by 3rd May.]

The 7th, being Sunday, I was engaged according to custom to dine with my officers in the Gunroom. After divine service I went ashore. I had scarcely mounted the steps of the Mole when I was accosted by the General's Secretary and aid-de-camp, Kennedy. They acquainted me that Sir John had received some important intelligence from Cherbourg. I instantly accompanied them to his house, where he informed me that a confidential spy had just arrived, announcing that Bonaparte intended to send out some ships of war from that harbour: and an impression existed that he might be embarked in one of them himself. He assured me that he placed confidence in the person who had brought this intelligence, and I made up my mind to take station off the port of Cherbourg. Three of my squadron were away. One, the *Leven*, I had sent to receive the Duke de Bouillon, an Admiral in our service, who was residing at Jersey and had applied for one of my squadron to give him a passage to England. Only the *Sapphire* remained with me. Having made known my plans to His Excellency, I withdrew.

When we reached the Mole, to my astonishment I met several ladies and gentlemen, engaged, as I understood, to the *Horatio* to dinner. All my ship's boats were in waiting to receive them. This was a most unpleasant affair, as I was obliged to order them back to the ship instantly. I acquainted one or two of the gentlemen whom I knew that the *Horatio* would soon be under sail, but the party was extremely annoyed at this information. The ladies being wrapped up in shawls, the veils covering their faces, I passed them without speaking, not being aware that I knew them. That act, not intended, gave great offence to the fair ones: and, I was informed by one of the officers when on board that a lady whom I passed without acknowledging her exclaimed in ill temper that she hoped the ship would strike on the rocks that evening. However, I reached the *Horatio* about 2 o'clock, and immediately made the *Sapphire's* (Capt. Brown)[1] signal to quit the roads and take certain station. She left in half an hour, but I kept my own ship quiet till the evening, being fully aware that all our motions were watched from the coast of France. I could not resist calling the officers to an account for having invited such a party without giving me any notice of it, as the incident had no doubt caused a very unpleasant sensation to my prejudice. However, the urgency of the case, when known, must have convinced all those who were disappointed of their entertainment that unexpected circumstances had occasioned the whole proceeding.

The Pilots, being consulted as to the best channel for my ship to pass out, recommended the Little Russel Passage, by which means the *Horatio* would be clear of the island by dark, without being seen from the French shore. But the wind was lulling, which completely altered the plans of our Pilots. They requested me to get under way without loss of time, fearing, if it fell calm, the ship could not be moved that night. Upon that information, the hands were turned up to weigh the anchor, and in 17 minutes we had all sail set, steering the course agreed upon. This was an act performed with so much order, regularity and quickness, which the Ship's Company had not hitherto accomplished, that I publicly thanked them for their exertions, anticipating therefrom the most favourable results for the future.

Whilst some of the officers were complimenting me upon the improved discipline of the crew, our attentions were suddenly intruded upon by a violent shock, which threw all the sails aback, and, before I had time to look about, another one shook the ship in a most alarming manner. In fact, she had struck upon a needle rock. A part of the false keel was seen floating alongside, and the sea was entering below at a fearful rate. The Pilots were sadly dismayed, stating that the current, being stronger than the wind, had carried the ship on to the rock. I believed this assertion, as the wind was light at that moment.

All hands were now turned to the pumps, the Carpenter reporting that the water was coming in at the rate of 8 inches in a minute. Here was an unlooked for calamity! There was no anchoring, but it required the utmost exertion to prevent the ship's sinking. Many signal guns were fired to recall the *Sapphire*, which she at last noticed, and closed upon us. Her Captain coming on board, I desired him to keep near to us during the night, and to send me 24 men to

[1] Adam Brown, Lt. 6/4/1811; Cdr. 28/4/14; not promoted.

assist in working the pumps. After the first quarter of an hours' hard work at them, there was every prospect of being able to keep the ship afloat. The next thing to be done was to thrum a sail with oakum, to place over the leak, which, it was ascertain, existed near the step of the mizen mast in the bread room. When I had given all directions that this critical event required, I made my appearance at the pumps, encouraging the men to exert themselves to the utmost. They cheered me. Then, taking off my coat, I wished to lend a hand at the winches. But the tars vociferously called out, 'That can't be, Capt. D. You must not exhaust yourself by bodily labour. You are here to command us. We will obey you to the last moment of our lives.' Several of them closed near, and entreated me to put my coat on. When I witnessed this determined conduct of these fine fellows, I left them at their work, giving orders that they were to be fed every two hours with beef and grog. Fortunately we had received several bullocks the day before, so that I was able to grant the nourishment mentioned, and to that lucky circumstance I attribute the ship's being saved. The tars frequently told me afterwards that they could not have stood the work, had it not been for the food which strengthened them when fatigued.

A course was shaped for the coast of England, I intending if possible to reach Spithead. The weather was favourable, and as the exertions of the crew continued with the utmost determination, I had every reason to expect reaching that anchorage. Every soul on board, down to the smallest boy, had to take his share in the arduous labour of the pumps. It required 24 men to work them to the full extent. They were divided into 12 reliefs, every hundred making four, that number being changed every two hours. They performed wonders. They kept going the rounds with the winches in a most extraordinary manner till some of them literally dropped, and were covered with the water coming out of the spouts, their companions lifting them up and placing them upon a dry spot, where refreshment was administered. There were several women on board[1] who rendered essential service in thrumming the sail. About 11 o'clock it was finished, and by degrees secured under the bottom. When it was properly placed, a change was felt at the pumps. The sea did not enter so rapidly, which caused a sensible relief to the working party's labours. But unfortunately, in getting that sail over, one of the best seamen of the ship, a Boatswain's Mate, Jackson, fell overboard. A boat was instantly lowered to pick him up, and I

---

[1] Quite contrary to regulations, in an 'operational' frigate.

shortened sail. The seamen, noticing this, addressed me with anxiety. 'Only one man, Sir. We are upwards of 300. Pray save us. We have no time to lose.' 'Surely,' said I, 'you can afford a quarter of an hour to save the life of a good seaman?' But it was evident that the majority were against the delay. After several minutes' search in the boat, he could not be found: sail was again made and we resumed our course. His wife was on board, and in sad distress at her loss.

We saw the Caskets Lights as we passed, and on Monday afternoon were closing with the Isle of Wight. When near Dunnose, I sent the *Sapphire's* men back to that ship, directing her Captain to return to Guernsey, and ordering Capt. Bluett of the *Leven* to take command in my absence. I also wrote to Sir John Doyle, regretting that I had not had it in my power to make some return for the many kind and hospitable attentions received from him and the principal inhabitants. I wonder what the lady mentioned felt when informed that her wishes had been fulfilled!

Our anxious moments were now drawing to a close, as we were nearing a port where we could receive assistance. Luckily the pumps did their work to perfection. Had any one of them failed, it is impossible to say what might have been the consequence. In nearing St. Helens', with every stitch of sail set, I fired guns and made signals for assistance. As I approached Spithead, the various ships of war sent boats full of men who, as they came on board, were placed at the pumps to relieve mine. The *Prince*, Flag Ship, sent 150. By ½ past 8 o'clock the ship was at anchor in the harbour, and shortly afterwards lashed alongside of the *Perseverance*, hulk. What a relief to an anxious mind! Although eased from care and responsibility, I could not sleep, as the noise of the pumps prevented it. The next morning, the 9th, a fresh supply of 150 men was sent to relieve those who had worked all night, and I began to prepare the ship for going into dock. One lighter took away the powder, another received some of the guns. Most of the Ship's Company moved their effects, chests and bedding, into the hulk. At ½ past 10 the Dock Yard officers made their appearance, the lashings were slipped from the *Perseverance*, and by 12 o'clock the *Horatio* was safe inside one of the Docks of the Arsenal. When we got under way from Guernsey Roads on the Sunday evening, it never was contemplated that we should be in the Dock at Portsmouth on the Tuesday morning.

I now hastened to pay my respects to the Admiral, Sir Richard Bickerton. After a long conversation with him, he, to my astonishment, expressed himself perfectly satisfied with all my proceedings during the short command I had held in the Channel Islands. All the information I had transmitted had been duly appreciated, and the whole of my conduct approved. I confess, when I heard those words from the lips of Sir Richard, I was rather in doubt whether I could place any reliance in them. But as they were repeated in a deliberate tone, I could not help feeling some degree of satisfaction at receiving those encomiums from a Flag Officer who had, for a long period, shown a disposition to annoy me in every professional transaction that had occurred between us.

When the water had been let out of the dock, the damage sustained was easily seen. There was 25 feet of the main keel knocked off, and as many of the garboard streaks, that is, the plank above the keel. The Dock Yard officers were all astonishment when they examined this injury, declaring that they had never witnessed so large a fracture in a ship's bottom, and expressed the highest praises of the crew who had kept the *Horatio* afloat under such circumstances. It appeared miraculous that the rudder had not been carried away. This accident, having taken place under the Bread Room, was rather a lucky affair, as the biscuit swelled by the admission of the water, and in some shape contributed to fill up the vacuum. For several days crowds of officers of all ranks came to take a look at the broken keel, everyone passing eulogiums upon the extraordinary exertions of the crew in saving so fine a frigate from sinking.

I wrote to Sir Geo. Hope at the Admiralty, entreating him not to take away any of my seamen. He did not reply to that letter. Consequently I continued in a state of uneasiness, as it was generally the custom, when a ship went into Dock, to take away a certain portion of her men to supply other vessels of war. But he did not touch one of mine. A Court of Inquiry now assembled on board the hulk, to examine the Pilots and ascertain the cause of the *Horatio's* having struck upon the rock in the Little Russel Passage. It was allowed that the accident occurred owing to the wind failing, by which the ship, not being under the influence of the rudder, was drifted on the rock by the strength of the current: and no blame was attributed to the Captain or the Pilots. So all anxiety on that head terminated. While the ship was in the Dock, I unstowed the hold, swept it clean, and restowed it upon a plan of my own, as I thought, by her propensity to roll, the ballast had been too much winged up, instead of being more confined in a centrical position. It turned out to great advantage. On the 26th the Dock Yard officers terminated their labours, the ship was floated out into the harbour, then secured alongside of the hulk, and every exertion made to get her ready for sea.

It was about this time that Sir Richard Bickerton was relieved in his Command by Sir Edward Thornborough.[1] This was an agreeable change for me, as in him I had a friend. He had had his Flag flying for a short time in the *Africaine*, and afterwards, when in command of a squadron off the coast of Holland, he had availed himself of an opportunity to represent to the Dutch Authorities the unjustifiable act of detaining me with a Flag of Truce. But they threw the blame upon the French. On the 30th the Pilot came aboard, and we sailed for Spithead, receiving many compliments from the Admiral for the expeditious manner in which the docking, refitting and undocking had been managed. When I inquired if I should be sent back to Jersey, he acquainted me that Rear-Ad. Sir Thomas Freemantle[2] had been appointed to succeed me in that command. That officer soon afterwards made his appearance at Portsmouth, and I had some long conversations with him relating to the Channel Islands.

['In some shape a perfect idler', he awaited orders for several weeks, and he gives a long account of how, at a friend's house, he was criticised to his face by some fellow-guests who did not know who he was, for alleged tyranny in not granting leave to a young Midshipman acquaintance of theirs. On the same occasion he was also, much to his amusement, mistaken for a clergyman—*by* a clergyman—and offered 'in a jocular mood' to change places with him: the more especially as the cleric in question, the son of the Bishop of Dublin, was of the wealthy, sporting type, and possessed of a fine stud of horses. He also reports a remarkable natural phenomenon, observed off Boston, U.S.A., by Capt. Hayes[3] of the *Majestic* on August 27, 1814, who saw 'at the sun's rising the complete figure of a man in the centre of that luminary, with a flag in his hands divided by three lines. As the sun advanced from the horizon towards the Pole, the body, which lay flat, gradually assumed an erect posture, and at midday stood upright. Towards the evening he as regularly declined, descending with his flag head foremost. On the

---

[1] See Vol. I, p. 343, note.
[2] Thomas Francis Freemantle, Lt. 13/3/1782; Cdr. 3/11/90; Capt. 16/5/93; R-Ad. 31/7/1810; V-Ad. 12/8/19. Died, C. in C., Mediterranean, 19/12/1819.
[3] John Hayes, Lt. 7/10/1793; Cdr. 1/3/99; Capt. 29/4/1802; R-Ad. 10/1/37; died 7/4/38. Member of a well-known family of shipwrights, and himself a naval constructor of note.

28th the same outline was apparent, but had become a skeleton. On the 29th the figure was disjointed, and its appearance was that of six separate flags united in a circle resembling a cord. After this, nothing more was observed on the sun's disk but a few small spots. As all the officers and most of the Ship's Company saw this extraordinary phenomenon, they could be appealed to for its veracity. . . . Whether these figures had anything to do with the destiny of Bonaparte is a question I cannot attempt to solve. But 'coming events cast their shadows before' is an old saying, and many events occur in this sublunary Planet that lead the reflecting mind to place some sort of reliance on these extraordinary visions.']

The glorious news of the Battle of Waterloo put a termination to all our anxiety, and we heard that the Admiralty had issued orders not to detain any more of the French ships at sea. Who can describe the state of excitement throughout the land? But our expenses had been immense, as all Europe had been subsidized by us. What a happy termination to the Duke of Wellington's exertions! And the extraordinary gallantry displayed by our brave soldiers will emblazon the Page of History to the honour of Old England to the latest generation.

It was just then that I was accosted one morning in the street of Portsmouth by the principal East India Agent residing there, Lindegreen. He stated that he had some important communications to make to me. Consequently we entered what was considered a public library, Motley's shop. He selected a retired corner, and addressed me nearly as follows:—'I am directed by the Secretary of the East India Company to propose to you to receive two thousand pounds for any quantity of money that may be sent on board of your ship, on freight to India.' When I heard this, I was, I confess, completely taken by surprise, and the idea instantly presented itself to me that my friend General Abercromby had been to Lord Melville in my behalf. Before I replied, I pondered, and at last said: 'The *Horatio* is a very large frigate, and capable of receiving a very considerable sum of money. The proposal you are making has all the appearance of a hard bargain. I do not approve of it. This is all made in secrecy. It does not appear to me to be fair to try and take advantage of an officer in my position.' He replied that the East India Company was desirous, on an occasion like this, to contribute its mite to the benefit of the Navy: that they might put the money on board their own ships, but, in the present instance, an unexpected demand had come home for cash, and that time would be saved by transmitting it in a fast-sailing man of war. 'Very well,' I observed, 'if that is the case, a due allowance ought to be made for the safety and the speed with which the money would be conveyed.' The Agent frequently repeated that his employers had no wish to take an unfair advantage, that I should find in the end that they would be just in their proceedings. On that point I differed from him, remarking that the offer of 1 per cent., which he had mentioned, was not the usual freight in wartime on board of a King's Ship: that $2\frac{1}{2}$ per cent. at least was what I understood to be the general rule going to India. He replied that it could be sent on board their own ships free of all expense. 'I shall give you,' he added, 'a couple of hours to think of my proposal, but I must know your decision before the post starts this evening. Recollect that there are, at this moment, 19 fine frigates lying at Spithead, and any one of their Captains would be too happy to have such an offer made to him.' I replied, in conclusion, that I had never received a freight,[1] and that I would not yield to what appeared to me to be unfair. 'Besides,' I observed, 'how do I know but, if I accept your offer, that an advantage may be made of it on other occasions, and I shall be blamed by my brother officers for having acted contrary to the regulations of the Navy in such cases; and all for some trifling benefit to myself?' Upon that we parted. Left to myself, I could not apply to any friend for advice, as all this transaction was upon honour and in the strictest secrecy.

The two hours having elapsed, the Agent came again: but very little change could I discern in his proposal. 'I can understand your feelings,' he observed, 'but rest assured that the Directors of the E.I. Company will not submit to be dictated to in these money affairs by the officers of the Navy. You had better accept the freight, and I will write to them, to explain your hesitation in agreeing to their terms. I make no doubt that, when you deliver your dollars at their destination, you will be satisfied.' 'Oh, very well,' said I. 'That makes an improvement in the proposal, and if you will fulfil your promise, to explain fully to the Directors in writing all that has passed between us relating to this freight, I shall yield to your offers.' Thus we parted, the Agent repeating in decided terms that he would represent most energetically what he thought was injustice to me. Two or three days now passed without my hearing anything further on this subject, nor did I receive any letters from my friend General

---

[1] Not strictly true (see *e.g.*, p. 229). But he probably meant a 'private' freight (see p. 271), in which case, so far as he has informed us, it was true.

Abercromby. I began to have my doubts upon the realization of this trip to India.[1]

My expectation relative to my taking the freight was now interfered with in a most unlooked for manner. On the 29th of June, Sir Edward Thornborough's Captain called on board to see me, and insisted upon my accompanying him to the Flagship to lunch with him. I very quietly yielded to his request, and when that ceremony terminated he kindly took me on shore. We landed on Common Hard. I had left the *Horatio* at midday, and on reaching my lodgings, about ½ past one o'clock, I found a letter inviting me to dinner with friends at Havant. I ordered my servant to lose no time in procuring a single-horse gig, intending to start immediately. I had changed my uniform coat for a plain one, and was in the act of stepping into the gig, when I was leisurely accosted by the usual messenger—it was then two o'clock—announcing that the Admiral wanted to see me. 'Why did you come so soon?' I demanded. 'Had you been five minutes later I should have been out of Town, beyond your reach. Had you any particular message to deliver?' 'No, Sir,' he replied. 'I was ordered to find you and let you know that Sir Edward wished to see you.' I dropped the reins, soon resumed my uniforms, and made the best of my way to the Admiral's.

When I was admitted to his presence, he said, 'Dillon, your ship is unmoored, and you must go to sea without loss of time.' I was never so completely astounded. I replied that most of my officers were on shore on leave. 'They are all on board,' said he. 'Your launch is in, your orders will soon be ready, and I expect you will be under way in less than a couple of hours.' This information floored me. The Admiral, who was watching the effect his statement produced, very goodnaturedly remarked, 'When you know where you are going you will be overjoyed with delight.' 'Pray, Sir,' said I, 'have the goodness to explain yourself.' 'I cannot,' he replied. 'You are proceeding under secret orders. You will only know where you are going when you are at sea. There is a sloop of war under your orders. She, as well as the *Horatio*, has her topsails sheeted home. I have settled all these affairs for you, so sit down and wait till my Secretary has finished writing your instructions.' Worse and worse,

---

[1] In a long note he records a private visit paid to the *Horatio* by Earl Spencer, 'so long First Lord of the Admiralty' (1794–1801). His Lordship was, of course, 'delighted with all he saw, especially my portable library, where he noticed French and Spanish books, saying, "we don't see these books in many naval officers' cabins."' He then dined with Lord and Lady Spencer 'at his country villa at Ryde', where he met, among others, 'my old friend Mr. Marsden of the Admiralty.'

I thought. 'But I have no stores on board, Sir Edward,' I said. 'I have nothing to eat but the ship's provisions.' 'I am sorry to hear that,' he replied. 'There is my boat's crew at the door. You may dispose of them as you please, but you must not quit my house until you receive your instructions.' Fortunately I had ten guineas in my purse: then, sending for the Admiral's Coxswain, I desired him to procure for me two or three joints of mutton, a bag of potatoes, some vegetables, half a dozen head of poultry and two or three loaves of bread. As I had no boat of my own on shore, the Admiral placed his barge at my disposal, and those articles were to be deposited in her as soon as purchased. Being again alone with Sir Edward, I requested permission to communicate to him, in the strictest confidence, the proposal that had been made to me by the East India Company's Agent; and that, if the *Horatio* was sent away, I might lose a handsome freight. He listened very patiently, then in reply observed, 'I cannot interfere in that matter. All I can tell you is that, when you know what you will have to perform, you will be overjoyed at having been selected. I see,' he added, 'you are annoyed. But cheer up. Depend upon it, you will be satisfied.'

In the course of a few minutes the Secretary made his appearance. The Admiral signed the document and, having sealed it, handed it to me. But 'Most Secret' was written on the cover. I now hastened down to the Sally Port. The first person I met—a wine merchant, whose house adjoined the Admiral's—said, 'I wish you joy, Capt. D. You are going after Bonaparte.' 'That's very strange,' I replied, 'that you should know of my orders before I do.' 'It is true. You may rely on it,' he added. Having been so taken up with the East India Agent I had not troubled myself much with Bonaparte. He was a fallen Hero, and was sinking in my opinion daily. However, this brought all the acts of that extraordinary man fresh into my memory. The Admiral's barge took me off to Spithead, where of course the first object that I noticed was my ship, her topsails sheeted home, as well those of a brig of war, the *Griffon*, lying close to her.

When I reached my Quarter Deck, all the officers were in a state of excitement. 'We are going after Bonaparte,' they said: 'we wish you joy, Sir: we hope you will catch him.' I was all amazement, and of course in some sense annoyed, to find, as Captain of the ship, that everybody seemed to know better than I where my ship was going. They told me that I had not left the ship half an hour before the Admiral had made the signal to unmoor, to collect all officers aboard, hoist the boats in and prepare for sea. All this, they said, had been accomplished in a very satisfactory manner, and they only waited for my orders to make sail. 'Then,' said I, 'you shall not wait long. Turn the hands up, and let us see how quick you will be in weighing the anchor.' By ½ past 5 the *Horatio* was loosened from her holding ground, standing towards the Needles passage. But, the wind failing, she was obliged to anchor in Yarmouth Roads shortly after 10 o'clock at night. By daylight of the 30th we got under way with the *Griffon* in company, and went to sea through the Needles. When clear of the land, I opened my orders, which directed me to proceed off the harbour of Cherbourg, and watch the motions of the men of war brigs lying there. It was supposed, from information our Government had received, that Bonaparte intended making his escape from this port. In fact, my instructions appeared to be a counterpart of the secret intelligence communicated to me by Sir John Doyle on the day that I left Guernsey Roads. I was directed to secure the person of the Corsican if I fell in with him, and bring him to England. I stood close in to Cherbourg, and made a strict examination of the vessels mentioned. All my thoughts were occupied with the chances of my nabbing the fallen Emperor. It would have been a most gratifying circumstance to me after all the annoyances I had undergone by his unjustifiable detention. While here the brig of war *Harrier* joined us.

All the officers and Ship's Company now came forward as volunteers, and begged me to run into the harbour that night, and cut out the French brigs. I at last assented to their entreaties. When all my preparations were made, I stood in towards the port: but, at 2 o'clock in the Middle Watch, a violent squall came on which split the fore topsail into shreds and deranged all my plans for that night. The next morning we observed a vessel coming out from Cherbourg. We instantly made after her, but a fog came on so thick that I lost sight of her. This was a most anxious moment, as I had no means of knowing who might be on board. In the afternoon I stood close in with the land, and took a good look at Fort Pelée. It was crowded with soldiers. I backed the main topsail, to let them see we were not afraid of their guns. I thought they meant to salute me with a few shot, but nothing of the kind happened. Whilst going to an fro along the shore, we were all highly delighted at the improvement in the ship's sailing. My plan of stowage had succeeded beyond all expectation. Her motions were buoyant, the rolling more easy: she did not pitch so heavily. Altogether, we thought ourselves on board of another vessel. 'What a pity,' was the daily remark, 'that the war is over, and we can't have a chance of chacing an enemy's frigate.'

The Captain of the *Harrier* came on board, but no information could be obtained from him. Soon after he left me, a strange sail was observed standing towards us, and at noon of that day, the 2nd of July, I exchanged numbers with the *Hyacinth.* Her Captain, Sharpe,[1] came on board. He had orders to relieve the *Horatio,* and delivered to me instructions to return to Spithead. Thus terminated all my anxiety at catching Bonaparte. I suspected that he might have been on board of the vessel which evaded us in the fog. However, when back in port. I ascertained that she had been examined by one of our cruisers. She was bound for America, with a cargo of the Paris plaster.[2]

As I made sail for Spithead, there being a commanding breeze, I was determined to try what the *Horatio* could do. We were upon a wind, close hauled, and when the sails were trimmed the log was hove. To our astonishment, and delight, the ship was dashing through the waves at the rate of ten knots an hour.[3] The most agreeable part of this was that, with the exception of the leeward inclination, no motion was felt, and the sea foaming as white as snow gave the most ample proofs of the advantage gained by the alteration in the stowage. Our rapid progress soon took us across the Channel, and by 6 o'clock that evening we were not far from St. Catherine's Point. But as we neared the land the wind became variable. Consequently I kept out at sea during the night, and made sail for Spithead next morning, anchoring on the evening of the 3rd.

Sir Edward Thornborough received me with great kindness, regretting my not having caught Bonaparte. 'You have now,' he said, 'other affairs to occupy your attention. The dollars are arrived, and you have to prepare to receive them.' On the 5th I received orders to fit for foreign service. But I was not hurried.

As Sir Edward had lately married his former wife's sister, there was a great deal of chat in Society. However, as soon as I was prepared to receive the Commander in Chief, I proposed to him to take a déjeuner à la fourchette on board of my ship. He accordingly came with his family and staff. By one o'clock they were all at table, with a party suitable to the occasion. The repast being over, the company repaired to the Quarter Deck, which had been prepared as a Ball

---

[1] Alexander Renton Sharpe, Lt. 8/12/1806; Cdr. 25/3/09; Capt. 22/1/13; R-Ad. 1/6/48.
[2] Napoleon actually arrived at Rochefort—not Cherbourg—on the day after Sharpe took over from W.H.D.—3rd July—but he did not go on board the *Bellerophon,* Capt. Maitland, till the 15th.
[3] *Cf.* Vol. I, pp. 368, 381.

room. The Admiral was much pleased: so was the lady, as this might be considered her first appearance in public since her marriage. She did not dance, but there was no lack of spirit with the rest of the company, who figured away on the light fantastic toe till 6 o'clock in the evening. I was much gratified at this attention of Sir Edward's. It made an impression in the naval circles of the place, it being his first naval entertainment upon his assuming the Port Command, which was considered a marked compliment to me.

So soon as the Ship's Company knew that they were going to India, several of my men deserted. Precautions were immediately adopted which were of course very unpleasant to me, as well as to my crew. The next act that drew my attention was an Order relating to the Midshipmen and Mates. The youngsters could no longer be received into the Navy and entered on the Ship's Books without the sanction of the Admiralty. I was glad to find that some kind of regulation was to be enforced in that direction, as it was well known that many Captains had placed improper youths on the Quarter Decks of the King's Ships. The Navy has much improved in consequence of that arrangement, and now you are nearly certain of having young gentlemen in the profession, whereas formerly there were many of very doubtful character in it.[1]

Being aware that we should be exposed to stormy weather when rounding the Cape of Good Hope, I resolved to have some eyebolts fitted in the ship's side, by which I could howse the Main Deck guns. I consulted the Master Shipwright of the Dockyard, who showed no inclination to supply the iron required, saying that he had never heard of the guns in a frigate being so secured. However, as I had received a friend of his as carpenter of the *Horatio*, who at times was fond of his glass, I gave the Dock Yard officer a few hints on that propensity of his friend's, and made him understand that there was a chance of his being tried by a Court Martial on the next trip he committed in that way. That threat had the desired effect, and I obtained the iron, which was soon turned into the bolts mentioned.

No satisfactory news had yet reached England of the proceedings of Bonaparte. He had left Paris on his way to the sea coast. Some supposed that he would embark at Rochefort, as there were two frigates ready for sea lying there. We had cruizers watching in every direction. Consequently his escape was a doubtful case. I now understood that I was to take the dollars to China, a part of the world I had long been most anxious to visit. The Admiralty sent me a couple of

[1] See above, p. 273.

Masters who had served on that coast, that I might take my choice. However, the Master of the *Horatio* stated that he had been in an Indiaman and felt himself capable. As he begged so hard, having a wife and family to maintain, I therefore kept him. I had to regret that measure afterwards. On the 13th, 211 cases of dollars were sent on board by the Agent, and the Secretary in London wrote to me authorizing me to draw for £1,000, being one half of what I was to receive for my freight, which would be two thousand on the sum embarked, two hundred thousand pounds sterling. He supposed that I might require some cash to fit out for so long a voyage. He was quite right in that instance. I made use of the £1,000. He also supplied me with a book of charts which I stood much in need of. The East India Directors also authorized the officers of my ship to draw for £300, to lay in some stock for their mess. That was a generous act, which was much appreciated by them. From a retired East India Captain who happened to be on a visit to his brother, Ad. Halkett, at Portsmouth, I obtained some very useful information, and followed his advice in procuring Horsburgh's book of instructions for the India and China Seas. As I could not trust my boats on shore, fearing the men might desert, the Admiral gave directions to the *Puissant*, Receiving Ship at Spithead, to supply me. On the 15th I shifted the *Horatio* further out from among the shipping. On the 16th I put to sea, but, when outside of St. Helens, the wind not being fair and my ship so deeply laden, I was obliged to put back and anchor there. I had made preparations for a three-year's station in India, and was in a great state of anxiety, as I had never rounded the Cape of Good Hope. On the 18th the weather moderated, which enabled me to get under way, but as the wind hung in the western quarter, I had to beat down Channel.

I must allude to the transactions passing on the coast of France at the period of my departing for China. When Bonaparte reached Rochefort, he found the two frigates at his disposal, but, having consulted their Captains, was informed that there were several English men of war outside: that the port was blockaded. He at last entered into a negotiation with Capt. Maitland[1] of the *Bellerophon*, which ship hoisted a Flag of Truce. Ad. Henry Hotham,[2] in the *Superb*, soon appeared there with some smaller vessels of war. When the Corsican Hero found that he was driven to the last extremity, he

[1] (Sir) Frederick Lewis Maitland, Lt. 3/4/1795; Cdr. 14/6/99; Capt. 21/3/1801; R-Ad. 22/7/30. Died 30/11/39.
[2] Hon. Sir Henry Hotham, Lt. 6/6/1794; straight to Capt. 13/1/95; R-Ad. 4/6/1814; V-Ad. 27/5/25.

surrendered himself to Capt. Maitland. His letter to the Prince
Regent may be worth your notice. I give it to you in English:—

                                          Rochefort, 13th July
Your Royal Highness,
    Exposed to the factions which divide my country, and to the
enmity of the great powers of Europe, I have terminated my political
career, and I come, like Themistocles, to throw myself upon the
hospitality (m'asseoir sur le foyer) of the British people. I claim from
your Royal Highness the protection of the laws, and throw myself
upon the most powerful, the most constant and the most generous
of my enemies. . . .
                                          Napoleon.

Bonaparte had with him a numerous suite, not less than 50
persons including servants. They were received on board of the
Bellerophon. During the time that he was there he expected all the
homage due to a Sovereign Prince, as he still considered himself the
ruler of Elba. He invited Capt. Maitland to dine with him. These
pretensions were winked at by our officers. He was perfectly free in
his conversation, and replied to all the questions put to him, having
always a reason for the whole of his conduct. To Ad. Hotham he said,
'I have given myself up to the English; I would not have done so to
any of the other Allied powers. Had I done so, I should have subjected myself to the caprice and will of an individual. In submitting
to your nation, I place myself at its mercy.' The *Bellerophon*, in the
first instance, went over to Torbay.
    When our Ministers were informed of this hero's surrender, a
Cabinet Council was held, and instructions were sent to prevent his
landing. On the 26th that ship proceeded to Plymouth Sound and
anchored inside the breakwater. Two frigates, the *Eurotas* and *Liffey*,
were stationed near her to keep off the numerous boats that had
anxiously hastened from the shore to obtain a glance at the Emperor.
Among the visitors were Admirals, Captains and the most distinguished gentry. But all were refused admittance, and obliged to be
content with a distant view of his person, as he occasionally gratified
the spectators by showing himself from the Poop and the Gangway.
Bonaparte, hearing that Sir Richard Strachan was alongside in his
barge, appeared and took off his hat to him. Ad. Lord Keith, at
Bony's request, had a short interview with him. It was then that
orders had been given to treat him as a prisoner and a foreign general.
The Plymouth breakwater was crowded beyond all expectation with

visitors watching to get a peep at the Imperial Magnet. Here, to their surprise, they found a supply of fruit, biscuit and porter.

On the 28th the fate of Bonaparte was finally decided at a Cabinet Council, and the following morning Sir H. Bunbury, the Under Secretary of State,[1] accompanied by the son of Earl Bathurst and Mr. Guy, the King's messenger, set out for Plymouth to communicate to Napoleon that he was doomed to captivity at St. Helena. They were to superintend all the arrangements necessary for his departure, and in all the orders issued relating to him he was designated as General Bonaparte. When Col. Bunbury read the Commission acquainting him with his destiny, and that he would be removed into another ship to be conveyed to his future residence, he exclaimed, 'You may take my body to St. Helena, but you shall never take my spirit.' Afterwards he frequently repeated to Capt. Maitland, 'You shall never take me over this ship's side alive.'

On the 4th of August the *Northumberland*, commanded by Sir George Cockburn,[2] was ordered to proceed to Plymouth Sound, with the *Ceylon*, and *Bucephalus*, troopships, to receive Bonaparte and his Staff for conveyance to the island mentioned. On that day some British Bonapartist obtained a writ of Habeas Corpus, addressed to Lord Keith, to deliver up the body of Napoleon whom he had in custody. His Lordship, having had timely notice of it, instantly embarked for Plymouth Sound. There, finding the *Prometheus* under sail, he went on board of her, hoisted his Flag and stood out beyond the breakwater, making signals to the *Bellerophon, Eurotas* and *Tonnant*, 80, to follow him to sea. When he was clear of the Sound, he removed his Flag to *Tonnant*,[3] and cruized between Eddystone and the Start until the *Northumberland* made her appearance.

On the 7th Bonaparte was taken from the *Bellerophon*, accompanied by Lord Keith, Sir George Cockburn, two French ladies and two French generals, then placed on board the *Northumberland*. On quitting the *Bellerophon*, he took a very respectable leave of Capt. Maitland and his officers. When the barge shoved off from that ship, he took off his hat to him. Lord Keith returning to his own ship to superintend the transhipment, a fast sailing schooner and cutter were kept on the watch, to prevent boats getting too near. Lord

[1] Of the Colony and War Department.
[2] Then R-Ad. of the Red (4/6/1814). See Vol. I, p. 33.
[3] Note the absence of the definite article, which makes W.H.D. appear to conform to a modern, and oft-criticised, practice. But as it is the sole example of an omitted article, and as it must be set against at least a thousand cases where it is included, it may certainly be taken as a mere slip of the pen.

Lowther and the Hon. Mr. Lyttleton went to the *Northumberland* and remained in conversation with Napoleon for two hours. Bertrand expressed himself in strong terms against the measure of sending the Emperor (as he always styled him) to St. Helena, as his wishes were to live quietly in England under the protection of the British laws. Lord Keith and Sir George Cockburn declined entering into any discussion upon the subject. Sir George went on board the *Bellerophon* to examine the luggage, etc. All Bonaparte's private arms, pistols, etc., were secured, to the great annoyance of his officers. Those of his Staff who were not to accompany him were sent to the *Eurotas*. The separation caused a very unpleasant sensation, as they had all reckoned on residing in England. They remarked with vehemence that faith had not been kept with their Emperor. Sir George sent to his ship two services of plate, several articles in gold, a superb toilet, books, beds, etc. The persons to accompany Napoleon were thus selected: Gen. Bertrand with his wife[1] and children, the Count and Countess Montholon and child, Count Las Casas, Gen. Gourgaud, nine men and three women servants. Bonaparte's Surgeon refused going to St. Helena, upon which the Surgeon of the *Bellerophon*[2] offered to supply his place, and his offer was not only accepted, but allowed.

Bonaparte appeared in a cocked hat, much worn, with the tri-coloured cockade. He wore a plain green coat, buttoned close up, with a red collar and several orders. He was excessively indignant at being addressed as a General. 'You have sent ambassadors to me,' he would repeat, 'as a Sovereign Potentate, and you have acknow-ledged me as First Consul.' With Mr. Lyttleton and Lord Lowther he entered most fully into conversation. When they asked him how he came to commit such an unpolitical act as attacking Spain, his motives for the Berlin and Milan Decrees, the war against Russia, his refusal to accept the terms of peace offered to him before the first capture of Paris, etc., to all these questions he gave full answers, not avoiding but rather encouraging discussion. Whilst he remained on the *Northumberland's* Quarter Deck, occasionally noticing some of the officers near him, one of them said, 'Had you remained another hour at Rochefort, you would have been taken, and sent off to Paris.' Bonaparte fixed his eye steadfastly on the speaker without uttering a word. He then, addressing Sir George, asked several questions relating to St. Helena—'Is there any hunting or shooting there? Where am I to reside?' Then abruptly changing the subject, he

---

[1] Née Dillon: see Vol. I, p. xix, and below, pp. 411 and 456.
[2] Barry E. O'Meara, 1st Warrant, 10/6/1812. See below, p. 411.

burst into invectives against our Government. But no notice was taken of it. He afterwards retired into the after cabin, where he took leave of those who were not accompanying him. That parting, I heard, was a very interesting scene. He embraced his first wife's nephew. Next came a Polish Colonel, Pistowski, who had received 17 wounds in his army. He would have followed Napoleon in any capacity, but he was obliged to quit the ship. The Hero took a great deal of snuff upon this trying occasion.

When all the arrangements were nearly completed, Sir George asked if he wanted anything more, previous to putting to sea. Bertrand replied that 50 packs of cards, a backgammon board and a domino table would be useful. Madame B. required some necessary articles of furniture. They were promised forthwith. On the 8th, the *Tonnant* returned into the Sound, the *Northumberland* lying to, waiting for a store ship, the *Weymouth*, which joined the next day. She then made sail with her consorts for St. Helena; and I now take my leave of Bonaparte till we meet at that island.

XIV
VOYAGE TO CHINA

July 20, 1815–January 10, 1817

(*aet.* 35–36½)

INTRODUCTION

PEACE has come, and the Narrative can no longer be a war-record. So, if the war itself had been its sole interest, it would have been logical to stop at this point, and print no more of it. But, throughout, the Navy of Dillon's day has held a place in his story which is of at least equal interest with the hostilities described, and that interest is by no means at an end. It is both interesting and important to see what happened to the Navy when peace came. It had been grossly overswollen by the influx of in- numerable officers whom, nowadays, we should class as 'Hostilities Only': and, having taken from the start the precaution of labelling them 'R.N.R.' or 'R.N.V.R.', we should have discharged them quietly back into their respective peacetime pursuits. But, since that had not been done, there they were—all full R.N. commissioned officers, unretired and, in a vast preponderance of cases, literally unretirable, there being practically no retirement machinery in existence. The pattern of all the rest of the Narrative is shot through with the threads of this problem, so all-important and personal to the individuals concerned: and we shall have to return to it again.

Meanwhile, W.H.D. was very fortunate in actually having a command when hostilities ended, and so not becoming a victim to the glutted market so soon as most. Indeed, he escaped from the dangerous area—home waters—only just in time, and, once away in the East, could hardly be brought back and 'put on the beach' immediately. Even so, he was recalled before his full time, and seems to have had no illusions as to what awaited him on his return. The strangest thing of all, as will later appear, is that in these gloomy forecasts he was wrong. He did receive another, and unexpected, appointment.

The plan, hitherto followed, of omitting non-naval matter has not been strictly adhered to in this Part. The exceptional passage is the long one describing his visit to Canton. It is felt that the China of 1816 was sufficiently unknown to Europeans to make any account of it by an Englishman of more than usual interest. The story is biographically important too, as revealing our officer's character and education—and its limitations. His attitude towards the Roman Catholics may be cited as one example: especially his reiterated, and blandly ill-informed, compari- sons between the rites of that Church and those practised in the temples of Fo: above all, perhaps, when he bluntly (though probably not de- liberately) accuses the Catholics of straight polytheism (p. 376).

To anyone familiar with the Far East of today, but not so well up in its history, it might come as a surprise to find W.H.D. going up to Canton, and passing quite close to the island of Hong Kong without so much as mentioning it. It lies only some 40 miles from Macao, on the eastern shore of the estuary. In 1816, however, it was nothing to us, or indeed to anybody, being all but deserted. We occupied it only in 1841, and then it developed rapidly. Its rise, naturally, meant the serious decline of Macao, which we only used, as it were, on sufferance—indeed on *double* sufferance. It was the original European foothold, first leased by the Portuguese in 1557; but the occupiers continued to pay an annual ground-rent for it right up till 1886, and the Chinese, as Dillon shows, still regarded themselves very much as its masters. None the less, the Macao he saw was still a prosperous commercial centre, with no 'European' rival. Indeed, its importance had been growing during the last few decades since the East India Company had been stretching out its hand towards China.

In 1816 it had a peculiar importance. It was only in 1813—three years before—that the 'John Company's' great citadel of Monopoly had been broken into: in fact, so far as the Indian trade was concerned, demolished. Now her only remaining monopoly was the China Trade. This serves to explain the correspondence between W.H.D. and the Company's Chairman, Sir George Staunton (p. 391). The English trader *Columbia* was, in Sir George's view, trespassing: and, if she tried to trade, she was breaking the law, for she was not a Company's ship. W.H.D. did not want to intervene because his arrangements would thereby be upset, but it is rather surprising that Sir George was not more insistent upon his doing so. The Company's China Monopoly was ultimately abolished too, but not until 1833.

On the other hand, W.H.D. mentions (p. 397) 'the Straits of Sincapore': but not the town of Singapore, in 1816 as unknown to fame as Hong Kong. But here he is only just too early, for it was founded by Sir Stamford Raffles within three years of his passing the site.

That W.H.D.'s interview with the exiled Napoleon did not come off must be a disappointment to us, as it certainly was to himself, in spite of his protestations to the contrary. Indeed, his off-hand yet persistent allusions to the whole affair provide as good an example as one could hope for of 'sour grapes'. Napoleon's refusal to see visitors, especially English ones, was in any case not unnatural, since the motive behind such visitations must have looked to him uncommonly like that which takes people to the lion-house at the Zoo. But it was also, without doubt, a part of his set 'martyr-policy'—that same which succeeded in bringing discredit upon his amiable and cultured gaoler, Sir Hudson Lowe.

There is one omission, at the very end of this Part, which has caused the Editor some misgiving, on the score that, possibly, justice was not being done to W.H.D. There is a long passage (p. 419) in which his officers, at their last dinner together, praise him and his captaincy. The fulsomeness of the language used and the smug meticulosity with which it is all recorded are not very seemly, and as such demand omission. Yet unquestionably the passage has an importance of its own as representing W.H.D.'s own idea of what the Perfect Captain (*e.g.* himself) should be. Therefore the three main headings of the praise are recorded here:—

1. He has saved their lives several times (all named) by his prudence, forethought and seamanship.

2. Whenever wanted he is always to be found—apparently a rare quality in a Captain.

3. He is always a 'perfect gentleman' and a most 'correct' officer— meaning, presumably, that all his actions are governed by the Regulations, so that all his subordinates, if they know those regulations, will know exactly what he will do under any given circumstance, and exactly where they are with him.

Now unkind doubts may flash through our minds as to whether the officers really said all these things in the hyper-enthusiastic terms alleged. They probably did not: or, alternatively, if they did, they were perhaps 'laying it on thick' from motives of flattery. Yet students of W.H.D. will surely not, at this late hour, leap to the other extreme, and accuse him of inventing the whole thing. That would be quite untrue to type. He had his faults, but sheer lying was never one of them. What is far the more likely hypothesis is that they *did* say these things in substance, and did, in substance anyway, believe them: but that W.H.D., with his essential vanity and passion to appear perfect, has exaggerated the reporting of them. And what impels the Editor to accept this particular interpretation is that he believes it to be, not only what the officers said, but also the actual truth. He believes that W.H.D. did possess these very qualities. He *was* a good and prudent seaman, with a real gift of looking ahead for trouble: he *was* invariably on the spot when wanted, because his heart was always, and obviously, in his professional work, which was his life: he *was* a tiger for 'correctness', and, though a martinet, a very just one according to his lights. In short, he *was* a good frigate captain.

But he was not a great one. He lacked two qualities which his officers did not mention—and, in fairness let us note, he does not say that they did. These qualities were Imagination in its wider sense, and Humour, in almost every sense. It may indeed be a paradox to affirm it, but the fact is that he was often *too* correct to be great. The ultimate object of his worship was, not Greatness, but Correctness—and, of course, Perfect Gentility.

XIV
VOYAGE TO CHINA

JULY 1815–JANUARY 1817

(*aet.* 35–36½)

(1) H.M.S. *HORATIO* (Outward Bound)

JULY 20, 1815–JANUARY 9, 1817

ON the afternoon of the 20th I had cleared the Channel, and was able to set studdingsails to shape a course for Madeira. This was to me the most interesting voyage of my life. I was under Admiralty Orders[1]: therefore on the seas I was at liberty to act as became most convenient to me. While crossing the Bay of Biscay I fell in with my old companion the *Tiber* who made many signals to me. But as I was under secret instructions, and not wishing to lose time, I telegraphed to her Captain explaining my anxiety to proceed. Consequently we soon parted company. On the morning of the 27th we made the island of Porto Santo, having on our way boarded several vessels of different nations. The next day we were close to the island of Madeira, and on the morning of the 29th anchored in Funchal Roads in 29 fathoms. Having paid my respects to the Portuguese authorities, and to our Consul, Mr. Veitch, I employed the boats in procuring fresh water, live stock, fruit and vegetables. The Consul invited me to his house, where I experienced the most kind hospitable entertainment. Here I met a Mrs. Douglas, the widow of my Verdun companion. He had lately died, a Captain in the Navy. I had many orders from my London friends to purchase Madeira wine for them, and from Mr. Veitch, who cultivated that vine, I made purchases to a good amount, not forgetting to lay in an ample stock for myself. Having settled these affairs very satisfactorily, not omitting to take a peep at some of the pretty nuns,[2] I left the island on the morning

---

[1] *I.e.*, not attached to any Admiral's Flag, but directly responsible to the Admiralty. For other advantages of being in this position, see Vol. I, p. 75, for its effects on 'Prize'. The same advantage applied in the case of 'Freight'.

[2] Perhaps from that one of the four convents where, he tells us in his description of the island, nuns 'may marry when they like and quit the monastery'.

of the 30th all hands being in good spirits as far as came under my observation.

[He gives a description of the island, omitted here.]

So soon as I had cleared the land, my first object was to attend to the health of my Ship's Company. The Surgeon,[1] though well provided with medicines, had none to spare. Consequently I suggested to him the propriety, as we were approaching the warm latitudes, of administering cooling draughts to the men. It was therefore decided that they should take every morning a tumbler of salt water under the direction of his assistant. This plan, having been recommended by me to the crew, they most willingly agreed to, and every morning they came in succession to the pump, helping themselves to a glass of the briny deep, which they called, jocosely, 'splicing the main brace' (that term alluding to a dram of spirits). These arrangements produced the most beneficial effects, as in our progress no sickness occurred by the change of climate. We passed close to the island of Palma, and as we decreased our northern latitude, we came into the region of the dolphin, the albacore, the flying fish, the bonetta; not forgetting the sharks.

Strange vessels were seen almost daily, but I did not take much notice of them. I had my ship disfigured in her painting to make her look like a foreign man of war, and occasionally boarded a craft under the expectation of obtaining some information, however small. It was something to talk about when alone in the midst of the ocean. Not far from the island of Brava I sent my boat to examine an American from the Isle of May bound to Philadelphia. On the 12th we were approaching the rainy regions. The weather became cloudy, and we were visited by drenching showers of rain. On Friday the 25th we crossed the Equator and performed the usual ceremonies. When Neptune came on board, he recognized me as an old acquaintance. I frequently sent my boat to try the current and ascertain its influence upon our reckoning.

I have now to relate an event which, if it had not been properly attended to, might have ended in the most fatal consequences. On Sunday the 27th we were still in the calm latitudes. It was my general practice to read the Divine Service on that day, and to refrain from all unnecessary work, that the Sabbath might be duly observed. As the weather was fine, the white hammock cloths were spread, out of respect for the church ceremony. I was sitting at my table with

[1] The new one was Simon Davidson, 1st Warrant, 9/3/1810.

the Common Prayer Book and Bible, selecting the lessons, etc. It only wanted a few minutes before the bell would be tolled for the seamen to assemble. My cabin door was open—always kept so during the day—there being a sentinel at it to prevent improper intruders. The most perfect silence reigned: there was not a breath of wind. But how shall I express my astonishment when I heard the Alarm Bell pealed with energy. I demanded of the sentry if the ship were on fire. 'Yes, Sir,' he replied. 'Where?' I inquired. 'In the Magazine, Sir,' was his answer. Such information was enough to cause the most serious apprehensions, because there was the probability of the ship being blown up, and the whole of us sent to our last account in quick time. However, not to show anything like fear, I put my hat on, and coolly walked forward. When I left my cabin, I beheld a column of smoke rising up the Fore Hatchway. Having reached that place I saw on the Lower Deck the Master,[1] who, the instant he noticed me, said, 'Don't be alarmed, Sir. The fire is out.' 'Well done,' I replied. In fact what he stated was true. Now must be explained the advantage derived on this occasion by my regulations.

In the early part of these adventures I have alluded to the horrid scene I had witnessed on board of a transport in Cowes Roads, which had caught fire[2]: and from that circumstance I had established in all the ships I commanded the plan acted upon in this emergency. It was a general order on board, if anyone saw the ship on fire, no matter where, he was instantly to repair to the Bell and ring it with all his strength. Then the crew were instantly to repair to their quarters at the guns, the carpenters to the pumps, and the Master, with a certain number of fire men attended by a party of Marines, was to set to work and extinguish it. The officers and men, having been frequently exercised at this work, knew what to do when the critical period arrived. There was no hurry, scurry or confusion. Every person repaired to his duty with the most perfect coolness and self-possession. On this occasion, from the first noise of the Bell to the termination of the danger, two minutes had not elapsed. So much for care and discipline: but this alarm stopped the Church ceremony as I determined, previously to releasing the Ship's Company from their quarters, to ascertain how the fire had originated. It turned out that the Sailmaker's Boy had, in quitting the Boatswain's storeroom, when taking away the hammock cloths, thrown down the lantern. Although he had blown the candle out, the wick, being thick, set

---

[1] Charles W. Taylor, 1st Warrant, 9/6/1810.
[2] Vol. I, p. 227.

fire to the horn surrounding, which, coming in contact with a tarry rope, instantly ignited it, and the ship was on fire in a most alarming position close to the Magazine. The Storeroom, being in a most confined position, was not of easy access, and had any delay occurred in going to it, no one could have got there, as the density and heat of the smoke would have rendered the place unapproachable. As it was, the Master assured me that he had the greatest difficulty in penetrating through without being smothered. The next day the youth in question was punished, to teach him to be more careful in future. All hands declared that my plan had saved the ship. 'We owe our lives to you,' they all said.

In due time we got into the trade winds, and shaped a course for Rio Janeiro. We had fine weather, and nothing to do but occasionally exercise the seamen at the guns and the Marines at small arms. On the 9th September we struck soundings, and the next day the coast of Brazil was in sight. We passed the islands of St. Anna: the following morning Cape Frio was seen, and on the morning of the 11th we received a Pilot and in the afternoon anchored in the harbour of Rio Janeiro, saluting the fort with 15 guns, which was returned. We found a Spanish frigate lying here the Captain of which called to pay his respects. The news of the Battle of Waterloo, which I communicated, made a favourable impression at the Court and among the inhabitants. Our Minister, Mr. Chamberlayne, received me with much kindness and hospitality at his country residence. An arrangement had been made for my being presented to the King of Portugal,[1] but by some mismanagement of the lord in waiting it failed. I had so many affairs to attend to that I was not particularly anxious to be devoting my precious time to the Palace.

The ship now underwent a hasty refit and received abundant supplies of water, horned cattle, vegetables and fruit. Several of my seamen deserted from the boats that communicated with the shore. I was not prepared for this contretemps, which obliged me to hasten my departure. There being several English ships here, I sent my boats to press a few hands to make up for those lost. I also recovered a couple of my deserters. Having therefore taken my leave of all who required that attention, we quitted this interesting port on the 16th.

---

[1] John VI. In 1815, however, he was not King, but still Regent for his deranged mother Maria. On Junot's invasion of Portugal in 1807, he had transferred himself and his government to Rio, where he remained during the whole of the Peninsular War. On Maria's death in 1816 he became king, but remained at Rio long after he might have returned; doing so, in fact, only in 1821, as a result of a revolution in the home country. He left behind his son Pedro as Regent, who, in 1822, proclaimed Brazil independent and himself Emperor. John VI died in 1826.

It is situated about four miles from the entrance of the harbour. Although generally called Rio, its proper name is St. Sebastian. It is built on a projecting tongue of flat land, with all behind it composed of high rising mountains, rocks, broken hillocks, woods, etc.

[A four-page description of Rio follows, of which one passage only is retained here. 'In another part of the harbour is a place called Val Longo, wherein are buildings for the reception of slaves, brought from Angola and Benguela on the African coast, the usual quantity being about 20,000 annually. There are about 600,000 negroes in the territory of Brazil, the white population being something more than 200,000. Many of the slaves belong to the Crown. The Benedictine monks have at least 1,000 upon their plantations, as the natives of Brazil can not be reduced to a state of slavery. They are a strange race, and will not be taught the domestic usages of civil society. In their persons they are generally under the middle size, muscular, stout and active, of a light brown complexion, black strong uncurling hair, very little beard, but long dark eyes indicating intellect. They never offer themselves for hire, giving the preference to their original habits of a savage life. However, they make good boatmen, and labour at the oar in a wonderful manner.']

Quitting the harbour was no easy matter. Although we began early, the land wind which generally takes a ship away from the roads failed us. Consequently I was obliged to employ the boats to tow us. The Spanish Captain kindly sent me his boats, and the officer in command of them, finding me conversant in his native tongue, remained with me to the last. After a very heavy tug, the narrow entrance was neared, and the strong castle of Santa Cruz drew all our attention. It is perpendicular, and has six fathoms water under its walls. A small fortified island called Lucia lies nearly abreast of it, and between these the ship passed, the strait being about a mile wide. There are about 50 heavy guns on the fort of Santa Cruz, and other batteries in the neighbourhood, so that no enemy could penetrate in that direction if the guns were well worked.

Once clear of the land, we had nothing to do but shape a course for the island of Tristan da Cunha. The weather was variable, but all sail that could be conveniently carried was constantly set. Our next landfall was a very distant one. I cannot pass by unnoticed a great feat of sailing by the *Horatio*. On the afternoon of the 27th, with a strong breeze from the northward on our larboard beam, the ship was dashing through the waves at an extraordinary rate. My cabin windows were open, and I lay reclined, deeply occupied in perusal of an interesting book, when, about 7 o'clock in the evening, the Officer of the Watch came in, announcing that she was going 14 knots. The ship lay over about 15 degrees, but had no pitching motion. I was quite astonished at this information. The sea foaming had all the appearance of snow. I went on deck, the sail set being the courses, double reefed topsails, topgallant sails, jib and driver. The log was hove and, sure enough, out went 14 knots of the line. I had never before seen anything of the kind. However, the wind was increasing and, not wishing to carry anything away, I took in a reef of the topsails and furled the topgallant sails. We had every reason to be satisfied with the ship's sailing qualities. By noon the next day, 282 miles had been realized by our reckoning, although the log only gave 261.

We were now approaching the latitude of the Cape of Good Hope, where we might expect some of Boreas's boisterous visitations, and our rate of going, I found, averaged 1,000 miles per week at the least, sometimes much more. On the 12th of October we were assailed by a regular storm, out in the midst of the Southern Ocean, with a tremendous swell, and the ship laboured woefully. It was now that I housed all the Main Deck guns, the doing of which eased her so much that all hands were astonished. The Carpenter in particular, who had had many years of experience, was loud in his praises. On that occasion I made him promise to report the advantage gained by such an arrangement, in a gale of wind, to the builder at the Dock Yard, Portsmouth, Mr. Didhams, who had made every possible objection to supply me with iron to make the bolts which, upon trial, were so useful. However, the swelling, rolling seas were so high that many broke upon the ship and did damage, but fortunately no serious injury. On the afternoon of the 21st we saw the island of St. Paul's, and at 10 o'clock that night passed within a few miles of it. Some adventurers occasionally visit this desolate place to catch seals, and take their skins for sale at the Canton markets, where they produce a good profit. St. Paul's cleared, a course was set for the N.W. Cape of New Holland, South Australia. We kept in the latitude of about 39 South, steering to the eastwards.

As I had never been this way before, my whole time was devoted to the charts and to Horsburgh's Directions. I had a long consultation with the Master, who did not appear overconfident. Some time elapsed before we could come to a settled plan for our course to China. There were two routes open to us, one by the Straits of Sunda, and the other the circular one round New Holland. After mature deliberation I determined to take the passage through one of the straits, in preference to the immense circle we should have to make in passing to the South of Australia. Having fixed upon the perpendicular course, I selected all the charts, and, with the assistance of my Clerk, Roe, who was a clever draftsman, I drew out a sketch of our passage, intending to pass through the Straits of Macassar, keeping the Borneo shore on our left. There appeared some dangers and obstacles in that direction, but one satisfaction remained—I might anchor if necessary. In course of time the Clerk completed his labours, and the chart by which we were to regulate our proceedings extended several feet in length. As we drew near to the coast of South Australia, we gradually kept more to the northwards. We had with few intervals very fine weather, our ship constantly attended by the birds of these regions. I tried my fowling piece at many of them without success.

On the forenoon of the 8th November we saw high land in the neighbourhood of Lombock. We closed upon it, entered the Straits of Alles, and by 7 o'clock in the evening anchored in Bali Roads[1] about two miles from the town of that name. Here was a change in our affairs. There was a small native vessel at anchor not far from us. I sent my boat to examine her, but nothing could be obtained from people whose language we did not understand. My officer reported that all her crew were armed. Probably it was a pirate, as they abound in those seas. Next morning a strong party, attended by some Marines, was sent on shore to collect good fresh water. We had crossed the ocean with scarcely a sick man on board. The scenery of this mountainous country was highly interesting. I landed, but could not speak to the natives, who were naked except for a wrapper round the loins. Their skins were yellow. The next forenoon I got under way. Whilst that operation was performing the Prince of the place came alongside, but I was in too great a hurry to receive him. However, I made him a present of the Union Jack, as he appeared anxious to express his admiration of Great Britain. He remained close to us till the ship made sail. The hoisting in of our boats seemed to make a great impression upon him. With extended arms he evidently wished to convey feelings of astonishment.

Between the high land the winds were light and variable, and we made slow progress. Through the straits the lead was constantly hove. On the 15th we were standing towards Pulo Laut. Next, we

---

[1] 'Bally' in MS.

saw the Alika Islands. The next day we were in sight of the high land of Borneo. The ripplings on the surface of the sea gave proofs of the setting of the current. The boats were lowered and sent to ascertain its direction—a southerly one. We were assailed by thunder and lightning, and passed through a great quantity of driftwood; also quantities of light lava, indicating an eruption from a volcano in the neighbourhood. The passage up the Straits of Macassar was a very anxious one. However, I succeeded in my progress beyond expectations, as I had performed in 7 or 8 days what I thought might have occupied as many weeks. By the 29th I cleared those straits and entered the Sulu Sea,[1] where the light winds and currents kept us constantly on the alert. On the night of the 20th the current was so strong against us that a commanding breeze had no effect. I remained on deck all night fearing our being cast on shore. The seas rose to the height of our Quarter Deck, frequently threatening to inundate us. But as the day dawned the swell diminished, and I shaped a course for the roads of Zamboanga,[2] Island of Mindanao, where I anchored in the forenoon of the 1st December.

The island belonged to the Spaniards. The fort was saluted with 13 guns, which was instantly returned. The Spanish Governor did his best to be useful, but he was in bad health. My Surgeon, Mr. Davidson, took care of him, and administered relief, for which he appeared most grateful. The boats were employed in procuring water, wood and vegetables. Some bullocks were obtained, but the town was a miserable place, and in constant dread of an attack from pirates. There were no temptations here: therefore, so soon as I had obtained supplies, we left the roads on Sunday afternoon of the 3rd.

The winds and currents were so uncertain that I was obliged to anchor at no great distance from where I had departed, but next morning the ship was again under way, standing towards Cape Balanganan. Up to this date I had considered myself extremely fortunate in having proceeded without any sickness. However, the case was now altered in a most serious degree. Whether the change was to be attributed to the water or the climate we could not decide, but in a few days I had 100 men laid up. We experienced some heavy gales, and another night was passed in extreme anxiety. We passed between the islands of Mindanao and Santa Cruz. Another

---

[1] 'Soolo' in MS. But—unless the names were different in his day—he was probably entering the Celebes Sea. The Sulu Sea lies well to the N. of it, and N. and N.W. of Zamboanga, his next port of call.

[2] 'Samboagan' in MS.

night, not being satisfied with the ship's position, I hove to till daylight. It was a lucky circumstance as, with the dawn, we saw an immense range of breakers directly in the course that would have been steered. One of our best seamen fell overboard and was drowned; two or three died, and were committed to the deep. Nothing but gloom prevailed on board. I had a slight attack of the liver complaint, but it disappeared in a couple of days, which I attributed to the constant perusal of Dr. Johnson's book upon the cure of that malady.

On the 13th we came in sight of Luzon,[1] the principal of the Philippine Islands. On that afternoon a strange ship hove in sight which had the appearance of a man of war. The private signals were exchanged and, to our satisfaction, she proved to be H.M.S. *Alpheus.* She closed upon us and her Captain, Langford,[2] came on board. This proved a most agreeable rencontre. When he had descended into my cabin, Capt. L. exclaimed in a most merry fit, 'I have been anxious to make your acquaintance for many a year. I owe my promotion to you.' That assertion startled me, as I could not understand his meaning: which, however, he explained in the following manner:—

'When I commanded the *Sappho*, I captured a Danish Privateer of more guns than I carried. When my report appeared at the Admiralty, no notice was taken of it. But when your official account of your action with the Danish brig of war *Lougen* was read to their Lordships, you were instantly promoted. My friend, the Hon. Henry Pierrepont, who had been our Minister in Sweden, heard of this and hastened to the Admiralty, demanding if it were true that you had received your Post Captain's Commission. He was answered in the affirmative. "Then," said he, "you must promote my friend Capt. L." To that he received the reply that my action was a very different affair to yours, mine being with a Privateer and yours with a man of war of very superior force: that you were severely wounded, and had fought one of the hardest battles of the war. However, my friend Mr. P. would not quit the Admiralty until he obtained my advancement. In short, if it had not been for the *Childers'* action I should not have been promoted. Besides, your name was mentioned to me by Mr. Yorke, when First Lord of the Admiralty, who offered me an acting command which I refused. "You must not complain," he said, "when such an officer as Capt. D. accepts everything that is offered to him." "Who is this Capt. D." thought I. "Shall I ever make his

---

[1] 'Luconia' in MS.
[2] George Langford, Lt. 16/12/1797; Cdr. 27/4/1808; Capt. 5/3/08.

acquaintance?" Our meeting in the China Seas is a strange one, but I am highly delighted at becoming known to you.'[1]

This was all new to me, but at the same time highly gratifying. I then acquainted my companion that Lord Manvers, Mr. P.'s Father, was my particular friend, and that I had met Mr. P. at Thoresby Park; but he had never said a word to me about the *Childers'* action, although it had been frequently mentioned during my residence there.

When Capt. Langford became acquainted with the sickly state of my crew, he advised putting into Manilla for their recovery. I therefore agreed to do so as, he being known to the Spanish authorities, he promised to have me well provided with everything necessary. He then returned to his ship, and, as he was my senior by one upon the list, I of course attended to all his motions. We made sail towards Luzon, and the next morning we tried the rate of our ships' sailing. To my great satisfaction the *Horatio* was considerably the better goer. As we approached the land, the Spanish guard ship came to us. I hove to and received the officer. Afterwards we stood into the Bay of Manilla, and at 9 o'clock that evening came to an anchor for the night. The following morning we stood into the roads of the town, where we took up a good position, anchoring opposite to a large fort, as did also the *Alpheus*. Upon my presenting my respects to the Governor, Don I. Gardoqui, who was an Admiral in the Spanish Navy and had been in the Battle of Trafalgar, I was most courteously received. But when he heard me address him in his own language, he was deeply pleased. My friend L. knew no other but his own, so that all the compliments fell upon me. When the Governor heard my account of the Battle of Waterloo, which was news to him, he was all astonishment, and extremely excited upon the downfall of Bonaparte. It was agreed that we on board should each fire a salute of 19 guns out of honour to that important victory, and the Spanish fort fired the same number. As I became acquainted with some of the principal authorities, they overloaded me with questions relating to that glorious event.

There was an English merchant residing here, Mr. R. Stevenson; upon durance, as the Spaniards did not allow any foreigners to settle in that colony. He was obliged to renew his permission every six

---

[1] The Navy Lists bear this story out in the main, the respective dates of posting being, Langford 5/3/1808, Dillon 21/3/1808. But Pierrepont had evidently succeeded not only in procuring promotion for his friend, but also in getting him antedated into his right place in the list: for the *Sappho's* action with the Danish Privateer *Admiral Yawl* had been fought on 2nd March, while the *Childers* and *Lougen* action took place on 14th March. Thus Langford figures next above Dillon on the Captains' List: but, unlike Dillon, he did not live long enough to reach Flag rank.

months. This gentleman threw his house open to me, and placed a
bed at my disposal during my stay. This was to me a great luxury as,
there being so many sick men on board, a change of air was very
desirable. There was a Dock Yard at the extremity of the bay on the
same shore as the town, called Cavite.[1] Thence I drew some supplies
that were much wanted. A survey was held upon my sick crew, when
it was decided to send 50 of them to the Hospital, the Spanish
Governor kindly directing that one of the wards might be occupied
by the English seamen. One of the Surgeon's Assistants took up his
residence there, and the 50 worst cases were landed. I also sent a
junior officer of Marines[2] with a few of his men to watch over the
premises, and prevent improper persons coming into the ward.

With the Governor I established a sort of friendly intercourse,
but he was of rather too sombre a type to be upon terms of familiarity. He was jealous of our power. But what seemed to cause a sort
of coolness towards us had originated in Capt. L.'s conduct. He had,
just before my arrival, been caught in the act of smuggling dollars.
The Governor sent out his armed launches, and Capt. L.'s barge
was captured, and towed in triumph up a sort of lagoon that ran by
the town. This was a most unfortunate affair, which had considerably
lowered Capt. L. in the estimation of the Spaniards. They used to call
him 'El Capitano de los patacos'—the Captain of the Dollars.

The climate was sultry, so that only the evenings were devoted to
the meetings of Society. The tertulias were held in accordance with the
customs of Spain. There was an esplanade outside of the walls where
the ladies and gentlemen used to assemble for recreation, the donnas
figuring away in their mantillas and the motions of their fans: as
well, their piercing black eyes could not escape notice. I became most
familiar with the Lieut. Governor, a very different character from
Gardoqui. I often dined with him, and he lent me books to read. He
was agreeable to perfection. I once or twice presented myself at the
Governor's evening parties. They were not well attended, nor were
they cheerful. I could not, from the sickly state of my ship, ask any
persons of consequence to dine with me, but one or two of the merchants belonging to the Spanish factory came to partake of my
cabin dinner.

There were some English seamen, deserters from one of our ships
of war, lurking about the place. His Excellency had promised to hand
them over to Capt. Langford, but he did not do so. My companion
advised me to try my luck, and, upon my applying to the Governor,

---

[1] Cavita in MS.   [2] Charles Webb Bridge, 2nd Lt. 9/4/1810.

he in a certain manner assented to deliver them up provided that I would not punish them. I agreed, remarking that I had no desire to inflict any severity upon the men, but that I claimed them as British subjects in right of the Law of Nations. Some days now elapsed without my hearing any more about them. I was then informed that they used to sleep on board of a Spanish ship that lay close to me fitting out for Acapulco.[1] Consequently I sent an officer to that ship to ascertain the fact. The Spanish Mate was very guarded in his replies, but he acknowledged that they slept on board, though none of them had come off from the shore at that moment. Upon this information, I wrote a letter in Spanish to the Governor, acquainting him with what I had done, emphasizing that my only object in sending an officer to the ship was to obtain intelligence concerning the seamen. However, the Mate reported that my boats were armed, and that threats had been used to take away the Englishmen by force. This statement was a shameful falsehood: but the Governor made use of it, indicating that I had insulted the Spanish Flag. Some discussion ensued, but the Spaniards are a stubborn set of fellows, and I plainly saw that my case was a hopeless one. I retired, leaving the Governor to understand that I had done my duty, and hoped he would not oblige me to represent his proceedings to my Government. In future I kept his Excellency at a distance.

At one of Capt. Langford's entertainments, the proprietor of the Acapulco ship was present with two or three other wealthy Spanish merchants. These gentlemen occasionally spoke to each other in their native language, little thinking that I understood it. Shortly before my arrival a French frigate had come to Manilla bringing a valuable freight of dollars from Acapulco. He had made himself extremely popular with the authorities by declining the usual freight money. One of them alluded in pointed terms to the Frenchman's liberal proceedings, dwelling with considerable encomiums on that officer's handsome conduct, proving that he did not care for money. 'Very true,' said another. 'I wonder if these English officers would have the generosity to follow the Frenchman's example?' This was a direct hit at my friend Langford, but as he did not comprehend the subject under discussion, he could not feel it. As the Spaniards seemed inclined to humble my countryman, I thought it high time to interfere, and addressed them as follows:—'I am much obliged to you gentlemen for the good opinion which you seem to entertain of the

---

[1] Capulcoa in MS.: but later he calls it Acapulcoa, and evidently means the Mexican terminal of the famous treasure-ship route.

British officers, but you seem to have entirely lost sight of what England did for Spain in this war. I for one, when stationed on your coasts to act against the French, saved many of your villages from being ravaged by their troops. The inhabitants were sheltered on board of my ship and fed. I was employed on that service for months, without ever receiving any acknowledgment from Spain. But,' I added, 'I will mention to you an English Captain who went from Cadiz in a small 64, to collect freight on the shores of Peru. He loaded his ship with treasure and brought it to Spain without receiving any pecuniary consideration. He had some millions more than your French friend, but he nobly declined claiming any remuneration for the service rendered.'* When these gentlemen heard my statement delivered with energy in Spanish, they were astonished and completely humbled. 'We were not aware,' they said, 'that you understood our language, and we solicit your pardon for our thoughtlessness.' I believe the owner of the Acapulco ship was a Frenchman. It was he who took the lead during the conversation here related. I communicated to Langford all that had passed. He was not much pleased, as he had frequently shown those guests attentions which he thought not well returned on this occasion.

I made the acquaintance of some of the Spanish officers. When they heard I had come up the Straits of Macassar and by the Palembang Passage[2], they expressed their astonishment in pointed terms, assuring me that it was a dangerous route at this season, and that none of their ships of war whose captains knew those regions ever attempted it. They considered that I had had a lucky escape. I was introduced too to the Bishop and some of the leading clergy. When I met his Holiness, I could not help recollecting the cunning proceedings of the priests when Manilla had been taken by us under the command of Sir William Draper and Commodore Cornish. The latter I had met many years before at my friend Gambier's house, when he was an aged Admiral. Sir William, being a good latin scholar,

* The officer alluded to was the Hon. Capt. Flemming.[1] Many years afterwards, when I made his acquaintance, I related to him this event, for which he kindly thanked me, not denying the statement. I have since heard, however, that his having declined accepting the freight mentioned was a doubtful case. If he had not, he certainly ought to have told me so.

    [1] This was the Hon. Charles Elphinstone, who, some time after promotion to Captain, took the name of Fleeming (sometimes spelt Fleming, but not, save by W.H.D., Flemming): see above, p. 321. This episode took place—if it ever did—when he was Capt. of the *Standard*, 64, to which he was appointed in 1811.

    [2] Unless there is another Palembang besides the well-known one in Sumatra, this is impossible. For Palembang, lying not very far S.S.E. of Singapore, is a long way *west* of Borneo, whereas the *Horatio* passed *east* of Borneo, up the Macassar Strait, and so quite 900 miles east of Palembang.

agreed to the terms of the Capitulation being drawn out in that language, as many difficulties had been made by the Spaniards, evidently on purpose, arising out of their ignorance of English. They were apprehensive, they said, of signing a document which they did not understand. The ransom of the island amounted to one million sterling. Bills for the payment of that sum were drawn upon the Treasury of Madrid, written in latin, and so worded that they directed the *non*-payment, not the honouring of them. Consequently the Manilla Ransom, as is well known, was never paid, and Commodore Cornish made himself noticed for his frequent repetition of his sorrow at having served with an officer of the Army who knew latin.*[1]

The Ship's Company gradually improved in health. Fresh meat, soft bread and vegetables were very conducive thereto. The starboard headrailing and bumpkin had been carried away by the violence of the seas, and were well replaced by the Spanish artificers: and I was agreeably surprised at the moderate charges made for these repairs, and the accommodation I had received in all quarters in respect of my refitting. Capt. Langford turned over to me 13 seamen which he had received from one of our sloops of war dismantled in India. This was a very useful help, having so many at the Hospital, and several having died. At Mr. Stevenson's I met a Spanish gentleman, one of the members of the factory, who made himself very useful in escorting me about the town. One of the greatest curiosities was the tobacco manufactory where cigars were made. Women were employed there to the number of 4,000. I was very glad when my visit was over. I could not say much for the *gentle* behaviour of the females—I should not call them fair, for they consisted of all colours, black, brown, dingy and yellow. The natives of Manilla are a diminutive race, and black. One of the odious sights to me was to see sitting at a door a female smoking a cigar as thick as my wrist, 8 or 9 inches long, the thick end taken in at the mouth so that she was obliged to open it to the fullest extent: and the difficulty appeared to be how to draw her

---

* I am not certain of having given you a correct version of that extraordinary occurrence, but in substance, I believe, I am not much out, as Sir William Draper acknowledged his having been defrauded of £25,000 by the Spanish Government's protesting the bills, and Cornish lost the same sum.

[1] The whole of this story shows signs of being purely derivative, and quite untrustworthy. This incident is recorded in Charnock (V. 139), but introduced as 'a ludicrous anecdote'. Nor can W.H.D. possibly have met Cornish, whose service career was: Lt. 12/11/1739; straight to Capt. 12/3/42; R-Ad. 14/2/59; V-Ad. 21/10/62: died, 30/10/1770. W.H.D. was born in 1780 (or at earliest, 1779). Cornish and Draper took Manilla 6/10/1762. Perhaps the man whom W.H.D. had met was Cornish's nephew and heir, Samuel Pitchford, who took the name of Cornish and died, Ad. of the Red, in 1816.

breath in and keep the cigar alight. But she did so, and, when satisfied with her smoking, she would hand it to another of the family, and so to another. A cigar of such dimensions would last the family a week or more.

When my Spanish friend heard of my preparations to depart to China, he requested me to give him and his wife a passage to Canton. I readily agreed. He, wishing to show himself useful, proposed to me to receive some dollars on freight to Macao, and offered to speak to his mercantile friends on the subject. I replied that I would not smuggle, but if they chose to send their cash to the *Horatio* it would be received. Many applicants soon came. If I smuggled, it would deprive the Custom House of the duties of exportation, and the proprietors would save that duty. When these gentlemen heard my determination not to assist in defrauding the Government of its revenue, they changed their plans. But various sums were sent off to the ship through the Custom House. The Spaniards were not prepared for this act of mine. They all expected that I would have followed Capt. Langford's plan. But they were mistaken. A naval officer sent off 4,000 dollars in bags, each containing a thousand. The officer on deck fortunately noticed that one of those bags appeared very light, and when he questioned the bearer was told that it was all right, having in it the proper number. However, he would not believe the assertion. He had the bag opened in my cabin, and ascertained that there were only 600 dollars inside of it. He instantly wrote me a note stating the circumstance and the deficiency. When I received it I happened to be on the Esplanade, and whilst in the act of perusing it I was accosted by the Spaniard to whom those bags belonged. I remarked that it was a lucky circumstance my meeting him at that moment, then acquainted him with the fact that there were 400 dollars minus in one of his bags. He appeared very much annoyed at this information, and circulated what I had told him to the company present. But, previous to my allowing him to leave me, I told him that I should send the bags back to him in the same condition in which they had reached my ship. He entreated me not to do so, as he would call upon his Bankers, and let me hear further from him next morning. After a searching inquiry at the Bank it was ascertained that a mistake had been made by one of the clerks, who had selected a wrong bag. This was all explained to me next day, and the 400 dollars were sent to make up the 1,000. This was a lucky find, as the English Naval Officers' character was on the wane in the town, and had any representation been made in Macao to the Spanish naval officer that 400 dollars were missing in one of his bags, he would instantly have imagined that they had been purloined on board of my ship.

Whilst these arrangements were going on, I invited my friend of the factory to dinner. He accepted, but at the same time assured me that some unexpected circumstances would prevent his going with me to Canton. He expressed himself with so much frankness that I had every reason to believe him, and when I mentioned this to my host Stevenson he declared that the Spaniard was too honourable a man to have attempted to trifle with me, after I had made preparations to receive him. My Spanish friend now confidentially acquainted me of his intention to send off to the *Horatio* some of the Manilla sweetmeats, preserves, dried fruits, etc., and requested me to place a couple of my boats at his disposal. As this information was conveyed in rather a jocular manner, it led me to suspect that there was something more in contemplation than the articles to which he alluded. His whole bearing, and a certain sarcastic expression of countenance indicated that the Don had in view some plan that was not altogether the thing, and I begged him to explain himself. It at length came out that he should send some jars of various sizes, which would be filled with dollars, in amount 60,000; that the fruits, etc., would be ticketed upon each jar. As this was in a certain sense a smuggling transaction, I most decidedly objected to the proceeding. This led to an altercation, which, at last, ended in his taking upon himself the whole responsibility of the act. He held, he said, an official situation under the Governor, and he would take care that the jars should find their way in safety to my ship. This was an act of kindness on his part towards me, as I was to receive 2 per cent. freight upon the sum mentioned. However, amongst the dollars there were two or three jars of real sweetmeats. The officer who took charge of them in my boats had orders to have them all conveyed into my cabin. Consequently, when we assembled at dinner, they were noticed by the company. When my friend, pointing to the labels, explained their contents, one of them with preserves in was opened and passed round to my guests. But the Spaniards, I believe, knew full well their true lading: yet, as their countryman was a person in power, they evidently indulged him by appearing to approve of the present which he said he had made to me. We had a very sociable meeting, and in the evening all returned on shore.[1]

---

[1] After such self-congratulation on the score of honesty, W.H.D.'s condoning of so flagrant an act of smuggling, so complacently admitted, is surprising.

The next morning, ascertaining that no more dollars had been sent off, I determined to quit the bay and proceed to China. I issued my orders accordingly, then called on the Governor to take my leave, explaining that I should return to reship my seamen. With the Secretary I made arrangements for the payment of all the expenses of the Hospital. Next I went to the Lieutenant Governor, and to all the Dons with whom I had established a friendly intercourse. Several of them had written to me in the romantic Spanish style. Mr. Stevenson promised to attend to the two officers left to watch the sick tars. That gentleman's kindness can never be forgotten. Capt. Langford's ship was not in the soundest condition. He intended to proceed towards the first point of our Indian possession to refit, then to England. Having parted with him upon the best terms I left the Bay of Manilla on Monday, the 1st of January, 1816.

His Excellency the Governor-Admiral Gardoqui had requested me to receive a Portuguese major belonging to the garrison of Macao. As he had not shown much disposition to be accommodating, especially on the subject of the deserters, I was not much pleased with this demand. However, to prove my desire of removing all unpleasant nationalities, I readily yielded to his wishes, and that officer appeared on board, the Lieutenants taking him into their Mess. I now proceeded, I confess, with considerable anxiety, as I had to contend against the N.E. monsoon. Had I followed the general rule of sailing on the circle, I should have reached the coast of China with a fair wind: but now I had to beat up against it. I had obtained all the information I could from Capt. Langford, who knew these regions. The Spaniards too contributed their share. They recommended my keeping close to the shore of Luzon until I reached the extreme northern Cape called Bajador, then stand over towards the Grand Lemma Passage. I acted accordingly. At our starting we had light, variable winds, making but very slow progress. The high, commanding land afforded some beautiful scenery. After 3 or 4 days of fine weather, we encountered some strong breezes, and the ship was tacked as often as necessary. One night I fell in with a strange ship, but I did not interfere with her as it came on to blow a gale. By the 8th I got a sight of the Cape mentioned, and left it to reach the land for which I was bound. We now felt the effect of the monsoon, but were under extreme uneasiness on account of the Pratas Shoal that lay in our way. It was a very dangerous one, as the currents in that neighbourhood ran in several directions with great strength. On the evening of the 12th we saw at a considerable distance what had the appearance of land. I now began to hope that all my cares were drawing to a close. The atmosphere was misty, which threw doubts upon all we saw. However, at sunset, we made out plainly the outlines of a rock called Pedro Blanco. The wind falling light, I anchored in 20 fathoms. We afterwards made out the Grand Ladrone.* This was satisfactory, as we now knew that we had crossed the China Seas in safety. We had the Grand Lemma Passage open to us.

In the night a Chinese Pilot boat came alongside, offering his services. But his demands were so exorbitant that I preferred trusting to our charts. At half past 2 in the morning the monsoon freshened. There was a fine moonlight, and I determined to weigh the anchor and run inshore. But when I sent for the Master, directing him to pilot us in, he refused to do so. I was much displeased with him. His objections to taking charge of the ship I thought unbecoming of an officer who had made such professions to me at Spithead, when the Navy Board had sent me a choice and skilful Master who had served long in these seas. When I found that my remonstrances had no effect, I said, 'Very well. I will undertake the task myself.' I then ordered the ship to be got under sail, and steered the course indicated by the chart. I kept in 18 fathoms water, taking every precaution by having the anchors and cables ready. When the officers noticed that I was piloting, they exerted themselves in an extraordinary degree. The oddity in this case was that I was trying to regulate the ship's speed at 5 knots per hour as, at that rate, the lead could be kept going. But we had not been long under way when the wind freshened and obliged me to reduce the canvas, till at last the topsails were lowered on the caps and braced by, the ship still going 6 knots. However, as we neared the land the breeze slackened, and as the moon disappeared we were in smooth water. The soundings were then correctly ascertained, and I stood on in full confidence. All sail was now made, studdingsails, etc., and as daylight dawned I found that I had taken the right direction, the ship being in the entrance of the Grand Lemma Channel. When the Master found that I had succeeded, he came to offer to take the responsibility off my hands. I allowed him to do so, but I did not fail to point out to him the

---

* The Ladrones are a cluster of islands lying at the southern extremity of this part of the coast of China.[1] They have a very barren aspect, they form the Grand Lemma Channel, and have been noticed for the residence of Pirates. I expected some annoyance from those fellows, but none of them were in the neighbourhood.

[1] Quite distinct, of course, from the better-known Ladrone or Mariana Group, far to the East, which contain Guam and Tinian where *Anson* was marooned.

impropriety of his conduct. However, we were in a distant clime, and
I was in some sense obliged to bear with him. He consequently piloted
us into the roads of Macao, where we anchored before 1 o'clock of
the 13th. As we had not selected a good position, the ship was moved
the next morning closer inshore, and saluted the fort, which compliment was returned. That you may understand the dexterity of the
Chinese at picking pockets, I had not landed 5 minutes on the beach
of Macao when one of these chaps carried off my pocket handkerchief.

(2) H.M.S. *HORATIO* (Macao and Canton)

JANUARY 13, 1816–FEBRUARY 18, 1816

The principal person to whom I now addressed myself, the
Chairman of the British Factory, the Hon. W. Elphinstone,[1] was
highly delighted when I related to him the amount of dollars I had
brought: but still more so when he heard the details of the Battle of
Waterloo. He very kindly lodged me in the house of an absent Factor.
The members of our Factory also paid me a formal welcome visit,
and invited me to Canton, as they passed one half of the year there
and the other at Macao. I inquired if the East India Directors had
sent them any instructions relating to the payment to me of any
additional freight. A negative was the reply. It would therefore
appear that the Agent at Portsmouth had led me to expect more
than was performed. I only received 1 per cent. instead of 2½—surely
an unfair proceeding towards an officer of my standing.

The first thing was to unbend the sails, strike lower yards and
topmasts, examine all the rigging and put it in good order. Regular
supplies of beef and vegetables came off to the ship, and in a few
days the seamen were improving in health and strength.

I was taken to the Portuguese Governor. He was only so by name,
as the Chinese nominate one also, who acts as he thinks proper. The
town has a good appearance. There is a battery commanding the
bay, and a respectable church. But the place itself is not of much
importance, excepting its utility to commerce. It is situated at the
extremity of an island, and forms a sort of tongue, the land on which
it stands being mountainous. It is not much more than 7 miles in

---

[1] William Fullarton Elphinstone, 3rd son of John, 10th Lord Elphinstone, and
elder brother of Ad. Lord Keith. He was, at this time, Chairman of the whole E.I.C.,
not the local head in China.

circumference, and is joined to a long narrow neck of sand not more than 100 yards across, which runs up towards Whampoa, about a mile from the high ground. There is a guardhouse with a sort of wall running across the sands. The length is about 3 miles from North to South. Here the Chinese have possession, and no one can pass that way, either to or fro, without their permission. It forms a part of the Province of Canton, being placed on the left entrance leading to that city.

Shortly after my arrival, I was requested by the Factory to take charge of, and convoy home, 13 large Indiamen deeply laden with cargoes of tea. These ships were lying at Whampoa, and could not be seen from the roads of Macao. They informed me that, by my complying with their request, a very handsome pecuniary present would be made by the East India Company to me. They thought there was a chance of some French men of war meeting these valuable ships: consequently they applied for protection. I explained to them that my crew were still in a very infirm state—50 of them left at Manilla—and that it was not in my power to comply with their solicitations: but they need not, I thought, be under any apprehension of the French intruding upon their China trade. Thereupon they formed their plans accordingly, and instructions were issued to the Captains of their ships to prepare for sea, Mr. Elphinstone intending to avail himself of this opportunity to proceed to England. These fine Indiamen now came down the river, and, as I noticed the Chairman pass my ship in an open boat, I saluted him with 11 guns. That compliment was much appreciated by his colleagues. These ships made an imposing appearance, very much resembling two-decked ships of war.[1] They were soon at sea on their way home,* and Sir George Staunton now filled the chair of the Factory.

When the Purser, acting upon my orders, tried to purchase provisions for the sea stock, the Chinamen would not provide them without the dollars being paid. It was not only this refusal that annoyed me, but the Comprador (as he was called by the Portuguese)

[1] *Cf.* the famous 'action' off Pulo A'or in February 1804, when Ad. Linois, with a regular French squadron, had a returning E.I.C. fleet at his mercy—but, mistaking a number of them for 64-gun men of war, sheered off.

* I became acquainted with some of their Captains. As they are generally very intelligent men, clever in their navigable pursuits, they were fully approving of the passage I had adopted for coming to China at this season, because it was the shortest, though a dangerous one. Amongst them was a Surveyor who was constantly sounding in all directions upon the Chinese coasts without the authorities being aware of it. By that means the most useful knowledge was acquired of navigation on these shores and in their rivers.

which meant the buyer or purveyor, had a demand upon the British
Government to the tune of 40,000 dollars. Consequently he declined
furnishing any more ships of that nation until the sum was refunded.
He had, it appeared, complied with the demands of several of our
small ships of war and had received bills upon the Navy Office for
payment of the same. These papers, he said, were of no use to him
and he would accept no more. In this dilemma I applied to Sir George
Staunton for assistance. In his reply, he stated that I had only to
sign my name to a piece of paper and there would be instantly
100,000 dollars at my disposal. That assurance removed all difficulties. The Comprador was directed to produce his bills, and when
he did the dollars were handed to him. After that, the *Horatio's*
wants were instantly completed.

Several demands were now made to me by the Factory, asking if
I had any particular orders regarding my proceedings with the
Chinese Authorities. On my replying that I had not, they expressed
considerable anxiety, as they remarked that all naval officers who
had hitherto come here had been directed to act under certain
regulations. 'What will you do,' they inquired, 'if any unpleasant
misunderstanding should occur between us and the Chinese? We do
not at present apprehend anything of that nature: nevertheless, it
is necessary that we should know what we can depend upon, having
a British man of war within our reach.' In answer I remarked, 'If
you suspect any untoward event, you must give me timely notice
that I may be prepared. But if I am caught on shore, here by myself,
I can do nothing. On the other hand, if I am warned, and can get to
my ship, you will then find that I will support the cause of my
country to the last extremity.' With that assurance they expressed
themselves satisfied.

There were two English residents at Macao, of considerable
wealth and respectability, who had nothing to do with our Factory.
They had by their management contrived to establish themselves
here, and were very hospitable and sociable companions: one by
name Magniac,[1] the other Beel.[2] One of my requisites was to have a
Chinese servant. I hesitated for some days. I knew nothing of their
language, and was strongly prejudiced against their propensity to
thieving, lying and deceit. However, one of the gentlemen of the
Factory interested himself in my behalf, and had one engaged for
me who spoke a few words of English, in the Chinese fashion. This
fellow had not been long in my service when I missed a small

[1] In MS., here, Maniac; but elsewhere as above.   [2] ? Beet.

spy-glass which was of the utmost use to me. It formed the upper part of a handsome walkingstick, with the telescope screwed on to the upper part. When walking on the beach, I could use it to notice what was passing in the bay, or on board of my own ship. I left it on my sopha one morning on being called upon to make a ceremonial visit. On my return the glass had disappeared. When I questioned my Chinese about it, his countenance convicted him: but I was informed that there was no remedy. I could not better myself by discharging him. They were all alike, and my only security was to keep all my articles under lock and key.

The arrival of H.M. Ship the *Tyne*, of 20 guns, made a little change in the common routine. Her Captain, Allen,[1] was a great invalid. He applied to me for an officer to fill up a vacancy in his ship for a Lieutenant. I accordingly selected one of my Mates, Mr. Ford[2] and, being the Senior Officer, appointed him Acting Lieutenant to the *Tyne*. The Admiralty confirmed him to his rank—the fourth Mate I had promoted out of the *Horatio*. One day I met the Portuguese major whom I had brought from Manilla. He appeared most anxious to acknowledge my kindness to him. However, I was informed that he was so proud at having had a passage in a British ship of war, and wishing to turn that event to account with his countrymen, that he acquainted them at his landing that the salute fired by the *Horatio* was out of compliment to him. So much for vanity, as every person must have known that it was intended to the fort of the town.

The gentlemen of the Factory, having settled all their affairs at Macao, had others to occupy them at Canton. They invited me to accompany them thither, where I was to be shown all the curiosities of that celebrated city, and to be introduced to some of the principal Chinese merchants of the Hong. A nice junk was prepared, and we set off one morning, having embarked the previous evening. Instead of proceeding up through the Bocca Channel, we selected another, a back passage, on the other side of Macao. We had to round the southern extremity upon which stood that town, and wend our way up a narrow passage. This was nearly a two-day's job. We were stopped by the Custom House Officers of a large village who made themselves very consequential. The Mandarins are inclined to be very troublesome. They all expect some pecuniary consideration from their inferiors. There are about 50 grades of them: therefore

---

[1] John Allen, Lt. 16/9/1807; Cdr. 4/2/14; Capt. 20/9/15; Ret. Capt. 1/10/46.
[2] Not identified. The name is written in, as an afterthought, above the line.

you may easily imagine the numberless ceremonies they impose upon each other. We occasionally saw a small square building, erected for religious purposes. As the junk neared it, one of the crew lit some small pieces of rosewood, and circular pieces of paper covered with tinfoil, and threw them towards the structure, called by the English a Joss House. The Chinese were very strict in these observances, as belonging to the sect of *Fo*. The management of the junk was something new. The mat being used for a sail attracted my attention. However, they made good progress and turned the creeks well. The crew were clever at their meals, and a bowl of rice disappeared in no time. We had come up a branch of the river Pe-kiang, on the eastern shores of which is situated the renowned Canton. Having cleared the narrow stream, we beheld it in all its splendour. The day was fine, and the approach to the city by water is imposing. My attention was first directed to the buildings of the factories of the different nations of Europe, extending along the banks of the river outside of the walls, each with its national flag displayed: but that of Great Britain was certainly the most conspicuous. The various pagodas seen at a distance gave ample proof of the regions to which I was a stranger. The waters opposite to the town are expansive, and the currents rapid.

We were soon on shore, when I was introduced to the other members of our factory, then taken to a residence fitted up solely for the use of the Captains of the Navy by the East India Company. It is but justice to those Directors that their attentions to our naval officers should be most warmly acknowledged. A ready-furnished house is placed at our disposal at all the Presidencies, with fire and lights, so that, upon landing in India or China, you have only to provide the necessaries of the table. In addition, the Admiral having the Chief Command has an allowance of £5,000 per annum, the Post Captains £500 and the junior officers a sum in proportion, by which means your respectability is maintained without injury to your Government pay. The number of strangers to be met here in the suburbs while their ships are loading and unloading, their various languages and dresses, as well their characteristic bearing, give to the whole an appearance of novelty of a most interesting description. On the river, the motions of the various junks, large and small, the boats going to and fro, with the Chinese jargon striking the ear, create an effect of a very enlivening nature. The environs of the foreign factories are occupied by storehouses for the reception of European goods, until disposed of to the natives. They are mostly built of brick and painted blue, not more than two stories high as the Chinese are not fond of going up and down stairs.

So soon as I had taken charge of my quarters, I met the principal members of the Factory at dinner, given in a large hall of their establishment, their entertainments being in perfect character with the respectable station that is maintained here. The attendants were chiefly Chinese, and as I could not speak their language I was obliged to make known my wants by signs. However, as I was seated between two English gentlemen, they took care that I should be well served. The great blank was the absence of the ladies at these meetings. Some of the factors occasionally had their wives, but as the Chinese Authorities were not favourable to their presence they were not often to be seen. Sometimes there were a few musicians, such as they were, who broke in upon the monotony of those parties. The various members, about 30 in number, were not always present, as they all had separate apartments. It was only on selected occasions that they attended. Besides, many were absent in England on furlough, so that the table was not crowded, but the social intercourse well maintained.

Aware that I should pass some days in these quarters, I prudently, to avoid attracting too much notice from the natives, dressed in a long, plain blue coat with a round hat, and only used my uniforms on ceremonial occasions. I had brought my English valet with me, and two or three of the officers of my ship, who were most kindly attended to by the Factory. Not being accustomed to the usages of the place, I was attacked with a violent bowel complaint, arising from my not being supplied with the pure water. The principal Surgeon, however, gave instructions to my Chinese servant, who laid in a quantity of the proper fluid. I was soon rid of the torment. Aware that my pocket would be picked as I rambled about to lionize, I desired my valet to keep at a certain distance behind me, and, the instant he saw a native make an attempt upon the skirts of my coat, to give him a good blow with the broom stick with which he was armed. He had only once to strike a delinquent, who was in the act of taking hold of my dress. The bystanders and the lookers-on from the ship were so fully convinced of the fellow's guilt that they all approved of my valet's proceeding, and appeared to enjoy the chastisement received, as they laughed most heartily. No further annoyance ensued, and finally I found that I could pass along the streets alone without being followed.

In my frequent mixing with the rabble, I could not help noticing

CANTON, 1805

the cheerful countenances of all the lower classes. I do not recollect ever meeting with a sorrowful or downcast look, which is so common among the labouring classes in England. However, there is this difference: a Chinaman can be amply supplied during the 24 hours for three halfpence of our money, but that pittance would not produce such a result with us. This impression of their easy tempers made such an effect on me that I was determined at all risks to put one of the mob to the test. I mentioned this to some of my Factory friends, who did not approve of it. However, one day, in passing through a very narrow lane known as 'Squeeze Gut Alley', I caught hold of a Chinaman's tail. They pride themselves upon its length, as it generally reaches within two or three inches of the ground, and it is considered insulting for anyone to touch it. When I gave it a pull he turned round, but, instead of rebuking me, burst out a-laughing. I made my bow to him and walked off—a proof of their goodnatured dispositions.

Although with us the month of January had nearly expired, the Chinese devote five days at this period to celebrate the New Year, during which time ceremonial visits among the upper classes are in constant vogue. But with the lower ones you become familiar with their complimentary bows to each other in the streets. They close both hands and raise them in an horizontal position: then, lowering them with a low bend of the head, as well the body, they say, 'Chin chin', meaning 'How do you do? I am glad to see you.' Then there is the 'cum shaw'—a trifling present generally tendered on these occasions. One day I bent my steps towards the gates of Canton, but when I got there the entrance was crowded, the passers-by addressing me in a tone and style which I did not understand. Their features had more the appearance of menace than of friendly attention. Consequently I soon retired, never returning that way again.

At the Factory mess there was one of our missionaries, a Mr. Manning[1], who had contrived to adopt the Chinese costume, but he could not succeed in penetrating any distance into the interior of the country. The gentleman who most engaged my attention was Doctor Morrison[2]. His labours in producing a Chinese dictionary proved him to be a person of the first talent. It was a most elaborate work. The Chinese language is composed of 40,000 characters, but

[1] Thomas Manning (1772-1840), Chinese authority, traveller and first Englishmen to enter Lhasa. In 1816 he was living in the Factory at Canton.
[2] Robert Morrison (1782-1834) His *Dictionary of the Chinese Language* (1815-23) was for long the standard one, and earned him his election as F.R.S. He, not Manning, was a missionary.

the knowledge of 20,000 will answer every purpose required for the common transactions of society. I accepted one day an invitation from Sir George Staunton to breakfast, with great pleasure, as I had not had an opportunity hitherto of entering into confidential communication with the leading members of the Factory. One gentleman, I. Cotton, had kindly devoted much of his time to me; but I wanted something more—to make the acquaintance of some of the upper class Chinese; to see their gardens in the environs, and obtain information relating to their family occupations. When I kept Sir George's appointment, there were fortunately two Chinese gentlemen with him. He presented me to them, and they invited me to their houses. When they retired, we sat down to some of the best flavoured tea in the country. It was then that Sir George inquired if I knew Mr. Mervyn Dillon. 'He is only my uncle,' I replied. 'Indeed,' said he, 'I wish I had known that before.' The conversation now turned towards your Father and Sister, with whom, as you know, he was intimate. At the end of our breakfast, Sir George promised to devote all his leisure hours to me, to show all that an English officer could be allowed to see at Canton.

The first move was to escort me to the other side of the river to see one of the Chinese temples. As we left the Factory to embark in their state boat, I noticed an immense crowd of the natives and many of the upper classes. This assemblage at first occasioned in me some uneasiness, and I alluded to it to Sir George. He replied that he imagined it was nothing more than curiosity. They wished to see what was going on, and, as I happened to be in my uniforms, 'you,' said he, 'are the object of attraction.' He had scarcely dropped these words when a Chinese youth, of respectability by his dress, caught hold of my sword and attempted to shove himself between my legs. This was so sudden and unexpected an attack that I seized him with both hands, intending to throw him into the water for his abrupt intrusion. But Sir George, seeing what I was going to do, entreated me in the most urgent terms to set the boy at liberty. I did so, and he scampered off to his party. 'It is a lucky circumstance,' said Sir George, 'that you let him go. If you had thrown him into the river, our lives were in danger.' 'The act,' I remarked, 'was a very improper one.' 'Very true,' he replied. 'But we are obliged to submit to many unpleasant affairs with these people.' I got into the boat with two of my officers, and Sir George, having placed us under the care of a guide, withdrew.

Upon our arriving at the opposite shore we hastened to the

Temple, a building of some extent, of the architecture of the country. We were received by a priest, and when we entered the sanctuary, we saw several others at prayers, chaunting and making genuflections very similar to what may be seen in a Roman Catholic church. When they noticed the presence of strangers, they retired from the altar, which lay on our right covered with fine white linen and decorated with flowers and articles of glass. The light fell direct upon this part of the premises, all the rest having a most sombre appearance. On our left was to be seen, on a substantial pedestal, Jupiter, the God of Thunder, a most horrid-looking monster of immense stature carved in wood; the body polished with a dark brown mixture, the head ornamented with sprigs of gold. The roof, of wood, appeared to be of a good height. As we proceeded, several more deities were noticed, the most prominent being the God of the Winds, of equal dimensions to the former, and another of Neptune, a very different character to ours. He had no trident, but in one hand a dolphin, in the other a magnet. All the males had countenances intended to inspire fear instead of adoration. Next we noticed a female, intended to represent Providence. In her hand she held a circular plate with an eye depicted on it. This figure made a graceful appearance. Next, behind a screen, we saw another female with a child in her arms. This was the Sacred Mother, and might be compared to the Virgin Mary.

Having seen as much as we thought worth our while, we were in the act of quitting this holy mansion when in came a female, large in the family way, attended by a friend who, in a long gown and with cords round his waist, resembled a friar of the order of St. Francis. Upon perceiving us, she became alarmed, evidently wishing to retrace her steps. However, the priest soon set all to rights. The woman took her station near the altar, and he placed us close to the Thundering Deity. The fair one now gave the priest two small conical pieces of wood very like muscles [*sic*. mussels?] He took them to the altar, and, after some motions not readily understood by us, returned them to her. She then, twisting her right hand two or three times over her head, threw them over her left shoulder on to the floor. The priest, examining their position, shook his head, signifying that the omen was not a good one. Upon this the woman's countenance showed despair, and a long pause ensued. However, a few words passed in a whisper between the parties, and the priest again gave the fallen articles to the anxious mother. She repeated the same operation, and, this time, the priest, after stooping to ascertain the turn they had taken, after a few moments of hesitation nodded an assent, and with a smile handed them to the excited female, whose countenance brightened up with the prospects of a safe delivery. So soon as she had recovered the trying moment, she gave the priest a fee and retired in high spirits, bowing to us most gracefully.

The temples of Fo abound with more deities than may be seen in Roman Catholic churches. In this building, I was told, there is a figure very similar to that of Lucina,[1] particularly addressed by unmarried women wanting husbands and married ones wanting children. The Chinese of the lower order are extremely superstitious. They have their household gods to whom they constantly apply in cases of necessity. If their supplications are not complied with, they frequently punish these penates. When any important enterprise is about to be undertaken, the disciples of Fo attend the temples to consult the superintending deity. Some place a parcel of consecrated sticks, differently marked and numbered, which the suppliant shakes in a hollow bamboo until one of them falls on the ground. Its mark is then referred to a corresponding one in a book which the priest holds open. Polygonal pieces of wood are by others thrown up in the open air, each side having its particular mark, and the uppermost when fallen is referred to in the book. The religion of Fo professes the doctrine of the transmigration of souls, and the Chinese wear long tails, to be hauled up by them into another existence when they depart this life.

Upon coming out of the temple into a small square, we saw two or three priests lounging at the door of a small dwelling. As I approached, I made my bow and they returned it. I was struck by the extremely benign countenances of those men. Their eyes conveyed the most perfect contentment. I then hastened away to my boat, and heard the noise of the gongs in every direction, evidently alluding to some national ceremony. When I reached my apartment, I found that my Chinese servant had lit several bunches of the scented rosewood in performance of a religious observance. The rooms were full of smoke. He received a terrible scolding, and no more repetitions of that nature occurred. I had scarcely got myself to rights when I received a visit from a Chinese gentleman of consequence named Fat Quaw, a button on his cap, with a peacock's feather, indicating a man of rank. Tea was soon presented to him which, when he tasted, he said was not good. He spoke sufficient English to make himself understood. He told me that he came to invite me to a Sing Song. There was no refusing such a compliment. At parting he promised

---

[1] *I.e.* Juno Lucina, who presides over childbirth.

to send me a case of choice tea, and sure enough in the course of a couple of hours a very handsome ornamented chest arrived full of delicious Pekoe.

Two Chinese gentlemen, brothers, were in constant communication with the English: their names Ponque Quaw. The elder was advancing in years and had considerable wealth: the younger was styled by us 'the Squire', as he tried all he could to imitate the English customs. But generally the upper class of the Chinese were not much inclined to be sociable with us foreigners. They were jealous of our power, and our Factory underwent many trials, and strict circumspection was necessary to keep upon good terms with their authorities. I was taken by Sir George to the house of the senior Ponque Quaw who received me very graciously. He was fond of literature, was considered a good scholar, and fond of poetic flights. The long nails of his hands indicated his gentility. He was particularly anxious to know if I had been at Court and noticed by my Sovereign. When he learnt that I had been well received there, his attentions were more marked, and he invited me to see his garden. Here he invited my attention to the branch of a tree that had united itself with an opposite one across the path, for which reason it was called 'the alley of union'. It is characteristic of these people to give names to various objects. He pointed next to a large round stone in the shape of a globe. It had been sent to him by the Emperor, of which he was very proud. But that lump of stone cost him probably its weight in gold as, when his Imperial Majesty sent a present to a subject, an ample return was expected. Having viewed the grounds, which were well wooded and abounding with flowers, we returned to the Hall of Reception, which had no closing doors to it. The house was surrounded by a good wall, but the room in which we sat was entirely open on one side and only sheltered by the lowering of a mat. The cushions on the sophas were small and very hard, appearing to be made of wood. After passing about an hour with Ponque Quaw, whom I shall never forget, we retired, Sir George remarking that many of his wives had seen me, although I had not seen one of them. He had 300, which was the general number for a man of independent fortune. But one of them was his legal wife by marriage, and she ruled over the rest.

Now for a curious Chinese dinner. A tea merchant, a regular bon vivant, by name Tin King, had come to Canton to dispose of his produce. This was the 40th year that he had left his plantation 1500 miles off in the upper provinces, and had carried away, each time, 40,000 dollars. As he had no private dwelling in this locality, Sir George, four other gentlemen of the Factory and I, with Tin King's son, made up the party in his tea warehouse. We met on the first floor, where we found a table and just sufficient room for us to be seated, the rest of the space crowded with chests of tea. All the dishes and the wine came from a small partition on our right. It is the Chinese system of good breeding for the guest to be placed on the host's left. The master of the house then tastes the dish before him, using his chop sticks. If he is satisfied with its good quality, he hands a small portion to the invited friend. That part of the ceremony was not at all to my liking, and my English friends enjoyed my embarrassment. However, I yielded, and took into my mouth the piece of meat tendered. It was highly seasoned. On the table were several plates with dried sweetmeats, and the soy sauce was in great request. My host was a man of 60, the fore part of his head shaved according to the custom of the country, with a long tail hanging from the back of it. His son, of 40, was a stout well-limbed man. The rosy tint in their cheeks indicated their being of tartar blood. The father's hair was perfectly black, he had a youthful appearance, and no one would suppose him of the age mentioned. He was very fond of the bottle, taking his quantum daily. He instantly filled my glass— properly speaking, a metal cup, not holding so much as a table spoon, in shape like a large thimble, and fitted upon an article resembling a saucer turned bottom upwards. During the dinner, father and son contrived to draw off my attention, filling this little cup so often that I soon made out their object. They called me a 'Man of War Mandarin', and, as I had tolerable square shoulders, they considered me a person capable of indulging in their beverage, the Sam Shu, which was served warm and not unpleasant to the taste. They tried very hard to lay me under the influence of the fluid, but they failed. The food was served in bowls and cut up in small pieces about an inch square, clear of bone. We had in succession the shark's fin, the bird's nest and all the variety for which the Chinese are famous.* The wine was poured out of a leaden mug, very similar to what our barbers use when shaving. There were nearly 200 bowls brought in in quick succession. My English friends, who were accustomed to these entertainments, regulated their proceedings accordingly, so that the host devoted his whole time to me, and a hard trial I underwent.

---

* There was also abundance of fruit—plums, pears, apples, grapes, apricots, and, most delicious of all, the Mandarine Orange, the skin of which is quite loose. Consequently you tear it off, and the interior is exquisitely sweet, cooling and void of pips.

However, shortly after 10 we were allowed to retire. This was a plain merchant's entertainment, without fuss or ceremony.

The next day I was invited to a flower show, where the ladies assemble at stated periods. Almost the first person I met there was Tin King, but I found him very different in public to what he was in his own house. He scarcely acknowledged me, and I of course kept him at a distance. He indulged amazingly in the bottle, and never failed, having found a gentleman of the Factory with a similar propensity, of being *non compos* daily. I hardly know how to describe the fair ones. Their faces were all thickly bedaubed with flour, and as they went tottering along with their cramped feet, they caused a most unpleasant impression. Their heads were well decorated with flowers, the hair well fastened up and secured with several long pins with large pearls or metal balls at the outer ends. As their gowns are fastened close round the neck, there is no forming an opinion of their shapes. I cannot say much of their beauty and little eyes. The garden was crowded with both sexes and the weather was fine, which gave to the scene a degree of exciting interest. There were some refreshments, such as lemonade and cakes for the ladies. After staying upwards of an hour, I withdrew.

One of my officers brought me a couple of beautiful white mice, purchased under the supposition that they were Chinese. However, we afterwards discovered that they came from England, which proves the cunning of those chaps. But one of our countrymen, some years ago, turned the Chinamen's fondness for clocks to good account. He brought out a cargo of the cuckoo kitchen ones, and produced a very handsome, remunerative profit. But in the course of time the cuckoos left off the hourly song, and when this Master came back to Canton with goods, he was seized by the purchasers, who intended to throw him into prison because all the cuckoos had done calling out when the hour struck. 'Oh,' said he. 'That's easily explained. That bird only sings in the Spring, and we are now in the winter.' He was liberated. But he knew he had imposed on the Chinese, and when he got clear he never returned to the Celestial Empire.

Now for my entertainment at Fat Quaw's. That gentleman sent a palanquin for me at 4 o'clock—a very unusual attention from the Chinese. My friends warned me to be on my guard, that I might be prepared for a somerset. Sure enough, I experienced some very unpleasant jolts, being scarcely able to keep my seat. Under this trial I insisted upon being set down, got out, and at last made the bearers understand that if they would not carry me with an easy motion, I would walk. As I was in my uniforms, all the passers-by stopped to take a look at me. Finally I resumed my seat, and the vehicle was taken onwards quietly till I reached the mansion, premises of considerable extent. Mr. Fat Quaw introduced me to his father, whose whole deportment proved him to be an accomplished gentleman. There was much ceremony, and when it was terminated I was taken to the Hall where we were to dine. The table was spread for upwards of 40 guests, though four is the usual number at a Chinaman's dinner table. Opposite it was erected the stage for the theatricals. After examining the arrangements for the Sing Song, which generally lasts three or four days, I went into a garden laid out with much taste with flowers of every description. I frequently heard a great deal of tittering, evidently from female voices, but all my attempt to catch sight of any of them failed: except in my returning to the hall, and that was quite accidental. The fair one, unconscious of my being near, was coming into the garden, and almost ran on board of me before she was aware of a stranger being there. Then she uttered a shriek, and was out of sight in no time. Some of her companions had noticed this recontre from the windows. Laughing from them I plainly heard.

The banquet being served, we took our places. Most of the dishes were dressed and cooked in the English style. There were joints, poultry and two or three substantial pieces of roast beef. Port and sherry abounded. Then came their own dishes, with the Sam Shu, so that you might indulge your appetite either in English or Chinese cookery. There was a great display of lamps, in which the Chinese take great pride. In about an hour the noise of a gong announced the appearance of the actors. The curtain being drawn, the theatricals commenced, but I could not make out what they alluded to. The performers were either boys or eunuchs. They cut a very good figure, but the music was of that screeching description that had an effect of anything but harmony upon my senses. At the conclusion of every act, additional dishes were produced, so that there was ample means of satisfying one's appetite. Tea was served every two hours in cups, with the leaves of the plant at the bottom, a saucer being placed over to keep it warm. There was neither milk or sugar added. After two hours, we rose from the table and lounged about, then returned to our places. At 11 o'clock I had witnessed enough, and proposed to Sir George to quit the premises. But he did not approve, observing that the least compliment I could pay to Mr. Fat Quaw would be to remain until daylight. But the pains in my wounded legs attacked me so violently that I requested my friend to explain my sufferings to our host, who finally allowed me to retire. The palanquin was sent for, and, taking my leave of Mr. Fat Quaw and the company, I withdrew. The bearers behaved, I noticed, with more propriety than before, and I was in the act of taking a snooze when suddenly the vehicle was landed, some doors were opened, and to my astonishment I beheld my host, surrounded by several servants with lights. Fat Quaw, with many courteous bows and salutings from his joined hands, gave me to understand that I had arrived at the outlet of his premises and that he had come to wish me a good night. I had been more than a quarter of an hour reaching the gate from the Hall! That being over, the bearers lifted up the palanquin and carried me off. Thus terminated my Chinese hospitality, and I witnessed another proof that there are what are designated 'gentlemen' in every part of the globe. Sir George told me that, soon after my departure, all the members of the Factory came away, and he supposed that Mr. Fat Quaw put an end to the Sing Song, which had been given solely out of compliment to me.

Next day I received ceremonial visits from two Chinese gentlemen named Chunqua and Qoqua: but as their names on the cards were in cyphers I could not make them out. My friend Fat Quaw had his written in English. These cards were thin pieces of red paper, 10 inches long and 5 broad, enclosed in a sort of envelope open at one end. On the outward cover the visitor's name is glued on, on a small slip extending its full length.

As the time for my departure was drawing near, I had to make purchases, intending to take home some of the rich productions of this country to all those friends who had been useful to me in my profession. Sir George recommended me to the best shops in the suburbs where I could be understood in my own language. When making a bargain, if I thought myself overcharged, I attempted to lower the price. But the Chinaman would say, 'Me no hab two word,' and shut up the article bid for. Articles of ivory, pearl cardmarkers, silks, nankeens, china jars, shawls and gold and silver ornaments were selected, as well some beautiful thread work in both metals. The Chinese ivory productions surpass all other nations'. I had directions from a friend to purchase a complete set of china, and he decidedly told me to select the *Maker* china. However, I could not find any bearing that name, nor had the gentlemen at the Factory ever heard anything of the kind, but told me that a regular set of the best would cost about £300, as it generally consists of 1,000 or

1,200 pieces. Upon this information, I gave myself no further trouble in my friends' commission, as he had not supplied me with any cash. When they heard of my returning to Macao, they, according to custom, made me some presents —as they said, 'Cum Shaws'. The most prominent were large cases of tea and some lacker work from Sir George. They were embarked on board one of the Company's ships, in my name. I was to be the merchant, and the Captain promised to take care of my interests at the Custom House in England.

Silver was the coin in constant use in shops. I never saw gold in circulation. The shopkeeper makes use of a 'Swanpan', a sort of board with deep edges, upon which balls are strung on wires on different rows, and arranged upon a plan of their own. Those in the first row represent units, with a lowering diminution of the others from right to left. The decimal multiplication and subdivision of quantities used by these people simplifies their calculations. For instance, a liang, which may be considered an ounce of silver, is divided into 10 chen, the chen is 10 fen, the fen into 10 lee. The ideal subdivision of money descends much lower, but always, as well as in increasing quantities, in the same decimal proportions. A lee, or the thousandth part of a liang, is an actual coin of copper, far from pure and of brass colour. It is of circular form, with a hole in the middle for the convenience of being strung upon a sort of packthread. This coin is very convenient for the lower classes, who can thus buy as small quantities as are suitable to their stations in life. Tea in China is sold like beer in England, in every village and along the public roads. In the upper provinces silver is often used in making bargains by the lump, but in the South the Spanish dollar has the most extensive circulation. The probity and punctuality of our Factory is so well known to the Chinese, that their goods are always taken as to quality and quantity according to the invoice, and sent into the interior without examination.

The science of Physic and Surgery are at an extremely low level, there being no public schools or teachers in that line. A youth who wishes to become a physician must engage himself as an apprentice, and improve himself by attending to his master's practice. A copper coin corresponding to an English sixpence is the usual fee to a doctor among the people, and perhaps four times as much from a Mandarin. Those of high rank have one constantly in their families, who travels with them. No male physician is allowed to attend a woman in her pregnancy. There are many quacks, who make money by selling nostrums and distributing hand bills. The Canton artists are extremely clever in imitating European works. They mend and even make watches, copy paintings and colour drawings with the greatest nicety. They supply strangers with coarse silk stockings and socks, knit or woven in that city. I laid in a good supply of these, as I found them cool to the feet and of long duration.

The Chinese in easy circumstances marry early and generally have large families. With the poor, marriage is a measure of prudence, because the children, particularly the sons, are bound to maintain their parents. In no country is the father more respected than in China. Even when the son has made himself independent, his submission to his parents' will is manifest to the last moment. Very little room is occupied by a family, at least by the middle and lower classes. In their houses there are no extra apartments. The dwelling is generally surrounded by a wall within which a whole family, of three generations, with all their wives and children, will frequently be found. One small enclosure is made to serve for the individuals of each branch, sleeping in different beds, separated only by mats hanging from the ceiling, and one common room is used for their meals. This custom is attended with important effects. It renders the younger temperate and orderly in their conduct under the example and control of the Parent, and by subsisting in one mess economy is maintained. Yet notwithstanding this the labouring poor are reduced to vegetable food with a very scanty relish of meat, the price of labour generally bearing as small a proportion to the price of provisions as the common people will consent to suffer. Yet in appearance they are contented. Great order is preserved amongst them, and the Police watches over them with great strictness within the walls of the city. In the suburbs only public women are registered and licensed. They are not numerous. It is reckoned that at least one million, of both sexes, reside upon the rivers in junks, and a child may frequently be seen floating down the stream, with a gourd slung round its neck to keep it from being drowned, by superstition committed to the Holy Spirit: and a faint hope is entertained by the parent that they may be preserved from untimely death, and that those who are appointed by the Government to rescue these miserable objects will finally provide for them if found alive. This can not be considered more criminal than what is occurring almost daily in France, a Christian country, where children are left exposed in the streets by the mothers, and then conveyed to the foundling hospitals.

I went one day to visit a junk in the river. The Master of it received me very courteously. The rudder is the most awkward machine, as it is not fixed down the stern post, but secured by ropes. The Chinaman now drew my attention to some plates of dried sweetmeats, sugarplums, etc. These are kept in constant readiness for their god, Joss, that he might eat whenever it suited his convenience. But Joss never made his appearance, and after waiting a certain time, they took them away and laid out another set, under the expectation that the Deity would help himself, that event never taking place.

There are no hereditary titles in China, but there are three classes from which the Mandarines are chosen, viz. Men of Letters, Landed Proprietors who cultivate in a large way, and clever Mechanics, including wealthy Merchants. All honours come from Pekin, awarded by the Emperor. Military rank is also conferred upon those who excel in war-like exercises. There being no hereditary dignity, the delegated authority of the Government often falls more heavily upon the unprotected rich than on the poor: and it is a common observation among the Chinese that fortunes, by being divided among many heirs, or lost in commercial speculations, gambling or extravagance, or extorted by oppressive Mandarines, seldom extend beyond the third generation: so that it is necessary to ascend again into ambition, to devote a life to long and laborious study and to be noted in the learning of the country, which alone qualifies the individual for public stations. There are nine degrees of Mandarine, distinguished by the colour of the button on the cap.* The 'Katoo' is the ceremony observed when presented to the Emperor. The subject goes on his knees and touches the floor nine times with his forehead. This ceremony created so much difficulty when Lord Macartney had to make his appearance at Court, that it was settled, I believe, by a Chinese Mandarine making a similar prostration to the portrait of our King. Then matters were arranged very amicably.

Their cemeteries are held in high veneration, and their tombs generally built of stone, some in the shape of small houses six or eight feet high, fronted with white pillars. These burying places are not joined to the temples, but in open spaces: those of persons of high rank are often upon a slope of rising ground or on a terrace of

---

* The Princes wear the transparent red button, and some Mandarines have three peacock feathers attached to their caps. A Chinese General, writing to the Governor General of Bengal, styled his Emperor, 'The Flower of the Imperial Race, the Sun of the Firmament of Honour, the Resplendent Gem in the Crown and Throne of the Chinese Territories.' Yellow is the imperial colour.

semicircular form, and supported by breast walls of stone. The doors, inscribed with the names, qualities and virtues of the deceased at full length, are of black marble. Sometimes obelisks are erected, surrounded by different species of the cypress, whose deep and melancholy hue seems to fit them for scenes of woe. A night seldom passes without a visit from relations with torches, to pay respect to the departed, whose tombs they decorate with slips of silk or painted paper, strewing flowers and burning perfume before them. There is no Sunday in China, or even such a division as a week. But their temples are open every day to receive devotees. There are no tithes for the maintenance of the Clergy, but there is a sort of Poll Tax proportional to the income of the individual.

Their dress is not unbecoming, though very awkward in appearance—long gowns or cloaks trimmed with fur in winter, and heavy solid shoes or boots. The Mandarines make use of fans—in fact, all gentlemen do—and some of them have very indelicate figures painted thereon. The Chinese are held in complete submission and apprehension by their superiors, but when free from constraint they are cheerful and confident. Dress is not regulated by fashion, but according to what is thought suitable, or the season of the year. Even among the ladies there is little variety, except in the flowers or ornaments for the hair, to which they devote great attention. They do not, as do our females, wear shifts, but a silk netting in lieu; then a waistcoat and drawers of silk trimmed or lined (in cold weather) with furs. Over these a long satin robe is worn, tastefully gathered round the waist and secured with a sash. The dress is varied in colour, in the selection of which the fair display their judgment to a nicety. Corpulence in the male is considered equal to good looks in the lady, and—by the gentleman—a proof of his wealth and independence, as by his rotundity it is evident he is not subjected to labour. But the ladies consider anything like a large shape a great blemish in their own sex. Their whole object is slimness and a slight figure. If they allow their nails to grow to a great length, they reduce their eyebrows to a small arched line, and the small angular eye is the desideratum for perfect beauty. Every nation has its peculiarities. The labouring women exert themselves in a most extraordinary manner, and contribute most effectively towards supporting the wants of the family. A farmer at the plough is assisted by his wife. Married women are distinguished from maidens by the latter allowing the hair on the forehead to hang down near the eyes, whilst the former have all theirs bound up on the crown of the head.

The women of every condition are little better than slaves. Few receive any education, and they have no chance of acquiring knowledge by observation or travel. Their ignorance, their retirement and their awe of those whom they consider their superiors disqualify them to a certain extent from becoming good companions. They do not mix with the men. Consequently refinement, delicacy of taste or sentiment, and the play of the passions, liveliness or wit cannot be brought into practice. Again, the demeanour of the men is very ceremonious, consisting of various evolutions of the body, inclinations of the head and bending of the knee; then the joining of the hands and disengaging them, all which motions are considered necessary for gentlemen of good breeding. But when these formalities are terminated the performers relax into familiarity.

Want of offspring is not well considered in China. Therefore those parents who are without any adopt those of their friends, and they become theirs exclusively, inheriting the property, etc. If a wife proves barren, a second may be espoused in the lifetime of the first. The opulent are allowed concubines without reproach, and children by them are brought up in sentiments of duty and affection, benefiting in all rights of legitimacy. There are missionaries in China, but they do not make many converts.

I did not see many soldiers in China. The military profession is not much esteemed. Men of literature have the preference. Their troops are gaudily dressed, and the fan is used in the Army. After exercise their regimentals are laid aside and the men work in the fields. They are thus useful in time of peace, but cannot be considered well disciplined. Their pay and allowances exceed those of the labourer, so that there is no difficulty in recruiting the Army. There are learned lawyers, but there are no juries. It seldom happens, however, that a capital sentence is enforced without confirmation of the Emperor, though the Viceroy of a Province may, in case of rebellion, order an execution. Their punishments are numerous and cruel. The infliction of the bamboo is ordered very summarily upon anyone below the rank of Mandarine. Theft is not punished with death, nor is robbery, unless the act be accompanied with personal injury. Strangulation is considered less infamous than beheading: the separation of one part of the body from another is considered particularly disgraceful. The confinement in a sort of pillory, in which both head and hand are secured, lasts sometimes for weeks and months, according to the bodily strength of the culprit. The administration of the jails is said to be good. The debtor and the felon are separated, and the two sexes likewise. A man may sell himself in certain cases, such as to discharge a debt to the Crown or assist a Father in distress. No property is safe in this country, however, against the claims of the Emperor.

The bamboo is turned to immense account. It is not only beautiful in appearance, but useful in a hundred ways. It flourishes most in dry ground in the neighbourhood of running water, and is at once light and solid. The natives reckon more than 60 variations of it. It rises out of the ground with a trunk hollow and jointed like a reed, and will attain the height of 20 feet in as many months. It is used in building, and in all sorts of furniture: its pulp is turned into paper and its tender branches used as food. Next come the mulberry trees. They are planted in rows about 10 feet apart in loamy earth. From the leaves are produced the silk worm. The eggs are deposited upon paper and preserved till the time of hatching. Artificial heat is applied when an early brood is required, the insects being suffocated previous to reeling off the silk by placing the cocoons or silk-balls in a basket, and exposing them to the steam of boiling water. No country produces finer silk than China.

I took my departure, in the Company's launch which served me as a Yacht, on the afternoon of the 8th February, passing the island of the Dutch folly, Whampoa, etc. At night I anchored to wait daylight, and the next morning, it being a calm, I made my way to the shore in the boat attached to my launch. I was in the neighbourhood where Commodore Anson had anchored. Not wishing to expose myself to any unpleasantness among the Chinese, I landed at a place which appeared lonely. I soon found a path which I used, but had not been long upon it when I fell in with a female, dressed in a large blue cotton gown, trousers of a similar colour down to the calves of her legs, no stockings or shoes, and a basket on her head. She was tramping along at a good pace, a sturdy person and good looking, but perfectly yellow. At first she was rather alarmed at my appearance, but as I did not interfere with her proceedings, she did not seem to mind me. This was evidently a female of the lower class, as she had large feet and an altogether strong and healthy deportment. I next came in contact with a Duckboat. The Chinese keep some hundreds of ducks in boats prepared for that purpose, afloat on the river. They are landed occasionally, there being a large board launched from the boat's side to the shore. The last duck always receives a castigation both in going out and in returning, and it is a curious sight to see these birds quitting the boat and returning. They display their desire not to be punished by quacking, treading and jumping over each other. The keeper showed me what he fed them with—a sort of dry grass which the birds swallowed with great avidity. I now hastened back to my yacht, and reached my frigate by the evening, having passed through the Bocca Tigris.

I rejoiced to find all in good order, the crew improved in health, the ship clean, painted, and making a very imposing appearance. The crew had regained strength, and were ready for any service. But my cabin was full of cases and toys, sent by the Chinese purveyors, who had, I was told, brought them on board themselves. I sent for them next day, and desired them to take the articles away. But this they would not do, exclaiming that they supposed I had plenty of children and at least 150 wives to whom the cum shaws would be acceptable. Finding I could not persuade these compradors to remove this lumber, I distributed it among my officers, and some I took to Manilla and gave to my Spanish friends. By that means I entirely cleared my cabin.

[He entertained Messrs. Beel (?Beet) and Magniac, and presented to Sir George Staunton 'a quarter cask of choice Madeira, out of which, odd enough to say, not long since I drank some in Devonshire Street.' He visited some curious gardens in Macao, and a cave on a high hill in which tradition said that 'the Portuguese poet Camoens had written his celebrated poem of the Lusiad.' It is indeed quite likely that the first six books of the poem were written while Camoens was in exile at Macao.]

There is an extensive prospect from here. I now beheld the islands forming the Lantao Passage, or the Grand Lemma Channel, as well the island in which is the harbour of Typa. It is here that ships take refuge in stormy weather, as the roads of Macao are not considered safe when the typhoons come on. But as, I believe, there is only 18 feet of water in the Typa, it is not sufficiently deep for the *Horatio*.

When the Chinese allowed the Portuguese to settle on the island of Macao, they carried on a considerable trade with Japan, Eastern Asia, China, Cochin China and Siam. They soon made splendid fortunes, the proof of which still remain in many large and costly buildings, public and private. But the times are much altered, and Macao is now in a neglected state. Luxury followed wealth, the spirit of enterprise declined, the Portuguese became enervated by the climate, and the settlement has gradually fallen from its former prosperity. However, there is still a proportion of trade carried on by the Portuguese, who lend their names to other foreigners from the Canton Factories, by whom various speculations are made. The town's population may be considered near 12,000: there may be 4,000 Portuguese, and the rest Chinese who do all the laborious work of the colony. The market is well supplied from the Chinese part of the island. Whenever any misunderstandings occur between the Portuguese and Chinese authorities, the latter lay an embargo upon all provisions. Consequently the Europeans are obliged to give in. The Portuguese attend only to commerce and navigation. The military Governor is assisted by a Senate consisting of a Bishop, a Judge and a few of the principal inhabitants. There are many small churches or chapels besides the Cathedral already mentioned. There are at least 50 ecclesiastics. The garrison does not consist of 400 men, principally mulattoes and blacks. They are commanded by a large proportion of officers. The Bishop bears the character of a worthy man, but is a bigot, and has great sway in the Government. There are three monasteries for men and a convent for 40 nuns. There are as many females of a loose character who are confined, and can only obtain their liberty by marriage.

There is a striking contrast between the busy and unceasing industry of the Chinese and the marked indolence of the Portuguese. They may be seen sauntering about the square of the Senate, and the English gentleman is often accosted by one of these loungers in threadbare finery, with a bag and sword, demanding charity. On the other hand, in the bay you may see a Chinaman, single handed, managing a boat, with one hand at the tiller steering, and one foot at the oar, which he feathers with skill. He has a pipe in his mouth, and with the other hand he trims the sail. So much for economy of time! The windows of the houses at Macao are fitted with oyster shells instead of glass. The oysters here are large, and when divided and polished are a good substitute.

My Chinese valet, taking me for a merchant, came to me one morning with a long narrow slip of paper, and inquired if I could supply a Mandarine with 'lum.' Not knowing what he meant by 'lum', I took him with me on shore, and, mentioning this to a gentleman of the Factory, requested him to explain. He very kindly told me, laughing all the time, that a chinaman could not articulate the letter R, but pronounced it like an L. 'He wants rum,' said my friend, 'Have you any to sell?'

You may judge what he would have made of 'rice'!

One of my friends proposed to me to take a ride outside upon the sands, to the Chinese barrier. We had to descend from the high land at the back of the town, and took a good gallop to the guard house. But the sentinels would not allow us to pass through. Though I could not understand one word of what they said, I was determined to let them know that I could return the Chinese civilities to us in Canton, where the natives are in the habit of addressing foreigners by the style of 'Fan qui lo', which means 'Foreign Devil'. I therefore repeatedly made use of these words to them, then retreated. When we re-entered the town and were riding quietly along the streets, two or three urchins got some squibs of gunpowder and set them off under our horses. I gave one of them a good slap with my whip, which astonished the lookers on. Had not my horse been a quiet one, some accident might have happened. This shows how ready all the rabble in China were to be mischievous when they thought they could be so with impunity.

At this time, my friend Ponque Quaw, 'the Squire', was particularly attentive, and frequently invited me to his house at Macao. But I declined going unless he would promise to introduce me to his wife. I knew that my request was contrary to the usages of the country, but as this gentleman had so often expressed a desire to comply with the wishes of the English, I made my application so often that he at last agreed to present me to her. When I called at the appointed time, Ponque Quaw told me that he had contrived to smuggle me into his house unknown to his wife, and that we must remain quiet below until the lady should go to take tea in a small room directly over our heads. Presently we heard footsteps passing over us. He then led me out of the Hall into a dark passage, in which there was a staircase, with no matting or carpet on it. We ascended with extreme caution, under the impression that we had reached the landing without being noticed. But we were mistaken. When Ponque Quaw opened the door with the utmost care, the wife had disappeared. He was very much annoyed—at least, pretended to be so— and let loose some observations relating to the ladies that were not very complimentary. The room was very small, and not elegantly furnished. The teapot was of black ware and the cup and saucer of the commonest china, and nothing in unison with the other parts of the premises. There being nothing to be done under this disappointment, we returned to the Hall below.

Like all Chinese gentlemen, Ponque Quaw was very fond of clockwork. There were several examples, their works entirely open to view. He wore a very elegant repeater, which he frequently set in motion; then several of the clocks, one of which had a horizontal balance resembling a perpetual motion. The walls were adorned with many paintings in water colour. The objects, principally landscapes, appeared correctly drawn, but the perspective was not properly attended to, which I noticed. But when I did so he merely replied, 'Chinese custom': and to any other remark I might make on things which did not agree with our rules of propriety, he always made that answer. Light and shade were entirely omitted in some of these drawings. One in particular, a lake, was represented with trees and houses near it on every side. But it would have been a great error in the Chinese artist if he had made the shadows of any of these objects perceptible on the water. Altogether, his house was a very handsome establishment, quite fit for a man of fortune. Although in easy circumstances, however, he was not as rich as his elder brother, who was the first Chinese to purchase a European-built vessel, and send her to England with a cargo of goods upon his own account.

[Ponque Quaw next took him to the Senate House and showed him ' some columns of granite with Chinese characters cut into them, which alluded to the solemn cession of the island of Macao, made by his Emperor to the Portuguese. But the authorities of the Celestial Empire do not, on many occasions, show proper respect to the grant made, as they often exact duties on the Portuguese, punish individuals within the limits of the town, and, what is still more offensive, march in idolatrous procession through the streets, causing serious annoyance to their religious ceremonies.' Next they visited a pagoda, and a not very erudite commentary follows on that type of building. Then follows a brief, and far from illuminating, dissertation on the tea-plant.]

The appearance of an English schooner now caused some delay in my proceedings. During my absence H.M.S. *Tyne* had left Macao, and two of my crew had died. It was therefore necessary for me to procure men from any English vessel that came in my way. This schooner had come from the N.W. coast of America. She was called the *Columbia*, and by rights had no business in this part of China. Sir George sent me, in a roundabout way, some secret information to inform me that, according to the East India Company's charter, no British vessel but those of the Company could trade here, and that I should be justified in detaining her. The hint was probably correct, but the arresting of a vessel of this description would oblige me to man her and send her to some port in India for adjudication. I was not at all prepared for such a measure, being anxious to return to Manilla to recover my men left there. Consequently, when I met Sir George, I inquired if he were in earnest. He merely stated that he did not wish to take a decided part in the case, as it might be attended with very serious consequences to the owner of the schooner. 'But,' he said, 'I thought it my duty to acquaint you with the powers of our charter, that you might adopt such a line of conduct as best suited your convenience.' I candidly owned that, if I acted upon his communication, all my arrangements would have to be set aside. We therefore agreed not to interfere with the *Columbia*, but I sent my boat to examine her, and took four good seamen, leaving her to manage as her Master thought best.

The weather had suddenly changed to heavy showers of rain. I had to complete my water. Consequently I bid adieu to my friends at Macao, including the Chinese Comprador who, in coming to take his leave of me, produced several drawings of the Imperial Dragon. When he handed them to me he said, 'You English gentlemen place no faith in these animals.' 'There may be,' I replied, 'dragons of other shapes, but those with wings here represented are not known to us. However, if you will show me one alive, I shall alter my opinion.' To this replied that he had never seen one alive, and had his doubts as to their existence. In conclusion, it was 'Chinese custom'. Those dragons are delineated on all the Emperor's property, and are on all occasions the Imperial seal.

On the afternoon of the 12th I weighed anchor and stood over to the opposite coast, Tyho Bay, where we anchored again to complete our water. But we had not got into the right position for the springs, and next morning we moved to the proper place. A select party of seamen and marines was landed to commence operations. The spring was situated upon an eminence of at least 300 feet: therefore some tact was required to obtain the supply of water. By the evening of the 17th we had completed our wants. According to my usual habits I attended to all the labours of the watering party daily. On this day, having ascertained that there was no delay, I took my station on the top of the rising ground. I had a spy glass in my hand, and after examining the premises in the neighbourhood of the spring, I returned to it. There being none of my party near it, I thought I felt something behind, and, turning, I beheld a Chinaman who was attempting to look through my telescope. I instantly shoved the fellow off, but he closed upon me and struck me on the breast.

I then gave him a blow with my clenched fist in the face, and called out to a couple of my marines not far off, who instantly came to my assistance. My assailant took to his heels and escaped over the brow of the hill about 50 yards away. I ordered one of the marines to fire his musket, and there immediately appeared a crowd of heads just over the rise mentioned. They commenced chattering to each other, but made no advance. They had evidently been watching me, and the fellow who had struck me had been sent forward to reconnoitre. At the sight of so many men, so near and so unexpected —for up to this third day at the spring no native had appeared—I did not feel very easy at this apparition. I therefore called up all the marines and those seamen not attending the hoses, drew them up in marching order and went towards the assembled Chinamen. They retired very peaceably, and I became satisfied they would not disturb our proceedings. Another musket was fired, to let them see we were prepared and then I returned with my men to their occupations. Had I not been prepared, some skirmishing might have taken place. A very awkward affair had occurred to the watering party of one of our frigates at Linting in this neighbourhood. Luckily, however, on this evening our watering labours terminated.

(3) H.M.S. *HORATIO* (Homeward Bound)

FEBRUARY 18, 1816–JANUARY 9, 1817

We were still visited by plenty of showers of rain, but by the 18th we were sailing through the Lantao Passage on our way to Manilla. When we had cleared the land, we felt the effects of the N.E. monsoon, and the ship made rapid progress on a favourable wind. But the nights were biting cold, and, not having sufficient covering in my cot, all my limbs were painfully chilled. I was obliged to turn out and procure blankets, but did not recover my natural warmth for at least a couple of days. On the afternoon of the 21st we made the land of Luzon. We were standing into the Bay of Manilla, but did not reach the usual anchoring ground till the evening of the 23rd. After paying my respects to the Governor, I took up my quarters at Mr. Stevenson's, then received my men from the Hospital, only 19 being left out of 50—a serious reduction to an active frigate's crew. There being still a few sick on board, I sent them ashore, determined if possible to have a healthy Ship's Company. It was a good opportunity to black the rigging and paint the ship. My intercourse with the Spanish authorities remained on a good footing.

The arrival of H.M.S. *Hesper*, Capt. Campbell,[1] caused a pleasant change in our society. The effects of the climate were still felt by some of the crew, but on the whole the ship was in a very superior condition to what she was on our first arrival. Several offers had again been made to me, indirectly, to receive smuggled money: all to no purpose, as I had declared that I would not commit any act of the kind. I was therefore very much astonished one afternoon to be addressed by a Spanish member of the Factory, requesting me to convey, on the behalf of their Establishment at Macao, about 100,000 dollars. Explanations ensued, and I at last agreed to take charge of them, but upon the understanding that the specie was to be sent off to my ship in Spanish boats. The gentleman with whom the agreement was made was a very intelligent person, of a most amiable disposition. Consequently our terms (payment of freight, etc.) were soon brought to a very satisfactory conclusion. In collecting bills for expenses here, I was rather annoyed by the Government Secretary, who demanded ready cash for the use of the Hospital; altogether £1,200. I explained to him that an officer in my position could only give bills upon my Government. He refused to accept them, but next day changed his tone, and the affair was settled.

Having made up my mind to take the Spanish Factory's money to Macao, I renewed my offer to the gentleman already mentioned, to give him a passage in my Cabin to China. To my disappointment he again declined, but when I mentioned the circumstance to Mr. Stevenson, he exclaimed, 'What would I give to have such an offer made to me!' I was, I own, completely taken by surprise, and re-marked, 'Had I known that you had any desire to go to China, I should certainly have given you the preference. But you have never given me the slightest hint on the subject.' 'Very true,' he replied, 'But it is the greatest object I have in view. I have long been anxious to see that country, and to go there in a British ship of war would be the most gratifying event of my life.' 'Then,' said I, 'you have now the power to fulfil your inclination. Let my Cabin be yours, and to China I will take you.' My friend readily, in the highest flow of spirits, closed with me and agreed to prepare himself for the voyage. All this occurred at breakfast. 'When do you intend to quit the Bay?'

---

[1] Robert Campbell, Lt. 5/11/1803. Properly 1st Lieut. of the *Hesper*, the Navy Lists showing Michael Matthews as her Captain up to Oct. 1816, when they show Campbell. This 'acting' post did not secure him promotion, for he was not made Commander till 12/7/1821.

he demanded. 'By one o'clock today,' I replied. 'Then,' said he, 'I must go to the Governor and obtain his permission to quit the island, and shall be back in less than an hour.' 'Very well,' said I. 'Please to present my respects to His Excellency and tell him that I will take charge of any dispatches he may wish to send to Macao, and bring him a reply to them in three weeks. I shall not call upon him myself, as I feel he has not conducted himself properly towards me. But I commit my case into your hands, to convey to the Don all manner of compliments in my behalf, etc., etc.' I now called to take leave of all my Spanish friends, among the number a Señor Urroz, who made me a present of a most splendid edition of Don Quixote—the one published by the Royal Academy of Madrid, full of beautiful prints; in fact, the best in Spain. When I met Mr. Stevenson at 11 o'clock, he acquainted me that the conversation of the whole town turned upon my upright proceedings relating to not smuggling the dollars. 'You are,' said he, 'the only English officer who has acted thus at Manilla. Moreover, the Collector of the Customs is in rapture with you. He is most anxious to make your acquaintance.' I assured him of my readiness to meet him, and requested Mr. Stevenson to bring him on board. However, when the hour of one struck, Mr. Stevenson was on board with the Governor's dispatches, but no Collector of Customs. A calm was now a serious annoyance, as it placed my undertaking to return in three weeks in jeopardy. However, by 5 o'clock of the 11th March, the *Horatio* was under sail, standing out of the Bay of Manilla.

We were teased with light winds beating up on the coast of Luzon till the 16th, when one of the crew fell overboard. When, fortunately, we had picked him up, the wind had freshened, enabling us to make better progress. But then there were the Pratas Shoals in our way. On the 18th the coast of China was seen in the distance, and we were considerably leeward of the Grand Lemma. Several Chinese boats were in sight, and it was on this occasion that I noticed the difference between their mats used for sails and our canvas ones. The pitching of our ship, in the heavy swell which was on, threw all the wind out of the sails, whereas the mats merely yielded to the motion of their vessels without striking against the mast. We now had to beat against the wind the whole day, and finally entered the Lemma Channel late in the afternoon—a sad drawback in my time—coming to anchor in the roads of Macao only at 11. But our position was not good, and next morning we moved nearer in shore.

I now had to deal principally with the Spaniards, as I had brought them some money. Mr. Magniac, however, received me hospitably into his house, and devoted much of his time to my guest, Mr. Stevenson. On this occasion I could not visit Canton. I had not been lucky in my passage from Manilla. The N.E. Monsoon was drawing to its close, and I was anxious to be out of the China Seas before the S.W. one set in. I was solely occupied in my preparations to quit these regions when I was taken by surprise by a proposal from Mr. Magniac that, if I could make it convenient to stay a few days, he would secure me a freight in dollars that would produce £1,200. When I came to weigh all the circumstances, I thought I could not be acting with propriety to delay the *Horatio* any longer. My refusal on this occasion completely astounded Mr. Magniac, who remarked that, by accepting the cash mentioned, I should be doing a part of my duty in forwarding the commercial interests of my countrymen. He could not understand my punctilios, and repeatedly observed that I was blind to my own interest. To all of this I merely replied that I preferred doing my duty to all other considerations.

Having decided not to wait for the freight offered, I requested Mr. Stevenson to settle his affairs without loss of time, and, on the afternoon of the 23rd my ship was under sail standing out towards the Grand Ladrone passage. I had been 12 days away from Manilla, and was all anxiety to return there at the time stated. The case appeared a doubtful one, as the monsoon was on the wane and the ship made very slow progress. However, we made the land (of Luzon) on the morning of the 30th, and were soon inside of the Bay. Before midnight of the 31st the ship was anchored opposite to the town, this being the twentieth day of my having quitted it. I thus arrived one day sooner than I had engaged to do publicly. The next day, with the dawn, Mr. Stevenson landed and found his way to the Governor's Palace before 7 o'clock. He was received by His Excellency in his dressing gown, who thus addressed him:—'Well, Don Robarto, you see how it is. You have not been to China. You have been detained off Cape Bajador and obliged to come back again for want of a fair wind.' Mr. Stevenson, having patiently listened to Don Gardoqui's remarks, quietly handed to him the replies to his dispatches. 'Your Excellency,' said he, 'may now form another opinion of Capt. D's proceedings': and, sure enough, when he opened his letters, he found he had received replies in so short a time. Such an event never having occurred to the Spaniards before, he overloaded me with compliments as to the discipline of my ship and my honourable bearing in refusing to smuggle the dollars. 'In short,' said he, 'we have never met anyone like him, and I pray you to offer him the expressions of my highest consideration.'

There was no bound, too, to the greetings I received from my Spanish acquaintances. They were gratified to learn that their dollars had been safely deposited. These compliments over, my first object was to learn whether the Governor intended restoring to me the English seamen remaining here. But as no satisfactory reply came from that quarter, I prepared for my departure. Moreover, there was a letter from the Commodore, Sayer,[1] who had taken the naval command in India in consequence of the Admiral, Burlton's,[2] death, stating that my detention in the China Seas might become the subject of inquiry. Therefore on the morning of the 3rd April I made sail from the Bay of Manilla.* Mr. Stevenson knew no bounds in his expressions for the agreeable trip he had had with me. I received many letters from him afterwards, but the climate did not suit his constitution and he soon became one of its victims, not living another year afterwards.

I now had to return by a very different route from that by which I had come to Luzon. I shaped a course for the island of Pulo Sapatu, off the coast of Cochin China, intending to reach India through the Straits of Malacca. We had light and variable winds and did not make the land till the afternoon of the 12th. The lead was kept going. On the 17th we were near the island of Pulo Aor, and stood towards the Straits of Sincapore.[3] Several men died, and were committed to the deep with the usual ceremonies. On the evening of the 19th we anchored off the coast of Malacca: the next morning, again under sail, but a calm obliged us soon to anchor. A few hours afterwards we were under way, then anchored on the 20th off St. John's Isles. After plenty of this tedious work we reached the roads of Malacca on the 22nd, and found H.M.S. *Orlando*, Capt. Clavell,[4] with an East

---

[1] George Sayer, Lt. 23/8/1790; Cdr. 11/5/96; Capt. 14/2/1801. Succeeded Sir Samuel Hood as S.O., India, 12/1813, remaining so till relieved by Sir George Burlton, 6/15: on the latter's death, 9/15, he acted again till nearly the end of 1816.

[2] Sir George Burlton, K.C.B., Lt. 15/9/1777; Cdr. 5/7/94; Capt. 16/3/95; R-Ad. 4/6/1814.

* I availed myself of my knowledge of the productions of Manilla to lay in a good stock of the Manilla rope, made out of the cocoa nut coverings. It completely surpassed our hempen ones both in strength and durability. I made my reports to the Admiralty, recommending their Lordships to give directions for its being used by our ships of war in India. Their Lordships approved of my suggestions.

[3] See above, p. 347.

[4] John Clavell. His name appeared on the books of various ships from the time he was five until, 11 years later, he went to sea (11/11/1792): Lt. 6/7/97; Cdr. 22/10/1805 (promoted the day after Trafalgar, in which action he served as Collingwood's First Lieut. in the *Royal Sovereign*); Capt. 4/2/08. Originally four above W.H.D. in the Post Captains' List, he was even less lucky than Dillon (see below, p. 497). He missed promotion to Flag rank by one on 23/11/41, remaining Senior Captain in the Navy. But whereas W.H.D. lived to receive his Flag, Clavell did not, dying 11/3/46—eight months too soon.

Indiaman under her convoy, both laden with treasure. In my first intercourse with the Captain of the *Orlando*, I was reproached for having made so bad a bargain with the East India Directors on the subject of the freight. He in plain terms told me that I had sacrificed the interests of the Navy by yielding to their terms. I in reply explained the whole proceedings as they had been proposed to me by their Agent. But the only satisfaction that I could get from him was that my naval friends were highly displeased at the agreement I had made. It now turned out that the monies embarked on board those ships was the amount originally intended by the Admiralty to be placed on board the *Horatio*. I was determined to lay the case before the Admiralty as soon as I could, as, evidently, an advantage had been taken of me.

The town of Malacca belonged to the Dutch, who took it from the Portuguese many years ago. The fort saluted my ship, which compliment was returned. After presenting my respects to the Governor and the authorities, I was entertained by an English merchant who kept up a very hospitable establishment. The *Orlando* parted company with us next day with her convoy bound to China, and I left the bay on the morning of the 25th. Malacca is the principal town of the Malay peninsula, about 600 miles in length. The natives are under the sway of the Dutch who possess all the strong places on the coast, and compel them to trade on their own terms, to the exclusion of all the other nations of Europe. The native Chief is styled King, or Sultan, but his subjects, the Malays, are considered the most restless people on earth. They are noted for their treachery and ferocity. Piracy seems to be their principal occupation. The climate is a fine one: the lands are fertile, abounding with delicious fruits. The city lies on a flat surface close to the sea and very convenient for commercial purposes. The houses are tolerably well built, some of them with large gardens. The streets are broad, but badly paved. The walls and fortifications are carried up to some height, the lower parts washed by the sea. Besides the Dutch and the natives, there are many Chinese, Moors and other Indians inhabiting Malacca.

On quitting Manilla, I had taken charge of several parcels and many letters for Pulo Penang, otherwise called Prince of Wales Island, situated at the other extremity of the Malayan straits. Consequently I felt it my duty to proceed there. As the winds continued light and variable, our progress was very slow. We were visited with storms of thunder and lightning. The ship was several times shaken by those peals, but fortunately no casualties happened.

The passing through those straits is generally marked by some accident, either by thunder or lightning. We anchored two or three times and finally reached Pulo Penang on the afternoon of the 30th. My stock of water required replenishing. As soon as we anchored, we were saluted by Fort Cornwallis with 11 guns, the compliment being returned. Here I was again among my countrymen. The Governor, Mr. Petre, resided at that time upon the topmost pinnacle of the island. Therefore he sent off to me his aid de camp, who invited me in his Excellency's name to dinner at the Government House. I accordingly attended him, after which I was installed in the house allowed to the naval Captains—a most delightful spot. I was in what is called in India a 'Bungalo', suited in every way to the climate and close to the sea. At breakfast next morning, to my extreme surprise, there entered my room a fine old gentleman dressed in black and with powdered hair, who closed upon me with the utmost respect. Then, showing me his card (upon which I noticed 'Sir Edmund Stanley'), 'If I mistake not,' said he, 'your name is Dillon. I know all your family well. I am the Lord Chief Justice of this island, and as my bungalow is close to yours I have brought a palanquin to take you to my quarters, with no fuss or ceremony, there to make my house your home whilst you stay here.' This proposal, the handsome manner in which it was made, and the whole deportment of this accomplished gentleman left me for a moment in a complete dilemma. Recovering myself, however, I expressed my apprehensions of incommoding Sir Edmund. But he would not listen, and, so soon as I had finished my breakfast, I ordered my servants to pack up, and was conveyed to his house, about 100 yards away. Such a reception in a distant climate was without exception one of the most agreeable events of my life. The individual from whom the proposal came gave to the whole proceeding a romantic effect that I shall never forget. Innumerable questions relating to all the Dillons ensued. He had, he said, often heard of me in the Navy, and was delighted at having an opportunity of receiving me under his roof. I had been mixing chiefly with wealthy merchants who, though often persons of superior attainments, generally tended to converse on commercial pursuits, loss and gain, etc. But Sir Edmund's company was another affair. He had mixed in our first circles of society. Stowe and its proprietor were familiar to him, and many other notable places. He would entertain me upon politics, law and literature. He knew India well, acquainting me with many particulars to which I was a perfect stranger. Poetry would flow from his lips in a most agreeable manner. I wrote to the Government Secretary, acquainting him that I had left the bungalow placed at my disposal, that no extra expense might be incurred to the E.I. Company.

After a couple of days with Sir Edmund, I persuaded him to dine on board the *Horatio*, where he enjoyed himself to his heart's content. I now received an invitation from the Governor to pass a few days with him at his residence among the clouds. He sent some horses, that I might bring some of my officers with me. We set off next day under the care of a guide. The ascent was of two hours' duration, but the road not bad, and sheltered all the way by trees which were crowded with monkeys. Their noise and chattering was most extraordinary. Several of them threw branches at me as I passed along. On reaching the Residence, several thousand feet above the level of the sea, I was received in all the etiquette of Indian magnificence. As I had in the course of my travels made the acquaintance of the Governor's married daughter, I was not considered a perfect stranger. The evenings here were so cool that we had fires, drank Port wine and slept under blankets—a luxury indeed in so hot a climate. The second evening we were visited by a storm of thunder and lightning which took effect about one third of the way down the mountain. We, above it all, saw the lightning and heard the thunder, but experienced no annoyance whatever. This was riding over the storm in reality. My three officers were in raptures. These electric and noisy visitations occurred nearly every night, without any alarm to us.

All the invalids of India repair to this island for the benefit of their health. Situated only two miles from the Malay peninsula, this charming spot lies not more than five degrees north of the equator. It is about 7 leagues in length and 3 in breadth, and runs nearly parallel with the main land. In between, a channel is formed where might lie in safety the largest fleet in the world. As the height of the surrounding mountains is a barrier against the prevailing winds, the thermometer is seldom above 80 degrees in the heat of the day. There is a constant ventilation occasioned by perpetual breezes, and the soil is dry. Beautiful mountains covered with evergreens attract the eye. Many rivulets flow from these eminences, their waters noted for transparency and coolness. The gardens are well supplied with vegetables and choice fruits, and most of the plantations of Europe grow here in perfection. Nature has been truly bountiful, the hills ornamented by forest trees of a stupendous height, and the stranger or invalid enraptured by the breezes impregnated with the fragrance of the valleys. There are no tigers or ravenous beasts to be found here, but the domestic ones arrive at the best quality. The crocodiles that float about, however, are of immense size. One that I noticed outside my boat I took to be at least 24 feet long. The sea abounds in fish, the finest turtle and plenty of oysters. The commercial advantage of this island cannot be too much extolled. I passed five days here, and I confess, when taking my leave, that my heart beat, wishing that I could establish myself for the rest of my life in such a romantic locality. However, after presents exchanged with my hosts and under the most friendly feelings, I took my leave, and reoccupied my apartments under the roof of Sir Edmund's bungalow.

After completing the ship's water, I took my departure from Port Cornwallis on the afternoon of the 11th. We had scarcely made sail, however, when a calm obliged the ship to be anchored, to prevent her drifting on the coast. But next day, there being a commanding breeze, the *Horatio* was under way. I boarded a couple of country ships from Bombay bound to China. Having nothing to do with warlike operations beyond the necessary exercise, some of the marines took a fancy to theatricals, and requested my permission to make the attempt. This feeling I encouraged, and lent them my books to assist them. Consequently, a company of about 16 men and two or three boys, both seamen and marines, commenced operations under the Half Deck. Playbills were distributed, and the first performance turned out better than I expected. Others followed, which caused a very agreeable sensation throughout the ship. So soon as we were clear of the Strait of Malacca, a course was shaped for Madras. On the 26th we passed the Nicobar Islands.

On the 6th of June we were nearing the roads of Madras. H.M.S. *Cornwallis* was lying there, and I anchored close to her, the surf of the beach beating and rolling in a most extraordinary manner. The next day I called on the Captain of that ship, King,[1] he being my senior, and we agreed to take our passage to the beach in the same boat. Landing here is no joke. The heavy, swelling breakers extend upwards of $\frac{1}{4}$ mile from the sandy shore. There are native boats in attendance, called Masulo Boats, manned by Indians. Their sides

[1] Certain minor errors appear here. O'Byrne records that Edward Durnford King, a Capt. of 8/1/1801, was appointed to the *Cornwallis* 14/11/14, but resigned the command owing to ill-health in Dec. 1814. The Navy List confirms the date of appointment, but calls the Captain J. D. King—an officer who did not exist. The man who *was* Captain of the ship when W.H.D. was at Madras was Robert O'Brien, a Capt. of 1/5/1804. It seems probable that W.H.D., when he came to write up this part of the Narrative, had forgotten the man's name, and refreshed his memory by looking it up in a Navy List, of a slightly earlier date, which still showed King as being in command.

are about 10 feet high, about 30 in length and square at each end. The rowers are seated on benches fitted close to the gunnel, and, if the men sing in proceeding towards the shore, it is a proof that they apprehend no danger. But when they become silent and pensive they are in expectation of some untoward event. I confess that my first trial was rather a nervous one. However, I soon observed that I stood the test much better than my companion. When the men stop pulling, and place the boat with its broadside towards the raging sea, they wait for its striking against the side. It comes with great violence, some part breaking in and the rest hurling on, almost oversetting you. When that is over, the crew get the boat end on till another rolling wave follows. This operation happens four or five times, when the last surge sends the craft on the beach, where several men are waiting who instantly seize hold of you, and carry you safely beyond the reach of the waves. You seldom get a wetting. These boats are quite hollow, with generally about a foot of water in the bottom, in which there is brushwood where parcels are laid if necessary. The crew are perfectly naked excepting round the waist —and the turban. The boats which attend the ships of war are paid by the E.I. Company, but the Naval Officer always gives a douceur, of the same amount, to the men who land him.

I soon paid my respects to Mr. Elliot, the Civil Governor. As there is a sort of Dockyard here, I found plenty of work for the artificers in setting the *Horatio* to rights. Commissioner Puget[1] had control over the naval department. I took possession of my apartments at the Captains' House. King was a good companion. Our Commander in Chief, Commodore Sayer, was at Trincomalee, to whom I communicated my arrival at Madras, requesting him to let me know my destination.

[W.H.D. now had trouble with his Steward, whom he 'had brought up from boyhood to that responsible position'. He repaid his master's many kindnesses by giving a party to all the servants he could find, 'entertaining them with my choice wines, clarets, etc.' Dillon's Indian servant reported the incident, and the Steward, being sent for, tried to bluster his way out of trouble by asserting 'in the most barefaced, impertinent manner, that every servant drinks his master's wine.' As he remained quite unrepentant, and apparently indifferent to the consequences, W.H.D., who on this occasion showed remarkable moderation, discharged him, still defiant, from the ship.]

[1] Peter Puget, Lt. 15/11/1790; straight to Capt. 29/4/97.

He cared little about that, as he thought, being in India, he would get a good situation. However, in these expectations he met with the keenest disappointment. No English gentleman would engage him, so that in the course of a few days he came to me in a most abject manner, entreating me for a recommendation: which I could not consent to give. However, the Commander of a sloop of war lying in the roads, being in want of a servant, took him. So no more of that chap for the present.

In addition to the *Cornwallis*, 74, the *Iphigenia* frigate, the *Tyne* and the *Cameleon* were lying here, so that there were five of us living at the Captains' House. We had our round of invitations. The Governor, the General, the Naval Commissioner, the Judge, and various gentlemen gave hospitable entertainments, as well the Military Mess at the Mount. There was not much stirring until about 4 o'clock, when all the fashion was out, in all sorts of carriages, to enjoy the fresh air; the ride being constantly from the sands of Madras to the Mount. Horsemen were also in repute. Then, in addition to balls and picnics, there were the jugglers, the palanquins and ships arriving from England with cargoes of beautiful girls to be married,[1] which caused a variety and plenty of chit chat. However, the War being over, no further excitement existed on *that* side of our profession. The 'Tiffing,' or lunch, about 3 pm, was considered the substantial meal of the day, but the 8 o'clock dinner, with the puncas, was more a matter of ceremony than of real enjoyment. It was at a tiffing one day, at Commissioner Puget's office, that the following extraordinary circumstance occurred:—

[The conversation turned on the subject of gratitude, and W.H.D. told the story of the young man, Hood, whom he had bought out of prison at Leith by paying £10 for him (see above, p. 101): 'whom, when I could no longer be of service to him, I turned over to Sir Thomas Hardy.' Having told his tale, W.H.D. stepped out on to the balcony, and was instantly accosted, most respectfully, by an officer who held out his hand and said, 'There, Sir, is the £10, with which I have made my fortune. I am the Purser of that ship' (pointing to her). 'My name is Hood, and I am come with grateful heart to express to you my warmest acknowledgements. . . . I owe all to you.' . . . 'Well then,' said I, 'since the £10 has been of so much use to you, to complete the act you had better keep it'—which, after a little argument he did. But this was not quite the end of Mr. Hood.

[1] Not, happily, an early instance of the White Slave Traffic, but a phenomenon not unknown to Anglo-Indians, right to the end of the British Raj.

On leaving Dillon, he attempted to reach his ship without tendering the customary 'douceur' to the masulo boatmen, who thus took their revenge:—]

When they had shoved off from the beach, they kept the boat in the midst of the surf for a considerable time, with the sea washing over him. The people on the shore crowded to the sands to watch the proceedings, and shouts and huzzas indicated the approbation of the lookers-on. These noises reached our ears in the back apartments of the Commissioner's office, and we hastened to the balcony. I took hold of a spy glass and saw an individual stooping so low that a pool of water had formed in the hollow of his back between the shoulders. He had on a blue coat, which led me to believe that he was a Naval Officer. I therefore requested the Commissioner to send off one of his catamarans to inquire the reason of the boat's being kept in that position, and he instantly complied. When the messenger got alongside of the masulo boat, the crew, hearing from whom he came, instantly plied their oars and proceeded clear of the surging waves to their destination. Upon the catamaran's returning, we were informed that Mr. Hood was the person thus treated, for not having paid the crew the usual allowance. This act did not say much in that gentleman's favour, considering that, a few minutes previously, I had made him a present of £10. I have never seen or heard of him since.

On the 20th the *Cornwallis* and *Iphigenia* left the roads, by which I became Senior Captain. Two days afterwards the *Elk*, sloop of war, arrived with the news that Ad. Sir Richard King[1] was coming to India as Commander in Chief. This sloop had no permanent Commander, and, as my Second Lieutenant, Mr. Dennis,[2] had been brought up under that chief, I thought it would be a good opportunity to place him in the temporary command of the *Elk*. The Admiral might be enabled to do something for his old shipmate. However, my Senior Lieutenant, Mr. Mackenzie,[3] showed a great deal of temper, thinking that he had a right to the appointment. I shall not trouble you with all the details, but my reasons for not placing Mr. M. there were that he was a perfect stranger to Sir Richard King, who could not feel any interest in his behalf.

[1] See above, p. 226.
[2] Properly Lardner Dennys, Lt. 6/2/1812. His—and W.H.D.'s—hopes were not fulfilled. He brought the *Elk* home as Acting Captain, but was not employed again. Greenwich Hospital Pension, 1852; Ret. Cdr. 1853; living 1855. Provides a good illustration of what the Peace meant to the more junior officers.
[3] See above, p. 323.

When Lieut. Dennis had established himself in his command, he found he was short of Mids. There were two or three of mine who had by their misdeeds lost my good opinion, and I offered him a couple of them, and he most willingly accepted. One of them, Vaughan by name, had, when I was on the point of quitting England, literally contrived to talk me over into taking him into my ship. His Irish connections, he repeated, knew mine very well. I declined receiving him unless he could prove that he had an allowance of £50 a year. The next day he produced an Irish Banker's letter, which made it appear that he had an allowance to a greater amount than that. He was accordingly received on board, and I endorsed his draft on the Bankers for £35. Shortly after sending him to the *Elk*, I received letters from England acquainting me that Mr. Vaughan's bill had been protested. Here was a regular take in. I sent for Lieut. Dennis and consulted him. I thought that he had better send the young gentleman back to the *Horatio*. He agreed, but Mr. Vaughan declined returning to the ship, no doubt knowing that he had drawn in England for more money than lay in the Banker's hands. The result was my losing the £35. Many years afterwards, when in Dublin, I called upon these Bankers, but never obtained a farthing from them.

[He now volunteered to give a passage home to Commissioner Puget's family, but soon discovered that he had undertaken rather more than he had bargained for, since . . .]

Mrs. Puget was attached to a maiden lady of a certain age, Miss Jeffreys, and she could not embark without having her as a companion. This, I confess, startled me. However, after a few words of explanation, I placed my Cabin at the Commissioner's disposal. By doing so, I had to receive his wife, two young daughters, the maiden lady mentioned and a certain proportion of servants. I wrote to the Commodore, and requested the Commissioner to do the same, to sanction my receiving his family. In the meantime, he came on board, and gave such directions as he thought necessary in partitioning off apartments for the accommodation of his wife and children. It was at a moment when Capt. Puget called to take me home to dine with him that I discovered the loss of a very handsome gold snuff box, which had been extracted from my writing desk. The act was brought home to my Indian valet. The debash, whom I had engaged to attend my affairs, had provided me with this servant. When I acquainted him with the robbery, he very quietly came upstairs and, after a searching inquiry, assured himself that the Hindoo valet had purloined the missing article. Puget advised me to bring an action against the debash. However, that person gave in. Luckily, I had borrowed £100 of him—a general practice in this country when engaging such men, to guard against acts similar to that which had befallen me. Therefore, as I had that sum in my hand, the debash paid the value of the gold box. It was a very beautiful one, costing near £20. It was intended as a present to my friend General Abercromby.

It so happened that Puget wanted a clerk. This, I thought, was a good opportunity to provide for mine, who had been with me for six years. The Commissioner willingly took him out of acknowledge-ment for my taking home his family. Consequently Harley, such being his name, was discharged from the *Horatio* and established in the Dockyard, with a salary of £300 a year: which finally led to his being the Secretary of the Seamen's Hospital on the Thames.

The *Horatio* left the roads of Madras on the 16th of this month, with the passengers already mentioned. When I left England, I had prepared for a three years' stay in India, but the ship, being on a war establishment, was ordered home. Though disappointed in my expectations, I was not sorry to quit the country, whose climate did not agree with me. The heat of Madras is at times insupportable. The principal town is named St. George, and is fortified. There is a Mayor and Council. The fortified part is principally occupied by the Europeans and is called the White Town: that part inhabited by the natives is styled the Black Town. The principal ride for equestrians in the cool of the evening is to the Mount, about four miles off—or, more properly speaking, Mount St. Thomas, as it is supposed that that saint once visited the locality. There have been found diamonds in the neighbourhood, and, if I mistake not, from this place the celebrated Pitt Diamond came. The purest water is to be found close to the beach by digging to a certain depth. I took care to lay in a good stock of it for my own private use. The rainy season lasts from October to April, when the place is drenched. Then the dry sets in, and, although the town is close to the sea, the breezes do not suffi-ciently cool the air. Madras was taken from us by the French in 1746, but restored to Great Britain at the peace of Aix la Chapelle.

We had delightful weather on our homeward-bound course, but I had become extremely anxious at the fixed position of my baro-meter. It had been struck in moving some of the furniture, and I apprehended that some mishap had befallen it: but more of this by and by. Our theatricals were kept up with good spirit, to the agree-able entertainment of my guests. On the 26th we crossed the Equator into South Latitudes. On the second of August we chased a strange sail which proved to be a schooner. We went on our course very quietly, nothing of consequence occurring. One of the seamen fell overboard, and, though a boat was sent after, the poor fellow sank to Eternity. A strange sail was seen on the afternoon of the 20th. At that moment we were changing the main topsail, which operation was performed in eight minutes. The strange vessel proved to be the *Alpheus*. We exchanged numbers and agreed to keep company. She had been to the Mauritius, Isle of France, to refit, but she was in a very crazy state. When the weather permitted, we visited each other, which caused an agreeable change in the monotony of a sea life. As we were nearing the coast of Africa, the weather began to change, and to my astonishment the barometer began to fall. We had no wind of consequence and all sail was set. However, the third morning after the quicksilver had gradually lowered, the ship was rolling most woefully. Turning out of my cot at daylight, I sent for the officer of the watch, and questioned him upon the state of the weather. He replied that there was hardly a breath of air, but an immense heavy, rolling swell. 'We have all sail set,' said he, 'and not a cloud to be seen.' I told him that the barometer, provided it had not been injured, indicated a storm, and ordered him to begin with the watch on deck and take in the sail as fast as he could. By 9 o'clock it blew a perfect hurricane, and it became very evident that, if I had not reduced the sails, one of the masts—or probably the whole of them—would have been carried away. At that moment all hands were aloft close reefing the topsails and the courses. The storm raged in the greatest fury and the rain came down in perfect torrents. In lowering our top-gallant yards, the wind blew one of them away, so that we were obliged to lower it into the water, whence it was hauled on board. I do not recollect a more violent gale, and the ship was reduced to the storm sails. It raged without remittance till 4 o'clock in the afternoon. As we were now in a different climate, approaching the Cape of Good Hope, we prepared for bad weather.

On the afternoon of the 27th we had a distant view of the African mountains. We were visited with thunder and lightning, the gale again increased, and seas of tremendous height kept us in perpetual motion. I found that Capt. Langford kept under very easy sail, which I attributed to the defective state of his ship's hull. I therefore, availing myself of a change of wind, made more sail and parted company from him. The weather continuing most boisterous, many sails were split, and the yards, booms, etc., all suffered more or less;

but they were repaired as well as our means allowed. At noon on the 2nd September we were only 61 miles from Cape Agulhas.[1] On the 4th the gales were boisterous, but we sounded in 45 fathoms and the land was seen. On the morning of the 6th the weather moderated and I shaped a course for False Cape: by ½ past 8 I was running into Simon's Bay, where I anchored, and found lying there H.M. ships, *Revolutionaire, Spey, Racoon, Zebra, Zephir,* and *Cameleon.* This was a happy relief to our anxiety. Here I found an old friend in the Commissioner—Brenton,[2] who had been with me at Verdun. The next day the *Alpheus* arrived.

Commissioner Brenton very kindly invited my guests to put up at his house, which enabled me to have my ship put to rights. As these ladies were placed under my care, I supplied them with cash, etc., and attended to all their wishes. The ship had not been long at anchor when I was attacked by a violent inflammation in both eyes, the result of a cold caught in the late gales. The Surgeon attended me constantly, and inflicted upon me some painful trials. Both the lower eyelids were scarified, my right temple opened, which only produced temporary relief. As I suffered so much, I applied to the family physician of the Governor, Lord H. Somerset. This gentleman was in the Army, and considered extremely clever. Many surmises were in circulation relating to him; from the awkwardness of his gait and the shape of his person it was the prevailing opinion that he was a female. He was extremely assiduous, but did not approve the remedies resorted to, plainly telling me that a milder treatment would have sufficed. Having written down his instructions, and explained fully the system I was to follow, he took his leave, and only demanded his travelling expenses to the ship and back. It was a long time before I could leave off wearing a green shade over my eyes: in short, my left eye has never recovered its natural strength since the infliction mentioned.

After about three weeks in Simon's Bay, I reshipped my female friends, taking on board some Government stores for Cape Town. On our way round to Table Bay, we had fine views of this coast. The mountain called the Lion's Hump and the Table Mountain were objects of deeply interesting notice. On the evening of the 29th the *Horatio* anchored in Table Bay. Being still a great invalid, I took lodgings in Cape Town, Mrs. Puget and her companions occupying apartments in the same house, and we submitted to the Dutch

---

[1] Spelt throughout 'Lagullus.'

[2] Sir Jahleel: see vol. I, p. 156, note, and above pp. 38 *et seq.*

customs. I soon waited on his Excellency Lord Somerset at Government House and made the acquaintance of his amiable daughter, but I could not accept any dinner invitations. I hired a carriage, and took the ladies up the country to see the celebrated vineyards of Constantia, some productions of which, with other choice wines, the product of the African Continent, I purchased. The scenery was splendidly magnificent during two or three excursions over the mountains.

[A description of Table Mountain and the other hills is omitted, and the use of cloud-formations round it as an indication of coming weather.]

The houses of Cape Town are generally built of stone, but not more than two storeys high, on account of the high winds that prevail. The streets are well placed at right angles. One of my curiosities was to watch the motions of the waggons coming in from the country. The Hottentot driver would have 10 horses to this machine —sometimes 16 or 18, but generally oxen. His whip was so heavy that it required the strength of both arms to wield it. Yet he would manage all with the greatest nicety, an accident seldom if ever occurring. The climate is delightful, and the soil produces abundantly, but not in all parts. There is a wooden pier where the boats can deposit their passengers, as the surf is at times too high to admit their landing on the beach.

[In landing at this pier, Mrs. Puget allowed a very valuable bracelet to fall into the sea, much to W.H.D.'s annoyance. 'Why put it on then?' he asks. 'Who was to notice it I could not make out.' It was not recovered.]

Close to the pier stands the Castle, a strong extensive work with ample accommodation for the troops. The coast is well defended, but all the fortifications have been much improved since the colony has been in our possession. I found the Dutch inhabitants very sociable during my short visit, but, by being an invalid, I lost the opportunity of mixing much in their company. The Cape of Good Hope is a most valuable acquisition to us. A splendid garden attached to the Government House is open to the public. There is also a menagerie which I visited, and saw some enormous ostriches, lions, tigers, etc. There are two good churches. The Calvinists occupy the larger, and the smaller is for the Lutherans.

We quitted Table Bay on the evening of the 8th October. During my stay at the Cape, the subject of Bonaparte's detention at St. Helena was often the theme of conversation, and my being bound there gave rise to many surmises. General Bertrand had married a Dillon, and I had heard that the General had already been making inquiries about me among the naval officers. Nothing of consequence occurred on our way to that island. On the 18th we got a sight of it, and spoke H.M. Brig *Podargus* which was cruising off the place. As we neared, we showed our number to the Signal Station, and by ½ past II am were safely anchored off St. James's Town. The *Phaeton* was lying here, also the *Cameleon*. The Captain of the former, Capt. Stanfell,[1] held all the responsibility during the absence of the Admiral, Sir Pultney Malcolm.[2] He was under apprehensions of my interfering with the Port duties, as being the Senior Officer. However, I soon quietened him on that subject, declaring that I would not meddle with any of the transactions going on.

I soon found my way to the Governor, Sir Hudson Lowe, who requested me to take up my residence at his house—a mark of attention for which I was not prepared. However, I accepted it, and placed the ladies at snug quarters on shore. Here I made the acquaintance of Mr. O'Meara,[3] the Marquis de Montchenu, the French Commissioner, Baron Sturmer the Austrian, and Count Balmain the Russian. Lady Lowe was a very accomplished interesting person, and my pastime was one continued scene of excitement at Plantation House. Some of the foreigners took me for Sir Sidney Smith. That mistake was soon explained, but I found myself most agreeably placed. Col. Read, afterwards Sir Thomas, managed all the affairs in the town, and I had placed at my disposal the horse which had been used by Bonaparte upon his first arrival here. It was at this critical moment that Bonaparte had refused receiving any visitors. His misunderstanding with Sir Hudson Lowe became so well known that I shall enter into no particulars, but merely relate what happened to myself.

Sir Hudson was anxious to break the monotony that the Corsican had imposed upon himself, and thought that my appearance (I being a sort of connection of Madame Bertrand)[4] would be a good opportunity to make the trial. He in consequence proposed to me to visit Longwood, and attempt to obtain an interview with the Hero.

---

[1] Francis Stanfell, Lt. 31/7/1795; Cdr. 4/2/1803; Capt. 19/3/10.
[2] Sir Pulteney Malcolm (G.C.B., G.C.M.G.), Lt. 3/3/1783; Cdr. 3/4/94; Capt. 22/10/94; R-Ad. 4/12/1813; V-Ad. 19/7/21; Ad. 10/1/37. Died, 20/7/38.
[3] The *Bellerophon's* Surgeon. See above, p. 343.
[4] See Vol. I. Introduction, xix.

The next morning at about 11 o'clock I was to ride over and present myself for an interview. At the hour appointed a dragoon was in attendance at Sir Hudson's, from whom I had received my instructions, with a saddle horse. Capt. Stanfell, it seems, was to accompany me. In short, I was to be placed in his leading strings. When this circumstance was communicated to me, I at once frankly declared that I would not submit to such terms. 'What the Devil do I care about seeing Bonaparte?' said I. 'I have seen him often enough in France, and now I go merely for the object of inducing him to continue receiving visitors. Therefore, if you cannot trust me by myself, after all the proofs I have given of attachment to my country, I shall stay where I am. The horses may be removed.' On hearing this declaration, Capt. Stanfell, who was the only officer present, retired.

There was a very thick, heavy, wet fog, and the dragoon, wrapping me up in a cloak, assisted me to mount my charger. I started under his guidance for Bonaparte's habitation, where in due time we arrived, the fog still as thick as it could be. We first went to Gen. Bertrand's cottage—Hut's Gate, close to Longwood—but, as he was out, Madame B. did the honours. She was a fine person, possessing all the accomplishments of a well-brought-up lady. There was a fire in the room, at which I was very glad to warm myself. I had a long conversation with her previous to the General's appearance. He had been in attendance upon the Emperor, he said. When he heard the object of my visit, he plainly told me that His Imperial Majesty was not well, and could not that day receive visitors. Therefore all my expectations of seeing the great man vanished.

The conversation now turned to other matters, during which the General and Madame made many inquiries about Lord Dillon, Ditchley, etc., and their children were brought in and introduced to me. Madame B. wrote a letter to her mother which I promised to take care of, and, after passing a couple of hours with these interesting people, I retired. Madame B., hearing that I had lady passengers with me, with children, ordered her servant to pack up several parcels of bonbons for them.

On my quitting the premises the fog had cleared away. I therefore told my groom that I did not require his assistance any longer, requesting him to put me on the right path. My guide did so, and I gradually descended from the high grounds, keeping the thorny hedge[1] close on my right. I had not gone far when suddenly, at a small opening in the hedge,[1] appeared Mr. O'Meara. He accosted me

[1] 'Edge' in MS.

in the most friendly terms, and inquired if I had seen Bonaparte. I replied that I had not, upon which he offered, if I would come inside of the grounds, to afford me at least an hour's conversation with him. This I declined. 'It will never be known,' he said, 'unless you proclaim it.' 'That is of little consequence to me,' I rejoined. 'I certainly should like to have a few moments' conversation with the Hero, who has been the cause of so much personal injury to me. I am one of his victims: I lost my promotion and a good deal more through his ordering my detention with a Flag of Truce. And not only that, but he would not allow me to quit France when a French officer of superior rank to mine was sent over from England in exchange for me. It is impossible to calculate the mischief he has done me.' O'Meara listened to all I said, and again urged me to place myself under his guidance, to be presented to the Emperor. But to all this gentleman's proposals I turned a deaf ear, telling him that, as I could not see him in the way originally intended, I would not see him at all. I then put the spur to my steed and hastened down the hill. When I arrived in the town I met Col. Read, who invited me to dine. The select party present all thought that I had had an interview with Bonaparte. But I plainly told them all that had passed, and that I had not been admitted to his presence. We had a very friendly dinner, and I retired a full hour after all the passes of the garrison were closed, and took my boat to the *Horatio*.

The next morning, the 23rd, my ship was under sail, bound to England. I determined to try the experiment of sailing on the Meridian, instead of the Circle, and the result will be noticed. The *Alpheus* had been at St. Helena, and had left shortly before my arrival. On the 27th we made the island of Ascension. By the afternoon we had exchanged numbers with H.M. Sloop *Racoon* and anchored about one mile from the fort. As I had not been here before, I landed to examine the place we had taken possession of, and Capt. Rich[1] of the *Racoon* favoured me with his company. I supplied the garrison with bread and water, and at noon of the 28th quitted the island so celebrated for turtle. We had not long been the occupiers,[2] and the turtle continued to land in the uninhabited bays to deposit their eggs. This barren island, of considerable height, is healthy, and the garrison was occupied in gardening. It lies in latitude 7 South, about 17 degrees west longitude, and was originally discovered by the

[1] George Frederick Rich, Lt. 30/12/1805; Cdr. 26/10/13; Capt. 1/7/23. It was he who had established the new settlement on Ascension.

[2] Since 1815, when we occupied it as a safeguard against possible attempts to free Napoleon from St. Helena.

Portuguese. The high rising ground is called the Green Mountain, whence there is a small spring of water. Otherwise it is all lava, and must have proceeded from some volcano. Capt. Rich was particularly inquisitive relating to my interview with Bonaparte. I merely mentioned that I not had seen him. He stated that some of Capt. Langford's guests in the *Alpheus* had contrived, with Mr. O'Meara's assistance, to be admitted to his presence and have a long conversation with him. They were so highly pleased that they could speak of nothing else whilst they remained at the island. My feelings on that subject were of a very different nature. Capt. Rich appeared to be of the same opinion as myself in adopting the meridianal course. It was worth a trial therefore. On our departure a northerly course was shaped. On the 31st we crossed the Equator into the Northern Latitude.

We now had cloudy weather with rain. On the 4th November, we chased and boarded a French merchant brig from Marseilles: on the 10th we passed the island of Brava at no great distance, but without seeing it owing to the haze. So far all had gone well in my experimental course. We proceeded in good order. One or two vessels were boarded, but no news of consequence obtained. On the afternoon of the 26th we saw the island of St. Mary's, one of the Azores, or Western Islands, distant about 12 leagues, and next day I anchored in the roads of Ponta del Goda, Island of St. Michael's. It is not usual for ships from India to stop here, but I did so as a novel case. I landed the ladies and paid a visit to our Consul, the Portuguese Governor, etc. As the cow which I had brought with me from Madras had become dry and no longer of use, I made a present of it to the Consul, who handsomely in return sent me a small cask of St. Michael's wine. I received some bullocks, took in a few casks of fresh water, and on the afternoon of the 28th the ship was at sea, for Old England. There are here seven islands. The one I visited is very mountainous, and has the remains of some large craters worth the traveller's notice. They are all volcanic. I had as yet no cause to regret the course I had adopted in traversing the ocean.

On the 3rd and 4th of December we were assailed by a violent gale, which brought on heavy rolling seas. The head rails were washed away, and one tremendous wave struck us on the stern, stove in the windows, and frightened my female passengers woefully. They received a regular wetting. However, no accident of consequence occurred, and all was set to rights in due time. My eyes were very troublesome. On the evening of the 5th we struck soundings in 90 fathoms. As the weather continued windy and hazy, we did not make the islands of Scilly, but at 3 o'clock on the morning of the 7th the Gasket lights were seen ahead, by which we shaped our course so that, by daylight, the west of the island of Alderney was seen. We then shaped course for the Needles, which we entered in the afternoon, and by 5 o'clock the ship was safely anchored at Spithead. The *Alpheus* was lying here, and the *Akbar*. I had been only 40 days from Ascension, so that my trial upon the Meridian answered well. The *Alpheus*, which had left that island eight days before us, had only arrived at Spithead two days previously. She had sailed on the Circle; therefore I had the advantage, for I touched at St. Michael's where I remained 24 hours, thereby gaining six days upon that ship. Besides, I had taken in water, and anchored at Spithead with fresh beef on board. No ship from India had ever done so before.

Whilst the ladies were packing up their trunks ready to land. I thought I perceived some articles liable to seizure. This was only a surmise. However, as a Naval Officer whose duty it was to protect the revenue of the country, I could not be passive. I therefore pointed out to my fair friends the extreme impropriety of taking anything in my boat which might be detained by the Custom House officers. I explained to them, with pointed energy, my being no favourite with the authorities at Portsmouth: that they would be too happy to catch me tripping in any part of my professional calling: that unfortunately I had had several misunderstandings with them, and that I had on every occasion got the better of them all—the Customs, the Victualling Office, the Magistrates and others. They would delight in having the opportunity of exposing me. 'I entreat you,' I frequently repeated, 'not to take any article in my boat that has been manufactured in India.' They declared, over and over again, upon their honours, that I need not give myself the least concern upon the subject, as they had put up in the trunks no seizable article. Upon this assurance we left the ship. When we arrived at the Sally Port, there were two Customs House officers in attendance. They inquired if I were not Capt. D. of the *Horatio*. I replied in the affirmative. 'We perceive,' they said, 'that you have a great deal of luggage in your boat.' 'Yes,' said I, 'they belong to these ladies.' 'They cannot be moved unless you will pledge your honour that there is no contraband article in them,' was their reply. The ladies heard this. 'Very well,' I replied, 'I give you my honour there is nothing seizable here. The trunks only contain the ladies' soiled linen.' Upon this statement I left my boat, giving my arm to my fair companions, and we were allowed to pass freely. Near the house of the Admiral, Sir Edward Thornborough, who was an old friend, I directed the ladies to the George Hotel, whilst I went to deliver to him my despatches, etc. He was at dinner, but received me with open arms, insisting upon my sitting down and taking something. Of course I could not refuse a glass of wine. After having been with him half an hour, and satisfying him with all he wanted to know, I retired, and went over to the hotel.

There I saw a large crowd, portending that something had happened. Then I beheld Mrs. Puget, attended by the landlady of the house, surrounded by several Custom House men and two officers from that place directing their proceedings. They had opened the ladies' trunks, and found a large quantity of Indian articles, which were seized. Here was a regular mess. Mrs. P., a fine, handsome woman and of a good figure, was most sadly cast down, her hair hanging over her shoulders. When she saw me, she beckoned, requesting my assistance. But the officers told her I could be of no use to her. All the detainable articles were removed to the Custom House, and Mrs. P. made an arrangement with the landlady that she was to rebid for and repurchase them when they would be put up for sale. This was without exception one of the most unpleasant occurrences I had ever encountered. When Mrs. P. rejoined me upstairs, I could not help pointing out the responsibility that would be attached to me. Having taken tea, we retired to bed.

The next morning, coming down stairs, I saw the Custom House officers examining some articles landed from the *Horatio*. So soon as he noticed me, the senior of them addressed me in a loud voice, stating that he should report me to the Treasury. 'You are at liberty,' I replied, 'to do as you please. But as yet you have not examined any of my property.' When he perceived the off-hand way in which I treated him, he became silent, and I heard no more of him. Whilst I was at breakfast, however, my bedroom was searched, all the drawers opened, the clothes inside turned topsy turvy, my bed thrown upon the floor. The same was done to all the apartments occupied by my officers, proving that no mercy would be shown to me or mine. However, no further annoyance was inflicted upon me, nor did the official make any report to the Treasury.

To complete the tale, an old friend, a Naval Officer, told me that the Custom House officers had assailed Capt. Langford of the *Alpheus*, from whom they had made some seizures. And he had given them to understand that they would not find anything on board of his ship, but there would be abundance on board of the *Horatio*, as that ship had visited China. This was a most unpardonable proceeding of that officer's, especially as, whilst we were in company at sea, I had made him several trifling presents for his children. It was this statement of his that occasioned the strictness of the search visited upon every parcel that came from my ship. Besides, the Custom Officers sent off to the *Horatio* had orders of the most stringent kind regulating their duties while on board. This was not the kindest return from a friend.

An old friend living in the neighbourhood, Capt. Dashwood,[1] called, with his wife, to offer me the use of their house during my stay at Portsmouth. This was certainly an act of friendship, and most acceptable. The Admiral's Captain, Bourchier,[2] who had instructed me to purchase him a set of china (to which I have already alluded), insisted upon my taking dinner with them, instead of going off to my ship after my attendances in the Dockyard, etc. These proposals were very suitable to me at this season of the year, as I had only a five minutes' row on a cold day instead of nearly an hour's off to Spithead. At one of these dinners, I called upon Capt. B. to hand me £300 for the set of china which I had purchased according to order. My friend was evidently disconcerted at this remark. He tried to make it appear that I had misunderstood him, whilst I proved that he had directed me to purchase the 'Maker' china. After some discussion, wherein I got the best of the argument, I told him he might consider himself a lucky fellow, as I had not been able to discover any china of that name. This information caused a very agreeable change in the Captain's temper. He now asked if I had procured any chinaware for my own use. I told him that I had, not only for myself, but for some of my friends. 'Then,' said he, 'are you inclined to part with any of it?' I replied that the china in use for my table was at his disposal, but the more select, which I kept in reserve, was not come-at-able. Consequently, upon his first visit to the *Horatio* my steward received orders to hand over to Capt. B. all the loose china that could be spared without depriving me of a bare sufficiency for daily use. Besides this donation I added some other articles of curiosity, to be placed in a museum which he was occupied in collecting. Knowing that my ship was to be paid off, I gave away a great many articles, little thinking I should want them again.

---

[1] (Sir) Charles Dashwood (K.C.B.), B. 1765: as Mid., aide-de-camp to Ad. Rodney at the Saints (12/4/1782): Lt. 20/6/94; Cdr. 3/8/99; Capt. 2/11/1801; R-Ad. 22/7/30; V-Ad. 23/11/41. The great bulk of the Narrative was written at Dashwood's house in Havant.

[2] Henry Bourchier, Lt. 1/5/1804; Cdr. 20/4/08; Capt. 22/8/11.

My friend the Admiral and the Commissioner of the Dockyard[1] were both extremely courteous. There were ladies in both families, and some china relics, which I left at their disposal, were much appreciated. I had a large supply of wine, which I was anxious to deposit in safety. Sir Edward Thornborough requested half a pipe of Madeira, Sir Thomas Lavie[2] another: Mrs. Puget requested a whole pipe, by which means I was eased of nearly half my stock. But when our connection and friend, Major Robert Dillon of the 32nd, which regiment was quartered here, heard that my wine was for sale, he applied for all the port wine, which I was but too glad to spare him, and his messmates (he told me) to obtain. It was a choice wine, and, my health was toasted many a day in the 32nd.

Mrs. Puget requested me to invite the ship's officers to accept a parting dinner. I did the honours for her. During the evening she never ceased repeating her most grateful thanks for all the acts of kindness she had experienced on board. The next affair was to square accounts with me. I had placed my purse at her disposal at the Cape of Good Hope, and even in England had handed to her my last pound—altogether nearly £200. Knowing that her husband was in easy circumstances, I naturally expected that she would give me a check upon his Banker. But I was sorely disappointed: she handed me two bills on the Navy Office of £90 each, at a three months' date. I had therefore to wait all that time for my cash. This act I thought so ill judged that I could not help mentioning that she had received all my ready money, and, for repayment, I had to wait the time mentioned. She coolly replied that she was acting according to her husband's instructions. I must in conclusion add a few more words relating to this lady. When her husband the Commissioner heard at Madras that I had offered her my Cabin, for several days he continued to bestow upon me the warmest acknowledgements. He had, he said, powerful friends in Parliament. 'When you reach England they shall call upon you, as I am anxious to prove how sensible I am of your kindness in my behalf. I consider you now as a friend of the family, and we shall notice you accordingly.' All these sayings appeared to come from the heart: but I had asked nothing—only regulated my conduct by what I thought due to an individual in his official station. You will hear how all these fine promises terminated. She gave me the Banker's address at parting.

I now received orders from the Admiralty to proceed to Deptford to be paid off. I saw no hope of any further employment, and was

---

[1] Still Sir George Grey.   [2] See above, p. 52.

therefore deeply meditating my arrangements for the future. During my absence the Admiralty had ordered an extension of pensions to wounded officers. The Surgeon of the *Childers* wrote to tell me that my wounds would entitle me to one, and urged me to apply. At that period, in fact, I suffered most intense pain. I had nearly entirely lost the use of my left leg, being a perfect cripple, though I contrived to attend to all my professional duties. My friend Capt. Dashwood made me promise to pass some time with him when my ship was paid off.

I left Spithead on the afternoon of the 13th, under the surveillance of two Custom House officers. Next morning I was off Dover, and made the signal for a Pilot. One was sent, and away we went through the Downs. The Pilot was a character. In the afternoon we got into what is called the Queen's Channel, and were obliged to anchor. The appearances of the weather were not of the most favourable, and my friend the Barometer indicated a gale. About 9 o'clock in the evening, finding the winds increasing, I sent for the Pilot and questioned him on the weather for the night. He said that there would not be much wind, and gave himself some very consequential airs, saying he was the Pilot: he would take care of us, and be answerable for all consequences. 'I suppose,' said I, 'that you will obey my orders?' He stared, not being, it would seem, prepared for such a question. 'I am going,' said I, 'to order the top gallant masts to be struck, as we shall have some bad weather tonight.' When he persisted in his opinion, I told him that the barometer, which had never failed, indicated a storm. To all this he turned a deaf ear. 'Well,' said I, 'as Captain of this ship I shall in this instance order the masts to be struck, and you may withdraw.' I then, according to custom, offered him a glass of grog. 'No, I thank you, Sir,' he replied, 'I don't drink grog, but claret.' 'There is no claret open,' I rejoined, 'and I shall not send for any on this occasion.' Upon this the Pilot left the Cabin.

I sent for the Senior Lieutenant, telling him that we should be assailed by strong gales, and to prepare accordingly. I had not been long in my cot when the gale came, and I ordered the topmast to be struck. We were close to the Margate sands. The Pilot, very much annoyed at this, came into my Cabin to tender his opinion. But I would have nothing to do with him. The gale increased to extreme violence. The Pilot was bewildered, and seemed perfectly lost. More cable was veered and another anchor let down. The rain poured in torrents and all hands got thoroughly soaked. The middle watch from 12 to 4 was one of intense anxiety. Fortunately the tide set to windward, which eased the strain upon the cables, but sent a turbu-

lent sea breaking over the ship to our annoyance. Had it been a lee
one, our position was not the most enviable. After 5 o'clock the wind
began to moderate—a great relief to my anxiety. The Pilot had so
completely committed himself that the officers no longer attended
to him.

This Hero had been the Master of a Dover Packet, and, not long
before, had given a passage to Lord Dillon. His Lordship had had
some unpleasant words with one of the passengers which nearly
ended in a duel, the Master being called upon to be the Lord's
second. When he heard my name, he naturally supposed that we
were connected, and told this adventure to the officers, with many
additions. With daylight the weather continued to moderate, and
one of the anchors was hove up. It was a Sunday. In the afternoon
the topmasts were fidded, and I went to dinner with my officers.
Having the shade over my eyes, I could not see well, and as the day
was dark, the Gun Room had a very sombre appearance. During our
repast I could not help expressing my displeasure at the Pilot's
conduct. 'He is not fit,' I said, 'to take charge of a ship of war. He
is a d——n fool. Moreover, he couldn't drink a glass of grog. Nothing
would suit him but claret. But I had none up to give him.' These
words had scarcely escaped my lips when I heard the motion of a
chair trailing away from the table, and the person who occupied it
instantly left the Gun Room. 'Who's that?' I asked. 'It's the Pilot
Sir.' 'Very well,' said I. 'He has got what he deserves.'

[Several of the officers now made speeches—reported verbatim
and at length—praising W.H.D. to the skies, as a man and a Captain..
These are omitted: but see above, p. 347.]

. . . As I was not prepared for all these compliments, they were
the more acceptable, and I had reason to believe, from the manner
in which they were delivered, that they were sincere.

The next morning—the 16th—we were under way for the Thames,
and next morning anchored off Gravesend. Next day, in going up the
river, the ship took the ground for a short while on the mud, but we
soon got her off. On the 18th we came to an anchor at Greenhithe,
getting rid of our guns and powder. On the afternoon of the 21st, we
were lashed alongside of the *Abundance*, storeship, lying off Deptford.
Now commenced unbending sails, stripping ship and clearing holds
—all this to be done at Christmas. That day I spent at Lewisham
with my friend Capt. New[1] and family. My Coxswain, Herdsman,

[1] Thomas New, Lt. 9/6/1794; Cdr. 10/8/1801; Capt. 27/2/12.

an old shipmate, was drowned, I suspect from drunkenness. I took lodgings at Deptford, and you will recollect the letters that passed between us. Several pieces of my plate were stolen from my lodgings, but, being an invalid, I could not take any decided measures. My loss was somewhere about £40. All my furniture, crockery, cooking utensils, etc., were put up for sale, and at last I got £8 for what cost me upwards of £100. Next I arranged with the Custom House officers to take all my India and China articles safe to London for £40. By that means I saved a vast deal of trouble.

On the 9th of January (1817) the ship was clear, and the next day —a winter's one—the crew were all landed at Deptford Dock Yard to receive their pay. As I passed by them, to my utter astonishment they gave me three cheers. Then many of them surrounded me, requesting the honour to shake me by the hand. I did so to many. They were not sparing in their praises of the seamanlike manner in which the ship had been handled. 'We have seen some hard service,' they said, 'but you, Capt. D., guided us safely through all dangers. God bless you, Sir.' These words were repeated rather too often, I thought.

By the afternoon of the 10th the *Horatio* was paid off and out of commission. I held the command of that fine frigate nearly three years, going in her over three parts of the globe. My officers took a most affectionate leave of me, and I became a private gentleman.

XV
VOYAGE TO INDIA

JANUARY 10, 1817–OCTOBER 29, 1819
(*aet.* 37½–39)

INTRODUCTION

THIS was an unexpected command, and W.H.D. was certainly lucky to obtain it. He was financially lucky, too, with his Freight, and lucky with his weather, which enabled him to make a very fast trip to India and back. But, according to himself, all this good fortune was more than cancelled by the incident of the Bandsmen and his consequent loss of the command.

This is the only time in his career in which he seriously 'incurs Their Lordships' displeasure', and it is a curious story. All consideration of it should, perhaps, be prefaced by noting one stark fact, to which he himself never alludes—that is, the desperate competition among his contemporaries for a command of any kind. Under such circumstances, with Their Lordships' desks littered with lists of deserving officers awaiting appointments, it clearly behoved any officer who *had* an appointment to be more than ordinarily careful: for did he but make the smallest slip, it would be only human for the Admiralty to seize upon it as a pretext for working one more name off its swollen lists. Modern officers, competing for promotion through inconveniently narrow bottlenecks, will be well aware of the essential similarity between their position and that of Dillon, though the one concerns promotion and the other appointment. It may well have been just as simple as that. W.H.D. 'blotted his copybook': whether the whole inkpot was spilt or whether the blemish was microscopic probably mattered very little in 1819.

But of what size was the blot? Or was there—as W.H.D. so loudly claims—no blot at all? He certainly does not help us to decide. His persistent adherence to his story that he knew nothing of the matter from first to last has had the unfortunate effect of preventing *us* from knowing. To the end we remain in ignorance of many things, including what Lieut. Geary was really up to, and what he hoped to gain from receiving the deserters. His reference to the Deputy Judge Advocate suggested to the Editor the idea of consulting that officer's successor of today, Capt. A. P. Atwill, C.B.E., R.N. To him, therefore, he submitted the whole of that part of the Narrative which deals with the affair, *and nothing further*. This was, perhaps, rather more than fair to W.H.D., for the Deputy Judge Advocate of the Fleet was thus able to read nothing but the 'defence' side of the case: nor was he otherwise acquainted with Dillon's general character, even to the extent that the Editor is. He most kindly read it all with the utmost care and, with even greater kindness, went to the trouble of writing a full report on it. His findings were most instructive and, very slightly abbreviated, are printed as an Appendix at the end of this Part.

There is but little to add. The ordinary layman's view will surely be much the same. He will probably have two comments to make:—

1. 'Qui s'excuse s'accuse'. He protests too much!

2. His chosen line of defence was not only dangerous, but highly unimaginative. 'I know nothing whatever of all these irregularities which were going on in my ship.' Sooner or later he was bound, surely, to receive the answer for which he was so baldly asking—that, as Captain of the ship, he *ought* to have known. And ultimately he received it, from his tearful friend the Admiral—'*Were you not Captain of the ship?*' (p. 471). To the last W.H.D. stubbornly pretends not to understand the purport of these words. Yet they probably touch the heart of Their Lordships' views. He had fairly forced them to a dilemma, either of whose horns was fatal to him—'Either he knows more than he cares to own to, or, as Captain, he *ought* to.'

The record, as it survives, of Lieut. John Geary, so emphatically cast by W.H.D. as the villain of the piece, is very far from bad. He came of a good naval family, being connected not only with the Admiral Francis Geary of American War days, but also with Sir Cloudesley Shovel. He was born in 1787, entered the Navy in 1797, and saw a great deal of service. He was present, and wounded, at Trafalgar, and in 1806 was in two severe actions, in both of which he was wounded again. He was promoted Lieutenant, May 29, 1807. Then after much more hard service in which he figured, among other appointments, as senior Lieutenant of the *Neptune*, 98, his leg was badly mauled in a gunboat action on the Elbe (July, 1813).

After being dismissed his ship in 1819, he was not employed again—by the Admiralty—till 1828. But this was not bad—he might well consider it good—in that age of 'block': W.H.D. himself had to wait nearly twice as long. Once he secured re-employment, he did very well indeed as First of the *Madagascar*, being for a time its Acting Captain, and most gallantly rescuing a large number of troops wrecked in a transport off Sicily. For these services he was promoted Commander, 17/2/1831 After that he had no more R.N. appointments: but this did not prevent him from taking the command of several East Indiamen and private steamers. On 24/11/49 he was appointed a Commander of Greenwich Hospital, no mean honour in his day. His whole record seems to show a tough, industrious and enterprising man, and certainly not lacking in courage and initiative— incidentally, during his career he saved three lives by jumping overboard.

A charitable guess—though a guess it must remain—would be to suppose that his four separate wounds had upset the balance of his character and stability, rather more so, perhaps, than his biographers knew or cared to admit; and that they may have had something to do with his 'bandsmen' activities: which, even if we do not believe W.H.D. implicitly, still (to say the least) stand in need of explanation.

W.H.D.'s account (p. 462) of how he introduced 'the blue cap with a gold band' to the Prince Regent, who as a result ordered it to be worn in his yacht, has considerable importance in the story of naval uniform. If he is right—and we can have no reason to doubt him—this was by far the most enduring contribution that he ever made to the Navy. For that cap is, in essence, the ancestor of all subsequent naval officers' caps, including the present one. It was officially adopted only in a Memorandum of the 8th September, 1841, and even then for undress wear on shipboard only. But it was certainly extensively used, in practice, well before that. The Regulations of the 20th June, 1833, which, perhaps more than any other one set, are landmarks on the road to modern uniforms, do not mention it, but ordain one form of headgear only—the cocked hat—for 'dress' or 'undress', afloat or ashore alike. Yet L. Mansion's almost 'fashion-plate' lithographs of uniforms, published soon afterwards (c. 1835), show an Admiral, a Captain and a Commander, all in 'undress', and all wearing the 'blue cap with a gold band'.

This is just how such uniform evolutions invariably came about. Somebody invented them originally, out of his own head, for unofficial wear in his own ship. The idea 'caught on', and finally, when the moment came, the Admiralty confirmed the fait accompli. Common sense played a conspicuous part. A cocked hat for day-to-day wear at sea—whatever the regulations might or might not ordain—was clearly unsuitable, and experience had long since discovered the fact. There can be no doubt, therefore, that officers afloat had been wearing various forms of round hats of a much more sensible design for a long time. These, being quite outside Uniform Regulations, would naturally vary from ship to ship at the entire whim and discretion of the Captain. It is obvious, then, that *someone* must have been the first to hit upon the particular form which was destined to become, first the 'prevailing fashion', and then, when backed by Authority, the 'uniform'. W.H.D. claims that he was this 'someone', and we have no evidence to the contrary.

XV

VOYAGE TO INDIA

JANUARY 10, 1817–OCTOBER 29, 1819

(*aet.* 37½–39)

(1) UNEMPLOYED (London and the Continent)

JANUARY 10, 1817–APRIL 14, 1818

[*Summary in square brackets.*]

[HE took rooms at the Spring Gardens Hotel, but, finding it 'the dearest hotel in London,' he soon 'moved into a boarding house.' He now, through his friend Sir George Hope, the Senior Naval Lord, tried again for his pension. He was examined before a Board, but it reported that 'Capt. D. has been seriously injured in his left leg, but the wound is not equal to the loss of an eye or a limb.' He protested, talking rather grandly of his influential friends, but was informed that, if he insisted upon some recompense, he would be given a civil appointment. But that he refused. He also made an attempt to mobilise his 'interest' in order to obtain the C.B.]

During my absence from England, the Order of the Bath had been enlarged, and divided into three distinctions, the Grand Cross being the first, the Knight Commander the second, and the Companion the third. All my letters were addressed to me as a C.B. It was therefore the feeling of my profession that I was entitled to the third order. When I mentioned this to Sir George Hope, he very kindly recommended me to bring my case before the First Sea Lord. He plainly told me that the distribution had given great disatisfaction in the Navy, and that he had not had much to do with it. . . . The next move was to try the First Lord's feelings on the subject of the C.B. His Lordship explained that it lay principally with the Prince Regent. To his observations I stated that the Duke of York was my friend, and, through H.R.H.'s interference, I made no doubt that the honour would be conferred. His Lordship was not prepared for that assertion, and I plainly saw that he did not approve of it. I consequently did not think it prudent to take any steps with H.R.H. In fact, I heard so much dissatisfaction in all quarters relating to the ill-judged award of the Order that I thought my best plan would be to remain quiet; and I gave up all hope on the subject for the present.

[He now reopened the subject of his freight-money, spurred on, he says, by the adverse criticisms of his naval colleagues. But he had no success whatever. He was again sent by Sir George Hope to the First Lord, and by him to the Secretary of the East India Company. The latter received him with a lack of sympathy amounting to downright rudeness; whereupon W.H.D. bridled, and retired, giving up all hope of success.

He also suffered several more blows to his amour propre—and his pocket. The first came from Commodore and Mrs. Puget. The latter failed even to write and thank him for his many services to her. The former failed entirely to implement his promise of getting his influential friends to call upon W.H.D. Further, though the Admiralty paid him the expenses which he had incurred in connection with Mrs. Puget and her children, it turned out that her companion, Miss Jefferys, was not eligible to be transported at Government expense, and W.H.D. found himself obliged to defray her expenses out of his own pocket. Then he called on the French Ambassador, the Marquis D'Aumont, armed with an introduction from the Duchess of Orleans, and was almost snubbed in the entrance hall of the Embassy. Finally, trying to secure the notice of yet another Prince of the Blood—the most worthwhile, from his point of view, of them all—he had no better luck.]

An influential friend who had seen all my Chinese paintings, advised me to send the designation of some beautiful lamps of that country to the Prince Regent. H.R.H., he said, was fond of such things. 'He may be pleased with your attention, and it may bring you under his notice. I followed his advice. I saw Sir B . . . Bl . . .d,[1] and requested him to deliver the lamps to the Prince. He promised to do so; but I never heard another word on the subject. As a naval friend of mine had recently sent a present to H.R.H. who, when he received it, sent him an order to wear his button, entitling him to the entrée of the palace, why the same favour was not bestowed upon me

[1] Sir Benjamin Bloomfield, Chief Equerry and (in 1817) Private Secretary to the Prince Regent.

I never knew. This proves that, in all these transactions, there is some tact of which I was in ignorance.*

[But he had two consolations. He called, of course, upon the Duke of Sussex, who not only received him with great kindness but also forwarded him, with an introduction, to the Duke of Clarence. The Sailor Prince, like his brother of Sussex, seems to have taken a real fancy to W.H.D.]

I very soon obtained an audience of Prince William Henry, who, when he heard all I had to say, and noticing my lameness, took a very decided part in my favour. He assured me that he would not lose sight of me, and at parting stated that, whenever I wished to see him, I should call at half past ten in the morning. . . . As I was limping along a few days afterwards and passing by St. James's Palace, I felt a sharp rap on the right shoulder, and, turning round to see who had accosted me, to my utter surprise I beheld the Duke of Clarence. His R.H. would not allow me to take off my hat to him, but addressed me as nearly as I can recall as follows. 'D., I have been to Lord Melville about you and have explained all your case to him. He has promised me to give you the command of a ship.' I returned my warmest acknowledgments for his kind advocation of my cause, but, pointing to my lame leg, said, 'How can I, Sir, take command of a ship in this crippled state?' 'Recollect what I have said,' rejoined the Prince. 'You are to have a ship.' He then gave me a hearty shake by the hand, and left me. H.R.H.'s proceeding in my behalf was highly gratifying, and led me to reckon on the Prince's support when required.

[His other success was particularly gratifying to a man of his make-up. He was informed by Sir George Hope that he had been elected a member of the most exclusive Naval Club, 'which is held at the Thatched House, St. James's'. He instantly attended a dinner there, and, though the only Captain there, was (he declares) made much of by every one of the distinguished Flag Officers present. He reports the evening's entertainment at ecstatic length, closing with the words:—'However, there is a term to all the good things of this sublunary planet. The hour of parting had arrived, and Sir George [Hope] most kindly gave me a lift in his carriage.'

Late in February he left Town, and went to stay with his friend Capt. Dashwood at Havant, but soon left to visit his old Captain

* (In a much later hand) My being a friend of the Duke of Sussex was the reason, I was confidentially informed some time afterwards.

of the *Africaine*, Manby,[1] in Norfolk. Thence he proceeded to Chel-tenham for a cure, sharing lodgings with Capt. Duncan.[2] But, deriving little benefit from Cheltenham, he decided to go to the Continent. On his way thither through Town, he reached, all unknowing, a landmark in his career:—]

Just previous to leaving Town, I received an invitation to dine with the Duke of Sussex. H.R.H. literally—if I may use the expres-sion—overloaded me with kindness, the result of which was the Duke nominating me as one of his Equerries. That was an honour I was not prepared for, but it was bestowed with so much good will and cordiality that I could not help feeling the compliment. H.R.H. did not require my immediate presence, and approved of my accept-ing the Duchess of Orlean's invitation to repair to Paris. Having therefore settled these matters, I repaired to Ostend.

[Here he spent two months with his old Verdun friend, Mr. Sevright, proceeding thence, in July, to Paris, where he was welcomed with open arms by the Duchess of Orleans, and lived for several months in high style, meeting all the élite of the Restored Court, including the King, his brother and nephews.]

I thought it proper to present myself at the Court of Louis XVIII: more especially as he had resided six weeks at Ditchley under Lord Dillon's hospitality, and there was a chance, when he heard my name, of his noticing me. I attended at the Tuilleries on the day fixed. We were drawn up in a circle in the Hall of Reception, and the King took his place in the centre, having every individual presented to him separately. Sir Charles Stuart mentioned my name in so low a tone that I much doubt whether His Majesty heard it. He merely made his bow and passed on. The King was very corpulent, and bore an unwieldy appearance. His legs were enveloped in black leather gaiters, buckled up from the ankle to the knee. Altogether there was not much dignity, compared with what is generally expected in the presence of Royalty. I heard the vulgar French pass many jokes— 'Louis Double-neuf', as they called him. We were next taken to the Saloon of the Count D'Artois, styled 'Monsieur, the First Gentleman of France'. I had no reason to be satisfied with that Prince's notice of me. As he had long resided in England, I naturally supposed the naval uniform of that country would be familiar to him, and was

---

[1] See Vol. I, pp. 445 *et seq.*, and above, pp. 15 *et seq.*
[2] Hon. Henry Duncan, 4th and youngest son of Ad. Lord Duncan, Lt. 21/4/1803; Cdr. 6/11/04; Capt. 18/1/06.

not prepared for what passed. Monsieur was a tall, well limbed man, and of good appearance. When he approached, he demanded in a sharp tone, 'D'où venez vous?' Not quite at my ease at the way in which the question was made, I was in the act of replying, but the demand was repeated so peremptorily that I had no resource left than to answer in rather a loud voice, 'D'Angleterre.' He then fixed his eyes upon me and passed on to my neighbour.

[On the other hand, this brusque treatment from the future king, Charles X, was to some extent cancelled out by the genial reception which W.H.D. experienced from 'Monsieur's' sons, the Dukes of Angoulême and Berri. He also met Mr. C. A. Mackenzie, the Agent appointed by our Government to look after the interests of all our 'détenus', and the exchange of Prisoners of War. He also tells the story of the passage of arms which Mackenzie had with Napoleon, who insisted upon including Wellington's army among the British prisoners in French hands. 'Take it first,' was Mackenzie's laconic reply, and negotiations broke down completely. In October W.H.D. revisited Verdun, where he met many old friends. Thence he went to Metz and Thionville, to stay with his stepmother Lady (?) Dillon and her kinsman Mons. Dinot. He gives some account of the Prussian occupation of this district. In November he returned to Paris.]

It was at this period that an act of some clever Frenchmen was played off on Sir Sidney Smith. It occupied all the conversation of Paris for some days. It was well known that, after our having by our gallant exertions before Algiers under Lord Exmouth put an end to the Christian slavery, Sir Sidney had placed himself in communication with the different sovereigns of Europe, to establish a Society to prevent the renewal of Christians being seized and carried to Algiers. He was principally supported by the King of Prussia. He had frequent audiences with Louis XVIII on that subject, and maintained a correspondence with the Pope, relating to the propriety of His Holiness conferring some distinguished Orders upon a few individuals who had exerted themselves in that cause. At last Sir Sidney received from the Pope a case containing three orders of knighthood—Grand Cross of the Keys for himself, the other two of minor dignity for his friends. He accordingly distributed the two— one of them to a naval officer, Arabin.[1] This act of the Pope's, the theme of all the salons of Paris, came under the notice of the King,

---

[1] Septimus Arabin, a devoted follower and connection by marriage of Sir Sidney Smith, Lt. 4/8/1807; Cdr. 27/7/14; Capt. 20/3/23.

who requested to be informed what His Holiness had done. Sir Sidney gave His Majesty a full account of all that had passed between himself and the Pope. Louis XVIII then expressed a wish to see the letter written by His Holiness, as he was himself, he said, in constant correspondence with him and knew his handwriting well. Sir Sidney produced the case and the parchment letters: which, having examined them with attention, His Majesty declared to be forgeries. This was a terrible blow to Sir Sidney, who would have made any sacrifice to have discovered the author: but he never did. One of the French Ministers, it was supposed, planned and carried out the whole proceeding. Sir Sidney, who had fixed his residence in Paris, had taken such a decided lead in the higher circles of Society over ending Christian slavery that he exposed himself to what happened. He was considerably lowered in the estimation of all, as his share in the transaction had been nothing but writing. Lord Exmouth was the hero who levelled the fortresses of Algiers to the ground, and opened the prisons of the unfortunate captives.

[He left Paris in February, 1818 and went to Boulogne.]

The Army of England had been encamped here. The harbour that contained the Flotilla was in existence, and numerous forts upon the surrounding heights gave ample proof of the energy of the Corsican Hero. The scaffolding upon one of them, to erect a monument upon the successful invasion, I often ascended, and had a commanding view of the Channel and the coast of England. There was a strong division of the British Army quartered round Boulogne, and as some quarrels had occurred between individuals of both nations, it was a regulation that the English officers should appear at the theatre and ballrooms without their swords.*

[In March he returned to England, intending to stay again with his friends the Dashwoods at Havant. But in passing through London. . . .]

. . . I thought it would be proper to report myself at the Admiralty. I sent my card up to Sir George Hope, from whom I experienced a hearty welcome. I was still limping upon my unfortunate leg, but in other respects I had improved amazingly in health. 'What a resurrection!' said Sir George. 'I am glad to see you so much improved. What do you mean to do?' I felt inclined to be communicative, and explained that a French friend of mine had

* One of the officers—Major Grant—was then the terror of the place. I have often heard the French gentlemen say in a whisper, 'Prenez garde! Grant est ici.'

offered to lend me secret information of the smuggling transactions across the Channel, if I could obtain an appointment to watch their motions. Sir George did not seem to approve of my plan, but added, 'There are two fine frigates about being commissioned. I do not think that any Captain has yet been selected for them.' He gave me the names of the ships, one at Plymouth, the other at Portsmouth. A long conversation ensued, I fearing that I had not recovered strength to go to sea in an active frigate. 'Besides,' I said, 'I have no influence in Parliament. Will, you, Sir George, give me a lift?' 'There's the rub,' he replied. 'I cannot interfere with the First Lord's patronage.' However, it was settled that I was to send in my application to the First Lord. We shook hands, and I retired. I now felt it necessary to consult Lord Melville's Private Secretary, who received me with marked attention, and told me that he thought I might have the command of a fine frigate if I would only apply. I particularly requested him that he would prevent my being sent to Devonport, as I had very urgent reasons for not going there. Returning to the Hotel, I wrote to him, to lay my claim before Lord M. for the command of a frigate. Then, taking a turn in the Park, to bring on the dinner hour, I met Lord M., to whom I made my bow. 'Still lame,' said his Lordship as he passed. After dinner, without loss of time, I was seated in the mail on my way to Havant, where I arrived next morning.

Having communicated to Dashwood all that had passed, I found he concluded decidedly in my favour, and instantly pounced upon me to take both his sons to sea with me, as they had just finished their naval college education. Then came similar demands from others. But I was obliged to decline making any promises until I knew my fate. Ten days passed, and I wrote to the Secretary. By return of post he replied, saying that the frigate for which I had applied had been given to another officer, but one would soon be found for me. This set an end to all my doubts. I instantly packed up, and next day made my appearance at the Admiralty, where, to my agreeable surprise, I found myself Captain of the *Phaeton*, one of our crack frigates. I did not expect such an early appointment. The compliment was a marked one, and my friends on all sides tendered their congratulations, among the number Lord Gambier. It was the *Phaeton* that took the *Defence* in tow at the termination of the action of the First of June[1], 1794. I little thought on that day I should ever become her Captain.

[1] See Vol. I, p. 137.

(2) H.M.S. *PHAETON* (Spithead and Passage to India)

APRIL 14, 1818–MARCH 1, 1819

The *Phaeton* was lying in the basin of Portsmouth Dock Yard under the hands of the artificers. There was no hurry. The first difficulty was to find a First Lieutenant, the next, to collect fittings and furniture for my Cabin. Could I have foreseen the event, all that I disposed of when paying off the *Horatio* might have been preserved, which would have saved me a considerable expense. My Commission to command the *Phaeton* was dated the 14th of April. It took me a week to select a Lieutenant. Several were recommended, but I was still in hesitation when Capt. Langford wrote to me such a letter in behalf of a Mr. Geary[1] that I took it to the Admiralty and consulted Sir Graham M.[2] on its contents. He spoke so favourably of that officer that I instantly applied for him. He was residing in the neighbourhood of Portsmouth and was directed to repair thither and hoist the Pendant on board the *Phaeton*. He did so on the 20th of the month.

When I arrived, the congratulations of my friend Sir Edward Thornborough were extremely gratifying. 'What a resurrection!' he exclaimed. 'What a change for the better has taken place in your health!' After staying a few days at Portsmouth, I was obliged to return to London, to attend to the necessaries for my outfit. No doubt you recollect our meetings on that occasion, as well Sophy's[3] recommendation of a steward, who turned out to be a regular scamp. There was plenty to do, with very few men, as volunteers came in slowly. The equipment upon the Peace establishment was a very different thing from that of the War. Economy was the order of the day—the old rigging repaired, old sails mended, and every possible shift resorted to to save expense.

I called upon the Duke of Clarence in Town, but failed in seeing H.R.H. I then attended the Queen's Drawing Room at Buckingham Palace. It was the most crowded one that had ever been held in England. Many carriages failed in arriving, and the Queen was obliged to retire. Prince Homburg, who had just married the Princess Elizabeth, drew all attention. Having settled my affairs in London,

---

[1] John Geary, Lt. 29/5/1807; Cdr. 17/2/31. See above, p. 423.
[2] Sir Graham Moore, a member of the Board of Admiralty, 1816–20. See above, p. 160.
[3] Henrietta Sophia, sister of his correspondent (Sir) J. J. Dillon.

I hastened down to Portsmouth. Some progress had been made, but very few men presented themselves. To my regret Sir Edward Thornborough, whose time of command had expired, left us, and on the 21st May was relieved by Ad. Sir George Campbell.[1] Many reports were in circulation relative to the service upon which the *Phaeton* was to be employed. Some rumours sent me to St. Helena, but I ascertained from the Admiralty that it was not to be so. The prevailing opinion placed me upon attendance on the Royal Yacht, the Prince Regent having of late taken a fancy to cruizing about the Channel. Lord Byron did not fail to pass his strictures on the Regent's mixing among naval officers, it being well understood that H.R.H. was partial to the Army. That prejudice against the Navy arose, I have been told, from the following circumstance. After the Dogger Bank action with the Dutch in 1782,[2] the King went down the river to meet Ad. Sir Hyde Parker.[3] H.M. was attended by the Prince of Wales. When the Admiral presented himself to his Sovereign, he emphatically expressed himself to the King, saying, 'If Your Majesty's ministers had done their duty, I should have brought the whole Dutch fleet into port.' The Admiral was noted for not being of the most amiable temper, always being styled 'Old Vinegar'. The Prince was seriously annoyed at the abrupt manners of the veteran, and in future regulated himself accordingly to most of the naval officers. Very few were favourites with him. I only mention this, but do not vouch for its veracity.

I had to regard now the indisposition of Sir George Hope. He was obliged to retire from the Admiralty,[4] and his place was filled by Sir George Cockburn. At about this period Sir George C. was returned member for Portsmouth. I attended the election, and partook of the splendid entertainment given by him to the principal inhabitants of the town. His brother Alexander, who had been with me at Verdun, assisted him.

On the 5th of June the ship was removed out of the Dock Yard basin and lashed alongside of the *Brave*, a hulk in the harbour. As volunteers did not come in freely, I had to send a couple of Mids to the Thames, where a rendezvous was established to enter seamen. My residence at this time was at Havant, but, having a horse and gig at my disposal, I was in Portsmouth every morning by 10 o'clock, and returned in the evening to dinner and rest. It was here that I was

[1] See above, p. 139.
[2] The correct date is 5/8/1781.
[3] The elder: father of W.H.D.'s C. in C. in the W. Indies: see Vol. I, pp. 369 *et seq.*
[4] He died this same year.

accosted almost every morning by a seaman, sometimes two, who expressed a desire to enter for the *Phaeton*, but they could not, they said, find their way to the ship without a little cash. I would then give each of them a shilling, with a line to the First Lieutenant desiring him to receive them. But those fellows coolly pocketed the money, never in one instance going to Portsmouth. I lost at least £10 in that way, and at last refused giving any more shillings. On the 19th the guns came alongside and were hoisted in, but the seamen did not enter as fast as required. In the streets I met by chance the East India Company Agent, and recalled to his recollection the conversation we had had about the freight received on board the *Horatio*. He fairly acknowledged that justice had not been done me and offered to represent the case to the Directors. But I declined having anything more to say about it.

On the 24th of July H.R.H. the Duke of Clarence came here and embarked on board the *Spartan*, which frigate soon put to sea. On the 19th of August we left the harbour and anchored at Spithead, still 40 seamen short of the peace establishment, viz. 250. Rear-Ad. Otway[1] had asked me a few days before whether I had any objections to hoist his Flag and convey him and his family to Leith, where he was appointed to the naval Command. I had known this distinguished officer when he was Captain of a frigate in the West Indies, and was but too happy to render him any service. It was at this period that a steamer made its appearance at Spithead. All the naval officers of note went to examine her. Her powers were not very great, but she made a strong impression upon all who went on board of her. It was on her deck that I met Lord Spencer and Mr. Marsden, who had been Secretary of the Admiralty. The former acknowledged me in very gracious terms, the latter considered me an old acquaintance. Ad. Otway now hoisted his Flag on board, and the next day, the 22nd, with fine weather, we got under way. I had given up the whole of my Cabin to the Admiral's family, and had fitted for myself a small canvas berth outside. In going out of Spithead, I set the studdingsails, but unluckily one of the booms slipped out of the irons and fell overboard. The Duke of Buckingham, who was keeping company with us in his yacht, most kindly shortened sail, picked it up and brought it to us. We reached the Downs on the 24th.

[After an uneventful passage, he reached Leith on the 31st. Here he met, and became friendly with, a certain Capt. Smith (probably

[1] Sir Robert Waller Otway. See Vol. I, p. 394.

Thomas, Lt. 1/9/1807; Cdr. 15/6/14; not Capt. till 16/8/25; then commanding the *Cherokee*, sloop.) Also, he met at the Admiral's table Ad. Sir Philip Durham[1]—]

who, being a character, entertained us with anecdotes without end. But I shall not vouch for the veracity of many of them. He was well known to George III, and when any tale was related at Court which was of a doubtful nature, the King would say, 'That's a Durham.' It was at a dinner party here that Capt. Smith made an unwarrantable attack upon my friend Sir James Yeo[2], then holding the naval Command on the coast of Africa. I could not allow such an event to pass unnoticed. I requested him to retract the offensive part of his statement. Instead, he added something offensive towards me, which obliged me to tell him that he must be answerable for such assertions. I withdrew, and in due time sent a friend to Capt. S. I will not intrude upon you the details of an unpleasant affair. In the end it was made up by the Captain making two apologies, one for his improper remarks upon Sir James, and another to me. Capt. S., I ascertained, was a very thoughtless character. The most extraordinary part of the affair was that, whilst my second and I were at breakfast, the newspapers were brought in, wherein was announced the arrival of Sir James Yeo at Spithead from the coast of Africa—a corpse.

I quitted Leith Roads on the 6th September, reached the Downs on the 9th, and anchored at Spithead on the morning of the 11th. I was astonished to find that Sir George Campbell had been informed of my affair with Smith, as I thought the affair had been secretly managed. The Admiral, and his Captain, B——s,[3] complimented me in handsome terms upon the decided manner in which I had acted. I soon heard that I should have to attend upon the Prince Regent, when he went a-yachting. That was a very desirable position to be placed in, I thought, with an independent income, but as that was not my case, I should be led into expenses beyond my means. Our attention had been drawn to three Russian frigates that came here. Their officers were often on shore, but they were suddenly ordered away, which prevented my becoming acquainted with any of them.

All my surmises relating to the Prince Regent were set aside by the unexpected news to prepare for foreign service. I had expressed a desire to serve abroad, and an offer had been made to remove me

---

[1] See Vol. I, p. 343.
[2] See above, p. 42.
[3] (Sir) Thomas Briggs, Lt. 28/9/1797; Cdr. 30/1/1800; Capt. 24/7/01; R-Ad. 27/6/32; V-Ad. 23/11/41.

into one of our frigates ordered to the West Indies for a period of three years. Had I not experienced the uncomfortable effects of that climate it is probable that I should have accepted the proposal. However, I preferred holding on for coming events, being finally inclined to give up the command of my ship, and retire into private life. The First Lieutenant, who had already failed to show proper attention to Ad. Otway, in attending to the removal of his luggage at Leith, now conducted himself in a most offensive manner towards one of our senior Captains who had called upon me. He insisted upon an apology. Consequently I sent for Mr. Geary, and acquainted him of the complaint made of his indecorous behaviour, and plainly told him that, if he did not make ample amends, I would instantly lay the whole case before the Admiralty, and request his removal from the ship. He attempted to shuffle out of it, but, having an opportunity, as I thought, of getting rid of a troublesome fellow, I ordered pen, ink and paper, and told him to wait a few minutes, when he should hear my representations to the Admiralty. The Cabin door was open, and it is probable that the Sentry might have heard some of my words. Mr. Geary, observing this, requested the door being shut, which I would not allow, giving him to understand that, the ship being ordered on foreign service, I wished for a more correct officer as my Senior Lieutenant. My firmness completely humbled him. He entreated me to make, in his name, the apology demanded, and promised to be more circumspect in future, his only object being to obtain my good opinion. As he declared himself so anxious to give satisfaction in his professional duties, the breach was made up. But mind the result.

For foreign service it was necessary to receive on board the whole of our great guns, viz. 46. We had only 22, and we had to collect 40 seamen. The Admiralty sanctioned my establishing a rendezvous at Portsmouth, and I appointed Mr. Geary to that station, which gave him an addition of 8s. a day. He had a wife and three children: therefore I proved to him my feelings in his welfare, and expected in return that he would prove himself deserving of the consideration. The guns were soon taken in, and as our preparations were nearly completed, I understood that I was to receive treasure on board and proceed to Calcutta. When we were expecting to attend on the Prince Regent, Lieut. Geary had come to me, as he said, in the names of the other officers, who offered to subscribe a certain sum to maintain a band of musicians. To that proposal I would not consent, but merely remarked that if a band were established on board, it should be solely at my expense. Moreover, he stated, he could procure a set of instruments, second hand, for £27 at a shop in Portsmouth.

The *Tartar*, with Commodore Sir George Collier[1] on board, was lying here. He was most seriously annoyed at my having to receive Treasure for India. He was to assume the Command on the Cape Coast. My presence was required in Town, not only at the Admiralty, but also at the India Court of Directors. I accordingly repaired to London, having given Lieut. Geary £50 to purchase the musical instruments. 'Here,' I said, 'are the means for you to procure what you require, and I trust to your economical arrangement.' At the Admiralty I had a long conversation with Sir George Cockburn, who thought it probable that I should take the Marchioness of Hastings to India. Then I went to Leadenhall St., then waited upon the Duke of Sussex at Kensington Palace. H.R.H. sent his servant with my carriage to show me the way to the Marchioness's residence not far off. After a short interview, she declared she could not be ready to proceed to join her husband with me. I returned to the Duke, who gave me plenty of commissions, also a letter to Lord Munster, directing him to write to the Marquess of Hastings about me.

Whilst staying at the Salopian, I was called upon by Sir Benjamin Hobhouse,[2] to me a perfect stranger: but he knew your Father. I inquired the object he had in view. 'I understand,' said he, 'that your ship is ordered to India. My son holds a responsible situation there under the Government, and it may be worth your while to give him a passage. Your doing so would be productive of some advantage to you.' I replied that he had made a great mistake in addressing a Captain of a ship of war upon such terms, as they were not in the habit of receiving passengers in the way he alluded to. 'You had better think of it,' he rejoined, and acted under the impression that he was perfectly justified in making his proposal. I requested his son's age, which he stated to be about 25. 'He would be no companion to me,' I said. 'I keep no table: but if you approve of it, I will insure his reception with my officers in the Gun Room.' Sir Benjamin was not overpleased with my suggestion, but I would not yield. Then, after a long conversation, during which he frequently made use of Mr. Barrow's name—the Secretary of the Admiralty—but produced no change in my determination, he withdrew, promising to call again in a couple of hours. So soon as he had left me, I went to the Admiralty, saw Mr. Barrow, related to him what had passed, and inquired if he took any interest in the son. If he did, I promised to

---

[1] See above, p. 283.   [2] 1757–1831, Politician.

receive him in my Cabin. Mr. B. was extremely annoyed at the way in which Sir B. had made use of his name, telling me that the son had a wife with several children, and that he could not be ready in time. 'He would put you to great inconvenience,' said he, 'and I disapprove of the troublesome manner in which you have been intruded upon.' At the same time he thanked me in handsome terms for my offer. I then withdrew. At the lapse of two hours Sir Benjamin reappeared, and stated that his son could not accept my offer of messing with the officers. 'Very well,' said I. 'There's an end to your proposal. But, Sir Benjamin, you reside, I believe, in Parliament Street? How would you like my rapping at your door and asking for six months' board and lodging?' 'Very true,' he observed. 'I have laid myself open to that, but I was determined to take my chance.' He retired, and I never heard more of him.

I now repaired to Portsmouth. I had not been more than an hour at the hotel when I received a note from two or three individuals who stated themselves to be musicians, and offered themselves for my band. I directed the bearer of it to call at the Rendezvous and apply to the officer there. When I went on board, I found the ship loaded to the utmost, but all in good order. I paid the waterman 40 halfcrowns for bringing me 40 seamen. I then fixed the hour for sailing, but first invited two or three of the Captains who had their sons, Mids, on board to dine with me and meet them at my table. On Monday the 19th, they were all united in my Cabin, and a very sociable repast we had. Lieut. Geary was of the party. He had taken care not to purchase the secondhand instruments, but others from London, and, by way of proving his desire to economize, put me to considerable expense. Our dinner over, he requested permission to go on shore to take leave of his wife, promising to be on board by daylight. But, previous to quitting the ship, he told me that he had made an arrangement for two or three men who would come on board that evening to be placed under the Half Deck, as he had not been able, during our hurry, to procure sleeping plans for them on the Lower Deck. The Second Lieutenant received my instructions to attend to his suggestions.

The rest of the evening was passed with great cheerfulness, little thinking what would happen the next morning. With the dawn the ship was unmoored. Lieut. Geary made his appearance and attended to the duty. But how shall I express my surprise at seeing an Army officer come alongside about 7 o'clock? He said that he came to claim some deserters from his regiment, the 18th Royal Irish, who had entered for the *Phaeton*. In the meantime one of these men who had joined the preceding evening had put on his regimentals. He was a spy, and, delivering himself over to his officer, told him that two others, his companions, were on board the ship and hid away below. This was a transaction altogether so unexpected that I was astounded beyond measure. I appealed to Lieut. Geary. He denied the charge in the most positive terms. I then ordered the Ship's Company aft on the Quarter Deck and inquired if they knew anything of the men sought for by the officer. They all denied in the most positive manner their knowledge of any such men. All the officers did the same. The Army officer, attended by some of mine, was then allowed to examine every part of the ship: but they could not be found, he still persisting that they were on board. Here was an awkward dilemma, to be told to my face that there were men on board who, after the strictest search, could not be discovered in any part of the ship.* The details of this affair are of such an unpleasant nature that I can scarcely describe them. However, I wrote to the Admiral stating what had passed. At the time the topsails were sheeted home, and in a few minutes the ship would have been under sail, but for this officer's visit—Major Hammil.

It ended upon my going on shore to explain matters to the Admiral. The Governor, Lord Effingham, was with him, and there the matter was discussed, not in the most pleasant manner. But what could I do or say? I knew nothing of what had occurred, and the deserters could not be found on board my ship. It was at last agreed that two of the Senior Captains of the Squadron should go on board the *Phaeton*, attended by the Colonel of the Regiment, and examine the ship most strictly. Accordingly Capts. Hollis[1] and Briggs[2] came on board with the Colonel. The first person spoken to was Lieut. Geary. He was asked whether he knew anything of the men in question. Mind you, he laid his hand across his breast and declared upon his honour that he did not. His conduct was so impressive that it had its effect upon everyone who heard him. To me, who was completely in ignorance of what had been going on, it confirmed me in the opinion that nothing out of order had taken place. The other officers were questioned, all declaring their total ignorance of the men sought. Then the Ship's Company, individually, were asked what they knew

---

* They slept on board, but escaped, unknown to me, in a shore boat that happened to be alongside at that moment. So I was told—but so many falsehoods were put into practice on that occasion that I never knew the truth.

[1] See p. 249 above.

[2] The Flag Captain, see above, p. 435.

of the matter. They replied in the same way as their officers. The ship was then most strictly searched, even to the Magazine, but no strangers turned up. This last act was conclusive. The Naval Captains left the ship, and I took the Colonel on shore, with whom very unpleasant words passed.

It was just getting dark when I landed the Colonel. I hastened to the Admiral, who was perfectly satisfied with the result of the inquiry. 'Now,' said he, 'I have reported to the Admiralty that your ship has sailed. Therefore, if possible, contrive to get away in the night. If you cannot, have your topsails at the masthead tomorrow morning, that I may notice your proceedings accordingly.' He then gave me a written order, in the event of these deserters being concealed on board, to deliver them up to the first ship I might meet, and send them to England. Then I parted with Sir George Campbell on friendly terms. I got on board to a late dinner, and settled with the Master that, if possible, we should quit Spithead during the night. Then I turned in. But, about 10 o'clock, I was awakened by Lieutenant Geary, stating that the two men had come alongside, requesting admission. I was extremely angry with him for disturbing me, and forbid their being received, telling him that the ship had been reported by the Admiral as having sailed. Consequently, she could not be at Spithead. The soldiers returned, I suppose, to the shore.

On the morning of the 21st, in the Middle Watch, the wind favouring us, the ship was soon under sail and went through the Needles. So far I was content, little thinking of what was to happen on my return. I had on board 1,200,000 dollars, most of which was for the East India Company, and a small portion for one or two of the principal merchants of Calcutta. I naturally called Lieut. Geary to account for the annoyance and delay he had caused by receiving the two men belonging to the 18th Regiment. However, the explanations he gave of his conduct appeared to me so satisfactory that I could not take further notice, at that moment, of his proceedings. When I had called upon him, on the morning that the Army officer came on board to claim his deserters, he had very coolly given me a statement which I had set down in writing and sent to the Admiral. It completely removed any unfavourable impression relating to him, but in the end it proved to be a direct falsehood. We soon passed the Lizard Lighthouse, but as the ship was so deeply laden, all manner of contrivance was resorted to that her equilibrium might be maintained. My friend Dashwood had favoured me with what I considered some wholesome advice: which however, when acted upon, proved fallacious. We had scarcely cleared the Channel when we met strong westerly winds. My friend's last advice urged me to stand to the Westward. By doing so there was no getting on. Consequently I shaped a course to the Southward, and gradually reached a milder climate, with a clearer sky. Had Ad. Christian adopted that plan in the winter of 1795, when bound to the West Indies, he would have made better progress and succeeded with the voyage.[1] In the present instance, therefore, I acted upon my own judgment and experience. It is now well understood, when bound for the East or West Indies, that it is desirable after quitting the British Channel to stand to the Southward, and, when nearing Cape Finisterre, you encounter Northerly winds which lead you into the Trades. However, I have now to give an account of one of those extraordinary escapes that the Divine Providence occasionally extends to seamen upon the Ocean, which mercifully prevent shipwreck and the loss of life.

We proceeded tolerably well till Sunday the 25th, when we were assailed with strong winds from the S.E. The topgallant masts were struck, the mainsail handed, and the topsails close reefed. I dined with the officers that day, but as the gale increased in the evening, I was obliged to attend on deck. The topsails, being old canvas, were split and furled. We were reduced to the storm staysails, the rain coming down in torrents. However, suddenly the dense, thick clouds began to lighten, and by degrees moved off to the Westward like the drawing of a curtain, leaving the ship totally becalmed, with a clear sky, moonlight, and the brilliancy of the planets and stars, causing a sensation after storm hardly possible to describe. The ship had laboured so much that the handlines had been laid, secured to the guns, to enable one to move along the Quarter Deck. The wind having left us, the ship rolled about woefully. The topsails were set. A rumbling noise now attracted attention. The men in the maintop gave warning of a foaming sea coming towards us rapidly from the Southward. It gradually approached with an appalling roar. It was seen by all of us extending along the horizon. There was not a breath of wind to steady the craft, and she had no steerage way. At last the white rollers came so near that the deepest apprehensions were entertained by the crew. The ship lurched over towards them, and everyone thought we must be submerged. The sea was on a parallel with the main yard. What an awful moment! The Lieutenant, Geary, gave me his hand saying, 'God bless you, Capt. D. It is all over.

[1] See Vol. I, p. 176.

Nothing can save us now!' Everyone was silent, and at the critical moment which I thought would close our fate, the ship appeared to rise, and went over with a sudden inexpressible roll upon her starboard broadside, the sea coming in upon the Quarter Deck. The cutter hanging on the quarter was filled, and, as the ship righted again, was carried away, but, still holding by the after tackle, it was cut to get clear of it. The boat was lost. One of the studdingsail booms came down from the larboard main topsail yard and went right through the Quarter Deck on the opposite side. In the midst of these disasters a gust of wind of the utmost violence assailed us. The topsails, which were wet through, were at once blown from the yards in the way that a candle would be put out. The roaring of the wind was beyond all description for a couple of minutes, then became more steady, with lightning and rain. Here was an escape! Voices were heard from the seamen and officers congratulating themselves upon their happy release from the danger that had threatened us. The next thing to be done was to bend new topsails and put the ship to rights. The main topmast was sprung. On the afternoon of the 27th the wind moderated. Sail was made, and we proceeded on our voyage towards Madeira.

On the morning of the 3rd November the islands of Porto Santo were seen, and not long afterwards we exchanged numbers with H.M.S. *Tartar, Iphigenia* and the *Fly* sloop of war, all making their way towards Madeira. The *Phaeton* anchored with the chain cable in Funchal Roads about 3 o'clock. The Portuguese fort was saluted with 15 guns, which compliment was returned. All hands were now employed in setting the rigging to rights, getting in supplies, etc. I soon received a complimentary visit from our Consul, Mr. Veitch, whom I saluted with 13 guns. When I met Commodore Collier we had a long conversation on the gale off Finestere. He had experienced a part of it, and had his main topsail sprung. The *Fly* had also been a sufferer. Upon a strict examination of our log-books, it would seem that the storm extended over upwards of 50 miles, and the reports in the Logs of all three vessels tallied so minutely that the Log of one ship would have answered for the whole. With Mr. Veitch I visited the highest peak of the island. When we reached it, we were enveloped in a thick mist. Thus deprived of any extensive view, we soon retraced our steps, and had to descend some very steep precipices. We passed some of the vine districts, where I saw the method adopted for refining the choice wine.

On the 6th the *Creole* arrived. I was very deliberately making my arrangements for quitting the island, when I unexpectedly received a message from Sir George Collier, requesting me to delay my departure till the next day. The principal merchants, it seemed, wished to entertain the Commodore at dinner, and I was included in the invitation. This proposal was by no means suitable to my plans. However, I yielded. When I saw Sir George, he thanked me for complying with his wishes, and entered into a long conversation of what would be thought at the Admiralty when the ship's logs were examined, if I had left the island before him: with many other remarks which I thought quite out of place. To all these I merely replied, 'You are here on your station. You are the Commanding Officer, and it is not likely, in my opinion, that their Lordships will be displeased with your proceedings. It is more probable that I should be the first found fault with of the two, as I am employed upon a particular service, and unnecessary delays may be improper.' Thus terminated the affair for the moment. But Sir George had let it out that he was annoyed at my taking the dollars to India, and had in other ways beneath him, I thought, conducted himself in rather a strange manner towards me.

The Commodore had dined on board with me the previous day, when he took particular notice of a light white wine, the produce of the Hock grape, grown at Madeira. It was in hot weather most delicious. There was no end to his praises of it. Consequently it flowed in abundance. It had only been put on board that morning, in quantity about 12 dozen bottles. As he contrived to turn the conversation to it, and remarked that it must be high priced, it became quite evident that some crotchetty humour had seized on Sir George. I therefore, with his permission, directed my Steward to put one dozen in his boat when it came for him. He was much pleased with that act, which quite changed his temper. 'But now for payment,' said he. 'As to that part,' I replied, 'you may make yourself easy. It stands me in about 15 pence per bottle, and I beg you to accept it as a trifling present from me.' He finally agreed to do so, astonished at its cheapness. But to return to the proceedings of the following day. So soon as he had ascertained that I had sent orders not to quit the roads that day, it being about 11 o'clock, he directed his own ship to get under sail. That act I thought so truly ungenerous, taking an unfair advantage of me, that I instantly sent off instructions to Lieut. Geary to up anchor and keep close to the *Tartar*, trusting to the Commodore's taking me in his boat off to my ship in the evening.

Our Consul escorted me to the gentleman's residence where we were to be entertained. It was truly gratifying to meet such a patriotic reception in a foreign island from our countrymen. The banquet was a splendid one, and the hour of 9 struck. But the Commodore gave no symptoms of moving. It was a dark night: both our ships lay under sail in the offing. I at last rose, and, expressing to the company my warmest acknowledgements for their friendly and hospitable attentions, left the table. Sir George was now obliged to follow, and we wended our way to the beach. But, to my astonishment, there was no boat in waiting. This appeared to me a most unpardonable proceeding on the part of the Commodore. I had in a certain sense placed myself under his guidance, and by doing so, had not ordered my boat to be in attendance. We rambled about, trying to find some conveyance off to the *Iphigenia*, from which we could obtain a boat to our ships. In this we failed. However, we at length picked up a Portuguese sailor, who offered us a miserable sort of canoe. Here was a pleasant position for two Captains of the British Navy ! Just as we were stepping into it, the guard on the beach arrested us, saying we were his prisoners. We thought it prudent to yield, then sent the Portuguese to let Mr. Veitch know what had happened. He soon made his appearance, but he could do nothing for us at that hour of the night except liberate us from the guard. We then made a bargain with our foreign seaman to assist us off to the *Iphigenia*. We were soon afloat, and the Commodore and I took it in turns to pull an oar, by which means we reached that ship. I now expected that a boat would be instantly supplied to us. But no such thing. When in the Cabin, the Commodore called for pen, ink and paper, and began writing letters for England. It was midnight: so I sat down very quietly, waiting his pleasure. Five quarters of an hour were occupied at the pen, and finally a boat was announced, ready to convey us to our destination. Our ships had lights up, but we could not discern which was which. Away we went, and after a long pull we luckily reached the *Tartar* first. In taking leave, we agreed to keep company for a few days.

When I reached the *Phaeton*—at 2 o'clock—Lieut. Geary remarked, 'We soon found out you were under the wing of the Commodore. I didn't expect to see you till morning. Sir George does not attend to punctuality like you.' The next morning, Sunday, we kept close to the *Tartar*, and the following day Sir George came on board, wishing me to dine with him. There was no refusing. I explained to him that I had put to sea several tons of water short, in consequence of his having got under sail sooner than I expected: that I had weighed anchor contrary to my intentions, as I had reckoned upon his waiting at Madeira one day longer. He instantly offered to supply me with the quantity of water I wanted, and I received several tons from the *Tartar*. 'What a change,' I thought. 'His feelings and temper have improved towards me!' When the morrow came, the *Tartar* was so far off, appearing to be in chace, that I did not try to join her: but, instead of dining with him, I requested permission to part company, which he sanctioned: and there ended our visiting, as the ships were soon out of sight of each other. That gallant officer appeared to be an odd compound in his temper and disposition.

We now proceeded in good order. I contrived to keep my crew in perfect health by recommending drams of salt water. They readily complied, and there was no sickness on board. On the 11th we saw the island of Teneriffe, and, the next day, the island of Palma. On the 16th we fell in with an English ship bound to India. As she kept company with us—rather an unusual occurrence for a merchant ship—I naturally concluded that the *Phaeton* was out of trim. I instantly shifted some of the specie, and we soon widened our distance. We were, in fact, too much by the stern. On that day we passed the island of Bonavista. On the 19th we were assailed by rain —we were approaching those wet, squally regions. On the 28th we boarded an English ship from Bengal bound to London, and next day we crossed the Equator with the usual ceremonies, Neptune and his Myrmidons acquitting themselves perfectly well. We soon reached the Trade Winds.

On the afternoon of the 7th December, we boarded a Swedish ship from India bound to Stockholm. By the mismanagement of the Officer of the Watch, Lieut. Chevalier,[1] in the middle of the night of the 8th, both topgallant masts were carried away in a squall. One of the seamen, who was furling the royal, fell overboard. All sail was shortened, and a boat sent to look for him, but he could nowhere be seen. The poor fellow was drowned. Another in his fall got entangled in the loose rigging hanging over the fore topsail, and remained there many minutes without giving notice below of his perilous position. He was in due time relieved, and brought down without injury. We now had to replace the broken spars, etc. Nothing of consequence occurred till the 27th, when the high land in the neighbourhood of the Cape of Good Hope was seen, and on

[1] George Chevallier, Lt. 17/3/1815. Third Lieut.: died 20/8/1819 (see below, p. 458.)

the afternoon of that day we anchored in Simon's Bay. Here were lying H.M.S. *Fowey, Trincomally* and *Carron*. The latter, to my surprise, was a ship alluded to by an India officer who had dined with me in Portsmouth as having a freight of treasure for India. Though she had sailed some time before me, I had overtaken her. When her Captain, Furneaux,[1] came on board, he expressed in vivid terms his astonishment at seeing me at the Cape. 'What will be said at the Admiralty,' he remarked, 'at your arriving here previous to my quitting?' He appeared much disconcerted at the event. I tried to ease his mind, and thought I had, as he became more composed. He owned to never having been to India, and I proposed to him to wait a few days for my refit, that he might avail himself of the opportunity of going with an officer who knew those regions. He seemed inclined to do so. The next day being Sunday, nothing could be done in the way of stores, etc. I therefore called on my old friend, Sir J. Brenton the Commissioner, and some of the inhabitants whom I knew when last here.

On the following day all exertions were made to refit. My first visitor was Capt. F. who repeated his uneasiness at my arrival. Nothing could persuade him that the Admiralty would not censure him for his delays. Finding him in that trim, I declined all further interference. He soon quitted the ship, and was shortly under sail for India.

We had now to usher in the New Year, and, after labouring without a moment's rest, my ship was thoroughly put to rights by Saturday, January 2nd. Next morning there was not a breath of wind in the bay, but two miles in the offing I noticed a fine breeze. I instantly unmoored, and, ordering all the boats of the ships of war to assist my own, I took my departure. By 1 o'clock I had a fair wind which enabled me to proceed. The *Carron* had one week's start of me, and it was now a question among the officers which ship would reach Saugur Roads first. I availed myself of every favourable change by night or by day: and—without intruding upon you all the details of our proceedings—on the 27th February we had entered the Bay of Bengal, and spoke an English ship from Calcutta bound to Madras, which proved that our reckoning was strictly correct. The weather was hazy, so that we could not discern an object at any distance. The lead was hove occasionally, the soundings indicating our approach to the sand heads. A fog came on, which obliged me to fire guns as a signal for a Pilot. We heard the report of many in the

---

[1] John Furneaux, Lt. 13/6/1812; Cdr. 19/7/14. He was thus a fairly junior Commander at this time, and was not made Post until 16/3/29.

evening. About 10 o'clock we were in 9 fathoms water: consequently I brought my ship to anchor, still enveloped in a fog. But, strange to say, when the topmen went aloft to furl the royals, they saw a light over the fog, which proved to be the light vessel on the Saugur Sands. The mist clearing away enabled us to ascertain our true position. To my great satisfaction the chronometers and the lunar observations had conducted us to the sand heads with a precision probably never surpassed. The Master, Mr. Town,[1] I complimented upon the occasion.

At dawn on the 28th several vessels were seen, and guns fired to bring a Pilot, but without success. As I had never been here before, I was at a loss how to proceed. At length I noticed a vessel which had all the appearance of those containing a Pilot. I upped anchor and followed him at considerable risk. As she seemed to avoid me, a shot or two sent over the craft induced the officer in command to close upon the *Phaeton*. It proved to be a Pilot vessel, and I ordered one to be sent to my ship. When he came on board he received a rowing for not paying more attention to a King's ship wanting a Pilot and with treasure on board. He was a thick headed fellow. I gave him to understand that his neglect would be represented to the authorities at Calcutta. He took charge of the ship, and we began working our way, tacking often, beating up to Saugur Roads. But as the winds were so light and variable we were obliged to anchor in the afternoon. And here it seems that the Pilot would have kept us all night, off the jungle of Saugur: but, noticing many small Indian ships passing us, I got under way upon my own responsibility, directing the Pilot, who cut but a miserable figure, not to run the ship on shore. We were obliged to anchor at 9 o'clock in the evening. The next morning, the 1st of March, we were again under way, tacking as necessary until near noon, when the ship was anchored in Saugur Roads. The *Carron* had not arrived. Many bets relating to her were lost and won.

(3) H.M.S. *PHAETON* (India and Passage Home)

MARCH 1, 1819–SEPTEMBER 5, 1819

I have now to relate my reception by the Marquess of Hastings and my proceedings at Calcutta, the city of palaces. My first object was to have the ship moored in a place of security. I landed the mails,

[1] John Town, 1st Warrant, 5/12/1812.

and then had to engage the Pilot vessel that had attended the *Phaeton* to convey me to the Seat of Government, nearly 100 miles up the Hoogly. I had considerable difficulty in establishing a good understanding with the Pilot. In outward appearance he was heavy. There was nothing possessing about him. However, I at length explained to him the necessity of my being conveyed to the Governor General without loss of time. I embarked on board his craft with some of my officers and in the afternoon he weighed, and made sail up river. We were obliged to anchor for the night. About 2 o'clock in the morning, one of Lord Hasting's messengers made his appearance on board, bringing, among other things, an invitation from the Marquess to pass a few days with him at Barackpoore. His Excellency had also given directions for my being lodged in the Government House at Calcutta. The messenger also inquired whether the Marchioness had arrived, and was told that she had not come out. He explained to me what to do. The approaching of Calcutta is a most interesting sight, and my feelings as an Englishman may be easily understood—our possessing such an Empire as India.

I landed at the wharf of Calcutta about 10 o'clock on the morning of the 2nd. I first paid my respects to the Naval Department established there, to acquaint those in authority what I had done relating to the Pilot. He himself had much improved upon acquaintance, and had conducted himself with extreme propriety. We therefore parted better friends than when we first met. Some coolies now took charge of my luggage, and I hastened to the Governor's Palace. I was received by the Steward, who installed me in the Marchioness's apartments. When he noticed the bearers of my effects, 'Good God, Sir!' he exclaimed. 'How did you manage to allow these fellows to have anything to do with your trunks?' 'I know nothing about it,' I replied. 'I thought it was all right, as they made themselves so handy at the landing place that I concluded they were the proper people to be employed.' 'You are lucky, Sir,' said he, 'if you have escaped being plundered. You had better examine your luggage previous to their quitting.' I acted accordingly, and missed a very nice boat cloak. 'You will never see it again, Sir,' he said. In short, he was quite disconcerted at seeing the men in the Palace. He instantly sent for a Police Officer to get rid of them. In the meantime I requested him to pay the coolies what was necessary. He did so, and I ordered the bearers out of my room. Presently the Policeman arrived. He saw the Hindoos out of the premises, but he gave me no hopes of recovering my new cloak.

The Government Secretary now made his appearance. He was all courtesy when he saw the Marquess's invitation for my repairing to Barackpoore. He first of all ordered some tiffin—lunch—then a carriage to convey me up country. About 4 o'clock in the afternoon I reached Barackpoore and was presented to the Governor General. After my first introduction, 'If I mistake not,' said His Excellency, 'you are the son of Sir John Dillon?' 'Yes, My Lord,' I replied. 'I am very glad to see you,' said the Marquess. 'Give me your hand. Your Father was a very old friend of mine. What can I do for you?' This reception was so kind and flattering that I confess I was rather startled. 'Sit down,' said his Excellency. 'I want to have some conversation with you.' I obeyed accordingly. Then ensued a very familiar chat. 'You have brought me a million of dollars, I understand'? 'Yes, My Lord.' 'I do not want them,' said the Marquess. 'This is some job, all got up without my knowledge, when I was in the Upper Provinces. Therefore, to prove to these gentlemen that I can do without their money, I will put another million on board of your ship and send it to England. The Treasury here is full.' Upon this statement my spirits were excited. What a lucky turn up, thought I. Of course I expressed my obligation to His Excellency. The conversation having lasted for some time, the Marquess sent for one of his aids de camp to escort me to my apartments and to mind that I wanted nothing. Then I retired till dinner time.

It was a beautiful day. I therefore, accompanied by the aid de camp, took a ramble round the premises, then prepared for an Indian entertainment. Wishing to show respect to the Governor General, I took some pains in my toilette, and, instead of boots, appeared in shoes and buckles. We had a very recherché dinner—only a small party, which was to me the more acceptable. Thousands of questions were put to me concerning passing events in England. My replies were, so far as I could judge, satisfactory. Before dark His Excellency rose, and the rest of the evening was passed out of doors. I had during dinner felt some stinging pains round my ankles. Consequently, looking downwards when I left the table, I found my stockings overflowing with blood. This was the effect of the mosquitos. One or two gentlemen, noticing my unpleasant position, instantly accompanied me upstairs. Bandages were produced and, steeping them in brandy, they applied them to my ankles. By the next morning all inflammation had disappeared. After breakfast I was able to go about in a palankeen. But I took good care, that day at dinner, to put on my boots. Barackpoore was the Marquess's country residence. There were no formal parties, but I met here an old Verdun acquaintance, Col. Pine, and also one of my shipmates in the *Glenmore* in 1798—a Mr. Swanton, one of the youngsters then, who now held a good civil appointment. He was married and had children.

In the evenings the Governor invited me to accompany him in his rounds on the Elephant. My first mounting the Houdah was rather a nervous affair, as the animal, perceiving me to be a stranger, fixed his eyes upon me in so marked a manner that I could not help feeling myself an intruder. However, the Marquess led me by the hand, and I was soon seated. The motion of my first trip nearly brought on sickness. In fact, I had the same feelings in the stomach as produced by the motion of a vessel at sea. Luckily, it went off. I noticed that the Elephant's walk kept an officer in attendance on horseback at a trot. The Marquess had just terminated the wars with the Pindarees, and all our possessions in India were in a most peaceable situation. His Excellency was highly esteemed in all quarters, as his government had proved his capabilities. The ceremonies attending the Governor General were not upon the scale of the Marquess of Wellesley's, when he held sway in Hindoostan. A certain attention was due to such an elevated station, but not more than necessary. I stayed a week with Lord Hastings.

When the time for returning to Calcutta arrived, we started with the dawn, a thick, dewy fog attending us which made it very cold. The Marquess took me in his carriage—four horses and outriders. We had 14 miles to go. Just as we got near the capital, the sun burst forth and set our clothes a-smoking. The dew had made an impression on them.

Being now installed in the Government House, I had to call upon many of the officials. One of the principal merchants, Mr. Palmer, to whose firm I had brought bullion, was the first to offer his assistance. Another was the brother of Sir Charles Adam of the Navy. It appeared that the E.I. Company, at that time, were paying 10 per cent. interest for their money. Under these circumstances they could not transmit any home. When the Marquess made this communication to me, he said, 'Since I can't send to England the million which I intended, I will not remove from your ship the dollars you have brought here: but you shall take them to Madras, for which you will receive a double freight. I regret that I have not been able to do more. However, so it is.' That arrangement added £2,000 to about £3,000, which I was to receive for my first freight. Although I was a little disconcerted in my calculations, I had no reason to be dissatisfied with the Marquess's kind attentions towards me. Had I taken home the million, I should have realized about £10,000. But there was no cause to complain, as, upon my leaving England, I only reckoned upon receiving £3,000. I had no idea of meeting such a friend as the Marquess proved to be.

What was to be done with the cash which would be handed over to me by the Indian Government? It could be disposed of with security at 10 per cent. I consulted Mr. Palmer, and, odd enough, whilst I was examining his premises, I saw several ingots of lead, as I took them to be, and inquired of him what use they were to him. 'Lead?' said he. 'It is silver—what you brought out in your ship.' 'Well done,' I rejoined. 'That is the way you have done me out of a part of my freight. Had they been in dollars, they would have taken up more room, and I should have had to claim additional payment in consequence.' 'Very true,' he observed. 'But we have paid what is due, and you have no further demand to make upon me.' These sayings ended in a laugh, and nothing more transpired. But Mr. Palmer offered me 10 per cent. for the use of the dollars, if I would lend them to him, making allowance for the rate of exchange upon the rupees. After some discussion, I told him that I did not want 10 per cent., but I was willing to let him have on loan upwards of £4,000—for there were my expenses to be deducted out of the gross sum which I had to receive—for a couple of years at 8 per cent., and he was to pay me at the same rate of exchange at which the loan was contracted. He willingly accepted that proposal. It was a capital bargain for him. In fact, I was desirous of showing him some acknowledgments for his friendly and hospitable attentions. He in most suitable terms appreciated my intentions. By this agreement, when my money came home after nearly three years, I had not realized more than 5 per cent. instead of 8 per cent. Therefore Mr. Palmer had every advantage in that transaction. I shall know better another time.

The Hon. Mr. Moore, who appeared to be the Master of the Marquess's household, took me under his especial care. He certainly did the honours to perfection. The Governor General requested me to receive in my Cabin a Major C. of the E.I. Company's service, who was charged with despatches of importance for England. Commodore Hayes, the E.I. Company's naval Commander-in-Chief, invited me to a splendid dinner. But my greatest delight was the familiar conversations I had with the Marquess at his table. Many anecdotes were related of Bonaparte: but, although he allowed him talent, capacity and enterprise, he did not adjudge to him the qualities of a great man.

I had now been about three weeks in Calcutta, and I threw out my hints to Lord Hastings that my departure was near. His Excellency with all kindness and condescension ordered his yacht to be got ready to receive me. At that period all conversation turned upon the fate of the *Carron*, which had money on board for several merchants. Bets were making on the Exchange whether she would appear or whether gone to the bottom. However, at last the news arrived of her arrival in Saugur Roads, and soon afterwards her Captain made his appearance in the Indian capital. He had quitted the Cape exactly 8 days before me, and had not arrived for upwards of 14 days after the *Phaeton*. He had left England many weeks before me. The explanations which he gave of his proceedings proved that he had not made sufficient East longitude previous to altering his course to the Northward. By not doing so, he encountered variable winds and lost much time.[1] Horsburg's India Directory explains all these matters very clearly, so that anyone attending to it is nearly sure of performing a quick passage, barring accidents.

On the afternoon of the 25th I embarked on board the yacht, accompanied by the Major. There was also a Clergyman, Mr. Shep—d, to whom I had given a passage to England. We were obliged to anchor a few miles below Calcutta to wait for the tide, and I wrote to the Marquess, expressing my warmest acknowledgments for his friendly attentions. I never saw him more. A gentleman's bungalow being near, he persuaded myself and party to partake of an hospitable dinner under his roof. About 10 o'clock we all returned to the yacht. There was during the night a rush of the river called a 'boar'. Luckily it was not a serious one. Those swellings of the waters often capsize a vessel lying in their way, occasioning the loss of life. The whole of the next day was taken up in beating down to Saugur Road, but the yacht was compelled to anchor 4 or 5 miles from the *Phaeton* in the evening. My barge soon arrived. In the middle of the night, when the tide changed, the Master of the yacht persuaded me to take the barge, and proceed to my ship. Her lights were distinctly seen.

---

[1] The worst fears of this apparently timid navigator were realised next year, when, 6/7/1820, the *Carron* was lost in the Bay of Bengal, and himself barely saved. He had been badly wounded in the face when serving as Midshipman in the *Royal George* during her passage through the Dardanelles with Sir John Duckworth, 19/2/1807. Perhaps this had affected his nerve.

I did not, I confess, see much necessity for proceeding so far in the
dark, especially as the sandsheads, upon which the surf beat tremendously, were not far off. However, the India officer made such
light work of it that I started in my boat, all the party being against
my doing so, especially the Major. After about two hours' hard
rowing, I thought we were widening our distance from the frigate's
lights. The roaring noise of the sea began to attract my attention.
I had settled that when the *Phaeton's* lights could not be seen, it
would prove my being on board. Whilst my apprehensions of our
dangerous position were augmenting, I suddenly heard the report of
a musket, and beheld the yacht, under sail, coming after me. I was
hailed, evidently with great anxiety, and requested to make every
exertion to get hold of the yacht. We soon did so. When I reached the
vessel's Quarter Deck, all my friends, in a state of the greatest
excitement, said, 'We thought you were lost. Not seeing the lights
hauled down on board the *Phaeton*, we insisted upon the yacht's
going after you. And it is lucky we did so, for we are now on the edge
of the breakers. A few minutes longer, and you would have been
swallowed up by them.' This was all true. They gave the Master a
fine jobation for having persuaded me to quit the vessel. In about
½ an hour we got near the frigate and, daylight appearing, I rejoined
the *Phaeton*. 'All's well that ends well.'

A Pilot vessel was obtained to attend us, and on the 27th the
anchor was weighed. But we did not get clear to sea till the afternoon
of the 29th, the ship's crew all in good health and homeward bound.
We had some passengers for Madras. To the officers I made a present
of a good supply of sherry wine. We had fine weather, and reached
Madras on the evening of the 11th of April. Here, next day, I had
to undergo the nervous trial by landing over the surf in a Massulo
boat. When I reached the beach, there were two palanqueens waiting
for me. Not being prepared for such a compliment, and not used to
the dialect of the palanqueen's bearers, I could not exactly make out
from whom they came.

[The first came from the lawyer son of an old friend, the second
from another old friend, Sir Edmund Stanley (see p. 399), now
'Chief Judge at Madras.' He also renewed acquaintance with several
other friends made during his previous visit.]

The day after my arrival here, we received the news of Queen
Charlotte's death. Minute guns were fired in consequence. Here I met
the first Bishop sent out from England, bound to Calcutta, who was

saluted when he embarked. The specie was soon landed, and as I was anxious to be on my way, by the 17th I made sail from the Roads. We had very fair weather, and nothing of consequence occurred during this voyage. In 19 days we ran 4,000 miles. On the 3rd June we made the coast of Africa, and were then visited by some heavy gales. But, the *Phaeton* being a capital sea boat, we weathered the storms without accident of any moment: but the fore yard was sprung. On the morning of the 8th Cape Hanglip was plainly seen, and a course was shaped for Simon's Bay. We exchanged signals with H.M. Ships *Dauntless*, *Nautilus* and *Redwing*, and at 4 o'clock p.m. we anchored in the bay mentioned.

We had not been long here when some letters from England prepared me for some unpleasant inquiry relating to the deserters from the 18th Regiment who had offered themselves as musicians in the band. I could ascertain no decided information, but enough oozed out to lead me to believe that some underhand work had been in practice. I had the First Lieutenant and the Master at Arms, who it seems had a great deal to do in that affair, in my Cabin. A strict investigation ensued, but I could not obtain any insight into what had been going on. Therefore nothing could be done until we reached England. The procuring of a spar for a new fore yard took some time. Consequently I determined, in return for many civilities from the principal gentlemen in office and several of the inhabitants, to give a Ball. The Commissioner assisted me with planks and canvas, for the season was wet, and it was necessary to have the Quarter Deck proof against the rain.

[His description of the Ball itself is omitted, but one portion of it —how he transformed the ship for the occasion—is retained.]

The after part of the ship, from the main mast to the taffrail was roofed over, and covered with canvas. The gun ports were fitted with transparencies, and chandeliers were hung in various directions. But the Ballroom was not accessible till the hour of dancing had arrived. One side of the Half Deck was fitted up for a dinner party of about 30 persons, the Cabin being employed as a drawing room. At 5 o'clock all the guests were on board, without their wives. When dinner was announced, the gentlemen went out of my Cabin to the banquet. They were astonished to behold a place on shipboard so nicely fitted, decorated with flags, festoons and evergreens and well lit up. By 9 o'clock the ladies appeared in the Cabin, overloaded with flowers. When they were well supplied with partners, the lights were put out,

and they were led upstairs on to the Quarter Deck, still in darkness
except for the transparencies. When they were all up, the signal—
three claps of the hand—was given, and instantaneously the Ballroom was illuminated by innumerable lights. The band struck up
'Rule Britannia'. This sudden and unexpected shock surpassed all
description, and caused some of the fair sex to faint. However, soon
they all recovered their buoyancy of spirit. There was nothing to be
seen, excepting the planks of the deck, that could lead anyone to
suppose they were on board of a ship of war.

The We were now surprised by the arrival of H.M. Ship *Malabar* from
Bombay. Capt. Clavell.[1] This was a 74 built of teak. As the frigate
commanded by Capt. C.—the *Orlando*—proved worn out, he had
removed his officers and Ship's Company into the line of battle ship,
without guns, and was navigating her home. He had also on board
the timbers of a large frigate. The appearance of this ship caused a
considerable change in all our operations. He being the Senior
Officer, all the work of the dock Yard for the *Phaeton* was at a stand,
to accelerate what was required for the *Malabar*. An unfortunate
misunderstanding took place between that officer and me, almost too
trifling to mention. However, he assumed a degree of arrogance that
led to a correspondence in which that gentleman got the worst
of it. The Commissioner kindly interfered and in some shape
set affairs to rights. I had never experienced any meddling so ill-
judged.

The *Malabar* having taken her departure, by the 4th of July a
new foreyard had been received, and by the morning of the 5th we
were under sail. The weather was wet and cloudy as we beat out of
the bay. We had not been long out when I was informed that the
Master at Arms had been left behind. When I inquired of Lieut.
Geary how this all happened, he had his story ready. He had been
sent, he said, to look for one of the liberty men. All this was a pre-
arranged plan, as it proved afterwards, to prevent his being examined
on our arrival in England touching the deserters from the 18th
Regiment. I now began to suspect that there had been some very
improper proceedings going on, but I could only suspect, as I could
learn no particulars from those around me. Our progress was slow.
However, on the morning of the 22nd the island of St. Helena was in
sight. Shortly afterwards we exchanged numbers with H.M. Ships
Eurydice and *Tees*. The island made a very conspicuous appearance,
and about 2 o'clock the *Phaeton* was anchored off James' Town.

[1] See above, p. 397.

There I saluted the Flag of Ad. Plampin[1] on board the *Conqueror*. As we had brought cattle for that ship, they were sent to her. The Admiral was an old friend, from whom I experienced a hearty welcome. Sir Hudson Lowe now resided at the Governor's residence in the town, so that I had not to proceed to Plantation House. The invitations to dinner came in so rapidly that I was at a loss to know how to manage without giving offence. Col. Read would have a day, but with extreme regret I was obliged to decline that pleasure, having decided to dine only with the Governor and the Admiral. My first was with Sir Hudson, as he secured me the instant I landed. At his table I related all my adventures in Paris, my having seen Mme. Bertrand's mother, as well the relations of the French Commissioner at St. Helena, the Marquis de Montchenu. I had so many anecdotes to mention and so many questions to answer that our sitting was a late one. At parting, Sir Hudson promised me a pass to Longwood the next day. On the following morning I had a long chat with the Admiral, who sanctioned my going to Longwood. But the Governor somehow or other delayed giving me the required authority for admission. I urged my request, when, to my astonishment, he, with a long preamble, began to scrutinize all I had said the previous evening. 'You must not,' he said, 'repeat any of those sayings with which you entertained us last night. They won't do up there, and may cause some unpleasant feelings.' 'Good God, Sir Hudson,' I observed. 'Do you take me for a fool? Don't I know what I am going about?' After a few more ill-judged hints, as I thought, the pass was handed to me, but by that delay I did not reach Longwood until near 3 o'clock. I found great alterations in the premises since I had been there. The house was surrounded by scaffolding, undergoing considerable improvements in the accommodations, and Gen. Bertrand had removed from Huts' Gate into a more suitable residence.

Upon my requesting admission at the General's, I was informed that he was occupied with the Emperor, and that his wife had had a miscarriage that night. However, so soon as she heard of my arrival she insisted upon seeing me. Her medical attendant now made his appearance, stating that she had undergone great suffering, and he could only allow of my being admitted upon the decided condition of my not staying more than five minutes. I readily consented to those terms, as all I wished to tell her was that I had seen her Mother

[1] Robert Plampin, Lt. 3/12/1781; Cdr. 30/8/93; Capt. 21/4/95; R-Ad. 11/6/1814; V-Ad. 27/5/25.

before her death, and that I had forwarded the letters she had
entrusted to me, as well as those of the General. I was then permitted
to enter the room. Poor soul! She was extended upon her bed, but
in apparent high spirits. I very soon delivered all I had to say,
keeping my watch in hand not to mistake the time fixed upon: and
I found that a great deal might be said in so few minutes. When the
time expired, the medical friend appeared at the door, but she
insisted upon a few more seconds, during which she requested that
Mr. Dillon, one of my Mids, might be allowed to see her that evening.
Having left her, I was ushered into the presence of the General, who
was in his dining room, the table cloth laid. It was 4 o'clock, and as I
was engaged to dine with the Admiral, there was no time to spare.
The General pressed me to dine with him, but I could not well accept
it, and I told him how I was situated. He was satisfied with my
explanation. I then availed myself of the opportunity to inquire if I
had any chance of seeing his Emperor. 'I think not,' he replied. 'He
is not well.' 'Then,' said I, 'I suppose I shall never see him again. I
have frequently seen him when in France. This is the second time I
have visited St. Helena. It is not likely I shall come a third time.
Therefore have the goodness to present my respects to him. It was
through his means that the greatest calamity of my life befell me. I
was sent with a Flag of Truce into one of the ports of Holland in
1803. I was made a prisoner of war by your countrymen, lost my
promotion, detained in France nearly five years, and obliged to
dispose of some landed property in Ireland to cover my expenses.
Pray tell him all this. And now it is his turn. He is paying for all the
evil he has inflicted on mankind.' When Bertrand heard my statement, 'What!' he exclaimed. 'Detained with a Flag of Truce?'
'Parlementaire!' He repeated the last word two or three times, and
stared with astonishment. 'I cannot make that out,' he said. 'It is
all true,' I remarked, 'and I am one of the victims.' I then rose and,
shaking his hand, retired.

When I left his house and mounted my nag, I met Sir Hudson
Lowe, who, I thought, had been watching my motions. I hastened
to the town to dress for the Admiral's dinner, and sent a message off
to the ship for young Dillon to repair to Longwood. He went, was
admitted, and kindly entertained by the General and his wife. I had
a very agreeable entertainment at the Admiral's, and it was agreed
that I was to leave the island next morning. The ship was under sail
next morning, the 25th, but an unexpected message from Sir Hudson
Lowe kept me waiting for his despatches. While we sailed to and

fro, anxiously awaiting them, a heavy gust of wind took the ship aback, and drove us on the board *Sophie*, sloop of war, which received some injury: and the *Phaeton* lost her stern boat. However, at 3 o'clock the Governor's boat came alongside and delivered the letters, parcels, etc. All sail was then made towards home.

The weather, though cloudy, was accompanied by a strong favourable breeze, and the *Phaeton* dashed along at the rate of 10 and 11 knots an hour in good style. At daylight on the 29th the island of Ascension was seen, and we shortened sail to communicate with H.M. sloop *Leveret*. On the 2nd of August we boarded a Portuguese schooner bound to Rio Janeiro, and the Equator was passed this day. On the morning of the 9th the island of Brava was discernable at the distance of about 14 leagues. The Master, Mr. Town, proved himself very correct in his reckoning. His lunar observations tallied with the chronometers. On the 20th, the Third Lieutenant, George Chevallier, departed this life, and was committed to the deep next day, with the naval funeral ceremonies usual on such occasions. By his death I was enabled to fill up that vacancy, and appointed one of the Mates, Mr. Groom,[1] Acting Lieutenant. But I could not afterwards prevail upon the Admiralty to confirm the promotion—an act of injustice on the part of the Board, as it was an understood privilege for the Senior Officer to fill up the death-vacancies on a foreign station. On the 29th we boarded an American ship from Liverpool bound to Philadelphia. On the 3rd of September we were nearing the entrance of the British Channel, and in the evening sounded in 92 fathoms. The morning of the 4th, Scilly was seen. We soon got into the Channel, and the next morning entered the Needles passage. Next day the ship was anchored at Spithead, and saluted the Flag of Sir George Campbell.

(4) H.M.S. *PHAETON* (The Bandsmen)

SEPTEMBER 5, 1819–OCTOBER 29, 1819

When I landed at Portsmouth, I met Capt. Briggs, the Admiral's Captain, who had been anxiously looking out for my coming. He addressed me with much earnestness, and stated that, during my absence, there had been a voluminous correspondence with the

---

[1] John Groom. He had been with W.H.D. to China in the *Horatio*, and followed him into the *Phaeton*. Though Dillon failed to secure his confirmation, he did obtain his lieutenancy, 22/10/1823.

Horse Guards relating to the deserters already mentioned. 'The Admiral,' said he, 'is your friend, and I sincerely advise you to let him know all about it. Mind, whatever you do tell him the truth.' I was, I confess, completely astonished at all his remarks, and very coolly told him I knew nothing about it. He would barely credit my assertions. He accompanied me up the street, during which he complimented me upon my speedy return. This led to particulars, by which it appeared that the *Phaeton* had been to Saugur Roads and back in a few more days than 10 months. Out of that time, 70 days had been passed at an anchor, so that the period of being under sail made as near as could be eight months. That was considered good sailing in those days.

I hastened to the Admiral's House. Sir George was waiting for me, attended by his Secretary, in a private room upstairs that we might not be interrupted. He bestowed some handsome remarks upon the good sailing qualities of my frigate, my good health, etc. 'But look here,' he said, pointing to a bundle of letters at least 4 inches deep. 'These all relate to the deserters from the 18th Regiment, the Royal Irish. I have had plenty to do on that account.' 'I am sorry for it,' I replied. 'They did not go to sea in the ship. I have had no hand in the transaction. I knew nothing about it. All that I can say is that these deserters made an attempt to come alongside about 10 o'clock at night, after the inquiry which you ordered relating to them: but I would not receive them.' Upon this the Admiral drew back. 'What?' said he. 'Not detain them according to orders?' 'You had, Sir George,' I replied, 'reported the *Phaeton* to the Admiralty as having sailed. Consequently, she was not supposed to be at Spithead. When the officer made their appearance known to me, I told him that the ship was officially at sea, and that I would have nothing to do with them.' 'Take your words back,' said the Admiral. 'I do not hear them! There will soon be another inquiry into the case, and let things stand over till then.' I retired, of course very uneasy upon his communication.

My friend Capt. Dashwood was soon with me. I made a hasty visit to Havant, allowing his son to go there, then hurried back to the ship. When the officers heard of the inquiry that would take place, it seems they reproached the Senior Lieutenant for all his doings in this affair, and gave him to understand that, if he would not confess the whole to me, they would expose him, as they had no intention of being lugged into dirty work to please him. Two or three days after this, Lieut. Geary came into my Cabin and declared that the transaction was all his own doing, and that he came to acknowledge the whole to me. 'Very well,' I replied. 'Will you make that declaration to the Admiral?' 'Yes, Sir. I am ready to do so,' was his answer. I instantly had my boat manned, and took the Lieutenant to the Admiral's. When I was admitted, I told Sir George that I had brought Lieut. Geary with me, and that he acknowledged his being the principal actor in the affair. 'It must be made to me in writing,' was his reply. I hastened downstairs, and told the Lieutenant. When he heard this he shuddered, and with a woeful countenance declared that he was a ruined man. 'Whilst you have been upstairs,' said he, 'I have had some conversation with the Admiral's Secretary who tells me that, if the charge against me be proved, I shall be broke. Pray, Sir, have mercy upon me! I have a wife and three children. I appeal to your feelings in my behalf.' He went upon this strain for some time. 'Very well,' I observed. 'You have made a nice mess of it. Had you declared this to me upon our arrival, I would have written to the Duke of York, who I have reason to believe is well disposed towards me, and I might have persuaded H.R.H. to lighten the proceedings towards you. But it is now too late.' However, he continued to entreat my remaining passive, and allow him to take his chance at a Court Martial: and at parting, as I was still in ignorance of what had been going on, I agreed to remain quiet, that his Commission might not be taken from him.

Among many letters from London was one from the Duke of Sussex with a cordial invitation to repair to the Palace to see him. However, the Prince Regent was expected daily, and I could not quit my station. When the *Phaeton's* lower rigging was examined, it was found to be rotten. This was the supply of the Peace Establishment. The ship was ordered into Portsmouth harbour to undergo a regular refitting. Therefore on the 9th the *Phaeton* was brought into the harbour and lashed alongside of the *Skiold* hulk. Soon afterwards the foremast and bowsprit were found to be sprung, and the ship was taken to the sheer hulk to have them removed. It was now that I made Lord Liverpool's acquaintance. His Lordship went on board the Flagship, and as I had to transact some duty with Sir George Campbell, he introduced me to the Peer. But as Sir George had rather a guttural pronunciation, I did not exactly make out the name of the Earl. Hearing that I had just returned from India, he asked many questions, and I replied with great freedom, not being aware that I was addressing the Prime Minister of the country. This was the period when we had occupied Singcapoore, and in alluding to it I said, 'There will be some nice work for the diplomats.* We have taken possession of Singcapoore.' The instant those words had escaped my lips, the Lord made off. Being on the Poop, he descended to the Quarter Deck. The abruptness of his leaving of course made its effect upon me, and I inquired of Sir George who he was. Then he stooped and whispered in my ear very distinctly, 'Lord Liverpool.' 'Oh,' said I, 'a pretty mess I have made of it!' Sir George laughed, and I quitted the ship.

Not long afterwards the Prince Regent arrived to enjoy yachting excursions. The arrival of the *Phaeton* from India had absorbed considerable conversation at Portsmouth, and the Regent desired the Port Admiral to present me. It was arranged therefore that Sir George was to take me in his barge next day to the Royal Yacht. Accordingly I accompanied the Admiral to the yacht, then under sail but lying to. The Regent received me most graciously. The presentation being over, H.R.H. took me under the arm and led me aft. He was most simply dressed in a plain blue frock coat with a small star on the left breast, an old round hat, etc. Addressing me with the utmost cordiality and freedom, he desired me to put my hat on, and to consider myself as speaking to a friend, and no ceremony. I accordingly felt perfectly at ease, and replied to all his questions. We rested upon the quarter rail netting abaft the mizen mast, but the arrival of some persons of distinction put an end to our conversation for the moment. However, the instant the Regent felt himself free, he again took me by the arm, returning to our former position. We had a long chat about the Marquess of Hastings, his particular friend. Another interruption ensued for a short while. When at leisure H.R.H. took me a third time to the same place. On that occasion the conversation turned upon St. Helena, Bonaparte, Sir Hudson Lowe, etc. He praised the Governor for his management and tact in his difficult position. 'I feel for him,' said the Regent, 'more than for any subject of my dominions. His trials are great.' Another arrival called off the Prince. By this time the Regent thought it necessary to make sail, and the visitors all took to their barges and withdrew. When it came to my turn, he gave me a hearty shake by the hand, took off his hat, made a low bow, and said, 'I am very glad to have made your acquaintance.' I was soon over the side, and returned to my ship.

* Previous to my quitting Calcutta, it was whispered about at the Government House that Sir Stamford Raffles, whom I afterwards knew, had acted upon his own responsibility, and had put himself at the head of an expedition and occupied Singcapoore.

The yacht was under the command of Sir Charles Paget,[1] and Ad. Sir H. Neagle[2] and Ad. the Hon. Blackwood,[3] besides others, were on board. The Regent noticed that I had adopted for the officers of the *Phaeton*, at sea, the blue cap with a gold band. He approved of that system, and ordered that all his yacht's crew should be supplied with them. By that means they became in general use in the Navy. I shall here merely allude to what had originally passed between me and Sir George Campbell relative to these caps. I had established them merely for sea service, but not to be used on shore as they were not belonging to the naval uniforms. When the Goodwood races took place the preceding year some of my Mids attended with these caps on. The Admiral noticed them, and inquired what ship they belonged to. He was told, the *Phaeton*. He then sent for me, and in certain terms expressed his displeasure at their being worn. I explained to him that I had only sanctioned their being used at sea, and then ordered all these youths on board for disobedience of orders. He little thought that, in a short while afterwards, they would become in use throughout the Navy. But so it was.[4]

A Court of Inquiry was assembled on board the Hulk to ascertain all the particulars relating to the reception of the deserters on board the *Phaeton*. The Master at Arms not being present, Lieut. Geary had it all his own way, and the result of that enquiry was that the Lieutenant was the culprit. When the order arrived for the Court Martial, the Deputy Judge Advocate wished to include me as one of the members of it, but I objected, thinking that I might be called upon as a witness to transactions which had been going on on board of the ship under my command. It was finally decided that I should not form one of its members.*

On the 8th of October the Court Martial assembled on board the Flag Ship, the *Queen Charlotte*, to try Lieut. Geary for secreting two men belonging to the 18th Regiment on board the *Phaeton*, and the Major who had been on board to claim his men appeared to

---

[1] Sir Charles Paget, Lt. 12/12/1796; Cdr. 27/6/97; Capt. 17/10/97; R-Ad. 9/4/1823; V-Ad. 10/1/37.

[2] Presumably Neale (not Neagle), Sir Harry Burrard, Lt. 29/9/1787; Cdr. 3/11/90; Capt. 1/2/93; R-Ad. 31/7/1810; V-Ad. 4/6/14; Ad. 22/7/30.

[3] Hon. Sir Henry Blackwood, Lt. 3/11/1790; Cdr. 6/7/94; Capt. 2/6/95; R-Ad. 4/6/1814; V-Ad. 27/5/25.

[4] See above, p. 424.

* When the trial was about to take place, one of the Senior Captains of Greenwich Hospital, Edge, who resided at that period at Ryde, came over to see me. I had served with him in the *Prince George*. [See Vol. I, pp. 175–204]. He stated that I had given early proof of uprightness and honourable feelings, and that he was ready to rebut any charge of that nature brought against me. In expressing my grateful acknowledgements, I plainly told him I had nothing to do with the trial.

support the charge. I was one of the first witnesses called. Lieut. Geary put into my hand the piece of paper which I had sent to him when I had received it from the two men in question. It merely stated, 'There are two of us who wish to join your ship.' Mr. Geary had the assistance of Mr. McArthur, who had already published a very useful production on the subject of naval Courts Martial.[1] He could not have had a better adviser. The President desired me to state all I knew relating to the charge. I then demanded to which time he alluded. 'Am I to answer your question at the time the occurrence took place, when he himself had formed one of the Court of Inquiry, or now, of what I knew since the ship had arrived in England?' He answered, 'When the deserters went to your ship, last October.' 'My reply to that is soon made,' said I, 'for I know nothing whatever of the men in question. I never saw them, and only know that they wished to join the ship under my command by this piece of paper. But I have heard a great deal about them since my return home.' Upon this reply, the President said, 'You may withdraw.' On my retiring, it was evident that a sensation of surprise became visible upon the listeners. The first day's trial did not produce much to guide the Court. I retired to Havant at its closing. The next day the trial was continued without termination, and, whilst I was quietly reading a book in a back room by myself, my friend Dashwood came in, and in a tone of extreme anxiety said, 'My worthy friend, you do not seem to be aware of the danger you are in. The impression has gone abroad with the public that you are sacrificing your First Lieutenant. No one will believe that a Lieutenant would act as yours has done without authority.' 'I cannot help what the public may think,' I replied. 'I know nothing about it, and when the trial terminates that ignorance will be made clear.' However, all that I could say would not quiet my host. He had heard all that had passed on the second day's trial, and there was a very strong feeling existing against me. Moreover, his brother had dined with the Admiral the preceding day, and the impression was unfavourable to me. 'Have you any objection,' he demanded, 'to renew your evidence?' He then began putting a certain number of questions— 'Can you say so-and-so?' I forget the principal questions, but it

---

[1] John McArthur, or M'Arthur (1755–1840). Originally a Purser (1st Warrant, 22/3/1779). Lord Hood's secretary, 1791–3: a pioneer of naval signals. Author of *Principles and Practice of Naval and Military Courts Martial*—the book mentioned here, and for long the standard work on the subject. Founder, with the Rev. James Stainer Clarke, of the *Naval Chronicle* (1799), and, again with Clarke, author of *The Life of Nelson*, 1809.

ended in my writing to the Judge Advocate to request him to solicit the President and members of the Court to allow me to renew my evidence on the following morning. When the Court was opened next day, I made my appearance, and the President demanded what was my object in again appearing. I replied that all sorts of reports had been circulated to the prejudice of my character, and I begged leave to offer a few statements which would set me right in the estimation of the public in general. 'You are not under trial,' he observed, 'and we have nothing to do with the reports in circulation.' However, when the Court was satisfied that a great deal of falsehood, injurious to me, had gone abroad, I was allowed to make my statement. I told the Court in a clear decided tone all that had passed between me and Lieutenant Geary relating to the band: of his having applied to me in the behalf of his messmates—which, by the bye, was all a falsehood—and of his being able to procure a set of instruments, second hand, at a very moderate price. I entered into full details of every circumstance, and clearly proved to those most prejudiced against me that I had nothing to do with the deserters, or knew anything about them. In conclusion, I stated that I had mentioned to the Admiral upon my arrival that the deserters had made an attempt to come on board during the night, but, the ship being reported as at sea, I would not allow them to come on board. During all this statement Lieut. Geary never offered a single remark or demanded any question. The result was a buzz of approbation from all present, and I withdrew. However, when the Admiral heard that I had used his name, he took the alarm, sent for me, and with tears in his eyes went on in an extraordinary manner. He said that he must report to the Admiralty the words that had passed between us on the day of my arrival. 'Very well, Sir,' I replied. 'Anything sooner than see you in your present state on my account. All I can say is, the deserters did not go to sea in my ship, and I cannot suppose that the Admiralty will be much displeased upon such a trifling affair.' I then retired.

The charges were fully proved against Lieut. Geary, and he was dismissed the ship. I did not hear the sentence, but as the Court terminated Mr. Geary happened to pass me, and I gave him my hand, expressing my fears that he would have been cashiered, thinking him well clear of his difficulties. That act of mine was reported to the Admiralty. But with his dismissal all my intercourse with him terminated, and I hastened in completing the ship's fittings for sea. I then wrote to Capt. Langford and pointed out his mistake

in recommending Lieut. Geary to me in the strong terms he did. He
had proved himself to have neither honour nor principle, nor was he
entitled to the denomination 'gentleman.'

During all these proceedings the First Lord of the Admiralty was
in Scotland. I heard that I should proceed to Halifax, taking Sir
James Kempt who was to be the Governor of that place. All my
naval friends complimented me upon the termination of all the
annoyance I had experienced, and concluded that I should hear no
more on that subject. Some others calculated otherwise, and thought
the Duke of York and the Army would not be satisfied with the
simple dismissal of the First Lieutenant.

Days passed on, and the ship was ready to quit the harbour when
I received an invitation to dine with Capt. Hollis, who had been the
President of the Court Martial. Capt. Briggs and Mr. Glover, the
Admiral's Secretary, were of the party, a most sociable and elegant
entertainment at Gosport. On our return, the evening was excessively
boisterous and very dark. Our boat was a small one, and, as the tide
was at the flow, the swell coming in with the wind made us hesitate
as to the safety of crossing over to the Point. However, we determined to run the risk, but, when we had reached half channel over,
a large fishing smack came towards us so rapidly that all our calling
and shouting appeared not to be heard. We instantly, most fortunately, laid in the oars, and rose to our feet to repel the bow of the
vessel in the act of running over us. By that act we prevented being
upset, but we got a thorough drenching. Having cleared ourselves
of the danger, we proceeded to the shore, congratulating ourselves
upon the lucky escape. As I walked up the street with Capt.
Briggs, he in the most warmhearted terms shook me by the hand,
expressing how delighted he was that all my troubles were over,
saying that, after the lapse of so many days, I should hear no more
about it.

How then shall I express my surprise and wounded feelings when
next morning, I received a message desiring me to call at the Admiral's office. Upon my reaching it, I was ushered into a private
apartment, and found Sir George Campbell in a most depressed
mood. 'I have most unpleasant news for you,' he said. 'I have
received orders from the Admiralty to pay your ship off, all standing.
I never expected anything of the kind. You have had no chance of
clearing yourself of any charge brought against you. You must write
to the Board: they may change their minds. It is one of the severest
measures I ever heard of,'—and the tears came trickling down his

cheeks abundantly. He held his head down for some moments before he recovered himself. I could not say much, as I was at a loss to know upon what grounds the Admiralty had acted. He advised me to appeal, or to apply for a Court Martial, but he finally recommended that I should request a reconsideration of their Lordship's decision. It was evident that he was more affected than I was. In the course of an hour I received the official letter announcing that, as several improper acts had taken place on board of His Majesty's ship under my command relating to the deserters from the 18th Regiment, their Lordships thought it proper in consequence thereof to pay the ship off, and directed my losing no time in preparing the books, etc., for that measure. I accordingly communicated to my officers the substance of the letter. They were all astonished, the crew also, saying, 'As the principal delinquent has been tried, proved guilty and punished, the rest of us are entirely blameless in the whole transaction.' I then wrote to the Admiralty, pointing out in strong terms that I knew nothing of what had been going on, dwelt upon my character, my long and faithful services, and that the decision visited upon me was more severe in its bearings than that visited upon the guilty Lieutenant, and hoped that their Lordships would rescind the order. However, in due time, their Lordships replied that they could not rescind the order given, and I must prepare to receive another Captain.

Nothing could be done but submit to my fate. I had purchased stock, painted my Cabin, and been at the expense of some hundreds of pounds to prepare for a foreign station. All these were now useless: all my wine, furniture, library, etc. were to be landed. The expressions of the officers and seamen of attachment to me can never be forgotten, as I had, by supplying the sick on all occasions from my table saved the lives of many: and the Mids, when ill, were allowed to sleep in my Cabin. Sheep were killed to supply them with the food recommended by the Surgeon. By that means there was scarcely any sickness on board, and the *Phaeton's* having performed the voyage out and home with so few casualties was a constant theme of all hands. By the 29th the crew received their wages, and I left her, understanding that Capt. Montagu[1] would take the command.

[He hurried to London, and found every officer he met loud in his praises and in their condemnation of the Admiralty's action. His

---

[1] (Sir) William Augustus Montagu, Lt. 14/11/1804; Cdr. 31/10/05; Capt. 12/10/07; R-Ad. 23/11/41. He commanded the *Phaeton* for the rest of her commission—all but three years.

first official call was upon Sir George Cockburn, still principal Naval
Lord, who . . .]

to my astonishment addressed me in the following words, generally
speaking in the plural number:—'We have no fault to find with you,
and had it not been for the Admiral's letter which he wrote about
you, we should merely have written to express our displeasure at
the proceedings relating to the secreting of the deserters. We cannot
allow such things to take place on board of the King's Ships. We
must support our Admiral. . . . All was reported to Lord Melville
in Scotland. His Lordship will be in Town tonight. All will blow over.
Remain quiet. Lord M. will give you another ship.' That assertion,
I confess, made its impression, and I omitted saying many things
which I had intended to dwell upon—the severity of the act and the
injury my character might sustain. Sir George appeared in perfect
good temper. He frequently demanded why I did not put the
Lieutenant under arrest. I replied that he had so completely thrown
himself on my mercy, since, as he had a wife and three children,
nothing but ruin stared him in the face: and upon those feelings I
allowed him to take his chance. 'If he had had 100 children,' observed
Sir George, 'you should have put him under arrest. However, Lord
M. will settle all with you when you see him.'

[He next waited on the First Lord's Private Secretary, who gave
him his indignant sympathy too, and arranged for him to see Lord
Melville himself.]

I accordingly presented myself, and was admitted to an audience
with his Lordship. When he desired me to state particulars, I explained all that I thought necessary, observing that, as Sir George
Cockburn had stated to me only a couple of days before what his
Lordship's intentions were towards me, I supposed he did not wish
me to enter into minute detail. He nodded. 'But,' said his Lordship,
'those two men, what became of them?' When I related what had
happened, 'Well,' said he, 'I do not see how you could have acted
otherwise.' That assertion, I confess, startled me to the quick.
'Then,' said I, 'my Lord, please to restore me the command of my
ship. You have taken her from me without hearing what I have to
say, and the consequences to me in my profession may be of the
most serious injury. Please to reinstate me in my command.' He
replied that the Duke of York had taken a very decided measure in
the proceeding: that during the number of years he had held office,

several Captains of the Navy had abstracted away from the regiments of the Army their bands, to the great annoyance of their officers: that mine was the only ship in which a proof had been established of the bandsmen having been found on board, and that he was determined to visit the utmost severity in his power to prevent any future recurrence of such acts. 'All your Lordship's remarks,' I replied, 'may be correct: but to me it is altogether a new case. I know nothing of what other ships had been doing, still less of how my Lieutenant had been going on. The men did not go to sea in my ship: and moreover, you have approved of my conduct.' At this reply his Lordship was startled, but again repeated the name of the Duke of York in support of his argument. 'If that is the case, my Lord,' I observed, 'H.R.H. is a friend of mine, and in less than 48 hours your Lordship will receive proofs of it.' That assertion was a regular settler upon the Peer. His countenance changed and, leaning back upon his chair, he seemed at a loss what to say. I then demanded whether he had any objection to my writing to the Duke. His Lordship made no immediate reply, but, rising from his chair, alluded to other matters. He most gracefully told me that he had received Lady M.'s instructions to thank me for a case of India muslins which I had sent her. 'You,' said his Lordship, 'call them trifles, but she considers them splendid and of great beauty. Besides, there are some furs very difficult to be procured in this country, and she values them accordingly. She is highly pleased with your attentions. Then,' added his Lordship, 'I am equally sensible of the Pipe of wine which you placed at my disposal. But you have done enough already, and no doubt you have other friends to whom it would be more acceptable. I must decline accepting it.' I could only bow, regretting that it would not be admitted into his cellar. He then inquired whether I had realized anything from my freight. I owned in grateful acknowledgment that I had, but it was still in India. Perceiving that the Peer was anxious to close the interview, before withdrawing I requested permission to lay my case before the Duke of York. That question, I noticed, was not to his liking. 'Very well,' he said. 'You may apply if you wish it.' Thus terminated an interview which I shall remember to the latest day of my life.

[He next met, in the Waiting Room below, his successor, Capt. Montagu, who, indignant like the rest, declared that he would refuse the command if, by doing so, he could assist W.H.D.'s reinstatement. Montagu now went up for an interview with Lord Melville, but on his return admitted that he had accepted the command, having ascertained that, even if he refused it, it would not return to Dillon. Next, he offered to take over a number of W.H.D.'s midshipmen, who were 'all fine young men of good connections'. He even agreed to buy his predecessor's wine, furniture, etc., and later in the day they met in W.H.D.'s club to put the various agreements down on paper. Another long passage now follows in which he further enlarges upon his wounded feelings and his friends' indignation, in which first Capt. Montagu, then Capt. Duncan and finally Ad. Otway commiserate, and try to comfort him. Capt. Montagu even relates how he has very nearly fought a duel with an Army officer who spoke slightingly of W.H.D. The latter closes his indignant outburst with a characteristic note:—'It is well understood in the naval circles of that day that, if I had possessed sufficient parliamentary influence to be useful to the Minister, I should not have had my ship paid off.']

Two or three days having elapsed, I received a letter from Capt. Montagu quite at variance with all the assurances he had made of relieving me of the articles previously agreed upon. Excuses were made; among others, the wine that had sustained a long sea voyage generally turned out to be sour. I did not reply to that letter. However, one of the Mids, Mr. Thompson, had in the kindest manner when I quitted the ship offered to take under his care all the articles of value. He had made a list of them so that I could not be a sufferer. I turned the wine over to my wine merchant who willingly took charge of it. My Cabin, of which Capt. Montagu became the possessor, had been most comfortably arranged, fitted out and painted, etc. He in the first instance approved and admired it, but in the end he would not reimburse me my outlay. His conduct brought on a coolness between us, and I never spoke to him for many years. He had received Lieut. Geary, and, by appearances, that officer, who had accepted the situation of Mate in a merchant ship lying at Spithead, had prejudiced him against me. I shall not relate all the underhand work reported to me by Mr. Thompson, when he applied to Capt. M. for the payments he had agreed to make. But the worst part of the story is that Lieut. G., who had been dismissed his ship for encouraging deserters from a regiment, had committed a similar offence with some of the seamen of the *Phaeton* to whom he had taken a liking, wishing them to serve in the ship of which he was the Mate. It became known to Capt. M. that two of his seamen had been enticed on board of Geary's vessel. They were searched for and recovered. But Capt. M. never reported the Lieutenant's conduct to the Admiralty. This was the officer who had disapproved in such strong terms of my having been deprived of my command!

An audience to see the Duke of York was immediately granted, and I was most graciously received at the Horse Guards. The Duke listened with great attention to all I had to say, and I clearly explained that the principal delinquent had been the Lieutenant.

[The whole tale is poured out again.]

The Duke then assured me that he was satisfied as far as the Army was concerned, and that he would not lose sight of me. As this was a most critical moment for me, I could not help calling upon him to make ample allowances for me on such an occasion. To all my remarks the Duke responded most nobly, repeating three times his promises to write to Lord M. in my favour. Nothing could be more gratifying than the interview, and I retired with hopes that were never realized. However, I proved to Lord M. that I had a friend in the Duke of York, as H.R.H. wrote to him immediately in my behalf.

[He next visited his special Prince, the Duke of Sussex, and a very similar scene followed. In this yet another of the Royal brothers participated—the Duke of Kent—the father of Queen Victoria having the whole story unfolded to him again. He too joined the chorus of sympathy. But—interesting and significant commentary—' They both declared that they could not interfere, notwithstanding their wishes in my behalf.']

On my return to Portsmouth, I availed myself of the first opportunity to have an interview with Ad. Sir George Campbell, to whom I explained that he was the cause, by his representations, of my having been removed from the *Phaeton*. When Sir George heard this he appeared very much annoyed, and without hesitation promised to remove any unfavourable impression his report might have made. That declaration was in keeping with his expressions when he conveyed to me the Admiralty's orders to prepare my ship for being paid off. I must do Sir George the justice to say that he acted a most honourable part. He repeated the shock of his feelings which the Admiralty order had produced, and that he would do his utmost to reinstate me in the good opinion of that Board. At our parting he said, ' I am going to Town in the course of a few days. I shall take up your cause at the Admiralty, and if any unfavourable feeling exists there, I will remove it as far as it lies in my power. The rest you shall hear on my return.'

He very soon went to London, and, shortly after his return to Portsmouth, he sent for me and entered into a statement, if such it may be called, of what had passed at the Admiralty. Tears came flowing down his cheeks, and all I could collect from him was a few incoherent words—'Were you not the Captain of the ship?' As I could not obtain any other kind of explanation, I made my bow and withdrew. That was all the service rendered me by Ad. Sir George Campbell.

Having in a few days settled many affairs in Portsmouth, I returned to Town, determined to leave no stone unturned to reinstate myself on my proper footing in my profession.

APPENDIX

REPORT ON THE 'BANDSMEN' CASE

By Capt. A. P. Atwill, C.B.E., R.N.

DEPUTY JUDGE ADVOCATE OF THE FLEET

28th July, 1954.

I have read these pages with much interest and the general impression I gain from the narrative is that either Dillon knew a great deal more about this affair than he describes in his notes or he was lacking in his application to keep himself conversant with all that transpired on board his ship.

The points which I find particularly revealing in regard to his conduct are—

1. The first information we have about these musicians is when they appeared at his hotel and sent in a note to him. Having received the note and given certain instructions to these would-be bandsmen, he seems to have done nothing further. I would have expected him either to make enquiries from the applicants at the time or to make enquiries about these men later, particularly as some suspicion about bandsmen deserters from the 18th Regiment appeared to fix on the ship.

2. When Lieutenant Geary, before going ashore in the evening, reported that he had arranged for two or three men to come on

board and sleep on the half deck, I would have expected the Captain of the Ship to make enquiries as to what these men were and where they were coming from.

3. Major Hammil appears to have come on board armed with the information that his deserters have entered 'for the Phaeton'. From where did he get this information? Someone must have had knowledge of what had been going on and presumably this information was communicated to Dillon who does not appear to have followed up the chain of circumstances.

4. Dillon states that all the officers in the Ship's Company denied that they had knowledge of any men being on board. I cannot believe that deserters can have been brought on board one of His Majesty's Ships without someone sighting them or being concerned in hiding them. The denial of *all* officers and men seems to indicate that Dillon had not the complete loyalty and confidence of his officers and men.

5. The note on page 439 suggests that the men slept on board and escaped in a shore boat, presumably in the early morning. Here again, I cannot but believe that the watch on deck must have seen something of what was going on.

6. The man who surrendered to the Major in his 'regimentals' must have been in a position to give very valuable information, but here again Dillon does not seem to have followed it up. His action in allowing the two men to escape again after coming alongside at 10 o'clock at night to try and get on board the ship is, I think, blameworthy. If he did not wish to embarrass the Commander-in-Chief over the sailing time he could have turned them over to another ship and no doubt the official reports could have been cleared so as not to drag in his own sailing time.

7. Dillon states that the explanation given by Lieutenant Geary when Major Hammil came on board turned out to be entirely false. Either Geary must have been a very expert liar or Dillon must have been very slow in checking up on his statements when he had one deserter already in his custody for interrogation and presumably had a background of information brought by Major Hammil which had led that officer to the ship.

As regards Dillon's evidence at the court-martial, I feel he would have been much better advised to have made a fuller statement when first called as a witness. It seems to me the court got the impression he was 'hedging' in his evidence and withholding information. Even in his second statement to the court he was rather foolish in that he dragged the

Admiral into the question, and brought out the fact that deserters had made an attempt to come on board during the night. He would have been well-advised to leave that out entirely.

Without fuller information under the various headings noted above, it is difficult to say whether a court-martial charge could have been brought against Dillon under Section 9 or Section 43 of those days: *i.e.*, 'neglect of duty in that he failed to . . .', or 'neglect to the prejudice of good order and naval discipline in that he failed to . . .'. I have a general opinion that Dillon did not come up to the standard of intelligence and application expected in such matters from an officer in command of one of His Majesty's Ships: and although he may have been morally innocent of any action in connection with these deserters, I do not think he acted in such a way that Their Lordships could have felt a great deal of confidence in him. From their point of view the problem seems to have been how best to resolve a difficult situation, in that, although the negligence of Dillon might not have been so tangible as to form a court martial charge, yet this officer's handling of the situation was a disappointment to the authorities, and caused them to feel that he had better be replaced.

A. P. ATWILL.

XVI
THE WILDERNESS

NOVEMBER 1819–JULY 9, 1835
(*aet.* 39–55)

XVI

THE WILDERNESS

NOVEMBER 1819–JULY 9, 1835

(*aet.* 39–55)

(Summary of 294 pages of manuscript omitted)

ALL was in vain. The unfortunate Dillon was not given employment for nearly 16 years. This is not surprising. Indeed, had there been no 'bandsmen case' at all, his fate might well have been little if any better. For the worst of all periods of frustration had overtaken the profession of Naval Officer. Owing to the absence, not only of all regularised Retirement, but also of those modern means of reducing post-war overcrowding, the R.N.R. and the R.N.V.R., the number of commissioned officers still nominally 'on the Active List' exceeded many times over the number of available appointments. Experiences like Dillon's were not only common, but inevitable, and his 16 years is by no means a record sojourn in the wilderness.

Yet, by any criterion, 16 years is a long time: and, though W.H.D. made constant efforts to secure appointment, mobilising every scrap of influence at his disposal, including that of no less than four of the Royal Brothers, he could not spend *all* his time in the Admiralty Waiting Room or on the doorsteps of the great. The result was that, in effect, he ceased to be a naval officer at all. So did many another. But, faced with this unpleasant situation, the officers concerned tended to join one or other of two well-defined groups: the one which gave it up as a bad job, and went right out of the Service, into quite other professions—often other navies—and the other which revolved round and round the Admiralty, waiting with what patience it could muster for something to turn up. W.H.D. was essentially a member of the latter class. He made no attempt whatever, at any time, to change into another profession. He never for a moment relinquished his professional ambitions. In a word, he did no work at all, but clung tenaciously to the belief that, sooner or later, employment would come his way again. It did: but, in the meantime, it is hard to escape the conclusion that he was wasting his life in more or less complete idleness. It was a tragedy only too characteristic of the times and shared by all too many of his generation. It must not be forgotten that, even now, he was only 39, with all but half his life still before him.

No attempt will be made here to follow his detailed career during these years, still less to print his Narrative in full. While much of it is of considerable interest for other reasons, most of it cannot be classified as 'Naval' at all. The policy adopted has been to present, as far as possible, a chronological summary—not always easy, since hereabouts, he departs from his previous practice of inserting months and years in the margin—and to transcribe only such excerpts from the Narrative as seem to be of naval, or particular personal, import: much the same treatment, in fact, as that accorded to the 'Captivity' epoch and the other shorter periods of unemployment.

The early part of 1820 he divided between quiet residence with his friends Captain and Mrs. Dashwood at Havant and several sojourns to the Salopian Hotel in London. He was still struggling with his fate. He prevailed upon the Duke of York to write direct to Lord Melville asking the latter to employ him, and was for a moment full of hope. But nothing came of it. Then, in November, he met by chance the Master at Arms of the *Phaeton* who had been (according to W.H.D.) deliberately excluded from the Court Martial (p. 455). This man, at Dillon's request, made a full statement on oath of all that had occurred, and W.H.D. sent it, with some confidence, to the Admiralty. The latter, however, 'in acknowledging its receipt, merely observed that it was an affair of the past, and that their Lordships did not wish to be troubled any more on the subject.' These two setbacks defeated him for the moment, and he resigned himself to a long wait.

Under February 1821 he gives a long account of the First Lord's treatment of Captain Dashwood, who, appointed Flag Captain to Admiral Sir Archibald Cochrane at Devonport, was after a bare six months jockeyed into the inferior command of a 74 by Lord Melville, who wanted the 'plum' appointment for a friend. Yet, W.H.D. reports with glee, this shabby treatment redounded to his friend's advantage: for his two-decker, the *Windsor Castle*, was by sheer chance detached in a hurry to Portugal. Here Dashwood was able to secure the person of 'the rebellious Don Miguel,' and to receive the Royal Family on board, where it remained till the troubles were over: for which services Dashwood and his officers acquired both kudos and substantial rewards.

It is immediately after the recording of this incident that the major date-change in the writing of the Narrative occurs. We have now reached MS. Vol. V, p. 408. (See Vol. I, Introduction, p. xxv). W.H.D. has been whiling away his hours of enforced idleness at Havant by writing to his first cousin, Sir John J. Dillon, the series of letters which has constituted the Narrative so far: and, by February 1821, he has got right up to date. The Dashwood incident has just happened, and for the moment there is no more to say. Now comes the new series. The next letter is headed 'Harbour of Ferrol, Spain,' and dated 1836. In the notebooks (which furnish the only surviving text of the Narrative), this time-lapse of all but 15 years passes unnoticed, save for the change in the address-heading from 'Havant' to 'Harbour of Ferrol' and a brief reintroductory passage. But it must be recorded because it affects closely the relative contemporaneity of all his evidence. As this question has already been discussed in the Introduction to Vol. I (pp. xxix–xxx), all that need be added here is a reminder that W.H.D.'s account of the whole *Phaeton* episode was, in effect, a recording of all but current events, and hardly 'History', in the usual sense of that word. This alone accounts, perhaps, for some of the many ill-considered accusations which Dillon hurls about so wildly, and for much of the sense of intolerable injustice under which he so obviously labours. Thereafter the Narrative becomes altogether quieter in tone: which is but natural, since he is once again reviewing events of relatively long ago. Once more reinstated in his profession, and Captain of the *Russel*, 74, he reopens the new series to his cousin in the following words:—

> As I had brought my Narrative to the years 1820 and 1821, the dates at which I commenced it, all I can now do is to send you an account of the incidents that occurred between that date and the period of my being appointed to the command of the *Russel*, 74, in 1835, a lapse of 14 years. As I happen at present to be a perfect idler lying in the Spanish harbour of Ferrol, I transmit this to you.

He now suffered two misfortunes, the one to his health, the other to his pocket. First he fell ill, coming as a result into contact with a well-known naval figure.

> Suffering from a violent and tormenting headache, I . . . fell under the care of Dr. Beatty, who had been Lord Nelson's Surgeon. He . . . promised to cure me, and would not accept the usual fees. The Doctor evidently mistook my complaint. My having rather a sanguine complexion, and being, in body, of square frame, he thought

that Plethora was the cause of my suffering, and reduced me to the lowest degree of debility, but would not change his system.

After three months of progressive deterioration brought on by semi-starvation, W.H.D. was reduced to a mere shadow, and 'The worthy Doctor decided that I should be bled in the jugular vein.' Fortunately, three hours before the operation was due, W.H.D. received a chance visit from another old friend, Dr. Freeman, who instantly pronounced emphatically against plethora.

'Can you,' said he, 'afford to put yourself into a post chaise and take a trip to the Continent?' 'What?' said I. 'Without waiting to be bled?' 'Certainly,' he replied. 'Leave this place as soon as you can.'

Freeman had scarcely left when Dr. Beatty arrived 'attended by an apothecary with lancets and bandages.' Thereupon Dillon not only refused to undergo the treatment, but answered back with more spirit than politeness.

I then showed him one of my legs, the calf of which had disappeared. 'When I placed myself under your care,' said I, 'I had a good stout limb. It is now a broom stick. Pray let me know what I am in your debt.' . . . The Doctor, in spite of all his professions, made me pay more than the usual fees.

Following Dr. Freeman's advice, he instantly went to Ostend, and thence to Dunkirk, where he put himself under a Surgeon called Macfarlane. The latter's prescription was the very reverse of Dr. Beatty's—plenty of food and wine, and sea bathing. In a few weeks Dillon was in perfect health again. Returning to England in January 1822, he met Beatty by chance at his club, and once again—this time in public—did not spare him.

'There,' said I, pointing to a pint of Port Wine on my table. 'Since I have renewed my former habits, I have recovered my health and strength.' My medical friend retired in very ill humour, and never forgave that observation of mine.

The other misfortune was financial—and twofold. First, it seems, he had lent to a Mr. Stackhouse a sum of £2,000 which he could not get back, and, having spent another thousand in the effort, lost £3,000 altogether. Then his freight-money—£5,000—was remitted to him from Calcutta. (See above, p. 451). Prudent friends advised him to invest it in the new Danish Government 5 per cent. Loan. This he did; but unfortunately, soon afterwards, he allowed himself to be persuaded by his own Agent, Mr. Peyton, to sell out and to give the latter carte blanche in reinvesting it—'to bring in 15 per cent. to 20 per cent.' Very shortly afterwards he learned 'of Mr. Peyton's becoming a bankrupt to the tune of £130,000.' For a time he lived in the fear that the creditors might have some claim on him too, and faced complete ruin. But from this danger he was saved by Mr. Peyton's father-in-law, and finally he actually received back a few hundred pounds. But he was seriously impoverished. 'I had', he records sadly, 'my half pay to fall back upon, and no outstanding debts.'

W.H.D. reveals himself throughout as something of a simpleton in money matters. His financial affairs are often, indeed, rather mysterious. He complains from time to time of being hard up, yet poverty is never reflected in his mode of life. He always seems to have enough on which to live comfortably and 'support the character of a Gentleman': to travel when and where he wants, even, at times, to keep a carriage. He had received all his Father's estate in 1806, but the inference from his words quoted above is that, in 1822, he had nothing but his half pay left. He had not won much, according to his own account, by Prize Money, and though he had done well out of Freight Money, the inference again is that he had now lost it. It was only after 1832, when he married 'a lady having an independent fortune' that we obtain any certain clue as to what he lived on: but even then, needless to say, he nowhere confesses that he is living on his wife's income! It may be noted, however, that until his marriage, and especially in the years following Peyton's bankruptcy, he spent a considerable percentage of his time staying with his many friends. Indeed, his life is divided into two roughly equal halves—flitting about the Continent, where living was obviously cheaper—a significantly numerous band of his fellow-officers doing the same—and residence in England, a good deal more than half of which he spent in rounds of visits. It was while on one of these, to Dr.—now Sir Thomas—Grey[1] at Ramsgate, that he made his first trip by steamer.

> Packets of that description began to ply upon the Thames. The one that attracted most notice at that time was called the *Hero*. She certainly was a most magnificent craft. The weather was delightful —the first week in June (1822)—and I embarked early that I might

[1] See Vol. I, pp. 337, 343, and index to this volume. The defective eyesight which made his patients nervous of his surgical ministrations evidently had not seriously affected his professional career.

examine all the machinery relating to steam. Whilst I was doing so, I was astonished to be accosted by Lord Exmouth. . . . We both put questions to the Engineer in attendance, but our interrogations were suddenly stopped by the ringing of a bell. We immediately hurried on deck to witness the casting off and the Paddle wheel set in motion, the whole proceeding a very interesting sight. We reached Margate by 5 o'clock pm, having left the pier in London at 8 in the morning: quite a feat at that time, and I was much gratified in my expectations of the power of steam when employed in our Navy.'

At the time of Peyton's failure, Dillon had been on the point of paying a visit to Russia. This he had now to forego, and went instead to Ireland, staying first at Dublin with a Verdun friend, and then with the Dillons of Lismullen (see Vol. I, Intro., pp. xiv, xv and xix), the resident holder of the baronetcy at that time being General Sir Arthur Dillon. Here, too, he met the younger brother, that other William—later Sir William—Dillon, whose certificate of service in the Navy had been offered to him by the old Sir John of Lismullen. (See vol. I, pp. 9 and 10). While here, too, he made a pleasure trip with Counsellor Sweney to the Isle of Man in a 12-ton boat, encountering a storm which all but drowned them, and in which—a most unusual confession of mortal frailty—'I suffered much from sea sickness.'

He was tempted to settle in Dublin, 'but the discords arising on the religious differences drove me away.' He gives one example of these 'discords.' As he drove in the country with a Protestant clergyman, they were greeted with two volleys of—fortunately very inaccurate—musketry. His return to England strikes quite a modern note. 'I quitted Dublin on the 7th of November (1822) by steamer to Holyhead, where we arrived in 7 hours.'

Early in 1823, the Duke of Sussex invited him to take up his residence in Kensington Palace, to become, in fact, a full-time employé of that Prince. But W.H.D., feeling as ever that his independence might be endangered, refused, though not without regret. That he was really fond of the Duke, and the Duke of him, there can be no doubt. He has much to say of this often comical but by no means unlovable Royal Brother, and it is all entirely to his credit. Even the fact that the Duke preened himself upon his liberalism and regarded himself as a leader of that party, while W.H.D. was, at heart, a dyed-in-the-wool Tory made but little difference, primarily because Dillon's conservatism was instinctive and hereditary, and he was always very careful to give politics a wide berth. In spite of his refusal to become personal equerry to the Duke, however, he still put in quite long spells of residence at Kensington Palace during the next few years. Here from time to time he came in contact with the Duke of Clarence—on one occasion in a very literal manner.

> One morning when at breakfast with the Duke [of Sussex], a particular bell was rung, and the Duke said to me, 'D., you must be off. Here's one of the Royal Family coming—one of my sisters, I believe.' I instantly rose and, in opening the door, came in immediate contact with the Duke of Clarence. Our stomachs touched as I passed out.

This led to an invitation to Bushey Park, where he was very well received by the future William IV. The latter expressed himself very strongly—and with his usual lack of reticence—on the subject of the First Naval Lord (Cockburn), whom, it seems, he regarded as an upstart. He also warmly promised Dillon his help. This was in 1825. In the previous year W.H.D. had been led to expect that an appointment was immediate, and had actually made a journey to Portsmouth to inspect the frigate which he was sure would be his. But nothing had come of that. Now he was sanguine again, for he thought—and who can blame him?—that interest in such a quarter would be irresistible, especially when that patron became, two years later, the first Lord High Admiral that there had been for over a century, and, three years afterwards, actually Monarch. Yet in spite of these things the Sailor Prince did not secure an appointment for W.H.D.: and the latter never makes it clear—indeed perhaps never knew—whether it was a case of 'would not' or 'could not.' It is hard to say. There are several possible explanations, of which two are the most likely:—

(1) That Dillon was altogether overestimating the degree of personal interest that Clarence was taking in him. He is always apt to regard himself as one singled out for special ill treatment: as—and he often says so—'the most ill-used officer in the Navy': whereas the fact was that he was only one of many whom a bad system had grievously harmed, and not necessarily even the worst-harmed. So, without much more and wider evidence, we need not convict H.R.H. of hypocrisy or deceit, or even serious failure to keep his word. We might even extend our sympathy to him, and even to Melville and Cockburn, as men called upon to solve the impossible and very disagreeable problem of getting a quart into a pint-pot—a problem which was none of their making.

(2) Alternatively, it may be that William *did* try hard to help him, and failed: that, insofar as the making of appointments was political, he simply did not carry the requisite—*i.e.* the political—weight of guns: that he was deliberately excluded by the political holders of Admiralty patronage, which was still a very tight vested interest. It is significant, and well known, that, even when Clarence appeared to have stormed the fortress, and had assumed the obsolete yet still glittering title of Lord High Admiral, his powers were so curtailed, controlled and hedged around with safeguards that they remained largely illusory. Anyway, whatever be the true answer—and perhaps it is a blend of both—the Lord High Admiral came and went, William IV was crowned King, and still Dillon got no appointment. It was not, in fact, until two years before that monarch's death that the spell was at last broken: and there is no hint, even then, that the King had any hand in breaking it.

The same remarks apply, in a minor degree, to the efforts of W.H.D.'s especial patron, the Duke of Sussex. Here at least there can be no doubt that H.R.H. was doing his best for his protégé. But there can also be no doubt that he was failing. Possibly, even, as the unfortunate Dillon sometimes suspected, he was *hindering*: for he was always a very vociferous Whig, while Melville and the party he represented at the Admiralty were emphatically Tories. Yet, that his exertions and influence were not entirely ineffective is made clear from an episode which Dillon describes under the year 1830. In the January of that year the Duke sent for him, and announced triumphantly that he had secured him an appointment. This was the command of the Ordinary—the ships out of commission—at Portsmouth. According to W.H.D., he instantly took his well-worn path to the Admiralty, where he was greeted by a smiling Cockburn, who himself, and without solicitation, offered him the job. He accepted at once, and a very friendly interview was closed by Sir George saying, 'Very well, at Portsmouth next March.'

Yet March came, and, hearing nothing, he sought a further interview. All was now changed. A very frigid Sir George referred him to an even more frigid Lord Melville, with whom he got nowhere: and, 'in April the *Ordinary* at Portsmouth was given to another officer who turned out to be one of Sir George's followers.'

At this not only Dillon, but also the Duke was furious. 'I was astonished when I heard the reproaches uttered by H.R.H., who went on in a stream of abuse that cannot be repeated.' He was indeed so angry that he put W.H.D. into a very invidious position. 'Go to him from me,' he said, and ordered me to deliver a message to Sir George —not a very agreeable one—accusing him of double dealing, etc. W.H.D. was scared. He could hardly disobey the Duke's direct orders, but he blenched at the thought of giving mortal offence to a well-entrenched pair like the First Lord and his senior Naval Adviser. So he hedged, shirking the personal interview, and writing a letter instead, in which, no doubt, he watered down some of the harsher Hanoverian asperities.

The result was interesting. Cockburn did not give way, but he thought it advisable to make a personal call on the Duke and try to justify his actions. We can hardly hope, here, for dispassionate reporting, but this is what W.H.D. tells us:

> He made it appear to the Duke that he had not promised Ports-mouth to me, but 'one of the ports.' As the Duke had not been present at the conversation between me and Sir George, he could not deny the assertion. Therefore the Naval Lord told his own tale and got out of the scrape: but not honourably. Such are the doings of men in power. Here ended all my expectations from the present Admiralty.

Then there was the Duke of York. This Prince, who had played such a large, if impersonal part in W.H.D.'s loss of the *Phaeton*, 'had written about me every year since I was paid off.' He had no more success than his brothers, and, early in 1827, his efforts ceased, for he died, having, according to Dillon, sent off his last letter to the Admiralty on his behalf only 10 days previously. W.H.D. was summoned to his funeral, but 'I could not go, being lame from a bad foot—probably a lucky circumstance for me, as several gentlemen who were at it were taken ill and died.'

That year—1827—was spent mostly at Kensington Palace. He also stayed with his old friend the Marquis of Hertford, where he met Prince Esterhazy. Later in the year he met another old colleague— the Mate of the *Crescent*, Thomas Fellowes,[1] now Sir Thomas, knighted for bringing home the Navarino dispatches. W.H.D. has nothing to say of this action itself, but, later on, under 1831, he gives a curious account of what happened at a very high level soon after the battle.

---

[1] See Vol. I, pp. 367, 374, 389. This officer (dates of whose career were omitted in Vol. I) started late, having first served as a Mid. in the E.I.C.'s service, and entering the R.N. as a Mate. Though two years older than W.H.D., and not lacking in 'interest' —he was no tarpaulin—he was 29 when promoted Lieut. (29/6/1807); Cdr. 6/9/09; Capt. 4/3/11; R-Ad. 26/7/47. He had a particularly gallant and distinguished career, specialising in small craft—flotillas, fireships, boats, etc.

Dillon, it appears, received a letter from a brother officer who had been in the action, in which he remarked that all Sir Edward Codrington's officers were under the impression that he fought it against orders, and would certainly be court-martialled when he returned home: and that they were immensely surprised, not only when they received a very generous distribution of honours, but even more when Sir Edward was given the G.C.B. This letter W.H.D. read to the Duke of Sussex, saying that he, too, in common, he thought, with almost everyone in the country, held the same view and shared the same surprise. At this H.R.H. was furious, exclaiming loudly that the Admiral had *not* disobeyed orders; and he packed Dillon off then and there to his famous library to read an article in the *Foreign Quarterly Review*, wherein some foreign diplomatist had 'betrayed his trust' and blurted out the true nature of the instructions given to the Admirals of the British, French and Russian fleets. Having read it,

I returned to H.R.H. and acknowledged to him the impression favourable to Sir Edward produced by the perusal of this article, observing at the same time that I could only be guided in my judgment by the information conveyed to me from the British Squadron. However, the Honours distributed to the Naval Officers present at the Battle of Navarino surpassed in proportion those given to the heroes of Trafalgar: and many comments were the consequence of that act. The fact was that the Duke of Clarence, being then Lord High Admiral, upon the receipt of the account of that victory, repaired instantly to his Royal Brother, the King, and they settled quietly between themselves the honours to be awarded without consulting the Minister.

Early in 1828, despairing of the Lord High Admiral's help, W.H.D. left England, to visit his mother-in-law in France, visiting first Paris, where he became intimate with the Duc de Bourbon, and met Talleyrand : on to Vendome, where Lady Dillon lived, and thence to Tours. Here he proposed to pass the winter, but, hearing, with undisguised relief, of the death of his 'troublesome wife,' he returned to England, arriving in November. He spent the spring of 1829 at Southampton, and the summer and autumn in Town, mainly with his Duke, and varied by a visit to Lord Dillon at Ditchley.

The year 1830 brought renewed hope—two separate hopes, in fact. The first, the chance of the Portsmouth Ordinary command described above, was still-born. The second, however, had more long-term promise. On the 26th June George IV died (W.H.D. attending the funeral): William IV succeeded, and shortly afterwards Earl Grey succeeded Wellington. But, more important from Dillon's point of view, Melville's long term at the Admiralty came to an end. Of his successor, Sir James Graham, W.H.D. has a great deal to say, largely critical. Yet his appearance at the Admiralty undoubtedly made an appointment for Dillon possible: for he had now come to the conclusion, probably rightly, that he had nothing to hope for from the old firm. At the same time, too, Sir Thomas Masterman Hardy relieved Cockburn as First Naval Lord: and Hardy was an old shipmate and, as he thought, an old friend of his. Moreover, his patron, Sussex, though he had constantly quarrelled with the old King, was on much better terms (at first) with the new. Better still, 'as Sir James G. was considered an intimate friend of the Duke of Sussex, and one of the members of his Masonic Lodge, the Alpha, everyone complimented me upon my prospects.' The faithful Sussex pushed him into the new King's presence whenever he could, and everything looked rosy enough. The King even sent to the Admiralty and asked the Second Secretary, Mr. (afterwards Sir John) Barrow, to draw up a report of W.H.D.'s services, which Mr. Barrow, having completed the task, pronounced as highly favourable. So did Hardy, when Dillon hastened to visit him: indeed, he went so far as to say he was sure that Dillon would get anything he asked for. Thereupon W.H.D.'s ambitions soared. He even settled with Sir Thomas, at one moment, to ask for the Command at the Cape, then held by a Commodore. But he soon changed his mind, and decided for the Coastguard Command at Newhaven. His decision, he frankly admits, was coloured by the pay—£1,400 a year—'I wished to make up for the many thousands I had lost through the villany of agents and my long captivity in France.'

Yet nothing happened. The Cape Command was given to an Admiral: the Coastguard Command was abolished by Sir James Graham as a measure of economy. Then, in 1831, he was (he affirms) actually appointed Captain of the *Dublin* by the Board in full conclave, and remained so 'during the space of about two hours': at the end of which Sir James allowed himself to be persuaded (by a naval officer who was also an M.P.) to rescind his decision and give the command to Captain Lord James Townshend,[1] 'to whom, [said the M.P.] he owed his seat in Parliament.'

This is interesting, for Lord Grey and Sir James Graham had both, says W.H.D., made a real effort to clean up the choking undergrowth of 'Interest.'

[1] Lt. 31/1/1806; Cdr. 14/11/06; Capt. 2/6/09. Died *c.* 1841, unpromoted.

Lord Grey began by reducing 250 appointments. His Lordship intended, he said, to govern the Country by public opinion. However, he soon found out that he had miscalculated, for he had scarcely been in power 10 months when he found himself obliged to alter his plans, and to provide for those who supported him in Parliament. The paid Magistrates and other nominations made his Government as expensive as that of the Tories.'

There follows some comment on Graham's well-known reforms—'Economies' is how he describes them.

The First Lord, wishing to make it appear that he had saved the Country a good round sum, began by reducing his own salary £500 per annum. He then did away with the Navy Board, next turned over the Coast Guard, which was considered as a certain number of seamen kept in readiness to be called upon at a minute's notice to man our ships of war, from the Admiralty to the Treasury. Consequently the Admiralty lost all power over them. He then paid off the Marine Artillery—without exception the finest body of men in the whole Kingdom. The Guards were but too glad to enlist them. That was one of the most ill-judged acts. After this, the Naval School of Architecture in Portsmouth Dock Yard was done away.[1] Hitherto we were in the habit of following the foreign lines of construction for our ships of war. Great Britain, the most powerful naval Country in the world, had no naval School of design. It was wanted, and one had been established which was beginning to prove its ability. But it was paid off—for economy. Then the Transport Board. The next reduction was the Royal Yachts. When Lord Grey made that proposal to the King, his Majesty was sensibly annoyed, and exclaimed emphatically, 'What? Take away the Royal Yachts? Then take away the furniture of this room, as one is connected with the other!' This decided tone of the King's led to some discussion, and it was finally decided that three of the yachts were to be dismantled, and the three remaining to be commanded by officers who were to perform a double duty—Captains of the yachts and Superintendents of the Dock Yards. The command of these Royal yachts had been bestowed, six in number, upon very meritorious Naval Officers as a reward for their distinguished services. But under the Whig Administration the whole system was changed. All our Dock Yards were well supplied with stores, and none were purchased during the first 12 months of his administration. All for economy, but this in the end, it was proved, did no good. However, he did establish an office for the registration of seamen, at an annual expense

---

[1] This was retrograde, and short-sighted. The first school of Naval Architecture had only been established in 1810—about a century after the first French one. Abolished in 1832, it was several times restored and re-abolished before the final establishment in 1883 of the Royal Corps of Naval Constructors.

of £3,000. Sir Thomas Hardy, I thought, yielded too much to his Chief's propensities. The poor unfortunate Mates in the Navy who, when deaths occurred, were ordered to act as Lieutenants in their places, were deprived of the pay for which they did the duty.[1] Such an oppressive act had never before been enforced.

This diatribe is, of course, by no means fair to Sir James,[2] some of whose reforms, notably those connected with the Navy Board, and the Registration of seamen, were of the utmost importance, and destined to usher in, almost, a new era. But it is not very surprising that the oft-disappointed Dillon, diehard Tory as he was, should take so poor a view of Graham and his economies. For it all militated —or he thought it did—against his chances of a job. And in Graham's time he did not get one.

Thus frustrated, W.H.D. now turned his attention to securing comforts and honours of a different character. First, he made another determined effort to be made a Companion of the Bath (see above, p. 425). On the occasion of the King's Coronation (September 1831), twenty C.B.'s were to be distributed to naval officers, and, on the advice of his old friend Sir Robert Otway, he wrote and put in a strong claim to be included in the list. Then, hurrying to the Admiralty, he persuaded Hardy to acknowledge the justice of that claim, and indeed, learned that his name stood twelfth on the list. But—alas— 'the next day I received an answer from Sir J. Graham that His Majesty had decided that the honour should only extend to Capt. A. King,[3] just two above me.' Poor Dillon was angry: but angrier still when first the King and then Sir James each added a name of his own choosing to the lucky ten. So twelve got it after all—but W.H.D. was not one. 'So much,' he comments bitterly, 'for Court favour. I was thrown out, and have never received the honour here mentioned.' O'Byrne, in his *Naval Biography*, asserts that Dillon was nominated K.C.B. on the 13th January 1835, thereby promoting his subject to an even higher grade. But he is wrong, and Dillon is

[1] This injustice, another legacy of a hopelessly overcrowded profession, was partly redressed in 1840 by the creation of the new substantive rank of 'Mate,' between 'Midshipman' and 'Lieutenant,' to be renamed, in 1861, 'Sub-Lieutenant.'

[2] It is not even quite fair, for instance, to infer that Sir James abolished the Royal Marine Artillery. That magnificent body, established by O. in C. 18/4/1801, was, it is true, reduced in 1831 to two companies, to be annexed to the Portsmouth Division. But the operative order of 2/12/1831, having decreed the retention of these companies, goes on as follows:—'. . . in order to prevent the total extinction of Artillery science and skill, *and as a nucleus whereon to form a greater body which may hereafter be judged desirable*'. (Editor's italics.)

[3] Andrew King, Lt. 11/8/1797; Cdr. 22/1/1806; Capt. 13/11/07. Died, 30/6/35. An officer with a fine record: at the First of June, Copenhagen (1801 *and* 1807), Trafalgar (Fourth Lieut. of the *Victory*) and Walcheren.

right: he never received even the lower one. The 'K.C.B.' is clearly a misprint for 'K.C.H.' (see below).

Yet another year passed, and no appointment came: then W.H.D. made a wiser and much more successful move of a different nature altogether:

> . . . therefore, as a favourable chance presented itself, I took unto myself a wife, who having an independent fortune, we were united in the month of September (1832).

He took her off to Blois and Tours for the winter; and, though the lady remains a complete shadow throughout the Narrative, the match was clearly a not unhappy one. Her name—which he never mentions —was Isabella Willan, eldest daughter of John Willan, Esq., of Hatton Gardens, and there are many small indications that that 'independent fortune' was coming in handy. Now, when he goes abroad, he travels in his own carriage with his own horses, and takes 'a pleasant furnished house for the winter' instead of staying in hotels. They returned to England in May 1833, and went into residence 'in my own house.'

Still his hopes were unsatisfied. A year passed, and, in June 1834, he and his wife decided on an extensive continental tour. They were just about to start when Sir James Graham suddenly left the Admiralty, to be succeeded by Lord Auckland. The persevering Dillon instantly postponed his departure, in order to make himself known to the new Chief, and obtained an interview. He was very well received, and though he got nothing for the moment, he was not altogether dissatisfied: for Auckland, evidently a novice, was betrayed into admitting that 'my colleagues tell me there is no officer before you.' W.H.D. pounced on this, and promptly replied, 'If that is the opinion of me at the Admiralty, how is it that I can not get employed?' But his Lordship instantly covered up. 'Very true, very true,' he replied. 'But there are conflicting interests which you can not possibly understand.' And this was probably about as near the truth as any of the answers with which Dillon had been fobbed off for the last dozen years. The old scramble was still on. The man-on-the-spot—the man who got in the last word, particularly if he happened to be an M.P.—was always successful.

Disappointed once more, W.H.D. now tried a move in the other, the social, game. It was in this year—1834—that he put in to the King his request to be 'allowed to assume the title, so long in our family, of a Baron of the German Empire.' We have seen (Vol. I,

Introduction, p. xi) how the King reacted to this rather naïve request, and the probable reason. Yet now, at long last, Fate—and the King—relented, for William having said in effect, 'No, not in England,' added, 'However, if he chooses I will knight him and give him the Star of Hanover.'

It need scarcely be mentioned, perhaps, that W.H.D. *did* choose, and it was arranged that 'His Majesty would knight me within the year.' He was highly gratified. He could even, he felt, afford it now.

> I found that I had sufficient income to support the title about to be conferred on me, and I thought that I was right in taking it, as my Father and others of our family, yourself in the number, had borne one.

Then, in a happier frame of mind than had been his for many years, he bore his wife off on their extended tour. It lasted one year less six days. They explored Italy with remarkable thoroughness, and he expends 171 MS. pages of Vol. VI in recording it. He covered, he writes, 4,152 miles.

From the moment that he set foot again in England on 18th June, 1835, things began to happen. The old King had not forgotten his promise. W.H.D. received from the Hanoverian Minister 'the Second Order of the Hanoverian Knighthood'—that, is Knight Commander, (K.C.H.), below G.C.H. but above K.H.—and on June 24th, 1835, the accolade from His Majesty, 'who knighted me with a cheerful countenance . . . and desired his Private Secretary to let me know that he felt great pleasure in bestowing that order upon me. . . . The tide had taken a turn in my favour.'

It had indeed: for, in addition, his great ambition was about to be fulfilled. His days in the wilderness were over.

It is not clear to the last who was primarily responsible. Everyone, all of a sudden, seemed to smile upon him. The First Lord, Auckland, was so lavish in his praises as to reduce him in an interview to an incoherent and unaccustomed stammer. At his club he was accosted by 'the Hon. Admiral Fleeming,'[1] a complete stranger to him, who volunteered the information that he would be given the choice between two ships, the *Rodney*, a new 90-gun ship at Portsmouth, and the *Russel*, an ordinary 74 at Sheerness, and urged him to take the latter, simply because 'she is lying at Sheerness where I have the Port Command.' (He was C.-in-C., Nore, at the time.) 'But don't you accept the *Rodney*,' he went on. 'If you do, you will repent it. She is built upon what are considered improved principles,

[1] See above, pp. 321 and 361.

and you will be worried out of your life with letters, experiments and the Lord knows what.' No sooner had the Admiral moved on than his Flag Captain took his place, and besought Dillon to come down to Sheerness and take the *Russel*, offering to give him a bed indefinitely in his house. The Captain had hardly left him, gasping, when one of the Lords of the Admiralty, Troubridge,[1] bore down upon him, and literally stood over him while he wrote to Lord Auckland to ask for the *Rodney*: which W.H.D., by now almost dithering, did. But his luck was still in, for the knotty point was decided for him without anyone's feelings being hurt. At 6 next morning, the 9th July, he found an official letter on his table, and 'was informed of my being appointed Captain of the *Russel*, 74, at Sheerness.'

So there it was at last, the precious scrap of paper! He had been 'on the beach' for 15¾ years, but his dream had come true at last. He had been honoured by the King: he had been reinstated: he had become, in his own right, Captain of his first—and, as it was to prove, his last—battleship. He was nearly 55 years old, and he had been Post Captain for 27⅓ years—by a curious coincidence almost exactly half his total lifetime. He was somebody again, both socially and professionally. He was very happy.

---

[1] Sir Edward Thomas Troubridge, Bart., C.B., M.P., at this time still a Captain. Only son of the famous Sir Thomas Troubridge. Lt. 22/2/1806; Cdr. 5/9/06; Capt. 28/11/07; R-Ad. 23/1/41.

XVII
LAST COMMISSION AND AFTER

JULY 9, 1835–SEPTEMBER 9, 1857
(*aet.* 55–77)

XVII
LAST COMMISSION AND AFTER

JULY 9, 1835–SEPTEMBER 9, 1857

(*aet.* 55–77)

THE narrative of W.H.D.'s last commission in the *Russel*, consisting of 251 pages, is entirely omitted here. As this is a radical departure from previous practice, some explanation is necessary.

That final command, so long and so eagerly awaited by himself, must prove a great disappointment to the reader, whether his interests are primarily nautical, historical, political, literary or just 'general'. It is probably true that the author tended to become more prosy and prolix as he grew older, and this does not help the two last-named interests. But he also tended to convey less and less information about life afloat, and the day-to-day working and administration of a ship. In lieu of such matters he substitutes, more and more, accounts of his social relations—especially 'grand balls', 'splendid banquets' and sightseeing excursions—with the various people whom he meets. They are, it is true, rather more important and influential people—mainly foreigners—than he consorted with before. Yet, even so, they are none of them people of much historical significance, nor are they, for the most part, people with any serious naval connections.

Thus far, the absence of interest and importance in this part of his Narrative may be laid as a fault at his door. But the fault is by no means entirely his. Circumstance plays its part. The geography of the *Russel's* cruises was, as it happens, much the same as that of the *Leopard's*, so that he had but little topographical novelty to help him eke out his pages. Moreover, when the *Leopard* was cruizing in a wartime Mediterranean, off the Iberian coast much of which was occupied by the enemy, and where, any day, something of true naval interest *might* happen, the *Russel* was rather 'showing the flag' in a period when Great Britain at any rate was wrapped in profound peace, and when anything of a warlike nature was most unlikely to happen. Nor again is there any real political significance in his pages. Here he might have done more, for events of at least local political significance were not entirely absent. Indeed, he does from time to time refer to the Carlist troubles, and even maintains, a trifle half-heartedly, that the very presence of his 74 did on occasions assist the Spanish Government: and probably he was right, though that assistance never amounted to anything in terms of action. He mentions, too, a joint Anglo-French demonstration at Lisbon in November, 1836, against the subversive Septembrists. But here, as usual, his essentially unpolitical outlook intervenes, and he actually excuses himself from giving any details 'as I never exactly understood or had explained to me the exact bearings of the case.' Again, the 1830's contain for the naval historian much that is of interest and importance in the way of the evolution of ships, armament and equipment, even then gaining impetus. Yet Dillon is of no use whatever here: not once does he touch upon the subject.

The three topics upon which he spends most time—apart from 'elegant collations' etc.—will perhaps best serve to justify the Editor's decision. There is, first, a very long-drawn-out account of a stupid misunderstanding, leading to a bitter and rather obscure wrangle, which he had with the British Ambassador to Portugal, Lord Howard de Walden; in which, of course, he was entirely in the right, and from which the Ambassador emerged second-best. Then there is a long account of the trouble which he had with his very well-connected but (he says) highly unruly quota of Midshipmen. This ended with seven of them being removed from the ship, and one—the son of an old friend—from the Navy. He mentions no names. The third topic is an even longer-drawn-out diatribe against Sir John Ommaney,[1] the Admiral Commanding the Lisbon station during the latter part of the commission. W.H.D.'s complaints centre upon the impoliteness, boorishness and lack of consideration of the C.-in-C. for his Second in Command—Dillon—which he illustrates with endless and mostly trivial instances. It is dreary because, in essence, we have heard it all before, and regrettably true to type as a recurrence of that persecution-mania with which we have long been familiar. To reproduce it all again would enhance neither our knowledge of the man nor the esteem in which we hold him. Indeed, the

---

[1] Sir John Acworth Ommaney, K.C.B., Lt. 20/5/1793; Cdr. 6/12/96; Capt. 16/10/1800; R-Ad. 22/7/30; V-Ad. 23/11/41; Ad. 4/5/1849. A fair example of 'the Block' in its later stages. In 1854 he was still employed—as C. in C. Plymouth in wartime, aged 81! The anxiety of fitting out the Baltic Fleet caused his breakdown, and he died in 1855.

only evidence that such things provide is that his weaknesses had not diminished with age.

One other factor made the Editor's decision easier. Space would not have permitted the inclusion of this *Russel* part and all the other parts. Had this been included, some other must have been excluded, and there is certainly no better candidate for omission.

His command ended early in 1839, and he left the ship finally on the 18th January. He was now in a very different frame of mind from that usual to him upon paying off. No longer did he rush straight off to the Admiralty in search of a new appointment. Far from it: he had evidently made up his mind beforehand that his active career was over. Whether he had been officially told so or whether the initiative came from him is not made clear. He never discusses the point. He just assumes that his sea-time is done. Yet he probably knew more about future arrangements and prospects than he mentions. The King had told him, before he took command of the *Russel*, that 'when your command expires, I shall take care that you will be provided with an appointment for life.' But, 18 months before this happened, the old Sailor King had passed on his Crown to the young Queen, and W.H.D. does not refer again to this promise. Yet he was evidently expecting the Good Service Pension to be awarded to him on his return; and when it was offered, he promptly accepted it, with a sense neither of gratitude nor of being done out of his deserts, but simply as the inevitable reward for one who had been so good and faithful an officer.

Yet these pensions were by no means automatic grants to deserving officers. They were rather special awards—only about half a dozen Flag Officers and perhaps a dozen Captains were receiving them. Their history, then just beginning, is interesting. Until two years before—1837—the well-known 'sinecures' of Generalships, Lieut.-Generalships, Major-Generalships and Colonelcies of the Royal Marines had been in existence, and under a sporadic fire of criticism, for many years. They had been distributed to well-known, or well-placed, naval officers, primarily upon the principle of 'unto him that hath shall be given.' But now—12/7/1837—an Order-in-Council had abolished them, and, taking over the fund which had gone to pay them, had established Good Service Pensions out of it for a few Flag Officers and Captains. The former were to receive not more than £300 a year, the latter not more than £150. But there were conditions attached which serve to show the object underlying the new scheme. A Flag Officer was to relinquish his pension upon securing a command, whilst a Captain was to forego his, not only when appointed to a ship but also when promoted to Flag rank. The whole thing was just another small contribution towards relieving the existing block in promotion and appointment. Indeed, the sequel seems to show that it was the promotion rather than the appointment delay which Authority wanted to alleviate, for a further Order of 27/4/1842 laid it down that Good Service Captains should retain their pensions even when employed, though not when promoted. Thus an employed Good Service Captain would now endure more readily the tedium of waiting for his Flag in that he was receiving both full pay and pension.

But this did not, as it happened, affect W.H.D., who was not employed again. So he went on drawing his pension until 1846 when, upon promotion, he relinquished it. And he did not, nor by the rules could he, receive the larger Good Service Pension of the Flag Officer.

It is very probable that he wanted no more service. He was 58, and had suffered a good deal both from the effects of his wound and from more general ill health. He had a sharp attack of ague in 1837, and at Christmas-time in that year he was suffering from stomach trouble, and felt so ill that he tried to arrange an exchange into a ship which would bring him home then and there. This fell through at the last moment, but it was very likely then that he made up his mind to apply for no further appointment afloat when his *Russel* time was up.

He must have realised, moreover, that his prospects of hoisting his Flag at sea—the prime ambition of most naval officers—were extremely slender. The dreadful promotion-block had not nearly resolved itself. His early failures in reaching Commander's rank, coupled with his unfortunate captivity at Verdun, had handicapped him grievously in the gruesome promotion-stakes. The process of waiting for one's seniors to die was slow and tedious, and elevations to flag-rank, made in batches, were few and far between. Even now the Captains made post after Trafalgar were only just receiving their flags: and thereafter there must be, he knew full well, another weary wait before any of them, and even then only the very select among them, would fly them afloat. If he thought along these lines—and he almost certainly did—the actuality certainly bore him out. He did not have very much luck. There was a large promotion on the 23rd November, 1841, which reached down all but, but not quite, to him. He found himself left third on the Captains' List, and it was five years before the next promotion happened. Then, on the

9th November, 1846, he became a Rear Admiral at last, being 66 years old and having 38½ years in as a Captain.

But now—now that, for all practical purposes, it was too late— two factors were at work resolving the block. First, the veterans of the Wars were all growing old, and rapidly dying off: and second, the long overdue reforms which brought in a more modern and equitable system of Retirement were already under way. So he did not have to wait nearly so long for his next step—he was promoted Vice Admiral on the 5th March, 1853. He would have become full Admiral on the 20th January, 1858: but, four months before, on the 9th September, 1857, he too fell out of the race. He died, one month after his 77th birthday.

We know little of his later years, and that, such as it is, has already been recorded in the Introduction to Volume I of this work (pp. xxiv–xxvi). He himself had no more to add after leaving the *Russel.* He had contracted in his letters to his cousin to give a 'Narrative of my Professional Adventures,' and these adventures were now over. So he stopped writing his letters.

Yet, though the letters end here, the Note Books (into which he copied them) go a little further. There are three short notes, clearly intended to be explanatory, or additional, to the main Narrative. These are given in full here, the first for its bearing on the composition of the whole, the second for its intrinsic interest, and the third as being the very last words that we have from Admiral Dillon's pen.

I.

Some years after this Narrative was written, my cousin Sir John Dillon being dead, all my letters were returned to me by his sister the Baroness, who has also departed from this life: and I transcribed them as they now appear. They were addressed to him in confidence: therefore many parts alluding to various individuals ought to be left out—their names, etc.—should the Narrative ever appear in print.

The gallant Author made some sporadic attempts to implement this decision by omitting, in the later part of his work, many letters in many personal names. The Editor's apologies are, possibly, due to him for having disregarded this directive: but he hopes that he may be regarded as having in some measure expiated his guilt (if any) by the extra labour, not inconsiderable, involved in refilling the blanks.

II.

I took a very lively interest on many occasions in the fate of Horatia, Nelson's daughter, now Mrs. Ward; and, assisted by others, I headed a deputation to the Prime Minister, Lord Aberdeen. Mr. Hume took a very decided part in this instance in behalf of Mrs. Ward, and the result obtained a pension for her from the Queen's Bounty of £300 per annum, to descend to her three daughters at her decease. A sort of public subscription had been previously set on foot to which I contributed, but it was not a successful one. However, Lord Aberdeen's influence as Prime Minister gained the object desired. This transaction is alluded to in the Illustrated London News of the 17th June, 1854.

III.

[Written, probably, in 1856 or 7.]

When Lord Grey's administration came into power, allusion is made in this Narrative to the reductions made by the First Lord of the Admiralty. Sir James Graham returned to that Board in the year 1853. In the following year we were at war with Russia, and, as our troops were sent out to the Crimea, we had not Government transport vessels sufficient to convey them thither. Consequently we were obliged to hire from the Merchant Service. Some were bought at an immense expense, and the ill-judged effects of the paying off of that Board [*i.e.* the Transport Board] was seriously felt by the nation. So much for economy! In a country like Great Britain, with numerous colonies, transports are always wanted, peace or war, to send out military there, as well for other purposes. And Sir J. Graham was under the necessity of re-establishing the Board which he had dismissed—a decided proof that the economy intended was a complete failure.

An attempt was made in the Introduction to Vol. I (pp. xxxii–xxxiv) to assess the qualities of W.H.D., mainly as a naval officer. Little more need be added. Yet one particular quality in his make-up has been rather startlingly underlined in the later pages of the Narrative. We still note certain traits which, to the ordinary man, are extremely irritating. Yet it would be very wrong, and a real injustice to him, to end upon so critical a note. Let us rather, as we take our leave of him, stress one quality of his which is altogether good: one which, throughout the history of the Royal Navy, has been almost as common as it is good—an intense loyalty to the Service of his choice. No one who has read these pages can doubt for a moment the intensity of that loyalty. The Navy was in a very full sense his whole life. Forty-nine years passed between the day when he first set foot on the deck of the *Royal William* and that on which he left the *Russel's*: and, though his service was by no means continuous, that, we must readily admit, was no fault of his. Far from it! Not once in this near-half century did he refuse a chance to go afloat: on the contrary, whenever he was not afloat there is no missing his fretful eagerness to remedy so unnatural a situation. Even when, in the depths of the Wilderness, other officers, and good ones too, became disheartened and gave up with an unhappy shrug, not so W.H.D. Be there the merest whiff of a rumour that something is going, there, as sure as fate, is W.H.D. 'hastening to the Admiralty', and, it must be owned, pestering the life out of officialdom residing there.

There is another manifestation too of this same wholehearted loyalty. W.H.D., it can hardly be denied, is by nature a censorious person. People can be, and all too often are, exceedingly blameworthy in his eyes. Politicians and diplomatists may err—in fact, it would appear, usually do. First Lords are by no means exempt. Even naval officers, individually, are targets for some of the severest criticisms. But THE NAVY, in the abstract, is never wrong: is never bad: is never beaten: is never beatable: is, in his every thought and word and deed, the prime object of his affection, his veneration, his worship. The legion of criticised persons resolves itself upon examination into just two categories: those who wrong or decry W.H.D., and—an even larger group—those who are (in his opinion) acting contrary to the interests of the Service.

So his critics, I believe, especially if they be Naval Men, will, in their final judgment, rally to his defence. To him who loves much, much is forgiven.

INDEX

2 K

INDEX OF SHIPS

Note: the letters in brackets after a ship's name indicate as follows:—(Dan), Danish; (Du.), Dutch; (Fr.), French; (Hu.) Hulk; (Mer.), Merchant; (Pri.), Privateer; (Sp.), Spanish ; (St.), Storeship ; (Tr.), Troopship; (U.S.), United States.

Navy Records Society.

(Founded 1893.)

The Navy Records Society was established for the purpose of printing rare or unpublished works of naval interest. The Society is open to all who are interested in naval history and any person wishing to become a member should apply to the Hon. Secretary, Royal Naval College, Greenwich, London, S.E. 10. The annual subscription is two guineas, the payment of which entitles the member to receive one copy of each work issued by the Society for that year.

The annual subscription for members under thirty years of age is one guinea.

MEMBERS or NON-MEMBERS requiring copies of any volume should apply to the Hon. Secretary.

The price of volumes published before 1950 (*i.e.* Vols. I–LXXXVII inclusive) is 21/– to members and 25/– to non-members. Volumes published after that date are available at 42/– to members and 45/– to non-members.

The Society has already issued :—

Vols. I. and II. *State Papers relating to the Defeat of the Spanish Armada, Anno* 1588. Edited by Professor J. K. Laughton. (Vol. I. *Out of Print.*)

Vol. III. *Letters of Lord Hood*, 1781–82. Edited by Mr. David Hannay. (*Out of Print.*)

Vol. IV. *Index to James's Naval History*, by Mr. C. G. Toogood. Edited by the Hon. T. A. Brassey.

Vol. V. *Life of Captain Stephen Martin*, 1666–1740. Edited by Sir Clements R. Markham. (*Out of Print.*)

Vol. VI. *Journal of Rear-Admiral Bartholomew James*, 1752–1828. Edited by Professor J. K. Laughton and Commander J. Y. F. Sulivan.

Vol. VII. *Hollond's Discourses of the Navy*, 1638 and 1658. Edited by Mr. J. R. Tanner.

Vol. VIII. *Naval Accounts and Inventories in the Reign of Henry VII.* Edited by Mr. M. Oppenheim.

Vol. IX. *Journal of Sir George Rooke.* Edited by Mr. Oscar Browning. (*Out of Print.*)

Vol. LXIV. *The Journal of the First Earl of Sandwich.* Edited by Mr. R. C. Anderson.

Vol. LXV. *Boteler's Dialogues.* Edited by Mr. W. G. Perrin.

Vol. LXVI. *Papers relating to the First Dutch War,* 1652–54 (Vol. VI. ; with index). Edited by Mr. C. T. Atkinson.

Vol. LXVII. *The Byng Papers* (Vol. I.). Edited by Mr. W. C. B. Tunstall.

Vol. LXVIII. *The Byng Papers* (Vol. II.). Edited by Mr. W. C. B. Tunstall.

Vol. LXIX. *The Private Papers of John, Earl of Sandwich* (Vol. I.). Edited by Mr. G. R. Barnes and Lieut.-Commander J. H. Owen, R.N.

Corrigenda to *Papers relating to the First Dutch War,* 1652–54 (Vols. I. to VI.). Edited by Captain A. C. Dewar, R.N.

Vol. LXX. *The Byng Papers* (Vol. III.). Edited by Mr. W. C. B. Tunstall.

Vol. LXXI. *The Private Papers of John, Earl of Sandwich* (Vol. II.). Edited by Mr. G. R. Barnes and Lieut.-Commander J. H. Owen, R.N.

Vol. LXXII. *Piracy in the Levant,* 1827–8. Edited by Lieut.-Commander C. G. Pitcairn Jones, R.N.

Vol. LXXIII. *The Tangier Papers of Samuel Pepys.* Edited by Mr. Edwin Chappell.

Vol. LXXIV. *The Tomlinson Papers.* Edited by Mr. J. G. Bullocke.

Vol. LXXV. *The Private Papers of John, Earl of Sandwich* (Vol. III.). Edited by Mr. G. R. Barnes and Commander J. H. Owen, R.N.

Vol. LXXVI. *The Letters of Robert Blake.* Edited by the Rev. J. R. Powell.

Vol. LXXVII. *Letters and Papers of Admiral the Hon. Samuel Barrington* (Vol. I.). Edited by Mr. D. Bonner-Smith.

Vol. LXXVIII. *The Private Papers of John, Earl of Sandwich* (Vol. IV.). Edited by Mr. G. R. Barnes and Commander J. H. Owen, R.N.

Vol. LXXIX. *The Journals of Sir Thomas Allin,* 1660–1678 (Vol. I. 1660–66). Edited by Mr. R. C. Anderson.

Mavy Records Society

LIST OF MEMBERS

1956

Asterisk denotes membership paid by Covenant.

———◆◆———

Allen, Lieutenant (S.) A. E., 12a Castle Street, Christchurch, Hants.
*Allenby, R. F. H., Esq., The Beacon, Shanklin, Isle of Wight.
*Ampthill, Captain The Lord, C.B.E., R.N., 6 Springfield Road, St. Johns Wood, N.W.8.
Anderson, R. C., Esq., Litt.D., F.S.A., 32 Dartmouth Row, London, S.E.10.
*Angerstein-Burton, Commander E. A., R.N., The Old Rectory, West Lexham, Kings Lynn, Norfolk.
Appleby, Sub-Lieutenant (Ex. S.) John S., R.N.V.R., Cranford House, Elmstead Market, Colchester, Essex.
Armytage, Captain R. W., A.M., R.N., Foxlease, Limpley Stoke, Near Bath.
*Arrowsmith, Lieutenant H. C., R.N.V.R., Moorings, Grove Road, Southlands, Stone, Staffordshire.
Atkinson, C. T., Esq., 16 Chadlington Road, Oxford.
Andrewes, Vice-Admiral Sir William, K.B.E., C.B., D.S.O., Royal Naval College, Greenwich, S.E.10.
Austin, E. D., Esq., 17 Earls Court Road, Penylan, Cardiff.

Baddeley, Sir Vincent W., K.C.B., 60 Harley House, Marylebone Road, London, N.W.1.
*Barlow, Captain T. E., R.N., Boswells, Wendover, Bucks.
*Barnes, Sir George R., The Clock House, Keele, Staffs.
Barnes, Lieutenant-Commander H. J., R.N., H.M.S. *Ceres*, Wetherby, Yorks.
D. F. Barton, Esq., Henslow Close, Fyfield, Abingdon, Berks.
Bateman, C. J. L., Esq., Caixa Postal 416, Santos, Brazil.
Bax, Allan E., Esq., Prudential Buildings, 39 Martin Place, Sydney, Australia.
Beale, Commander P. S., R.N., 21 Palmyra Street, Honolulu 18, Territory of Hawaii, U.S.A.
Beattie, Captain S. H., V.C., R.N., A.C.R. Dept., Queen Anne's Mansions, S.W.1.
Beeston, P. S., Esq., c/o National Bank of Australasia Ltd., 308 Queen Street, Brisbane, Australia.
Bell, Captain L. H., C.B.E., R.N., c/o The Admiralty, London, S.W.1.
Bellairs, Rear-Admiral Roger M., C.B., C.M.G., Wyvenhoe, Farnham Royal, Bucks.
Benbow, Colin H., Esq., B.A., 33 Heathfield Gardens, London, N.W.11.

LIST OF MEMBERS

*Bennett, Captain G. M., D.S.C., R.N., c/o National Provincial Bank Ltd., The Hard, Portsmouth, Hants.

Besford, C. H., Esq., 4 Vine Cottages, Grove Footpath, Surbiton, Surrey.

Besnard, Lieutenant P., R.N.N., c/o Marine Post Kantoor, Amsterdam, Holland.

*Bevan, Lieutenant W. J., R.N. (Retd.), De Montalt, Lyncombe Hill, Bath.

*Blair, Lieutenant Arthur W., R.N.V.(S.)R., 22 Thorn Drive, Bearsden, Glasgow.

Blake, Vice-Admiral Sir Geoffrey, K.C.B., D.S.O., Fiddlers, Beaulieu, Hants.

*Blundell, Captain G. C., O.B.E., R.N., c/o National Provincial Bank Ltd., 95 Chancery Lane, London. W.C.2.

*Booth, Lieutenant Norleigh, R.N.V.R., Stanner's Close, Corbridge-on-Tyne.

*Boultbee, Lieutenant-Colonel W. R. P., R.N., 38 Priestfields, Rochester, Kent.

Boyer, Francis L., Esq., 299 Alabama Road, Towson 4, Maryland, U.S.A.

Bright, Captain B. N. F., (Retd.), B.Hist., Richmond Manse, Tarporley, Cheshire.

Broadbent, Lieutenant-Commander (E.) W. D., R.N., Gower House, Stockbridge Road, Chichester, Sussex.

*Brock, Rear Admiral P. W., R.N., c/o Bank of Montreal, 47 Threadneedle Street, London, E.C.2.

Brock, Thomas L., 31 Hyde Park Gate, London, S.W.7.

*Brocklebank, Captain H. C., C.B.E., R.N., Charlton House, Shaftesbury, Dorset.

*Brockman, Captain (S.) W., c/o Barclays Bank Ltd., Saltash, Cornwall.

*Bromley, John S., Esq., M.A., Keble College, Oxford.

Brooke, Mrs. Cecil, Hampton Court Palace, Middlesex.

Brooks, Lieutenant-Commander C. E., R.C.N., 25 Finchley Road, Hampstead, Montreal, P.Q., Canada.

*Brown, Thomas W. F., Esq., D.Sc., Dumbreck, Wylam, Northumberland.

Buckland, J.V., Esq., Honer House, South Mundham, Near Chichester, Sussex.

*Buckle, Lieutenant F. A., D.S.C., R.N.V.R., The Secondary County School, Midhurst, Sussex.

Bulley, Lieutenant H. C. E., R.N., St. Edmund's School, Hindhead, Surrey.

*Bullocke, Professor J. G., 5 Dartmouth Grove, Greenwich, S.E.10.

*Burden, Lieutenant (S.) H. S., R.N.V.R., 63 Eastfield Road, Waltham Cross, Herts.

Burnford, J. M. W., Esq., Borough Farm, Pulborough, Sussex.

*Burns, Lieutenant-Commander George, 201 Bath Street (Second Floor), R.N.V.R., Glasgow, C.1.

*Burrough, Admiral Sir Harold M., K.C.B., K.B.E., D.S.O., c/o Westminster Bank Ltd., 21 Clarendon Road, Southsea, Hants.

Butler, Professor J. R. Montagu, O.B.E., M.V.O., M.A., Cabinet Offices, Great George Street, London, S.W.1.

*Butler-Bowden, Captain M. E., O.B.E., R.N., 6a North Grove, Highgate Village, London, N.6.

*Carr, Frank G. G., Esq., National Maritime Museum, London, S.E.10.

Caufield, W., Esq., B.Sc., M.R.C.V.S., 26 Regent Place, Rugby.

*Carter, Captain T. G., O.B.E., R.N., c/o Glyn, Mills & Co., Kirkland House, Whitehall, S.W.1.

*Catlow, A. J., Esq., " Sunnydene," Bounds Cross, Biddenden, Ashford, Kent.

*Chandler, Commander R. B., R.N., Recruiting Office, Royal Navy and Royal Marines, 7 St. John's Lane, Liverpool, 1.

LIST OF MEMBERS

Charig, Commander (E.) Peter, R.N., St. Peter's Cottage, Nunney, Frome, Somerset.
*Chatfield, Admiral of the Fleet the Rt. Hon. Lord, G.C.B., O.M., K.C.M.G., C.V.O., D.C.L., The Small House, Farnham Common, Bucks.
*Chichester, Commander M. G., R.N., 83 Barkston Gardens, London, S.W.5.
Child, Commander D. W., O.B.E., R.N.V.R., Lavenir, Wellington Parade, Walmer, Deal, Kent.
*Cleveland-Stevens, W., Esq., Q.C., Winchet Hall, Goudhurst, Kent.
Cleyndert, J. B. De J., Esq., 4 Strand on the Green, London, W.4.
*Cole, Commander (S.) J. H. Melvin, R.N., c/o Westminster Bank Ltd., 26 Haymarket, S.W.1.
Cole, Commander P. F., R.N., H.A.F. Med., F.M.O. Malta.
*Congleton, The Rt. Hon. Lord, Minstead Lodge, Lyndhurst, Hants.
Costeker, Miss E. P., 15 Marlborough Road, Bournemouth West.
*Cottesloe, The Rt. Hon. Lord, C.B., The Old House, Swanbourne, Bletchley, Bucks.
Coulehan, N., Esq., Burke Road North, Ivanhoe, Melbourne, Australia.
Cox, Lieutenant-Commander I. N. D., D.S.C., R.N., Royal Naval Barracks, Portsmouth.
*Creswell, Captain John, R.N., Ellerslie, Gattistock, Dorchester.
*Crick, Commander T. G. P., O.B.E., D.S.C., R.N., c/o Barclays Bank Ltd., Peterborough.
*Critchley, Lieutenant (S.) W. L., R.N., Royal Naval College, Dartmouth, Devon.
Cunliffe, Captain R. L. B., C.B.E., R.N., Pakenham Lodge, Bury St. Edmunds, Suffolk.
Cunningham-Graham, Vice-Admiral Sir A. E. M. B., K.B.E., C.B., Ardoch, Cardross, Dumbartonshire.
*Curry, The Rev. Jim, R.N., H.M.S. *Daedalus*, Lee-on-Solent, Hants.

Daly, Associate Professor R. W., U.S. Naval Academy, Annopolis, Md, U.S.A.
*Davidson, The Rt. Hon. The Viscount, G.C.V.O., C.H., C.B., Norcott Court, Berkhamsted, Herts.
*Davis, B. J., Esq., F.C.A., 101 Ridgway, Wimbledon, S.W.19.
Daw, Instructor Commander L. J., R.N., Fair View, 414 Crownhill Road, Higher St. Budeaux, Plymouth.
Dawson, Instructor Commander E. R., M.A., R.N., 9 Guest Road, Cambridge.
Dee, Mrs. Stephanie, Adisadel College, Cape Coast, Gold Coast.
*De Pass, Lieutenant-Commander Robert E. F., Inchyra House, By Perth, Scotland.
de Beer, Esmond S., Esq., F.R.Hist.S., 11 Sussex Place, London, N.W.1.
de Cosson, Lieutenant-Commander C. Anthony, R.N.V.R., 3062 Mathers Avenue, West Vancouver, B.C.
Dewar, Captain A. C., C.B., O.B.E., B.Litt., F.R.Hist.S., R.N., Junior Army and Navy Club, Horse Guards Avenue, London, S.W.1.
*Dick, Rear Admiral R. M., C.B.E., D.S.C., R.N., 52 Old Church Street, Chelsea, S.W.3.
Dixon, Lieutenant-Commander (S.) D. B., R.C.N., U.S.N. Supply Depot, San Diego, California, U.S.A.
*Dowell, Squadron Leader W., Restenet, Lenzie, Glasgow.
Denizet, M. Jean (*Corresponding Member*), Comité Central, 41 Rue De La Bienfaisance, Paris 8.
Dorling, Captain H. Taprell, D.S.O., R.N., 97 Rivermead Court, Hurlingham, S.W.6.

LIST OF MEMBERS

Drake, K. M., Esq., 17 King's Drive, Birstall, Leeds.
Draper, A. S. Esq., Westfield, Wigginton, York.
*Driscoll, The Reverend W. J., R.N., St. Joan of Arc's, Torpoint, Cornwall.
Dye, Commander Ira, U.S.N., 3200 Raymond Street, Seattle 8, Washington, U.S.A.

Eastwick, Miss C. L., Curlew Bank, Brittas Bay, Co. Wicklow, Eire.
Eccleshall, Leslie C., Esq., 148 Priory Road, Hardway, Gosport, Hants.
Eckford, Lieutenant (S.) P. J., R.N., c/o Lloyds Bank Ltd., Sparkhill, Birmingham.
Edwards, Messrs. Francis, Ltd., 83 High Street, Marylebone, W.1.
Egerton, Rear-Admiral Brian, The Manor House, Ringwood, Hants.
*Ehrman, John, Esq., M.A., Sloane House, 149 Old Church Street, London, S.W.3.
*Elphinstone, Kenneth V., Esq., Artillery Mansions, Westminster, London, S.W.1.
Ensor, Lieutenant Moreton J., U.S.N.R., 30 Charles Street, Lexington 73, Mass., U.S.A.
*Erskine, The Honourable David, 50 Argyll Road, Kensington, W.8.
Evans, Commander (S.) L. C., V.R.D., LL.B., F.C.A., R.N.V.R., 1 Windsor Place, Liskeard, Cornwall.

Fardell, Commander K. M., R.N., Hartfield, Littleham Cross, Exmouth, Devon.
Farrington, Instructor Lieutenant-Commander L., H.M.C.S. *Venture*, H.M.C. Dockyard, Esquimalt, British Columbia, Canada.
Fenwick, K., Esq., 22 Grosvenor Road, Scarborough.
Ferrigno, Anthony V., Esq. 29 Caldy Road, Aintree, Liverpool 9, Lancs.
Feteris, Vice-Admiral P. J., C.B.E., Van Boetzelaerlaan 57B, The Hague.
*Fisher, Captain B. J., D.S.O., R.N., Courtfield, Haslemere, Surrey.
*Fisher, Lieutenant-Commander R. C., R.N., c/o Westminster Bank Ltd., Clarendon Road, Southsea, Hants.
Foxley, G. H., Esq., 10 Westcraig Avenue, Moston, Manchester 10.
*Fremantle, Admiral Sir Sydney, G.C.B., M.V.O., 30 Bullingham Mansions, Church Street, London, W.8.

*Gascoigne, Instructor Commander J. C., O.B.E., R.N., H.M.S. *Dryad*, Smethwick House, Near Fareham, Hants.
*Gathorne-Hardy, Surgeon Lieutenant-Commander The Hon. A., Royal Naval Air Station, Yeovilton, Somerset.
Gibbs, Professor N. H., All Souls College, Oxford.
Gilbert, Commander (S.) A. D., R.N., H.M.S. *Gannet*, R.N. Air Station, Eglinton, Co. Londonderry, N. Ireland.
Gilchrist, Lieutenant W. L. R. E., R.N., Sherborne Hill, Near Basingstoke, Hants.
Gill, Lieutenant-Commander G. Hermon, R.A.N.V.R., Inveresk, 258 Beaconsfield Parade, Middle Park, Melbourne, S.C.6.
*Gillespie, Commander (S.) T. P., M.B.E., R.N., c/o The Manager, Lloyds Bank Ltd., Commercial Road, Portsmouth.

LIST OF MEMBERS

Glossop, Lieutenant-Commander J. J., R.N., H.M.S. *Dryad*, Southwick, Near Fareham, Hants.
*Godfrey, Admiral J. H., C.B., White Stacks, Wilmington, Near Polegate, Sussex.
Goodenough, Captain M. G., C.B.E., D.S.O., R.N., Lower Woodlands, Shiplake, Henley-on-Thames, Oxon.
Goulding, Lieutenant B. H., R.N., H.M.S. *Whirlwind*, c/o G.P.O., London.
*Graham, Professor Gerald S., M.A., Ph.D., University of London, King's College, Strand, London, W.C.2.
*Graham, N. W., Esq., Suilven, Kings Road, Longniddry, East Lothian.
Grant, Alistair Ian, Esq., c/o Grant & Cia Ltda., Rua XV de Novembre 194, P.O. Box 707, Santos, Brazil.
Grice, C. E. O., (AR) H.R.C., R.N., The Oast Cottage, South Binns, Heathfield, Sussex.
Gwilliam, R., Esq., 9 Eccleston Avenue, Handbridge, Chester.
Graves, Miss Marjorie, Cocknowle, Wareham, Dorset.

Hale, Colonel F. W. H., Box 913, G.P.O. Melbourne, Victoria.
*Hall, Instructor Rear-Admiral Sir Arthur E., K.B.E., C.B., 10 Liskeard Gardens, Blackheath, S.E.3.
*Hamilton, Admiral Sir Louis H. K., K.C.B., D.C.O., c/o Messrs. Coutts & Co., 440 Strand, London, W.C.2.
Harding, Gilbert, Esq., 43 Hamilton Road, Dollis, Hill, N.W.10.
*Hanson, Lieutenant-Commander R. J., D.S.O., R.N., 30 Ledmore Road, Charlton Kings, Cheltenham, Glos.
Hazel, Senior Commissioned Gunner E. W., Ward Room Mess, Royal Naval Barracks, Chatham, Kent.
Hegarty, Lieutenant-Commander (E.) R. D. M., R.N., 475 Maidstone Road, Wigmore, Gillingham, Kent.
Herbert, M., Esq., The White House, Perry Street, Chislehurst, Kent.
Hill, Mrs. S. F., 181 Rayleigh Road, Hutton, Essex.
Hill, Surgeon-Lieutenant-Commander R. C. J., R.N.V.R. (Retd.), 606 Essenwood Road, Durban, Natal, South Africa.
*Hinton, Captain E. P., D.S.O., M.V.O., R.N., Puckington, Near Ilminster, Somerset.
Holder, Sub-Lieutenant D. K., R.N., 24 Crooks Lane, Alcester, Warwickshire.
*Hood, The Viscount, c/o The Foreign Office, Whitehall, London, S.W.1.
Hope, Admiral Sir George, K.C.B., K.C.M.G., Common House, Plaistow, Billinghurst, Sussex.
*Hume, J. M., Esq., c/o The Royal Northumberland Yacht Club, Blyth.
Hordern, Lieutenant-Commander M. C., R.A.N.R., B.A., c/o Hordern Brothers Ltd., 19 Basinghall Street, London, E.C.2.
Hornsby, F. L., Esq., Bletchley, Moulyining, Western Australia.
Horsburgh, George D. L., Esq., c/o Messrs. Swift Levick & Sons Ltd., Clarence Steel Works, Sheffield 4.
*Horton, Captain C. Ivan, R.N., Fenwick Cottage, Emsworth, Hants.
Howieson, Lieutenant L. S., R.N., 98 Shandon Road, Broadwater, Worthing, Sussex.
Hughes, Arthur J., Esq., Pages, Chigwell Row, Essex.
Hughes, Professor Edward, The Manor House, Shincliffe, Durham.
Humphreys, Commander L. A., R.N., Elm Lodge, Biddestone, Chippenham, Wilts.
Hussey, John, Esq., 47 Northaw Road, Cuffley, Potters Bar, Middlesex.

LIST OF MEMBERS

*Ingram, Captain Sir Bruce S., O.B.E., M.C., Ingram House, 195/198 Strand, London, W.C.2.
Irrmann, Professor Robert, Ph.D., Department of History, Beloit College, Beloit, Wisconsin, U.S.A.
Ivliev, N. V., Esq., 89 Addison Road, London, W.14.
*Iveagh, The Rt. Hon. The Earl of, C.B., C.M.G., Pyrford Court, Woking, Surrey.

*Jackson, Instructor Captain T. E., R.N. (Retd.), 131 Gudge Heath Lane, Fareham, Hants.
*Jackson, Rear-Admiral W. L., D.S.O., Soberton Mill, Swanmore, Hants.
*Jacob, Lieutenant J. C., R.N., The Red House, Woodbridge, Suffolk.
James, Admiral Sir William M., G.C.B., The Road Farm, Churt, Surrey.
*Jennings, Lieutenant E. D., R.N., Meadow View, Bathampton, Bath.
Jenson, Lieutenant-Commander L. B., C.D., R.C.N., 22 Revelstoke Drive, RR2, Billings Bridge, Near Ottawa, Canada.
Jewell, J., Esq., " Tamar," Southpark Road, Tywardreath, Par. Cornwall.
Jobson, Lieutenant P. A., R.N.V.R., 117 Eton Avenue, North Wembley, Middlesex.
Johnston, S. H. F., Esq., University College of Wales, Aberystwyth, Cards.
Jones, Lieutenant-Commander (S.) A. M., R.N., Suffield, Albert Drive, Deganwy, Caernarvonshire.
*Jones, Commander C. G. Pitcairn, R.N., Royal Naval College Staff, Greenwich, S.E.10.
*Jones, Commodore Gerald N., C.B.E., D.S.O., R.D., R.N.R., Westwinds, Deganwy, N. Wales.

Kelsey, J. A. C., Esq., 46 Ambleside Gardens, South Kenton, Wembley, Middlesex.
*Kemp, Commander P. K., R.N., Malcolm's, 51 Market Hill, Maldon, Essex.
Kennedy, L., Esq., 26 Church Row, London, N.W.3.
*Kinnahan, Admiral Sir H. R. G., K.B.E., C.B., Southwater, Lee-on-the-Solent, Hants.
*Kingsford, The Rev. Maurice R., M.A., B.Litt., The Rectory, Nuneham Courtenay, Oxford.
Kirk, Admiral Alan Goodrich, U.S.N. (Retd.), The Dalcota, 1 West 72 Street, New York, 23, New York.
Knight, R. W., Esq., P.O. Box 56, Port Louis, Mauritius.
Knox, Captain D. W., U.S.N., Naval Historical Foundation, c/o Navy Department, Washington, 26, D.C., U.S.A.

Ladner, Thomas E., Esq., 4610 Connaught Drive, Vancouver, B.C., Canada.
*Laing, E. A. M., Esq., 73 Barrow Point Avenue, Pinner, Middlesex.
Lambe, Vice-Admiral Charles, Knockhill House, Newport, Fife.
Lambert, Commander Douglas, M.B.E., D.S.C., R.N.V.R., Caixa Postal 941, Sanots, Brazil, South America.
*Lampen, Commander D., D.S.O., O.B.E., R.N., White Rocks House, Garway Hill, Hereford.
Lang, Sir John G., K.C.B., The Admiralty, London, S.W.1.
Lavett, Lieutenant J. L., R.A.N., c/o Department of External Affairs, Canberra, A.C.T., Australia.

LIST OF MEMBERS

*Law, H. G., Esq., Spring Grove, Ranelagh Drive, Bracknell, Berks.
*Lawder, Lieutenant-Commander (S.) M. C., R.N., Brook House, Wrington, Near Bristol, Somerset.
Larsson, Hans, Esq., c/o Svenska Dagbladet, Stockholm, Sweden.
*Leck, John E., Esq., M.R.S.T., 3 Stanley Avenue, Latchford Without, Warrington, Lancs.
*Lemon, H., Esq., 48 Moutcharles, Belfast.
Lenox, Patrick G., Esq., Suite 401, The Canadian Bank of Commerce Building, 640 West Hastings Street, Vancouver 2, B.C., Canada.
Lester, Lieutenant Richard M., R.C.N. (R.), 20 Chipping Road, Don Mills, P.O. Ontario, Canada.
*Lewis, Captain A. F. P., R.N., The Captain of the Fleet, Mediterranean Fleet, c/o Fleet Mail Office, Malta.
*Lewis, Professor Michael A., C.B.E., M.A., F.R.Hist.S., Royal Naval College, Greenwich, S.E.10.
Lewis, J. Parry, University College, Cathays Park, Cardiff.
Lister, R., Esq., Grey Friars, Kent Road, Harrogate.
*Little, Admiral Sir Charles J. C., G.C.B., G.B.E., The Old Mill, Ashurst, Near Steyning, Sussex.
*Lloyd, Professor Christopher C., M.A., F.R.Hist.S., Royal Naval College, Greenwich, S.E.10.
Lloyd, Mrs. K. B., Pilgrims House, Knockholt, Kent.
Lloyd, Commander L. G. B., R.N.V.R., Perriswood, Parkmill, Swansea.
Lloyd, Lieutenant-Colonel W. A. S., M.B.E., Mucklowe House, 53 Strand-on-the-Green, London, W.4.
Loram, R. G., Esq., Land House, Blind Lane, Mersham, Ashford, Kent.
Love, Major Stuart, D.S.O., M.C., 31 Irving Road, Toorak, Melbourne, S.E.2.
Lowe, Brian S., Esq., 1877 Hare Street, Vancouver, B.C., Canada.
Lucas, J. C., Esq., Holly Lodge, Croxfield Green, Petersfield, Hants.
Lorimer, Surgeon Commander J., M.B., Ch.B., R.N.V.R., Hazelwood, Creetown, Kirkudbrightshire, Scotland.
*Lowther, Lieutenant L. W. H., R.N.V.(S.).R., Abbotsbury, Greenways, Abbots Langley, Herts.
Lindsay-Macdougall, Miss K., 25 Hans Place, London, S.W.1.

McCormick-Goodhart, Commander L., O.B.E., V.R.D., R.N.V.R., 610 East Boulevard Drive, Alexandria, Virginia, U.S.A.
McClure, Professor William H., P.O. Box 543, Saginaw, Michigan, U.S.A.
McDougall, Commander A. R., R.N.V.R., Stone House, Highmoor Cross, Near Henley-on-Thames, Oxon.
McKeown, Commander (E.) R. J., R.C.N., c/o Principal, R.C.N. Technical Representative, Harland & Wolfe, Belfast, N.I.
*Martin, Captain C. J. P., 41 Lish Avenue, Whitley Bay, Northumberland.
Mason, Colonel F. van Wyck, Enfield, Ely's Harbor, Somerset, Bermuda.
*Mason, Cecil C., Esq., O.B.E., Beverley, 14 Bentley Road, Cambridge.
Mathieson, Writer A. H., 12 Eglington Street, Saltcoats, Ayrshire.
Mathew, The Most Rev. Archbishop, M.A., Litt.D., F.S.A., Athenaeum, Pall Mall, S.W.1.
Mendenhall, Professor T. C., 128 High Street, New Haven, Connecticut, U.S.A.
Merriman, Commander R. D., D.S.C., R.I.N., Somerdown, 26 Somers Road, Reigate, Surrey.
Minchin, Sub-Lieutenant P. D., R.N., H.M.S. *Centaur*, c/o G.P.O., London.
Moir, Lieutenant-Colonel A. C. D., Woodham, Manor Road, Chigwell, Essex.

LIST OF MEMBERS

McKee, Lieutenant Fraser M., R.C.N.(R.), 242 Castlefield Avenue, Toronto 12, Ontario, Canada.
Monsarratt, Nicholas, United Kingdom Information Office, 275 Albert Street, Ottawa, Canada.
*Montgomery, Commander J. R. C., R.N., Kinnabus, The Oa, Port Ellen, Isle of Islay, Scotland.
*Moore, Sir Alan, Bart., Hancox, Whatlington, Battle, Sussex.
*Moore, Admiral Sir Henry R., G.C.B., C.V.O., D.S.O., Junior United Service Club, London, S.W.1.
Morgan, John M., Esq., 910 Sybil Street, Am Arbor, Michegan, U.S.A.
Morpurgo, J. E., Esq., New Hall, Bradwell-Juxta-Mare, Near Southminster, Essex.
*Morse, Rear-Admiral Sir John A. V., K.C.B., C.B., D.S.O., Union Club, Carlton House Terrace, London, S.W.1.
Mote, Captain Paul, M.C., U.S.N.R. (Retd.), Box 1275, Fairhope, Alabama, U.S.A.
Mountbatten of Burma, Vice-Admiral The Right Hon. the Earl, K.G., P.C., G.C.S.I., G.C.I.E., G.C.V.O., K.C.B., D.S.O., 2 Kinnerton Street, London, S.W.1.
*Moxly, Commander S. H. S., Fontabelle, Belmore Lane, Lymington, Hants.
Muderlugu, Deniz Muzesi, Dolmabrahce, Istanbul, Turkey.

Naish, Lieutenant-Commander George P. B., R.N.V.R., National Maritime Museum, Greenwich, S.E.10.
Nicholson, Lieutenant H. E., R.N.V.R., 66 Durban Road West, Watford, Herts.
Nijhoff, Mr. Martinus, Lange Voorhout 9, The Hague, Holland.
Nugent, Vice-Admiral R. A., C.M.G., The Field House, Lee-on-Solent, Hants.

Ommanney, Lieutenant J. L. N., R.N., Fordes, Ropley, Hants.
*Overton, E. M., Esq., 54 Somerset Road, Edgbaston, Birmingham 15.
*Owen, Commander J. H., F.R.Hist.S., R.N., 41a Roland Gardens, London, S.W.7.

*Packer, Vice-Admiral Sir H. A., K.C.B., C.B.E., 4th Sea Lord, Admiralty, S.W.1.
*Parker, Lieutenant-Commander E. V., V.R.D., R.N.V.R., 61 Marlborough Crescent, Sevenoaks, Kent.
Parker, Lieutenant V. A., R.A.N., 14 East Crescent Street, MacMahons Point, Near Sydney, Australia.
Parkinson, C. Northcote, Esq., Ph.D., D.R.Hist.S., Department of History, University of Malay, Cluny Road, Singapore.
*Pearsall, A. W. H., Esq., 6 Pemberton Drive, Morecambe, Lancashire.
Pelling, John L., Esq., Messrs. T. Bickerstaff & Son, A9 and 10 Queen Insurance Buildings, 10 Dale Street, Liverpool, 2.
Penn, C. D., Esq., F.R.Hist.S., 4 Grantley House, 30A Florence Road, Boscombe, Bournemouth.
*Penney, Major-General W. R. C., C.B., C.B.E., D.S.O., M.C., Brooks House, Stanford Dingley, Berks.
Penny, K., Esq., Department of Pacific History, The Australian National University, Box 4, G.P.O. Canberra, A.C.T.

LIST OF MEMBERS

Petree, J. Foster, Esq., 36 Mayfield Road, Sutton, Surrey.
Perren, G. E., Esq., 64 High Street, Burnham-on-Crouch, Essex.
*Petrie-Hay, Lieutenant-Commander (S.) A. J., R.N., H.M.S. *Harrier*, Kete, Near Haverfordwest, Pembrokeshire.
Petyon-Burbery, Rev. Canon R. J. P., S.G.M., R.N., St. Mary's Rectory, March, Cambridgeshire.
Phillips, Bertram, Esq., 7a Crown Circus, Dowanhill, Glasgow, W.2.
Phillips, Sub-Lieutenant J. M., R.N., 4 Molyneux Court, Tunbridge Wells, Kent.
Phillips, Lieutenant-Commander M. H., V.R.D., R.N.V.R., The Bombay Company Ltd., P.O. Box 201, Bombay.
Plunkett-Ernle-Erle-Drax, Admiral The Hon. Sir Reginald A. R., K.C.B., D.S.O., Charborough Park, Wareham, Dorset.
Pool, Bernard F., Esq., C.B.E., Contract Department, Admiralty, London, S.W.1.
*Powell, The Rev. J. R., 3 Lennox Gardens, London, S.W.1.
*Price, Lieutenant G. D. A., R.N.V.R., Barlow Fold, Heybridge Lane, Prestbury, Cheshire.
Pring, Commander (S.) L. W., R.N., Stoneways, 60 Aldenham Avenue, Radlett, Herts.
Pullen, Rear-Admiral H. F., O.B.E., R.C.N., Admiral's House, H.M.C. Dockyard, Esquimalt, B.C.

*Raikes, Commander Iwan G., D.S.C., R.N., Mantley, Newent, Glos.
*Ranft, B. McL., Esq., Royal Naval College, Greenwich, London, S.E.10.
Rau, Professor Virginia (*Corresponding Member*), 75 Av. da Republica, Lisbon.
Rayner, Commander D. A., R.N.V.R., Earlstone Manor, Burghclere, Near Newbury, Berks.
Regnart, Lieutenant H. J., R.N., R.N. Air Station, Ford, Sussex.
Reid, Captain W. R. G., R.N., Bordein, West End, Woking, Surrey.
Rivers, P. J., Esq., c/o The Chartered Bank, Singapore.
Robson, Brian, Esq., Albria, Wayland Avenue, Brighton, Sussex.
*Rodger, A. B., Esq., Balliol College, Oxford.
*Roper, Captain E. G., D.S.O., D.S.C., R.N., Polmayne, St. Minver, Cornwall.
*Roskill, Captain Stephen W., C.B.E., R.N., Blounce, South Warnborough, Basingstoke, Hants.
*Rowbotham, Commander W. B., R.N., 22 Ashley Gardens, London, S.W.1.
Rust, L. R., Esq., One Tree House, Honor Oak Rise, London, S.E.23.
*Rutherford, Miss G., 2 Phillimore Place, London, W.8.
Ryan, Anthony N., Esq., 8 Prince Alfred Road, Liverpool, 5.

*Sanders, Commander C. B., V.D., R.N.V.R., 59 Winchester Court, London, W.8.
*Sandwich, The Right Hon. The Earl of, Hinchinbroke, Huntingdon.
*Sarell, Captain R. I. A., D.S.O., R.N., Braeside, Ashurst Road, East Grinstead, Sussex.
Saunders, Lieutenant-Commander Raphel, D.S.O., R.N.V.R., 6 Douglas Mansions, Quex Road, London, N.W.6.
Saxby, R. C., Esq., 7a South Park, Sevenoaks, Kent.
Schurman, D. M., Esq., Research Fellow, Sidney Sussex College, Cambridge.
*Scott, Surgeon Lieutenant-Commander W. I. D., M.D., Ch.B., R.N.V.R., 30 Curzon Park, Chester.

LIST OF MEMBERS

Scrivenor, Lieutenant-Commander R. J., R.A.N., c/o Navy Office, Melbourne, Australia.

*Sergeant, Captain T. A., R.D., R.N.R., No. 1 The Brow, Friston, Near Eastbourne.

*Sheen, Commander C. E., D.S.C., R.N., H.M.S. *Dodman Point*, H.M. Dockyard, Devonport, Devon.

*Shelley, Rear-Admiral R., C.B., C.B.E., The Pickeridge, Stoke Podges, Bucks.

Shelmerdine, Malcolm G., Esq., 36 Moncktons Avenue, Maidstone, Kent.

Shute, Lieutenant-Commander R. H. N., R.N., c/o Commercial Bank of Scotland, Campbeltoun Branch, Campbeltoun, Scotland.

*Smith, Admiral Sir Aubrey C. H., K.C.V.O., K.B.E., C.B., Hay's Wharf and Dock, Southwark, London, S.E.1.

*Somerville, Lieutenant-Commander J. A. F., R.N., Hoefield House, The Leigh, Coombe Hill, Gloucester.

Sommerville, Commander I. F., R.N., c/o National Provincial Bank Ltd., Portsea.

Spicer, Captain S. D., R.N., Salt Mill House, Fishbourne, Chichester.

Southcott, Lieutenant-Commander T. Ian G., c/o Mrs. E. Spencer-Niarn, Burham, Cupar, Fife.

Stanford, Peter, Esq., Essex, Connecticut, U.S.A.

*Stanhope, The Rt. Hon. Earl, K.G., D.S.O., M.C., D.L., Chevening, Sevenoaks, Kent.

Steeves, Lieutenant M. P. T., R.N., 22 Ashley Road, Aberdeen.

*Stephens, Lieutenant Richard Alan, R.N., The Old Vicarage, Easebourne, Midhurst, Sussex.

Stuart, Lieutenant W. D., R.N., North Lodge, Swarland, Felton, Northumberland.

Stubbs, Lieutenant R. D. S., R.N., Chelmsford Hall, Eastbourne, Sussex.

Sturdee, Lieutenant-Commander A. R. B., D.S.C., R.N., 98A, Addison Road, Kensington, London, W.14.

*Style, Lieutenant-Commander G. W., D.S.C., R.N., Gilhams Birch, Harvis Brook, Near Crowborough, Sussex.

Swinson, B. H., Esq., c/o Canadian Shell Ltd., 600 University Avenue, Toronto 1, Ontario, Canada.

*Symes, Lieutenant-Commander E. D., R.N., Dymoke House, Easton, Winchester, Hants.

Swinley, Lieutenant J. G. B., R.N., Lypiatt Hill House, Near Stroud, Gloucestershire.

Talbot, Vice-Admiral Sir Cecil P., K.C.B., K.B.E., D.S.O., Little Hafton, Pine Road, Woking, Surrey.

Tanner, Commander (E.) G. W., R.N., Royal Naval Air Station, Yeovilton, Somerset.

*Taylor, Rear-Admiral A. Hugh, C.B., O.B.E., The Manor House, Diss, Norfolk.

Taylor, T. G. T., Esq., B.A., Cobblers Last, Holy Cross Green, Clent, Near Stourbridge, Worcs.

*Thistleton-Smith, Commodore G., G.M., R.N., H.M.S. *Vanguard*, c/o G.P.O., London.

Thorndycraft, John, 87 Chester Drive, North Harrow, Middlesex.

*Thursfield, Rear-Admiral H. G., F.S.A., Creake Abbey, Fakenham, Norfolk.

Timings, E. K., Esq., M.A., Public Records Office, Chancery Lane, London, W.C.2.

*Tizard, Sir Henry, G.C.B., F.R.S., Keston, Hill Head, Fareham, Hants.

LIST OF MEMBERS

*Tolley, Lieutenant-Commander R. P., R.N., 37 Edenfield Gardens, Worcester Park, Surrey.

*Townsend-Green, Commander A., R.N. (Retd.), Waltham Lodge, 47B Netherhall Gardens, Hampstead, N.W.3.

Toy, Ernest W., Esq., Jr., 5456 Wayman Avenue, Riverside, California, U.S.A.

*Trentham, Captain David, R.N., Red House, Yateley, Hants.

Trevelyan, Professor G. M., O.M., C.B.E., F.B.A., Litt.D., L.L.D., F.R.Hist.S., The Master's Lodge, Trinity College, Cambridge.

Trier, Commander P. A., R.N., 77 Bambra Road, Caulfield, Melbourne, Victoria, Australia.

*Trotter, W. P., Esq., 78 Kenilworth Court, Putney, S.W.15.

*Troubridge, Lieutenant Peter, R.N., Middle Oakshott, Hawkley, Liss.

Walker, Lieutenant E. P. K., R.N., Navy House, Palazzo Lloyd Triestine, Trieste.

*Walker, Commander (Sp.) G. E., O.B.E., R.I.N.V.R., 26 Rutland Street, London, S.W.7.

*Walling, Captain R. V., R.A., Three Ways, Ledstone, Near Kingsbridge, S. Devon.

*Weir of Eastwood, The Rt. Hon. Viscount, G.C.B., LL.D., D.L., Holm Foundry, Cathcart, Glasgow.

White, E. A., Esq., B.A., 1 Park Avenue, Deepdale, Preston, Lancs.

*White, L. R. B., Esq., Gavanrie, Ersham Road, Hailsham, Sussex.

*Whiting, Instructor Commander R. O., M.A., R.N., Berwick Lodge, Barnham, Bognor Regis, Sussex.

Wallis, Frederick A. E., Esq., 3 Leith Avenue, Portsmouth, Hants.

Wickham, Captain E. T., O.B.E., R.N., Rokeby Lodge, Bathford, Somerset.

*Wiggins, Harold P., Esq., Hans Cottage, Henley-on-Thames, Oxford.

Willis, H. C., Esq., Boulders House, Simon's Towns, C.P., South Africa.

*Woodrooffe, Commander T., 11 Allen House, Allen Street, London, W.8.

Woodward, Chief Officer S. M., 43 Shaftesbury Road, Southsea.

*Wright, Rear-Admiral (S.) Noel, C.B., O.B.E., The Thatched House, 27 The Avenue, Alverstoke, Hants.

*Wyatt, Lieutenant (E.) A., R.N., Wharfedale, Innox Hill, Frome, Somerset.

LIST OF MEMBERS

LIBRARIES, INSTITUTIONS, ETC.

Aberdeen University Library.
Admiralty Library, London, S.W.1.
Amsterdam, Nederlandsch Historisch Scheepvaart Museum.
Antiquaries, Society of, Burlington House, Piccadilly, London, W. 1.
Ariel, H.M.S., Wardroom Mess Committee, Winchester, Hants.
Athenæum, The, Pall Mall, London, S.W.1.
Australia, Commonwealth National Library, Canberra, Australia.
Australia, S., Public Library of, Adelaide, S. Australia.

Baltimore, The Enoch Pratt Free Library, Baltimore, Md., U.S.A.
Baltimore, Johns Hopkins University Library, Baltimore, Md., U.S.A.
Bath Club, The, 74 St. James's Street, London, S.W.1.
Bath, Victoria Art Gallery and Municipal Library, Bath, Somerset.
Belfast, Linen Hall Library.
Belfast, Queen's University Library.
Birmingham Public Libraries (Reference Library).
Birmingham University Library.
Bolton Central Reference Library.
Boston Athenæum, Boston, Mass, U.S.A.
Boston Public Library, Boston, Mass., U.S.A.
Bristol Public Library, College Green, Bristol.
Bristol University Library.
British Columbia, The University of, The Serials Division S-3170, The Library,
    Vancouver 8, Canada.
Brown University Library, Providence, Rhode Island, U.S.A.
Bureau Des Acquisitions De La Bibliothèque Nationale, 58 Rue de Richelieu,
    Paris 5.
Burgersdijk & Niermans, Leiden, Holland.

California, University of, Berkeley, California, U.S.A.
California, University of, The Library, c/o Messrs. B. F. Stevens & Brown
    Ltd., New Ruskin House, 28–30 Little Russell Street, London, W.C.1.
Cambridge, Christ's College Library.
Cambridge, St. John's College Library.
Cambridge, Seeley Historical Library.
Cardiff Public Libraries.
Chicago, The Newberry Library Chicago, Illinois, U.S.A.
Chicago, University of Chicago Libraries, Chicago, Illinois, U.S.A.
Chichester, West Sussex County Library, County Hall.
Cincinnati Public Library, Cincinnati, Ohio, U.S.A.
Cincinnati, The University of.
Columbia University Library, New York City, N.Y., U.S.A.
Congress, Library of, Washington, D.C., U.S.A.
Conservative Club, St. James's Street, London, S.W. 1.
Copenhagen, The Royal Library, Copenhagen, Denmark.
Copenhagen, The Library of the Royal Danish Navy, Overgaden oven
    Vander 60, Copenhagen K.
Cornell University Library, Ithaca, N.Y., U.S.A.
Croydon Public Libraries.
Cruising Association, Chiltern Court, Baker Street, London, N.W.1.

LIST OF MEMBERS

Dartmouth College Library, Hanover, N.H., U.S.A.
Dolphin, H.M.S., Ward Room Mess, Gosport.

Edinburgh Public Libraries.
Edinburgh Society of Writers to H.M. Signet, The Signet Library.
Edinburgh University.
Excellent, H.M.S., Portsmouth.
Exeter City Library.
Emory University Library, Georgia, U.S.A.

Folger Shakespeare Library (Washington D.C., U.S.A.), c/o George Harding's Bookshop Ltd., 64 Great Russell Street, London, W.C. 1.

Glasgow, The Mitchell Library, Glasgow Corporation Public Libraries.
Glasgow, Institute of Chartered Accountants in Scotland.
Glasgow University Library.
Guildhall Library, The Librarian, E.C.2.

Hague, The, Holland, The Royal Library.
Halifax Memorial Library, Halifax, Nova Scotia, Canada.
Harrier, H.M.S., Kete, Haverfordwest, South Wales.
Harvard College Library, Cambridge, Mass., U.S.A.
Hull Public Libraries.
Huntington Library and Art Gallery, San Marino, California, U.S.A.

Illinois University Library, Urbana, Illinois, U.S.A.
Implacable, H.M.S., c/o G.P.O., London.
Indefatigable, H.M.S., c/o G.P.O., London.
Indiana University Library, Bloomington, Indiana, U.S.A.
Iowa State University Library, Iowa City, Iowa, U.S.A.
Ireland, National Library of, Dublin.

Johannesburg Public Library, Market Square, Johannesburg, Transvaal, S.A.

Karlskrona, Kungl. Örlogsmannä Säliskapet Bibliotek, Karlskrona, Sweden.

Leeds University Library.
Liverpool Public Libraries.
Liverpool University Library.
London Library, St. James's Square, London, S.W. 1.
London University Library, Senate House, Bloomsbury, London, W.C.1.
London University, Institute of Historial Research, Senate House, Bloomsbury, London, W.C. 1.
Lords, House of, Library, Westminster, S.W. 1.
Lund, K. Universitets-Biblioteket, Lund, Sweden.

Malta, The Commissioner of Police, Valetta.
Malta, Royal Malta Library, Valetta.
Maida Vale Library, The Librarian, Sutherland Avenue, London, W. 9.
Maine Library, University of, Orono, Maine, U.S.A.
Manchester, John Rylands Library, Deansgate, Manchester.

LIST OF MEMBERS

Manchester Public Libraries, St. Peter's Square, Manchester.
Manchester, Victoria University of Manchester.
Manitoba, University of Manitoba Library, Winnipeg, Canada.
Marine Nationale, Bibliotheque Principle, Dupont Delorient, Morbihan.
Mariners' Museum Library, Newport Mews, Virginia, U.S.A.
Massachusetts Historical Society, 1154 Boylston Street, Boston, Mass., U.S.A.
Melbourne, Public Library of Victoria, Melbourne, Australia.
Melbourne University Library, Melbourne, Australia.
Michigan University Library, Ann Arbor, Michigan, U.S.A.
Minnesota University Library, Minneapolis, Minn., U.S.A.
Missouri University Library, Columbia, Mo., U.S.A.
Montreal, Redpath Library, McGill University, Montreal, Canada.

Nadem, H.M.C.S., Command Education Officer, Esquimalt, B.C., Canada.
National Defence Librarian, Royal Military College of Canada, Kingston, Ontario, Canada.
National Maritime Museum, Greenwich, S.E. 10.
National Portrait Gallery, St. Martin's Place, Trafalgar Square, London, W.C. 2.
Nebraska University Library, Lincoln, Nebraska, U.S.A.
Newcastle-on-Tyne Public Library.
Newcastle University College, The Librarian, N.S.W. University of Technology, Tighes Hill, 2N, N.S.W.
New South Wales Public Library.
New York Public Library, Fifth Avenue and 42nd Street, New York City, U.S.A.
New York Public Library, The Librarian, c/o Stevens & Brown, 28/30 Little Russell Street, London, W.C.1.
New York, University of Rochester Library, Rochester 3.
New York State Library, Albany, New York, U.S.A.
New York University Library.
New York Yacht Club, 37–41 West 44th Street, New York City, N.Y., U.S.A.
New Zealand, Alexander Turnbull Library, Bowen Street, Wellington, C. 1, New Zealand.
New Zealand General Assembly Library, Wellington, New Zealand.
Nottingham Central Public Library.

Ocean, H.M.S., c/o G.P.O., London.
Ohio, Ohio State University Library, Columbus 10, U.S.A.
Ottawa, Departmental Library, (Naval Section) " C " Building, Department of National Defence, Ontario, Canada.
Ottawa, Library of Parliament, Ottawa, Canada.
Oxford, All Souls College Library.
Oxford, Exeter College Library.
Oxford, Rhodes House Library.
Oxford, Trinity College Library.

Paddington, The Librarian, Maida Vale Library, Sutherland Avenue, W.9.
Pennsylvania Historical Society, 1300 Locust Street, Philadelphia, Pennsylvania, U.S.A.
Pennsylvania University Library, Pennsylvania, U.S.A.
Perth, The State Library of Western Australia, James Street, W. Australia.
Pittsburgh, University Library, Room 517, Cathedral of Learning, University Library, Penn, U.S.A.

LIST OF MEMBERS

Plymouth Central Library, Tavistock Road, Plymouth, Devon.
Portsmouth Central Public Library.
Portsmouth, H.M. Navigation School, Portsmouth, Hants.
Princeton University, Princeton, New Jersey, U.S.A.
Public Record Office Library, Chancery Lane, London, W.C. 2.

Queensland University Library, Brisbane, Australia.

Reading Central Library, Reading, Berks.
Reading University Library, Reading, Berks.
Rice Institute Library, Houston, Texas.
Royal Cruising Club, 1 New Square, Lincoln's Inn, London, W.C. 2.
Royal Empire Society, Northumberland Avenue, London, W.C. 2.
Royal Historical Society, 96 Cheyne Walk, Chelsea, S.W. 10.
Royal Institution Library, 21 Albemarle Street, London, W. 1.
Royal Naval Barracks, Devonport, Devon.
Royal Naval Club, Portsmouth.
Royal Naval College, Dartmouth, Devon.
Royal Naval College, Greenwich, S.E. 10.
Royal Naval Engineering College, Maradon, Plymouth.
Royal Naval Port Library, R.N. Barracks, Chatham, Kent.
Royal Naval Port Library, Devonport, Devon.
Royal Naval Port Library, Portsmouth.
Royal Naval Staff College, Greenwich, S.E. 10.
Royal Roads, H.M.C.S., The Librarian, Victoria. B.C., Canada.
Royal United Service Institution, Whitehall, London, S.W. 1.

San Francisco Public Library, Civic Centre, San Francisco, California, U.S.A.
Scotland, University Library, St. Andrews.
Secretary, The, Royal United Service Institution, Whitehall, London, S.W.1.
Suedè, Bibliothèque, de l' Université, Uppsala.
Service Historique de la Marine, 3 Avenue Octave Greard, Paris 6eme, Seine, France.
Sheffield University Library.
Stadacona, H.M.C.S., Command Reference Library, Halifax, Nova Scotia, Canada.
Stanford University Libraries, Stanfori, California, U.S.A.
Sweden, Universitetsbiblioteket, Uppsala.
Swets and Zeitlinger, Messrs., Amsterdam C, Keizersgracht 471, Holland.

Tamar, H.M.S., Ward Room Mess, Hongkong.
Tecumseh, H.M.C.S., Wardroom Mess, Calgary, Alberta, Canada.
The Official Secretary, Agent General for Tasmania, 457 Strand, W.C.2.
Theseus, H.M.S., c/o G.P.O., London.
Toronto Public Library, College and St. George Streets, Toronto 2b, Ontario, Canada.
Toronto Legislative Library, Parliament Buildings, Toronto 2, Ontario, Canada.
Travellers' Club, 106 Pall Mall, London, S.W. 1.
Trinity House, Tower Hill, London, E.C. 3.

Union College Library, Schenectady, 8, New York.
United Service Club, 116 Pall Mall, London, S.W. 1.
United States Naval Academy, Annapolis, U.S.A.

LIST OF MEMBERS

Vernon, H.M.S., Ward Room Mess, Portsmouth, Hants.
Venture, H.M.C.S., Secretary Treasurer Recreation Fund, H.M.C. Dockyard, Esquimalt, B.C., Canada.
Victoria Provincial Library, Victoria, B.C.

Wales, University College of, Aberystwyth, Wales.
Washington University Library, Seattle, Washington, U.S.A.
Westminster Public Library, St. Martin's Street, London, W.C. 2.
Winchester College, Moberly Library, Winchester, Hants.
Winconsin University, General Library, 816 State Street, Madison 6, Wis., U.S.A.
Witwatersrand University Library, Milner Park, Johannesburg, S. Africa.

Yale University Library, New Haven, Conn., U.S.A.

Printed in Great Britain
SPOTTISWOODE, BALLANTYNE & Co. LTD.
London & Colchester